FIFTY WESTERN WRITERS

FIFTY WESTERN WRITERS

A Bio~Bibliographical Sourcebook

edited by FRED ERISMAN
and RICHARD W. ETULAIN

GREENWOOD PRESS
WESTPORT, CONNECTICUT • LONDON, ENGLAND

Library of Congress Cataloging in Publication Data
Main entry under title:

Fifty Western writers.

Includes index.
1. American literature—West (U.S.)—Bio-bibliography.
2. Authors, American—West (U.S.)—Biography. 3. West
(U.S.) in literature—Bibliography. 4. American litera-
ture—West (U.S.)—History and criticism. I. Erisman,
Fred, 1937-   . II. Etulain, Richard W.
PS271.F5   810'.9'978   81-13462
ISBN 0-313-22167-7 (lib. bdg.)   AACR2

Library of Congress Catalog Card Number: 81-13462
ISBN: 0-313-22167-7

First published in 1982

Greenwood Press
A division of Congressional Information Service, Inc.
88 Post Road West
Westport, Connecticut 06881

Printed in the United States of America

10 9 8 7 6 5 4 3 2 1

TO

Edwin R. Bingham
Earl Pomeroy
Mulford Q. Sibley
George G. Williams

Scholars, Teachers,
Mentors, and Friends

CONTENTS

INTRODUCTION

The American West is many things. It is a place, defined loosely by the Mississippi River to the east, the Pacific Ocean to the west, Canada to the north, and Mexico to the south. It is a state of mind, a circumstance created by the slow but inexorable interaction of landscape, climate, and diverse cultures, coming together over a period of more than two centuries. It is a cliché, a never-never land created in the minds of persons who take their impressions from the movie screen or the television, a region paradoxically a place of dusty streets and promiscuous violence, of lavish cities and unscrupulous wheeler-dealers. And it is, finally, a locale peculiarly rich in the diversity of literature and literary forms that it has generated.

That the West has given rise to a widely varied literature is unquestioned. From the region have come works acknowledged as significant by critics of all regions—the poetry of Robinson Jeffers and Theodore Roethke, the essays of John Graves and Bernard DeVoto, the fiction of Willa Cather, Wallace Stegner, and John Steinbeck. It has given rise to literature highly traditional (the novels of Owen Wister or George R. Stewart, for example) and works notably experimental (those by Ken Kesey, perhaps, or Gary Snyder). And it has evolved—and given its name to—an entirely new form, the Western.

The Western, a stylized tale of conflict and high adventure set in the environs of the West, stands as one of America's contributions to world literature. As delineated by Max Brand, Zane Grey, Louis L'Amour, Jack Schaefer, and other writers lesser and greater, the Western offers a view of American life and ideas found in no other literary genre. It builds upon themes central to American life: the difficulties of settling a hostile environment; the tensions existing between natural freedom and civilized limits; the manner in which persons of other cultures have been absorbed into, and have contributed to, the course of American civilization. It deals with problems still current in American life: those of individual liberty, its rights and its responsibilities; the question of progress, and

Richard W. Etulain is indebted to the Research Allocations Committee of the University of New Mexico for financial support in the preparation of this volume.

its cost; the many-faceted relationship of the individual to the land; and others. And perhaps most significantly of all, it crystallizes once and for all that most characteristic of American literary figures, the Western hero—the solitary, laconic individual who time and again turns his back upon domesticity and the easy way because of his individual perceptions of rightness and the way of the world. Uneven in quality though it may be, the Western is the literary form most readily recognized as American. As such, it deserves attention.

Fifty Western Writers exists to help call and direct attention to the many forms of western American literature. It is an introductory reference and research guide, intended for the beginning researcher who is interested in the West and for the literary specialist who seeks to branch out into new areas of study. Its contents, although selective, are assembled to supply narrative introductions and bibliographical guides to the study of fifty leading authors whose work emanates from—or is associated with—the West. As such, it fills a long-standing gap in literary and historical guides, for no other work has yet focused attention upon this region and these authors in this fashion.

In developing *Fifty Western Writers*, we have built upon the well-established scholarly pattern of limited research guides. Our way has been prepared by such works as Floyd Stovall's *Eight American Authors* (1956, 1971), Jackson Bryer's *Fifteen Modern American Authors* (1969), and *Fifteen American Authors before 1900* (1971), edited by Robert A. Rees and Earl N. Harbert. These guides have amply demonstrated the utility to researchers of specialized guides of limited scope. None claims comprehensiveness; instead, each endeavors to supply its users with sound, specific, balanced information about the topics and persons included. *Fifty Western Writers* shares this goal.

Also helpful to us in our planning have been guides to regional materials, such as Ralph L. Rusk's *The Literature of the Middle Western Frontier* (1925), Louis D. Rubin's *A Bibliographical Guide to the Study of Southern Literature* (1969), and *Southwestern American Literature: A Bibliography* (1980), edited by John Q. Anderson and others. We have, in addition, been encouraged in our work by the increasing interest in the literature and culture of the American West. Organizations such as the Western Literature Association (which publishes the invaluable journal, *Western American Literature*); major commentaries like Henry Nash Smith's *Virgin Land* (1950) and John R. Milton's *The Novel of the American West* (1980); and comprehensive studies like the forthcoming *Literary History of the American West* attest to the substance and vitality of Western studies. *Fifty Western Writers*, we believe, will serve as a useful adjunct to these other works.

The authors represented in *Fifty Western Writers* reflect the variety of the West. They range from figures of the nineteenth century (Bret Harte, Joaquin Miller) to those of the present (Edward Abbey, A. B. Guthrie). They include authors eastern born (Owen Wister, Mary Hallock Foote) as well as western born (Andy Adams, H. L. Davis). They speak for diverse groups—the Native American (N. Scott Momaday), the Frisian-Dutch (Frederick Feikema Manfred), the

Slav (Mari Sandoz), the Scandinavian (O. E. Rølvaag), and others. They write of times stretching from the primitive (Dorothy Johnson) to the modern (Larry McMurtry). They embrace points of view extending from the conservative to the radical. They do not limit themselves to any particular form of expression but employ them all—fiction, nonfiction, poetry, journalism, the popular Western. Yet varied though they are, all speak at length of the American West, and all have contributed to the development of western literature as we know it.

The essays constituting *Fifty Western Writers* are intended to call attention to those authors associated with the West who should be known to all students of American literature and culture. Each essay is the work of an expert in the general field of western studies, and often that of a person who is a specialist in the writings of the author concerned. Because they are intended to be as helpful as possible to the individual beginning an investigation of western literature, the essays follow a uniform pattern. Each opens with a brief overview of its subject's life, emphasizing the literary development of that person. This is followed by an analysis of the major themes and ideas that characterize the author's work—their nature, their origin, and their most significant expressions. Closing the essay is a review of selected scholarship dealing with the particular author, focusing upon those works that seem to be most important in shedding light upon the author's place in, and contribution to, western literary history. A separate bibliography provides selective listings of primary and secondary works, with full publication data. The essays themselves are arranged alphabetically by the last name of the author discussed.

Two specialized usages perhaps need discussion. First, in the bibliographies, the abbreviations "SWS," "WWS," and "TUSAS" refer, respectively, to the Southwest Writers Series published by the Steck-Vaughn Company, the Western Writers Series issued by Boise State University, and the Twayne's United States Authors Series published by Twayne Publishers, a division of G. K. Hall. Second, throughout the book we use the term *Western* (capitalized and standing alone) to refer to the works of those authors working in the popular, formulaic tradition—for example, the books and short stories of Luke Short, Ernest Haycox, or Zane Grey. Conversely, we use "western" literature (uncapitalized and often modified) to refer to a broader body of writing—that which deals with more sweepingly universal human concerns against the backdrop of the American West. Into this category would fall the works of such authors as Willa Cather, Conrad Richter, and Walter Van Tilburg Clark. We consider this distinction a matter of definition only. We make no evaluation of the comparative worth or merits of the two forms and acknowledge the importance of both to the genre.

Western literature and western studies have been consigned to secondary status for too long. Too many scholars, seeing the admittedly visible flaws of the most familiar forms of western writing, have condemned the entire genre out of hand. "Nothing good," the traditionalists say, "can come from Medicine Bow." Perhaps. Yet the authors represented here do much to give the lie to the generalization. In the diversity of their works and the variety of their concerns, they have created a body of writing that can stand without apology. It is writing that speaks to a time, a place, and a people. It is writing that needs to be recognized. The essays comprised in *Fifty Western Writers*, we believe, do justice to the authors represented, making their works and their ideas available for the careful study they deserve.

Fred Erisman
Texas Christian University

Richard W. Etulain
University of New Mexico

Ann Ronald

EDWARD ABBEY
(1927-)

"vulture: a large bird of prey that lives on the flesh of dead animals"
—Oxford American Dictionary

"Even the buzzards were present, two of them, hovering high in the blue, meditating in space, but the savage eyes missed nothing that stirred in the desert below—belly, beak and claws taut with hunger and desire. Next time around, I thought, if we get the choice, I too want to be a long-winged, evil-minded predatory bird."
—Billy Vogelin Starr, in Edward Abbey, *Fire on the Mountain*

"For a lifetime or two, or three, I think I'll settle for the sedate career, soaring and serene, of the humble turkey buzzard."
—Edward Abbey, from "Flights of Reincarnation"

Melancholy, humble, serene, then arrogant, predatory, and fierce—Edward Abbey soars above the desert landscape with his pen a vulture's talons and the twentieth-century West a vulture's prey. Watching the carrion waste that technocracy is making of the land, Abbey flies in ever-widening circles, calling attention to the carnage he sees below. In strong, pictorial prose, both factual and imaginative, he pinpoints the sins that modern man commits against the environment and predicates the evils that, as a result, man causes. Some call this literary buzzard an eco-freak, others a prophet of doom; but no one denies the impact he has made upon his readers, those other aficionados of wilderness, of freedom, of sanctity for the individual and for the land. More directly than most other contemporary western writers, Abbey confronts present-day problems and predicts future ills by analyzing the mistakes of the past. The result is a curious blend of old and new, the traditional and the radical welded in a sometimes brilliant, sometimes bleak, vision of what the West was, and is, and perhaps will be.

Biography

Not a corpse but an incarnation of possibilities was Abbey's first characterization of the western landscape. That did not occur until 1944. Born on 29 January

1927, he did not even see the West until seventeen years later, when he left his Pennsylvania home to hitchhike around the country before serving in the army. A 1970 essay reprinted later as the opening chapter of *The Journey Home*, "Hallelujah on the Bum," describes the three-month adventure in retrospect. For Abbey, the trip began a love affair with the West that has been crucial in both his intellectual and his literary development. His first sight of the Rockies, he wrote later, "struck a fundamental chord in my imagination that has sounded ever since"; his first view of the desert seemed "full of a powerful, mysterious promise." And seeing the silent emptiness, he felt for the first time that he "was getting close to the West of my deepest imaginings" (*Journey Home*, pp. 1-11). The source at once of early optimism and his later despair, the western landscape became the catalyst of his career.

After World War II he returned to New Mexico—to study philosophy at the University of New Mexico, to flirt with the boundaries of radicalism as editor of the student literary magazine, but most of all to explore the southwest desert country as intimately as possible. On occasion he ventured away from his now-adopted land, but the treks east frustrated him, and by the mid-1960s he settled "permanently" on a succession of western homesites. During those years, too, he worked as a part-time ranger and then as a fire lookout in a number of western parks and national monuments. Such random seasonal jobs, coupled with his personal explorations of the western scene and his observations of the people and places that he saw, provide the materials for most of what Abbey has written, fiction and nonfiction, both frivolous and serious. But no matter what the format, the author, as buzzard, wings above the landscape in predatory circles and strips naked those who would destroy its beauty.

Major Themes

Abbey's earlier books are less aggressive than his later writing has been. *Jonathan Troy* (1954), his flawed first novel of a painful Pennsylvania adolescence, hardly counts in any discussion of its author's career. Only its use of the West as metaphor—a place of possibilities—and of the West as literal fact—where the protagonist can physically escape—indicates that the book was written by the same young man who saw in the West "the land of his deepest imaginings." Otherwise the story is overly introspective; the characters, eccentric; and the prose, for the most part, dull. By contrast, Abbey's second novel, *The Brave Cowboy* (1956), finds the author firmly controlling his materials while writing from a carefully managed point of view. The buzzard, this time, has found his prey.

Both *The Brave Cowboy* and *Fire on the Mountain* (1962) show the individual pitting his wits and his energies against the establishment. Neither the cowboy nor John Vogelin of *Fire* succeeds, unless we consider their efforts pyrrhic victories in the sense that they have stirred our moral outrage, but their battles underscore Abbey's growing uneasiness with the forces of government and law.

Jack Burns, "the brave cowboy," tackles the county sheriff in a quixotic attempt to free a draft-resisting friend from jail. Vogelin fights a greater foe when he refuses to let the United States Air Force condemn his ranch for a guided-missile test site. Legally, of course, the two men are outlaws; spiritually, however, they are remnants of an older West, a time when individual freedom prevailed over the ostensible law of the land. Together they voice their author's frustrations in a West no longer expanded by possibilities but instead constricted by a closed frontier.

To picture better his view of the chameleon West, Abbey next changed his medium to the broader canvas of nonfiction. *Desert Solitaire* (1968), perhaps his best-known book, followed. Drawing from the designs of Henry David Thoreau and Joseph Wood Krutch, Abbey collapsed three years as a seasonal park ranger into one and mixed the pigments of Arches National Monument onto a fresco of desert color. The result blends his unique descriptive talents—"a kind of waking dream, gliding beneath the great curving cliffs with their tapestries of water stains, the golden alcoves, the hanging gardens, the seeps, the springs where no man will ever drink, the royal arches in high relief and the amphitheatres shaped like seashells" (*Desert Solitaire*, p. 187)—with his innate love for the landscape and his disgust at the changes modernity is making. We find him seeking intimate corners of the desert, now-forgotten bends of the Colorado, and still-to-be-discovered catacombs of the Maze. We hear him trying to define its essence, like modern music, "a-tonal, cruel, clear, inhuman, neither romantic nor classical, motionless and emotionless, at one and the same time—another paradox—both agonized and deeply still" (*Desert Solitaire*, p. 286). And we feel him repeat that deep agony as he speaks out against the rush of industrialized tourism, the onslaught of computerized technocracy, the endless building of voracious dam(n)s.

His next piece of nonfiction, *Appalachian Wilderness* (1970), looks back at the East he abandoned, lamenting the encroachment of man and his machines there, too. Nowhere is that intrusion so personally offensive to him, though, as in the West, where Abbey now focuses his journalistic and propagandizing talents. He wrote *Slickrock* (1971) for the Sierra Club as an overt argument for environmental protection. *Cactus Country* (1973), although more subtle because it was commissioned as a Time-Life publication, carries a similar banner. Both books examine the desert Southwest, the slickrock country of southeast Utah and the Sonoran Desert of southern Arizona respectively, to show the reader its beauty and to reveal its fragility. Neither volume possesses the literary merit of its predecessor, the more original *Desert Solitaire*, but these books together helped build Abbey's reputation as "a nature writer," "an environmentalist," even "an ecological anarchist," all inaccurate tags that he flatly dismisses. Rather, he mournfully insists, what he writes is "not a travel guide but an elegy. A memorial. You're holding a tombstone in your hand." And so the buzzard circles, ready to throw "a bloody rock. . .at something big and glassy" (*Desert Solitaire*, p. xii).

Meanwhile, in fictional form, the buzzard flies toward a partial feast on the body of man himself. *Black Sun* (1971), the least understood of Abbey's novels but surely the most introspective, focuses microscopically on a single individual, Will Gatlin. A middle-aged dropout who prefers life in a fire tower to mere existence as a college professor, Will finds and then loses an idyllic relationship with a woman half his age. The climactic scenes of the book come when he searches for her deep in a parched and burning Grand Canyon, an allegorical descent into hell itself, while vultures soar above. At the very least, *Black Sun* is a serious consideration of one man's agony of self; at most, it is a weighty examination of primordial relationships between human beings and, concomitantly, between man and his environment. Certainly the book asks more questions than it answers, but in so doing it opens those elemental issues of self about which Edward Abbey cares the most.

Impossible to categorize as man or author, he surprises us with his next novel, *The Monkey Wrench Gang* (1975). It pivots almost 180 degrees on an imaginary "scale of seriousness" and argues hilariously for an activist approach to ecological warfare. The band of anarchists four attacks heavy equipment, trains, bridges, any human construct that vilifies the land, in a vigilante campaign to preserve the sanctity of the southwestern desert. Outgunned and outmanned, they fight on with nonviolent violence, determined to carry their cause to a successful conclusion. Meanwhile, Abbey's playful imagination turns their deeds into a modest proposal of comic proportions. The result angers not a few readers but delights even more.

So, too, in his more recent nonfiction, has Abbey stirred lighthearted laughter into a negativistic brew that critiques modern man's impulse to destroy the land. Sometimes the irony works; sometimes it does not. Abbey speaks in *The Journey Home* (1977) with resignation, with dismay, with anger, with cynicism, all modulated by hyperbole and humor. Unable to stop "the rape of the West" with gang warfare, he tries to derail it with words, exposing the desecration of specific spots like Telluride, Colorado, and objecting more generally to civilization's propensity for choking the life force from freedom and wilderness. *Abbey's Road* (1979), a less effective although no less predatory sequel, continues the verbal onslaught with more somber specifics and glib generalities. For a new twist, Abbey transports himself to Australia and Mexico, where endangered open spaces remind him of the rapidly disappearing American West of a century ago, and then he returns to his own desert where he draws pointed comparisons. Reiterating the same cautions and concerns found in his other books, *Abbey's Road* is unfortunately repetitive and unnecessarily strident on some pages, although its prose still enchants on others.

By contrast, two other pieces of nonfiction written in the late 1970s sound like the Abbey of old, treating the desert wilderness in milder tones and with considerable affection. Designed as coffee-table embellishments, *The Hidden Canyon* (1978) with John Blaustein and *Desert Images* (1979) with David Muench are meant to emphasize the photographer's art rather than Abbey's. The prose in both books complements the camera work of the two collaborators while affirming Abbey's personal commitment to the hostile beauty of the desert Southwest.

For readers who relish pictorial make-believe, the books hold a special kind of magic.

Sadly, his latest piece of fiction prophesies the devastation of the land he loves. *Good News* (1980) postdates the holocaust, after the West has consumed itself. The time is the future; the place is Arizona; the dream is gone. Jack Burns, the brave cowboy come to life again, rides into the ashes of Phoenix on still another futile quest, searching for his long-lost son. Encountering only the failed— sadists, idealists, misfits—he and an Indian comrade blunder through episodes designed to reveal the paucities of the fallen world. The apocalyptic vision of *Good News* underscores Abbey's own horror at the directions in which modern America seems to be moving. Its naturalistic descriptions of the carrion West expose brutally the entrails of a putrefying civilization, one overly ripe for a buzzard's beak. Using his pen to tear into the body, as he has repeatedly done in his other prose, Abbey rips open the twentieth century's impending disintegration.

If we were to listen to Abbey talk about himself, though, we would hear a more benign literary buzzard. "I plan to return in future incarnations," he explains in *The Journey Home*'s introduction, "as a large and lazy soaring bird" (p. xii). Or so he says. But his prose belies his disclaimer, since it suggests instead a more activist animal, an "Agrarian Anarchist," to be specific. Such a creature chafes at the strictures of contemporary society, would overthrow most traces of technocracy if possible (except for the electricity that makes ice cubes), and might be happiest living a life of Emersonian self-reliance. Although he recognizes the difficulties inherent in going down this road, Abbey still seeks its route and destination. The characters in his books, both real and imagined, undertake his quest as idealistically as knights-errant of old, and about as effectively.

Both Jack Burns and John Vogelin tilt at the windmills of the law, but neither leaves so much as a footprint on the landscape. The loquacious ranger of "Arches Natural Moneymint" picks up the lance but, like the "ironical anarchist" of *The Brave Cowboy* who sees "clearly enough the utter hopelessness of the anarchistic ideal" (*Brave Cowboy*, p. 110), he changes nothing in the park service's promise to coddle overweight tourists in giant recreational vehicles. Gang warfare does not work for Abbey either. Although a few bridges totter, the detonations are more symbolic than significant. And while the angry narrator-persona of *The Journey Home* and *Abbey's Road* pursues similar quests too, he jousts only verbally, shaking a fist at the establishment rather than moving conglomerate mountains. Anyone who finds in Abbey's world a prescription for violence misreads his books completely. For the "ironical anarchist" as well as for his author, anarchy is a "metaphor" not a political description; it is "just a sentimentality," although one with a purpose (*Brave Cowboy*, p. 110).

Abbey intends, with his verbal fists, to shake his readers awake, to advocate such a metaphorical subversion to the system as might lead to a resuscitation of the American dream. At his best, he promises a better tomorrow if one only respects the land and acknowledges man's secondary relationship to it. The "agrarian" part of the "agrarian anarchist" says of himself, "He fell in love with the planet earth, but the affair was never consummated" (*Abbey's Road*, p. 184). Whenever Abbey writes of man touching the land and the landscape, he is trying fervently to reverse that epitaph. His later fiction does so directly. *Black Sun*'s protagonist experiences fully the possibilities of love in an intimate wilderness setting, and even though external forces prevent a permanent consummation, Will Gatlin's personal changes argue for the efficacy of the dream. The monkey wrench gang members come even closer to an agrarian serenity when they retire to rural Utah at the close of the novel. But they, like Sam and Dixie of *Good News* and like their author, recognize the futility in blocking out the rest of the world; the Enchanted Mesa will not suffice.

Perhaps this is why Abbey, in his nonfiction, so carefully integrates the agrarian ideal with his metaphorical anarchism. Episodes like *Desert Solitaire*'s two "Cowboys and Indians" chapters, *The Journey Home*'s aborted climb of Wilson Peak, and the exploration of Isla de la Sombra in *Abbey's Road* combine fears for the landscape's fragility with more positive assertions about the potential for happiness whenever and wherever one touches it. Transposing the literal twentieth-century West into a figurative one, Abbey creates an environmental hothouse for dreams. The power of his prose makes this possible. By internalizing the exterior world, he restructures a western landscape more vibrantly alive than most nature writers', more infinitely complex than most cowboy novelists'. In *Cactus Country* he acknowledges his goal:

What I hope to evoke through words here is the way things *feel* on stormy desert afternoons, the exact shade of color in shadows on the warm rock, the brightness of October, the rust and silence and echoes of human history along dusty desert roads, the fragrance of burning mesquite, and a few other simple, ordinary, inexplicable things like that. [P. 21]

This emphasis on "the way things feel" enables Abbey to put readers in touch with his environment and in contact with his dreams. So when he describes a hostile or indifferent desert universe, he captures its infinite perfectibility too:

Hills like melted elephants. Hills like crumbling castles. Buttes like skyscraper pipe organs. Cathedrals of stone, carved by wind and rain and frost and ice into an intricate tracery of lace and filigree, with gargoyles out of a gothic nightmare squatting on surreal pedestals of petrified mud. Moonlight scenes to horrify the innocent. Visions of eternity frozen in stone, hallucinations fixed in rock specters, enough to jolt the most hardened opium eater into permanent insanity—or back to earth. [*Desert Images*, p. 68]

And as he pulls us back to earth, he works to fuse the imagined West with the real one, to wed the old West with the new. Out of untold dichotomies he builds a composite, one first suggested to him by the desert in 1944 when he felt he "was getting close to the West of my deepest imaginings—the place where the tangible and the mythical become the same" (*Journey Home*, p. 5) and one repeatedly promised by subsequent views. Unlike pulp writers whose western landscapes form escapist backdrops and unlike environmentalists whose nonfiction reproduces the world exactly, Abbey takes the best from both. His visual and verbal sense of the land, outstanding among western writers, leads him beyond his peers. It enables him to redesign a modern-day American dream, one that can withstand the relentless onslaught of technocracy and the sad persistency of cynicism.

The essence of Abbey's dream is twofold, appearing throughout his writing under the rubric "Freedom and Wilderness, Wilderness and Freedom." In the introduction to *The Journey Home*, a book that includes the duo as a chapter title, he explains how he is attempting "to make sense of private experience by exploring the connections and contradictions among wildness and wilderness, community and anarchy; between civilization and human freedom" (p. xiv). A huge mouthful for a buzzard perhaps, but one essential for the writer-philosopher-agrarian-anarchist-dreamer to chew on. His novels, as well as his nonfiction, pit the individual versus the corporate West of the modern age, set against a backdrop of desert landscape and overlaid by a mist of imaginative idealism.

Beginning with the personal adventures of *Desert Solitaire* down canyon corners and river rapids and then continuing through each of the "personal histories" that follow, Abbey-as-narrator first advocates man's inherent need to discover himself in the wilderness. He creates his own persona to lead the expedition, a colorfully genial, egocentric soul, not a misanthrope but a hater of man-centeredness, not an anarchist but a hater of false constructs, a man who remains constant in his belief in personal freedom and his irritation at corporate constraints. "What good is a Bill of Rights," he asks, "that does not include the right to play, to wander, to explore, the right to stillness and solitude, to discovery and physical freedom" (*Abbey's Road*, p. 137)? His novels answer, "No good at all."

Individualism means freedom to Abbey, and we "cannot have freedom without wilderness" (*Journey Home*, p. 235), he insists. "No, wilderness is not a luxury but a necessity of the human spirit, and as vital to our lives as water and good bread. A civilization which destroys what little remains of the wild, the spare, the original, is cutting itself off from its origins and betraying the principle of civilization itself" (*Desert Solitaire*, p. 192). To build something like the Glen Canyon Dam—Abbey's giant symbol of governmental shortsightedness and corporate greed—is to tear down a greater edifice. So his books are consistent arguments against that betrayal of what is wild and free and for an expression of loyalty to the land. In an effort to isolate society's corruptive instincts and to distinguish between those ills and a higher good, he juxtaposes civilization against culture. "Civilization," he writes, "is the vital force in human history; culture is that inert mass of institutions and organizations which accumulate around and tend to drag down the advance of life" (*Desert Solitaire*, p. 276). Abbey's nemesis, the Glen Canyon Dam, exemplifies the difference between the two. "Civilization is the wild river," he affirms. "Culture, 592,000 tons of cement" (*Desert Solitaire*, p. 277). The goal of his writing is to explode that cement verbally and to erect in its place a freeform superstructure of possibilities.

His nonfiction books plant those charges that metaphorically dynamite the failures of the twentieth century. *Desert Solitaire* attacks the government's need to tame the wilderness, while *The Journey Home* and *Abbey's Road* demolish any remaining belief that a wilderness can exist much longer without the strongest protection. *Slickrock* and *Cactus Country*, too, elevate the fragile beauty of the desert and undermine corporate needs that would maim it for profit. His novels, on the other hand, set off individual detonations under the massive body of technocracy, imaginatively specifying courses of action that jolt and jar. In them, Abbey suggests not so much a brand of "agrarian anarchism" as a breed of "nihilistic libertarianism," seeking true liberation through the destruction of a ponderous system that has betrayed itself. Paradoxically, he couches his nihilism in idealistic phrases, so that his promise of a better dream than the American one that has failed becomes the most attractive aspect of his writing. To be sure, Abbey's dream never quite succeeds either, but he keeps going after it in true knight-errant fashion. And a host of readers ride at his side.

Survey of Criticism

It would be a mistake to interpret Abbey's books as rehashes of the escapist-fiction formula or even as inversions of the ever-popular pulp Western. Although his novels bear elements of both—a distant and magical setting, a lonely individual who pits himself against insurmountable odds, damsels (or ranches or landscapes) in distress, villainous machinations that must be overcome—the key to interpreting those novels lies in an understanding of his nonfiction. Abbey's world comes in two shapes and sizes; his readers must consider them complementary, since to understand either is to understand both.

Neal E. Lambert's Introduction to the Zia paperback edition of *The Brave Cowboy* best acknowledges this inseparability. Integrating lines from *Desert Solitaire* with his interpretation of Jack Burns's quixotic quest, Lambert necessarily advances one's appreciation for both books. Equally as provocative are William T. Pilkington's two essays, "Edward Abbey: Southwestern Anarchist" (1966) and "Edward Abbey: Western Philosopher, or How to Be a 'Happy Hopi Hippie' " (1974). The former exuberantly attacks Abbey's early books, while the latter tempers the youthful criticism with a strong argument for the growing sacrality of Abbey's prose.

The only extended study is Garth McCann's *Edward Abbey* (1977). A solid overview, it sidesteps critical controversy while providing generally thoughtful comments about Abbey's world. The most tantalizing, however, are the rhetorical ones.

To be avoided are the countless "popular" reviews that have accompanied Abbey's book-length publications. Too many of these ill-conceived snippets reveal extraordinary gaps of understanding, dubbing Abbey a "nature writer" while chastising him for anarchist leanings not compatible with the reviewers' political biases. (A pleasing exception is Edwin Teale's "Making the Wild Scene"

[1968].) Also to be avoided are partial critiques found in books devoted to other literary figures or subjects. Often these one-liners, too specialized to merit citations in the accompanying bibliography, are products of haste rather than of thoughtful consideration.

Little solid academic criticism exists to counteract the excessive popularization of Abbey's prose. A victim of the times, perhaps, he has fallen prey to reviewers' talons that cannot handle the complexities of the bird they hold. To combat their flights of fancy, more probing essays like Lambert's and Pilkington's need to be written. Abbey's irony, his anarchism, his political and philosophical points of view, and more about his rhetoric, need to be examined by appreciative but thoughtful readers, although Abbey himself would scoff at the exercise. Indeed, his Introduction to *Desert Solitaire* disdainfully prays that "serious critics, serious librarians, serious associate professors of English will if they read this work dislike it intensely" (p. x), but of course he is speaking more as the "lazy soaring bird" than as the predatory buzzard who flaps his wings in order to be heard. Useful, too, would be more detailed studies of the individual books created by this winged westerner, for none of them has been meaningfully isolated.

Most significant would be a critical attempt to consider Edward Abbey in the context of other western writers. Because of his occasional frivolity and his reputation as an eccentric curmudgeon, because of his miscast role as an environmental activist or "pop" philosopher rather than as a serious analyst of the desert scene, and because of his dogged unwillingness to adopt the "frontier mentality" as an acceptable way of looking at the West, Abbey too often is relegated to the wrong stack of authors. As profoundly committed to the land as John Wesley Powell or Joseph Wood Krutch but as imaginative as the most fanciful novelist, Abbey shapes his writing so that his books restructure the reality he sees. Whether he wears an idealist's garb or an anarchist's, or whether he cloaks himself in both disguises at once, he communicates to his readers not only a prophecy of the wilderness's doom but a happier perception of possibilities for its salvation. In so doing, this "philosophical vulture on indolent wings" (*Good News*, p. 60) sees salvation for us all, a new American dream of freedom on the land.

Bibliography

All citations in the text refer to the paperback edition, listed second, whenever one is available.

Works by Edward Abbey

Jonathan Troy. New York: Dodd, Mead, 1954.

The Brave Cowboy: An Old Tale in a New Time. New York: Dodd, Mead, 1956; Albuquerque: University of New Mexico Press, 1977.

Fire on the Mountain. New York: Dial Press, 1962; Albuquerque: University of New Mexico Press, 1978.

Desert Solitaire: A Season in the Wilderness. New York: Simon and Schuster, 1968; New York: Ballantine Books, 1971.

and Eliot Porter. *Appalachian Wilderness: The Great Smoky Mountains*. New York: E. P. Dutton, 1970.

Black Sun. New York: Simon and Schuster, 1971.

and Philip Hyde. *Slickrock: Endangered Canyons of the Southwest*. New York: Sierra Club/Charles Scribners' Sons, 1971.

Cactus Country. New York: Time-Life Books, 1973.

The Monkey Wrench Gang. Philadelphia: Lippincott, 1975; New York: Avon, 1976.

The Journey Home. New York: E. P. Dutton, 1977.

with John Blaustein. Introduction by Martin Litton. *The Hidden Canyon: A River Journey*. New York: Viking Press, 1977.

Abbey's Road. New York: E. P. Dutton, 1979.

and David Muench. *Desert Images*. New York: Chanticleer Press, 1979.

Good News. New York: E. P. Dutton, 1980.

Studies of Edward Abbey

Abbey, Edward. "From the Lookout [Flights of Reincarnation]." *Outside* 13 (November-December 1978): 18-24.

————. "On Nature, the Modern Temper, and the Southwest: An Interview with Joseph Wood Krutch." *Sage* 2 (Spring 1968): 13-21.

Erisman, Fred. "A Variant Text of *The Monkey Wrench Gang*." *Western American Literature* 14 (Fall 1979): 227-28.

Haslam, Gerald. Introduction to *Fire on the Mountain*, by Edward Abbey. Albuquerque: University of New Mexico Press, 1978.

Lambert, Neal E. Introduction to *The Brave Cowboy*, by Edward Abbey. Albuquerque: University of New Mexico Press, 1977.

McCann, Garth. *Edward Abbey*. WWS. Boise: Boise State University, 1977.

Pilkington, William T. "Edward Abbey: Southwestern Anarchist." *Western Review* 3 (Winter 1966): 58-62.

————. "Edward Abbey: Western Philosopher, or How to Be a 'Happy Hopi Hippie.' " *Western American Literature* 9 (May 1974): 17-31.

Ruess, Everett. *On Desert Trails*. El Centro, Calif.: Desert Magazine Press, 1940.

Standiford, Les. "Desert Places: An Exchange with Edward Abbey." *Western Humanities Review* 24 (Autumn 1970): 395-98.

Teale, Edwin W. "Making the Wild Scene." *New York Times Book Review*, 28 January 1968, p. 7.

Wylder, Delbert E. "Edward Abbey and the 'Power Elite.' " *Western Review* 6 (Winter 1969): 18-22.

Don Graham

ANDY ADAMS
(1859-1935)

Biography

Born in Indiana on 3 May 1859, Andy Adams came to Texas in the 1880s where he worked on ranches, participated in numerous horse drives (but only one cattle drive), and generally lived the life of a cowman. He listened to the talk of cowboys and cattlemen; he absorbed the images and rituals of the open-range cattle industry during its heyday. In 1891, with the cattle kingdom on the wane, Adams moved to Colorado, where gold had been discovered at Cripple Creek. Making his home in Colorado Springs, he dabbled in mining ventures and ran unsuccessfully for county sheriff. Then in 1898, he saw Charles Hoyt's play *A Texas Steer*, and, appalled at the drama's "ludicrous and false" absurdities, he resolved to write the truth about western life. So Adams launched into a new career, and from then until his death in 1935 he pursued "the writing game" (Hudson, *Life and Writings*, pp. 51, 190). His first efforts were short stories. After placing a couple in national magazines, he was approached about a book. The result, in 1903, was *The Log of a Cowboy*, universally esteemed as a classic of its kind and thought by major authorities on the West, such as Walter Prescott Webb, Charles M. Russell, and J. Frank Dobie, to be the best book ever written on cowboy life.

Unfortunately, Adams never again matched the accomplishment of his first book, though he kept doggedly at the job of writing for the next thirty-odd years. In 1904 he published *A Texas Matchmaker*, a novel that tried to merge the themes of courtship and ranch life. The next year, 1905, saw the publication of another trail-drive novel, *The Outlet*; the following year, a collection of short stories, *Cattle Brands*; then, in 1907, a novel disguised as autobiography, *Reed Anthony, Cowman*. This succession of five books in as many years represented the best writing Adams was to produce, and the rate of his publication in the years to follow fell off sharply. A boys' book about cowboys and ranching appeared in 1911, *Wells Brothers: The Young Cattle Kings*, but its sequel, *The Ranch on the Beaver: A Sequel to Wells Brothers: The Young Cattle Kings* did not appear until 1927. Two books edited by biographer Wilson M. Hudson were published posthumously: *Why the Chisholm Trail Forks and Other Tales of the Cattle Country* (1956) and *The Corporal Segundo* (1968), one of the numerous plays that Adams was unable to get produced or published during his lifetime. Although Adams never published anything that did not treat the cattle industry, he tried to write about two other western subjects that he felt had not been truthfully explored: mining and the new oil industry. Such efforts survive, along with other unpublished cow country narratives, among Adams's manuscripts.

Of Adams's life outside his twin vocations of cattleman and author, there is not a great deal to be said. A bachelor, he appears to have been a man thoroughly comfortable with the terms of existence. The self-portrait of himself as a cowboy that he recalled a year before his death on 26 September 1935 seems to be accurate: "a good horseman always, a favorite with my employees, and a hail fellow with my vagabond cronies" ("Autobiographical Sketch," p. 4). Adams may be thought of as much like the persona of his cowboy narrator in *The Log of a Cowboy*: sunny in temperament, dutiful, honest, hard working, pragmatic, humorous.

Major Themes

As an author without a deep fund of personal experience to draw upon and with little education, Adams faced a literary problem that proved insolvable. After *The Log of a Cowboy*, Adams did not want merely to repeat himself. The problem was how to write about what he knew best without duplicating *Log*. His third novel, *The Outlet*, best illustrates the difficulties. It attempts to exploit the same materials that proved so successful in *Log* but with a telling difference. In *Log* Adams relied upon natural obstacles—arid terrain, river crossings, storms, stampedes—to provide impediments to the successful conclusion of the cattle drive. All are overcome, though not without human loss. *Log* is a magnificently matter-of-fact account of group man contending against and triumphing over the forces of nature to carry out a meaningful piece of work. But in *The Outlet* Adams turned from nature to human obstacles. This novel is filled beyond credibility with schemes, plots, and economic conspiracies to thwart the honest plans of Lovell, Flood, and Tom Quirk, all major characters first introduced in *Log*. But Lovell is craftier than any renegade cattle syndicate and hatches elaborate counterschemes involving disguises and deceptive stratagems to move not one but three herds to market. Such invention kills the reader's interest, which is whetted only in those sections where the book replicates the natural obstacles present in the first novel.

Adams's two other book-length attempts to deal with the cattle industry (discounting the two juvenile novels, which add nothing to the canon) are more interesting than *The Outlet*. The second of these, *Reed Anthony, Cowman*, portrays the managerial or capitalistic side of the cattle business. Cowboys were day laborers, no matter how much they might have enjoyed the vigorous life of the trail. But the men who owned the cattle and hired the cowboys were capitalists, and Reed Anthony is Adams's most sustained look at such a figure. Couched as autobiography, *Reed Anthony* gets bogged down in economic details and suffers, as do all of Adams's less satisfying works, from a lack of omission, a lack of shaping design. With greater conciseness and narrative focus, *Reed Anthony* could have been one of Adams's best books.

Reminiscent of the life of Charles B. Goodnight, the legendary Texas Panhandle rancher and empire builder, *Reed Anthony* recounts how a young man, hard working, intelligent, and resourceful, rises from a cowboy to become a large landowner and dealer in cattle. Reed Anthony makes and loses several small fortunes but eventually achieves his patriarchal ambition. Yet the novel lacks any dramatic buildup; it is a success story without a climax. It also contains almost no character depth; in fact Adams intentionally makes his hero's private life sublimely happy, surrounding him with a wife and numerous children but leaving them entirely in the background. Cows and deals are all that interest him, and these are not enough to sustain a novel, even if it is called an autobiography.

A Texas Matchmaker, Adams's second book, is also second in interest. Here Adams took the narrator of *Log* back to his pre-trail-driving days and placed the action on a large ranch in south Texas, in the Nueces country. About half of the novel deals with cowboys and ranching materials, about half with courtship and social sorties that would not have embarrassed Sir Walter Scott. There is, for example, an account of a chivalric tournament, and there are hunts aplenty, not to mention numerous social gatherings where young folk meet to engage in courtship rituals. Presiding over the festivities is Uncle Lance Lovelace, a large ranch owner who in his ripened years devotes himself almost inordinately to overseeing the romances of his young attendants. One of the curious sidelights of the novel is the dismay Uncle Lance experiences over the failure of the Anglo-Saxon population to marry well and populate the good earth. By comparison the Mexican population gratifies him with its vital institution of matrimony and bountiful reproduction. Another interesting perspective is the sense of elegiac loss that permeates the novel; old Lance, who helped settle the country, avidly continues to purchase land whenever he can in order to forestall the encroachment of new settlers. The pastoral atmosphere of the trail that Adams captured in *Log* is here transferred to a setting even more pastoral in effect; though there is plenty of work in this novel, there is also a vast sense of time's expansiveness, of seasonal rhythms and social harmonies that remind one of eighteenth- and nineteenth-century English novels. Also surprising, given one's genre expectations concerning how courtship novels end, is the conclusion Adams provides. The young hero, guided by the old patriarch, fails utterly; he does not marry the girl of his dreams. Instead she marries a no-account sharpster, and the hero, after engaging the husband in a gunfight, is wounded and forced to flee the wonderful country. *A Texas Matchmaker* remains an interesting novel despite the usual problems of unity and focus. Temporarily ignoring the fallacy of imitative form, one can find in its meandering structure a sense of a vanished era of amplitude and country pleasures.

Adams's short stories exhibit the same tendencies toward loose structure and episodic effect that weaken everything but *Log*. This is not to say that his short stories are without interest. *Cattle Brands* is an agreeable collection, much better, say, than any collection of Adams's contemporary, Alfred Henry Lewis. Certainly Adams is much superior to Lewis in creating believable dialogue. Adams's cowboys sound convincing, their remarks laced with homely ranching metaphors and colloquial turns of phrase. Often Adams lets his cowboys tell entire stories, which he called campfire tales and which, taken individually, represent some of Adams's best writing. But as narratives set within the larger structure of a short story, the campfire stories often seem disruptive. "At Comanche Ford," a story or sketch in *Cattle Brands*, illustrates the problem. The story begins with a chase; a detachment of Texas Rangers is sent to apprehend a stolen herd of cattle being moved across the border into Mexico. The Rangers ride a great distance, then camp at a lovely water hole. Before turning in for the night, two Rangers tell campfire stories. The frame story then resumes and ends without the Rangers catching the thieves. Realistic? Probably. Interesting or artistic? No. Such a story is either an aimless sketch or an unrealized piece of fiction. But *Cattle Brands* also contains stories such as "The History of a Poker Steer," which show what Adams could do when he let his imagination have a freer rein. The story is a biography of a steer from birth on a south Texas ranch to a cattle drive to death on an Indian reservation. Although somewhat too anthropomorphically conceived, the steer's tale has more imaginative force than many of the tales that seem to have come from actual experience or true stories heard by Adams. The short stories aside, Adams's campfire tales, which appear in all his books, represent, along with *Log*, his primary contribution to the literature of the American West.

Although Adams began his literary career in opposition to palpable lies about the West, he soon found himself in competition with formulaic fiction. During his writing career he saw the rise and immense popularity of such Western romancers as Owen Wister, Zane Grey, and Emerson Hough, the latter a friend of Adams. Indeed, Hough gave Adams literary advice on how to enhance his stories' marketability. Under Hough's influence Adams created a woman character to accompany the men in another trail-drive novel, "Army Beef," but unlike Hough's popular *North of 36*, Adams's novel was not accepted for publication. From the viewpoint of popular success, Adams had a fatal tendency to ignore or subvert formulaic requirements. Thus in "Army Beef" the young woman masquerades as a male, thus losing any sentimental benefit of having a female on the trip in the first place; in *A Texas Matchmaker* the young hero is thwarted in his attempts to marry the woman he loves; and in stories like "At Comanche Ford" Adams almost perversely avoids the staple requirements of formula fiction—successful chase, shoot-out, defeat of villains.

Striving always to write fiction "as convincingly as fact," Adams held to a literary doctrine that stressed authenticity, simplicity, and honesty. This is a good enough credo, provided it is enlivened by imagination. Certainly Adams did not shrink from using invention to aid the facts, as Wilson M. Hudson has amply demonstrated. Indeed, his finest book, *Log*, is made up; Adams himself never went on a trail drive such as the one he describes. Yet most early readers, and many latter-day ones, have had no doubts that in *Log* they were in the presence of the real thing. Adams's notion of authenticity committed him as a writer to a special vision of experience. "Fiction must be a reflex of life, hence the homely setting, the fire on the hearth, the cattle in the fields, after which human imagination peoples it with men and women who are fictional, but are a mirrored reflection of those we know in the flesh" (Hudson, *Life and Writings*, p. 107). Such an aesthetic actually leads to something rather different from realism—a species of pastoral, an idealization of rural or cowboy life. The essential dialectic of pastoralism informs Adams's work; in *Log*, for example, towns are exciting but diabolical places where the innocent camaraderie of cowboy life on the open range is threatened by such complexities as gamblers, sharpsters, and women. The only good life is that of the open range, where there is world enough and time for simple work, good stories told around the campfire, trust among fellow cowboys, and the beneficial tending of the beasts of the field.

Survey of Criticism

During his lifetime Adams was fortunate in having his work acclaimed by both the famous and the soon to be famous. In 1903, for example, Emerson Hough said of *Log*: "Andy Adams is the real thing, and the first time the real thing has appeared in print" (Hudson, *Life and Writings*, p. 67). By the 1920s when J. Frank Dobie began to correspond with Adams, all of Adams's works were out of print. Dobie, a tireless champion of southwestern range literature, wrote a major essay on Adams for the *Southwest Review* in 1926, wherein, after judiciously appraising Adams's canon, he proclaimed *Log* to be the "best book that has ever been written of cowboy life, and the best book that ever can be written on cowboy life" ("Andy Adams, Cowboy Chronicler," p. 93). Walter Prescott Webb shared Dobie's enthusiasm, and together they spread the word at every opportunity.

As heir to the Dobie-Webb legacy, Wilson M. Hudson consolidated their work on Adams and produced a carefully researched critical biography, *Andy Adams, His Life and Writings*, in 1964. In 1967 followed his pamphlet *Andy Adams* for the Southwest Writers Series, essentially a distillation of the longer book. Hudson remains the leading Adams scholar. His biography contains ample material regarding Adams's life, the sources of his works, his literary notions, and critical estimations of his work. Still, Hudson must be seen as operating within the circle of the Dobie-Webb view of Adams, which is essentially celebratory. Their valuation of Adams is founded upon their belief in his absolute fidelity to life (though Hudson, of course, is fully aware of Adams's reliance upon invention). For them, Adams is valuable because he shied away from formula Westerns and because he expressed himself in supple, Bunyanesque English prose. Like Dobie,

Hudson says of *Log*, "It is the best piece of fiction that has been or can be written on the subject" (*Storyteller*, p. 30). But Hudson also rates the campfire stories very high. His fullest critical response to these may be found in his introduction to *Why the Chisholm Trail Forks and Other Campfire Stories* (1956).

Critical response to Adams's work is largely confined to *Log* and divides into two distinct categories. The first, and certainly the majority opinion, follows the tradition of acclaim fostered by Dobie, Webb, and Hudson. Dayle H. Molen, for example, in a comprehensive but unoriginal overview of Adams's life and writings, "Andy Adams" (1969), praises *Log* as "the finest volume written about the old cattle trail days," citing in particular Adams's refusal to sensationalize the West with shoot-outs and other familiar devices of pulp Westerns (p. 25). A more useful look at *Log* may be found in " 'Sailors' and 'Cowboys' Folklore in Two Popular Classics" (1965), Jan Harold Brunvand's discussion of Adams's work in relation to an earlier American classic, Charles Henry Dana's *Two Years Before the Mast*. Often cited as strikingly similar books, here the two are definitively compared. Brunvand finds many correspondences, including narrative reliance upon oral style and proverbial language, attitudes toward nature, and similar experiences relating to work, dangers, and male camaraderie.

One of the few articles not centered on *Log* is Levette J. Davidson's descriptive survey, "The Unpublished Manuscripts of Andy Adams" (1951), of the contents of stories and novels left among Adams's unpublished papers. Davidson's summary of Adams's shortcomings stands as a representative statement that would not be seriously challenged by Adams's most ardent fans:

He was unable to contrive an original plot, he did not understand feminine character, he rarely penetrated below the surface in depicting motivation and emotion, and he lacked interest in all philosophy (except rules for material success in life and a simple code for ethical behavior in personal relationships). ["The Unpublished Manuscripts of Andy Adams," p. 107]

It should not be overlooked, however, that Davidson also declares *Log* to be the "best book yet written about the West's most popular folk character" (p. 107).

Three critical articles on Adams take a revisionist tack. One of the most interesting is by Benjamin Capps, himself a distinguished southwestern novelist of the present day. Capps, in "A Critical Look at a Classic Western Novel" (1964), seeks to redefine *Log* as nonfiction rather than fiction. Judged as a novel, *Log* has too many weaknesses, Capps asserts; it lacks character depth and contains an episodic structure unrelated to character change or growth. The year Capps published his essay, he also published a fine cattle-drive novel of his own, *The Trail to Ogallala* (1964). Thus his essay must be seen in the light of a novelist's reexploring the terrain of a classic predecessor. Perhaps the best overall critique of Adams's work is Barbara Quissell's study of what she terms Adams's "restricted realism." In "Andy Adams and the Real West" (1972), Quissell examines the attempts Adams made after *Log* to come to terms with popular formulas of the period, including Wisterian romance in *A Texas Match-maker* and Jack London-type naturalism in an unpublished story, "Nature in the Raw." But Quissell's major point is her perception that *Log*, so often praised for its prosaic, unvarnished realism, should really be seen as a version of American pastoral. She states, "All the specific and vivid facts of the cattle drive days meet the literary not historical demands because they provide the illusion that life in the West was once meaningful, free, exciting and uncomplicated." ("Andy Adams and the Real West," p. 219). Her conclusion is also worth quoting: "The 'real West' that Adams recorded in *The Log of a Cowboy* is an ideal life, a golden age" (p. 219).

The most recent critical commentary on Adams extends the revisionist view by comparing Adams's accomplishment with that of Benjamin Capps's *The Trail to Ogallala*. Don Graham, in "Old and New Cowboy Classics" (1980), takes issue with the claim of Dobie and others that *Log* is the definitive trail-drive novel. By pointing to fictionalized elements, the dominant pastoral mood, and certain previously unnoted Wild West flourishes in *Log*, Graham directs attention to issues different from that of authenticity. Finally, Graham argues that *Trail* is a superior novel because of three qualities: authenticity as convincing as that achieved in *Log*, a deeper historical perspective, and the interrelation of motivation, incident, and character development in the narrative movement.

It is unlikely that future consideration of Adams will alter the status of his best book as a classic of its kind or produce a revival of interest in his other works. There is need, however, for more literary analyses of the art of *Log of a Cowboy* and fewer repetitive assertions of its validity as a historical document.

Bibliography

Works by Andy Adams

The Log of a Cowboy: A Narrative of the Old Trail Drives. Boston: Houghton Mifflin, 1903.

A Texas Matchmaker. Boston: Houghton Mifflin, 1904.

The Outlet. Boston: Houghton Mifflin, 1905.

Cattle Brands: A Collection of Western Camp-Fire Stories. Boston: Houghton Mifflin, 1906.

Reed Anthony, Cowman: An Autobiography. Boston: Houghton Mifflin, 1907.

Wells Brothers: The Young Cattle Kings. Boston: Houghton Mifflin, 1911.

"Western Interpreters." *Southwest Review* 10 (October 1924): 70-74.

The Ranch on the Beaver: A Sequel to Wells Brothers: The Young Cattle Kings. Boston: Houghton Mifflin, 1927.

"Autobiographical Sketch of Andy Adams." In *The Junior Book of Authors*. Ed. Stanley J. Kunitz and Howard Haycraft. New York: H. W. Wilson, 1935, pp. 3-4.

"The Cattle on a Thousand Hills." *Colorado Magazine* 15 (September 1938): 168-80.

Why the Chisholm Trail Forks and Other Tales of the Cattle Country. Ed. Wilson M. Hudson. Austin: University of Texas Press, 1956.

The Corporal Segundo. Ed. Wilson M. Hudson. Austin: Encino Press, 1968.

Studies of Andy Adams

Brunvand, Jan H. " 'Sailors' and 'Cowboys' Folklore in Two Popular Classics." *Southern Folklore Quarterly* 29 (December 1965): 266-83.

Capps, Benjamin. "A Critical Look at a Classic Western Novel." *Roundup* 12 (June 1964): 2, 4.

Davidson, Levette J. "The Unpublished Manuscripts of Andy Adams." *Colorado Magazine* 28 (April 1951): 97-107.

Dobie, J. Frank. "Andy Adams, Cowboy Chronicler." *Southwest Review* 11 (January 1926): 92-101.

Graham, Don. "Old and New Cowboy Classics." *Southwest Review* 65 (Summer 1980): 293-303.

Hudson, Wilson M. *Andy Adams, His Life and Writings*. Dallas: Southern Methodist University Press, 1964.

————. *Andy Adams, Storyteller and Novelist of the Great Plains*. SWS. Austin: Steck-Vaughn Company, 1967.

Molen, Dayle H. "Andy Adams: Classic Novelist of the Western Cattle Drive." *Montana* 19 (January 1969): 24-35.

Quissell, Barbara. "Andy Adams and the Real West." *Western American Literature* 7 (Fall 1972): 211-19.

T. M. Pearce

MARY HUNTER AUSTIN
(1868-1934)

When Mary Hunter Austin was writing her autobiography, *Earth Horizon* (1932), she returned to her birthplace in Carlinville, Illinois, where she found many changes in both the community and in Blackburn College, from which she had graduated in 1888. For a major study, she had chosen the sciences instead of literature because, as she stated, "English I can study by myself; for science I have to have laboratories and a teacher" (*Earth Horizon*, p. 167).

With almost petty faultfinding, Austin complained that the new buildings at Blackburn failed to preserve the trophies and memorials she recalled from her student days. She was also displeased that tenants in the house where she had been born had remodeled the interior by joining rooms and then altered the exterior by adding a second porch. These details are of interest because they point to Mary Austin as a conservative, holding to a past that was familiar and to a tradition with values that should be retained. Her mind treasured experiences from her childhood, and her autobiography records them in vivid details.

Biography

Mary's father, George Hunter, came to Illinois from Yorkshire, England, in 1852. He was eighteen years old and traveled in the company of his brother William who was several years older. They joined cousins in a group of English settlers at Alton, forty miles southwest of Carlinville. This was the year that the railroad completed its line from St. Louis, and Hunter was among the first passengers to arrive in Carlinville. He acquired legal training, as was customary, by reading law in the office of an established barrister, who also held a commission in the 122d Illinois Regiment of the Union Army. Hunter was admitted to the bar in 1858 and opened his office on the second floor of a building owned by a druggist, Milo Graham, whose daughter, Susanna, George courted and married in August 1861, several months after he had enlisted in the Seventh Illinois Volunteers. Hunter was promoted to the rank of captain, but malarial fever prevented him from field activity, and after three years in the legal branch of the army, he returned to Carlinville shortly after the war ended.

Mary Hunter was born 9 September 1868 in the house her father built on First South Street not far from the drugstore belonging to her grandfather. She had an older brother, James, who was born in 1866; and a second brother, George, was born eight years later. When Mary was four years old, her father moved to a farm located at the edge of town. He hoped to have a garden there and to raise cattle. A hillside nearby was a wonderland where children could pick hazelnuts and wade in a creek that drained the bottom land. Young people could find crayfish in its muddy banks and hide in brush heaps near Indian mounds, which stirred their fancy about earlier times.

Mary Hunter recalls especially a morning when she was six or seven years old. She walked in the sunshine on a spring day to stand under a giant walnut tree that seemed to extend into an infinite sky. Bees were in the wildflowers, and a gentle wind rippled the grass. In a child's world of wonder, she recalled the name she often heard in her Sunday school class. It was *God*, and it came to her in a moment of soundless thought. In later life, Mary Austin found various ways to describe this concept, calling it "the spirit in the fields" or the "communion of the stars." She became a naturist, as her books of both fiction and nonfiction confirm.

In the autobiography, Austin tells of social and cultural groups in her home community, such as the Literary Circle, the Debating Society, the Temperance Union, and other organizations in churches and schools in Carlinville. Spelling bees, candy pulls, picnics, and sleigh rides provided pleasure that youth desires. On the restrictive side were taboos against social dancing and frivolity in dress or deportment.

Captain Hunter's library was a day-by-day learning experience for his daughter. From the earliest period of her recollection, Mary tells of watching her father write speeches that he read at the Horticultural Society or at the grange. Books surrounded her in this library, and just gazing at their leather bindings with tracings of titles in gold gave her an impression of a world where she planned to live and find work. She wrote that her father was a "bookish" man and had first editions of the English and American classics on his shelves. When she asked him one time if he would leave her his books when he died, he inquired, "What would you do with them?" and she replied, "I would sell them and live on the money until I could write a book my own self" (*Earth Horizon*, pp. 70-71).

Mary's father died before she entered high school. Her mother sold the farm to move closer to Blackburn College where she could prepare meals for students attending the school and thus increase income from Captain Hunter's military pension. Mary's brother James received his diploma from Blackburn in 1886 and then taught in a country school for two years before an event occurred that was to change the destiny of the Hunter family. Letters from cousins in California came to Susanna, James, and Mary urging them to apply as homesteaders upon public lands in the San Joaquin Valley northwest of Bakersfield. In the summer of 1888, the family sold their Carlinville property and left for San Francisco en route to Los Angeles where they planned to fulfill the obligations to settle claims by living on the land. Mary, eager to make good her promise to "write a book about my own self," composed an account of the trip to their homesteads. She sent it to the *Blackburnian*, the college literary magazine, and it appeared in January 1889. The title was *One Hundred Miles on Horseback*. A reprint was published by Dawson's Book Shop, Los Angeles, in 1963.

Writing in the first person, Mary states that her family, with the exception of George, set out from Pasadena with a saddle horse and a white-topped "prairie schooner" pulled by two horses. Eight days later, the Hunters rode through Tejon Pass into the valley where their land was to be claimed. Susanna's quarter-section had a one-room cabin on it, with calico curtains and bunks along the wall. There was also a cabin on the claim held by James, which he shared with his younger brother, George, when he joined them. In the months ahead, Jim Hunter tried to cultivate some of the sandy soil but found it hospitable only to salt weed, sagebrush, and bunch grass. After six months, Susanna Hunter purchased a small farm with irrigated land near the stage line where it cut through the pass, and Mary obtained work teaching school in a community called Mountain View Dairy. Jim Hunter had to remain on the claim. At the end of the required period, homesteading became a memory for them all.

Mary Hunter became increasingly independent of her family. When her mother bought a vineyard near Bakersfield and moved there with Jim and George, Mary knew that her life was her own. She lived with a family whose children were among those she taught in the classroom, and she traveled in a cart around the country to instruct the children of other families. Among her acquaintances was another schoolteacher, who was the owner of a small vineyard. His name was Stafford Wallace Austin, and in the communities near Bakersfield he was addressed as the "Professor" because of his career as an educator. Austin came from a prominent Hawaiian missionary family that had contributed leaders in educational and political fields. He and his brother Frank came to the mainland when Frank represented the sugar plantation owners in Hawaii. He was also associated with an irrigation company located in San Francisco. Wallace at a later date sought employment with this company. However, at the time he met Mary Austin, he was a farmer as well as a schoolteacher. Their mutual interest in books, learning, and teaching brought them together. On 19 March 1891, they were married at Susanna's home, three miles from Bakersfield. Friends from Bakersfield hired a stagecoach with four horses to pull it and drove out on a moonlit night to fill the Hunter house and porch for the wedding.

Wallace and Mary went to San Francisco the following year so that Wallace could complete plans for work with the irrigation company north of Bakersfield. On this trip, Mary became acquainted with Ina Coolbrith, a poet and head of the City Library in Oakland, who knew many of the writers in San Francisco. Among them was Bret Harte, the earliest editor of the *Overland Monthly*, the magazine that accepted Mary Austin's first short story. Titled "The Mother of Felipe," it appeared in the November 1892 issue. The story was republished fifty-eight years later by the Book Club of California.

Publication and recognition underlay the spiritual and intellectual conflicts in

Mary Austin's life. She was obsessed with her search for literary fame, and although she loved her husband and bore a child, she discovered that both were a handicap to the time she needed to achieve her goal as a writer. The child, Ruth, born 30 October 1892, was mentally deficient. She needed nursing care, provided in private families and mental institutions until her death at the age of twenty-five. The project in which Wallace had been employed was abandoned, and he returned to the schoolroom, later becoming superintendent of schools at Lone Pine, California.

During this period, Mary Austin went to Los Angeles where she met Charles F. Lummis, city editor of the *Los Angeles Times*, who knew many of the important figures in the literary and educational community. Mary taught in the Los Angeles Normal School during 1899, and in the following year she went to Independence, California, where her husband had been appointed registrar of the Land Office. They built a house there in 1900, which, in *The Land of Little Rain* (1903), she refers to as "the little brown house under the willow tree at the end of the village street" and where she invites the reader to knock if he wants "news of the land." On 13 June 1954, this house was designated California Historical Landmark No. 229.

With the publication of this first book, Mary Austin became nationally known as a writer exploring a world hitherto largely untouched: the mesas, water trails, mining camps, pasture lands, desert spaces, Indian reservations, Spanish villages, the homes of prospectors, sheepherders, stagecoach drivers, basket weavers, faro dealers, barkeepers, priests, and missionaries in the open scenario of a vast part of the western United States. As her writing career developed, Mary Austin wrote fiction, criticism, poetry, and plays, but her early story sketches of the western land and its people remain her unique achievement.

In 1904, Austin visited the Monterey peninsula and found that artists and writers were building homes in this picturesque spot. She sold the Independence house and the following year built a forest lodge at Carmel-by-the-Sea, where she celebrated the success of her first novel, *Isidro*, in 1905 and a study of the California grazing country, *The Flock* (1906). With the royalties from these publications, she planned her first trip to Europe, which lasted from December 1907 until September 1910. She traveled first in Italy, where she collected material for the book *Christ in Italy*, which was not published until 1912. When she arrived in London, she was welcomed by the Herbert Hoovers, friends from California, who drove her to the country to greet Joseph Conrad and his wife. She met H. G. Wells and presented him with a copy of her new book, *Lost Borders* (1909). The friendship with Wells was a lasting one, although she disagreed with the freedom expressed in his novels toward extramarital sex and joined with critics who found him active in this respect himself.

While in England, Austin's allegorical novel, *Outland* (1910), was brought out by an English publisher. She used the pseudonym "Gordon Stairs" because the characters were fictional portrayals of well-known figures in the Carmel colony. The book was not published in the United States until nine years later. Mary

Austin returned to New York City when plans were announced for the production of her play, *The Arrow Maker*. The play opened at the New Theater on 27
February 1911 to unfavorable reviews, and the play closed after a few performances. Austin called the period between 1912 and 1924 an "interregnum" in her
life. Her husband divorced her at San Bernardino, California, on 9 November
1915, giving abandonment in defense of his action. Nevertheless, the Austins
exchanged letters until Wallace died on 13 September 1931. In his late years he
was a retired sales agent for the American Potash Chemical Company in Los
Angeles.

Mary Austin retained her house in Carmel, but during the interregnum she
speaks of, she lived in places as widely separated in New York City as the
Washington Irving House on Riverside Drive and 10 Barrow Street in Greenwich
Village, where in 1921 she was a neighbor of Willa Cather, who was then living
at 5 Bank Street. During the summer of this year, Mary traveled to England,
where she entertained the Fabian Society of Socialists by writing a satiric play,
Femina, poking fun at the "American Court of Domestic Relations." She states
that she took the leading part in the play and that G. B. Shaw was among the
actors in the cast.

In New York City, Mary often stayed at the National Arts Club in Gramercy
Park, where on 8 January 1922 she was honored by a large gathering of friends
and acquaintances that included the editors of many of the leading magazines and
publishing houses. She was active in a number of the city organizations, including the Mayor's Committee for National Defense during the war years from 1914
until 1917. She supervised the collecting of food reclaimable at markets and then
had it prepared at community kitchens in City College buildings on Twenty-third
Street. She lectured on women's rights before the New York Legislative League
and participated in the Woman Suffrage Association at 505 Fifth Avenue.

Mary Austin's explanation for her failure to adjust to the environment of New
York City is discussed in book 5 of *Earth Horizon* (1932). She reports that,
for her, New York lacked freshness, air, and light. She was accustomed to
searching for patterns in human activity because she believed that there was a
pattern in her own life. Convinced that there was an overall design in the growth
of individuals and groups, she found New York too complex. In the country west
of the Alleghenies, she could find an order she understood. Therefore, her next
and final move was to the southwestern United States, an area where human
history could be observed in archeological, village, and urban terms. She could
study the overlay of contemporary culture upon strata of aboriginal, European,
and Anglo-American development.

As early as 1918, Austin had visited in Santa Fe, New Mexico, where her
friend, Frederick Webb Hodge, historian and archeologist who directed the
Southwest Museum in Los Angeles, suggested that she would find the Indians of
Arizona and New Mexico interesting for study and investigation. From the time
that Mary Austin established her home in Santa Fe, she became a leader in the
"Colony" group of painters, musicians, and writers with studios and homes

along a street called El Camino del Monte Sol, or "the Road of the Sun Mountain." Mary was active in the organizations that worked to keep Santa Fe in the distinctive Spanish colonial tradition of architecture. Among her allies in promoting the contribution of Indians in American culture was Mabel Dodge Luhan, a friend from Mary's New York days. Luhan had moved to Taos in 1918, and there she entertained well-known creative people in art, theater, and publication. Mary met the D. H. Lawrences there in one of the periods they lived in Taos between 1922 and 1925. Lawrence left an unfinished manuscript for a play, "Altitude," which was edited, illustrated, and reprinted in a Taos, New Mexico, magazine, *Laughing Horse* (Summer 1938), with permission from Frieda Lawrence and the Viking Press. Mary Austin is introduced in the cast of characters as "a Woman with Ideas, who can also cook."

Austin expressed challenging ideas in the books she wrote in the last ten years of her life in Santa Fe. *The American Rhythm* (1923, 1930) dealt with the poetry of Indians as their epic, religious, and personal expressions were translated and reexpressed in English verse. *Everyman's Genius* (1923, 1925) introduced a novel view of unusual talents. *Experiences Facing Death* (1931) revealed the author's attitude toward pain and suffering. *Starry Adventure* (1931) was a novel in which love sought fulfillment. *Can Prayer Be Answered?* (1934) approached the subject through avenues in both Christian and non-Christian faiths. *Earth Horizon* (1932) was considered a notable addition to the bookshelf of auto-biographies in American literature.

Mary Austin appeared on the day before her death to read at the Poets' Roundup, an occasion when various local and visiting poets read their verses at a fund-raising benefit for the Indian Arts Fund. At this time, 9 August 1934, she read from her book of verses for and about young people, *The Children Sing in the Far West* (1928). The following day she died at her home on the Camino del Monte Sol. The funeral, held there on 14 August 1934, consisted of the ritual of prayers read by an Episcopalian minister, supplemented by several of her poems that were read by local poets who knew her well.

Following the funeral, Austin's casket was placed in a private vault at the Santa Fe Cemetery. More than two years later, the trustees of her estate ordered cremation with provision to inter the ashes in a rocky cairn on the summit of Mount Picacho, a massive pyramid several miles to the east of her home. The grave site is unmarked, but the rocky crypt is on the tip of a peak visible from her home and in view of a city she loved.

Major Themes

Austin's short stories appeared in magazines of both national and regional circulation. These pieces were assembled and reprinted in *The Basket Woman* (1904, 1910), *Lost Borders* (1909, 1910), *The Trail Book* (1918), and *One Smoke Stories* (1934). From each group can be selected reports and revelations of character that are masterful. Among the longer narratives, Austin's novel *Isidro* deals with a controversy between officials of the Mexican government and the Franciscan religious organization in mid-nineteenth-century California. The principal figure, Isidro Escobar, must choose either to manage his father's sheep ranch or to enter the priesthood. Murder, mystery, and intrigue are woven into his decision. Central to the plot is a young shepherd named El Zarzo, "the barb," who is a young woman disguised as a boy. The climax occurs when a giant forest fire destroys not only woodland but also Isidro's rival for the hand of the shepherdess in marriage. Austin's superb gift for description makes this novel one of her most effective achievements.

Austin's second novel, *Santa Lucia* (1908), concerned a fictional college where a new assistant professor of biology, Dr. Antrim Stairs, produces elements of discord and romance. The context is well documented, but no outstanding figure emerges in the unhappy developments. *Outland* is a curious novel because it portrays people in the Carmel colony who are identified as creative outlanders living near a group of free spirits, called woodlanders, who believe in communal living. Poet George Sterling, novelist Jack London, and journalist Lincoln Steffens are woodlanders (under other names) who take part in the search for the King's Treasure, or materialism in this world, which is buried and then lost after it is found.

Mary Austin's fourth novel, and perhaps her most widely read work of fiction, appeared two years later: *A Woman of Genius* (1912). The leading character, Olivia May Lattimore, is an ambitious but frustrated actress, who fights to succeed professionally against masculine attitudes toward career women. She surmounts all obstacles with courage and the help of a mystical outer force of power, which at times descends upon her with brightness and a singing sound. *A Woman of Genius* was dedicated to Lou Henry Hoover, and one critic has suggested that the portrait of Helmett Garrett, the engineer in the book, is drawn from the business career of Lou Henry's husband, Herbert Clark Hoover.

The Lovely Lady (1913), Austin's fifth novel, is disappointing because it seems to have been written to a formula, such as "How to Succeed as a Writer of Popular Fiction." The hero of the book, Peter Weatheral, rises from his position as a clerk in a department store to become partner in a real estate firm, but failing to climb the social ladder, he travels abroad and meets the daughter of former neighbors, recovering his self-esteem through a happy marriage.

The Ford (1917), Austin's sixth long narrative, was revised and completed while she was still commuting between Carmel and New York City. Its background involved the water situation in southern California, where the Austins lived during the early years of their marriage. "Tierra Longa" in the novel was a fictional name for the Owens Valley, which provided water for the Los Angeles aqueduct to irrigate the San Bernardino agricultural land. Central characters in the novel oppose the U.S. Reclamation Services, real estate agents, and political powers in the battle for land that controlled water. However, Austin changes the locale of the struggle from the area north of Los Angeles to a terrain east of San Francisco. *The Ford* is successful in characterization and narrative flow.

The title of Austin's next novel, *No. 26 Jayne Street* (1920), makes use of the name of a street as a clue to the nature of the plot. "Jayne," or "Jane," Street is a center for feminist groups. The household here, led by Neith Schyler, an aristocratic and socially prominent woman, enlists the support of Adam Frear, a progressive reformer whose surname signals him as a "freer" of human rights. The climax occurs when Neith becomes engaged to Adam and discovers that he previously had promised to marry a schoolteacher whom he met on a lecture tour. Neith decides that Adam has failed the test of integrity. His attitude of social reform is empty when interpreted in personal terms.

No. 26 Jayne Street was not a commercial success, and Austin did not write another novel for ten years. When she did, *Starry Adventure* (1931) became a summary of her life as a thinker and creative writer. At one time she had chosen to call the story "Love Is Not Enough," and central to the solution of this theme are four young people who overcome obstacles, including religion, social values, and sex as motivation, and finally reach the conclusion that despite conflicts their lives are starry adventures in a larger cosmos governing humanity. Austin was ill during the period in which she wrote this book, and errors in Spanish plus digressions into Indian, Spanish, and Anglo-American folklore interrupt the story line. Nevertheless, the book is remarkable in scope and coverage, as it illustrates the statement on the final page of her autobiography, "I have seen America emerging: the America which is the expression of the life activities of the environment, aesthetics as a natural mode of expression" (*Earth Horizon*, p. 368).

Survey of Criticism

In 1934, two years after Austin's death, the second volume of the California Literary Monograph Series, *Mary Austin*, was prepared by Joseph Baer, as a research project offering documentation about the author's life, with critical opinion and bibliography concerning her achievement. In the same year, Elizabeth Shepley Sergeant, who knew Austin well, published a tribute, "Mary Austin: A Portrait" (1934). Sergeant spoke of her friend as perhaps the most monumental of American women writers and one who embodied the pioneer tradition in her life and authorship.

William Allen White, the Kansas journalist and novelist, took his wife in 1931 to visit Austin in Santa Fe. He reports in *The Autobiography* (1946) that the Whites loved her and "took her to their hearts," but he adds that she had a "tough-fibred mind" and was a "strong, over-bearing woman" (pp. 370-71). He thought *A Woman of Genius* was a great American novel.

Van Wyck Brooks, in *The Confident Years, 1885-1915* (1952), states that Austin had transferred her knowledge of the Southwest through the magic of her pen. In *The Liberation of American Literature* (1932), V. F. Calverton calls attention to Austin's ability to describe Indian and Hispanic folk life, as well as Anglo-American regional folkways. Somewhat earlier, John C. Farrar, editor of the *Bookman* magazine, published *The Literary Spotlight* (1924), a book that contains evaluations of authors written by anonymous critics. The critic who wrote about Mary Austin stated that she belonged in the company of great minds but lacked one essential ingredient, the comic sense. For her, life was consistently serious, a view that robbed some of her novels of sustained interest.

Grant M. Overton, writing of Austin in *The Women Who Make Our Novels* (1928), calls her author, scholar, publicist, and citizen, contributing to all of the things that interested her. Carl Van Doren, in *Many Minds* (1924), describes her as a prophet and a mystic, who lived her life as close to the groundswell of the nation as she could get. Van Doren's essay was reprinted in *Mary Austin, A Memorial*, published by the Laboratory of Anthropology, Santa Fe, in September 1944. Fourteen other testimonials also appear in the volume.

Dudley Wynn's comprehensive survey of Austin's life and work is his dissertation, "A Critical Study of the Writings of Mary Hunter Austin," (1941). He stresses her place as a naturist who combines scientific and rational thought. Helen Addison Howard in *American Indian Poetry* (1979) presents Austin as one of the most eloquent interpreters of Indian songs, indigenous lyrics, and ritual chants. A tribute based upon friendship and literary inquiry appears in T. M. Pearce's *The Beloved House* (1940). He also contributed *Mary Austin* to the Twayne United States Authors Series in 1965 and edited *Literary America, 1903-1934, The Mary Austin Letters* (1979), which collects Austin's correspondence with seventy writers in her circle of friends and acquaintances.

Bibliography

Works by Mary Austin

The Land of Little Rain. Boston and New York: Houghton Mifflin, 1903; Albuquerque: University of New Mexico Press, 1974.

The Basket Woman: A Book of Fanciful Tales for Children. Boston: Houghton Mifflin, 1904.

Isidro. Boston: Houghton Mifflin, 1905.

The Flock. Boston: Houghton Mifflin, 1906.

Santa Lucia: A Common Story. New York: Harper and Brothers, 1908.

Lost Borders. New York and London: Harper and Brothers, 1909.

Outland (under the pseudonym Gordon Stairs). London: John Murray, 1910.

The Arrow Maker: A Play. New York: Duffield, 1911; rev. ed., Boston: Houghton Mifflin, 1915.

A Woman of Genius. Garden City. N.Y.: Doubleday Page, 1912; Boston: Houghton Mifflin, 1917.

Christ in Italy. New York: Duffield, 1912.

The Lovely Lady. Garden City: Doubleday, Page, 1913.

The Man Jesus. New York and London: Harper and Brothers, 1915; reprinted as *A Small Town Man*, 1925.

The Ford. Boston: Houghton, Mifflin, 1917.

The Trail Book. Boston: Houghton Mifflin, 1918.

No. 26 Jayne Street. Boston: Houghton Mifflin, 1920.

The American Rhythm: Studies and Re-expressions of American Songs. New York: Harcourt Brace, 1923.

Everyman's Genius. Indianapolis: Bobbs-Merrill, 1923.

The Land of Journeys' Ending. New York and London: Century, 1924.

The Children Sing in the Far West. Boston: Houghton Mifflin, 1928.

Experiences Facing Death. Indianapolis: Bobbs-Merrill, 1931.

Starry Adventure. Boston: Houghton Mifflin, 1931.

Earth Horizon: An Autobiography. Boston: Houghton Mifflin, 1932.

Can Prayer Be Answered? New York: Farrar and Rinehart, 1934.

One Smoke Stories. Boston: Houghton Mifflin, 1934.

One Hundred Miles on Horseback. Los Angeles: Dawson's Book Shop, 1963.

Studies of Mary Austin

Baer, Joseph. "Mary Austin." *Bibliography and Biographical Data.* Berkeley: California Literary Research, 1934.

Brooks, Van Wyck. *The Confident Years: 1885-1915.* New York: E. P. Dutton, 1952.

———. *From the Shadow of the Mountain, My Post-Meridian Years.* New York: E. P. Dutton, 1961.

Calverton, V. F. *The Liberation of American Literature.* New York: Scribner's and Sons, 1932.

Farrar, J. C. *The Literary Spotlight.* New York: George H. Doran, 1924.

Howard, Helen Addison. *American Indian Poetry.* Boston: Twayne, 1979.

Keiser, Albert. *The Indian in American Literature.* New York: Oxford University Press, 1933.

Kunitz, Stanley J. *Living Authors.* New York: H. W. Wilson, 1931.

Mary Austin, A Memorial. Ed. Willard Hoagland. Santa Fe, N. Mex.: Laboratory of Anthropology, 1944.

Overton, Grant M. *The Women Who Make Our Novels.* New York: Dodd, Mead, 1928.

Pattee, Fred L. *The New American Literature, 1890-1930.* New York: Century, 1930.

Pearce, T. M. *The Beloved House.* Caldwell, Idaho: Caxton Printers, 1940.

———. *Literary America, 1903-1934, The Mary Austin Letters.* Westport, Conn.: Greenwood Press, 1979.

———. *Mary Austin.* New York: Twayne, 1965.

Sergeant, Elizabeth Shepley. "Mary Austin: A Portrait," *Saturday Review of Literature,* 8 September 1934, p. 96.

Smith, Henry. "The Feel of the Purposeful Earth." *New Mexico Quarterly* 1 (February 1931): 17-33.

Tracy, H. C. *American Naturists.* New York: E. P. Dutton, 1930.

Van Doren, Carl. *Contemporary American Novelists.* New York: Macmillan, 1922, 1931.

———. *Many Minds.* New York: Knopf, 1924.

Wagenknecht, Edward. "Mary Austin, Sybil." In *Cavalcade of the American Novel.* New York: Henry Holt, 1952.

White, W. A. *The Autobiography.* New York: Macmillan, 1946.

———. "Women of Genius." *Saturday Review of Literature,* 12 November 1932, pp. 235-36.

Wynn, Dudley. "A Critical Study of the Writings of Mary Hunter Austin." Ph.D. disser-
    tation, New York University, 1941.
————. "Mary Austin, Woman Alone." *Virginia Quarterly Review* 13 (April 1937):
    243-56.

MAX BRAND (Frederick Faust)
(1892-1944)

"The emotion of art is impersonal," T. S. Eliot wrote in "Tradition and the Individual Talent." In no case does this statement apply so precisely (and with such irony) as it does in that of Max Brand. Brand, the King of the Pulps, an author of great familiarity to readers of popular fiction between the two world wars and one of distinct visibility even in the 1970s and 1980s, was in fact an entirely impersonal fiction himself. His existence began not as the result of human birth but of disguise. On 23 June 1917, in *All-Story Magazine*, Max Brand came to life as the first, and eventually the most famous, pseudonym of Frederick Schiller Faust.

Between 1917 and 1936 Faust used at least seventeen other pseudonyms, but "Max Brand" was his most prolific. It was also the one that stuck, the name that is invariably associated with Faust, the outward sign of a mass-cultural phenomenon in which the identity of an actual writer was not merely hidden but virtually obliterated by his pseudonym. The title of Faust's biography, written by his son-in-law, Robert Easton, is *Max Brand: The Big "Westerner"* (1970); selections of nonpseudonymous writing by Faust were published in 1957 as *The Notebooks and Poems of "Max Brand"*; Darrell C. Richardson's compendium of biographical and bibliographical information about Faust, including a careful accounting of all his pseudonyms, is entitled simply *Max Brand: The Man and His Work* (1952).

Although Faust presented Max Brand as the author of many kinds of pulp writing—including detective stories, historical adventures, the Dr. Kildare novels, even poems—the pseudonym took particular hold on the title pages of Westerns. Of the more than 350 book-length Westerns (serials and single-issue novels and novelettes) that Faust published in magazines—almost exclusively "pulps" rather than "slicks"—between 1918 and 1938, more than half appeared under the Max Brand pseudonym. Many published first under other names, especially that of George Owen Baxter, appeared during Faust's lifetime as Max Brand books. Since Faust's death in 1944, virtually all of his paperback Westerns have appeared as Max Brand novels.

Max Brand, then, represents not so much a simple pseudonym as it does that part of Frederick Faust that led to the production of hundreds of popular Westerns. Furthermore, it seems logical to refer to any of Faust's Westerns as a Max Brand Western, even if it has not yet appeared in print under the Brand pseudonym.

Frederick Faust was a consummate pulp writer. He wrote in a dozen genres under twenty names. His total published production, almost all of which was written between 1917 and 1938, totals more than 600 items, more than 400 of which are novels or novelettes. In some years he published nearly 2 million words; each word earned him between three and ten cents. He saw his pulp writing primarily in such terms—as a means to an end, a way of supporting his style of life. When the decline of the pulp market in the mid-1930s forced him to write with more sophistication for slick magazines, Faust found writing less enjoyable. In view of the nature of his pulp work, with Faust spinning out commercial fantasies with nearly unconscious ease, seldom writing with conscious thematic commitment or personal involvement, taking pride mainly in the accumulation of words and dollars, the facts of his life and personality might well seem irrelevant to understanding his contributions to popular Western fiction. But the "impersonal" works of Max Brand take on their greatest significance when they are seen not only as matters of formula and popular culture but also as reflections and even extensions of a remarkable American life.

Biography

Faust's life was extraordinary, perhaps even Faustian. His ambitions for material success and, ironically, for literary achievement of a much higher order than that of the pulps matched his physical size (he was six feet four) and his exuberant personality. Born in Seattle in 1892, orphaned by the time he was thirteen, Faust endured a youth of constant movement and hard physical labor, especially on farms in California's San Joaquin Valley. "He became filled with bitter hatreds, powerful resentments, giant ambitions," Robert Easton notes in his biography (*Max Brand*, p. 7), and sought both refuge and expression in literature. By working full time he managed to attend the University of California where he achieved fame as a drinker, a fighter, and a writer. His satiric attacks on university policies, especially in the student newspaper and the literary magazine, so infuriated the president of the university that Faust was denied his degree in 1915. He left Berkeley, started for India, worked briefly as a journalist in Honolulu, went to Canada at the outset of the war to enlist in the Canadian Army, deserted his American battalion when red tape prevented him from getting to Europe, and in 1916 found himself in New York City. Forced by poverty to seek employment where he could find it, he became a writer for Frank A. Munsey's pulp magazines, though he yearned for fame as a poet. His interest in poetry never died (he published two volumes of poetry in his own name, *The Village Street* in 1922 and *Dionysus in Hades* in 1931), but neither did it ever flourish. Poetic aspirations fell victim to his incredible ability—and willingness—to provide entertainment for the readers of *Argosy*, *Adventure*, *Double Detective*, *Dime Western*, *Star Western*, *Western Story*, and at least two dozen other pulp magazines.

In 1917 Faust married Dorothy Schillig, whom he had left in California two years before. In 1918 he enlisted in the American army, only to be prevented from infantry service first by influenza and then the armistice. He used his time instead to write his first Western, *The Untamed* (1919), and to establish Max Brand as a regular contributor to the pulps. Faust's entrance into the Western genre was motivated partly by his awareness of Zane Grey's popularity and, conceivably, by his own unfulfilled needs for action and adventure. In the West itself he took little personal interest. The West was "disgusting," he once wrote (*Notebooks and Poems*, p. 24), alluding to the frustrations and bitter memories of his youth. In 1919, when his publisher insisted that he soak up local color on a Texas ranch, Faust found cowboy life dirty and unappealing to the point where he spent much of the trip reading Sophocles in an El Paso hotel room. But he had no trouble exploiting the Old West in his stories. The availability of Street and Smith's *Western Story Magazine* after 1919 as a primary outlet for Max Brand Westerns was certainly a greater influence on Faust than any personal contact with or feeling about the actual American West.

The money that Max Brand and Faust's other "writers" earned made it possible for him to indulge in his appreciation of Europe and its culture. From 1926 to 1937, while he and his family lived lavishly in a rented villa in Florence, Faust collected art and books, wrote traditional poetry with great care and slowness (even using a quill pen), and typed out pulp stories with amazing speed (up to fifty pages a day). All the while he suffered from a fibrillating heart, a condition he felt was treated best by increased activity. The nature of that activity, and a firsthand glimpse of the personality that created Max Brand, can be seen in "Destry and Dionysus," a 1955 *Atlantic Monthly* article by Martha Bacon, the daughter of one of Faust's closest friends in Florence:

He lives like a medieval prince in his Florentine villa. His swimming pool and tennis court are the envy of the petty aristocracy for miles around. He runs a pack of Newfoundlands and keeps the stars in sight with a telescope on his terrace. He has a weak heart which threatens momentarily to kill him; and against the advice of a battery of doctors he puts the heart in its place by drinking deep, smoking like Vesuvius, playing tennis like a champion, driving an Isotta Fraschini a hundred kilometers an hour through the Rhone valley, and keeping a work schedule that would murder a stevedore. . . . And the novels are stacked like cordwood in the offices of Brandt & Brandt. He writes them faster than they can be printed. Faust is a one-man factory. [Pp. 73-74]

Faust's pulp writing declined after the mid-1930s, largely because of the effect that the depression had on magazines of that kind. He began thereafter to write for *Esquire*, *Collier's*, *Cosmopolitan*, *Saturday Evening Post*, and *Harper's*, often using his own name. In 1938 he moved to Hollywood where he began to write for MGM; Aldous Huxley, his personal friend, and F. Scott Fitzgerald were fellow MGM writers. Faust's greatest successes in Hollywood were the film adaptations of *Destry Rides Again* and his Dr. Kildare novels. His own screenwriting was not notably successful. Although his efforts at slick and even high-brow stories (in *Harper's*) were more fruitful, he drank heavily in Hollywood and grew increasingly uneasy about his career and his personal life.

In 1944 the man who had written hundreds of adventure stories out of his imagination became eager to write a firsthand account of American soldiers in combat. After an extended effort he managed to be assigned as a correspondent to the Eighty-eighth Infantry Division in Italy. There, not far from his beloved Florence, in middle age and with a bad heart, Faust found himself on the front lines. On 11 May 1944, he was wounded in the chest by a shell fragment. In his last words, and in a manner entirely appropriate for a Max Brand hero, he insisted that he was not in pain and that the army medics should take care of others first. He was almost fifty-two when he died.

Major Themes

By the time that Max Brand became a Western writer in 1918 (when *The Untamed* began appearing in *All-Story Weekly*) the Western was firmly entrenched as a genre of popular American writing. Owen Wister's *The Virginian* (1902) had demonstrated the wide appeal of the cowboy story, which before that time had been restricted mainly to dime novels intended for juvenile readers. Following Wister, B. M. Bower, Clarence Mulford, William MacLeod Raine, Charles Alden Seltzer, and—the most popular of all—Zane Grey established the Western as a medium of cultural mythology.

When Frederick Faust began writing *The Untamed*, he knew that he was writing for an established market. Logically, he would have modeled his Westerns closely on those that had proved successful. Although both Faust and his editor were aware of Zane Grey, in particular, and although the works of Max Brand share obvious qualities with other Westerns, the usual results were horse operas of another color.

The uniqueness of Max Brand lies in the absence of any serious pretensions to dealing with the actual West. Owen Wister wrote about a Wyoming that he had visited frequently for fifteen years, and Zane Grey wrote romantically about the western geography to which he was emotionally attached. Even Clarence Mulford, who wrote stories about Hopalong Cassidy from the safety of Brooklyn, did extensive research on western topography. In Max Brand, however, the setting is rarely an identifiable place in the West, plots almost never are based on historical events, and the trappings of the Western (for example: costume, architecture, and means of violence) are handled with considerable latitude.

There are hundreds of Max Brand Westerns, so any attempt to discuss them must fall seriously short of comprehensiveness. The problem of how to approach such a body of work is compounded by the fact that Max Brand never repeated himself. His novels are formulaic, to be sure. They emphasize action over contemplation; the hero, like those in most other Westerns, has a streak of wildness in him or in his past; description of settings, especially landscape, unlike most other Westerns, is severely restricted; and quite frequently the story contains or suggests elements from other literary genres—heroes and plots drawn from classical and northern European mythology and legend, gothic settings and devices, mysteries and urban characters more suitable for detective stories than Westerns. Action, which motivates the plot and permeates Brand's style, is the most ubiquitous quality. "Action, action, action, is the thing" Frederick Faust once said (*Notebooks and Poems*, p. 39). Formula, however, never served as much of an impediment to Max Brand's pulp imagination or kept Brand from coloring his stories with off-trail qualities.

A number of Max Brand novels are mentioned in the following paragraphs. For the sake of discussion, many of them could be replaced by others with no real loss of content or context. Even so, most have thematic importance; together they illustrate a wide range of achievement. All are pulp Westerns that were first published in magazines; the dates cited are those of first magazine appearance.

The Untamed was the first Max Brand Western. An unearthly hero who combines innocence and violence in equal proportions and a plot that develops out of a quest for revenge are its main features. Dan Barry, several times referred to as "Pan of the Desert," is an orphan of mysterious origin who becomes the adopted son of Joe Cumberland, a rancher in a region identified only as the "mountain-desert." Barry's natural innocence is reflected in his strange companionship with animals, particularly with a wolf named Black Bart and a horse named Satan, and in his equally strange whistling. According to Joe Cumberland, when he first discovered Dan Barry as a boy apparently following the flight of wild geese across his ranch, it was "a funny, wild sort of whistlin' that didn't have any tune to it that I recognized. It gave me a queer feelin'. It made me think of fairy stories—an' things like that!" (Pocket Books ed., pp. 8-9). "Whistlin' Dan," as he becomes known, shows an almost unperturbable, nonchalant personality until he is struck one day by Jim Silent, the leader of an outlaw gang. Having tasted his own blood, Dan Barry is overwhelmed by an instinctual desire for revenge. An unhuman yellow light begins to glow in his eyes, and he vows to kill Jim Silent. "That's the only way that I can forget the taste of my own blood," he explains (p. 44). His quest for revenge conflicts with his love for Kate Cumberland, the rancher's daughter with whom he has grown up. The plot climaxes when Barry kills Silent—not in a classic gunfighter showdown (although Whistlin' Dan possesses superhuman speed and accuracy with a six-gun) but by choking Silent with his hands. This act of violence stands in contrast to Dan Barry's physical characteristics; he is small, slim, even feminine in stature. At the end of the novel, just when the reader expects Barry to settle down and marry Kate Cumberland, he hears the call of wild geese and leaves the ranch following their sound. He is still untamed. "You've lost him, Kate," says Joe Cumberland (p. 186). The last paragraph of the novel reinforces the strange, mythological qualities of Max Brand's first Western hero:

Far off, above the rushing of the wind, they heard the weird whistling, a thrilling and unearthly music. It was sad with the beauty of the night. It was joyous with the exultation of the wind. It might have been the voice of some god who rode the northern storm south, south after the wild geese, south with the untamed. [P. 186]

The Untamed contains several features that may be taken as Max Brand hallmarks. Allusions to European mythology are an obvious one, as is the hero who acts instinctively and individualistically rather than contemplatively or for the sake of society. A western landscape of nonspecific denomination and a plot based on pursuit and discovery are also standard features. Although some stories marry off the hero at the end, the role of the woman in *The Untamed* is typical of Max Brand: to illuminate a sensitive side of the hero but not to consummate a union with him and thus add connotations of stability and generation to his character.

Dan Barry must have had a particular fascination for Frederick Faust, for two other novels continue his story and continue to emphasize his unearthly traits. At one point in *The Night Horseman* (1920), Barry is identified as a werewolf, at another as a wolf. Throughout the novel he is torn between his allegiance to Kate Cumberland (he has returned to the ranch) and the atavistic call of the wild that he hears. He spends most of his time roaming the landscape at night with his black horse and his wolf-dog. At the end of the novel, on an appropriately dark and stormy night, he forces Kate Cumberland, who both fears and loves him, to leave the ranch (and her dying father) with him. In *The Seventh Man* (1921) Dan Barry and Kate are married and living in a wilderness cabin with their daughter, Joan (whose later story is the subject of *Dan Barry's Daughter* [1923]). This apparently settled life is disrupted when a horse (not Satan) that Barry is riding is killed. Driven by his old rage, the yellow once again flaming in his eyes, he seeks revenge against the seven men responsible for shooting the horse; he kills six of them. But Dan Barry's untamed wildness finally triumphs over him. The seventh man (of the title) becomes Barry himself, shot to death by his wife in a strangely powerful and ironic moment of love and understanding.

In *Trailin'* (1919), the second published Western by Max Brand, the use of material from other literary sources is clear. Written at a time when Faust was reading Sophocles, *Trailin'* presents a character who, like Oedipus, comes into conflict with a man who turns out to be his father. Unlike Sophocles, however, Brand pulls strings at the last moment and identities are revealed. In this novel the West serves mainly as the setting of events in the father's early life and as a place to which the son, who begins as a rich and somewhat spoiled young man in New York City, must go in order to solve a murder. The hero, Anthony Bard, shows far less inner wildness than Dan Barry and thus demonstrates Max Brand's emphasis on action rather than characterization.

Brand often uses restraint to depict violence, especially after the Dan Barry novels. Blood that is shed is usually not the hero's doing. In *Singing Guns* (1928), for instance, the hero Rhiannon (the name comes from Celtic mythology) fires only two shots in the entire story, only one of which does any injury to another person. No shots at all are fired in *The Garden of Eden* (1922). Anthony Bard of *Trailin'* fails to kill anyone even though he almost guns down his father. The appeal of Max Brand has always lain in matters of plot, suspense, and style rather than in a vicarious interest in violence.

Max Brand set few limits on the kinds of furnishings appropriate for the pulp West that he created. One of the main characters of *The Garden of Eden* is a racetrack tout from the East; the novel also features a mysterious feudal estate staffed by black servants and governed by a man who claims to talk directly to God. *Border Guns* (1928) deals with powerful automobiles, border police, smuggling, and a castle-like house complete with secret passageways and mistaken identities. *Silvertip's Roundup* (1933) uses as its main character an eastern safe-cracker, a yegg complete with all the tools of his trade, who is eventually converted to decency by contact with Jim Silver, the hero of twelve other Silvertip novels, all published in 1933 and 1934.

The appearance of elements not naturally associated with the Western reflects Frederick Faust's understandably enormous need for fictional materials. (In 1932, for instance, Faust published something in every issue of the weekly *Western Story Magazine*.) Such elements also suggest a kind of narrative facetiousness that sets Brand apart from writers like Zane Grey and Louis L'Amour. In *The Streak* (1936), in fact, where an easy-going cowpuncher (whose ineptitude with a six-shooter is so dangerous to himself that he packs it around empty) gains a flagrantly undeserved reputation as a gunfighter, the novel seems like a spoof, even an anti-Western at times.

Yet Max Brand delivers serious messages on occasion. This fact may account for the importance and visibility of *Destry Rides Again* (1930), where the Max Brand revenge motif is oddly twisted at the end of the story. Harry Destry, stalking the twelve hypocritical members of a jury (of his peers) who sent him to prison, suddenly realizes the real meaning of the word *peer:*

Equal. For all men were equal. Not as he blindly had taken the word in the courtroom, with wrath and with contempt. Not equal in strength of hand, in talent, in craft, in speed of foot or in leap of mind, but equal in mystery, in the identity of the race which breathes through all men, out of the soil, and out of the heavens. [Gregg Press ed., p. 268]

Serious thematic implications are also found in some of Brand's stories about Indian-white conflict, one of the oldest subjects in American literature. The best of these stories are three novels—*War Party* (1934), *Frontier Feud* (1935), and *Cheyenne Gold* (1935)—in which the hero is a white boy kidnapped and reared by Cheyennes. Although these novels qualify easily as pulp literature because of their stereotyping and their emphasis on revenge, action, and mystery, they fail to resolve the dilemma of the central character, Red Hawk, who is drawn equally toward white and Indian cultures. Moreover, since the Red Hawk novels deal explicitly with white greed and duplicity, they provide suggestions, if not the substance, of social criticism. In places, much the same is true of *The White Cheyenne* (1926), although the novel ends much less ambivalently than does the final Red Hawk story.

As might be expected of writing designed to appeal to masses of readers during the Great Depression, many Max Brand novels in the 1930s show an awareness of social problems. In fact, in the last series of Westerns that Faust wrote, the Montana Kid novels published under the Evan Evans pseudonym, he produced a kind of neoproletarian pulp fiction. Had B. Traven written stories for *Star Western*, they might resemble *Montana Rides!* (1933), *Montana Rides Again* (1934), and *The Song of the Whip* (1936). The hero of these novels, set in Mexico, is the Montana Kid—or "El Keed"—a nonchalant Anglo roamer. "El Keed" eventually becomes a confederate of Mateo Rubriz, a Mexican revolutionary who battles constantly and joyfully against agents of the oppressive military dictatorship. The novels feature escapades appropriate for Robin Hood; one of Rubriz's followers, in fact, is a jolly, burly friar. *The Song of the Whip*, virtually the last pulp Western written by Frederick Faust, offers a revenge plot pitting peons, church, and bandits against upper-class landlords. Aided by the guns and wits of the Montana Kid, the lower class is victorious. Despite explicit scenes of violence and gore (for which Brand's Anglo hero is hardly ever responsible), the Montana Kid novels provide free-wheeling merriment (especially among Rubriz and his jolly men) and exotic characters. "My God, amigo!" Rubriz says to Montana at the end of the last novel, "What a wonderful thing it is that in such a little world there should be two such men as you and I" (American Reprint ed., p. 189).

Perhaps innocence is the most important feature common to Max Brand's hundreds of Westerns. They lack both literary and historical pretensions; they present themselves, without great seriousness, as public entertainments. They were written for the pulps, for uncritical readers, and meant to be read and then thrown away. Although some admirers of Frederick Faust regret that he did not take the time to shape his work into recognizably literary contributions, the kind of narrative freedom provided by the pulps—to stereotype, to exaggerate, to ignore many genteel standards of taste—found not only its most prolific but perhaps also its best and truest expression in Max Brand.

Survey of Criticism

There is little criticism of Max Brand, his Westerns hardly resembling the kind of literature that traditional scholars and critics feel compelled to analyze. The attitude of *Time* magazine in 1952—that Faust's writing was only "the gooey residue of boiled pulp," no more impressive than "an endless herd of buffalo stamping upside down across the sky in a mirage" ("Greatest Pulpist," p. 78)—may still be representative.

Although John Cawelti's work in both *The Six-Gun Mystique* (1971) and *Adventure, Mystery, and Romance* (1976) provides means of understanding and appreciating the formulaic nature of Westerns and their cultural significance, he pays little specific attention to Max Brand. John Milton's chapter on the popular Western in his *The Novel of the American West* (1980) also shies away from discussing individual Brand novels. In *The Unembarrassed Muse* (1970) Russel B. Nye devotes several paragraphs to Max Brand Westerns but ultimately dismisses them as "rubberstamped adventure fiction" (p. 298).

Robert Easton's biography of Faust, *Max Brand: The Big "Westerner"* (1970), is indispensable, as is the bibliographical information in Darrell C. Richardson's *Max Brand: The Man and His Work* (1952). Martha Bacon's short essay "Destry and Dionysus" (1955), offers a perceptive view of Faust himself.

Virtually the only scholarly article on Brand is Edgar L. Chapman's "The Image of the Indian in Max Brand's Pulp Western Novels" (1978), which presents a case for Faust's sensitivity to native Americans. The introductions to Gregg Press editions of *The Untamed* and *Destry Rides Again*—by Jack Nachbar and Richard Etulain, respectively—show that Max Brand is a popular literary figure who deserves far more attention than he has received, particularly by scholars who are neither Faust cultists (like some of the contributors to Richardson's collection) nor of such a bent as to reduce Brand instinctively to the essence of boiled pulp.

Bibliography

Works by Frederick Faust

The Untamed. New York: G. P. Putnam's Sons, 1919; New York: Pocket Books, 1955. Published first as a serial in *All-Story Weekly* beginning 7 December 1918.
Trailin'. New York: G. P. Putnam's Sons, 1920; New York: Warner Books, 1975. Published first as a serial in *All-Story Weekly* beginning 1 November 1919.
The Night Horseman. New York: G. P. Putnam's Sons, 1920; New York: Warner Books, 1974. Published first as a serial in *Argosy* beginning 18 September 1920.
The Seventh Man. New York: G. P. Putnam's Sons, 1921; New York: Warner Books, 1974. Published first as a serial in *Argosy* beginning 1 October 1921.
The Village Street and Other Poems. New York: G. P. Putnam's Sons, 1922.
The Garden of Eden. London: Hodder and Stoughton [1927]; New York: Warner Books, 1976. Published first as a serial in *Argosy* beginning 15 April 1922.
Dan Barry's Daughter. New York: G. P. Putnam's Sons, 1924; Roslyn, N.Y.: Black's Service, n.d. Published first as a serial in *Argosy* beginning 30 June 1923.
The White Cheyenne. New York: Warner Books, 1974. Published first as a John Frederick serial entitled "The White Wolf" in *Western Story* beginning 6 March 1926, then as a Max Brand book with the same title (New York: G. P. Putnam's Sons, 1926).
Border Guns. New York: Warner Books, 1975. Published first as a George Owen Baxter serial entitled "Riders for Fortune" in *Western Story* beginning 15 September 1928, then as a Max Brand book entitled *The Border Kid*. New York: Dodd, Mead, 1941.
Singing Guns. New York: Dodd, Mead, 1938. Published first as a George Owen Baxter serial in *Western Story* beginning 15 December 1928.

Destry Rides Again. New York: Dodd, Mead, 1930; Boston: Gregg Press, 1979. Published first as a serial entitled "Twelve Peers" in *Western Story* beginning 1 February 1930.

Dionysus in Hades. Oxford: Basil Blackwell, 1931.

Montana Rides! New York: Harper and Bros., 1933; New York: American Reprint Co., 1975 (with the author indicated as "Max Brand writing as Evan Evans"). Published first as an Evan Evans serial in *Western Story* beginning 14 January 1933.

Silvertip's Roundup. New York: Dodd, Mead, 1943; New York; Warner Books, 1970. Published first as a book-length novel entitled *Horseshoe Flat's Speedy Stranger* in *Western Story*, 10 June 1933.

Montana Rides Again. New York: Harper and Bros., 1934; New York: American Reprint Co., 1976. Published first as an Evan Evans serial in *Argosy* beginning 28 April 1934.

War Party. New York: Warner Books, 1975. Published first as a serial entitled "The White Indian" in *Argosy* beginning 9 September 1933, then as a George Owen Baxter book entitled *Call of the Blood*. New York: Macauley, 1934.

Frontier Feud. New York: Warner Books, 1976. Published first as a serial entitled "Brother of the Cheyennes" in *Argosy* beginning 17 March 1934, and then as a George Owen Baxter book by the same title (New York: Macauley, 1935).

Cheyenne Gold. New York: Warner Books, 1976. Published first as a serial entitled "The Sacred Valley" in *Western Story* beginning 10 August 1935.

The Streak. New York: Dodd, Mead, 1937; New York: Pocket Books, 1953. Published first as a serial in *Argosy* beginning 25 January 1936.

The Song of the Whip. New York: Harper and Bros., 1936; New York: American Reprint Co., 1976. Published first as an Evan Evans serial in *Argosy* beginning 28 March 1936.

The Notebooks and Poems of "Max Brand." Ed. John Schoolcraft. New York: Dodd, Mead, 1957.

Studies of Max Brand

Bacon, Martha. "Destry and Dionysus." *Atlantic Monthly* 196 (July 1955): 72-74.

Cawelti, John G. *Adventure, Mystery, and Romance: Formula Stories as Art and Popular Culture*. Chicago: University of Chicago Press, 1976.

————. *The Six-Gun Mystique*. Bowling Green, Ohio: Popular Press, 1971.

Chapman, Edgar L. "The Image of the Indian in Max Brand's Pulp Western Novels." *Heritage of Kansas* 2 (Spring 1978): 16-45.

Easton, Robert. *Max Brand: The Big "Westerner."* Norman: University of Oklahoma Press, 1970.

Etulain, Richard. Introduction to Max Brand, *Destry Rides Again*. Boston: Gregg Press, 1979, pp. v-xi.

"Greatest Pulpist." *Time*, 25 August 1952, p. 78.

Milton, John. *The Novel of the American West*. Lincoln: University of Nebraska Press, 1980.

Nachbar, Jack. Introduction to Max Brand, *The Untamed*. Boston: Gregg Press, 1978, pp. v-xii.

Nye, Russel B. *The Unembarrassed Muse: The Popular Arts in America*. New York: Dial Press, 1970.

Richardson, Darrell C., ed. *Max Brand: The Man and His Work*. Los Angeles: Fantasy Publishing, 1952.

James W. Lee

BENJAMIN CAPPS
(1922-)

Biography

The West of Benjamin Capps's novels is the Great Plains and, in all but one novel, the southern part of that great expanse of grass and desert. Capps was born, grew up, and has spent most of his life on the eastern edge of the south plains, an area larger than New England, which encompasses a large part of west Texas and the western third of Oklahoma. Benjamin Franklin Capps was born 11 June 1922 in the small town of Dundee in Archer County, Texas. He attended one-room schools in Dundee and Anarene and was graduated as salutatorian from Archer City High School in June 1938, the month he turned sixteen.

When he left Archer County in 1938, he went to Lubbock, Texas, got a job working on a Double Cola truck for 75 cents a day and found, and began preparing to enter Texas Tech University in the fall. He completed one year of college before financial straits forced him to leave and join the Civilian Conservation Corps (CCC). He spent a year in the CCC and then took a job as a surveyor and assistant engineer with the U.S. Army Corps of Engineers. Between his service in the Corps of Engineers and his enlistment in the Army Air Corps in 1942, he worked as a truck driver on the construction of Lake Texoma and was a partner in a chicken farm in Colorado. Shortly after World War II began, Capps joined the air corps, and from 1943 until 1945 flew forty-one missions as a B-24 navigator in the Pacific.

At the end of the war, Capps enrolled at the University of Texas at Austin, with English as his major field of study. He was graduated Phi Beta Kappa in 1948 and remained at Austin another year to complete the master's degree. His master's thesis, directed by Mody C. Boatright, was entitled "Mesquite Country" and was set in Archer County in the 1930s. The thesis-novel was the last in a series of fictional works that Capps wrote while he was at the University of Texas. Several of his short stories had won awards and had been published in the university literary magazine. He had determined before World War II began that he wanted to be a writer, and he thought that, after graduation, a job teaching English in college would be the way to pursue his career.

When Capps received the master's degree in 1949, he moved his wife and two children to Tahlequah, Oklahoma, to take a position as instructor of English at Northeastern State College. But the two years he spent in Tahlequah teaching freshman composition and supervising the school's student newspaper convinced him that an academic career was more harmful to a writer than helpful. He decided in 1951 to move his family to Paris, Texas, where his mother owned a house, and devote his full time to writing. He wrote steadily for a year, but nothing was published, and in 1952 he moved his wife, who was expecting another baby, and his two children to Grand Prairie, Texas, and took a job in the machine shop at Chance-Vought Aircraft.

Capps thought that his job as a tool-and-die maker would be a perfect complement to his writing career because of the jobs' dissimilarity. He would be able, he thought, to leave his work at the machine shop and go home at night to write. It turned out, however, that his work as a machinist was not much easier to put aside in the evening than the teaching had been; consequently, he did not write as much during the ten years of manual labor as he had hoped.

In 1961, Capps left his job and once again decided to become a full-time writer. This time, his plan was successful, for the following year he published his first novel, *Hanging at Comanche Wells*. The novel is not a success, for it falls somewhere between the formula Western and serious fiction, but it is not a complete failure either, for it shows Capps's ability to tell a story in an interesting and coherent manner and demonstrates his talent for creating character. Neither of those aspects of the novel, however, is fully developed, for Capps wrote the book for the paperback market, and its length was limited. In fact, he had hoped to sell the novel to *Saturday Evening Post* for serialization, but by 1962 the market for magazine fiction was quite small. The dearth of magazines that publish fiction also helps to account for his having over fifty short stories that have never been published.

After Capps left his job as a tool-and-die maker and published *Hanging* in 1962, he turned his attention to writing full time and produced five more novels before the end of the decade. Not only was Capps writing rapidly during the decade, but the novels that he produced are mature works of fiction. The rather immature and tentative *Hanging*, which has more merit than its publishing history would indicate, was followed in 1964 by the excellent *The Trail to Ogallala*, which won the Silver Spur Award of the Western Writers of America (WWA) and the Levi Straus Golden Saddleman Award.

The following year, Capps published *Sam Chance*, a novel about an old-time cowman, which was also selected by WWA as the best Western novel of 1965, and awarded the Silver Spur Award. *A Woman of the People* (1966), the first of Capps's three novels of Indian life, was one of the three finalists for the 1966 Spur Award and the first of his serious novels not to win. In 1967, *The Brothers of Uterica*, a novel about the establishment of a utopian colony in nineteenth-century Texas, appeared. Two years later, Capps's best-known novel, *The White Man's Road*, was published and won the Silver Spur Award and the Wrangler Award of the Western Heritage Center for the best Western novel of 1969.

During the 1970s Capps devoted much of his energy to nonfiction, writing only two novels. Two of his works are *The Indians* (1973) and *The Great Chiefs* (1975) in the Time-Life series on the Old West. Capps provided the text for these two books, and the editorial staff of Time-Life Books collected and arranged the material. The nature of the books makes them seem to be the work of a committee and not the work of one author. Capps wrote seven times as much text as was finally used, and what is left, though it often appears disjointed, is clear, informative, and accurate, but it is not likely to be considered an important part of Capps's work.

The Warren Wagontrain Raid (1974) is an important addition to the Capps canon. A notable history of a Kiowa raid in 1871, the book won the Wrangler Award and was a finalist for the Silver Spur Award. The book is an excellent historical account but goes beyond history and biography in its development of the central figures in the incident.

The two novels that Capps wrote in the 1970s lack some of the depth of his best work, but both are interesting and solid. *The True Memoirs of Charley Blankenship* (1972) and *Woman Chief* (1979) were finalists for the Silver Spur Award, but neither won. *Memoirs* is a humorous picaresque of a cowboy's adventures in the West. It purports to be the recollections of an old-time cowboy but is a novel. *Woman Chief* is based on an Indian woman in the Wyoming area who became a celebrated Crow war chief in the 1850s.

Capps has published nothing thus far in the 1980s, but he enters the decade with eight novels and three books of nonfiction to his credit, an impressive output for a career of less than twenty years. That he published eleven books in seventeen years is not as impressive as the quality of the books. Only one of them bears the marks of an apprentice writer, and even that novel, *Hanging at Comanche Wells*, is better than most first novels. Apparently he served his apprenticeship by writing fifty-five unpublished short stories, four unpublished novels, and *Hanging*. All his other works are the mature productions of a writer who has mastered his craft.

Major Themes

Benjamin Capps is a serious novelist whose main concerns are those of all other good novelists: the development of believable characters, the construction of coherent, unified plots, the exploration of significant themes, and the realistic rendering of a time and a place. Most of his novels are successful in all of the aspects of fiction, but he has few peers in the realistic rendering of a time and a place. The reader of a Benjamin Capps novel can be assured that the times depicted are accurate and that the places are minutely described. Capps creates a world of his own that no history of the period will belie.

The world of Capps's novels is the south plains in the second half of the nineteenth century; his Indians, the Comanches and the Kiowas; his settlers, the whites who carved Texas out of undiscovered country. He is a historical novelist in the best sense of that vague literary term; that is, he is not a writer of costume novels but an author who meticulously re-creates time past. He is a regional novelist in the best sense of the term, for local color is not his chief concern; the re-creation of a people in terms of their culture is.

The culture of a people is, to Benjamin Capps, the totality of their lives: their traditions, their beliefs, their folklore, their view of the world, their attempts to adapt to their environment. His depiction of the culture of the whites and the Indians makes Capps one of America's best historical novelists, as his many awards from western groups demonstrate. His sound historical account of the Warren wagon train raid of 1871 is proof of the accuracy of his knowledge of Indian life and of the confrontation between whites and Indians that informs much of his work.

Capps's three novels of Indian life—*A Woman of the People*, *The White Man's Road*, and *Woman Chief*—treat the culture of the plains Indians. Each focuses upon Indians and the life they lived. In both *A Woman* and *Woman Chief*, most of the action takes place before the whites have come in numbers large enough to drive the Indians from the plains. Therefore the two novels are interesting re-creations of the last years of freedom for the natives of the Great Plains. *A Woman of the People* is Capps's most complete rendering of south plains Indian life, and *Woman Chief* is his only novel about the Indians who lived in the northern part of the region. *A Woman* provides a detailed portrait of Comanche culture through its main character, an eleven-year-old white girl who is captured by a band of Indians and grows to maturity among them. Since the life of the Indians is an extreme shock to the girl, Helen Morrison, readers are equally shocked as they see, with her, the details of Comanche life. The device of having everything seen through the eyes of an outsider allows Capps to spend more time describing the customs of the band. We see as Helen sees, we accept as she accepts, and we become accustomed to the culture as she does. Every part of her work, her living arrangements, and her role in the band has to be explained to her and to the readers. The practices that seem barbarous to her, and to us, become normal. The way of life—the hunting, the cooking, the traveling, the fighting— begins to be as commonplace as the way of life of any other civilization.

Woman Chief gives an equally valid picture of the life of plains Indians. There is not the motif of adapting to a new culture that exists in *A Woman* and makes it a step-by-step revelation, but the culture of the Crows in *Woman Chief* is as fully realized as that of the Comanches in *A Woman*. In both novels readers are immersed in the life of an Indian tribe, and the thorough depiction of that life causes readers to accept certain premises that underlie Capps's novels of western life: Indian ways are neither better nor worse than the ways of the whites; the plains Indians had a world view that was not intellectually inferior to the world view of Americans and Europeans; Indian warfare was not more savage than that practiced elsewhere; and the civilization of the Indian, though different, was as valid as any other. In short, the Indian was not a different being despite a different culture. In his exploration of Indian life and culture, Capps does not sentimentalize the Indian. There is never a hint that the ways of the Indian are superior to the ways of the white or that the Indian is one of Rousseau's noble savages. Some of the Indians' ways are superior; some are not. Some of the individuals are greedy, some cowardly, some brutal; others are brave, kindly, generous.

When the Indian came into the great confrontation with the white man on the Great Plains, there was no doubt who the winner would be. In *A Woman of the People* it becomes clear as the novel ends that the buffalo have become almost extinct, that the settlers are inching ever nearer to the range of the Comanches, and that the soldiers are certain to herd the Indians onto the reservations. As the novel ends, the small band to which Helen Morrison, now Tehanita (Little Girl Texan), belongs begins the trek to join the soldiers who will take them to Indian Territory. The culture of the plains Indian is about to end, and now the Comanches can join the other "civilized" tribes in Oklahoma. The Mutsani band of which Helen-Tehanita has become a part faces facts, and Capps's portrayal of their choice is as matter-of-fact as it must have been to the real people who gave up their life of self-determination. Capps delivers no sermons, no paeans to a free life on the plains, no songs of lamentation. He tells it as it probably happened. It is his genius that he can leave a story alone to tell itself, that his characters do the talking, and that he allows himself no liberties of manipulation.

What Benjamin Capps does for the plains Indian, he does equally well for the white settler of northwest Texas. His novels treating the arrival of the whites are as unprejudiced as are those about Indians. *Hanging at Comanche Wells*, the one novel of Capps's apprenticeship, gives an accurate picture of small-town life on the frontier. The struggle in the novel is between the lawless elements of the region, represented by the old-time cowmen who had to bring their form of justice to the rough country, and the law-and-order advocates, who were concerned with a more regularized form of justice than had prevailed before. The judicial system of the West was changing from homemade law to statute law, and the changes brought on confrontation. The focus in the novel is on the new justice, but the reader can see, despite the brevity of the novel, that the old cattlemen were not so much villains as men who lived in the past. Despite *Hanging*'s shortcomings, it is a novel concerned with the culture that whites were bringing to the plains.

The Trail to Ogallala and *Sam Chance* also depict accurately the customs that frontiersmen lived by and the struggles that they faced in order to survive. Although *Trail* tells of a cattle drive and *Sam Chance* of the founding of a ranch, both go far beyond their main plot to establish a way of life. The men who built up the herds, as well as those who drove them north, brought a new culture to the south plains. Capps's interest in the ethic of the cattle empire includes its structure, its customs, its law, and its beliefs. The culture of the cattle kingdom laid the foundation for the culture of the present-day Southwest. Capps's historical novels of the settler on the frontier show the genesis of the modern West. The individualism, the rejection of governmental interference, the self-reliance—attitudes that modern westerners still cherish but that are fast disappearing—are all seen as the way of life created by men like Sam Chance, Billy Scott of *Trail*, and Charley Blankenship.

Another aspect of the culture of the West is evident in *The Brothers of Uterica*, which traces the foundation of a utopian colony in north central Texas, its abortive development, and its collapse. The characters in *Brothers* are attempting to bring the "high culture" of Europe and New England to the raw frontier and make socialism and high thinking flourish in a land too rough and too new for them. The culture that they try to bring is unsuited to the harshness of the elements and the ways of the neighboring Indians.

Any discussion of Capps's works inevitably returns to the matter of confrontation. If the culture of the West is to be explored at all, it can be explored only as confrontation. The history of the Great Plains is a history of war. The whites and the Indians were at war for more than a half-century; the inhabitants of the region have been at war with its elements forever; and the whites who finally won the West have never fully reconciled their own differences.

The most thorough treatment of the struggle between Indian and white appears in *The White Man's Road* and in *The Warren Wagontrain Raid*, a work of nonfiction. Both books are set at a time when the Indians have lost the plains and are sequestered on reservations. *The White Man's Road*, Capps's best-known novel, is his fullest fictional statement of the Indians' attempts to adapt to the ways of whites. Often funny but ultimately sad, *Road* narrates the attempt of Joe Cowbone to make a final stand as an Indian. Joe, in his twenties, knows only the life of the reservation, but he has heard stories about the times when the Comanches and Kiowas owned the south plains. The present is so unsatisfactory that he and some of his friends decide to steal a herd of horses from the U.S. Cavalry and head west to their rightful home. Against all odds, they bring off the raid and escape westward. As might be expected, they cannot avoid the cavalry, and the horses are retaken. But for one short span of time, the present is put aside and the young men are living the life remembered by Mad Wolf, the one-hundred-year-old Indian who never surrendered and who told Joe what real life for an Indian meant. The novel ends with Joe Cowbone married, back on the reservation, and preparing for a life on the white man's road.

The Warren Wagontrain Raid is similar in that a group of reservation Kiowas escape the Fort Sill area, go into Texas, and attack a small wagon train carrying supplies. The leaders, who remember the days of freedom, are returning to a way of life of which Joe Cowbone had only heard. They suffer a harsher fate than Joe and his friends. Satanta, who led the raid, is sentenced to death, has his sentence commuted to life, is paroled, and finally returns to prison where he commits suicide. Tsatangya, famous for decades among the Kiowas, does not stand trial because he attacks his guards and is killed before the prisoners leave Fort Sill for

Texas to be tried. The third of the leaders, Big Tree, is paroled when Satanta is and spends the rest of his life trying to walk the white man's road.

The confrontations on the plains are not all between Indian and white, though the transformation of the Great Plains from Indian land to white is the most dramatic part of the region's history. *The Trail to Ogallala*, *Sam Chance*, and *The Brothers of Uterica* devote little space to Indian problems but show the other hardships with which the early white inhabitants of the plains had to contend. *Sam Chance* traces the creation of a cattle ranch out of a harsh and unyielding land where nature wars with man and where homesteaders and government regulators cause constant disruption. In *Sam Chance* and *The Trail to Ogallala* man battles nature and wins—as far as such a victory is ever possible. But *The Brothers of Uterica* tells the story of a group that loses the struggle with nature because they lack the frontier spirit—which Sam Chance and the men who drove the cattle to market had. All three novels are good accounts of pioneer life in the south plains and show one of Capps's best features: his ability to give an authentic picture of the land and its perils.

Capps can delineate the ordinary working life of early Texas better than almost any other writer. *The Trail to Ogallala* is a much better depiction of life on the trail than Andy Adams's *Log of a Cowboy*, long considered the standard of the genre. Capps's descriptions of the terrain, the weather, and the hardships of those going north are excellent; in fact, Don B. Graham in a recent essay on the two novels, "Old and New Cowboy Classics" (1980), says that not only is *Trail* better than the *Log*, but it is more authentic. The authenticity of Capps's work impresses readers first. One may be impressed with the characterizations—always good, often outstanding—or the sophisticated handling of plot or the perfect rendering of dialogue, but one always comes back to the perfection with which Capps captures the life of the south plains. Only Capps and Elmer Kelton are writing realistic novels of plains life in Texas today. Both have been neglected by critics of contemporary fiction.

Survey of Criticism

Very little commentary on Capps's work has appeared. There are the usual newspaper reviews, and most of them have been complimentary, but such notices tend to be transitory and do little to assess the general quality of a writer's output. For a writer to be taken seriously by the critical community, it is imperative that essays on his works appear in journals of serious criticism.

Only in recent years has anything of lasting value been written about Capps's works in the quarterlies. A few reviews of his books have appeared in *Western American Literature* over the years; perhaps the best of those is C. L. Sonnichsen's 1970 review of *The White Man's Road*. Sonnichsen, long a sympathetic reviewer of Capps's novels in newspapers and journals, says that Capps "writes as well as anyone in his native state" (p. 304) and goes on to praise the novel as one of the best of its kind. A longer essay-review on the same novel appeared the following year in *Southwestern American Literature*. In that study, Richard Etulain devotes several pages to a full discussion of *The White Man's Road* and concerns himself with the various literary motifs that the novel has in common with other serious works of literature. *Road*, Etulain says, is Capps's best novel and is "ambitious, freighted with meaning, and well conceived. Nothing of the books [sic] seems 'made' but instead 'told' or 'pictured' " (p. 91).

The fullest study of one of Capps's books is Don B. Graham's recent study of *The Trail to Ogallala* in "Old and New Cowboy Classics" (1980), in which he praises the novel and argues that it is a better and more authentic work than Andy Adams's *Log of a Cowboy*. Intelligent and lengthy essays such as Graham's on Capps's work will form the basis for all future commentary.

There are several projected studies of Capps's writing that should do something to end the relative silence with which his novels have been greeted by the scholarly community. Ernest Speck, author of two excellent long works on Mody C. Boatright, is in the process of treating all of Capps's works in the Boise State Western Writers Series. James W. Lee's brief overview of Capps's work is scheduled to appear in *The Literary History of the American West*, a forthcoming publication sponsored by the Western Literature Association.

Some forgotten critic of southwestern literature is supposed to have said, nearly thirty years ago, that the fiction of this region will remain immature until writers abandon the cowboys-and-Indians motif. That attitude seems to prevail today, especially in Texas. Trivial novels about city life in Texas usually receive more space in the large state newspapers than do novels about early days. Benjamin Capps and Elmer Kelton, Texas's two best novelists of the 1970s, have apparently been dismissed by intellectuals as writers of pulp Westerns. Perhaps Kelton's early Westerns and Capps's *Hanging at Comanche Wells* helped shape the attitudes that seem to prevail, but both have long since abandoned the Western genre for serious fiction.

Bibliography

Works by Benjamin Capps

Hanging at Comanche Wells. New York: Ballantine, 1962.
The Trail to Ogallala. New York: Duell, Sloan and Pearce, 1964.
Sam Chance. New York: Duell, Sloan and Pearce, 1965.
A Woman of the People. New York: Duell, Sloan and Pearce, 1966.
The Brothers of Uterica. New York: Meredith Press, 1967.
The White Man's Road. New York: Harper and Row, 1969.
The True Memoirs of Charley Blankenship. Philadelphia: Lippincott, 1972.
The Indians. New York: Time-Life Books, 1973.
The Warren Wagontrain Raid. New York: Dial, 1974.
The Great Chiefs. New York: Time-Life Books, 1975.
Woman Chief. Garden City, N.Y.: Doubleday, 1979.

Studies of Benjamin Capps

Etulain, Richard. *"The White Man's Road*: An Appreciation." *Southwestern American Literature* 1 (May 1971): 88-92.

Graham, Don B. "Old and New Cowboy Classics." *Southwestern Review* 65 (Summer 1980): 293-303.

Sonnichsen, C. L. Review of *The White Man's Road*, by Benjamin Capps. *Western American Literature* 4 (Winter 1970): 304-5.

John J. Murphy

WILLA CATHER
(1873-1947)

Biography

Willa Cather was born on 7 December 1873 near Gore, Virginia, the first of seven children of Charles Cather and Mary Virginia Boak, both from established Virginia families. The farmhouse birthplace and the square brick house, Willow Shade, that the family moved into before Willa's first birthday are in verdant Back Creek Valley among the tree-covered Blue Ridge Mountains. This area, rich in Civil War lore, is the setting of Cather's last novel, *Sapphira and the Slave Girl* (1940), in the years before the outbreak of the war. In April 1883, Cather was uprooted from this familiar world and transported to the Nebraska prairies around the little town of Red Cloud. Her paternal grandfather and uncle had moved there with their families some years before, and now her father would try his hand at farming the new land.

In Nebraska, the land was the great fact; it was vast and barren, awesome and depressing. To overcome the heartache of alienation, Willa decided to contend with the country, "and by the end of the first autumn," she wrote, "that shaggy grass country had gripped me with a passion I have never been able to shake. It has been the happiness and the curse of my life" (Bennett, *World of Willa Cather*, p. 140). The western land itself would permeate her fiction from her early short fiction to her last story, "The Best Years" (1948).

Within two years, Charles Cather had given up farming and moved his growing family into Red Cloud, where he opened a loan office. The town proved as important an influence as the prairie country on Willa. It became Black Hawk in *My Antonia* (1918), Sweet Water in *A Lost Lady* (1923), Moonstone in *The Song of the Lark* (1915), and, in effect, every western town Cather wrote about. The Cather home at Third and Cedar became an important setting in *The Song of the Lark*, "Old Mrs. Harris" (1932), and "The Best Years." Her friends in and around Red Cloud inspired her characters. The Czech girl Annie Sadilek was the prototype of Antonia Shimerda in *My Antonia*, and the Miners, a neighboring family, became the Harlings in the same novel. Marian Forrester in *A Lost Lady* was based on Lyra Garber, wife of Nebraska's early governor, Silas Garber, and in *The Song of the Lark*, Willa's piano teacher, Professor Shindelmeisser, became Wunsch, Thea Kronborg's piano teacher. Willa and her friends explored every inch of town, picnicked on the Republican River, which flows through it, and roamed the river bluffs.

From 1890 to 1895 Cather attended the University of Nebraska in Lincoln, where she proved a brilliant student, albeit somewhat aggressive and masculine, and distinguished herself as a talented writer, serving as editor of the campus literary magazine, the *Hesperian*. The Cather family included seven children during Willa's college years, and the salary she earned writing her theatrical and literary column, "The Passing Show," for the *Nebraska State Journal* enabled her to provide for herself when the depression hit Nebraska in 1893. Lincoln in those days was a frontier capital feverishly transplanting culture to the prairies, and performers like Julia Marlowe, Helena Modjeska, Joseph Jefferson, Otis Skinner, and Lillian Nordika played to large audiences in two professional theaters. Even for a place where journalism was of the "hell-cat" variety, Cather had the reputation of being exceedingly frank, never hesitating to ridicule inferior performances and productions.

A year after graduation she moved to Pittsburgh to edit the *Home Monthly* magazine and later became a telegraph editor for the *Pittsburgh Leader*. She lived an active social life, was involved in club activities, met artists, writers, and the upper crust of the city, and was proposed to at least twice but never fell in love. By far the most important personal influence during these years and, according to her biographer James Woodress, the "one great romance of her life" (*Willa Cather*, p. 86) was Isabelle McClung, daughter of a prominent Pittsburgh judge. Isabelle was interested in promoting young talent, and in 1901 took Willa to live in the McClung family house. In that same year, realizing that editing took too much time from her writing, Cather began teaching Latin and English at Central High School.

During the *Home Monthly* and *Leader* years, she published numerous short stories and reviews. A high point was the acceptance of the Nebraska story "Eric Hermannson's Soul" by *Cosmopolitan*. In 1903 she published a volume of poems, *April Twilights*, and in 1905 a collection of stories of writers and artists, *The Troll Garden*, which included "Paul's Case" and led to an invitation by S. S. McClure for her to be an associate editor of his influential magazine in New York. During a Boston assignment for *McClure's* she met the Maine writer Sarah Orne Jewett, whose work and advice helped shape her career. Jewett told Cather to give up office work and devote herself to her art. Cather stayed with McClure for five years, becoming his managing editor in 1909. In 1911 she left to devote full time to fiction writing, and her major works began to appear regularly after 1912, when her first novel, *Alexander's Bridge*, appeared.

Cather took two vacations that were significant to her development as a writer. The first was during the summer of 1902, when she toured Europe with Isabelle McClung. Her response to France was particularly noteworthy, for France became a filter for her Nebraska experience. In the travel notes she sent back to the *Nebraska State Journal* (published in 1956 as *Willa Cather in Europe*) she notes mud and stone huts at Barbizon, prairies of wheat and Millet-type women of battered beauty who had raised large families and worked in the fields. The second vacation was ten years later, when she visited her brother Douglass, who was working for the Southern Pacific at Winslow, Arizona. She toured Indian missions, cliff dwellings of the Anasazi, and the Grand Canyon. Her experience of a western setting with more than a geologic past made a lasting impression, and she returned to the Southwest five times during the next fifteen years. On her trip back east she stopped in Nebraska and was able to see her childhood country with new vision. A year later, in 1913, she published *O Pioneers!*, her first Nebraska novel and the one she considered her first original work, "the first time [she] walked off on [her] own feet" (Bennett, *World of Willa Cather*, p. 200). This novel, she felt, would have pleased the now-deceased Jewett because it was about a country and a people its creator knew intimately.

The works that immediately followed, *The Song of the Lark* (1915), *My Antonia* (1918), *One of Ours* (1922), and *A Lost Lady* (1923), are based on Cather's Nebraska experience. In them she celebrates the heroic settling of the country during pioneer days and criticizes the growing materialism of subsequent generations. *The Song of the Lark* contains a section based on her southwestern experiences and thus indicates the direction of later works, *The Professor's House* (1925) and *Death Comes for the Archbishop* (1927), which is set entirely in the Southwest. The interest in Catholicism evident in *Archbishop* and *My Mortal Enemy* (1926) reflects her religious concern, apparent in her conversion from the Baptist to the Episcopalian faith in 1922. Several factors led to her conversion. She was approaching fifty and having health problems, and the war had upset her, as did Isabelle McClung's marriage in 1916. She remained an Episcopalian for the rest of her life.

Cather's career grew more nostalgic after the death of her father in 1928 and her mother's subsequent illness and death in 1931. New adventures were fewer. The summer cottage she and her living companion Edith Lewis built on Grand Manan Island was a comfort, and her first visit to Quebec City in 1928 inspired the writing of *Shadows on the Rock* (1931), which enabled her to continue her exploration of the Catholic past. *Shadows* has at its core a relationship between a father and daughter reminiscent of Willa's relationship with her father. *Obscure Destinies* (1932), a collection of three stories, is based on early family and Red Cloud memories. *Lucy Gayheart* (1935), her last Nebraska novel, proved a disappointment, although her Virginia novel, *Sapphira* (1940), is first-rate.

In 1941 she took her last long trip, traveling by rail through New Mexico and Arizona and staying a month in San Francisco. The last two stories she wrote, "Before Breakfast" and "The Best Years," are among her finest. Although her final years were marked by illness, they were filled with a sense of accomplishment. She had won a Pulitzer prize for *One of Ours*, an American Academy of Arts and Letters gold medal for *Archbishop*, and a Prix Femina Americaine for

Shadows; honorary degrees had been bestowed by Yale, Princeton, Columbia, California, Michigan, Nebraska, Creighton, and Smith. In 1937 Houghton Mifflin began a handsome library edition of her work. Before her death in New York on 24 April 1947, she was contemplating another trip west.

Major Themes

The predominant theme in Cather's fiction is response to the western land, including cultivating the earth, building towns, and developing in them the culture of Europe and the established American settlements. *O Pioneers!* presents these activities straightforwardly. Its heroine, Alexandra Bergson, a Swedish immigrant who has been left the running of the family farm by her father, detects the benign spirit of the new land and successfully cultivates fields her father found stubborn and killing. The optimism of Bergson's accomplishment is evident in her friend Carl Linstrum's vision of her coming from the milking at sunrise, as if she had walked straight out of the morning itself. Bergson's sympathy with the land is essential in making the new country: "For the first time, perhaps, since that land emerged from the waters of geologic ages, a human face was set toward it with love and yearning.... Then the Genius of the Divide... must have bent lower than it ever bent to a human will before. The history of every country begins in the heart of a man or a woman" (*O Pioneers!*, p. 65).

The relationship of Alexandra Bergson to the land is unique. She directs her sexual vitality toward the land and experiences a recurring fantasy of being carried away in the arms of an earth lover, which she tries to purge by pouring cold water over her body. This fantasy and her attempt to suppress it suggest the extension of her sexual self to the land, which at times represents her lover and at times is associated with her body; she felt "close to the flat, fallow world about her, and felt, as it were, in her own body the joyous germination in the soil" (*O Pioneers!* p. 204).

Although the tragic love affair and deaths of her brother Emil and best friend Marie Shabata challenge Bergson's positive approach to her world and plunge her into a dark night of the soul, the novel ends with her affirmation of the land, an appreciation of its universal dimension. She confides to Carl Linstrum, "We come and go, but the land is always here. And the people who love it and understand it are the people who own it—for a little while" (*O Pioneers!* p. 308).

Death Comes for the Archbishop is Cather's only other positive approach to the western experience. Its hero, Jean Marie Latour, inspired by Archbishop Jean Baptiste Lamy of Santa Fe, responds as intimately to the New Mexico landscape as Alexandra Bergson does to the prairies. The mesa country gives substance to his spiritual development, from the opening pages when he wanders among red hills in the desert and contemplates the thirst of the crucified Christ, to his discovery (on a ridge over the Rio Grande) of the golden stone from which will be built the cathedral to symbolize his work in New Mexico. Other responses include the unsettling night he spends in a dank cave in the Pecos mountains, where his guide Jacinto exposes him to challenging Indian mysteries; his recognition of the Ácoma mesa as the expression of human need, of the church and its idea of God; his sojourn in the Navaho desert during his period of aridity, and his discovery of the oasis, Agua Secreta, as a gift of grace, an answered prayer.

Latour's accomplishments include bringing order to his farflung diocese, where Catholicism is in decay despite the devotion of particular Mexicans. As the ecclesiastics who assign him stipulate, Latour "will have to deal with savagery and ignorance, with dissolute priests and political intrigue" (*Archbishop*, p. 8), in an area where revolutions, conquests, and uprisings have become customary. Like Aeneas, he is a civilizer, a carrier of gods to savage places. In the end he defines himself and makes a harmonious civilization in New Mexico by blending various European, Navaho, Pueblo, and established American cultural strains. He is Cather's most successful western hero, an atypical pistol-carrying horseman, rescuing those in need, righting wrongs, bringing law to lawless regions. Like Alexandra Bergson's, his story becomes an affirmation of the land itself. He lives out his retirement in New Mexico rather than his native France because he appreciates the eternal quality of the New Mexico landscape, the perpetual youth abundant "on the bright edges of the world, in the great grass plains or the sage-brush desert" (*Archbishop*, p. 275).

My Antonia, Cather's best-known novel, is thematically dualistic. Like *O Pioneers!* and *Archbishop*, this story of Jim Burden and Antonia Shimerda concerns responses to the land and the subsequent civilizing process; simultaneously it is the story of the orphan Jim's somewhat confused initiation into a disappointing adulthood and of the West's failure to fulfill pioneer hopes. It is revolt from the village fiction, and Jim, who betrays himself as a prime symptom of social decline, is Cather's critical voice. However, no introduction to the new land is more inspiring than his, and no Cather character has the mythic dimensions of Antonia. Jim's introduction to the prairies parallels Cather's own. He too is a Virginian and the age she was when she came to Nebraska, and the territory around Black Hawk (Red Cloud) is for him "not a country at all, but the material out of which countries are made" (*My Antonia*, p. 7). The land is the universal fact of Jim's Nebraska boyhood, and his response to it resembles Alexandra's. It is eternal reality, and to die and become part of it is to be "entirely happy," for happiness is "to be dissolved into something complete and great" (*My Antonia*, p. 18).

Although her verbal response to the land is limited, Jim's Bohemian friend Antonia is intimately associated with it. She plows it and plants it, returning to it for punishment and solace when she is abandoned with child by her lover, Larry Donovan. She is a manifestation of the earth itself: her eyes are "warm and full of light, like the sun shining on brown pools in the wood" (*My Antonia*, p. 23), and her neck "came up strongly out of her shoulders, like the bole of a tree out of the turf" (p. 122). During her first winter in Nebraska she sleeps in a hole in the black earth wall of the family dugout; later, when she is a "rich mine of life, like the founders of early races" (p. 353), her many children "came running up the [fruit cave] steps together, big and little, tow heads and gold heads and brown, and flashing little naked legs; a veritable explosion of life out of the dark cave into the sunlight" (pp. 338-39). The contributions of Antonia and Jim are complementary. She cultivates and populates the country, while he leaves to develop a world perspective from which to celebrate it, Antonia, and her achievements. Jim's reading of the classics enables him to see his "own naked land and the figures scattered upon it" (p. 262) in epic proportion. He brings the Muse into Nebraska, and Antonia consequently lends herself to "immemorial human attitudes which we recognize by instinct as universal and true" (p. 353).

Jim's version of the West, filtered through time and literature, contains some of Cather's harshest criticism of the post-pioneer period. The society that developed lost feeling for the land, became absorbed in business and creature comforts, eager to acquire money and the gimmicky products of American industry, and duplicated the injustices of Europe and the eastern states, although without cultural opportunities and distinctions. Jim's departure is actually a flight from Black Hawk, where established people ostracized foreigners like Antonia and the other country girls, where "respect for respectability was stronger than any desire" (*My Antonia*, p. 202) in youth who made love to foreign girls but married the vapid daughters of the established class, and where "every individual taste, every natural appetite, was bridled by caution" (p. 219).

Although Jim admits wanting "to get away as soon as possible" (*My Antonia*, p. 227), his townsmen's failings are obvious in him. When objections are raised to his attending dances with foreign girls, he stops going because "Disapprobation hurt me, I found—even that of people whom I did not admire" (p. 228). Like the "white handed, high-collared clerks and bookkeepers" (p. 204) he criticizes, Jim is afraid of spontaneity and sexually squeamish. When exposed to money lender Wick Cutter's lust for Antonia, he becomes "faint and miserable" and hates Antonia for letting him in "for all this disgustingness" (p. 250). While living in Lincoln he has an affair with the Black Hawk hired girl Lena Lingard but leaves her without regret to study at Harvard. After Antonia has Donovan's child, Jim tells her she is the most important woman in his life and then bids her farewell, returning twenty years later to make her a symbol of the pioneer West.

The pessimism in Cather's response to the West is evident in the novel's climactic image as Jim and the country girls watch a hand plow assume epic proportions in the setting sun and then sink back to insignificance. Through this image Cather symbolizes the short-lived potential of the pioneer West, a potential destroyed by social habit and small-minded, materialistic values.

This theme of the decline dominates *A Lost Lady*, which lacks the adventure that relieves *My Antonia*. Marian Forrester is an aging beauty married to an elderly railroad pioneer, Captain Daniel Forrester, and forced to depend on snake-like Ivy Peters, an ambitious young materialist, when the captain's health and finances fail. All this is witnessed and interpreted by Niel Herbert, from whose consciousness Cather narrates most of the story. Like Jim Burden, Niel is effete and ineffectual, given to viewing reality through books, and making the

captain and his wife into ideals they cannot satisfy. Marian is particularly important in Niel's development. Like Antonia to motherless Jim, Marian is mother,
sweetheart, sister, and, most of all, great lady to the impressionable, motherless
Niel. When he discovers that she has a lover among the men of her husband's
set, Niel condemns all beautiful women, "whose beauty meant more than it
said. . . . Was their brilliancy always fed by something coarse and concealed?"
(*Lost Lady*, p. 87).

Bereft of his ideal and powerless before the new breed of western men, Niel
transfers his disillusionment to the West: "The Old West had been settled by
dreamers, great-hearted adventurers. . . . Now all the vast territory they had won
was to be at the mercy of men like Ivy Peters, who had never dared anything,
never risked anything" (*Lost Lady*, p. 106). Here, as in *My Antonia*, the criticism
is manipulated through a character who is a manifestation of the decline he
laments.

Similar disappointment is evident in *One of Ours*, Cather's World War I
novel, in which Claude Wheeler, a farm boy with adjustment problems, fails to
conform to his society, botches his love life, and escapes into books and to the
war in France. The West frustrates him because it has been destroyed as a heroic
context. As he sits on the state house steps in Denver, contemplating the mountains and the statue of Kit Carson, he realizes that the West has vanished: "The
statue. . . pointed Westward; but there was no West, in that sense, any more. . . . Here
the sky was like a lid shut down over the world" (*One of Ours*, p. 104). The war,
however, represents a "Sunrise on the Prairie," an escape from claustrophobia.
The war enables Claude to become more than a clumsy dreamer and more than
Jim Burden and Niel Herbert. He can become heroic like the pioneers were;
during the train ride home before being shipped abroad, "Like the hero of the
Odyssey upon his homeward journey, Claude had often to tell what his country
was, and who were the parents that begot him" (p. 209).

The war could not retrieve the Heroic West, nor could it be a permanent
solution for idealists. Contending with their dilemma is Cather's final theme, the
attempt to find meaning in life and reason for living in a spiritually barren world.
The Professor's House depicts such a struggle. Godfrey St. Peter can no longer
find satisfaction in life; his materialistic family is indifferent to his cultivated
preferences, and the prairie university has lapsed from the liberal arts curriculum. St. Peter retreats into himself and relives his friendship with a deceased
student, Tom Outland, a cowboy turned scientist who studied at the university
before going off to war.

Tom's discovery of the cliff dwellings of the Anasazi at Blue Mesa (Cather's
version of the Wetherill discoveries at Mesa Verde) enables him to connect to a
valuable past. Like Jim Burden and Niel Herbert, Tom is an orphan in need of
parents, and the mystical experience he has on the mesa fulfills this need: "I had
read of filial piety in the Latin poets, and I knew that was what I felt for this
place" (*Professor's House* p. 251). Tom's response to the little city of stone
(Cliff Palace ruin) on the mesa is as to a holy city "looking down into the canyon

with the calmness of eternity" (p. 201). He is possessive about his discovery and fails to share its meaning with his cowboy companion, who sells the artifacts of the city to an enterprising German. Years later Tom returns to the mesa with the sympathetic Professor St. Peter.

The resolution of St. Peter's mid-life crisis long after Tom's death involves Blue Mesa in a curious way. Those dwellings in an earth cleft indicate something immortal to St. Peter and the fact that he will die: "He was earth, and would return to earth" (*Professor's House*, p. 265). Wilderness country like Outland's provides an image of the eternal dwelling against which temporal concerns pale, enabling one to pick up the pieces and survive in time. Earlier in *The Song of the Lark*, ruins in an Arizona canyon occasion singer Thea Kronborg's epiphany. Exhausted by flight from the small-mindedness of her prairie home town, Moonstone, and the disappointing conditions of life in Chicago, she discovers in the canyon the essence of art and its tradition and is able to prevail. The broken pottery, which once held living water, is comparable to her own throat as "a sheath, a mould in which to imprison for a moment the shining, elusive element which is life itself" (*Song of the Lark*, p. 378). She identifies with the efforts of the Indians who beautifully shaped and decorated their jars, and against this chain of endeavor "Moonstone and Chicago...become vague" (p. 380). Like Thea, Godfrey St. Peter is able to persevere from what the heart of the earth teaches him.

Cather used the West as a context of heroic struggle to bring civilization; then she criticized the West for failing to fulfill what seemed for a time a glorious potential; finally the earth and wilderness provided solace and insight that enabled her to conclude with strong, if battered, affirmation of the best that is in humanity. In "Before Breakfast," one of her final stories, an aging businessman with problems much like Professor St. Peter's watches a young girl, Venus-like, brave the icy Atlantic waters for a sunrise swim, and he concludes with relief that man will continue to evolve: "When that first amphibious frog-toad found his water-hole dried up behind him, and jumped out to hop along till he could find another—well, he started on a long hop" (*The Old Beauty and Others*, p. 166).

Survey of Criticism

The first book-length biography of Cather is E. K. Brown's *Willa Cather: A Critical Biography* (1953), completed by Leon Edel, an interesting, comprehensive introduction to the subject. Brown and Edel manage to interlace Cather's career with critical introductions to major works, making clear the autobiographical nature of much of the fiction and the concern for fiction as an art, evident in her two essay collections, *Not Under Forty* (1936) and *Willa Cather on Writing* (1949). Particularly well handled is Cather's response to personal crises after World War I through fiction involving Catholicism and the Indian past of the Southwest.

A good supplement to Brown-Edel is *Willa Cather Living: A Personal Record*, by Edith Lewis (1953). Lewis was Cather's living companion from 1909 to 1947 and provides, as is her intention, "the memories and impressions that came to me spontaneously out of my long friendship with Willa Cather" (p. v). Less self-effacing but in the same vein is Elizabeth Shepley Sergeant's *Willa Cather: A Memoir* (1953). Sergeant, who had a distinguished and varied literary career, from war correspondent to critic and translator, provides a more worldly view of Cather and intelligent comments on the fiction.

A different kind of book, valuable for the Nebraska background informing *O Pioneers!*, *The Song of the Lark*, *My Antonia*, *A Lost Lady*, and *Obscure Destinies*, is Mildred R. Bennett's *The World of Willa Cather* (1951, revised 1961). This book combines somewhat quaint items of local and family history with significant insights into the fiction and Cather's fierce dedication to art. Bennett quotes generously from previously untapped interviews, local sources, and letters. James Woodress authored the most recent biographical study, *Willa Cather: Her Life and Art* (1970). Woodress's work, although far from a definitive statement on Cather's life, benefits from the earlier biographical studies, from a thorough acquaintance with Cather's letters (which have not been released for publication), and from his knowledge of American literary history. This work combines the fiction and the life in the manner of Brown-Edel. Finally, in the biographical category, is a helpful guide to the Cather letter collections, scattered across the continent from New England to California, prepared by Margaret O'Connor (1974).

Bridging the biographical and essentially critical studies is Philip L. Gerber's *Willa Cather* (1975). Gerber provides a readable account of Cather's life and literary milieu. The book is excellent on Cather's critical principles, Gerber having profited from the publication by Nebraska of Cather's early reviews, criticism, and journalistic writings (*The Kingdom of Art*, 1966, and *The World and the Parish*, 1970). Much less satisfying is his treatment of individual novels; it is as if he neglected most recent criticism.

The first book-length critical study to examine Cather's entire career is David Daiches's *Willa Cather: A Critical Introduction* (1951). What his work lacks in originality it compensates for in aesthetic concerns, the effects managed in landscapes and interiors, and similar aspects of Cather's work. Daiches admits he is no expert in American literature and terms his work an "appreciation." In the next decade, John H. Randall III produced his controversial and elephantine *The Landscape and the Looking Glass: Willa Cather's Search for Value* (1960), the title suggesting the cultural disparity in Cather. But the study is blurred in focus, mixes life and art in a confusing manner, and fails to distinguish sufficiently between the critic's tastes and the subject's achievements. Nevertheless, Randall's is an important book; it contains the first thorough considerations of several novels and has generated many responses among scholars.

A more considered work is Edward Bloom and Lillian Bloom's *Willa Cather's Gift of Sympathy* (1962), which attempts an examination of Cather's themes and narrative techniques. Their chapter on literary theories and practices is valuable, as is the analysis of Cather's use of the Rev. W. J. Howlett's obscure biography of Denver's Bishop Machebeuf as a source for *Death Comes for the Archbishop*. Richard Giannone's *Music in Willa Cather's Fiction* (1968) examines formal aspects from the perspective of music—not only musical references but the structural dimension of musical techniques evident in the fiction. Giannone's approach is revealing in places but, like most other thesis-ridden approaches, does not apply equally well to every work. The most recent major study, and most thorough treatment of literary form in Cather, is David Stouck's *Willa Cather's Imagination* (1975). Stouck's application of epic, pastoral, and satiric modes illuminates several major works. His examination of *Archbishop* as a saint's legend is contributive, as is the sympathetic treatment given the four last books, somewhat neglected by critics.

Three essay collections deserve mention. *Willa Cather and Her Critics* (1967), edited by James Schroeter, while disappointing in many of its selections, brings together important general considerations (and protests) by H. L. Mencken, Granville Hicks, Lionel Trilling, Alfred Kazin, Maxwell Geismar, and others. Although several of these are more opinionated than objective, they indicate the reception afforded Cather by established literary arbiters. The 1973 centennial of Cather's birth occasioned two collections: *The Art of Willa Cather* (1974), edited by Bernice Slote and Virginia Faulkner, and *Five Essays on Willa Cather: The Merrimack Symposium* (1974), edited by John J. Murphy. The first gathers the major addresses and discussions from the international seminar sponsored by the University of Nebraska. Of particular interest are the contributions of novelist and short story writer Eudora Welty and Cather's publisher Alfred A. Knopf. The Merrimack collection, the outcome of a more modest commemoration, includes a perceptive essay by Bernice Slote on the complexities of Cather's mind and creative process.

Bernice Slote's exhaustive bibliographical essay in *Sixteen Modern American Authors* (1973) is the best guide to criticism through the 1960s. The annual essay by David Stouck, titled "Fiction: 1900 to the 1930s," in *American Literary Scholarship* provides an annotated guide to current criticism of Cather and other authors. Where earlier critics tended to be general, examining the range of Cather's career and applauding or condemning her traditional attitudes, contemporary critics are carefully exploring texts and sources, and mythic, sexual, and feminist aspects of the fiction. Essays by Charles, Gelfant, Helmick, Murphy, and Rosowski listed in the bibliography are representative.

Bibliography

The page numbers of sources cited in the text are from the paperback edition, listed second, when one is available.

Works by Willa Cather

Collected Short Fiction 1892-1912. Ed. Virginia Faulkner, with an introduction by Mildred R. Bennett. Lincoln: University of Nebraska Press, 1970.

The Kingdom of Art. Ed. with commentary by Bernice Slote. Lincoln: University of Nebraska Press, 1966, Covers Cather's dramatic and literary criticism, 1893-96.

Alexander's Bridge. Boston: Houghton Mifflin, 1912; Lincoln: University of Nebraska Press, Bison edition, 1977.

O Pioneers! Boston: Houghton Mifflin, 1913; Sentry edition, 1962.

The Song of the Lark. Boston: Houghton Mifflin, 1915; Sentry revised (1932) edition, 1963; Lincoln: University of Nebraska Press, Bison (1915) edition, 1978.

My Antonia. Boston: Houghton Mifflin, 1918; Sentry edition, 1961.

One of Ours. New York: Alfred A. Knopf, 1922; Vintage edition, 1971.

A Lost Lady. New York: Alfred A. Knopf, 1923; Vintage edition, 1972.

The Professor's House. New York: Alfred A. Knopf, 1925; Vintage edition, 1973.

My Mortal Enemy. New York: Alfred A. Knopf, 1926; intro. by Marcus Klein, Vintage edition, 1961.

Death Comes for the Archbishop. New York: Alfred A. Knopf, 1927; Vintage edition, 1971.

Shadows on the Rock. New York: Alfred A. Knopf, 1931; Vintage edition, 1971.

Obscure Destinies. New York: Alfred A. Knopf, 1932; Vintage edition, 1974.

Lucy Gayheart. New York: Alfred A. Knopf, 1935; Vintage edition, 1976.

Sapphira and the Slave Girl. New York: Alfred A. Knopf, 1940; Vintage edition, 1975.

The Old Beauty and Others. New York: Alfred A. Knopf, 1948; Vintage edition, 1976.

Willa Cather on Writing. New York: Alfred A. Knopf, 1949.

Studies of Willa Cather

Bennett, Mildred R. *The World of Willa Cather*. New York: Dodd, Mead, 1951; Lincoln: University of Nebraska Press, Bison edition, 1961.

Bloom, Edward A., and Bloom, Lillian D. *Willa Cather's Gift of Sympathy*. Carbondale: Southern Illinois University Press, 1962.

Brown, E. K., and Edel, Leon. *Willa Cather: A Critical Biography*. New York: Alfred A. Knopf, 1953.

Charles, Isabel. "Love and Death in Willa Cather's *O Pioneers!*" *College Language Association Journal* 9 (December 1965): 140-50.

Daiches, David. *Willa Cather: A Critical Introduction*. Ithaca: Cornell University Press, 1951.

Gelfant, Blanche H. "The Forgotten Reaping-Hook: Sex in *My Antonia*." *American Literature* 43 (March 1971): 60-82.

Gerber, Philip. *Willa Cather*. TUSAS. Boston: Twayne, 1975.

Giannone, Richard. *Music in Willa Cather's Fiction*. Lincoln: University of Nebraska Press, 1968.

Helmick, Evelyn. "The Mysteries of Antonia." *Midwest Quarterly* 17 (Winter 1976): 173-85.

Lewis, Edith. *Willa Cather Living*. New York: Alfred A. Knopf, 1953; Lincoln: University of Nebraska Press, Bison edition, 1976.

Murphy, John J. "Cather's Archbishop: A Western and Classical Perspective." *Western American Literature* 13 (Summer 1978): 141-50.

————, ed. *Five Essays on Willa Cather: The Merrimack Symposium*. North Andover, Mass.: Merrimack College, 1974.

O'Connor, Margaret A. "A Guide to the Letters of Willa Cather." *Resources for American Literary Study* 4 (Autumn 1974): 145-72.

Randall, John H., III. *The Landscape and the Looking Glass: Willa Cather's Search for Value*. Boston: Houghton Mifflin, 1960.

Rosowski, Susan. "Willa Cather's *A Lost Lady*: The Paradoxes of Change." *Novel* 11 (Fall 1977): 51-62.

Schroeter, James, ed. *Willa Cather and Her Critics*. Ithaca: Cornell University Press, 1967.

Sergeant, Elizabeth Shepley. *Willa Cather: A Memoir*. Philadelphia: J. B. Lippincott, 1953; Lincoln: University of Nebraska Press, Bison edition, 1963.

Slote, Bernice. "Willa Cather." In *Sixteen Modern American Authors*. Ed. Jackson Bryer. New York: W. W. Norton, 1973.

————. *Willa Cather: A Pictorial Memoir*. Photographs by Lucia Woods and others. Lincoln: University of Nebraska Press, 1974.

Slote, Bernice, and Faulkner, Virginia, eds. *The Art of Willa Cather*. Lincoln: University of Nebraska Press, 1974.

Stouck, David. *Willa Cather's Imagination*. Lincoln: University of Nebraska Press, 1975.

Woodress, James. *Willa Cather: Her Life and Art*. New York: Western Publishing, Pegasus edition, 1970; Lincoln: University of Nebraska Press, Bison edition, 1975.

Max Westbrook

WALTER VAN TILBURG CLARK
(1909-1971)

The apprenticeship of Walter Van Tilburg Clark does not predict his mature fiction. In the early 1930s while a graduate student, he was writing idealized poems that seem irrelevant exercises for the future author of *The Ox-Bow Incident* (1940) and *The Track of the Cat* (1949). In "The Death of Chuang Tsu, The Wise One," the opening poem of *Ten Women in Gale's House* (1932), Chuang Tsu is a mouthpiece for statements about truth: everything on earth is good except ugly thoughts; the truth is within each individual. "Dwight Marlowe" and "Youth Seeks for Truth" feature unsophisticated assertions about a vaguely romanticized aching toward truth. "A Note Dropped Through the Keyhole of Heaven" is a youthful simplification of themes about the immortality of the soul and the sweetness of love during our moment on earth, the soul's brief time apart from God.

Most literary artists have to purge themselves of some such beginning. Between youthful dreams and an aching sense of loss, between a desire for justice and a realistic recognition of injustice, artists tend to find ideas, messages, that block the stories they want to tell dramatically. Biography, then, at least in Clark's case, takes on an importance beyond our natural curiosity. How writers come to terms with the difference between dreams and reality may reveal insights into the best literature of their mature years.

Biography

Walter Van Tilburg Clark, born 3 August 1909, in East Orland, Maine, was raised in a home devoted to scholarship, the fine arts, and humanistic values. Young Clark could not be blamed if he developed an affinity for the ideal. His father, Walter Ernest Clark, was a distinguished economist who became a successful educator and administrator. After serving as head of the Department of Economics, City College of New York, he moved his family to Reno, Nevada, where he was president of the University of Nevada from 1917 to 1937. Walt's mother, Euphemia Abrams, was graduated from Cornell University, undertook advanced work in piano and composition at Columbia University, gave birth to four children in a six-year period (Walter was the first), and did settlement-house work at Greenwich House in New York City.

Later Clark would create some negative portraits of parents, but the more relevant portraits, for present purposes, are certainly those of parents, like the father in *The Watchful Gods* (1950), who are restrained, supportive, capable, and understanding. The best evidence of inherited idealism, however, is the product itself, and Clark was apparently a model youth.

After graduating from Orvis Ring Grammar School and Reno High School (1917-26), he entered the University of Nevada, where he participated in dramatics, played varsity basketball and tennis, wrote for campus publications, enjoyed a social life that ranged from dates and dances to mountain hikes, and developed his interests in music, chess, swimming, and poetry.

It is also clear from the record that Clark was a serious student. He earned the bachelor's and master's degrees from the University of Nevada (1927-31) and a second master's from the University of Vermont (1934). His interests included English literature, American literature, European and American philosophers, and Greek philosophers, poets, and dramatists. More revealing, perhaps, is the quality of his two master's theses, the first on the Tristram legend, the second on Robinson Jeffers. Both reveal extensive and careful reading, originality and independence of thought, and a mature capacity for judiciousness, suggesting that Clark's response to his academic family was a positive one.

The full story of how this young idealist was introduced to reality must await Clark's biography, which has not yet been written. We do know, however, that Clark was a lover of nature and of books who read both with remarkable courage and honesty. He was a "curable romantic," one whose fascination with ideals advanced by inclusions rather than by dichotomies. In *The City of Trembling Leaves* (1945), for example, Tim Hazard wrestles with Henry Adams's demonic pull toward nihilism, emerges as a champion of democracy, and does so with respect for nihilism and caution for democracy. It is the same with nature. Clark learned early that mountain and desert are indifferent to our species, often dangerous; yet his lifelong love of nature included affirmative and ontological implications.

Significantly, in his thesis on Robinson Jeffers, Clark defends Jeffers against the charge of negativism while admitting the merely scientific basis of Jeffers's beliefs. The conclusion, it should be emphasized, is that Walter Clark read nature, history, literature, and philosophy with love of their marvels and acceptance of their horrors. Like Buck at the end of *The Watchful Gods*, he confronted Jesus and the snake, wonders bathed in glory and terrors promising horror.

Externally at least, the facts of Clark's adult life suggest the high risk of honesty. Having married Barbara Morse in 1933, having taught high school English for ten years in Cazenovia, New York, having become the father of a son and a daughter (Robert Morse and Barbara Anne), he spent the last twenty years of his life in unproductive frustration, his brave confrontation of opposites having contributed to some fatal block. Almost all of his successful writing was done in a period of about twelve years: *The Ox-Bow Incident* (1940), *The City of Trembling Leaves* (1945), *The Track of the Cat* (1949), and *The Watchful Gods and Other Stories* (1950).

He moved about the West frequently, spending 1946 in Taos, New Mexico, for example, and 1949 on a ranch in Washoe Valley, Nevada. In 1950, he moved to Virginia City, Nevada, and taught creative writing at the University of Nevada, resigning in 1953 to protest the autocratic character of the administration. He taught briefly at Reed College, the University of Oregon, and the University of Washington. After a two-year stint at the University of Montana (1954-56), he taught creative writing for five years at San Francisco State College. In 1962, he made peace with his alma mater; Virginia City became his basic home, and he devoted himself once again to teaching creative writing, meanwhile editing the papers of Alfred Doten, an early settler in Nevada. He died 10 November 1971.

Major Themes

Clark's reputation with the critics, understandably, reflects both his accomplishments (primarily *The Ox-Bow Incident*, *The Track of the Cat*, and half a dozen short stories) and his twenty years of silence. He is widely respected as a literary artist. Among writers associated with the West as a region, he is considered the best or one of the two or three best. His short stories have been anthologized frequently. Although not a standard, he is taught in the schools. Still, Clark's critical reputation has suffered from truncation, from the long silence caused, at least in part, by his ironically successful honesty and courage.

With extreme variations in degree, the Clark "problem" is shared by writers generally. The romantic or idealist of whatever stripe who pursues the wonders of the world will encounter sins varying from the mundane to the demonic and thus be tempted to write stories with a message. Clark's special character here may be that, unlike Nathaniel Hawthorne, he made good critical judgments of his own efforts, pigeonholing the failures and publishing only those narratives in which he managed to find the concretions that contained the meanings he was after. One of the most recurrent and most indicative of those successful concretions is found in stories of the bully and in stories of a threatening force or energy.

Examples include Major Tetley, Mapes, and Farnley in *The Ox-Bow Incident*; Curt Bridges in *The Track of the Cat*; the cougar in "The Indian Well"; McKenny in "The Buck in the Hills"; and the forces of death in *The Watchful Gods*. In *The City of Trembling Leaves*, a contemporaneous and domestic novel, the brutal appears in a variety of appropriately subdued forms: first, for example, as the "threat" of sex, with young Timmy Hazard getting lessons he is not yet able to handle, and later as the frustrated or betrayed energies that appear within young artists and lovers, as well as in nature itself.

The question, obviously, is what can Major Tetley have in common with the forces of death? However evil or flawed, the Major is very much a human being.

Or what could the precocious Lucy (*The City of Trembling Leaves*)—for whom sex is fun rather than a threat—have in common with a cougar? In what way could such diverse concretions represent the evil that young Walter Clark discovered in his early readings of Chinese literature and translated, somehow, into dramatic stories of life in Nevada?

The early idealism of Clark featured a version of unity associated with oriental absolutes. The final reality, the only reality, according to Clark's rendition of Chuang Tsu, is spiritual. Later, when Clark translated that idealism into American and democratic terms, he emphasized the necessity of an ongoing dialogue between the spiritual and the practical. In brief, the brutal is a force that threatens because it is severed from the actual world. Major Tetley is therefore a successful concretion of Clark's mature values in that he is opposite the unity Clark was exploring, opposite, furthermore, in a way that is realistic to the particulars of ranch life in 1885. Tetley admires the code of Rome, the glories and manners of the Confederacy, and yet he lives on a ranch in Nevada. His powers are thus severed from the present. As shown by the horror of five deaths, Tetley's insensitivity to the agonies of his son, Gerald, and to the pleadings of Martin is dangerous indeed.

Mapes and Farnley, of course, as characters in search of a Hollywood movie, are also insensitive to the actual world in which they live. Smith paws ineffectually at the stolid Ma Grier, making sexist advances grossly severed from the awful context of three men awaiting their moment to die. And the supreme example of ideas and actions severed from their relevant context is the lynching itself.

In terms of the natural world—the cougar in "The Indian Well," the forces of death in *The Watchful Gods*—severed power takes the form of indifference to actuality. In the early chapters of *The City of Trembling Leaves*, sex play is, from Tim's viewpoint, a threatening power because it has no relation to love. Composers who cut themselves off from the history of music and from their audience are subjected to parody; Lawrence Black, who is offended by those who admire his painting, is self-destructive. In *The Track of the Cat*, Curt admits quite frankly that he has no love for the ranch but will use it to stake his escape to San Francisco. In "The Buck in the Hills," McKenny is oblivious to the horror of what he has done. In more subtle ways, "The Anonymous" is about a human being who severs himself from his own heritage and volunteers to become a trained toy for others.

Essential to Clark's translation of idealism into practical values, then, is his recurrent presentation of evil as an autonomous force that nonetheless involves human agents and therefore implies ethical responsibilities. After the lynching in *The Ox-Bow Incident*, after the deaths of Curt and Arthur in *The Track of the Cat*, one cannot say with Chuang Tsu that spiritual values are everything, that the present world is of no consequence. Major Tetley seems an inexorable force to Art Davies, but Tetley's suicide proves him to be, after all, a human being and not evil incarnate. Mapes is an eager bully, but he cannot lead. Farnley poses dramatically on behalf of blood vengeance, but in the end stares dumbly at the living Kinkaid. Curt is perhaps the emblematic version of this theme: granted the reality of sins that vary from domestic rudeness to the horror of lynch law, evil in human beings and in the amoral workings of nature has, in large measure, the power we permit it to have. Thus, from an interest in abstractions about pure spirituality, Clark changed to a practical and democratic insistence on the crucial role of self-reliance, of individual responsibility, with a touch of the Orient remaining in his vision of a unity beyond mere intellect.

With this framework in mind, Clark's characteristic themes can be seen to shape a coherent and realistic vision. We find, to begin with a puzzling instance, frequent examples of a willpower severed from any appropriate context. In *The Ox-Bow Incident*, Osgood and Tyler make speeches that are right—legally and morally—but seem wrong. Osgood and Tyler are parlor soldiers; they are afraid to join the community and fight. Their goodwill is abstracted from the challenges of actuality. Davies agonizes throughout the novel, powered also by will alone. He yearns to do the right thing but cannot bring himself to act, and thus his virtue is disenfranchised from the practical world. Davies's rationalizations about his physical cowardice notwithstanding, he is a fragmented if good man who makes speeches on the sidelines or in ill-chosen ways and at the wrong time. He fails on his own terms—his kind heart and good brain—and not because he is unable to do what a moral gunfighter would be obligated to do.

One of the most fully drawn versions of this theme occurs in *The Track of the Cat*, when Mrs. Bridges must assert her will to manage burial for one son and signal fires for another son she already knows in her heart to be dead or dying. Her will is severed from actuality because she is abstracted in mourning and in vague, troubled thoughts about righteousness sliding toward acrimony. She has nothing left to give just now, but the burden of leadership is handed to young Hal too suddenly, and, for the moment, she must assert herself. Mrs. Bridges is a person of many fundamental flaws, but the originally eastern concept of unity Clark worked toward democratic practicality included thereby an openness to variety. Much depends on the circumstances and on the intentions of the individual. A willpower severed from the practical world can be more or less strong, more or less moral.

Perhaps the most puzzling of Clark's themes is his frequent use of warnings, dreams, and apparently mystical signs, *The Track of the Cat* being the obvious example. This theme can be understood by reference to the framework described and to the role of family or community in Clark. In all three of his novels, Clark writes of people changing together, always in some strange way that is not understood by the characters themselves. Since Major Tetley, Lawrence Black, Curt Bridges, and so many others turn back in on themselves, the suggestion is that warnings exist—not for mystical reasons—but for the very practical reason that we ourselves are one of the sources of evil. The signs are there in our characters, our actions, and if they seem mystical or magical, it is because we seldom bring into focus what is there to be seen. Joe Sam's black painter seems as big as a horse, possessed of supernatural powers—until order is restored on the Bridges ranch. The black painter, then, is simply a dead cat.

Clark's extension of these themes includes the self-destructive idealist (Lawrence Black in *The City of Trembling Leaves*), the importance of ceremony (the icon Art Bridges does not prepare in time), the need for unlike males to find some type of harmony (the Bridges family, the Hazard family), the staggering variety of the world and the pain of confrontation with opposites (young Buck in *The Watchful Gods*), and the American dream as an essentially materialistic drive that has turned back in on itself. These themes and more cohere in terms of Clark's belief in a unity that must include individual responsibility, individual rights, democratic cooperation, human laws, the beauty and indifference of nature, and gods that vary from the energies of love to the powers of death.

Survey of Criticism

Such a bold amalgamation of ideas has proved to be a problem for Clark's critics as well as for Clark. What, the critics have asked, are his sources? The various answers to this question serve best to outline the criticism.

The first of four general types needs but brief mention. Edmund Wilson and Diana Trilling represent critics who fault Clark for not grounding himself in the literary fashions they themselves prefer. Since Clark did not accommodate that preference, Diana Trilling in "Fiction in Review" (1945) felt free to comment on *The City of Trembling Leaves* while admitting that she had not read it. In "White Peaks and Limpid Lakes" (1945), Edmund Wilson objects to the same novel, wanting something to happen—a marriage between Tim Hazard and Rachel Wells, for example. Criticism not based on knowledge of essential contexts requires no further comment.

The second type of critical response to Clark is a serious effort to identify techniques and sources but one that, unfortunately, selects the ancillary rather than the intrinsic. In "Form in Walter Van Tilburg Clark's *The Ox-Bow Incident*" (1969), Kenneth Andersen, for example, locates the strategy of *The Ox-Bow Incident* in extrinsic devices such as "sound usage" (p. 20). The men are responsive, he contends, not to rustling, not to news of Kinkaid's supposed death, but to the sound of Bartlett's voice. Donald E. Houghton, in "The Failure of Speech in *The Ox-Bow Incident*" (1971), also states that Bartlett is successful in "capturing the attention of the men and stirring them to action" (p. 1247); Art Croft's judgment, however, is that Bartlett arouses emotions but emotions that fade, prompting no action. Bartlett, in fact, is not a leader, and it is quite clear that the men are stirred by the rustling and by Kinkaid's reported death. The missing element is leadership. The mob will begin to act when Tetley arrives.

In a second essay (1970), Andersen locates the sources of *The Ox-Bow Incident* in stereotypical characters reshaped by Clark. The conclusion is that the "horror" of the "primitive soul" has been "glimpsed" ("Character Portrayal in *The Ox-Bow Incident*," p. 298); but it is at least equally valid to say that the novel is about a civilized horror that might have been prevented by a brave confrontation of the "primitive soul." Garth McCann takes a comparable approach, in "Patterns of Redemption and the Failure of Irony" (1974), but compounds the error by finding his definition of Cleanth Brooks's concept of irony in a literary handbook. Brooks's own and quite different definition is available in his "Irony as a Principle of Structure."

The third type of criticism, though also uninformed by demonstrated use or knowledge of Clark's sources, is redeemed by the saving grace of intelligent reading. Robert W. Cochran, for example, writes perceptively and helpfully in "Nature and the Nature of Man in *The Ox-Bow Incident*" (1971), arguing that Art Croft is representative of the good man who is realistically flawed, realistically virtuous. John Portz and Herbert Wilner also demonstrate the ability to read Clark and to help clarify his attempts to write of both unity and multiplicity.

The most successful of Clark's critics are represented by John Milton and L. L. Lee, two unusually perceptive critics who come to Clark as scholars in American literature who have specialized also in the literature of the American West. Both Milton and Lee read with sensitivity, and both know the relevant territory. Milton in *The Novel of the American West* (1980) emphasizes an aesthetic associated with vast space and unaccommodated land, while Lee in *Walter Van Tilburg Clark* (1973) is especially acute in analyzing Clark's handling of the American dream as a drive that has turned back in on itself.

Max Westbrook's criticism of Clark, in *Walter Van Tilburg Clark* (1969), is comparable to that of Milton and Lee, the major difference being that Westbrook sees archetypalism as being ontological to Clark rather than thematic. The advantage of Westbrook's approach—based primarily on his adaptations of C. G. Jung and Mircea Eliade—is a clarity and specificity unusual in literary theory and a lucid connection from theory to practice. Once Jung's implied but unstated ontology is extracted and modified, previously puzzling events in Clark's fiction can be analyzed (for example, the source of Tetley's uncanny power, the collapse into hysteria of the supposedly practical Curt Bridges). The chief disadvantage of Westbrook's theories is that no distinctions have been made between the American archetypalism of Clark and that of any other western writer. Westbrook is convincing when he argues that, for Clark, values normally thought to be impractical and unreasonable are in fact alarmingly practical and reasonable; it is highly improbable, however, as he keeps implying, that the same is true of, for example, Vardis Fisher.

Certainly for present and future critics of Clark, the door is open. There is a need for a biography of Clark and for a careful editing and republication of his works. His complete poems and complete short stories need to be collected and published in separate volumes. Robert Clark, his son, is reported to be at work on the unpublished materials, which are said to be extensive in quantity but to confirm Clark's wisdom in not offering for publication any but his best. For those interested in interpretation, the door is also open. No one, for example, has written an analysis of the obvious disparities in the characterization of Art Croft, who talks like a hick at one moment and like an intellectual the next, who is supposed to be just slightly known in Bridger's Wells yet possesses intimate and detailed knowledge of every significant character in the novel. No one, to mention just two more examples, has analyzed the musical structure of *The City of Trembling Leaves* or the recurrent and essential dreams in *The Track of the Cat*.

In spite of the fine work of Milton, Lee, and a few others, the total amount of quality criticism and scholarship on Clark is, in view of his high reputation as a western artist, surprisingly small. This is indicative, perhaps, of the curious nature of the Clark "problem." It is surely a challenge that young critics should accept.

Bibliography

Works by Walter Van Tilburg Clark

Ten Women in Gale's House and Shorter Poems. Boston: Christopher Publishing House, 1932.
The Ox-Bow Incident. New York: Random House, 1940.
The City of Trembling Leaves. New York: Random House, 1945.
The Track of the Cat. New York: Random House, 1949.
The Watchful Gods and Other Stories. New York: Random House, 1950.

Studies of Walter Van Tilburg Clark

Andersen, Kenneth. "Form in Walter Van Tilburg Clark's *The Ox-Bow Incident*." *Western Review* 6 (Spring 1969): 19-25.
————. "Character Portrayal in *The Ox-Bow Incident*." *Western American Literature* 4 (Winter 1970): 287-98.
Cochran, Robert W. "Nature and the Nature of Man in *The Ox-Bow Incident*." *Western American Literature* 5 (Winter 1971): 253-64.
Houghton, Donald E. "The Failure of Speech in *The Ox-Bow Incident*." *English Journal* 59 (December 1970): 1245-51.
Lee, L. L. *Walter Van Tilburg Clark*. WWS. Boise: Boise State College, 1973.
McCann, Garth. "Patterns of Redemption and the Failure of Irony: *The Ox-Bow Incident* and *The Man Who Killed the Deer*." *Southwestern American Literature* 4 (1974): 62-67.
Milton, John. *The Novel of the American West*. Lincoln: University of Nebraska Press, 1980, pp. 195-229.
Portz, John. "Idea and Symbol in Walter Van Tilburg Clark." *Accent* 17 (Spring 1957): 112-28.
Trilling, Diana. "Fiction in Review." *Nation*, 23 June 1945, pp. 702-4.
Westbrook, Max. *Walter Van Tilburg Clark*. TUSAS. New York: Twayne, 1969.
Wilner, Herbert. "Walter Van Tilburg Clark." *Western Review* 20 (Winter 1956): 103-22.
Wilson, Edmund. "White Peaks and Limpid Lakes: A Novel about Nevada." *New Yorker*, 26 May 1945, pp. 75-77.

Paul T. Bryant

H. L. DAVIS
(1894-1960)

Biography

By his own varying accounts, H. L. Davis lived several exciting, adventurous lives, punching cattle and herding sheep in Oregon, and pursuing Pancho Villa with Black Jack Pershing along the Mexican border. These and similar protean fictions were what Davis provided when asked for biographical information. More colorful than the actual facts, they have often been accepted as true. But they tend to mask some of Davis's creative achievements as a writer under a pretense of autobiographical derivation. The actual biographical facts are less colorful, but they do greater justice to his creative imagination.

Harold Lenoir Davis was the oldest of four sons of James Alexander and Ruth Bridges Davis. He was born on 18 October 1894 in the tiny settlement of Rone's Mill, near Roseburg, Douglas County, Oregon. James Davis was a country schoolteacher with some intellectual pretensions—he wrote poetry and read the literary journals. At the same time he was a skilled trainer of horses and a locally renowned marksman. These physical achievements are made more remarkable by his having had only one leg, the other having been lost in his early childhood in a sawmill accident.

The life of a country schoolteacher kept the James Davis family moving from community to community every year or two during Harold's early childhood. Until 1906 these moves were all among communities around Roseburg, between the Cascade Mountains on the east and the coastal range on the west. It is an area of plentiful rainfall, good timber, and mild seasons. In 1906, however, the family moved east across the Cascades to the town of Antelope, Oregon, in a high, dry plateau country of sagebrush ranches, dryland wheat farms, and occasional irrigation. The distances were greater, the climate harsher. Although Harold lived in Antelope for only two years (1906-8), and although he did not get the wide experience as cowboy and sheepherder that he later claimed, the region made a deep impression on his imagination. It appears repeatedly in his poetry, his fiction, and his sketches of Oregon. In addition, his career as a writer might be said to have begun with journalistic work, during the summer of 1907, for the *Antelope Herald* (no copies of the newspaper appear to have survived).

In 1908, James Davis became principal of the high school at The Dalles, Oregon, on the Columbia River. This brought an end to the family's frequent moves. Harold was to use The Dalles as his base for the next twenty years, leaving there finally only when he set out to make his living as a writer.

As a riverboating, railroading center of commerce, The Dalles helped round out Harold's experience of Oregon life. He was graduated from high school there in 1912, on schedule at the age of eighteen, although he was to imply later that his schooling had been casual and irregular. Casual though his attitude might have been toward the commercial course he studied in high school, Harold was a voracious reader with a prodigious memory.

After graduating from high school, Davis took a job as deputy county assessor for Wasco County, of which The Dalles was the county seat. Because in Wasco County the authority to collect taxes was vested in the sheriff, Davis was also made a deputy sheriff, but he never functioned as a law enforcement officer. In 1916 or 1917 he left the tax collection job and went to work for the U.S. General Land Office, surveying in the Mount Adams area of Washington.

In the fall of 1917, with fifteen hundred dollars in savings, Davis set out for Palo Alto, California, with the intention of enrolling as an engineering student at Stanford University. Although he later claimed to have been a Stanford student of engineering, Davis actually found that his savings were not enough to finance a college education, and he returned to The Dalles.

Davis later gave various interesting accounts of his military service, but the actuality was neither extraordinary nor exciting. He was drafted on 23 September 1918, assigned immediately to the Quartermaster Corps at Fort McDowell, California, and made a clerk with the rank of corporal. He was discharged fewer than three months later, 10 December 1918.

The most important event of those three months was not military in nature: Davis submitted a group of poems to Harriet Monroe, and she accepted them for publication in *Poetry*. This was the true beginning of Davis's career as a published writer.

This group of eleven poems appeared in the April 1919 issue of *Poetry* under the general title, "Primapara." Over the next fifteen years Davis published a total of thirty-nine poems, earning praise from Monroe, Carl Sandburg, and Robinson Jeffers. As his modest poetic reputation developed, Davis became acquainted with the literary scene in the Northwest, but as he was to do throughout his literary career, he remained an outsider. He confirmed this outsider's role in 1927 when he and James Stevens published a privately printed pamphlet, *Status Rerum: A Manifesto, Upon the Present Condition of Northwest Literature*, making a blunt attack on the region's writers, editors, and teachers of writing.

There apparently were other forms of collaboration with Stevens. In 1928 two short stories, "Occidental's Prodigal" and "Oleman Hattie," appeared in *Adventure* magazine under James Stevens's name, but these may have been by Davis.

At the same time, H. L. Mencken, who had published some of Davis's poetry, had been encouraging him to write fiction, encouragement that led in 1929 to publication of "Old Man Isbell's Wife" in the *American Mercury*.

Davis's personal life, as well as his literary life, changed in 1928. In May he married Marion Lay, a journalist and aspiring writer, and moved from The Dalles to Winslow, Washington. He never again lived in The Dalles.

Depending primarily on the sale of his short stories and sketches, Davis's finances for the next few years were precarious. Then in 1932 he won a Guggenheim Fellowship to Mexico to work on a long poem. In Mexico, however, he abandoned plans for the poem and began to pull together ideas for a novel he had been considering for some time.

This first novel, *Honey in the Horn*, published in 1935 by Harper, won the Harper Novel Prize that year and the Pulitzer Prize in 1936. Unfortunately, this success was not soon followed by another. Although he had an early version of *Beulah Land* completed in 1937, Davis did not publish another novel until *Harp of a Thousand Strings* appeared ten years later.

The hiatus in novel production arose from two crises in Davis's life—one marital, the other professional. Davis's marriage had been periodically in difficulty, beginning as early as 1931. In 1942 Harold and Marion separated for the final time and were divorced in June. On the professional side of his life, Davis was having a dispute with his publisher over royalties and publication rights. One result was that with two manuscripts of novels on hand, Davis could publish neither. During these years the only volume published under Davis's name was *Proud Riders and Other Poems*, a collection of poems, most of which had been published previously in magazines.

In 1947 this problem was finally settled, and Davis changed publishers, moving to William Morrow and Company. *Harp of a Thousand Strings* was published almost immediately, in 1947, and *Beulah Land* appeared in 1949.

Davis's fourth novel, and perhaps his best, *Winds of Morning*, appeared in 1952, with good reviews. *Team Bells Woke Me*, a collection of some of his previously published short stories, appeared in 1953, again with critical acclaim. His career was once again prospering. Then on 2 June 1953, Davis married Elizabeth Tonkin Martin del Campo. This marriage was a happy one.

In October 1956, in Mexico, Davis was hospitalized with acute arteriosclerosis, and his left leg had to be amputated. Never free from pain thereafter, Davis continued to work, completing a series of travel essays for *Holiday*, seeing his last novel, *The Distant Music*, through the press in 1957, and a collection of the essays into print as *Kettle of Fire* in 1959. He began work on another novel, tentatively named *Exit, Pursued by a Bear*, but on 8 October 1960, while visiting San Antonio, he suffered a heart attack. Still in the hospital, on 31 October, he suffered a second attack that was fatal.

The body of published work that he left at his death included forty-two poems, twenty-four short stories, ten sketches, eleven travel essays, a scattering of critical essays and reviews, and five novels. It is not a massive body of work, but it is increasingly being recognized as a major contribution to western American literature.

Major Themes

H. L. Davis is one of a handful of fiction writers who have reclaimed the American West for nonstereotypical artistic treatment as part of the universal human experience. His exploration of the western experience has established its vital connections both with the cultural past of the Westerners and the present of the modern West.

The universality of the western experience runs as a common thread through the whole body of Davis's work, but it is most explicitly presented in *Harp of a Thousand Strings*: "Stories change, and shift ground and directions and actors. . . but they can no more end than a river can change its identity by shifts of current" (p. 267). When these stories move into the American West, they do not lose their connection with a longer past elsewhere. By the same token, they do not end with the closing of the frontier; they continue into the present. Davis's insistence on such continuing connections is part of the immediacy, vitality, and realism of his work.

To establish the western experience as a coherent part of human experience, Davis uses a number of devices and thematic approaches. Among the most effective of these is western folklore. As folklorists have often demonstrated, western folktales derive from earlier folk materials brought west with the frontier. If, as Davis observes, "the stories of a land are the cumulative assertion of what it is, its character, its people, its individuality, its being" (*Harp of a Thousand Strings*, p. 266), the folk tales he uses to illustrate his novels represent a distillation of the human experience of the West. As such, they provide a sense of the universal in the concrete, an air of detachment from the harshness of immediate experience while universalizing that experience.

Much as they are "of the folk," many of Davis's protagonists become, to an extent, picaros, outsiders, alienated observers who must be brought back into society if the dramatic tensions of the story are to be resolved. The picaresque element is perhaps most obvious in *Honey in the Horn*, but it is significant also in such short stories as "The Homestead Orchard" and "The Stubborn Spearmen," as well as in *Beulah Land*. The theme is further developed into an ironic doubling of the picaro into a youthful realist and an elderly idealist, both of whom must regain a place in society through initiation, in "Open Winter" and his finest novel, *Winds of Morning*.

Underlying these patterns of alienation and initiation and extending beyond them is the basic human need for love. All of Davis's novels, and most of his other fiction and poetry, deal in some way with the problem of love. In *Honey in the Horn*, Clay's love for Luce makes it possible for him to accept her guilt and his, and therefore the basic imperfection of humanity. Through this acceptance, he is able to rejoin society. In *Harp of a Thousand Strings*, romantic love is one of the three driving motives for Tallien and later for the three Americans.

The many varieties of human love, and what each can cost, become the central theme of *Beulah Land*. Love of one's land, love for one's people, love between parent and child, and love between man and woman are all explored in this novel, along with the vulnerability that such forms of love create, the costs such vulnerability can exact, and the values that can outweigh such costs.

Love is the final, resolving affirmation in *Winds of Morning*, both for Hendricks, the old man who has been driven out of society by a failure of love, and for Amos, the young man whose adolescent cynicism has kept him from yet joining society.

Davis's last published novel, *The Distant Music*, explores what can happen when the love of a certain piece of land dominates and finally destroys the forms of love between humans. Finally the land holds the people prisoner, excluding them from ties and sympathies necessary for their fulfillment as humans. The land becomes a prison that destroys all hope for happiness.

With the various forms of love as a central theme, it is not surprising that Davis frequently uses Christian symbolism. Thus the problems of love with which Davis's characters struggle become also moral problems, problems of the human soul. The problems of love are resolved not only in terms of what the characters want to do but also what they ought to do. Generally the resolution comes when the character reaches that point at which what he or she wants to do and what he or she ought to do coincide.

In joining obligation with desire, Davis makes regular use of Judeo-Christian patterns of innocence and initiation (the Edenic pattern of "The Homestead Orchard," for example), the common human mixture of angelic and satanic (the divided face of Clark Burdon in *Honey in the Horn*), and the capacity of human love to atone through sacrifice (Pap Hendricks in *Winds of Morning*).

This traditionally Edenic West, into which the serpent eternally intrudes, offers therefore another but fully congruent theme for Davis: the problems of illusion and aspiration. From the first explorer to the newest western suburbanite, Westerners have acted more on their illusions of the West and their aspirations than upon any objective reality. Davis develops this theme especially effectively in his pairing of initiates: the idealistic old-timer who represents the early-day hopes of Westerners and the cynical youth who sees the disillusioning modern reality of what the West has turned out to be. This pairing reaches its fullest development in *Winds of Morning*. Here illusion becomes unimportant, and aspiration, if it is worthy, becomes its own justification even when it is not realized. As old Hendricks finally realizes, living according to one's sentiments is sufficient success in itself. He concludes that what a man puts into life is more important than what he gets out of it. For the idealistic old-timer, this means accepting the likelihood of failure without defeat. For the cynical youth, this means choosing not necessarily what is possible but rather what is worth the efforts of a man's life. This brings us again back to Davis's moral center: doing what one ought to do is more satisfying than doing what will always succeed.

Finally, the most obvious and often noted characteristic of Davis's fiction is his ironic humor. A distinction that is not always made is between the ironic humor with which he treats his characters and the lyric sweetness with which he presents the natural landscape. The "Virgilian sweetness" of his landscapes was evident early in his poetry, but he did not develop the ironic humor until he began to write fiction under the tutelage of H. L. Mencken. The difference is one of artistic distancing. The pastoral landscape he can present directly, but the innate reticence of a painfully shy man kept him from going directly to the heart of profound human emotions. As with all other great humorists, and certainly with Mark Twain, whom Davis resembles in a number of ways, humor becomes a mask for tragedy and terror. For Davis, the tragedy and terror of the human predicament can be presented only through the screen of humor and can be redeemed only through courage and love, living life according to one's sentiments.

Thus H. L. Davis, the ironic humorist, the debunker of the mythical West, the portrayer of disillusion, is really a romantic after all.

Survey of Criticism

Davis's poetry was well received from the first, but aside from brief praise by Harriet Monroe, Carl Sandburg, Robinson Jeffers, and others of the *Poetry* group, it received little critical attention during the 1920s and early 1930s. As he moved on to fiction and began to establish his reputation as a novelist, his poetry was almost forgotten, certainly neglected. Not until the 1970s, long after critics had begun to give careful attention to his novels, did the significance of his poetry begin to be appreciated in its own right and as a source of insight into his development as a prose writer.

In 1974, Robert Bain examined some of Davis's most successful poems, finding in them the "racy and vernacular language that is the hallmark of his best fiction" (*H. L. Davis*, p. 15). Then in 1978 Paul Bryant (*H. L. Davis*) traced Davis's development as a poet and examined a number of his poems in considerable detail. Bryant found that although Davis's poetry had been praised for its evocation of the western landscape, he used that landscape actually as a metaphor for an internal landscape of human experience. Thus Davis is not a poet of the West or of any particular locale but a poet of the human condition.

Renewed attention was also called to Davis's poetry in 1978 by the publication of *The Selected Poems of H. L. Davis*, with an introduction by Thomas Hornsby Ferril. This slim volume reprints a selection of poems already published and adds some previously unpublished work found in Davis's papers. The quality of a few of these new pieces suggests that had he not moved on to fiction, Davis might have become a major American poet.

At the time of publication, Davis's novels received the mixed and often supercilious reviews that have so often been the lot of serious American writers who set their work in the West. Although *Honey in the Horn* won the Harper Prize and the Pulitzer Prize, reviewers tended to praise it for the wrong reasons—colorful language, western landscapes—and thus to reduce it to a regional work in the narrowest sense. On the other hand, Robert Penn Warren, writing in the *Southern Review* (Winter 1936, pp. 639-41) saw that *Honey* was more than just "a Baedeker of Oregon back-country." Warren perceived that Davis's humor had a deeper purpose: "humor is simply the basic way in which he asserts his objectivity and his control of his material." (pp. 640-41).

Contemporary reviews of Davis's later novels were usually more generous if not always more perceptive. After World War II, writing about the West had begun to be accepted as respectable by some members of the literary establishment. The most favorable reviewer reaction came from *Winds of Morning*. *The Distant Music*, a more somber and less successful novel, was not so well received, but another novelist, Walter Van Tilburg Clark, saw clearly what Davis was doing in the use of the land as the motionless center of the novel.

Academic criticism of Davis has been notably sparse, although his work has attracted greater critical attention since the mid-1970s. Dayton Kohler, in his 1952 article, "H. L. Davis: Writer in the West," was the first academic critic to recognize clearly Davis's literary achievement. Kohler's article is still useful to students of Davis's work.

In 1963 George Kellogg provided a valuable bibliography of Davis. Although this was intended as an exhaustive bibliography, including all editions of Davis's novels, Kellogg lists minor mention of Davis in secondary sources and provides a long but incomplete list of book reviews. There are some errors in this bibliography, but it is the standard basic bibliographic resource for Davis. In 1970, Richard Etulain provided a supplement to the Kellogg bibliography; it fills some of the gaps in Kellogg's bibliography and brings it up to 1970. Two years later, Etulain provided a useful bibliography of secondary sources on Davis in *Western American Literature*.

John Lauber, in "A Western Classic: H. L. Davis's *Honey in the Horn*" (1962), was the first to provide a perceptive comparison between Clay Calvert and Huck Finn in their efforts to come to terms with society. A wider-ranging and very helpful discussion of the art of Davis's novels is provided by Phillip L. Jones in "The West of H. L. Davis" (1968-69).

Jan Harold Brunvand, in *"Honey in the Horn* and 'Acres of Clams'" (1967), has offered a good beginning to the needed study of Davis's use of western folklore. In "H. L. Davis: Viable Uses for the Past," Paul T. Bryant studies Davis's techniques for using the past to understand the present in the West.

Robert Bain, in his Western Writers Series booklet, offers in the form of an extended essay a critically perceptive survey of Davis's career, analysis of his principal works, and an assessment of his artistic achievement.

The only book-length work devoted to Davis is Paul T. Bryant's volume, *H. L. Davis* (1978). This book seeks to establish the principal biographical facts of Davis's life and to lay out the essential critical framework for the continuing study of Davis's achievements as a literary artist. It offers readings of his better poems and short prose and of all five of his published novels. Finally, it provides a bibliography of Davis's published works, including some items from the *Rocky Mountain Herald* not included in previous bibliographies. It also provides a brief bibliography of selected secondary sources.

Bibliography

Works by H. L. Davis

"Jeffers Denies Us Twice." *Poetry* 31 (February 1928): 274-79. Review of *The Women at Point Sur*, by Robinson Jeffers.
Honey in the Horn. New York: Harper & Brothers, 1935.
Proud Riders and Other Poems. New York: Harper & Brothers, 1942.
Harp of a Thousand Strings. New York: William Morrow, 1947.
Beulah Land. New York: William Morrow, 1949.
Winds of Morning. New York: William Morrow, 1952.
Team Bells Woke Me and Other Stories. New York: William Morrow, 1953.
The Distant Music. New York: William Morrow, 1957.
"The Elusive Trail to the Old West." *New York Times Book Review*, 7 February 1954, pp. 1, 17. Reprinted in *Kettle of Fire* as "Preface: A Look Around," pp. 13-18.
Kettle of Fire. New York: William Morrow, 1959.
The Selected Poems of H. L. Davis. Introduction by Thomas Hornsby Ferril. Boise, Idaho: Ahsahta Press, 1978.

Studies of H. L. Davis

Armstrong, George M. "H. L. Davis's *Beulah Land*: A Revisionist's Novel of Westering." In *The Westering Experience in American Literature: Bicentennial Essays*. Ed. Merrill Lewis and L. L. Lee. Bellingham: Western Washington University, 1977.
Bain, Robert. *H. L. Davis*. WWS. Boise, Idaho: Boise State University, 1974.
Brunvand, Jan Harold. "*Honey in the Horn* and 'Acres of Clams': The Regional Fiction of H. L. Davis." *Western American Literature* 2 (Summer 1967): 135-45.
Bryant, Paul T. *H. L. Davis*. TUSAS. Boston: Twayne, 1978.
———. "H. L. Davis: Viable Uses for the Past." *Western American Literature* 3 (Spring 1968): 3-18.
Clark, Walter Van Tilburg. "The Call of the Far Country." *New York Times Book Review*, 3 February 1957, pp. 5, 29.
Etulain, Richard W. "H. L. Davis: A Bibliographical Addendum." *Western American Literature* 5 (Summer 1970): 129-35.
———. *Western American Literature: A Bibliography of Interpretive Books and Articles*. Vermillion, S. Dak.: Dakota Press, 1972.
Jones, Phillip L. "The West of H. L. Davis." *South Dakota Review* 6 (Winter 1968-69): 72-84.
Kellogg, George. "H. L. Davis, 1896-1960: A Bibliography." *Texas Studies in Language and Literature* 5 (Summer 1963): 294-303.

Kohler, Dayton. "H. L. Davis: Writer in the West." *College English* 16 (December 1952): 133-40.

Lauber, John. "A Western Classic: H. L. Davis's *Honey in the Horn*." *Western Humanities Review* 16 (Winter 1962): 85-86.

Warren, Robert Penn. "Some Recent Novels." *Southern Review* 1 (Winter 1936): 624-49.

BERNARD DEVOTO
(1897-1955)

Biography

Bernard Augustine DeVoto was born 11 January 1897 at Ogden, Utah, and died 13 November 1955 in New York City. He remained in his native Utah for his first eighteen years, graduating from Ogden High School and attending the University of Utah for a year. He then went to Harvard University in the fall of 1915 and enlisted in the army in 1917, becoming a commissioned officer and an instructor in marksmanship. After the war he attended Harvard again, graduating Phi Beta Kappa in 1920.

After teaching history in Ogden for a year, DeVoto began teaching English at Northwestern University, where he remained until 1927. He married Helen Avis MacVicar in 1923. During the Northwestern years, he wrote book reviews for the *Evanston News-Index* and other newspapers, two western novels, an article for an anthology on the frontier, and his well-known article on Utah for the *American Mercury*. He also worked on *The Writer's Handbook*, a freshman English text, which was published in 1928.

In 1927 the DeVotos moved to Cambridge, Massachusetts, where DeVoto taught at Harvard University from 1929 through 1936 and edited the *Harvard Graduates' Magazine* for almost two years.

During these years he wrote introductions to western histories, an important book on Mark Twain, and one of his best novels. In November 1935, he published his first "Easy Chair" essay in *Harper's*; he continued to sit in what Wallace Stegner calls this "uneasy chair" until his death in 1955. He wrote 243 "Easy Chair" essays, three more than did William Dean Howells. From 1936 to 1938 he was editor of *Saturday Review of Literature*.

In 1938 DeVoto became curator of the Mark Twain papers, working with them until 1946. Out of these years came three more Mark Twain books. He also began, perhaps with his first Mark Twain book, a running argument with the literary critics. He wrote fiction under his own name and under pseudonyms.

Beginning in 1939, he taught at the Breadloaf School of English during the summers for several years.

In 1943 DeVoto published the first of his histories, and before his death he wrote two more major historical works and edited the journals of Lewis and Clark. *Across the Wide Missouri* won the Pulitzer Prize for history in 1948, and the Lewis and Clark journals won the National Book Award for nonfiction in 1953.

During his eastern years DeVoto published many articles on a variety of subjects in major magazines. His two books of literary criticism are also products of these years. His output was tremendous, his travels through the West provided many articles, but he was best known for his "Easy Chair" articles.

Major Themes

One of the better-known American writers, DeVoto himself was never quite sure what kind of writer he was. Sometimes he considered himself a journalist. Most frequently he spoke of himself as a writer of fiction. He is best known as a historian. He was a good literary critic, though he despised the tribe. He was editor of *Saturday Review of Literature* for a little more than seventeen months, though it could not be affirmed that he was a successful editor. His essays, both in the "Easy Chair" and elsewhere, observed and criticized almost every aspect of American civilization.

His writing was consistently varied; his perceptions were clear; his opinions, both the biting and the loving ones, were nearly always based on the facts, which he saw clearly and accepted. The broadness of his interests and the vigor of his viewpoints frequently distressed his contemporaries. But throughout it all he projected a clear image of man thinking. And like Emerson, he did not strive for "a foolish consistency...the hobgoblin of little minds." He was also man writing, interested in almost everything.

Between 1924 and 1947 DeVoto wrote five novels under his own name, all related directly or indirectly to the westward movement in American history. His lighter and more popular works of fiction were published under the pseudonym John August.

DeVoto probably would protest at being called a "western" writer, but the facts of his literary and historical publications make the label reasonable. Three of his novels, *The Crooked Mile* (1924), *The Chariot of Fire* (1926), and *The House of Sun-Goes-Down* (1928), deal with the frontier experience, the westward movement, and the influence of the frontier on American civilization. The fourth, *We Accept with Pleasure* (1934), contrasts the intellectual life of the effete East with the more meaningful life of the West and the Midwest. The fifth, *Mountain Time* (1947), presents a theme similar to that of *We Accept with Pleasure*: the superiority of the simpler western frontier ethic to that of the more complicated, corrupted East.

The Crooked Mile is a careful study of the frontier town of Windsor (actually, Ogden, Utah); it tells of the deterioration of the third generation of the Abbeys and describes the "new West," which was controlled by rapacious corporations, which had (have?) destroyed or at least weakened the frontier ideal. His third novel, *The House of Sun-Goes-Down*, elaborates on and describes earlier phases of frontier development; the time of the action precedes that of *The Crooked Mile*.

The second novel, *The Chariot of Fire*, previously entitled *The Burning Bush* and *The Great God Boggs* (Stegner, *Uneasy Chair*, pp. 63-64), is a treatment of the life of a frontier religious fanatic previously described in *The Leatherwood God* by William Dean Howells.

In DeVoto's novels the westward movement is revealed in the lives of men of three generations of the Abbey family. The frontier, a place of hardships and problems, is an ever-present force in their lives, with some of the family never becoming reconciled to the problems. The struggle in the first generation was against the land itself; in the second generation, against the encroachment of a tainted capitalism; in the third generation, against a highly organized, dominant capitalism. DeVoto emphasizes human relationships rather than violence; in fact, unlike most other western novelists, he has firmly avoided most of the usual clichés. His novels are filled with long philosophical discussions; this and the absence of the clichés probably accounts for their lack of popularity. But his analysis is valid and interesting.

In *The Crooked Mile* DeVoto provides John Gale, frontier historian, with a bibliography, a believable one, and a theory about the development of the frontier. Gale believed, for instance, that no millennium would spring from the frontier because energy had declined. He believed that the pioneer was "not a superman dominated by visions of empire, but a hell-ridden calvinist [*sic*] driven west by economic pressure" (*Crooked Mile*, p. 149). Moreover, "not God's whisper urged him out, but bankruptcy among his stronger brothers. He sought not something lost behind the ranges, but free land by which he might repair his fortunes" (p. 149).

The frontiersman is more clearly pictured as an individual in *The Chariot of Fire* than in the other novels. His characterization of Jeff Brashear, one of the "hell-ridden calvinists," is of the frontiersman as historian John Gale pictured him, but Joe Stevens, another type, could have come from the pages of Franklin J. Meine's *Tall Tales of the Southwest* or from DeVoto's own *Mark Twain's America* (*Chariot of Fire*, pp. 20, 27). A memorable character is Thomas Chadborne, "a bewildering infidel," always on the side of religious freedom (pp. 46-47).

DeVoto's frontiersmen in his novels were not romanticized so much as they were in his later histories. His historian, John Gale, decried the myths of "the Pioneer and the Frontier." Gale wrote, "Freedom was conditioned by the inheritance of the race, a heritage not devoid of justice, mediocrity, tyranny and fear. And the true individualist on the frontier is to be found at one end of a rope whose other end is in the hands of a group of vigilantes" (*Crooked Mile*, p. 23).

Whether DeVoto was a good novelist is controversial. Wallace Stegner, though admitting that the novels are honest, states that the thrill of life is missing, that they are too contrived and perhaps too witty, too packed with ideas (*Four Portraits*, pp. 100-101). But I believe that when one compares them with the novels of DeVoto's contemporaries and with the growing tide of cliché-ridden Westerns, they are better than Stegner and others think. DeVoto's novels deserve reprinting. It says something about modern tastes that some of the John August novels were put into paperback editions, while the DeVoto novels were not.

DeVoto's interest in the frontier ethic influenced his essays on the plundering of the West by private-interest industrial forces, and his experience as a fiction writer was a continual aid in his writing of history. The style of DeVoto the historian was continually reflective of the imagination of DeVoto the novelist, although his love for the facts subdued or at least controlled his imagination.

DeVoto was always a historian of the American West, even when he was writing fiction, literary criticism, or social criticism. In the June 1939 *Harper's* "Easy Chair" DeVoto noted Allan Nevins's suggestion that historians were pretty dull writers. DeVoto had always thought of them as "splendid as the blond Indians who, in the legends of the Southwest, were some day going to appear and free the Zuni and the Pueblo and restore the ancient glories of the race" and was disheartened that Nevins considered the blond gods as "only Diggers coated with whitewash" ("What's the Matter with History?" pp. 109-12).

DeVoto defended the professional historian, although few historians are lively writers. For example, he cited Frederic Logan Paxson's *History of the American Frontier* (1924), a pedestrian work, as an example of interesting history. He did not believe that many literary men could write good history because the historian's love for facts would preclude such writing. He did believe, however, that the American historian was deficient in the exploration and synthesis of historical facts and was averse to making value judgments. It is one of the paradoxes of DeVoto's writing that he later wrote the kind of history that in 1939 he considered impractical. In general, his methods involved use of his recommended exploration and synthesis of facts, and he was not averse to drawing strict conclusions about the facts of history or to making extrapolations.

It is possible that DeVoto will be remembered for his histories rather than for his fiction. This likelihood, ironically, is due to the literary qualities of his historical works. Historians tend to consider DeVoto too literary, and literary men prefer to classify him as a historian. It should be an obvious truth, although neither historians nor literary critics hasten to accept it, that the best historians utilize literary skills. The line between belles lettres and good history is not clearly drawn.

By 1939 DeVoto was already working on the periphery of history, having contributed a thirty-five-page essay to Duncan Aikman's *The Taming of the Frontier* (1925) and having reviewed numerous books about the frontier, including Paxson's history.

Although DeVoto did not consider *Mark Twain's America* (1932) as history, it is social history of the finest kind, filled with minute detail about the life of the frontiersman. More importantly, it provided DeVoto with a technique for the writing of history.

In the order of their writing, DeVoto's histories are *The Year of Decision: 1846* (1943), *Across the Wide Missouri* (1947), and *The Course of Empire* (1952). He also edited and wrote an introduction to *The Journals of Lewis and Clark* (1953).

The first three books, which make up the bulk of DeVoto's historical writing, are really a trilogy with a changing focus of narration. The trilogy explains the impact of the frontier on American civilization. *The Year of Decision*, a superior book, gives a thorough account of the events of 1846, plus some months preceding and subsequent to the year. The most important events of the year, which included the Mexican War, are described. Thoreau's activities at Walden Pond, Francis Parkman's life among the Sioux, the transcendentalists' agricultural fiasco at Brook Farm, the Magoffins' trip along the Santa Fe Trail, and the Donner party are all discussed. DeVoto's purpose, according to the preface, was literary. He sought to "realize the pre-Civil War, Far Western frontier as personal experience" (*The Year of Decision: 1846*, p. x). But he had to become a historian to provide the complete background, which had not yet been compiled.

In *The Year of Decision* DeVoto, as a novelist would, described his settings and characters fully, using the original sources instead of his own imagination as background. His structure, or plot, was the relating of the events leading first to national unity and then to schism. Emphasized are the westward movement and the Mexican War. And he shows clearly that Henry David Thoreau was psychologically involved in the westward movement. The theme of the entire book is the psychological influence of the idea of manifest destiny on westward expansion. The book constantly reveals DeVoto's wit, as well as his prejudices. He was not afraid to draw unpopular conclusions or criticize respected individuals. *The Year of Decision* is his most significant and interesting history.

Across the Wide Missouri is avowedly a history of the Rocky Mountain fur trade between 1832 and 1838. At the same time it is a work of literary art. It even includes eighty-one paintings by George Catlin, Carl Bodmer, and Alfred Jacob Miller. Its subjects include such mountain men as Francis Chardon, Jim Beckwourth, Jim Bridger ("Old Gabe"), Kit Carson, and the Sublettes, earlier described by George F. Ruxton and Washington Irving.

DeVoto gives full analyses of such men as Captain Benjamin Bonneville, U.S. Army (first written about by Washington Irving), and Captain William D. Stewart, "a globe-trotting Scotsman." Early missionaries and their wives are discussed in detail. DeVoto suggested that two completely different white women, plain Eliza Spalding and beautiful Narcissa Whitman, wives of missionaries, should be used as symbols of the white man's domination of the West rather than the Sioux chief's supposed citing of his first sight of the white man's plows as a symbol of doom for his people (*Across the Wide Missouri*, p. 247.) DeVoto believed that the early missionary attempts (for the glory of God) and the beaver trade (for the service of Mammon) combined to promote the manifest destiny concept.

DeVoto's development from belletrist to historian can be traced in his use of traditional scholarly devices. His first history contains only a general statement of his sources; DeVoto claimed that a complete bibliography was not possible. The second volume, in which he admitted to being a historian, contains an extensive bibliography. In the third volume, *The Course of Empire*, DeVoto provided a highly structured bibliography, divided into "documentary" and "secondary" sources, for each chapter, His footnotes for the most part are explanatory rather than documentary; he makes no claim that the source references or the notes are complete and expresses the plaintive wish of all impatient scholars that books could be written without notes.

In *The Course of Empire* DeVoto came closer to being the historian's historian than in the other two histories. In his Acknowledgments he admits to being a historian of the westward movement, but in his preface he calls his book the "last of three narrative studies." The scope of *The Course of Empire*, however, vastly differs from that of the previous volumes. It covers a period of 278 years. DeVoto admitted that the difference in time covered made necessary "the use of different conventions, historical as well as literary, and a different method" (*Course of Empire*, p. xiv). The different method was a switch from a chronological to a thematic structure, although he used a chronological order as much as possible. He described his overall theme as a combining of a description of the geography of North America, the ideas of Americans about this geography, right and wrong, the exploration of the United States and Canada and a discovery of a route to the Pacific, the struggles among four empires for the area now the United States, and the relationship of all these things to the various Indian tribes.

While *The Course of Empire* is still more historical in bent, DeVoto continues to use literary approaches. His presentation of facts is not merely a dry journey; he exemplified the truth that western history no longer needs to be dull, if it ever did. New ideas, techniques, and points of view, including his own, manifested "a revolution in historiography." DeVoto was a historian under strong literary influence; he was a belletristic historian constantly working in a world of ideas inspired by historical facts.

In his essays DeVoto was the kindly curmudgeon, a critic and defender of the American way. Unlike Mencken's bombast, DeVoto's adverse criticism was mainly of those influences he thought were destructive, and his defense of America was a loving one.

His most powerful analysis of the American past was *Mark Twain's America*, an excessively thorough answer to Van Wyck Brooks's *The Ordeal of Mark Twain*, in which Brooks pictured Mark Twain as a shrinking genius, harassed by a rude, rough, uncouth frontier people. DeVoto insisted with vengeance that Brooks understood neither Mark Twain nor the frontier and then proceeded to educate Brooks. The answer was devastating, though the generation of literary critics whose god is Henry James is not impressed.

Mark Twain's America eventually led to a discussion of literary movements, a dispute that culminated in the University of Indiana lectures which were finally printed as *The Literary Fallacy* (1944). Stegner's *The Uneasy Chair* gives the details of the controversy. DeVoto pictured the critics and some of the "major" writers as feeding on one another's ideas and ignoring the mainstream of American thought. He accused Henry James, as well as the "Lost Generation" writers, expatriates like James, of having lost touch with America.

DeVoto's literary criticism and his social history grew together and supported one another. They were a result of DeVoto's continuous plea for a sober examination of the facts. In both areas his was a sane voice, seeking to return American thought to reality and recommending leaving the trickling brooks of effete literary and social criticism and turning to the vigorous mainstream, the source of American strength.

DeVoto's best articles have been reprinted in *Forays and Rebuttals* (1936), *Minority Report* (1940), and *The Easy Chair* (1955). In order to get a complete picture of DeVoto's continual loving argument with American civilization, one would have to read the articles listed in Barclay's bibliography in *Four Portraits and One Subject: Bernard DeVoto* (1963), along with Wallace Stegner's two DeVoto books. A full study of De Voto in the "Easy Chair," perhaps compared with William Dean Howells's long, restless career in the same chair, would be both interesting and enlightening.

As a conservationist, DeVoto, in *Harper's* and elsewhere, battled continually with forces that he accused of destroying the West, which he called "a plundered province" in an article in *Harper's* in August 1934. He accused eastern forces of being the plunderers, writing harshly of the mine owners, the railroads, the banks, the land speculators, and the absentee owners of ranches who took their profits back east. He also attacked westerners who, he said, aided in the West's decline; he accused them of wanting federal money but at the same time demanding to be let alone. Few western groups escaped his ire.

Despite many attacks from the western press, DeVoto continued his close monitoring of western groups, including some federal bureaus, that he thought were not serving the real interests of the West. For three decades he was the most vociferous advocate in America of conservation of western resources.

Survey of Criticism

Critical studies of DeVoto's works have not been as numerous as one could expect; the reason for this neglect is unclear. For anyone who wishes to study his works in depth a necessary (and unusual) book is *Four Portraits and One Subject: Bernard DeVoto* (1963). It contains four essays: "The Historian," by Catherine Drinker Bowen; "The Writer," by Edith R. Mirrielees; "The Citizen," by Arthur M. Schlesinger, Jr.; and "The Personality," by Wallace Stegner. Included is a ninety-five page bibliography by Julius P. Barclay. The varied views of the essayists, as well as their varied backgrounds, and the excellent bibliography make *Four Portraits* a basic work.

Stegner's article in *Four Portraits* is reprinted, with few changes, in his *The Sound of Mountain Water* (1969). And anyone who wishes to know very much about DeVoto the man and writer must go to the later works of Stegner. Stegner, a friend of DeVoto's, has published two excellent books about him: *The Uneasy Chair: A Biography of Bernard DeVoto* (1974) and *The Letters of Bernard DeVoto* (1975). Both present extensive material from the DeVoto papers, held by the Stanford University library.

Orlan Sawey's *Bernard DeVoto* (1969), now out of print, is limited by the Twayne's United States Authors format and by the fact that it is really an extended essay on DeVoto and the West. The book has merit, however, on the grounds that DeVoto's face, like that of Thoreau, was always turned westward, and his thinking was shaped by western thinking, which some have characterized as more open and perceptive than that of the East.

In his essays in *Harper's* during the last years of his life, he did not stray from his interest in what was going on in the West. To understand him, one must understand this attachment. Few other writers of the West and Midwest joined the eastern establishment, as did Howells and DeVoto, and retained the westerner's viewpoint. But few had the wide understanding and interests of either man.

DeVoto contributed much to western literature and history, with the difference between the two not always clear. His books about the West are complemented by his vigorous, opinionated essays. His interest in the West was unflagging, and America has profited greatly from this interest.

Bibliography

Works by Bernard DeVoto

The Crooked Mile. New York: Minton, Balch and Co., 1924.
The Chariot of Fire. New York: Macmillan, 1926.
The House of Sun-Goes-Down. New York: Macmillan, 1928.
With W. F. Bryan and Arthur A. Nethercot. *The Writer's Handbook*. New York: Macmillan, 1928.
Mark Twain's America. Boston: Little, Brown, 1932.
We Accept with Pleasure. Boston: Little, Brown, 1934.
"The West: A Plundered Province." *Harper's* 69 (August 1934): 355-64.
The World of Fiction. Boston: Houghton Mifflin, 1934.
Forays and Rebuttals. Boston: Little, Brown, 1936.
"What's the Matter with History?" *Harper's* 79 (June 1939): 102-12.
Minority Report. Boston: Little, Brown, 1940.
Mark Twain at Work. Cambridge: Harvard University Press, 1942.
The Year of Decision: 1846. Boston: Little, Brown, 1943.
The Literary Fallacy. Boston: Little, Brown, 1944.
Mountain Time. Boston: Little, Brown, 1947.
Across the Wide Missouri. Boston: Houghton Mifflin, 1947.
The Hour. Boston: Houghton Mifflin, 1951.
The Course of Empire. Boston: Houghton Mifflin, 1952.
The Louisiana Purchase. Springfield, Ohio: Crowell, Collier, 1953.
The Easy Chair. Boston: Houghton Mifflin, 1955.

Studies of Bernard DeVoto

Four Portraits and One Subject: Bernard DeVoto. Boston: Houghton Mifflin, 1963.
Sawey, Orlan. *Bernard DeVoto*. TUSAS. New York: Twayne, 1969.
Stegner, Wallace. *The Sound of Mountain Water*. Garden City, N.Y.: Doubleday, 1969.
————. *The Uneasy Chair: A Biography of Bernard DeVoto*. Garden City, N.Y.: Doubleday, 1974.
————, ed. *The Letters of Bernard DeVoto*. Garden City, N.Y.: Doubleday, 1975.

Gerald Haslam

WILLIAM EASTLAKE
(1917-)

The western writer who most clearly, provocatively, and controversially bridges the gap between the modern western novel (Larry McMurtry out of Walter Van Tilburg Clark) and contemporary revisionist expression (Tom Robbins out of Samuel Beckett) is William Eastlake. As he has written more and more, he has moved further away from the realism of his earlier novels into a surrealism reflecting intellectual despair in a world shadowed by ecological disaster and nuclear devastation. As Larry McCaffrey has observed, Eastlake's "books really have more in common with the absurd, often bitterly humorous creations of contemporary writers like Pynchon, Vonnegut, and Heller than they do with the realistic works of most traditional Western Writers ("Absurdity and Oppositions," p. 62).

Such a move was augured in Eastlake's earliest published work and represents not a departure but a move along the continuum of his perceptions. Real or surreal, Eastlake's art seems to hover tantalizingly on the edge of greatness, never bursting fully into it, yet always providing readers with evidence of his considerable gifts.

From the arresting opening lines of his first novel, *Go in Beauty* (1956)—

Once upon a time there was time. The land here in the Southwest had evolved slowly and there was time and there were great spaces. Now a man on horseback from atop a bold mesa looked out over the violent spectrum of the Indian Country—into a gaudy infinity where all the colors of the world exploded, soundlessly. "There's not much time," he said. [P. 1]

—to the final, equally arresting lines of his most recent western novel, *Dancers in the Scalp House* (1975)—

The undiscovered country is love and compassion and an inkling into the sufferings of others and the smack of lightning and the tintinnabulation of a small rain on the hogan roof and the joy in the feeling for life. The undiscovered country is not the complications of and dismay at life's problems but the ease and wonderment at life's mysteries. It is the only country that abides. [P. 245]

—Eastlake describes a journey into contemporary consciousnesses: original, unconventional, possibly too trendy, but always rich, and without question unique.

Biography

Perhaps the strange trail that led him to the Southwest in the first place presaged his special perspective. William Eastlake was born in Brooklyn on 14 July 1917 and raised in Caldwell, New Jersey. He attended an Episcopalian boarding school, Bonnie Brae, in nearby Liberty Corners; its singular philosophy helped shape his later development. Bonnie Brae operated a farm, for it was the school's belief that boys should learn useful work early. As Richard C. Angell has pointed out, "Bill's most vivid childhood memories center around his school" ("Eastlake at Home and Abroad," p. 205).

Eastlake completed high school in Caldwell during the depths of the Great Depression and, like many other adventurous young men at that time, went on the bum, hoboing his way across the country, working at everything from migrant farm labor to radio announcing. It was a vigorous apprenticeship in life for a writer to be, and it ended at Stanley Rose's Book Shop in Los Angeles where Rose, a fixture in southern California's literary scene, encouraged Eastlake to write and introduced him to such luminaries as Theodore Dreiser, Nathanael West, and the irrepressible William Saroyan. While employed by Rose, Eastlake met an artist, Martha Simpson, whom he married.

He was trying to write during the early 1940s, struggling with the anonymous apprenticeship of his craft, encouraged all the while by Rose and Martha. None of his work was published during that early period, which was cut short by World War II.

Eastlake joined the army in 1942. After a prolonged tour of stateside camps, he was sent to England and then to France, where he first experienced combat. He also fought in Belgium and was wounded in the Battle of the Bulge.

Following World War II and convalescence in various military hospitals, Bill and Martha Eastlake lived in Europe, where his first story was published. Later he worked as a military training instructor in Israel and then returned to California, where his apprenticeship as a writer continued. Finally, in 1954, *Accent* published "Little Joe," and Eastlake's literary career was launched. He was thirty-seven years old, a relatively late starter by contemporary standards; he brought to his craft a perseverance and perspective that were to mark him from the beginning, as William James Smith observed, as "an original, thus disturbing talent" (*Commonweal*, 21 January 1963, p. 357).

In the early 1950s, Eastlake began spending time at the ranch of his brother-in-law, paleontologist George Gaylord Simpson, in New Mexico's Jemez Mountains. It was the beginning of an enduring love for the Southwest, and the Eastlakes settled in Cuba, New Mexico, on a 400-acre spread in 1955. While there, Eastlake was exposed to the ranchers and Indians who play such important roles in his novels. For the past ten years he has lived in Arizona.

Major Themes

William Eastlake has felt the meaning of the Southwest and has translated it into literature with freshness and vigor. As Angell observes, "For William Eastlake the high, lonesome country he has been writing about is really home" ("Eastlake at Home and Abroad," p. 207).

One other aspect of Eastlake's identity as a writer merits exploration, for although he is best known and most widely praised for his novels, that may be more a reflection of America's literary taste than of the author's genius. William Eastlake is a consummate short story writer, a great one. "Little Joe," for example, was reprinted by Martha Foley in *Best American Short Stories, 1955*. The 1956 and 1957 editions of the same collection saw the publication of two other Eastlake stories—"The Quiet Chimneys" and "The Unhappy Hunting Grounds" —and he has continued to excel at the shorter form.

On the other hand, many of Eastlake's novels have been criticized for their episodic quality. *Portrait of an Artist with 26 Horses* (1963), for example, is actually a series of tales, most of them previously published—including "What Nice Hands Held," "Portrait of an Artist with 26 Horses," and "A Bird on the Mesa"—strung along the spine of still another previously published short story, "A Long Day's Dying," converted successfully into a novelistic structure resembling the picaresque.

In defense of Eastlake's decision not only to write novels, but to convert many of his stories into parts-of-novels, it must be acknowledged that had he remained exclusively a writer of short stories no matter how excellent, he almost certainly would have been largely ignored by publishers and critics alike. Such is a reality of contemporary fiction writing.

Certainly Eastlake's art is nothing if not contemporary. His major thematic concern has been to expose the excesses of contemporary American civilization. Because of the complexity inherent in such a concern, Eastlake's writing has often seemed paradoxical, romantically yearning for a simplicity of life best symbolized by American Indians, while at the same time imposing a harshly realistic, often bitter, interpretation of present trends. As his novels increasingly reflect the perplexity and nihilism of many contemporary intellectuals, critical views have bifurcated; some reviewers find his work revelatory, while other critics consider it excessive and inaccurate.

It is unquestionably true that Eastlake's literary acceptance east of the Mississippi has been unique for an ostensibly western writer. In the five years following the publication of "Little Joe," his stories were printed in *Harper's Magazine*, *Collier's*, *America's*, *Hudson Review*, *Saturday Evening Post*, *Evergreen Review*, *Nation*, and *Kenyon Review*. Moreover, his critical reception in eastern review media was solid from the start; his version of the West is acceptable in the East.

One major reason for Eastlake's eastern success is that his consciousness has retained a sophisticated edge that is often manifested in flippant dialogue, especially that of his Indian characters. Moreover, he has succeeded in imposing his knowing, hip comments on situations previously protected by the code of the West. In *Portrait of an Artist with 26 Horses*, for example, the following exchange takes place between a white youth and a Navaho:

> "You're not the center of the world."
> "I suppose the Indians are."
> "That's nice of you, Ringo. I've always supposed they were too." [P. 27]

Such dialogue led a more traditional western author, Oliver La Farge, to admonish in a review of *Portrait* that readers should discard any thought of realism when entering Eastlake's world (*NY Times Book Review*, 28 April 1963, p. 5). But Eastlake's world is intensely real, though singular. It must be remembered that his books are as much about their styles as they are about their themes, for attitude, in its complex semantic totality, is what sets Eastlake's work apart.

When his first novel, *Go in Beauty*, was published in 1956, William Eastlake seemed an unusually talented product of a generation much influenced by Ernest Hemingway. In fact, the book's plot is composed of three distinct stylistic sections: an engrossing, strongly wrought opening set in the Southwest in which the essential relationships of the story are developed; a long, somewhat floundering middle section, which takes the story to Europe; and a powerful conclusion that returns to the Southwest.

Early in *Go in Beauty*, Eastlake introduced what has become a trademark: the crisp dialogue of perceptive, often prescient, Indians:

Below the post, the exact center and the capital of the world for The People, two Indians crouched at the massive stone root of the petrified wood house where it made its way into the ground.

"This crack—" Tom-Dick-and Harry said, tracing it with his brown finger.

"They can fix it," Rabbit Stockings said.

"No," Tom-Dick-and-Harry said..."And perhaps even The People cannot stop something coming apart and beginning here at the center of the world." [P. 2]

Central to the plot is that the marriage of George and Perette Bowman is coming apart, as is the relationship of George and his brother Alexander, who is cuckolding him.

As the novel ends, a Navaho pronounces benediction: "One of the Indians... looked up one final time to the long blue mesa. Now he raised his turquois-ringed arm to the sky and shouted into the deep, pure distance above, 'Go in beauty'" (p. 279).

Eastlake's second novel, *The Bronc People* (1958), remains in many ways not only his best but among the finest ever produced in the Southwest. Delbert Wylder ("Novels of Eastlake") has called it a classic. The novel reveals far more of the combination of insight and flashing wit that has characterized Eastlake's subsequent fiction than did his first book. Indeed, with *The Bronc People*, it becomes clear that Eastlake is, as William T. Pilkington notes in his important study, *My Blood's Country*, "perhaps the most interesting and accomplished writer of comedy the Southwest has yet produced" (p. 82). There is a bite in Eastlake's humor that renders it far more than merely funny.

The Bronc People opens, for example, with a gunfight between a white cattleman and a black rancher over a water hole. The names of their respective ranches tell much about their conflict: the white man (Circle Heart) feels that his need makes the water his; the black man (Circle R) reasons that the water is legally his. The white man has this understated exchange with two Indians:

> "I don't want to hurt anyone down there."
> "Then why are you firing the gun."
> "So he does not fire at me."
> The two Indians looked at each other.
> "Oh," they said. [P. 18]

The story line of *The Bronc People* might be summarized as a merging of contemporary realities with western values within the growing perceptions of Little Sant Bowman (son of the white man in the water-hole struggle) and Alastair Benjamin (son of the black combatant). The two boys function as coupled halves of the yin-yang symbol: Sant is white, emotional, and intuitive; Alastair is black, intellectual, and rational. They are, in total, humanity in search of meaning. Like many other modern people they are inextricably linked through a ritual of useless violence.

Ritual is a key word for this novel, since so many of its scenes are strongly ritualistic. Two years after that gunfight, Little Sant attends his first rodeo where he encounters the bronc people. Rodeos are mythic mergings of humans and animals: challenges and communions. This rodeo, with judges who "pulled on their chins and stroked their thighs and squirted down wild brown juice on lesser heads as wise men will," is powerfully religious (*Bronc People*, p. 25). Lemaitre (the master), a local cowpoke who has become the greatest of bronc riders, acts as chief priest.

While lesser men make offerings of greased pigs— "like Montezuma's men the golden mantle, like offerings to the gods, the animals flashing and screaming in the sun"—Lemaitre rides a killer horse ("Hell, that's not a horse, it's an electric chair") and hoists a human offering, Little Sant, in an intense replay of the humble offerings of mere mortals (*Bronc People*, pp. 25, 29). The man, the boy, and the horse are linked in a kind of rodeo trinity: the Father (Lemaitre), the Son (Little Sant), and the Holy Spirit (the wild horse). Such is the symbolic texture of *The Bronc People*, and Eastlake continues this rich tapestry until Alastair and Little Sant finally reconcile the tension between mind and heart.

It also becomes clear in *The Bronc People* that Eastlake's use of the land as symbol and form, his consistent employment of irony, and his use of Indians as contrasts to white excesses have developed into major elements of his writing.

As the opening lines of *Go in Beauty* demonstrate, the geological miracle that is the Southwest has not been lost on Eastlake. In *The Bronc People*, for example, the land places events in perspective:

> The mesa here was eroding away in five giant steps that descended down to the floor of the valley where the abandoned hogan lay. Each of the five steps clearly marked about twenty million years in time. In other words, they had been laid down twenty million years apart, and were so marked by unique coloration and further marked by the different fossil animals found in each. It took the four boys about twenty minutes to descend these one hundred million years but they didn't think that was very good going. [P. 83]

Eastlake's irony, however, is not complete until he adds (as the four riders—two Indians along with Sant and Alastair—scramble down a final slope), "They went down together and at once, creating a storm, a tornado of ageless dust, a hundred million years in outrage, that followed them all the way down to the level of the Indians" (p. 84). As John R. Milton has shown, "These passages provide a biting commentary on man and, more specifically, on the Europeanized non-Indian. The important thing is that the meanings of the incidents are derived directly from the landscape" ("Land as Form," p. 107).

Portrait of an Artist with 26 Horses is more a collection of stories and sketches strung along the spine of a tale than it is a novel. Yet it works, with some of very memorable episodes indeed. Eastlake "has remarkable control in a form which invites sloppiness and variation of tone. He achieves this smoothness against odds," writes William James Smith in a *Commonweal* review (21 June 1963).

The unifying story deals with Ring Bowman, suspended chin deep in quicksand at the bottom of a remote arroyo. The young man searches frantically for some meaning in his life, and the bulk of the book is concerned with memories he grasps, as though they may somehow keep him afloat. Many of those memories have been drawn from among Eastlake's finest short stories. The novel's major weakness is that several of the tales seem to have been included simply because they are good in themselves; they do little to move the plot and may actually distract readers' attention from Ring Bowman's dilemma.

The book opens with the return to Navaho country of the son of the man with twenty-six horses, referred to simply as Twenty-Six Horses. Although he has been away from his native land, he still communicates with nature. Squatting before a spring, the young Navaho, who is Ring's boyhood friend, listens to a strange sound, then decides he can "waste no more time talking to the ground" (*Portrait*, p. 10). He has heard Ring's cry for help.

Some of Eastlake's most comical writing is found in *Portrait*. The mother of Twenty-Six Horses, for example, opens a restaurant in Coyote City and hangs out a sign: "REAL LIVE WHITE PEOPLE IN THEIR NATIVE COSTUMES DOING NATIVE WHITE DANCES." A friend of the young Navaho's, Ben Helpnell, buys a new "Monkey Ward" pump: "'It is a hermetically sealed, self-contained unit, and without any fuss or bother or expensive plumbers or electricians, you just drop the whole thing in the well.' Ben had done that yesterday and, since, had been looking for it" (*Portrait*, p. 19).

When the young man finally returns home, he achieves spiritual unity. "What's wrong with talking to the ground?" asks his mother (p. 23). His father says simply, "The earth understands," an admonition that sets the tone for the book (p. 23).

The earth may very well understand, but Ring Bowman does not. Why is he trapped, inches from death, in quicksand? Help is not likely to arrive, so the boy's mind searches for an explanation. High above him on a cliff wall he sees one of Twenty-Six Horses' paintings: "Maybe it's supposed to be something but it's only the suggestion of something. The running bones of something" (*Portrait*, p. 20). The painting, it soon becomes apparent, is roughly analogous to Ring's perception of his own life—"only the suggestion of something"—and he fights to understand the life he is losing, inch by inch, to the quicksand.

What Ken Kesey has called "a sort of Indian Existentialism, an acceptance of the forgotten earth" (*N.Y. Herald Tribune Book Review*, 2 June 1963, p. 5), finally blossoms in Ring as an answer to his central question: "What is happening to me?" Finally, he realizes:

> . . .everything you do is part of yourself. We leave our imprint everywhere. . . . We are all painting a picture. . . .
>
> Look up there. It just came to me. I can see for the first time. I have been trying to see with my eyes and eyes are not for seeing—they are only a small part of seeing. You have got to feel. [*Portrait*, pp. 171-72]

Two major points are well symbolized by Twenty-Six Horses' drawing and what it elicits. One is that the structure of Eastlake's novel is paralleled by the drawing on the canyon wall; the individual stories that constitute the novel are like the slashes of red that constitute the drawing, each requiring interpretation yet merging to create a complete picture. The second insight offered by Ring's perception is one that Larry McCaffrey has made much of in his study of Eastlake's fiction. He points out that "in the three early novels, the main plot revolves around the struggle of. . .main characters to reject the destructive forces of the white man's world and to integrate fully into their lives the positive, mystical values of the Indians" ("Absurdity and Oppositions," p. 74). In his four southwestern novels, Eastlake has contrasted what he asserts to be white values (or the excesses of same) with red values.

Eastlake's Indians, in their contrasted relations with whites, reveal his writing at both its best and worst. If his Indians are, as McCaffrey argues, "more magical and more real than the stereotypes which have settled into our national consciousness," his straw-man caricatures of whites are often less real and negatively stereotypical ("Absurdity and Oppositions," p. 63). They are also quite funny, and he uses them to make important points. But the one-dimensional, easily exposed white stereotypes he favors also weaken Eastlake's presentation, for they correspond too perfectly with what concerned intellectuals would like to believe about the unenlightened masses. As a result, his satire too often degenerates into burlesque.

It is in the cryptic, sometimes flip approach that Eastlake employs when pointing out white absurdities that he most closely approaches (and frequently surpasses) the writing of such modern gurus as John Barth, Donald Bartheleme, and Richard Brautigan. In fact, Eastlake frequently seems a deeply concerned contemporary thinker, much disturbed by nuclear reality, environmental deterioration, and useless aggression (his Vietnam reportage was brilliant), and a little baffled that stewardship of the West has been left to insensitive westerners.

He has employed southwestern settings, with their special ability to throw into high relief problems that might elsewhere remain hidden, to alert his readers to continuing deterioration of the human condition. This perspective has also been evident in his nonsouthwestern fiction—*Castle Keep* (1964), *The Bamboo Bed* (1969), and *The Long Naked Descent into Boston* (1977)—all of which are powerfully symbolic, compellingly humorous, and richly imaginative, but none of which is as successful as the best of his work set in the Southwest.

Dancers in the Scalp House (1975), Eastlake's most recent southwestern novel, approaches his finest. Certainly it reaches close to the core of issues, especially ecological insanity. At his powerfully understated best, the author presents the Navahos of Checkerboard Mesa and their white teacher, Mary Forge (who, unlike so many of his earlier white characters, understands and accepts Indian values), and their opposition to the construction of a dam that will inundate the Four Corners. The novel contains the predictably cryptic, ironically humorous conversations that characterize Eastlake's fiction:

"You don't kill women and children."
"Why not? They're white, aren't they?"
"You could have been born a white person."
"Oh God, don't say that, please don't say that." [P. 69]

It also contains the same powerfully evocative, almost-mystical symbolic texture that sets his work apart:

Like the Indians, the ancestors of Sun had one time roamed a virgin continent abloom with the glory of life, alove with fresh flashing streams, a smogless sky, all the world a sweet poem of life where all was beginning. Nothing ever ended. [P. 17]

The book's most powerful linkage is between Navahos and eagles, animals that traditionally symbolize the human spirit's transcendence. This link is used as a motif throughout *Dancers in the Scalp House*, "Eagles and Indians at one time controlled this whole country," explains a helicopter pilot (p. 25). In no other of Eastlake's novels are the ravages of white excess so eloquently stated. The same helicopter pilot says, "It's as simple as this, Drago. You are for progress or against progress. Mary Forge claims progress is the enemy of progress" (p. 12). Later he argues: "Did you ever hear a poor person complain about the lack of eagles? Did you ever hear a poor person complain about a dam that brings them money money money? There is an outfit of rich gentlemen called the Sierra Club. They egg on Indian-lovers" (p. 18).

Dancers in the Scalp House, while revealing contemporary absurdity, does not slip into fantasy. Although it is as highly stylized and ironic as any of Eastlake's other fiction, the author is careful not to avoid the bitter reality: the Indians and Mary Forge cannot win. This book is perhaps most distinguished by the lyric quality of Eastlake's prose; it reaches an eloquent level of expression.

Survey of Criticism

Despite Eastlake's singular contribution to western letters, or perhaps because of his uniqueness, he has not received a great deal of critical attention. While his books have been reviewed by a distinguished crew—including Ken Kesey, Douglas Woolf, Oliver La Farge, Herbert Gold, Lon Tinkle, and Robie Macauly—serious critical studies have been few.

Not until 1965, when *New Mexico Quarterly* published Richard C. Angell's "Eastlake at Home and Abroad" and Delbert Wylder's "The Novels of William Eastlake," did significant biocritical studies begin. Angell's article is an intimate view of the writer as a human being, tracing his life and listing all of his publications. Wylder is the first critic to recognize the power and importance of Eastlake's fiction. He places Eastlake's work in the continuum of western writing, acknowledging his major themes and innovations, and pointing out that he is one of two (along with Edward Abbey) contemporary novelists "able to break from a description of the land, its people, and its traditions to interpret them in the novel form in a manner that breaks from the restriction of regionalism" (p. 203). Eastlake is, Wylder asserts, "capable of interpreting the old frontier and its values for the needs of the new" (p. 203).

John R. Milton's "The Land as Form in Frank Waters and William Eastlake" (1970) points out the importance of the land in Eastlake's work, as had Wylder, but goes further in recognizing a pattern: "The physical world, especially that part of it which lies low . . . , is the place of trials and testing." Salvation, then, is to be found "out and up . . . everyone can ride up, look up, achieve the heights in a physical way that strongly implies spiritual achievement" (p. 106).

That same year Gerald Haslam's booklet on Eastlake appeared in Steck-Vaughn's Southwest Writers Series. The brief study surveys Eastlake's life and work through the publication of *The Bamboo Bed*, pointing out his strong sense of symbols and rituals, his unique dialogue and humor, and his firm grasp of Indian concepts of reality. The author, Haslam argues, is "a most unusual intellectual, for he actively applies a tempering modicum of myth and magic to his work" (p. 41).

Eastlake's particular mode of magic is explored in Haslam's "William Eastlake: Portrait of the Artist as Shaman" (1971), which argues that Eastlake's "reintroduction of myth and magic may seem a step into the past, but these aspects of human experience are perpetually modern" (p. 12). It also points out that Eastlake "is a profoundly modern novelist, employing the kaleidoscopic techniques of the new novel in a kind of literary post-impressionism" (p. 6).

Larry McCaffrey's "Absurdity and Oppositions in William Eastlake's Southwestern Novels" (1977) further and more explicitly explores Eastlake as a postmodern spokesman who uses contrasts between whites and Indians to present his major theme: "The idea that the white man's version of progress is a 'disease' for which right-thinking men need to find a 'cure'" (p. 65). He also points out that many of Eastlake's most important white characters actually exist in a sort of middle ground between white and red worlds: "In the three early novels, the main plot revolves around the struggle of these main characters to reject the destructive forces of the white man's world and to integrate fully into their lives the positive, mystical values of the Indians" (p. 74). He concludes by pointing out that Eastlake's southwestern novels "possess a strong sense of both the absurdity and the poetry of life" (p. 75).

Although he is among the most original and gifted of contemporary fictionalists, William Eastlake has not yet been accorded the degree of serious critical attention his work merits. Perhaps that is because, at his best, he is less a writer of the American Southwest than of the undiscovered country.

Bibliography

Works by William Eastlake

Go in Beauty. New York: Harper Brothers, 1956.
The Bronc People. New York: Harcourt, Brace 1958.
Portrait of an Artist with 26 Horses. New York: Simon and Schuster, 1963.
Castle Keep. New York: Simon and Schuster, 1964.
The Bamboo Bed. New York: Simon and Schuster, 1969.
Three by Eastlake: Portrait of an Artist with 26 Horses; Go in Beauty; The Bronc People. New York: Simon and Schuster, 1970.
Dancers in the Scalp House. New York: Viking Press, 1975.
The Long Naked Descent into Boston. New York: Viking Press, 1977.

Studies of William Eastlake

Angell, Richard C. "Complete Bibliography." *New Mexico Quarterly* 34 (Spring 1965): 208-9.
———. "Eastlake at Home and Abroad." *New Mexico Quarterly* 34 (Spring 1965): 204-7.
Haslam, Gerald. *William Eastlake*. SWS. Austin, Tex.: Steck-Vaughn Company, 1970.
———. "William Eastlake: Portrait of the Artist as Shaman." *Western Review* 8 (Spring 1971): 2-13.

McCaffrey, Larry. "Absurdity and Oppositions in William Eastlake's Southwestern Novels." *Critique* 19 (1977): 62-72.

Milton, John R. "The Land as Form in Frank Waters and William Eastlake." *Kansas Quarterly* 11 (Spring 1970): 104-9.

Pilkington, William T. *My Blood's Country: Studies in Southwestern Literature.* Fort Worth: Texas Christian University Press, 1973.

Wylder, Delbert. "The Novels of William Eastlake." *New Mexico Quarterly* 34 (Spring 1965): 188-203.

James K. Folsom

HARVEY FERGUSSON
(1890-1971)

Harvey Fergusson, although he permanently abandoned his native New Mexico at the age of twenty-two never to return except as a visitor, is nonetheless a southwesterner to the core. His biography represents, as much as that of any other American writer, a regional expatriate, one who leaves his native hearth in order to reflect upon it through both geographical space and metaphorical time. The Albuquerque in which Fergusson was born in 1890 was already something of an anachronism, a village redolent more of New Mexico's past than prophetic of America's future. Fergusson's removal to the East Coast, then, and later to California, is—in terms of his artistic development—emblematic of a profound distancing of himself from the land of his youth, a distancing ultimately more important in terms of internal space than of statute miles.

Biography

Fergusson, the second of four children, was born 28 January 1890 to Harvey Butler Fergusson and Clara May Huning. All four were to make their mark on the literary world: the eldest, Erna, became a distinguished historian of the Southwest; the third, Lina, edited the papers of her grandfather-in-law, J. Ross Browne, the famous nineteenth-century western traveler; and the youngest, Francis, turned his talents to literary criticism. Significantly, none of Fergusson's siblings was an imaginative writer—that is, if we take "imaginative" in the usual literary sense of "fictional" or "poetic"—and this factual bent is also found in Harvey Fergusson, whose fictions are always very closely anchored to place. "I have had my feet on all the country I have written about," Fergusson was once to say (Milton, "Conversation with Harvey Fergusson," p. 45), and the remark is by no means unique. Indeed, in addition to his fiction Fergusson also wrote two books of popular political science, a biographical memoir, and a study, much in the manner of his sister Erna, of the area in which he grew up. This is not intended by way of denigration of Fergusson's fictional achievement but as explanation of it. It is impossible to imagine Fergusson as, say, a writer of science fiction or thrillers (although his novels are not devoid of adventure and even, on occasion, melodrama) simply because such stories do not have a sure sense of locale and, more importantly, of the author's place within that locale. "If I hadn't seen...New Mexico, I wouldn't write about it," Fergusson said (Milton, "Conversation," p. 45), and the emphasis of the sentence is at least as much upon *I* as upon *New Mexico*.

Of interest also in Fergusson's childhood is that neither parent was literarily inclined, although Fergusson was to discover a memoir written by his maternal grandfather, Franz Huning, which was to affect him profoundly. Although Fergusson knew his grandfather only slightly, he thought of him as "my spiritual ancestor and of his life as one the like of which I might have lived if I had been born in time" (*Home in the West*, p. 47).

In 1912, at the urging of his father, who wished him to make a public career of some sort, Fergusson moved to Washington, D.C. There he drifted into newspaper work and in 1917 met H. L. Mencken, who adopted him as a protégé. This apparently happenstance event had profound effects, for both good and ill, on Fergusson's literary development. On the positive side, Mencken encouraged Fergusson's artistic development. Not only did he allow Fergusson to see print in his *American Mercury*, but he was instrumental in having the distinguished publishing house of Alfred A. Knopf accept Fergusson's first novel, *The Blood of the Conquerors*. A more negative result was that for many years Fergusson took over Mencken's point of view, as well as his patronage. Perhaps, indeed, the two were inseparable. In any event, Mencken's intrusion is easy to spot in the pieces Fergusson wrote for the *American Mercury*, where it is perhaps justified on the grounds of consistency in editorial policy, and in Fergusson's early Washington novels (*Capitol Hill* and *Women and Wives*), where its presence is less salutary. Mencken's influence proved hard to shake, especially to a young author who, by his own admission, "did not love society." Fergusson obliquely comments on Mencken's influence when he remarks that "only sympathy makes the human spectacle tolerable and finally fascinating, even at its worst, but in me sympathy was a slow growth and a late one" (*Home in the West*, pp. 94, 95). Mencken's pervasive influence goes a long way toward explaining the reactions of many critics that Fergusson's fiction is intellectual rather than emotional, that at its worst it lacks imagination even though it is long on ideas. The "late growth" of sympathy in Fergusson's mind may also explain the obvious superiority of his last two novels (*Grant of Kingdom* and *The Conquest of Don Pedro*), a preeminence upon which most critics are agreed.

In 1923 Fergusson moved to New York City, where he eked out a precarious living as a freelance writer. He lived there until 1931 except for a tragic journey to Salt Lake City in 1927 where his bride of less than a year, Rebecca McCann, died of influenza. In 1931 he settled permanently in California, working part time for ten years as a scriptwriter for a number of motion picture studios while writing seriously on his own. The aggravations of the motion picture industry finally became too great, and in 1942 he separated himself entirely from it, moving to Berkeley, where he lived until his death 27 August 1971.

Major Themes

The major difficulty facing the critic who attempts an assessment of Harvey Fergusson's fiction is easy to state but hard to explain: although he has always been well received critically, his works have failed to attract much notice among the general public. Only his last novel, *The Conquest of Don Pedro* (1954) which was named a selection of the Literary Guild, lays any claim to being a popular success. Numerous explanations have been offered to explain the public's indifference toward Fergusson's work. He is simply too good for the masses to appreciate, some say; others voice the perennial complaint that the eastern literary establishment has somehow sabotaged another of nature's western noblemen—a point of doubtful validity at best and of even less value when applied to works that have already been published rather than to editorial decisions concerning which works to accept.

John R. Milton, in his recent analysis of western writing in *The Novel of the American West*, comes nearer the mark, it seems to me, in his careful distinction between the formulaic cowboys-and-Indians story beloved of newsstands everywhere and the serious novel that, although set in the American West, transcends the formulaic nature of cowboys-and-Indians stories. One thrust of Milton's argument is that readers of the former neither anticipate nor desire to be confronted with the artistic complexities of the latter, while readers to whom the latter might be more habitually congenial will often decline to read them because they have been put off by the formulaic and escapist nature of the former.

The point is particularly astute when applied to the best of Harvey Fergusson's western fiction, which often deals with the stock themes of the typical Western. *Wolf Song* (1927), as a clear example, is from a superficial viewpoint just another in that goodly number of stories concerning the whites (in this case a mountain man) versus the Indians, and *Grant of Kingdom* (1950), perhaps Fergusson's best and certainly his most ambitious attempt to probe philosophically (rather than merely to relate) the significance of the development of western America, can be insensitively dismissed as just another of the pseudoepics of the West beloved of the devotees of grade B horse operas.

Whether one totally agrees with Milton's point or not, the fact still remains that Fergusson handled his western themes in odd and disturbing ways, ways that are certain to unsettle those readers who would like to be more at home in a safer, or at least relatively predictable, fictional landscape.

Perhaps that point at which Fergusson's work is furthest from his readers' presumed expectations is in its attitude toward the past. Western writing has always taken a nostalgic stance, generally affirming at least speculatively the superiority of some way of life that is now gone. From its early nineteenth-century beginnings in the then "West" of New York State (the "Old York" beloved of Cooper's Natty Bumppo) through later developments among the Mississippi River "jolly flatboatmen," out onto the Great Plains and into the mines of California, the habitual stance of western writing has been nostalgic and retrospective. Although western writing has received a good bit of hostile criticism for this retrospective stance, it is worth noting that there is nothing inherently unworthy in it. Such fiction is not necessarily escapist, literal-minded critics to the contrary. Indeed, if one's true literary subject is the temporal present rather than the regional West, certain real advantages accrue from a retrospective point of view. For one thing, a representative of the old order can often make trenchant comments upon the deficiencies of the present that would be incongruous on the part of a more contemporary character; for another, the deficiencies of the present may be made to stand in glaring contrast to the presumed virtues of the past, even though those virtues may not in reality ever have existed.

Nevertheless, attractive though this method of presentation is, it is not Fergusson's. For him, excessive attraction to the past is almost always a sign of inability to cope with the present. In his Introduction to *Followers of the Sun* (pp. vii-viii) Fergusson provides a good capsule statement of his attitude toward the past, a statement that also includes a summary of his spiritual autobiography:

I began by worshipping the past. I thought of it as the home of my soul. It seemed to me that, like Miniver Cheevy, I had been born too late. Now the past interests me chiefly for the light it sheds on the present. I began by looking backward with longing. Now I look forward with hope. I began as a romantic, in the simplest sense of the word—as one who longed for an escape and believed that escape is possible. I have become a realist, at least in thought and intention. What engages my interest now is how to deal with the prickly stuff of the inescapable present.

Fergusson's point here is not so much paradoxical as unexpected. The past is not important in its own right, he says, but only insofar as it casts light upon the present. The further implication, though this point should not be overemphasized, is that the present may be of primary importance insofar as it foreshadows, however dimly, the future. A millennialist Fergusson most definitely is not; nevertheless, there is a strong futuristic bent to much of his writing, especially his nonfictional material. A striking metaphor in *Modern Man* (1936) makes the point explicit: "Again and again I read that we are losing our roots, and this is always assumed to be a catastrophe, but I think there may be a compensatory gain in the fact that we are finding our wings" (p. 206). He goes on to state that the advantage of the past—in this case, one's personal past—is that somehow one has experienced it; this does not mean that the past is necessarily of generalized intrinsic worth or that it should be repeated:

A man may have a genuine and lasting relationship to a certain region without feeling any necessity to confine himself to it.... A man who really knows mountains can see cities with a clearer eye, and he can return to mountains with a sense of release and refreshment, but one who lives up a canyon all his life knows nothing but its walls. [Pp.206-7]

The point is not limited to Fergusson's nonfictional statements. In *Women and Wives* (1924) Fergusson remarks that "a tired and discouraged human looks longingly back to the past and leans on old familiar things, but an unwearied and restless spirit looks to the future and searches for the new" (p. 166). Here is why Fergusson, even though he regarded his Grandfather Huning as his "spiritual ancestor," did not emulate him in any physical way, for he had not been born "in time." The times have changed, and Fergusson must change within them. The matter of Franz Huning's life must be adapted to the manner of today.

The notion of change in Fergusson's writing is inextricably entwined with another less obvious one, which Fergusson calls "destiny." Destiny for Fergusson is a complex idea, and its explication is made no easier because of Fergusson's use of the term in a more or less private context. By *destiny* Fergusson does not mean "fate," at least in any sense of "predestination." Nor does he use the word in the grandiose social sense that, say, westward expansion is "manifest destiny," and those who bring it about are "men of destiny." For Fergusson, somewhat confusingly, destiny is something that an individual may select. Moreover, the selection of one's destiny is not seen in terms of one irrevocable moment; it is, rather, a process of constant redefinition of one's goals, coupled with a constant series of choices that must be made as much as possible on one's own terms, free from outside pressures of any kind. In Fergusson's view, individual choice becomes increasingly difficult as social pressures mount. Moreover, Fergusson maintains that social pressures become greater as the particular social unit grows smaller. Consequently, the individual who wishes to realize his destiny will find greater opportunity in the city (where, though there are more people, there is nevertheless less control) than in the small town (where individual choices are virtually impossible).

Although this explanation may shed some incidental light upon Fergusson's decision to abandon Albuquerque for the large urban centers of the East and West, its importance in our context is that it serves to define more precisely his notion of destiny. Oddly, this term has turned out to mean something far more like "self-fulfillment" than "predestination." In fact, one of Fergusson's most deeply held beliefs is that people should be flexible, should have, as he would say, "balance." Inflexibility, as shown in Fergusson's fiction by inability or unwillingness to change, is not so much a fault because it renders a character unable to survive in a world of constant flux (although Fergusson would admit that this is in fact the case) as because inflexibility makes it impossible for a character to fulfill himself.

These two ideas are by no means completely distinct, and much of the complexity in Fergusson's fiction derives from their interaction. As a clear example, consider his first novel, *The Blood of the Conquerors* (1921). This story details the fortunes of Ramon Delcasar, the last of a long line of New Mexico *ricos* whose fortunes and political influence have been eroded almost completely by the encroaching Anglo settlers. Spurred by an infatuation for an Anglo girl, Julia Roth, Ramon attempts to recoup the family fortunes of the Delcasars. At first all goes well, but when Julia (whose family does not approve of Ramon) leaves for New York, Ramon loses his motivation for success and by the end of the novel has retreated into a life of easy indolence, indistinguishable from the lives of the other *ricos* he had hoped to supplant.

The thrust of this novel is external: Ramon is found wanting because of that lack of initiative emblematized by his inability to carry through with his original plans. Less easy to see is that this passivity itself represents for Fergusson a statement of an internal failing on Ramon's part. Finally his own unwillingness to change—or, as Fergusson would put it, to accept his destiny—is the cause of his decline. Had he changed, Fergusson would say, he would have developed; character is enhanced only by facing challenges.

The love plot with Julia Roth emphasizes the point. In discussions of this novel, criticism has often focused upon Julia's leaving of Ramon as the catalyst of the action, as that moment within the story where the world cruelly turns upon Ramon. But Fergusson's point is neither so simple nor so sentimental. Rather Ramon's failure to woo Julia successfully, despite her family's dislike, emblematizes his refusal to accept a challenge. It is not accidental, in terms of Fergusson's private symbolism, that Julia returns to New York while Ramon, after following her there, goes back to New Mexico, an action that embodies his refusal to accept his destiny. Ramon has not only failed externally but internally; he has refused the challenge of and the opportunity for internal growth as represented by the possibility of marriage to Julia and removal to New York.

I do not wish to be misunderstood as stating that somehow Fergusson asserts the value of the active life (however defined) as superior to the contemplative. The point has little to do with externals. Fergusson's interest primarily is in motivation. Contemplation or reflection is not the major demon in Fergusson's cosmology; passivity is. The distinction is a fine one but worth emphasizing. In fact, Fergusson approved of his "spiritual ancestor," Franz Huning, largely because of his contemplative nature. Huning was, Fergusson says approvingly,

of an intellectual and imaginative type. His shyness, his love of solitude and books, his aversion to routine are all characteristic of the kind of youth who usually becomes an artist or a scholar, but he had also a longing for adventure and an avid curiosity about life. These impulses conspired with the spirit of his time to carry him to a wild frontier and convert him finally into a pioneer and a man of action. [*Home in the West*, pp. 15-16]

That Huning was also a successful entrepreneur adds to the point. Fergusson sees no essential difference from the point of view of destiny (or self-fulfillment) between the active and the contemplative life. The basic difference among men is not to be found in the externals of the lives they lead but in their internal willingness to face challenges.

This concern for destiny is metaphorically summed up in the figure of Leo Mendes, the hero of Fergusson's last novel, *The Conquest of Don Pedro* (1954). Mendes is one of the few characters of whom Fergusson wholeheartedly approves. His career is obviously derived from Franz Huning's; like Julia Roth, he is a New Yorker and a Jew. (This point is admittedly arguable; Julia is nowhere defined as Jewish, though Milton, in "Conversation," points out that her name implies her Jewishness.) Mendes arrives in the town of Don Pedro shortly after the Civil War (as Franz Huning arrived in Albuquerque) and manages to build a commercial empire of considerable extent. Yet Fergusson emphasizes how Mendes is not so much of Don Pedro as in it: "at heart he was always and everywhere a stranger" (*Conquest*, p. 4).

Instead of the town, which is not conceived primarily as a final home but as a temporary resting place, Mendes loves the road. It is not too much to suggest that in this most parabolic of Fergusson's fictions the road represents the road of life on which we are all, like Leo Mendes, poor wayfaring strangers. Throughout the novel various characters remind Mendes that his growing attachment to Don Pedro is not in his personal best interest, however financially successful he has become. In one particularly sharp exchange his friend the Padre asks him, "Why do *you* stay here?" Answering his own question he continues, "Because it is easy." He concludes: "It is not good! . . . A man needs to struggle with his peers and sharpen his mind on other minds. Here we sleep in the sun!" (*Conquest*, p. 92). At the novel's conclusion Mendes symbolically affirms the primacy of the road, leaving Don Pedro for an unknown destination. His lover had suggested earlier (p. 64) that "perhaps you are a man of many lives" (Fergusson admired Thoreau, and the echo of Thoreau's explanation for leaving Walden Pond—"I have other lives to lead"—is too striking to be coincidental), and we take leave of Mendes, setting forth along the road toward an unknown destination: "He knew that once more there would be the pain the struggle of uprooting—*and then perhaps the discovery of a new self*. He dreaded what lay before him here, *but he did not taste despair*" (p. 239, italics added).

This discussion may have inadvertently implied not only that Fergusson is a didactic novelist—a charge of some validity, especially when applied to his less successful Washington novels—but that his world view is essentially one of simple optimism. Although it would be misleading to define Fergusson's work as deeply pessimistic in its thrust, it is even less justifiable to interpret it as nothing more than a bland statement of inevitable progress in a world filled with sweetness and light. Let us conclude, then, with a brief glance at the tragic dimension to Fergusson's work.

This dimension is most often emblematized by the inability or unwillingness on the part of a given character to change in order to meet the challenges of his world. Although such a character is often merely a fool, such is not always the case. Fergusson believes very strongly that the nature of life is such as gradually to limit the individual's ability to adapt. Sooner or later, in Fergusson's view, life itself creates the inability to respond to it successfully. Even Franz Huning, Fergusson's spiritual ancestor, was not immune to the inflexibility brought on by advancing years. As an elderly man, Fergusson relates, Huning withdrew into the Albuquerque residence he had built (and which was known locally as "Castle

Huning"), which "became more and more his refuge from a society he neither liked nor understood." For Franz Huning ultimately "belonged wholly to the old Southwest of the wagon trail" (*Home in the West*, p. 44), a Southwest that was, by the time of his old age, irredeemably lost.

Although Fergusson's work from its inception concerned itself with the theme of man's inability to adapt and occasionally combined this theme with the other theme of aging, nevertheless this metaphorical identification is peripheral to Fergusson's fictional world until relatively late in his literary career. The first novel in which the two themes are combined as a major preoccupation is *The Life of Riley* (1937), a novel of more interest than the relatively scant criticism it has received would indicate. The title, for all its admitted pun on the cliché, is to be taken seriously. The novel deals with the life of Riley considered as a whole, not only with some important incidents within it. This life itself is unremarkable, considered in external terms, as Riley admits at the novel's conclusion, flatly stating to himself that "he had failed." Yet Fergusson continues the passage by reminding us that the failure is not Riley's own. All men must fail, for "the nature of individual destiny...is always a defeat" (*Life of Riley*, p. 328).

The life of Riley, however, considered at least in external terms, never was much of a success. A more compelling statement of the same theme is to be found in the figure of Jean Ballard, the enigmatic protagonist (one hesitates to use the term *hero*) of the first section of *Grant of Kingdom* (1950). In *Grant of Kingdom* we watch Ballard's gradual aging while following his growing inability to adapt. At the beginning, Ballard is a confident, not to say brash, young mountain man who manages, against the will of her family, to marry the daughter of a family of New Mexico *ricos*. As a dowry he is given a huge land grant by his reluctant in-laws. They have no use for the grant, which they consider worthless, partly because it is far from their residence in Taos, but mostly because it is in the heart of the Ute Indian country, and the Utes are known to be quarrelsome. The *ricos* are rather pleased with themselves in having foisted some worthless property off on a son-in-law they did not want, but much to everyone's surprise Ballard makes an accommodation with the Utes, settles on the grant, and lives in royal style for upward of twenty years. Eventually, however, the "new" world of finance capitalism, represented by a shady character named Major Blore, acquires the grant from the once-dauntless mountain man. Another character, James Lane Morgan, clearly a spokesman for Fergusson, draws the moral. Of Ballard he says, "He knew the destroying power of change and he knew he sat in its path....I think what he wanted was the past, *as do most men over fifty*" (*Grant*, p. 113, italics added).

The tragic element in Fergusson's fictional world does not lend itself to strict definitions of tragedy, Aristotelian or other. Rather than a flaw in individual character, tragedy for Fergusson is inherent in the nature of life itself. "Only the land lasts forever," Fergusson reminds us in *Home in the West* (p. 4). The human tragedy is a longing for this kind of permanence in a world of flux.

Survey of Criticism

Only three attempts at a general assessment of Harvey Fergusson's literary achievement have appeared to date: James K. Folsom's *Harvey Fergusson* (1969), William T. Pilkington's *Harvey Fergusson* (1975), and John R. Milton's "Harvey Fergusson and the Spanish Southwest," in his *The Novel of the American West* (1980). Folsom's study attempts a survey of Fergusson's work as a whole, suggesting that *Home in the West* may profitably be read as a gloss upon it. It argues that Fergusson's spiritual development may be seen metaphorically in his depiction of the contrast between his maternal grandfather Franz Huning (whom he admires) and his own father (whom he dislikes).

Pilkington's work is the most comprehensive of the three and the only one to contain a complete bibliography. Pilkington includes a detailed biography, especially valuable because much of it is based upon interviews with Fergusson, as well as analyses in depth of all of Fergusson's works. Most thought-provoking is Pilkington's discussion of *People and Power* and *Modern Man*, uniformly ignored by other critics, which he uses as a tool for explication of the novels. Folsom's discussion of destiny in the body of this essay is heavily indebted to Pilkington.

Milton's essay is the most intriguing of the three. He argues, brilliantly, that Fergusson not only writes a history of the Spanish Southwest (something of a critical commonplace) but that his is a totally different kind of history from others. For Milton, Fergusson's genius lies in the combination of different levels of historic truth into a kind of metahistory (the term is mine, not Milton's) that is true both to historic fact and to historical process.

Most other critics confine themselves to literal discussion of Fergusson as a historian of the Southwest. The best is Cecil Robinson, although the approach is of limited value. H. L. Mencken's essay provides a useful view of Mencken's opinion of his protégé, though typically it is more about Mencken than Fergusson.

Bibliography

Works by Harvey Fergusson

The Blood of the Conquerors. New York: Alfred A. Knopf, 1921.
Capitol Hill: A Novel of Washington Life. New York: Alfred A. Knopf, 1923.
Women and Wives. New York: Alfred A. Knopf, 1924.
Hot Saturday. New York: Alfred A. Knopf, 1926.
Wolf Song. New York: Alfred A. Knopf, 1927.
In Those Days: An Impression of Change. New York: Alfred A. Knopf, 1929.
Footloose McGarnigal. New York: Alfred A. Knopf, 1930.
Rio Grande. New York: Alfred A. Knopf, 1933.
Modern Man: His Belief and Behavior. New York: Alfred A. Knopf, 1936.
Followers of the Sun: A Trilogy of the Santa Fe Trail. New York: Alfred A. Knopf, 1936.
    Contains *The Blood of the Conquerors*, *Wolf Song*, and *In Those Days*.

The Life of Riley. New York: Alfred A. Knopf, 1937.

Home in the West: An Inquiry into my Origins. New York: Duell, Sloan and Pearce, 1944.

People and Power: A Study of Political Behavior in America. New York: William Morrow, 1947.

Grant of Kingdom. New York: William Morrow, 1950.

The Conquest of Don Pedro. New York: William Morrow, 1954.

Studies of Harvey Fergusson

Cohen, Saul. *Harvey Fergusson: A Checklist.* Los Angeles: University of California at Los Angeles Library, 1965.

Folsom, James K. *Harvey Fergusson.* SWS. Austin, Tex.: Steck-Vaughn, 1969.

McGinity, Sue Simmons. "Harvey Fergusson's Use of Animal Imagery in Characterizing Spanish-American Women," *Western Review* 8 (Winter 1971): 46-50.

Mencken, H. L. "Essay in Pedagogy." In *Prejudices: Fifth Series.* New York: Alfred A. Knopf, 1926, pp. 218-36.

Milton, John R. "Harvey Fergusson and the Spanish Southwest." In *The Novel of the American West.* Lincoln: University of Nebraska Press, 1980, pp. 230-63.

————, ed. "Conversation with Harvey Fergusson." *South Dakota Review* 9 (Spring 1971): 39-45.

Pearson, Lorene. "Harvey Fergusson and the Crossroads," *New Mexico Quarterly* 21 (Autumn 1951): 334-55.

Pilkington, William T. *Harvey Fergusson.* TUSAS. Boston: Twayne, 1975.

————. "The Southwestern Novels of Harvey Fergusson." *New Mexico Quarterly* 35 (Winter 1965-66): 330-43.

Raper, Howard; Knode, J. C.; Woodward, Dorothy; Krohn, A. L.; and Kromer, Tom. "Modern Man and Harvey Fergusson—a Symposium." *New Mexico Quarterly* 6 (May 1936): 123-35.

Robinson, Cecil. "Legend of Destiny. The American Southwest in the Novels of Harvey Fergusson." *American West* 4 (November 1967): 16-18, 67-68.

————. *With the Ears of Strangers: The Mexican in American Literature.* Tucson: University of Arizona Press, 1963.

Joseph M. Flora

VARDIS FISHER
(1895-1968)

When Vardis Fisher died at age seventy-three on 9 July 1968, he was the acknowledged dean of the writers of the American West. He had been credited with writing the first major fiction to come out of the Rocky Mountain region, and in the 1930s he had earned a national reputation, culminating in 1939 with the Harper Prize for his historical novel about the Mormons, *Children of God.* Fisher's reputation declined sharply in the 1940s, however, once he embarked on his Testament of Man, a series of historical novels that sought to trace the religious heritage of western man from prehistoric times through Judaic-Christian times all the way to Fisher's own. The story Fisher told was paralleled by a personal drama of declining influence and conflicts with publishers who were increasingly reluctant to back a financially disastrous project. Fisher was generally ignored from the mid-1940s until 1956 when Alan Swallow took up publication of the Testament novels that other publishers had spurned. Shortly after, many of Fisher's titles were published in inexpensive paperback, and scholars began to look again at the writer Alfred Kazin had called "our last authentic frontier novelist." When the Western American Literature Association was formed in 1966, it gave Vardis Fisher its first distinguished achievement award; he gave an impassioned lecture to the association, attacking the eastern literary establishment for its failure to recognize writers of the American West, and Fisher's primary example of mistreatment was himself.

Some fifteen years later—after Fisher's death—it is possible to view his personality and his achievement with more detachment. Although his widow has brought out editions of several of Fisher's books under her name, his last novel, *Mountain Man,* is the only one by Fisher listed in the fall 1980 volume of *Paperbound Books in Print* that she did not publish. The listing under Fisher in *Books in Print, 1980-81* also suggests that Fisher has again become an item primarily for specialists and libraries. If these two sources are good barometers, then in popular appeal Fisher is far behind the widely held giants of western literature—Willa Cather and John Steinbeck—as well as Wallace Stegner, formerly Fisher's student at the University of Utah, and other writers in the generation after Fisher's. Fisher is not forgotten, but the Fisher revival peaked at the time of his death.

Biography

Vardis Alvero Fisher was born in a remote Mormon community, Annis, Idaho, on 31 March 1895—just missing April Fool's Day, he would later quip. He was the oldest child of Temperance Thornton Fisher and Joseph Oliver Fisher. His mother was proud of her English ancestry; she loathed her frontier life and dreamed of the successes her sons would achieve in the civilized world and worked almost fiendishly to make her dreams come true. She was morally rigid, and Fisher later emphasized her Puritan orientation by portraying her as Prudence Hunter in his novels. Fisher's father liked the frontier life, and the son later paid tribute to his father's orientation by dedicating *Mountain Man* to him: "For Joe who was one of them." But Temperance's will was stronger than her husband's, and Joseph Fisher bent his energies to her plans for their children. Fisher saw little affection between his parents, but he caught from them a fierce dedication to bigger tasks.

His frontier experience was surely authentic. When he was six, the Fishers (there was now a brother, Vivian Ezra, and a baby sister, Viola Irene) moved into the Big Hole mountain region of the South Fork of the Snake River, some thirty miles from civilization. Their only neighbor within eight miles was the Wheaton family, who lived across the Snake. The Fisher children scarcely saw anyone other than the Wheatons for five years. To Vardis, the world seemed lonely and unfriendly, a reaction heightened by the few contacts he had with the hedonistic and untamed Wheaton boys. Vardis's first schooling came from his mother. Later he and Vivian boarded a year with relatives so that they could attend school. Neither the experience with the relatives nor the school was pleasant. The Fisher boys were morbidly shy; additionally, Vivian was cross-eyed, and Vardis had to protect himself and his brother from numerous "enemies."

When Fisher was sixteen, he and Vivian moved to a small hut outside Rigby, Idaho, so that they could attend high school. Fisher began to make progress at overcoming his shyness, but distrust of the stranger was strong in him. In high school he began to dream of being a teacher, and he wrote poetry and worked on a novel. He also fell in love with a part-Indian girl, Leona McMurtrey. Sexuality was frightening to Fisher. He was tortured by the conflict between his desires and the emphasis on purity instilled in him by his mother, and he fiercely imposed these views on McMurtrey. Fisher was thankful for the understanding and aid of a high school teacher, who helped him to see the absurdity of his fears over masturbation and to get a better perspective on the intellectual conflicts he faced. Fisher made a significant gesture to claiming his individuality by rejecting the Mormonism that was the faith of his parents and the community in which he had grown up: he would not go on any Mormon mission. Fisher's rejection of Mormonism did not cost him what it might have cost other renegade Mormons, precisely because his early years had been so isolated; the family and community sense that play so great a role in Mormonism had not been nurtured. Yet Mormonism was so much in Fisher's background and region that he had to give the movement a lot of thought. There is surely something very personal in Fisher's statement to John R. Milton about the writing of *Children of God*: "I also wanted to come to terms with Mormonism."

In the fall of 1916 Fisher enrolled at the University of Utah, with the intention of becoming a high school teacher. But Utah stimulated Fisher to give further thought to writing, and he became a regular contributor to the university's literary magazine, the *University Pen*. He also enrolled in a course in play writing, a genre rather public for the introverted and private Fisher.

While by outward standards Fisher was having a good measure of success in college, he was inwardly tormented. Much of his torment was caused by Leona McMurtrey, whose more earthy ways perplexed him. She agreed to marry her tortured suitor, with what misgivings the readers of Fisher's novels can imagine. The marriage took place on 10 September 1917, but the partnership had few moments of calm.

Meanwhile, there was the continued possibility of participation in World War I, and shortly after the birth of his son Grant in 1918, Fisher was drafted into the U.S. Army. He was, however, too late to get overseas. After the war ended he was back at Utah where he finished the bachelor of arts degree in 1920. Writing and teaching were on his mind, and he began work on the master's degree at the University of Chicago. The birth of a second son, Wayne, in 1921, complicated life for the Fishers, and since Leona did not at first accompany her husband to Chicago, the separation added to the complexities. After she joined her husband, it was clear that their differences were not reconcilable: Fisher longed for an intellectual mate. He was awarded the master of arts degree in 1922 and began studying for the doctorate. But Fisher's academic progress brought Leona little happiness, and she committed suicide on 8 September 1924. Shaken by guilt, Fisher contemplated suicide himself. Fortunately, however, his brother, now a student of psychology, helped Fisher to find renewed purpose, and Fisher immersed himself in his doctoral work and a series of sonnets modeled on the idea of George Meredith's *Modern Love*. Fisher had long identified with Meredith's struggles over an unhappy and tragic marriage, and he wrote his dissertation on Meredith. Fisher's sonnets were published in 1927 as *Sonnets to an Imaginary Madonna*. The publisher was Harold Vinal, whom Fisher eventually considered a vanity publisher and whom E. E. Cummings satirizes in "Poem: or, Beauty Hurts Mr. Vinal." The sonnets did nothing to give Fisher a literary reputation (he later minimized their literary value), but they did give him a first book, and their writing had been useful therapy at a difficult time.

Degree in hand, Fisher returned to the University of Utah in 1925, where he taught English from 1925 through 1928. Not surprisingly, he did not fit easily into the academic structure, and his views of life often came into conflict with the dominant Mormon culture in which he lived. In 1928 Fisher married Margaret

Trusler, whom he had met and courted in his Chicago days. He sought intellectual companionship in her (she also had the Ph.D. degree from the University of
Chicago) that he had not received from Leona. Margaret bore a son, Thornton
Roberts, in 1937. Fisher and Margaret were divorced in 1939. In 1940 Fisher
married Opal Laurel Holmes, whom he had met while he directed the Idaho
Writers' Project for the Works Progress Administration; the marriage endured
until his death in 1968.

Major Themes

In 1928, the year that Fisher married Margaret Trusler, Houghton Mifflin
published *Toilers of the Hills*, Fisher's first novel. It was an important beginning,
for although the novel is not a masterpiece, it was set in the Antelope Hills
country that had formed Fisher, and it suggested the possibilities for other fiction
set in this land. The rendering of life on one of the last frontiers would be a major
vein for Fisher; his fiction probed the loneliness of other characters before he
wrote about his own. In *Toilers of the Hills* the loneliness of the frontier is made
apparent through the consciousness of Opal Hunter, who is married to Dock
Hunter. Dock, determined to make the dry Antelope Hills prosperous farm
country, fights a reluctant nature, while the lonely Opal wonders about his
tenacity. Like Fisher's last novel, his first is a novel of male and female in the
American West. Convincing and colorful because of Dock's rich humor, *Toilers
of the Hills* received good reviews and surely made Fisher seem attractive to
Washington Square College of New York University, where he began to teach
English in the autumn of 1928.

Fisher taught at Washington Square College for three years, then turned his
back on the East and, except for summer assignments at the University of
Montana, on teaching. In 1931 Houghton Mifflin published *Dark Bridwell*, in
many ways Fisher's most successful novel. The novel, by recounting the story of
Charley Bridwell and his family, captures the wild and haunting isolation of the
river basin that was such a formative influence on Fisher. Charley is based on
Charley Wheaton, the only neighbor anywhere near the Fishers. In the novel
Charley becomes a legend to the Antelope people, and the narrator seeks to
present that legend with stark clarity, seeking to understand the motivations and
consequences of Charley Bridwell's decision to live in his river basin home in
isolation from the rest of the world. In *Dark Bridwell* Fisher created a work with
a force akin to tragedy, for the narrator's guiding hand is not overly obtrusive, as
Fisher's narrative voice would become in later works when he restored legends
based on historical research. The Antelope Hills country provided Fisher with his
richest material.

Fisher was obviously aware of the potential of this Antelope heritage, for
among the minor characters of *Dark Bridwell* was Vridar Hunter, nephew of the
Dock Hunter of *Toilers of the Hills* and a member of a clan based on the Fishers.
In *In Tragic Life* (1932) Fisher portrayed Vridar Hunter and his family, a family

very different from the hedonistic Bridwells. But it became obvious that Fisher's primary motivation was not the exploration of the Idaho frontier, even though *In Tragic Life* portrays this environment powerfully. Fisher's real subject was himself. The novel emphasizes the lonely childhood of Vridar Hunter and ends with his determination to conquer his morbid fears. The novel was the first of the tetralogy that helped give Fisher a national reputation in the 1930s. The other titles of the tetralogy, like the first, come from Sonnet XLIII of George Meredith's *Modern Love*.

Passions Spin the Plot (1934) carries Vridar through his college days in Salt Lake City and recounts his courtship of and marriage to Neloa Doole, who is based on Leona McMurtrey. *We Are Betrayed* (1935) charts the doomed marriage and Vridar's struggle to become a scholar; the novel ends with Neloa's suicide. *No Villain Need Be* (1936) treats Vridar's recovery, his marriage to Athene (based on Margaret Trusler), and his teaching career and final dedication to truth and writing. Written in a direct, realistic manner, the tetralogy nevertheless shows Fisher's more poetic side when he deals with the Idaho country. The last two volumes, however, deal only slightly with Idaho and are less appealing, for although Vridar wishes to be reasonable, he often misses that goal. Fisher meant for the reader frequently to judge Vridar as ridiculous, but, in the final analysis, he wanted the reader to approve his hero's honesty and courage. Identification with Vridar does not come easily after *In Tragic Life*, for Vridar's lack of humor is but a part of his rigidity. Any position that Vridar holds at any moment is the only position admissible, it seems. Vridar is a great haranguer, especially of Neloa, and the tetralogy becomes increasingly a matter of Vridar's intellectual debates—blunt talk about ideas. The structure of the whole (based on a symphony) works to counteract these drawbacks. Although readers may often find Vridar a frustrating protagonist, his is a suffering that matters.

All of Fisher's novels of the Antelope Hills frontier emphasize the loneliness of the environment and the anguish it can cause certain temperaments; the Charley Bridwells who thrive in the isolation are few. In *April: A Fable of Love* (1937) Fisher treats a different kind of loneliness in Antelope, a loneliness that is heightened, in part, because the region is not as isolated as that which Opal Hunter, Lela Bridwell, and Prudence Hunter found. *April* presents a peopled Antelope, a sense of community and the drama of lives not so restricted to the main character's immediate family. June Weeg's loneliness is rooted in her extraordinary homeliness. Because she is physically so unappealing, only the homeliest man in the Antelope Hills courts her. June dreams of herself as a lovely April, but she finally realizes and acknowledges that love, while necessary, needs to be based on realities. Fisher's fable avoided the stridency that sometimes marred the tetralogy, and it was his favorite among his works.

Fisher's greatest popular reputation came from *Children of God* (1939), a novel that depended not on re-created memory and the Idaho of his youth but on researched history. This is not to suggest that the exercise was purely or even mainly academic; Fisher was probing the history of the religious heritage that

more than any other had been part of his youth and world. He was also responding to the milieu of the 1930s, which favored American historical subjects, and
Fisher's subtitle, *An American Epic*, carried some weight. It had surely been one
of Fisher's assumptions in the depression years that Americans needed a better
grasp of their history and heritage. Fisher's success with his Antelope novels and
his tetralogy had led to his appointment as director of the Idaho Writers' Project
for the Works Progress Administration, a position he held for the four years it
took him to research and write *Children of God*. (Fisher worked with a vigor to
match Brigham Young's; he was intent that Idaho's would be the first of the
WPA American Guide Series, and it was.) And after his novel won the Harper
Prize, Fisher eventually saw the popularity for his novel dealing with an American theme as an entry to a market of American historical novels, novels that he
could write to support himself while he wrote a different kind of historical novel,
his Testament of Man.

For *Children of God*, Fisher—his insistence on the "truth" almost dictated his
method—chose to write his epic (his longest novel to that date) by focusing his
attention on the actual personages of Mormon history. *Children of God* chronicles the rise of Mormonism through the career of Joseph Smith and Brigham
Young's leadership after Smith's martyrdom. Only the final third of the novel
focuses on invented characters as Fisher portrays Mormonism after Young's
death when the church had to come to terms with federal opposition to plural
marriage. Although Fisher distrusted Smith, he admired Young a great deal, but
neither portrait is memorable as characterization. It was the movement more than
character that carried Fisher's novel; perhaps his realization of his failure to make
his characters live was part of his distaste for the novel his readers most often
praised.

The response of the critics to *Children of God* was mainly positive, however,
in part because Fisher's "objective" method suggested that he had left behind the
heavy didacticism of the tetralogy, especially that of *No Villain Need Be*, and of
the satiric *Forgive Us Our Virtues: A Comedy of Evasion* (1938). Fisher followed
his Mormon novel with a historical novel of a western enterprise that was totally
material. *City of Illusion* (1941) is also based on actual people, although not of
the importance of Smith and Young. The novel describes the heyday and decline
of Virginia City, Nevada, and the famous Comstock silver mining. Although it
had some deft touches, the novel seems too easy. Fisher was writing too fast, and
he and his publisher, Harper and Brothers, parted company.

Fisher needed more to identify with than the Comstock story gave him, and he
found it in the account of the entrapment of the Donner Party in the Sierra Nevada
Mountains during the severe winter of 1846-47. Since he had portrayed women
such as Opal Hunter and June Weeg with great understanding, it is not surprising
that Fisher would find his most important story in the narrative of pioneer
mistakes and eventual cannibalism to be the mother courage that would preserve
the children, if no others, from starvation. Although *The Mothers* (1943) has a
large cast, the focus of the narrative on survival in a crisis that covered a

comparatively short time span gives an intensity to the novel that makes it more dramatically satisfying than either *Children of God* or *City of Illusion*.

The year of the publication of *The Mothers*, 1943, also saw publication of the first novel of Fisher's Testament of Man. *Darkness and the Deep* portrayed earliest man man with only the rudiments of speech. *The Golden Rooms* (1944) depicts the birth of man's notions of ghosts or spirits and of his sense of religion that came with a conviction that death is not an end. Since Fisher was dealing with prehistoric peoples in these novels, a literate narrator was a necessary vehicle, and Fisher's voice is subdued enough, not strident or overly insistent. The stories Fisher told, while based on extensive research, were imaginatively convincing. Beginning with the third novel of the Testament, however, the imaginative force of the series declines. The reader gets the feeling that man is going to have to discover a good deal (farming, boating, and so on) before Fisher is done with his more important vision of man's spiritual progress. The instructing voice becomes more evident. The societies of the third and fourth novels are matriarchal rather than patriarchal; unfortunately Fisher does not make the matriarchal world as believable as that found in the Testament's first two books.

Fisher's burden of sharing his research with his reader increased significantly after he got into historic times. For the sixth volume, *The Valley of Vision* (1951), Fisher appended notes and commentary to justify or expand his rendering of the life of King Solomon. Notes of explanation also accompany volumes seven through eleven. Fisher's notes are a revealing symptom: he was more intent on having his readers reach his conclusions than in creating satisfactory novels. His scholarship interfered with his novelistic responsibilities. Fisher believed unquestionably in the necessity of such pilgrimages to the past as he was making, and his research was a means for his self-discovery—as he explained the motivation for writing the Testament and his retelling of Vridar's story as the final volume of the Testament, *Orphans in Gethsemane* (1960). The Vridar of *Orphans*, like Fisher, goes through great agony over the publishing and critical reception of the Testament that he, like Fisher, was writing. In a moment of despair, Vridar wonders about his artistic merit. That is the one doubt that his third wife, Angele, will not allow him to entertain, and he quickly dismisses it. The trouble, Vridar and Angele agree, is surely with the eastern establishment and man's reluctance to face truth.

While the Testament of Man is an ambitious series, it is not well known because it is also as didactic a series as can be found. It could have been, and should have been, more aesthetically rewarding. When he worked on the series, Fisher was immersed in reading scholarship. By his own admission, he read little fiction once he had embarked on the series. He thought too little about what a novel ought to be.

The publication of Fisher's short stories in 1959 as *Love and Death* revealed more of the author's self than it was designed to reveal. The book is fairly slender (some 211 pages), and it was necessary to borrow segments from five novels to achieve that length. Most of the stories were written in the 1930s; the last to be published was "Mr. Graham Takes a Bath" (*Rocky Mountain Review*, Autumn 1945). The stories show range of method and some experimentation with point of view. Many are set in Antelope. They are good enough to make readers wish that Fisher had written more short stories, especially since they suggest greater concern with the art of fiction than most of what Fisher wrote after 1945. When Fisher ceased writing short stories, he had left behind his greatest achievement: his novels of the Antelope Hills and his tetralogy.

While the Testament led Fisher to retell Vridar's story—and to expand it to take Vridar to the end of the writing of his Testament—*Orphans in Gethsemane* will make many readers more impatient with Vridar than did the tetralogy. While Vridar's agonies raise pertinent issues, he is to the end more emotional than intellectual, and the didactic bent is usually overdone. Vridar heaps an unconscionable number of quotations from many writers on the heads of his wives— and on Fisher's readers. John R. Milton judges parts of the expanded Vridar story as embarrassingly self-indulgent (*Novel of the American West*, p. 158). Imperfect as the tetralogy may have been, it had a degree of structure not equaled in *Orphans*.

For Fisher and the core of readers who stood by him there was a sense of relief that his Testament was finally concluded and a sense that he was again dealing with his proper material when he resumed writing about the American West. *Mountain Man* (1965), like most of Fisher's other western novels (the exception is *Pemmican*, the 1956 novel whose center is the conflict between Hudson's Bay Company and the North West Company), is based on a historic person, John Johnson—"Liver-Eating Johnson." But while Johnson's story gives Fisher a frame, he was up to something different in this novel, a fact made clear in the transformation of Johnson to Samson (or Sam) Minard. Fisher abandoned the realistic novel for something much more romantic and mythic. He thought of his novel as a symphony, and his mountain man was bigger than life. He had to bear a staggering fictional burden, however, by embodying love for great music and great art and the wilderness of the era of the western mountain men. The tension between Sam's love for opera and other music (tastes dependent on civilization and in constant need of refurbishment) and his love for an untainted wilderness works against a convincing narrative, making readers too aware of the author's unresolved conflicts. While *Mountain Man* is consciously dealing with legend, it often presents those legends awkwardly or bookishly. The habit of instructing was too ingrained in Fisher, and he felt compelled to work in accounts of many mountain men. Too, Sam is Fisher's means of indicting twentieth-century civilization. Sam has to be both himself and Fisher, and readers are likely to resent the intrusion of the modern. Probably *Mountain Man* has had more readers than any other Fisher novel since *Children of God*, but that fact probably owes more to the movie *Jeremiah Johnson* (which is based as much on Raymond W. Thorp and Robert Bunker's 1958 account of Johnson's legend, *Crow Killer*, as on Fisher's novel) than to the absolute merit of the novel. In truth, *Mountain Man* is not nearly as forceful a presentation of a legend as is *Dark Bridwell*. Fisher's last novel, like his Testament of Man, confirms the judgment that his most worth-while fiction comes out of the Antelope Hills background and most of it belongs to the 1930s. Fisher's preference for *April* was not very wide of the mark.

Survey of Criticism

The general reader of the 1930s likely would have been aware of Vardis Fisher, but George Snell's *The Shapers of American Fiction, 1798-1947* (1947) is the only history of the American novel that has treated Fisher as a major writer. More typical of the evaluation placed on Fisher is Harry Hartwick's *The Fore-ground of American Fiction* (1934) and Harlan Hatcher's brief comment in *Creating the Modern American Novel* (1935). Important overviews on Fisher from the 1930s are John Peale Bishop's essay "The Strange Case of Vardis Fisher" (1937) and E. Current-Garcia's "Writers in the 'Sticks'" (1938). David Rein's *Vardis Fisher: Challenge to Evasion* (1937) is an interesting period piece of criticism, analyzing Fisher in Marxist terms. Fisher answers Rein in the book's preface.

For most of the 1940s and 1950s readers and critics paid little attention to Fisher. Alan Swallow did more than anyone else to rescue Fisher from this neglect. He not only published Fisher's Testament but used his influence as a critic to help to establish Fisher's stature as an author. His "The Mavericks" (1959) is important as a call for a Fisher revival. Fisher's viability as an impor-tant writer was considerably enhanced when Doubleday published *Pemmican, Tale of Valor*, and *Love and Death*, all in the late 1950s.

By the 1960s, Fisher was considered important enough to be the subject for several doctoral dissertations (Ruel Foster's 1942 Vanderbilt dissertation had pioneered these by evaluating the influence of Freud on Sherwood Anderson, Theodore Dreiser, Thomas Wolfe, and Fisher). Three of these dissertations were published by Revisionist Press, but the choice of publisher did little to advance Fisher's cause, indicating ironically that Fisher was not in the mainstream; the books were expensive and their content was more economically available from University Microfilms.

In September 1963 the *American Book Collector* published a special Vardis Fisher number, and two years later Joseph Flora's *Vardis Fisher* was published. Since that time there have been several essays on Fisher, but they have come mainly from critics especially interested in the West. Boise State's Western Writers Series honored Fisher's pioneering role as a writer of the Rocky Moun-tain West by issuing Wayne Chatterton's *Vardis Fisher: The Frontier and Re-gional Works* (1972) as the first pamphlet of the series. Of later critics, John R. Milton's views are of especial interest; see especially Milton's chapter on Fisher in *The Novel of the American West* (1980). George Kellogg's bibliography (1970) gives a good listing of critical work and a nearly complete listing of Fisher's works.

Bibliography

Works by Vardis Fisher

Sonnets to an Imaginary Madonna. New York: Vinal, 1927.
Toilers of the Hills. Boston: Houghton Mifflin, 1928.
Dark Bridwell. Boston: Houghton Mifflin, 1931.
In Tragic Life. Caldwell, Idaho: Caxton, 1932.
Passions Spin the Plot. Caldwell, Idaho: Caxton/Garden City, NY.: Doubleday, Doran, 1934.
We Are Betrayed. Caldwell, Idaho: Caxton/Garden City, N.Y.: Doubleday, Doran, 1935.
No Villain Need Be. Caldwell, Idaho: Caxton/Garden City, N.Y.: Doubleday, Doran, 1936.
April: A Fable of Love. Caldwell, Idaho: Caxton/Garden City, N.Y.: Doubleday, Doran, 1937.
Forgive Us Our Virtues: A Comedy of Evasion. Caldwell, Idaho: Caxton, 1938.
Children of God: An American Epic. New York: Harper, 1939.
City of Illusion. New York: Harper, 1941.
The Mothers: An American Saga of Courage. New York: Vanguard, 1943.
Darkness and the Deep. New York: Vanguard, 1943.
The Golden Rooms. New York: Vanguard, 1944.
The Valley of Vision: A Novel of King Solomon and His Time. New York: Abelard, 1951.
God or Caesar? The Writing of Fiction For Beginners. Caldwell, Idaho: Caxton, 1953.
Pemmican: A Novel of the Hudson's Bay Company. Garden City, N.Y.: Doubleday, 1956.
Tale of Valor: A Novel of the Lewis and Clark Expedition. Garden City, N.Y.: Doubleday, 1958.
Love and Death: The Complete Stories. Garden City, N.Y.: Doubleday, 1959.
Orphans in Gethsemane: A Novel of the Past in the Present. Denver: Swallow, 1960.
Mountain Man: A Novel of Male and Female in the Early American West. New York: William Morrow, 1965.
"The Western Writer and the Eastern Establishment," *Western American Literature* 1 (Winter 1967): 244-59.

Studies of Vardis Fisher

Bishop, John Peale, "The Strange Case of Vardis Fisher." *Southern Review* 3 (Autumn 1937): 348-59. Reprinted in *The Collected Essays of John Peale Bishop*. Ed. Edmund Wilson. New York & London: Charles Scribner's Sons, 1948, pp. 56-65.
Chatterton, Wayne. *Vardis Fisher: The Frontier and Regional Works*. WWS. Boise: Boise State College, 1972.
Current-Garcia, E. "Writers in the 'Sticks.'" *Prairie Schooner* 12 (Winter 1938): 294-309.
Flora, Joseph M. *Vardis Fisher*. TUSAS. New York: Twayne, 1965.
———. "Vardis Fisher and the Mormons." *Dialogue, A Journal of Mormon Thought* 4 (Autumn 1969): 48-55.
———. "Vardis Fisher and Wallace Stegner: Teacher and Student." *Western American Literature* 5 (Summer 1970): 121-28.

————. "Westering and Woman: A Thematic Study of Kesey's *One Flew Over the Cuckoo's Nest* and Fisher's *Mountain Man*." In *Women, Women Writers, and the West*. Eds. L. L. Lee and Merrill Lewis. Troy, N.Y.: Whitston, 1979, pp. 131-41.

Kellogg, George. "Vardis Fisher: A Bibliography." *Western American Literature* 5 (Spring 1970): 45-64.

Milton, John R. "The Primitive World of Vardis Fisher: The Idaho Novels," *Midwest Quarterly* 17 (Summer 1976): 369-84.

————. "Vardis Fisher: The Struggle of Rationalism." In *The Novel of the American West*. Lincoln: University of Nebraska Press, 1980, pp. 117-59.

Meldrum, Barbara. "Vardis Fisher's Antelope People: Pursuing an Elusive Dream." *Northwest Perspectives: Essays in the Culture of the Pacific Northwest*. Ed. Edwin R. Bingham and Glen A. Love. Seattle: University of Washington Press, 1979, pp. 152-66.

Rein, David. *Vardis Fisher: Challenge to Evasion*. Chicago: Black Cat Press, Normandie House, 1937.

Snell, George. "Erskine Caldwell and Vardis Fisher—The Nearly-Animal Kingdom." In *The Shapers of American Fiction, 1798-1947*. New York: E. P. Dutton, 1947, pp. 276-88.

Swallow, Allan. "The Mavericks." *Critique: Studies in Modern Fiction* 2 (Winter 1959): 79-84. Reprinted in Swallow's *An Editor's Essays of Two Decades*. Seattle and Denver: Experiment Press, 1962, pp. 330-60.

James H. Maguire

MARY HALLOCK FOOTE
(1847-1938)

Like Bret Harte and Hamlin Garland, Mary Hallock Foote earned a considerable reputation for her stories and novels about the American West, but unlike Harte and Garland, she outlived her literary reputation. Yet when she grew older, she did not lose much of her creative power, as Harte and Garland lost theirs. In fact, her last work is her best. Unfortunately, by the time her last two novels appeared, she had entered her seventies, and many of the readers who had admired her earlier works had died. For years after her death, she was judged on the basis of her first efforts, and for that reason she shared the posthumous fate of writers such as Herman Melville and Kate Chopin, whose early works seemed unremarkable but whose later masterpieces either baffled or shocked their contemporaries. Although none of her novels can be ranked with *Moby-Dick* or *The Awakening*, Foote nevertheless offers literary artistry of a high order. Among the western writers of her time, she was one of the best, if not the best.

Biography

Foote's origins were thoroughly eastern, as were the origins of many of the other "western" writers of the nineteenth century, but she lived in the West for more than fifty years. Most of her works are set in the West and deal with western themes and characters, though she never forgot her heritage. Born on 19 November 1847 to Quaker parents in Milton, New York, Foote met many of America's most noted abolitionists and feminists during her childhood. When she became an art student at New York's Cooper Institute at age seventeen, she also began what was to be a lifelong friendship with Helena de Kay. Moving in the highest artistic and intellectual circles of the age, Helena and the man she married in 1874, Richard Watson Gilder, provided Mary Hallock with an entrée to the best of genteel society. Her own considerable talents as an illustrator gained Hallock a budding reputation in her own right.

She appeared to give up her friends and her promising career in 1876 when she married Arthur De Wint Foote, a young mining engineer whose career took the newlyweds to the golden but still wild West. Yet during her residence in New Almaden and Santa Cruz, California (1876-78), and in Leadville, Colorado (1879-80), Mary Hallock Foote's active correspondence with Helena Gilder strengthened their friendship, and publisher's commissions kept her busy supplying sketches for gift books such as a deluxe edition of *The Scarlet Letter*. So impressed were the Gilders with her verbal depictions of California that they urged her to revise some of her letters for publication as an article in the *Century*, a literary journal that Richard edited. Once she had published, Foote tried her hand at fiction, had a story accepted by the *Atlantic* (then under the editorship of William Dean Howells), and was promptly begged by the Gilders to submit all of her future work to her friends at the *Century*. For the next thirty years most of Foote's short stories and novels appeared first in the pages of the *Century* before being issued in book form.

While her husband sought a mining job in the West, Foote gained time for writing during visits to her family home in Milton. Arthur's search for a job led both of them to Morelia, Mexico, a romantic sojourn that had to substitute for a grand tour of Europe. Later, while investigating mining opportunities in Idaho, Arthur decided to undertake a risky venture: the irrigation of the Snake River plain near Boise. The Footes lived in Boise from 1884 to 1895, an experience that was largely a disappointment. Faced with the physical hardships of life in a small frontier town and critical of its crude cultural life, Mary also disliked many of Boise's residents, and the irrigation project was not completed while the Footes were there. But while Mary watched the collapse of Arthur's dream with the subsequent loss of his money, she managed to write a number of novels and short stories that soon established her as one of the leading literary interpreters of the West.

Written in Milton or Boise, Foote's first three novels portray the robust life of Leadville—at least as much of that life as could be experienced or surmised by a woman whose husband took it as his first duty to protect her from the coarser elements of life in a mining camp. At the core of most of Foote's fictions is a love story, but around that core she usually builds a tale based upon actual incidents. *The Led-Horse Claim* (1883), for example, is based upon a boundary dispute between the Adelaide and the Argentine, two Leadville mines whose workers armed themselves for a showdown. The guns were never fired, but Foote confessed that she was "afraid of secret shots"—and well she might have been, since her husband managed the Adelaide and rode each morning past the rifles of the Argentine. *John Bodewin's Testimony* (1886) also drew upon some of Arthur's Leadville experience—in this case his court testimony about the authenticity of a mining claim. Foote's own experience figured more centrally in *The Last Assembly Ball* (1889), a story about the social life of a Leadville boardinghouse. Published with that novel was the first of Foote's longer works set in the Snake River country, a novella entitled *The Fate of a Voice*. It is a skillful depiction of a young singer faced with the choice of going to the East for a career or staying in the West for a marriage.

The Colorado novels of the 1880s stand as the better-than-average results of her literary apprenticeship, but Foote's output during the 1890s consisted of potboilers, as she frankly called them in her reminiscences (*A Victorian Gentlewoman*, pp. 336, 359). Nevertheless, in spite of the sentimentality and despair that pervade Foote's Idaho works of the 1890s, they are among the first novels and stories to depict certain western scenes and themes. *The Chosen Valley* (1892) is clearly based on Arthur Foote's experiences in trying to build an irrigation system, and *Coeur d'Alene* (1894) presents Foote's propagandistic antiunion view of the Idaho mining wars between capital and labor. Much more effective than those novels are some of the Idaho stories that Foote collected in two volumes: *In Exile, and Other Stories* (1894) and *The Cup of Trembling, and Other Stories* (1895). Some of these fictional vignettes focus on local characters and customs: country dances, the tasks of a watchman on an irrigation ditch, the social code of an army garrison.

In 1895 the Footes moved to Grass Valley, California, where Arthur had accepted the managership of the North Star Mine. The move brought stability to the Footes' marriage, which Arthur's excessive drinking had shaken during the hard times in Idaho. With her increased financial and marital security, Mary Hallock Foote moved into a new phase as an author. Her work after the turn of the century displays less romantic sentimentality and more realism. Describing ordeals and tests of character that young men face in the West, *The Prodigal* (1900) and *The Desert and the Sown* (1902) are novels that also describe parental dreams and tribulations; and *A Touch of Sun and Other Stories* (1903) reveals Foote's increasing mastery of the short story form. She turned next to a historical novel about the American Revolution, but the death of her youngest daughter, Agnes, shattered her emotional equilibrium, and she put the manuscript aside for half a decade.

Published in 1910, *The Royal Americans* reads more like a historical treatise than a novel, perhaps because Foote researched her subject so thoroughly that her notes led her into writing almost straight history. Another historical novel, *A Picked Company* (1912), tells the story of a family that followed the Oregon Trail in the 1840s. Although not of the first rank, these historical novels gave Foote practice in recounting the events of several generations, practice she put to excellent use in the series of three autobiographical novels that mark the end of her career. *The Valley Road* (1915) is based on the Footes' experiences at Grass Valley' and also contains a section on the San Francisco earthquake of 1906. *Edith Bonham* (1917) goes back to the Footes' Boise days and is her best work, though it is almost equaled by *The Ground-Swell* (1919), an older mother's musings about her attempts to secure happiness for her three daughters.

Following World War I, Foote wrote an autobiography, but for the next fifty years only members of her family read the several manuscript versions of it. Superbly edited by Rodman Paul and published in 1972 as *A Victorian Gentlewoman in the Far West*, Foote's reminiscences "will probably"—in Lee Ann Johnson's view—"be judged her most enduring literary accomplishment" (*Mary*

Hallock Foote, p. 153). In 1932 the Footes moved to Hingham, Massachusetts, to live with their daughter Betty. Arthur died the following year, and Mary's death came on 25 June 1938 when she was in her ninetieth year.

Major Themes

Given Mary Hallock Foote's eastern birth and education and her more than fifty years of western residence and experience, it is not surprising that one of her major themes is the contrast between East and West. In her early works that contrast is stark and almost simple: the East is home, culture, a safe haven for women—civilized; the West is a place for masculine exploits, a social as well as a natural wilderness. In her later works the West holds the promise of settlement and eventual civilization. As in eastern novels such as *A Hazard of New Fortunes* (1890) by William Dean Howells, the characters in her works come from different regions and social classes. In the West, however, their differences rarely melt away. Some of her early work leads one to surmise that Foote was influenced by Hippolyte Taine's theory that culture is shaped by environment, whereas her last few novels present a much more subtle and complex view of the relationship between place and people.

One aspect of Foote's treatment of the West never varies. Beyond the hundredth meridian the forces of nature put people through ordeals that test their character; Colorado and Idaho mountain snowstorms, Idaho and California desert heat, raging rivers, and earthquakes either toughen or destroy the people who have to undergo them. Those who survive the tests are rewarded with a natural beauty that seems all the greater for the contrast with the danger. Edith Bonham says of that dangerous West, "I hated it, and so did Nanny. But it 'haunted' us both. It has tremendous force, concealed somehow; things may happen any time, but you don't know what, nor where to expect them" (*Edith Bonham*, p. 263). She eventually comes to feel that the land has an appeal, too, though "it wasn't beauty—it was a lofty loneliness that resembles the sea, far inland as we were. I began to feel how people who have lived in such places can never go back to the old values of life in villages and towns; they must forever be the 'gypsy-souls,' homeless in the paths of men" (pp. 170-71).

Edith's lament that those who have lived in the West "can never go back to the old values" did not mean that there was no longing to return, both to the values and to their setting. A recurrent pattern in many of Foote's works shows a young engineer and a young lady, both from the East, who meet and fall in love out West but whose romance does not end in marriage until they have returned to their eastern birthplace. A similar pattern appears in other western works of the period—Owen Wister's *The Virginian* (1902) and William Vaughn Moody's *The Great Divide* (1906), to name two well-known examples. This pattern suggests that these writers reacted to regions emotionally, feeling that the West offered freedom, opportunity, and adventure, whereas the East was a refuge, a haven, the source of tradition and legitimacy. Interestingly, the pattern of the return to the East does not appear in Foote's later works; and in "Pilgrims to Mecca," Foote even pokes fun at the notion that almost no culture of any value can be found west of the Alleghenies.

Foote's finest treatment of the contrast between East and West is conveyed in her portrayal of eastern women who must survive in the "haunting" immensity of western spaces. East is clearly more feminine, West masculine. Many of Foote's female characters who manage to survive the masculine West do so because of the support they receive from a sympathetic community of women, however small it might be. Edith Bonham's isolation on the mesa does not cut her off from such a community, for the memory of her friendship with Nanny sustains her, even though her friend has died. The mother-daughter love that sustains Mrs. Cope and her daughters in *The Ground-Swell* is similar to the bond between Edith and Nanny.

Feminine communities sustain many of Foote's characters, but when they agree to marry, many of them are forced to sacrifice their eastern friendships and homes or their hopes for a career. Lee Ann Johnson has called such unions in Foote's fiction "marriage by default," a theme that

depicts the romantic relationship between two young, attractive, and educated individuals. Born in the East but living in the West, the hero and heroine seem ideally suited because of shared interests and sympathies, yet there is always a complication which prevents them from achieving a satisfying relationship—a previous commitment, an obstacle presented by profession or family. It is only when the circumstances are suddenly altered through natural disaster, illness, death, or repudiation that they recognize the saving alternative each represents. Their resultant union is one of marriage by default. [*Mary Hallock Foote*, p. 34]

Many of Foote's women characters also face "marriage by default" because they lack adequate male protection; usually Foote shows that a woman's difficulties are caused by a father or brother whose drinking problem makes him incapable of giving his daughter or sister the kind of support she needs. Such situations should not be seen as simply sentimental, melodramatic frills, for what William Wasserstrom has said about the popular literature of the genteel tradition also applies to Foote's work: it "recognized that society could not competently fulfill its great tasks if men and women were themselves distraught, rendered incompetent to love" (*Heiress of All the Ages*, p. x).

Men's drunkenness constituted a betrayal of wives, daughters, and sisters— victims of male irresponsibility. Sober and responsible men in Foote's fiction sometimes seem at first to be ruthless, but what weaker, more ignorant characters think is hardness, is actually foresight based on a solid professional training and knowledge. Even Travis in "The Watchman" understands that "that talk against companies is an old politicians' drivel. This country is too big for single men to handle; companies save years of waiting" (*In Exile*, p. 233). Foote's heroes are responsible, well-educated members of the upper class, and when they are forced into duels or shoot-outs—as they often are in Foote's earlier works—they usually act from high principles. Yet in later characters such as Adam Bogardus in *The Desert and the Sown* and Tony Kayding in *The Ground-Swell*, Foote expresses considerable sympathy for the poor and the nonprofessional; and the dreams and schemes that drive her upper-class engineers often cause them to disregard the values of others, as in "The Harshaw Bride" when plans for a hydroelectric power plant call for the destruction of beautiful waterfalls.

In a number of Foote's later works, both men and women betray others by refusing to give of themselves. Emily Bogardus will not recognize her husband Adam; Peter Dalbert in *The Ground-Swell* lets his mistress die rather than endanger himself; Edith Bonham selfishly interprets Douglas Maclay's proposal in the worst possible way. Those later works show that even loving too well can ultimately betray, especially when parents such as Mrs. Scarth in *The Valley Road* and Mrs. Cope in *The Ground-Swell* meddle in their children's love affairs.

Foote's greatest gift—one that came to her late in her career—is her ability to portray parental emotions and concerns. And in sympathetically showing the different, sometimes opposing, views of the generations, she creates a counterpoint that enriches the work. Equally effective in her later work are the numerous allusions that strengthen the impression of a living cultural heritage, one that can be transported even to the western frontier. Her characters read George Washington Cable's *The Grandissimes* and George Meredith's *The Ordeal of Richard Feverel*, works whose themes offer readers mirror images of the situations Foote's characters are in; and lines from Alfred Tennyson and Robert Browning enter the narrative at equally appropriate points. In her use of allusions and of the parental viewpoint, she conveys a strong sense of tradition. The unfamiliar dangers of the new territory can be faced with the sustaining wisdom of the past.

Another of Foote's literary strengths is her style. Polished from the beginning, it grew in subtlety and power with the years, especially when she wrote in the first person as in her last two novels. Her style matched her temperament: a Quaker admiration of simplicity but an artist's eye for the rich beauty of sometimes elaborate symmetry, harmony, and color. A brief paragraph from *The Ground-Swell* illustrates the point:

And then I went out upon my usual beat, old wheel-tracks worn in the coarse grass and sand that already I had made into a path along the first bench above us. Eastward rose the moors, dark, wind-slanted grass against the sky, reminding one of Jane Eyre's drawing and Rochester's question, "Who taught you to draw wind?" [P. 43]

At its best, Foote's style is similar to Willa Cather's in her ability to evoke whole scenes with a few carefully chosen phrases.

Perhaps her style became more powerful because Foote's vision of life deepened and became richer and more complex. Even in some of her early works she spoke of victories that bordered on defeat, and she later came to see the tragedy in the restless pursuit of what she called the angle of repose, a phrase "which was too good to waste on rockslides or heaps of sand"; "one finds and loses [the angle of repose] from time to time but is always seeking [it] in one way or another" (*A Victorian Gentlewoman*, pp. 306, 309). Foote sometimes approaches, though she never enters into, the kind of philosophical probing that Melville made of the appearance-versus-reality theme in *The Confidence Man*. What she does arrive at is a kind of protoexistentialism that is expressed in the narrator's approving account of Mr. Cornish in *The Valley Road*: "He knew there is nothing in life but the meanings we put into it" (p. 348). Mary Hallock Foote came to see that there is no better way to put meanings into life than by weighing the ore of new experience (the West) in the scales of old wisdom (the East).

Survey of Criticism

Foote's own wisdom and talent made her well known not only as the Dean of Women Illustrators but also as a western writer. Her literary work was praised by writers and critics such as Charles F. Lummis and Owen Wister. By the time her best work appeared, however, she was virtually ignored. Most of the critics and reviewers who still mentioned her simply repeated the judgments they had come to in evaluating her fledgling efforts and her potboilers. A good example of such fixed notions can be seen in a brief review that appeared in the *Nation* in 1903: "Mrs. Foote long ago arrived at a pleasant mediocrity in the art of storytelling, and rarely rises above or falls far below her own standard. . . . There is a good deal to amuse, a good deal to skip, and nothing to do any harm" (24 December 1903, p. 508). A few critics recognized that Foote deserved more attention. Thomas Beer commented in *The Mauve Decade* (1926): "Mary Hallock Foote varied from sentimental romance to a sudden passage or two of bitter realism and critics neglected her to discuss something by Mrs. Humphrey Ward or William Black" (p. 92). Yet even Beer gives no indication that he was aware of the great improvement in Foote's work within the decade before his own observation.

Almost a quarter of a century after Beer's passing reference to Foote, Wallace Stegner wrote that in her work one finds "fine passages and fine single stories" but that her reputation was "likely to dwindle further rather than revive" (Spiller et al., *Literary History of the United States* [New York: Macmillan, 1948; rpt. 1964], p. 869). In 1958 Stegner tried to save her from total neglect when he included one of her uncollected short stories, "How the Pump Stopped at the Morning Watch," in his *Selected American Prose: The Realistic Movement, 1841-1900*, saying that hers was "the only serious writing after Bret Harte to deal with mining-camp society, and virtually the only serious fiction which has dealt with the camps from intimate knowledge" (p. 117). Also during the 1950s, in a master's thesis and several articles, Mary Lou Benn contended that Foote's early work is superior to her later efforts.

Stegner's prediction that Foote's reputation would dwindle further proved to be true until 1971, when he changed all that by writing *Angle of Repose*, a novel based in part on Foote's life and work and for which Stegner was awarded a

Pulitzer Prize. *Angle of Repose* follows Foote's life closely in the character of Susan Burling Ward from her courtship in New York to her early years in Idaho. Stegner uses direct quotations from the letters of Mary Hallock Foote to Helena de Kay Gilder, and many of his scenes and descriptions echo similar passages in Foote's work. But for the purposes of his novel, Stegner changes some of the events in Foote's later life: Susan Burling Ward has an encounter that the narrator strongly implies was adulterous, and the Wards' young daughter dies while her mother is neglecting her in order to see her lover. At the 1979 meeting of the Western Literature Association, Mary Ellen Williams presented a paper accusing Stegner of unfairly gaining credit for fine writing that is to some extent Foote's and of distorting Foote's life story in an unjust and degrading way. I see Stegner's intention and achievement much differently. *Angle of Repose* is a tribute to Mary Hallock Foote. Although he has made obvious changes in her life story, Stegner has faithfully used her literary accomplishment—not as Shakespeare used Holinshed, but more as Beethoven worked other melodies and harmonies into his own compositions, thereby adding resonance and deepening the meaning of both the old work and the new.

Only a year after the appearance of *Angle of Repose*, Rodman Paul published his edition of Foote's reminiscences, *A Victorian Gentlewoman in the Far West*, adding to it an informative introduction, many helpful notes, a useful bibliographical essay, and a discussion of the text and the illustrations. In 1976, referring extensively to Foote's unpublished correspondence, Paul published a biographical sketch of Foote, "When Culture Came to Boise," that adds to our understanding of her life. However, Paul also included in his article a brief discussion of *The Chosen Valley*; and he quotes out of context in his effort to establish what he says is the fact "that Mary Hallock Foote was an incurable romantic" (p. 12).

Arriving at a conclusion different from Paul's, Lee Ann Johnson says that Foote's romanticism gave way in her later years to realism. Johnson's *Mary Hallock Foote* (1980) answered the call for a "bio-critical study like those appearing in the Twayne United States Authors Series," a call issued by Richard Etulain in a bibliographical essay that appeared in *American Literary Realism, 1870-1910* 5 (Spring 1972): 145-50. Three years later, in an annotated checklist published in *Western American Literature*, Etulain commented favorably upon James H. Maguire's effort to introduce Foote's life and work to the general reader, but Lee Ann Johnson's Twayne Series volume now provides a more extensive introduction to Foote. In addition to perceptive and well-informed discussions of Foote's previously listed works, Johnson includes an analysis of "Gideon's Knock," one of Foote's uncollected stories that had escaped the notice of previous scholars and bibliographers.

A recent article on the friendship of Mary Hallock and Helena de Kay is not listed in the bibliography of Johnson's book. In "The Female World of Love and Ritual: Relations between Women in Nineteenth-Century America" (1975), Carroll Smith-Rosenberg uses the Foote-Gilder correspondence as evidence for her thesis that women of the nineteenth century lived in a world far superior to that which women of the 1980s must endure. Bari Watkins contends in "Woman's World" (1979) that Smith-Rosenberg has "surely exaggerated the autonomy of female culture—and proposed a new sentimentalization of womanhood—by presenting beliefs and behavior imposed on women from without as unalienated free choice" (p. 120). The differing views of Watkins and Smith-Rosenberg show how useful a published volume of Foote's correspondence would be in helping to answer questions about her life and work. Also needed is a full biography of Foote, paperback editions of her best works, and studies that will examine her accomplishments in relation to those of her contemporaries and fellow Westerners.

Clearly Foote's achievement deserves more recognition. *Edith Bonham, The Ground-Swell*, and *A Victorian Gentlewoman in the Far West* present a voice that can enrich our continuing discussion of woman's fate. Those works must be read by critics of western American literature who want to arrive at an informed understanding and appreciation of the masterpiece that is *Angle of Repose*. Other scholars and readers will find in Foote's work an imaginative world that examines honestly and clearly the results of rapid, bewildering change—an early view of what we now call *culture shock* and *future shock*. One of the most sustaining qualities of art is that it offers not the escape from the world that one finds in much popular entertainment but a momentary angle of repose; an angle of repose can be found in the best work of Mary Hallock Foote.

Bibliography

Works by Mary Hallock Foote

The Led-Horse Claim: A Romance of a Mining Camp. Boston: J. R. Osgood, 1883.
John Bodewin's Testimony. Boston: Ticknor, 1886.
The Last Assembly Ball, and the Fate of a Voice. Boston: Houghton Mifflin, 1889.
The Chosen Valley. Boston: Houghton Mifflin, 1892.
Coeur d'Alene. Boston: Houghton Mifflin, 1894.
In Exile, and Other Stories. Boston: Houghton Mifflin, 1894.
The Cup of Trembling, and Other Stories. Boston: Houghton Mifflin, 1895.
The Little Fig-Tree Stories. [children's stories] Boston: Houghton Mifflin, 1899.
The Prodigal. Boston: Houghton Mifflin, 1900.
The Desert and the Sown. Boston: Houghton Mifflin, 1902.
A Touch of Sun, and Other Stories. Boston: Houghton Mifflin, 1903.
The Royal Americans. Boston: Houghton Mifflin, 1910.
A Picked Company. Boston: Houghton Mifflin, 1912.
The Valley Road. Boston: Houghton Mifflin, 1915.
Edith Bonham. Boston: Houghton Mifflin, 1917.
The Ground-Swell. Boston: Houghton Mifflin, 1919.
A Victorian Gentlewoman in the Far West: The Reminiscences of Mary Hallock Foote.
    Ed. Rodman W. Paul. San Marino, Calif.: Huntington Library, 1972.

Studies of Mary Hallock Foote

Auerbach, Nina, *Communities of Women: An Idea in Fiction*. Cambridge: Harvard University Press, 1978.

Beer, Thomas. *The Mauve Decade*. Garden City, N.Y.: Garden City Publishing Co., 1926.

Benn, Mary Lou. "Mary Hallock Foote: Early Leadville Writer." *Colorado Magazine* 33 (April 1956): 93-108.

————. "Mary Hallock Foote in Idaho." *University of Wyoming Publications* 20 (July 1956): 157-78.

————. "Mary Hallock Foote: Pioneer Woman Novelist." Master's thesis, University of Wyoming, 1955.

Cady, Edwin H. *The Light of Common Day: Realism in American Fiction*. Bloomington: Indiana University Press, 1971.

Cragg, Barbara. "Mary Hallock Foote's Images of the Old West." *Landscape* 24 (Autumn 1980): 42-47.

Davidson, Levette Jay. "Letters from Authors." *Colorado Magazine* 19 (July 1942): 122-25.

Donaldson, Thomas. *Idaho of Yesterday*. Caldwell, Idaho: Caxton Printers, 1941.

Etulain, Richard. "Mary Hallock Foote (1847-1938)." *American Literary Realism 1870-1910* 5 (Spring 1972): 145-50.

————. "Mary Hallock Foote: A Checklist." *Western American Literature* 10 (May 1975): 59-65.

Foote, Arthur B. "Memoir of Arthur DeWint [*sic*] Foote." *Transactions of the American Society of Civil Engineers* 99 (1934): 1449-52.

Gilder, Helena de Kay. "Author Illustrators, II: Mary Hallock Foote." *Book Buyer* 11 (August 1894): 338-42.

Johnson, Lee Ann. *Mary Hallock Foote*. TUSAS. Boston: Twayne, 1980.

Maguire, James H. *Mary Hallock Foote*. WWS. Boise, Idaho: Boise State College, 1972.

Paul, Rodman W. "When Culture Came to Boise: Mary Hallock Foote in Idaho." *Idaho Yesterdays* 20 (Summer 1976): 2-12.

Schopf, Bill. "The Image of the West in *The Century*, 1881-1889." *Possible Sack* [University of Utah] 3 (March 1972): 8-13.

Smith-Rosenberg, Carroll. "The Female World of Love and Ritual: Relations between Women in Nineteenth-Century America." *Signs* 1 (Autumn 1975): 1-29.

Stegner, Wallace. *Angle of Repose*. Garden City, N.Y.: Doubleday, 1971.

————, ed. *Selected American Prose: The Realistic Movement, 1841-1900*. New York: Holt, Rinehart and Winston, 1958.

————. In Robert E. Spiller, et al., *Literary History of the United States*. New York: Macmillan, 1948; Rpt. 1964.

Wasserstrom, William. *Heiress of All the Ages: Sex and Sentiment in the Genteel Tradition*. Minneapolis: University of Minnesota Press, 1958.

Watkins, Bari. "Woman's World in Nineteenth-Century America." *American Quarterly* 31 (Spring 1979): 116-27.

Joseph McCullough

HAMLIN GARLAND
(1860-1940)

Hamlin Garland's place in the literary history of the United States has been assured by the historians of the past, for during a productive and varied, although sometimes controversial and paradoxical, literary career, he published nearly fifty volumes of fiction, poetry, plays, and essays. His reputation rests principally on his fiction written before 1895, and particularly on his book of short stories, *Main-Travelled Roads* (1891), and on one of his autobiographies, *A Son of the Middle Border* (1917). In these books, Garland demonstrated that it had at last become possible to deal with the American farmer as a human being instead of viewing him simply through the veil of literary convention. By creating new types of characters, he hoped not only to inform readers about the realities of farm life but to touch the deeper feelings of a nation. At times Garland was unable to integrate his social and literary theories with the materials he gathered from personal experience and observation; but whenever he was able to maintain a tension between his romantic individualism and the oppressive social and economic conditions that threatened this individualism, his work retained a compelling vitality. He showed a deep sensitivity toward persons attempting to cope with changes in modern America. His reputation is deserved, even if his specific achievements often fall short of their expectations.

Biography

Born on 14 September 1860 on a farm near West Salem, Wisconsin, Hamlin Garland was the second of four children. Because of his father's domineering nature, together with his migratory tendencies, Hamlin was drawn to his mother, Isabelle McClintock Garland, who accepted her husband's migratory nature with quiet resignation. The contrast between his parents was to leave Garland with a particular tenderness toward women, which he transformed into a recurring theme in his fiction in which he dealt compassionately with suppressed and exhausted farm women.

After spending his formative years on several farms, in 1884 Garland made the most crucial decision in his personal and artistic career: he journeyed to Boston, the intellectual and literary center of the country. While there, he immersed himself in the evolutionary writings of Darwin, Spencer, Fiske, and Helmholtz, and his reading of Henry George's *Progress and Poverty* quickly converted him to advocacy of the single tax. After meeting and striking up a significant friendship with William Dean Howells, he returned west in 1887 and, horrified by what he saw, vowed to depict his observations in fiction. He began publishing his work in the prestigious *Century*, edited by Richard Watson Gilder. But unhappy with the slowness with which his material was being printed, he looked elsewhere. He met Benjamin O. Flower, editor of the radical *Arena*, who immediately encouraged Garland to submit material to him regularly. At Flower's suggestion, Garland collected his stories and in 1891 *Main-Travelled Roads* appeared. In addition to his social and economic writings of the 1890s, he lectured frequently on George's theories and campaigned for Populist candidates.

By 1894 Garland, tired of the controversy surrounding his middle-border fiction, decided to look elsewhere for material. Feeling an emotional attachment to the "high country" of the West, he entered a long period—from the publication of *Rose of Dutcher's Cooly* in 1895 until 1916—in which he produced dozens of Rocky Mountain romances.

Finding himself unable to create new material, having exhausted his subjects, Garland again had to change his angle of vision for the final phase of his literary career, reverting to the middle border where he began; if he could not create new material, then he would re-create the past. Consequently, from 1916 until his death in California on 4 March 1940, he produced, in addition to some psychic material, a succession of autobiographies.

In recognition of his achievement in *A Son of the Middle Border*, he was elected to the American Academy of Arts and Letters; for *Daughter of the Middle Border* (1921), he was awarded the Pulitzer Prize for biography.

Major Themes

Garland's prolific literary career can readily be divided into three major phases, although each phase contains elements from the others: an early period of involvement in reform movements and middle-border fiction (1888-95), a period of Rocky Mountain romance (1896-1916), and a final period of literary autobiography (1917-40).

The years between 1888 and 1890 were prolific ones for Garland. In addition to writing plays and novelettes, he collected most of his stories during this time into *Main-Travelled Roads* and *Prairie Folks* (1893). Although several of the stories that constitute *Main-Travelled Roads* are flawed as individual pieces, the book as a whole is a powerful, evocative treatment of western farm life. It is a poignant portrayal of human struggles against the forces of nature and social injustice.

In it, Garland uses the metaphor of the western road as the symbolic structural center and provides an epigraph before each story to achieve unity. A prefatory statement to the book sets the dominant tone and hints at what is to follow:

The main-travelled road in the West (as everywhere) is hot and dusty in summer, and desolate and drear with mud in fall and spring, and in winter the winds sweep the snow across it; but it does sometimes cross a rich meadow where the songs of the larks and bobolinks and blackbirds are tangled. Follow it far enough, it may lead past a bend in the river where the water laughs eternally over its shallows.

Mainly it is long and wearyful and has a dull little town at one end, and a home of toil at the other. Like the main-travelled road of life, it is traversed by many classes of people, but the poor and the weary predominate. [*Main-Travelled Roads*, p. 5]

Throughout the volume Garland emphasizes that while farm life was sometimes tragic and generally desolate, it also contained moments of exhilaration. But unlike many other local-color stories of the time that sentimentally expressed the charm of quaint country villages and characterized American rural life as a pastoral idyll, his stories express outrage at the social and economic injustices suffered by farmers. Yet it is also possible to overstate Garland's disillusionment, for despite the pervasive deterministic forces present, a persistent strain of romantic optimism is evident. Throughout he stresses the strength of the individual will and moral responsibility set against these forces.

Generally Garland's treatment of farm life is anti-idyllic, and because of the harsh demands of the life that he attempted to capture, his treatment of the possibilities of romantic love is no less so. The emotional center of many of the stories is the demoralizing condition of the farmer's wife. While some may escape and while others are afforded temporary relief from the monotony, the point is always the same: the loneliness and hardships for which a prairie wife is destined serve as an ironic comment on the beauty of the landscape and finally defeat our expectation of romantic love.

Several stories suggest inequities in the economic system, but only "Under the Lion's Paw" explicitly makes use of Henry George's thesis of the harmful social effect of unearned increment. Garland believed that only through social reform could individual tragedies be averted.

Additionally, a spirit of guilt permeates several stories in the volume, a theme that unquestionably results from Garland's personal guilt over leaving his parents, the plight of his family, and especially his mother. Through a series of contrasts and tensions, he presents this theme: isolation and companionship, the beauty of the countryside and the paucity of beauty in the lives of the farmers, the contrasting life-styles of individual characters who escape the farm and those who are forced to stay behind, and the conflict between success and failure. The book, finally, despite its flaws, is not only a significant social and historical document but an illustration of Garland's capacity to transform feelings, attitudes, and experiences into compelling themes.

Garland produced other works during this period that were less successful artistically but that grew directly out of his reforming attitudes and activities. In *Jason Edwards: An Average Man* (1892), dedicated to the Farmers Alliance, he develops the discrepancy between the promise of the American dream and what the characters subsequently discover. Here he depicts the Alliance as a new political force that has arisen for the struggle against economic injustices in the West. He further develops his ideas in *A Member of the Third House* (1892), in which his main theme is the political corruption that seems inevitable given private ownership and monopoly ownership of land. Finally, in *A Spoil of Office* (1892), as in his other economic novels, he traces the economic suffering resulting from the effects of monopolies.

In January 1894, Garland announced that he was renouncing all controversial literature in favor of purely literary works. What he meant by this statement is open to speculation, but it seems clear that while he continued to treat such themes as women's rights in marriage and the injustices suffered by American Indians, he no longer intended to focus on controversial economic fiction as he had done before. He would choose instead the road of literary acceptance and respectability offered by Gilder rather than that of B. O. Flower, who encouraged him to use his art as an instrument of social protest.

Before turning to the "high country" for new material, however, Garland completed *Rose of Dutcher's Cooly* (1895), his most ambitious and best full-length novel, which he had worked on intermittently from 1890 to 1895. *Rose* provides a good transition from his earlier "realistic" works to his following "romantic" ones. As he worked on the novel, his themes grew more numerous and complex as the length of the work increased. While the novel initially intended to focus on traditional family conflicts between youthful horizons and familial roots, it gradually began to include also the nature and role of modern woman and an illustration of Garland's theories of art that he had expounded in his literary manifesto, *Crumbling Idols* (1894). The latter half of the novel in particular expresses his views on the true nature of art, the social injustices of the double standard, and the subservient role of women in marriage. Garland traces Rose's development from her first sexual awakening and shows that a woman who possessed vitality, intelligence, will power, and moral strength could triumph over personal and social obstacles. While Garland was always a romantic individualist to a degree, his earlier stories usually portray man as victimized by his environment. In *Rose*, Garland, unlike the naturalistic writers Theodore Dreiser, Stephen Crane, and Frank Norris, clearly minimizes the strong environmental determinism, emphasizing instead individual strength and freedom of will.

As Garland turned to the mountain West for new material, he attempted to deal with a variety of facets of western life and to create a multiplicity of types, but he usually focused on mountaineers, miners, foresters, and Indians. With few exceptions, most of his works during this period contain common elements: mild social themes, a sense of the glory of the mountain scenery, and a conventional love plot. *The Eagle's Heart* (1900), his "Colorado novel," was one of the first fruits of his western travels and is central among his romantic works because he attempts to put everything into it: the scene, the technique, the conventions, and, most of all, the types of characters that were to form the basis of his other western novels. It illustrates his new style and concerns and also exemplifies his strength and, ultimately, his failure as a romantic novelist. Here the bond is no longer the community but a single hero. Harold Excell, the novel's hero, emerges as a romantic individualist: strong, handsome, and self-reliant, belonging to a class of romantic noblemen who are in quest of the mystic mountains of the West.

Between 1903 and 1907 Garland published three novels—*Hesper* (1903), *Witch's Gold* (1906), and *Money Magic* (1907)—in which the scene shifts from the world of the mountaineer to that of the miner. These novels offer a continuation of the mountain pieces and, together with his Indian material, complete his picture of western life. Unlike his minor treatment of females in his mountain novels, however, here Garland shifts the main subject back to a woman. He combines mild social criticism, especially dealing with problems facing miners, with the themes of the power of money and the conflicts between desire and duty and the East and West. But the social background remains background only; his main interest is the development of a single heroine.

Although each novel is flawed in several respects, as was generally the case with Garland's novels as opposed to his short stories, which he could manage much better, his mountain fiction nevertheless contains some of his best writing. He was able to capture the romance that the West seemed to promise. His heroes and heroines are lured to a land holding a mystic promise, and Garland vividly portrays their excitement, anticipation, and disappointments.

Unquestionably the most successful writing Garland accomplished during this period was his treatment of the American Indian, particularly in the stories later collected in *The Book of the American Indian* (1923), which also contains a fictionalized biography of Sitting Bull, "The Silent Eaters," and *The Captain of the Gray-Horse Troop* (1902). Manifesting an engaging and genuine sympathy for the Indian, his work also has an authenticity unmatched in his other writings during this period. While indignant over the unjust reservation treatment of the Indian, he is not so concerned in these pieces with the forces that subjugated the Indian as much as with the conflicts that inevitably arose whenever he attempted to come to terms with an alien culture. Garland was able to combine sharp social criticism with the theme of the necessity of change; he was also able to present moving accounts of the inherent futility and tragedy of many Indians who attempted to retain their way of life in modern society.

By 1911, his interest in fiction declining, Garland began to feel the need to deal more directly and fully with the major events of his life. He had already experimented with autobiography in *Boy Life on the Prairie* (1899), a lively narrative of a pervasive American experience of growing up on a farm in the nineteenth century, told from the point of view of a boy. With *A Son of the Middle Border* (1917), Garland began a series of four autobiographical volumes, and four more of literary reminiscences, to close out a distinguished literary career.

Taken as a whole, the eight autobiographical volumes, which chronicle Garland's literary acquaintance with scores of writers, publishers, artists, and politicians and trace his family's history, are a rich record of the America of his day. But clearly *A Son of the Middle Border* and its complementary volume, *A Daughter of the Middle Border* (1921), are the most successful and the most interesting. Despite occasional sentimental lapses, factual inaccuracies, and bothersome digressions, *A Son* remains one of the most carefully conceived, searching, and complex autobiographies in American literature. Covering the period from 1865 to 1893, Garland was able to capture and record a universal pioneer epic. It is on one level a story about nineteenth-century immigration and the moving frontier, the pioneer spirit, and the gradual disillusionment of the pioneer ideal. Thus the book is, in one sense, a monument to the trials and hardships of "westering." On another level, however, the account takes the form of a personal history that chronicles the middle border as a child might have experienced it and from which he escaped, only to remain attracted to it.

Since the action in *A Daughter* moves into the region of middle age, depicting Garland's marriage to Zulime Taft (the heroine of the volume), the death of his mother and later his father, the births of his two daughters, and the beginning of World War I, its theme becomes more personal, its scenes less epic. But it serves as a significant record of Garland's literary and intellectual development. Not only are we able to see the sources and circumstances of the composition of his principal romantic works, but we are better able to understand his psychological moods, which were critical to his artistic evolution. We get a keen insight into his attempt to cope with middle age, the exaltation that he experienced in the mountains, followed by the painful task of writing about it, and the disappointment and depression caused by his lack of critical acceptance.

Survey of Criticism

Critical studies of Garland and his works abound. Not only did he receive a considerable amount of critical attention, at times unflattering to be sure, during his lifetime, but assessments of his work began to appear almost regularly after his death, and they have continued at a slower but steady pace ever since. For the most part, however, early treatments of his work are not particularly valuable as criticism. Rather they tend to be descriptive and appreciative, whereas later accounts probe more significantly his life and the nature and direction of his art.

An exception to the early treatments, and one with critical merit, is Eldon C. Hill's "A Biographical Study of Hamlin Garland from 1860 to 1895." Written as a doctoral dissertation in 1940, Hill's pioneer biography provided later researchers with valuable facts about Garland, even if the value of the literary criticism is limited. Since Hill had the advantage of corresponding with Garland, some useful letters are also contained in the study.

Excluding dissertations, four book-length studies have appeared that deal exclusively with Garland and his works. Jean Holloway's *Hamlin Garland: A Biography* (1956) presents a thorough chronology of the genesis and composition of Garland's works and includes as well critical reactions of his contemporaries and selected references to modern controversies. As an outline, the study is useful, but it does little to illuminate the complex cast of Garland's mind and his literary development.

Without question, the best examination of Garland's life and works between 1884 and 1895 is Donald Pizer's *Hamlin Garland's Early Work and Career* (1960). Pizer, who has produced much other significant Garland scholarship, places special emphasis on Garland as, successively, a local colorist, social reformer, theater reformer, Populist, arts reformer, and impressionist. Robert Mane's *Hamlin Garland: L'homme et l'oeuvre (1860-1940)* (1968) is the best comprehensive analysis of Garland's life and works. It discusses all of Garland's works and includes extensive bibliographies of writings by and about Garland. Finally, Joseph B. McCullough's study, *Hamlin Garland* (1978), gives accounts of Garland's life and analyses of his work. More concise than Mane's study, it also contains a useful primary and secondary bibliography. All of these studies should be supplemented, however, by Jackson Bryer and Eugene Harding's *Hamlin Garland and the Critics: An Annotated Bibliography* (1973), which, though dated, provides the most thorough listing of writings about Garland.

While most areas of Garland's life have received some attention and most individual works have been dealt with briefly and fully, a disproportionate amount of attention has been paid to his "decline from realism" after 1895. In each case the writers, drawing on the unpublished Garland-Gilder correspondence, have attempted to describe, explain, justify, or criticize this movement in Garland's career. In addition to the book-length studies mentioned previously, each of which deals with this aspect of Garland's development, several shorter pieces have probed the question. Claude M. Simpson, Jr., in "Hamlin Garland's Decline" (1941), believes that although Garland lived as many years in this century as in the last, he must inevitably be considered a nineteenth-century author who ceased to grow almost with the first appearance of real success. For Simpson, Garland's decline relates to the dichotomy between the desire for reform and that for literary success. Bernard Duffey, in "Hamlin Garland's 'Decline' from Realism" (1953), examines Garland's Boston years (1844-93), especially the Garland-Gilder correspondence, which, he argues, suggests that Garland was more concerned with literary and financial success than with reform. He believes, furthermore, that Garland seemed always willing to compromise in order to gain acceptance since reform and realism were never in themselves primary literary or intellectual pursuits of his; they were accessory to his campaign for literary and intellectual success. James D. Koerner, in "Comment on 'Hamlin Garland's Decline from Realism' " (1954), protests Duffey's view and disagrees with his interpretation of the Garland-Gilder correspondence and the genesis of Garland's work. Charles T. Miller, in "Hamlin Garland's Retreat from Realism" (1966), examines the differences between Garland's early fiction and the thirteen books published between 1900 and 1916 in an effort to show how, under the pressure to make money, Garland turned to romantic fiction.

Several other studies also focus on Garland's literary development, attempting to relate his literary creed to his life and works. One of the best treatments is Donald Pizer's "Romantic Individualism in Garland, Norris and Crane" (1958), which suggests that these authors belong not only to the naturalistic tradition but also to that of the American romantic individual, going back to Jefferson and the transcendentalists. Related to this study is Charles Walcutt's discussion of Garland in *American Literary Naturalism: A Divided Stream* (1956), which examines the traces of naturalism in Garland's works, particularly the evident strain of determinism and protest in them. Lars Ahnebrink, in *The Beginnings of Naturalism in American Fiction* (1950), also discusses Garland's naturalistic strain, but his main purpose is to provide an exhaustive study of European influences on American novelists, including Garland.

Other areas of Garland's literary career, as opposed to discussions of individual works, have also been studied. Particularly useful is Walter Taylor's discussion of Garland's economic fiction in *The Economic Novel in America* (1942). Albert Keiser discusses Garland's American Indian material at length in *The Indian in American Literature* (1933), as does James K. Folsom, in a more critically valuable way, in *The American Western Novel* (1966). And Donald Pizer's "The Radical Drama in Boston, 1889-1891" (1958) provides a good understanding of Garland's involvement with drama, as well as influences on his radical thought.

It is probably not useful, nor is it possible, to discuss all of the short studies of individual works. Clearly *Main-Travelled Roads* and *A Son of the Middle Border* have received the most critical attention. The discussions of these works listed in the bibliography are the most useful, but many other solid treatments also exist.

One area of Garland's life, which relates to many others and which continues to be investigated, is his prolific correspondence, some studies of which are cited in the bibliography. Letters to specific correspondents have been the subject of several short studies, and Joseph B. McCullough's forthcoming edition of the Garland letters will make available a great deal of previously unpublished material.

Clearly the amount of scholarship available on Hamlin Garland is an indication of his importance in American literary history. There are signs that this interest continues. The *Critical Essays on Hamlin Garland* (1982), edited by James Nagel, contains some of the best Garland scholarship available, as well as some original essays. Yet despite the amount of criticism already available, many fruitful areas still exist for examination.

Bibliography

Works by Hamlin Garland
Main-Travelled Roads. Boston: Arena, 1891.
Jason Edwards: An Average Man. Boston: Arena, 1892.

A Member of the Third House. Chicago: A. J. Shulte, 1892.

A Little Norsk: Ol' Pap's Flaxen. New York: D. Appleton, 1892.

A Spoil of Office. Boston: Arena, 1892.

Prairie Songs. Cambridge: Stone & Kimball, 1893.

Prairie Folks. Cambridge: Stone & Kimball, 1893.

Crumbling Idols: Twelve Essays on Art. Chicago: Stone & Kimball, 1894.

Rose of Dutcher's Cooly. Chicago: Stone & Kimball, 1895.

Wayside Courtships. New York: D. Appleton, 1897.

The Spirit of Sweetwater. New York: Doubleday & McClure, 1898.

Ulysses S. Grant: His Life and Character. New York: Doubleday & McClure, 1898.

Boy Life on the Prairie. New York: Macmillan, 1899.

The Trail of the Goldseekers. New York: Macmillan, 1899.

The Eagle's Heart. New York: D. Appleton, 1900.

Her Mountain Lover. New York: Century, 1901.

The Captain of the Gray-Horse Troop. New York: Harper & Brothers, 1902.

Hesper. New York: Harper & Brothers, 1903.

The Light of the Star. New York: Harper & Brothers, 1904.

The Tyranny of the Dark. New York: Harper & Brothers, 1905.

Witch's Gold. New York: Doubleday & Page, 1906.

Money Magic. New York: Harper & Brothers, 1907.

The Long Trail. New York: Harper & Brothers, 1908.

The Shadow World. New York: Harper & Brothers, 1908.

Moccasin Ranch: A Story of Dakota. New York: Harper & Brothers, 1909.

Cavanaugh: Forest Ranger. New York: Harper & Brothers, 1910.

Other Main-Travelled Roads. New York: Harper & Brothers, 1910.

Victor Ollnee's Discipline. New York: Harper & Brothers, 1911.

The Forester's Daughter. New York: Harper & Brothers, 1914.

They of the High Trails. New York: Harper & Brothers, 1916.

A Son of the Middle Border. New York: Macmillan, 1917.

A Daughter of the Middle Border. New York: Macmillan, 1921.

A Pioneer Mother. Chicago: Bookfellows, 1922.

The Book of the American Indian. New York: Harper & Brothers, 1923.

Trail-makers of the Middle Border. New York: Macmillan, 1926.

The Westward March of American Settlement. Chicago: American Library Association, 1927.

Back-Trailers from the Middle Border. New York: Macmillan, 1928.

Prairie Song and Western Story. New York: Allyn & Bacon, 1928.

Roadside Meetings. New York: Macmillan, 1930.

Companions on the Trail. New York: Macmillan, 1931.

My Friendly Contemporaries. New York: Macmillan, 1932.

Afternoon Neighbors. New York: Macmillan, 1934.

Iowa, O Iowa. Iowa City: Clio Press, 1935.

Joys of the Trail. Chicago: Bookfellows, 1935.

The Long Trail. New York: Harper & Brothers, 1935.

Forty Years of Psychic Research. New York: Macmillan, 1936.

The Mystery of the Buried Crosses. New York: Dutton, 1939.

Studies of Hamlin Garland

Ahnebrink, Lars. *The Beginnings of Naturalism in American Fiction, 1891-1903*. Cambridge: Harvard University Press, 1950.

Bledsoe, Thomas. Introduction to *Main-Travelled Roads*. New York: Rinehart, 1954.

Bryer, Jackson R., and Harding, Eugene, eds. *Hamlin Garland and the Critics: An Annotated Bibliography*. Troy, N.Y.: Whitston, 1973.

Duffey, Bernard I. "Hamlin Garland's 'Decline' from Realism." *American Literature* 25 (March 1953): 69-74.

Folsom, James K. *The American Western Novel*. New Haven: College & University Press, 1966, pp. 149-55, 180-84.

Gish, Robert F. *Hamlin Garland: The Far West*. WWS. Boise, Idaho: Boise State University, 1976.

Henson, Clyde E. "Joseph Kirkland's Influence on Hamlin Garland." *American Literature* 23 (January 1952): 458-63.

Hill, Eldon C. "A Biographical Study of Hamlin Garland from 1860 to 1895." Ph.D. dissertation, Ohio State University, 1940.

Holloway, Jean. *Hamlin Garland: A Biography*. Austin: University of Texas Press, 1956.

Keiser, Albert. *The Indian in American Literature*. New York: Oxford University Press, 1933, pp. 279-92.

Koerner, James D. "Comment on 'Hamlin Garland's "Decline" from Realism.' " *American Literature* 26 (November 1954): 427-32.

McCullough, Joseph B. *Hamlin Garland*. TUSAS. Boston: Twayne, 1978.

―――. "Hamlin Garland's Letters to James Whitcomb Riley." *American Literary Realism, 1870-1920* 9 (Summer 1976): 249-60.

―――. "Hamlin Garland's Quarrel with *The Dial*." *American Literary Realism, 1870-1920* 9 (Winter 1976): 77-80.

McElderry, Bruce R., Jr. Introduction to *Boy Life on the Prairie*. Lincoln: University of Nebraska Press, 1961.

Mane, Robert. *Hamlin Garland: L'homme et l'oeuvre, (1860-1940)*. Paris: Didier, 1968.

Miller, Charles T. "Hamlin Garland's Retreat from Realism." *Western American Literature* 1 (Summer 1966): 119-29.

Pizer, Donald. "The Garland-Crane Relationship." *Huntington Library Quarterly* 24 (November 1960): 75-82.

―――. "Hamlin Garland's *A Son of the Middle Border*: Autobiography as Art." In *Essays in American and English Literature Presented to Bruce Robert McElderry, Jr.* Ed. Max L. Shultz et al. Athens: Ohio University Press, 1967, pp. 76-107.

―――. *Hamlin Garland's Early Work and Career*. Berkeley: University of California Press, 1960.

―――. "Herbert Spencer and the Genesis of Hamlin Garland's Critical System." *Tulane Studies in English* 7 (1957): 153-68.

―――. Introduction to *Rose of Dutcher's Cooly*. Columbus: Charles E. Merrill, 1969.

―――. "The Radical Drama in Boston, 1889-1891." *New England Quarterly* 31 (September 1958): 361-74.

―――. "Romantic Individualism in Garland, Norris and Crane." *American Quarterly* 10 (Winter 1958): 463-75.

Saum, Lewis O. "Hamlin Garland and Reform." *South Dakota Review* 10 (Winter 1972-73): 36-62.

Simpson, Claude M., Jr. "Hamlin Garland's Decline." *Southwest Review* 26 (Winter 1941): 223-34.

Taylor, Walter F. *The Economic Novel in America*. Chapel Hill: University of North Carolina Press, 1942, pp. 148-83.

Walcutt, Charles C. *American Literary Naturalism: A Divided Stream*. Minneapolis: University of Minnesota Press, 1956, pp. 53-63.

Ziff, Larzer. *The American 1890's*. New York: Viking Press, 1966, pp. 93-109.

JOHN GRAVES
(1920-)

Although he has earned a considerable reputation for his craft, the art of John Graves is deceptively simple and disarmingly personal in its flavor. Despite the production of a small quantity of well-made narratives, some of them included within the framework of a larger rumination, a few fine essays in argument or observation on public questions such as conservation, and a little criticism, Graves's gift, and his characteristic manner, are lyrical. And both are rooted in his special relationship to the land of his birth. However large and transregional the implications of his discourse, Texas (and particularly rural Texas) is the setting, the subject, and the measure for human experience in his most representative work. In his two finest books we hear Graves talking about the traditional life of rural Texas: speaking usually to his hypothetical auditor or *adversarius*, who is expected to demur in obdurate but friendly modernity at so much emphasis on "country things." The result of this implicit encounter is sometimes heroic, sometimes elegiac, but most often pastoral—yet hard pastoral, recommending rural life as a discipline, not as a means of escape.

Biography

The details of Graves's biography reveal that the elements of his life that have contributed to the making of his authorial posture or persona as countryman are, his present residence on a stock farm in Somervell County notwithstanding, the results of conscious choice. For despite his pious affection for a bygone Texas of small towns, ranches, and farms, his ordinate pride in the heroic frontier beginnings and civil virtues of the state's essentially southern and agrarian order before World War II, John Graves grew up a town boy in Fort Worth, where he was born 6 August 1920. After completing his education in the public schools of that still provincial southwestern city in 1938, Graves enrolled at Rice Institute in Houston, Texas, from which he was graduated with honors, a Phi Beta Kappa key, and the bachelor's degree in English in 1942.

From college Graves went directly to the United States Marine Corps, whose peacetime officer training program he had joined in early 1941. After training, Graves did commissioned service with the Fourth Marine Division, fighting at Kwajalein and later at Saipan, where he was wounded. He left the service with the rank of captain late in 1945 after convalescence and some final duty in the United States.

For a few months Graves traveled in Mexico, returning to this country in 1946 to enter Columbia University. There he did graduate work in English and, with a thesis on William Faulkner, earned the master's degree in 1948. From 1948 to 1950, Graves was an instructor in English at the University of Texas. After leaving Austin, he passed through a period of artistic apprenticeship, wide-ranging travel, and personal uncertainty. He resided in such disparate places as New Mexico, New York City, Spain, Sag Harbor, New York, and (once again) Mexico, writing short fiction and articles for such magazines as the *New Yorker*, *Holiday*, and *Town and Country*. In the spring of 1957, Graves was drawn back to Texas by an illness in his family. It was a permanent relocation.

Once returned to Fort Worth, John Graves began to delve into the lore of his homeland, which had been an interest of his earlier years. In November and December 1957, he made a canoe trip down a heralded section of the Brazos River, which resonated for Graves, "ringing like a bell in my head" with the "old names" associated with the first settlement and early history of the region to which his family had migrated from Carolina, Mississippi, Missouri, and South Texas (*Goodbye*, p. 8). Out of this combination of experiences came Graves's most famous work, *Goodbye to a River* (1960). In 1958 he took a position as adjunct professor of English at Texas Christian University, a post in which he continued until 1965. In 1958, Graves married Jane Marshall Cole of New York, a designer and coordinator of special events for Neiman-Marcus. They have two daughters, Helen and Sally.

In 1960, Graves purchased 400 acres of land in Somervell County, an hour's drive south and west of Fort Worth, a remote and wooded area, where the state begins to tilt upward toward the high plains and the mountains beyond. He has improved and added to this holding, which has been his family residence (at first part time) for most of the last two decades. Furthermore, he has made of this home the subject of his second book. *Hard Scrabble: Observations on a Patch of Land* (1974) is both a title and a description of the chosen point of view for Graves's transactions with the modern world. It is also the focus for most of his subsequent creations. Indeed, in these years an intelligible shape, a pattern has emerged in Graves's career. He has received fellowships from the Guggenheim (1963) and Rockefeller (1972) foundations. Along with essays on a Texas writer of the previous generation, Colonel John W. Thomason, Jr., and on the hill country of south Texas, he has written powerful and persuasive commentaries on plans for water distribution in his native state and for cleaning up the valley of the Potomac River. Some of this discursive labor was sponsored by the United States Department of the Interior and by the Sierra Club. It has increased its author's deserved reputation as a naturalist. Yet he has done it while at the same time clearing and restoring land, building a house, fences, and a barn, raising cattle, goats, bees, horses, chickens, and dogs, and planting gardens and fields with corn, feed grain, and hay crops.

Graves has twice won the Carr P. Collins Award of the Texas Institute of Letters, has taught a little, and has served as advisory editor of the *Southwest Review*. After publishing a new series of rural reflections in the *Texas Monthly*, he gathered them in a new volume, *From a Limestone Ledge: Some Essays and Other Ruminations about Country Life in Texas* (1980). Yet despite the variety of his activities and the passage of years, he continues to cherish his location and establishment in the valley of the Paluxy River, in the cedar brakes and ledges along White Bluff Creek. "Rustication" (his choice of terms) is preferred to the usual life of the man of letters in our time, and for a reason that has to do directly with Graves's version of the literary vocation: a link between where and what he writes, connecting "the sacred Way" of living with, not in conquest of, the providential order of things and the literary assertion of the almost forgotten authority of that prescription.

Major Themes

Goodbye to a River has commanded a large audience and widespread critical approval from the time of its first publication and has been frequently reprinted. It is classic pastoral in structure: a journey from the city to a rustic setting followed by a return to the point where the journey began. What occurs following the trip out from Fort Worth westward toward Possum Kingdom dam and before the trip back is, however, the part of the pattern that signifies: Graves's three-week voyage of about 150 miles down the Brazos River, whose valley is the heartland of early Texas and the highway up which the original American settlement of the state penetrated into its interior and toward the edge of the Great Plains. The canoe trip Graves made down a section of the upper Brazos that he had come to know as a boy was a farewell to a setting, a people, and a way of life connected to memories of his youth: "young, I breathed in these, like pollen, from the air" (*Goodbye*, p. 287). With friends he had hunted, fished, and visited along that stretch of water at intervals throughout his adolescence. Twenty years of absence from Tarrant County and the rural communities surrounding it, and wider experience of the world made the rumor that some of his favorite haunts were soon to be dammed up into lakes and covered with water all the more poignant. But at these prospects he is moved by more than simple nostalgia. Recollections reaching far beyond his own possessed him—history at the personal level.

Yet though it is pastoral and dramatizes in the flow of his responses its author's conviction that we will be "nearly finished" when "we stop understanding the old pull toward green things and living things, toward dirt and rain and heat and what they spawn," *Goodbye to a River* salutes no static "green world"

(p. 262). Graves loves the pageant of the seasons and remembers with distaste living where the weather is always the same. "Without the year's changes, for me," he writes, "there is little morality" (p. 119). North-central Texas is Old Testament country, acknowledging a time for all things. In his Arcadia, winter usually arrives on schedule. Late fall is a time of great beauty and perfect for a last look at the Brazos. But it is necessary to be watchful of the coming shift, punctuated by rain, sharp winds, and (sometimes) early snow—difficulty of all sorts—which for John Graves is as it should be. Character and independence are not born in easy circumstances. Nature faced in solitude is a rigorous school, reminding us of our contingency and subservience before the ineluctable things. Old Man Willett of Parker County sums up the burden of Graves's evidence: "A man needs it hard. . . . He'd ought to have it hard a-growin' up, and hard a-learnin' his work, and hard a-gittin' a wife and feedin' his kids and gettin' rich, if he's gonna git rich. All of it. . . . [Then he not only appreciates it, but also] *does* it better" (*Goodbye*, pp. 173–74).

In the design of his river book, Graves gives all of the advantage to his representatives of the "Old Breed," men of "angry independence" who located the blood and (in an image that he borrows from Yeats) made the necessary myth that "married" their descendants to "rock and hill," shaping them into a "race" or people (p. 21). First he introduces his persona-speaker, then his setting, then a suggestion of the quality of their interdependence. Only then does he scatter his narratives with careful pacing: of the hermit Sam Sowell, Mrs. Sherman, the Birdsongs, Colonel Charles Goodnight, the McKee family (especially their fine women), White Bear, Big Foot Wallace, Satanta, Mr. Willett, and the Mitchells of Mitchell Bend. Finally, after much preparation, he urges the value of piety toward an inherited identity for those who know that the alternative is to be "half a man." His Brazos journey is thus calculated to encourage self-recognition among native Texans and to introduce the breed to curious outsiders. As this pattern concludes, the tone lifts a bit, inviting all to share the spiritual refreshment that the pastoral gesture is supposed to provide—and, in this case, does.

Graves's river journey was no "jaunt" to be embellished by a few "tall tales" of frontier violence and curmudgeon eccentricity. His intent was to recover perspective by comparing a made world full of mass men, anonymous beings, with a given order of things that once contained people like Colonel Goodnight and his black retainer, Bose Ikard—people who believed that "they did things to Fate," not the other way around, taking "no crap from nobody nowheres no more" (*Goodbye*, pp. 75, 199). Against herd-mindedness he strikes up the angry anthem of southerners during Reconstruction, "The Good Old Rebel": "I hate the Constitution and the uniform of blue;/ I hate the Declaration of Independence, too,/ And I don't want no pardon for what I was or am,/ And I won' be reconstructed and I do not give a damn" (p. 298).

The Promethean spirit of modern civilization will cover and tame much of the Brazos, but not John Graves or those who listened carefully to his report on the river before it was subjected to "praiseworthy purposes." Tribute issues in self-restoration, even if shared in vicariously: one task of the poet is to give to his culture a verbal incarnation of its identity. The proof of Graves's success is the order of history with which he surrounds the private acts of his thirty-seventh year—in what he could make of what he did that served the need for myth in his countrymen. One accomplishment sustains the other—trips back in time, out into the hinterlands, and down into the self: all finally made one.

The attitude toward the providential character of creation, "the ontological stance," of *Goodbye to a River*, like its "elegiac action" (an appeal to remember that implies a mandate to recover), points directly toward the position that Graves assumes in *Hard Scrabble*, almost as if writing gave an impetus to life. Graves's move to Somervell County followed from the logic of *Goodbye to a River* and also grew out of an aesthetic necessity. If, as Graves wrote in 1960, the "long bedrock certainty of thoughtful men that regardless of the race's disasters the natural world would go on and on is no longer a certainty," but rather "an improbability," then some testimony in behalf of a more "cooperative" attitude toward nature is in order—both as a public duty and as a precondition for preserving action into art, positioned but not strident (*Goodbye*, p. 296). In Deuteronomy we read, "Defile not therefore the land which ye shall inhabit wherein I dwell." In an epigraph Graves summons up that authority. Pastoral written by responsible countrymen for urbanites has a different purchase—a different claim on our respect—from that of pastoral made by one exile for another. As Graves tells us later in his career, he always has a "city reader" in mind, even when his symbolic auditor stands somewhere in between. Literally he has become something like the "Old Breed" characters who dot his first book; he is a provincial by choice but with results that have a universal significance. In his view, "the Antaean myth has meaning still" (*Goodbye*, p. 254).

One way to state the proposition examined in *Hard Scrabble: Observations on a Patch of Land* is (as Graves does) to announce "the possibility that archaism in times one disagrees with, may touch closer to lasting truth than do the times themselves" (p. 262). Graves offers us other, equally outspoken formulations of what he is about. But it is as conscious archaism that in his second book his voice acquires its force: as a representative of "disappearing quiet hard rural ways" (p. 4). He has achieved this status by moving to Hard Scrabble and adopting the traditions of his people, choosing, in the context of our hostile era, to sharpen the edge of his commitment to owning and making fruitful a restricted and "unmagnificent patch of the earth's surface," not in Cuero or the other gentle landscapes of his south Texas ancestors but rather among the fiercest, most particularistic sept in all the tribe, the closed, "schizoid," and xenophobic Texans of the cedar brakes, old fields, and creek bottoms (p. 5). "Mankind is one thing," writes Graves in *Goodbye to a River*, "a man's self is another. What that self is tangles knottily with what his people were, and what they came out of. Mine came out of Texas, as did I. If they were louts, they were my own louts" (p. 144). Somervell County is a fine place to perform an anachronism, to preserve an inherited, ancestral pattern of life and enjoy the effort. It is a rough land, which requires of serious residents all the character they can muster if they are to make it fruitful and bring it to "function" without doing violence to its built-in disposition and to earn in the process the right to a little ordinate pride. Only in such a fashion may a man participate in and contribute to the way in which the world was originally intended to operate.

John Graves has little patience with what he calls "the nonparticipant purity" of Henry David Thoreau (whom he calls "Saint Henry")—his scorn for hunters and farmers—or for the even more advanced sentimentality of Rousseau. From his first possession of the land, the author of *Hard Scrabble* has as his purpose that this inhabitation of this particular acreage will be different from all previous human use, for this occupation will depend upon a certain "lightness" of touch to move his operation toward function (p. 231). Or so he was determined from his first encounter with the place. The "Ownership Syndrome," the quality of will that justifies his self-description as "Head Varmint," is in Graves's view also compatible with "the sacred Way" of ontological modesty, the territorial imperative with "gentler human use" (pp. 58, 266). The Faustian impulse of post-Renaissance civilization need not end in "erasing us all" (p. 180). In "the trying itself," one is transformed into "a part of the land and the Way it works" (p. 248). Graves has it on authority from his "Anglo-Hibernian" forebears "that you were not whole unless you had a stake in [and daily knowledge of] crops and trees and livestock and wild things and water [which] mattered somehow supremely" (p. 42). He carries that faith into action in developing his stock farm: a belief in a "paleolithic golden time with its sense of the wholeness of natural things [which sank early] into our genes and memory" and also a belief "that sowed seeds and tended beasts and tilled dirt and their rhythms did likewise, for these things grew out of natural wholeness and our attachment to them is very old" (p. 194).

The variety of activities that define John Graves's life on Hard Scrabble gives to it a "tinge of 'being' " (p. 262). His owning carries with it the presumption of being owned himself. A spirit of possession for more than mere possession's sake, of working from the particular to the general distinguishes his proprietary labors (his husbandry) from the program of the standard variety of contemporary empire builder. In thinking about his motives in trying "to scratch through to an answer," Graves concludes that his aspiration is to experience a "glimpse" of the "old reality"—"indestructible" and able to "prevail"—"hiding among the creatures wild and tame and the stones and the plants, and in the teeming dirt" (p. 267). The process that embodies this dream is in one sense religious and entails a reaching after the numinous.

As a structure, the pattern of *Hard Scrabble* builds toward a final musing on freeholding as a contemplative exercise. Here the always functional voice of Graves's persona reaches a little above its customary genial, ironic tone, beyond a wry combination of the colloquial and the civilized that he sustains throughout the rest of the book (and in most of his work) and lifts toward the hieratic. We are rightfully reminded of Faulkner's *Go Down, Moses* and the ritual by which the woodsmen depicted there achieve a balance of "pride and humility." But the

dynamic that allows the persona to grow, to reach (as in lyric) toward generalizations and an envelope of thought within which his entire narrative may achieve
significance is not linear or direct but accumulative, giving him such authority
only after his enterprise in all of its particularities, in its proper setting, has been
unfolded completely. Inside the construction of the work, the voice grows with
what and how it says; after much reporting it has "earned" the status of advocate
and the right to exercise a direct purchase on our attention.

At times Graves plays the thread of his experience off against internal narratives concerning other people. There are four of these in *Hard Scrabble*, the most
important called "His Chapter." They are evidence of their author's artistic
range, his sense of form; their function is as counterpoint. But the action proper
is fully rendered, and to a point. Graves provides an introduction, concerning
purposes and aspirations; next a history of early settlements around Hard Scrabble; then an account of the first encounter with what was to be his—an encounter
that establishes the mutuality of man and land; then a topography; then trees and
animals and hired hands; and finally three chapters on the moving in, on the
pleasures of building house and barn and fence. Only when finished with all of
this does Graves rise to speak of larger themes, the great questions of human
stewardship over the earth.

As *Hard Scrabble: Observations on a Patch of Land* answers to imperatives
generated in *Goodbye to a River*, a book that made farewell to the old rural ways
too difficult to contemplate, the nineteen chapters of *From a Limestone Ledge:
Some Essays and Other Ruminations About Country Life in Texas* (1980) are a
natural sequel to *Hard Scrabble*'s denial that such a surrender is necessary. Or at
least they are an expected sequel when Graves's narrative voice shapes what he
calls "footnotes" to his previous work (*Limestone Ledge*, p. xiii). With the
question of the viability of traditional freeholding closed and "the sacred Way"
approximated, a more relaxed procedure becomes possible. In his second book
Graves insisted that some compromise with "the powers" was necessary if we
expected to cultivate "gardens" of our own—that "we need to learn lightness
again" (*Goodbye*, p. 230). The speaker in *From a Limestone Ledge* has "learned"
that he won't "get everything done" toward "restoring" the land, as he had once
planned to do. The book is clearly a collection, patched together by a common
focus on a "way of living" that he has "really cared about" as a "point of
comprehension" (p. xiv). Graves writes, "I hope I've got some small grasp of
overall principles relative to rural land everywhere and the events that take place
on it, but if I do I derived it principally from looking in individual spots in
specific places, especially in this part of the world and on this battered stock
farm" (p. xv).

In other words, to be "versed in country things" is to focus on a particular
country place—to be "provincial," or even "parochial." Spectatorial strategies
make for soft pastoral. But these nineteen chapters are still pastoral of the other
kind, like Virgil's *Georgics*, which deal with cattle plagues, hard work, and the
troubles of real farms—and also with bees and tended beasts and the virtue of

small holdings. Graves in the mild, less ambitious, reflective vein of his latest volume speaks a language reminiscent of his Roman prototype concerning "land and what people have done to it and what it's done to them [which] aren't things you can understand fully, but you come a little closer with time and you know more than ever that they matter greatly [with] weather and climate and stone and soil and wild creatures and plants [and] livestock and farming" (p. xiv). But Graves's interest in goats, chickens, and rural plumbing, and the ritual of butchering hogs is not sentimental. Indeed, at times he almost sounds like Marcus Cato or John Taylor of Caroline—practical advice, though in this case for stockmen. The finest essays, concerning his dog Blue and "Nineteen Cows," are, however, more affective than admonitory. Graves's delight in the creatures that inhabit Hard Scrabble is infectious. "Of Bees and Men" is a memorable performance, perhaps a small classic, as is his essay on weather. But the concluding chapter, a narrative of a visit to a farm outside his region where a sale is scheduled, has a power not found in the rest—a bite of fear, an edge of mortality. It is noteworthy that Graves chooses to end the book in this way. The mood of "A Loser" is elegiac. All human enterprise is subject to contingency. The farmer from the West Cross Timbers who was forced (probably by poor health) to sell out and lose his hold over the fruits of a lifetime's labor becomes, for Graves in this story, an object lesson, not just the source of a small Allis-Chalmers grain combine: a reminder that we are fortunate so long as something unexpected does not destroy our lives. The final truth concerning rural life is that it keeps us close to the uncertainties of our existence, humble and relieved to be, for the time, merely a spectator at the the misfortune of others: "The Loser had made us view the fragility of all we had been working toward, had opened our ears to the hollow low-pitched mirth of the land against mere human effort" (p. 228). Which is another way of saying "all flesh is grass." Country folk understand that verse. It is a touch of mastery for John Graves to conclude with evidence that he is of their company, even in this—self-described "dilettante" though he may be.

The components of John Graves's career not represented in the materials organized in his three books have only minor significance in any assessment of his literary achievement. There is only a little fiction and one poem, but three of his short stories have received the honor of collection in the O. Henry award series and in *The Best American Short Stories, 1960*. "The Green Fly" (1954) and "The Aztec Dog" (1960) reflect Graves's experience in Mexico. They are well made but lack the authority of "The Last Running," Graves's adaptation of the frontier tale sometimes connected to the old age of Colonel Charles Goodnight. According to Graves's redaction, nine Comanche warriors visit a Panhandle patriarch (here called Tom Bird) who is asked to contribute a buffalo bull from a small herd he had preserved so that the Indians may engage in a ritual hunt, a farewell to the old free life of the plains. Finally the old cowman agrees, but with accompanying choric comment on the passing of an heroic age, most of it directed to his nephew. "The Last Running" is thematically of a piece with

John Graves's extended meditations. It is beautifully designed and makes us hope for other fiction from his pen.

Survey of Criticism

Although his status among the writers of his region is unquestionable, there has been very little serious criticism of Graves's literary performance. This oversight proceeds in part from the formal problems presented by the design of his works. Thus, Margaret Hartley's review, "Southwest Chronicle" (1960), emphasizes Graves's place as inheritor of a tradition in Texas letters coming down from J. Frank Dobie, Walter Prescott Webb, and Roy Bedichek. On the other hand, M. E. Bradford, in "Arden Up the Brazos: John Graves and the Uses of Pastoral" (1972) and "In Keeping with the Way: John Graves' *Hard Scrabble*" (1975), strives to connect Graves's work to the tradition of "hard" pastoral. In "Western Writers and the Literary Historian" (1979), Fred Erisman places Graves alongside Edward Abbey, A. B. Guthrie, and John Steinbeck to consider the effect of place upon the works of all four authors. Of use also is "John Graves: A Hard Scrabble World" (1980), in which Patrick Bennett interviews the author and touches upon his work habits, major themes, reactions to other Texas writers, and his ideas.

Although Graves deplores the political intemperance so characteristic of our day, his discursive work and familiar essays are carefully constructed. Furthermore, as an advocate of water conservation, he enters the public arena with the well-earned credentials of the naturalist who is also a master of his craft. He is as persuasive in arguing for a policy to clean up the Potomac as he is in describing the beauty of the ranch left for the use of artists by J. Frank Dobie. Graves's perspective is always southwestern, the borderland that belongs to both West and South. And it is always in some degree lyrical, in a well-defined personal vein. The assumption behind this strategy is that he is able to speak for more than just himself, and in this he is correct.

Bibliography

Works by John Graves

"Quarry." *New Yorker*, 8 November 1947, pp. 89-90.
"The Lost Americans." *Holiday* 15 (February 1954): 72-73.
"The Green Fly." In *Prize Stories 1955: The O. Henry Awards*. Ed. Paul Angle and Hansford Martin. Garden City, N.Y.: Doubleday, 1955, pp. 215-24.
Home Place. Fort Worth: Pioneer Texas Heritage Committee, 1958.
Goodbye to a River. New York: Alfred A. Knopf, 1960.
"The Aztec Dog." *Prize Stories 1962: The O. Henry Awards*. Ed. Richard Poirier. Garden City, N.Y.: Doubleday, 1963, pp. 201-16.
"The Overlap Land, Gringo and Mexican Meet in the Rio Grande Valley." *Holiday* 35 (March 1964): 74-75.

"A River and a Piece of Country: A Potomac Essay." In *Potomac Interim Report to the President*. Washington, D.C.: Department of the Interior, Federal Interdepartmental Task Force on the Potomac, Potomac River Basin Advisory Committee, January 1966, pp. 51-61.

"The Old Breed: A Note on John W. Thomason, Jr." In *A Thomason Sketchbook*. Ed. Arnold Rosenfeld. Austin: University of Texas Press, 1969. pp. 15-27.

With Robert H. Boyle and T. H. Watkins. "Texas: You Ain't Seen Nothing Yet." *The Water Hustlers*. New York and San Francisco: Sierra Club, 1971, pp. 15-129.

"Recollections of Childhood." In *Growing Up in Texas*. Austin: Encino Press, 1972, pp. 65-75.

The Last Running. Austin: Encino Press, 1974.

Hard Scrabble: Observations on a Patch of Land. New York: Alfred A. Knopf, 1974.

With Jim Bones, Jr. "The Region and the Place." *Texas Heartland: A Hill Country Year*. College Station: Texas A&M University Press, 1975, pp. 11-31.

"The Hard Used Land." *Atlantic* 35 (March 1975): 91-97.

From a Limestone Ledge: Some Essays and Other Ruminations about Country Life in Texas. New York: Alfred A. Knopf, 1980.

Studies of John Graves

Bennett, Patrick. "John Graves: A Hard Scrabble World." In *Talking with Texas Writers: Twelve Interviews*. College Station: Texas A&M University Press, 1980, pp. 63-88.

Bradford, M. E. "Arden Up the Brazos: John Graves and the Uses of Pastoral." *Southern Review*, n.s. 8 (Fall 1972): 949-55.

————. "In Keeping with the Way: John Graves' *Hard Scrabble*." *Southwest Review* 60 (Spring 1975): 190-95.

Erisman, Fred. "Western Writers and the Literary Historian." *North Dakota Quarterly* 47 (Autumn 1979): 64-69.

Hartley, Margaret. "Southwest Chronicle." *Southwest Review* 45 (Autumn 1960): vii-ix.

Gary Topping

ZANE GREY
(1872-1939)

Probably no other western writer has ever been so widely read and so little understood as Zane Grey. The handful of literary critics who have deigned to comment on Grey's works have almost all castigated them either for alleged historical inaccuracies that they believe serious literature should not contain or for failing to transcend the confines of what they call the popular Western formula, a model they use in an attempt to explain an entire class of literature. On the other hand, the untold millions of Grey's devoted readers whose uncritical acclamation has remained strong since well before 1915, when his novels first began to appear on the best-seller lists, have done no more (and very little less) than the critics in the literary establishment toward achieving a balanced appraisal of Grey's place in American literary history.

Biography

Biography is a fundamental ingredient in any sound understanding of Grey's novels, most of which are fictional permutations of Grey's personal experiences in the West, heavily freighted with denunciations of the Gilded Age American culture that he had rejected in favor of western life. Grey, like Owen Wister, Frederic Remington, and other contemporary western writers, turned to the West as a refreshing, indeed redemptive, alternative to the perceived amorality, banality, effeminacy, and artificial social standards of the upper-middle-class eastern life to which he had been bred. To understand Zane Grey's West, one must first understand Zane Grey's East.

Zanesville, Ohio, where Grey was born on 31 January 1872, was founded in 1796 by an ancestor, Colonel Ebenezer Zane, a backwoods hero of the American Revolution who had successfully defended Fort Henry, on the site of present-day Wheeling, West Virginia, against the Indians and the British. Zane's Trace, a trail blazed by Colonel Zane from Wheeling to Zanesville, was a major route by which the Ohio River country was settled after the revolution. Young Pearl Zane Gray (he dropped the first name for obvious reasons and changed the spelling of the last name at the beginning of his literary career) grew up with his ears full of the legendary exploits of the frontier Zanes—how Colonel Ebenezer's sister Betty had carried a tablecloth full of gunpowder to the desperate defenders of Fort Henry through a fierce barrage of bullets and arrows, and how the grim Lewis Wetzel had sworn himself to a lifetime of Indian extermination for the murder of his family.

The reality of Zanesville in the late nineteenth century was very different from the romantic stories. Grey's father, Dr. Lewis Gray, had a comfortable income as a dentist and settled down to raise his family in an upper-middle-class neighborhood, the Terrace district of Zanesville. If the Zanesville of Grey's youth was devoid of romance, it was equally devoid of hardship, and a boyhood of fishing and baseball prepared him as poorly for the pressures of the professional life he was expected to enter as did the romantic tales of bygone days.

A baseball scholarship to the University of Pennsylvania opened the way to training for his father's profession, a choice he made rather by default than design. In the classroom Grey was adequate if not brilliant, but the folkways of Ivy League social life were far beyond the ken of the naive midwesterner, and Grey developed none of the old school ties that were part of one's initiation into the eastern establishment. Instead he became a loner, retreating to the library where he found in the works of Tennyson, Hugo, Stevenson, and the Social Darwinists a familiar world of romance in which inherent virtue and strength rather than conformity with artificial social rules were the keys to happiness and success.

Grey was graduated in 1896 and opened a dental practice in New York City but was no happier there than in college. He began to escape both literally and imaginatively from the big city pressures at every opportunity by going on fishing trips to nearby rivers and, most importantly, by beginning to write, both about his fishing trips and about the frontier experiences of his Ohio River ancestors. *Betty Zane*, which he published in 1903 on money borrowed from the woman he was to marry in 1905, was the first in a Zane family trilogy that later included *The Spirit of the Border* (1906) and *The Last Trail* (1909). Although none of the novels sold well enough to justify beginning a literary career, Grey believed that he had the ability to write novels that would sell, and he abandoned his dental practice in order to write.

A major turning point in his writing career occurred in 1907. Just as the funds from his wife's meager inheritance were almost exhausted, which would end his only income, Grey met Colonel C. J. "Buffalo" Jones, an old buffalo hunter who was in the midst of an unsuccessful lecture tour of the east, trying to describe convincingly some of his Wild West exploits. Grey talked the old man into letting him come to his ranch near the Grand Canyon to photograph and write about Jones's hunting trips where he roped wild mountain lions.

Grey's trip to the Grand Canyon that summer exposed him for the first time to the demanding conditions of the western frontier and the character of the people who lived there. He thought he saw in the West a social situation that vindicated the romantic and Darwinian ideas that he had learned at home and in college, and describing that West became his life's work.

Even so, success as a writer still eluded Grey. He continued to publish short stories and fishing articles, but his books met with repeated rejections. Even after *The Heritage of the Desert* found some success when published by Harper's in 1910, Grey had to take his next manuscript over the heads of the Harper's editors to the vice-president of the company to get it accepted. Time has vindicated Grey's persistence, for the book was *Riders of the Purple Sage* (1912), perhaps the most famous Western of all.

Harper's belated recognition of Grey's abilities was to pay spectacular and consistent dividends. Besides the sales of an average of two Zane Grey novels per year until his death in 1939, Harper's sold hardcover reprint rights to Grosset & Dunlap and paperback rights to Pocket Books, to say nothing of numerous movies and other peripheral sources of income. Grey even remained a lucrative property after his death, for he had written so many unpublished manuscripts that Harper's was able to bring out a new one every year from 1939 to 1963 and yet another in 1977.

Grey became very wealthy. Although he remained simple, even puritanical, in his tastes, his money enabled him to indulge his love for the outdoors, particularly fishing. Grey remained a loner who felt largely out of touch with the fast pace and technology of the twentieth century. He lived in a wealthy Los Angeles suburb overlooking the ocean and was inevitably involved with people in the movie and publishing industries, but he had few friends among the famous in either of those fields, preferring to chose his closest friends from among those with whom he fished. It was while fishing Oregon's North Umpqua River in 1937 that he suffered a heart attack from which he was barely able to recover, and he died of a similar attack in his Los Angeles home on 23 October 1939.

Major Themes

Zane Grey has attracted so little serious literary criticism that it is difficult to speak of a critical consensus regarding even the main outlines of his career and his place in American literary history. It does seem possible, nevertheless, to propose a tentative historical framework for his literary development.

Grey's works fall into three vaguely definable periods. The first period includes those works written before his trip in 1907 to Arizona and Utah with Buffalo Jones. The major writings of that period are the Zane family trilogy, which is characterized by obvious heavy debts to the dime novels and James Fenimore Cooper, although they do show early manifestations of Grey's characteristic love for the history and social diversity of the frontier.

Grey's middle period extends from *The Heritage of the Desert* in 1910 to roughly the mid-1920s; *Under the Tonto Rim* (1926) is a convenient point of termination. Grey attained his greatest narrative and descriptive heights and produced his best social criticism during this period. A prominent feature of the novels written during the middle period, a feature for which Grey has received scant credit, is his wide variety of character types. Mormons, miners, Mexicans, construction workers, prostitutes, and backwoods hermits occur almost as prominently as the better-known cowboys, rustlers, and schoolmarms. Unconventional themes as well as characters appear during that period. *The Desert of Wheat* (1919) and *The Day of the Beast* (1922) explore America's disgraceful treatment of World War I veterans; *The Man of the Forest* (1920), *The Call of the Canyon* (1924), and *Under the Tonto Rim* expound Grey's Darwinian theory of the significance of the West.

The final period extends from the mid-1920s until Grey's death in 1939. Grey had made his fortune and his literary reputation by that time and had said most of what he wanted to say about the West. Older themes and character types reappeared, and the freshness of the earlier periods became less noticeable. Although the novels of the final period tend to be more conventional Westerns, a few merit serious attention. *Wyoming* (1953), which was written in 1931-32, is an interesting view of the West from a feminine perspective, and *Boulder Dam* (1963; written in 1933) is significant as a contemporary Western, a subgenre pioneered by Grey in *The Light of Western Stars* (1914) and, once again, in the World War I stories.

The social criticism in Grey's novels is one of their most interesting aspects. While studying Grey's social ideas, though, one must not forget that Grey was not a systematic social theorist—he was primarily a novelist—and his ideas never appear in the thorough and consistent forms that intellectual historians would like to have.

The two fundamental components of Grey's social theory are a kind of secular Calvinism and Social Darwinism. Humanity can be divided roughly into two general categories: the elect and the damned, the fundamentally good and the fundamentally evil. Grey often recognized gradations in goodness and badness in spite of those whose superficial acquaintance with his novels has led them to believe that all of his heroes were paragons of virtue and all of his villains were fiends. But he did hold that a Calvinistic division of humanity into two groups was possible.

The basic law of social development, according to Grey, was the Darwinian survival of the fittest through natural selection. Those whose nature was fundamentally good would, under normal circumstances, rise to the top of the social ladder, while those whose nature was evil would sink to the bottom. The basic problem of modern civilization, according to Grey, is that somehow that natural winnowing process has been obstructed or subverted so that natural virtues and qualities are no longer allowed to flourish and be recognized. Consequently, spontaneous emotions, primitive strengths and capabilities, and stoical virtues have given way to artificial patterns of behavior, effeminacy, and materialism.

The importance of the West to modern civilization is that it is a more primitive environment, where the survival of the fittest is still the fundamental social law, and the basic tenor of life is determined by primitive emotions, strengths, and virtues. The West thus has, in Grey's view, redemptive potential; by following the western social model, modern civilization can be saved. The basic Zane Grey plot is a drama in which a jaded, disillusioned, and perhaps physically frail or ill member of eastern society comes west to find a complete reorientation of values. It was not a plot that Grey invented; it was a plot that he discovered: it was his personal experience, and he hoped that the rest of the nation would accept his discovery and find social salvation.

Grey's view of the West was thus more instinctual than intellectual, and historians find it full of intellectual blind alleys and inconsistencies. Grey failed to realize, for example, that he had blundered into one of the fundamental problems of American thought. Since colonial times, Americans have considered the wilderness to be at either the top or the bottom of two conflicting scales of social value. On the one hand, the wilderness produces the lonely, virtuous hunter and the noble savage whose innocence and freedom from worldly cares contrast favorably with the superficiality and corruption of civilized society. On the other hand, the wilderness produces the bloodthirsty savage and the social misfit who contrast unfavorably with the rational order of civilization. Menacing Indians and corrupt white men are as natural products of the West envisioned by Grey as are his virtuous, hard-riding cowboys, but his superficial Darwinism largely ignores the problem.

As a novelist, Grey was much more successful than as a social theorist. Grey was a writer of romances in the tradition of Sir Walter Scott, Victor Hugo, and Robert Louis Stevenson, a fact that has largely escaped his critics but that accounts in large measure for his appeal. The time-honored devices of the romance are as fully present in Grey's works as in those of his literary progenitors: the larger-than-life hero, the innocent heroine, the chase, the disguise, the colorful costume, the mistaken identity, the duel. Lassiter's dogged pursuit of Milly Erne's abductor in *Riders of the Purple Sage* calls to mind Ivanhoe's quest to recover his ancestral estate, and the flight of Lassiter and Jane Withersteen from Elder Tull's Mormon posse echoes the flight of Jean Valjean. Nor did Grey merely ape his predecessors; he proved himself to be a great master of the romantic mode in his own right. Although Grey's villains are much too corrupt to generate the appeal of the lovable rogue Long John Silver, even Scott's Sherwood Forest and Scottish Highlands can barely compete in pastoral beauty and physical challenge with Grey's southwestern forests and deserts, and where in all romantic literature can one find equine equals to Wildfire and Jane Withersteen's black stallions?

Grey's works contain literary as well as intellectual liabilities. For one thing, he was never able to capture dialect in print. The Texas drawl of Brazos Keene, the cowboy who appears in *Knights of the Range* and *Twin Sombreros*, is one example. Keene changes from a comical sidekick in the first novel to the romantic lead in the second, and while the small doses of comic relief work acceptably well, the impenetrable drawl becomes a liability when Grey tries to turn Keene into a romantic hero who woos not one but two heroines in the second novel.

Emphasizing that Keene's skill with fists and guns makes him dangerous when provoked cannot remove the stigma of comedy that is sustained by the awkward dialogue.

Another major liability is the emotional naiveté and intensity of Grey's characters. The worst examples of Grey's lack of subtlety in portraying emotion are embarrassing. The most embarrassing moments typically occur at the point of an eastern dude's conversion to western ways, which in Grey's mind had to occur with religious intensity. *Wanderer of the Wasteland* and *The Call of the Canyon*, in other respects two of Grey's best novels, are both seriously marred by scenes of gratuitous emotional intensity, though the superhuman demands of the desert environment that Grey delineates luridly but effectively in the former novel mitigate somewhat the embarrassment one tends to feel during the more emotional scenes. Readers are strongly tempted to leaf quickly through several pages of *The Call of the Canyon* where Carley Burch writhes on the ground as she discovers and accepts her feminine role as wife and mother in the great Darwinian order of nature.

Perhaps Grey's greatest literary flaw, into which he increasingly slipped as his career wore on, is the sameness and predictability in setting, plot, and character. The earlier novels, stories like *Riders of the Purple Sage*, *The Man of the Forest*, and even the earlier Zane family trilogy, are refreshing in their variety and not easily forgotten. It is true, of course, that our historical perspective is often a disadvantage in properly understanding and appreciating Grey. After six decades of black-clad gunslingers, it requires considerable historical imagination for us to recapture the thrill with which readers of 1912 greeted Lassiter. A different moral climate, too, sometimes prevents modern readers from appreciating the literary strengths in Grey's best works. Today's cynical readers, for example, will find it hard to believe that Milt Dale did not crawl under the tarpaulin-covered bedroll prepared for Helen Rayner on that rainy night when he rescued her from Snake Anson's kidnappers and took her to his forest hideout (*Man of the Forest*, 1920). Nevertheless, few readers cannot respond to the evil Jim Girty, the vengeful "Deathwind" Lew Wetzel, or the pastoral Eden of Surprise Valley and the earth-shaking avalanche when Lassiter rolls the balancing rock that will shut up himself, Jane Withersteen, and Fay Larkin in the valley, apparently forever.

Moments of such keen excitement become increasingly rare in the books written after the mid-1920s. There were, to be sure, occasional failures among the earlier works—*The Mysterious Rider* (1921), for example, is a conventional formula Western with few original elements—and occasional successes among the later ones—*Wilderness Trek* (written in 1936-37 though not published until 1944) deals with American cowboys in the Australian outback. But far more typical of the later period were such suspenseless pursuit stories as *The Fugitive Trail* (written in 1933, published in 1957) or *Shadow on the Trail* (written in 1933, published in 1946) and second-rate sequels like *Majesty's Rancho* (written in 1936, published in 1942), which attempted to revive the success of *The Light of Western Stars* (1914).

Most, perhaps all, of Grey's novels contain enough of what have become conventional elements of the Western story that those who dub him, usually pejoratively, the Father of the Western have a strong case for their point of view. If Grey actually invented few of the components of the Western, his productive career refined them and solidified them through repetition into a new literary genre. Perhaps even more important is the fact that Grey showed some of what the new Western formula could contain in the way of original character types, vivid prose, and philosophical significance. If it was a formula that he created, then it was a good formula, for he demonstrated to some degree that the formula was flexible enough to serve as a vehicle for works of literary, as well as merely cultural, significance.

Survey of Criticism

Students of Zane Grey have the ostensible advantage of a very large body of critical literature. That advantage, unfortunately, is illusory, for only a pitifully small part of that literature is based upon diligent research and careful reflection.

All Zane Grey research from now on will have to begin with Kenneth W. Scott's superb *Zane Grey, Born to the West: A Reference Guide* (1980), which is a nearly exhaustive, annotated bibliography of Zane Grey books and movies and critical writings about Grey since 1904. Scott's bibliography is thorough almost to a fault, for items of genuine significance tend to get lost in the underbrush of film and book reviews in the most obscure publications. Also, as one has to expect of a bibliography in a thriving field, the appearance of items of great merit since Scott's *Guide* went to press has already rendered it out of date. Nevertheless, it will remain one of the few truly indispensable works in Zane Grey scholarship, and Scott's occasionally outspoken annotations will help encourage further research.

Another indispensable, though much more seriously flawed, work is novelist Frank Gruber's *Zane Grey: A Biography* (1970). Gruber's bibliography supplements Scott, for he attempts to provide an exhaustive listing of Grey's magazine articles and stories, though one suspects that a bibliographer with Scott's energy could turn up yet more items in those categories. As a biography, Gruber's *Zane Grey* is erratic in quality. Gruber was the first of the few who have been fortunate enough to gain unrestricted access to the Grey manuscripts, most of which are not yet in a public repository. His biography gains much from his extensive quotations from those sources, but the general absence of literary criticism, of a consistent chronological foundation, and his penchant for irrelevant anecdotes seriously diminish the value of the work.

More recent book-length studies have added little to our understanding of Grey. Carlton Jackson's *Zane Grey* (1973), like Gruber's study, utilizes the Grey diaries and letters ineffectively, and while it concludes with some perfunctory intellectual history, it largely consists of plot summaries curiously grouped according to themes, which give little idea of Grey's intellectual and literary development. Joseph L. Wheeler's dissertation, "Zane Grey's Impact on American Life and Letters: A Study in the Popular Novel" (1975), is a troublesome example of inept use of the Grey manuscripts. Encyclopedic in scope, it discusses virtually every topic upon which Grey ever ventured an opinion with little analytical depth or interpretive integrity. Gary Topping's dissertation, "Zane Grey: Essays in Intellectual History and Criticism" (1977), is largely a collection of journal articles on disparate topics with no pretensions of exhaustive research or comprehensive coverage. Flawed by lack of unrestricted access to the Grey manuscripts, the essays nevertheless explore important aspects of Grey's intellectual and literary development and attempt to relate his career to its historical context and to the relevant secondary literature.

The better items of Zane Grey criticism have generally been brief articles and essays that have appeared over the 1970s. One important exception is T. K. Whipple's *Study Out the Land* (1943), which contains two essays on Grey and western literature that mark the first sympathetic analyses of Grey's works by a member of the literary establishment. Whipple's view of Grey's works as primitive epics similar to *Beowulf* and the Icelandic sagas may need to be reconsidered, but his work is an important landmark. Richard W. Etulain's "Dedication to the Memory of Zane Grey, 1872-1939" (1970) and Ann Ronald's *Zane Grey* (1975) are two useful brief introductions to Grey's work. Although Etulain's article is very brief, it is largely responsible for the recent rekindling of interest in Grey. Ronald's pamphlet is condescending in tone and superficial in analysis, rarely probing beyond the formulaic elements in Grey's books, but it provides a basically sound and thorough introduction to Grey.

Articles on specific novels or topics in Grey's work are perhaps the best part of the critical literature. The first article of real substance to appear in an academic journal is Kenneth W. Scott's "*The Heritage of the Desert*: Zane Grey Discovers the West" (1970). Based upon the excellent Zane Grey-Ripley Hitchcock letters at Wagner College, Scott's article explores Grey's initial contact with the West that led to his first genuine Western novel. Danney Goble's "'The Days That Were No More': A Look at Zane Grey's West" (1973) shows the effects of World War I on Grey's thinking—an episode perhaps second in importance only to his first western experience with Buffalo Jones.

Gary Topping's articles have dealt with limited topics of significance in understanding Grey and have called for a more sophisticated critical literature. "Zane Grey's West" (1973) was one of the first attempts to explicate Grey's social Darwinism, while "The Pastoral Ideal in Popular American Literature: Zane Grey and Edgar Rice Burroughs" (1977) uses a comparative approach to define Grey's theory of time. In "Zane Grey: A Literary Reassessment" (1978), Topping argues for a critical literature that will evaluate Grey according to his standards, as a writer of romances rather than epics or realistic novels. Two other 1978 articles, Topping's "Zane Grey in Zion: An Examination of His Supposed Anti-Mormonism" and Graham St. John Stott's "Zane Grey and James Simpson Emmett," offer new manuscript research and rereadings of Grey's important early novels.

Grey's writings on nature and sports provide a potentially significant field of study that has been largely ignored. George Reiger's enthusiastic anthology, *Zane Grey: Outdoorsman* (1972), will have to be reinterpreted in the light of Ernest Schwiebert's attack on Grey's personality, skill, and ethics as a fisherman in his recent *Death of a Riverkeeper* (1980).

No bibliographic essay on any popular Western writer seems complete without mention of the most important article in the field, Don D. Walker's "Notes toward a Literary Criticism of the Western" (1973). Although Walker does not deal specifically with Grey, he offers important new directions for criticism that have profoundly influenced current views of Grey.

Bibliography

Works by Zane Grey

All works listed in this highly selective section, unless otherwise noted, are published in New York by Harper's.

Betty Zane. New York: Charles Francis Press, 1903.
The Spirit of the Border. New York: A. L. Burt, 1906.
The Last of the Plainsmen. New York: Outing, 1908.
The Last Trail. New York: Outing, 1909.
The Heritage of the Desert, 1910.
Riders of the Purple Sage, 1912.
The Light of Western Stars, 1914.
The Rainbow Trail, 1915.
Wildfire, 1917.
The U.P. Trail, 1918.
The Desert of Wheat, 1919.
Man of the Forest, 1920.
The Mysterious Rider, 1921.
The Day of the Beast, 1922.
Wanderer of the Wasteland, 1923.
The Call of the Canyon, 1924.
Under the Tonto Rim, 1926.
Knights of the Range, 1939.
Twin Sombreros, 1941.
Majesty's Rancho, 1942.
Wilderness Trek, 1944.
Shadow on the Trail, 1946.
Wyoming, 1953.
The Fugitive Trail, 1957.
Boulder Dam, 1963.
The Reef Girl, 1977.

Studies of Zane Grey

Etulain, Richard W. "A Dedication to the Memory of Zane Grey, 1872-1939." *Arizona and the West* 12 (Autumn 1970): 217-20.

Goble, Danney. "'The Days That Were No More': A Look at Zane Grey's West." *Journal of Arizona History* 14 (Spring 1973): 63-75.

Gruber, Frank. *Zane Grey: A Biography*. New York: World, 1970.

Jackson, Carlton. *Zane Grey*. TUSAS. New York: Twayne, 1973.

Reiger, George. *Zane Grey: Outdoorsman*. Englewood Cliffs, N.J.: Prentice-Hall, 1972.

Ronald, Ann. *Zane Grey*. WWS. Boise, Idaho: Boise State University, 1975.

Schwiebert, Ernest. *Death of a Riverkeeper*. New York: Dutton, 1980.

Scott, Kenneth W. *"The Heritage of the Desert*: Zane Grey Discovers the West." *Markham Review* 2 (February 1970): 10-14.

———. *Zane Grey, Born to the West: A Reference Guide*. Boston: G. K. Hall, 1980.

Stott, Graham St. John. "Zane Grey and James Simpson Emmett." *Brigham Young University Studies* 18 (Summer 1978): 491-503.

Topping, Gary. "The Pastoral Ideal in Popular American Literature: Zane Grey and Edgar Rice Burroughs." *Rendezvous* 12 (Fall 1977): 11-30.

———. "Zane Grey: A Literary Reassessment." *Western American Literature* 13 (Spring 1978): 51-64.

———. "Zane Grey: Essays in Intellectual History and Criticism." Ph.D. dissertation, University of Utah, 1977.

———. "Zane Grey in Zion: An Examination of His Supposed Anti-Mormonism." *Brigham Young University Studies* 18 (Summer 1978): 483-90.

———. "Zane Grey's West." *Journal of Popular Culture* 7 (Winter 1973): 681-89.

Walker, Don D. "Notes toward a Literary Criticism of the Western." *Journal of Popular Culture* 7 (Winter 1973): 728-41.

Wheeler, Joseph L. "Zane Grey's Impact on American Life and Letters: A Study in the Popular Novel." Ph.D. dissertation, George Peabody College for Teachers, 1975.

Whipple, T. K. *Study Out the Land*. Berkeley: University of California Press, 1943.

Fred Erisman

A. B. GUTHRIE, JR.
(1901-)

Although not the most prolific of writers, Alfred Bertram Guthrie, Jr., is assured of a place among the notables of western American literature. The author of five major novels and three lesser ones, he has established himself as a perceptive commentator upon western ways and western life, from the era of the mountain man to that of the post-World War II years. He has dramatized key periods in the development of the West: the 1830s and 1840s, when settlement first began; the 1850s and 1860s, when the wagon trains traversed the plains; the turn-of-the-century period, when the frontier closed and the West turned inward upon itself; and others. He has written of the geography of the Rocky Mountain region, evoking its beauty and its spaciousness and demonstrating its impact upon those who settle it. And he has shown a deep sensitivity toward the inherent themes of westward expansion, from environmental exploitation to the human cost of progress. He is an author whose reputation is deserved.

Biography

Born on 13 January 1901 in Bedford, Indiana, A. B. Guthrie grew up in Choteau, Montana, where his father was principal of the Teton County Free High School. From his father he acquired several of the traits that later appear in his writings. Among them are a profound love for the spaciousness and beauty of the West and a keen awareness of its unavoidable emotional impact. His memories of his early life, recorded in his autobiography, *The Blue Hen's Chick* (1965), are undeniably colored by nostalgia; however, his account makes clear the family cohesiveness and stability that he experienced during his childhood.

Guthrie seems to have inclined toward a career in writing almost from his youth. As a teenager, he worked part time for the local weekly newspaper, the *Choteau Acantha*, learning the skills of typesetter and printer. In college (the Universities of Washington and Montana), he majored in journalism, earning his degree from Montana in 1923. After three years of working at a random assortment of jobs, he took a job as reporter with the *Lexington* (Ky.) *Leader*, where he remained for twenty years, moving from reporter to editorial writer to city editor to, ultimately, executive editor. Although he tried his hand at a suspense novel during the late 1930s (it was published, finally, as *Murders at Moon Dance* in 1943), he did not concentrate upon novel writing until 1945.

Stimulating his move to fiction was his winning, in 1944, a Nieman Fellowship at Harvard University. There, with free access to the Harvard curriculum, library, and faculty, Guthrie was able to focus his interest in the West; through his contacts with such persons as Bernard DeVoto of *Harper's*, Edward Weeks and Charles W. Morton of the *Atlantic Monthly*, and Arthur Schlesinger, Sr., and Theodore Morrison of Harvard, he sharpened his writing skills. Following his Nieman year in Cambridge with a session at the Bread Loaf Writers' conference in Vermont, he was able to make a substantial start on the novel that was to become *The Big Sky* (1947).

Although he returned to the *Lexington Leader* in 1945, Guthrie was determined to establish himself as a novelist. The success of *The Big Sky* and his second novel, *The Way West* (1949), which won for him a Pulitzer Prize, gave him the financial stability that he needed to give up journalism, return to Montana, and turn to full-time fiction writing. Also helpful was a sojourn in Hollywood in 1951, where he wrote the screenplay for the film of Jack Schaefer's *Shane*. Since 1953, he has lived in Montana, writing, in addition to other novels, a number of short stories and essays and a small amount of poetry. Honors he has received include an honorary doctor of literature degree from the University of Montana, and the Distinguished Achievement Award (1972) of the Western Literature Association.

Major Themes

Guthrie's book-length works fall into three readily discernible categories. The first, those books that fit no other grouping, includes three volumes. One is a juvenile story, *Once Upon a Pond* (1973), a minor fable with animal characters. More significant are a volume of short stories, *The Big It and Other Stories* (1960), and an autobiography, *The Blue Hen's Chick*. The first of these includes thirteen stories, most with western themes and Montana settings. The second, a nostalgic, conversational work, looks back over the author's life and career, providing a useful key to themes and characters that appear in the works written after its publication.

The second, somewhat larger, category in which he works is that of the detective story. His first book in this genre, *Murders at Moon Dance*, a breathless tale of lurid violence and half-breed villains, was a disappointment. Guthrie himself has spoken of it as not necessarily "the worst book ever written" but definitely "a contender" for the award (*Blue Hen's Chick*, p. 128). More successful and better received have been three books written after 1970: *Wild Pitch* (1973), *The Genuine Article* (1977), and *No Second Wind* (1980). Set in Midbury, Montana, the novels deal with the detective adventures of the local sheriff,

Chick Charleston, and his admiring young helper, Jason Beard, who narrates the tales. Although minor works by any critical standard, the three books are competent, entertaining excursions into the detective-story genre. Building upon the modern West and its problems, they show Guthrie exploring many of the themes present in his more significant books and reveal also his increasing use in his fiction of overtly autobiographical elements.

Most significant of all is the third category, the interrelated series of five western novels upon which his reputation is based. The first of these books, *The Big Sky*, deals with the West of the mountain man and the coming of civilization to the Rocky Mountain region. Focusing upon three characters, Boone Caudill, Dick Summers, and Jim Deakins, it introduces several of the themes that Guthrie employs throughout his work and provides memorable descriptions of the scenery and spaciousness of the early West. Closely tied to this work is his second novel, *The Way West*. The account of a wagon train journey from Missouri to Oregon in the 1850s, it reintroduces Dick Summers, now serving as guide to the emigrants. The major part of the book deals with Lije Evans, a farmer, his wife, and his son, Brownie, as they confront the recurring problems of human life within the context of day-to-day problems of the wagon train. Lije Evans appears briefly in *These Thousand Hills* (1956), but the emphasis now is upon his grandson, Lat Evans, as Guthrie writes of the establishing of the cattle industry in Idaho and Montana and suggests the effects of the coming urbanization in the last years of the nineteenth century.

The final two books, *Arfive* (1970) and *The Last Valley* (1975), continue the progression established by the three initial volumes but introduce a new set of characters. In *Arfive*, Guthrie details the problems faced by Benton Collingsworth, an Indiana-born schoolmaster, as he struggles to win the acceptance of the townspeople of Arfive, Montana. Collingsworth's efforts to reconcile western ways with his own austere rigidity are accentuated by his contrast with the book's other protagonist, the rancher, Mort Ewing, who speaks for tolerance and adaptability. Collingsworth and Ewing reappear in *The Last Valley*, but the time has moved from the early twentieth century to the period between World War I and 1945. The book itself follows the career of Ben Tate, who buys the Arfive newspaper and grapples with problems of local vice, fanatical patriotism, and the encroachment of big business into the region. Strongly autobiographical in tone and content, the two books reflect Guthrie's deep affection for Montana and his growing disenchantment with the effects of settlement and economic development.

Of the several recurring themes that permeate these works, the most obvious is that of the influence of the natural world upon those who live in the West. That influence stems from the physical geography of the West itself, a region, Guthrie believes, characterized by spaciousness, largeness, and great physical beauty. The effect of these qualities is to create in the persons who encounter them a distinctive breadth of vision and sense of personal freedom. Thus, Boone Caudill, the mountain man protagonist of *The Big Sky*, can muse to himself that life in the West was better than being walled in by a house, better than breathing in spoiled air and feeling caged like a varmint, better than running after the law or having the law running after you and looking to rules all the time until you wondered could you even take down your pants without somebody's say-so. Here a man lived natural. [P. 201]

A similar attitude emerges in Lat Evans of *These Thousand Hills*; looking about him at the Montana landscape, he thinks, "Here he was the land's. Miles, mountains, sky, waters, grass—they freed and claimed him" (p. 331). Although the two characters are separated by fifty years of history, their response to the landscape is the same.

The landscape itself, however, exercises another kind of influence as well, for it provides an arena in which the essential qualities of the individual are tested. Because the West throws individuals upon their own resources, pitting human nature against physical nature, it brings to the surface the basic deficiency or worth of each person. Some are broken by the West's immensity. One of the travelers in *The Way West* notes that "this here country puts its mark on a man, and the mark is that he ain't sure who he is, being littled by the size of it" (p. 173), and Lat Evans's wife, Joyce, finds in Montana "space that was a fear with nameless fears inside her" (*These Thousand Hills*, p. 272). Others, though, respond to the West's challenge and rise above themselves. Lije Evans's first response to the openness of the West is to realize that "he was humbled and set up at the same time and proud now with a fierce, unworded pride that he had put out for Oregon" (*The Way West*, p. 87), while Benton Collingsworth, the schoolmaster of *Arfive*, concludes that "here was a country to live in. All right. Be sensuous: it was a land a man wanted to wake up with" (p. 99). Whatever the individual's response to the region, it is not a neutral reaction. Good or evil, strength or weakness, whatever lies deep within the person will be brought out by the western experience.

A second characteristic theme of the works is that of progress and the coming of civilization to the West. From *The Big Sky*, which opens with the mountain man's penetration of the region and closes with the first wagon trains rolling across the plains, to *Arfive* and *The Last Valley*, which record the slow but inexorable encroachment of civilization upon the West, Guthrie is concerned with settlement. As he records the influx of settlers and all they bring with them, he presents two somewhat contradictory feelings regarding progress. One, a positive belief, deals with the growth of communities, for, as he suggests in *The Big Sky*, the course of human progress is from rampant individualism toward an interdependent society. Lije Evans, at last leader of the wagon train in *The Way West*, sees his compatriots as "Nation makers. Builders of the country" (p. 340). And the aged Sterling McLaine sums up the process for Arfive: "It is in the nature of things as camps grow older. First, lawlessness, then loose law and order, then churches and schools and social sanctions and, finally, a town, not a camp. The preacher and the schoolmaster are harbingers" (*Arfive*, p. 29). The nature of humanity is to form communities, Guthrie says, and the process, by and large, is good.

Balancing his attitude toward community but inseparably associated with it are his generally negative views on the cost of progress. He recognizes that nothing comes freely and that everything exacts its cost, a view stated succinctly in Mort Ewing's maxim, "Watch out for progress because you can't backtrack" (*Last Valley*, p. 31). One of the costs of progress is an unavoidable limitation of personal freedom as people crowd together into towns and make laws and rules for their own preservation. Boone Caudill chafes at the walls and stinks of the city; he can turn his back upon them, but others are not so privileged. In come "the wanters of new homes, the hunters of fortune, the would-be makers of a bigger nation, spelling the end to a time that was ended anyway" (*Way West*, p. 217). With settlement, moreover, comes complexity, until even the least undertaking is influenced by many concerns. Thus, Ben Tate, new owner-editor of the *Arfive Advocate*, discovers the interlocking relationship of the Anaconda Copper Company, the county administration, and his own bread-and-butter job printing service: "The company has its goddamn finger in every pie. Go against it, for instance, and you lose the county printing, without which you can't get along" (*Last Valley*, p. 44). What results, unavoidably, is a series of compromises; recognizing the need for community, Guthrie believes in the ability of the worthy individual to adjust and accommodate while maintaining a degree of principle. Boone Caudill cannot adjust and vanishes forever into the mountains; Lije Evans, Mort Ewing, and Ben Tate accept the realities of an increasingly complex world and endure.

An even more serious price exacted by progress is its effect upon the natural world. From the first of his novels, Guthrie is conscious of man's despoiling of the landscape; in his later books, the theme comes to the fore, dominating the concerns of the books and the characters. In the early books, the theme appears as a simple statement of fact: the coming of civilization, paradoxically, destroys the very qualities that drew human attention in the first place. "There was beaver for us and free country and a big way of livin'," Dick Summers tells a despondent Boone Caudill, "and everything we done it looks like we done against ourselves and couldn't do different if we'd knowed.... It's like we heired money and had to spend it, and now it's nigh gone" (*Big Sky*, p. 385). In the later books, Guthrie becomes more explicit, even didactic, giving scathing pictures of thoughtless exploitation of natural resources and the inevitable destruction that follows. Viewing the scars of highways, railway spurs, and decaying homestead shanties, Benton Collingsworth sees them "as impertinences, as violations of the first and true purpose, no matter the Christian ethic that the earth was created for man. Man would put it to his use, never fear. Let fellow creatures go hang. The land was there to tear up" (*Arfive*, p. 236). A similar attitude permeates *The Last Valley*, as Arfive is confronted with widespread mining and the building of a dam that, though initially thought to be beneficial, later proves inadequate and a threat to the community's safety. Again and again, Guthrie returns to this theme: desirable—and necessary—though progress and civilization may be, they come at the cost of terrible and irreversible changes in a way of life, and in the world itself.

Closely related to his concerns about progress is his last significant theme: the importance of individual growth and maturity. Just as the West must change, so must the individual, making the necessary transition from individualistic self-centeredness to the broader, more tolerant view of the truly mature person. This theme appears most explicitly in the three detective novels featuring Jason Beard. As Jason grows from brash youth to concerned adult, he learns of the complexity of life and the difficulty of the choices that must, nonetheless, be made. The three books, therefore, constitute a *Bildungsroman* cycle illustrating Jason's growth to maturity. The theme also forms, though, the basis of the five major novels, so that it becomes perhaps the most fully developed of all of Guthrie's ideas.

Acknowledging the attractiveness of the innocence of youth, Guthrie goes on to suggest that innocence is not necessarily all good; it can lead to egocentricity and a disregard for consequences. Thus, in characters such as Boone Caudill, Lat Evans, and, to a degree, Benton Collingsworth, he presents persons who in one way or another blunder their way through life, largely unaware of the results of their actions. Caudill opens the West to settlers and too late recognizes what he has done. Evans keeps his eye on the main chance, sacrificing friendships to his ambition as he plays financial and political games. Collingsworth, though older and more educated than either Caudill or Evans, is smug and aloof in his moral assuredness, even as he slowly adjusts to the realities of western life. All contribute to or participate in actions that have undesirable consequences, consequences farther reaching than any suspects.

Balancing them are those characters, still older and more experienced, who have accepted the world for what it is and have accepted the responsibility—personal and social—that goes with true maturity. Such a one is Dick Summers, who learns that "there was the first time and the place alone, and afterwards there was the place and the time and the man he used to be, all mixed up, one with the other" (*Big Sky*, p. 194). Such is Lije Evans, who as leader of the wagon train at last realizes that "he had had to take his choice, and he had taken it and stood by it, and the taking and the standing had made him a wholer man" (*Way West*, p. 236). Such is Mort Ewing, who surrenders his illusions and becomes part of "the head and the hoof and the haunch and the hump" of Arfive (*Last Valley*, p. 5). All accept the realities of life and strive within these realities to make of life as much as is realistically possible.

In their views of life, these characters share Guthrie's mature awareness that existence is complex. Guthrie himself, writing in 1954, notes that "one of the tragedies of the lives we have to lead" is that "we never have the clean choices that our youth and innocence have led us to expect; and not having them, weaken or lose our attachments in the compromises we can't avoid" ("Historical Novel," p. 3). Some never recognize the absence of clean choices and cause untold damage as a result. Others, seeing the absence of clean choices, collapse into cynicism or expediency. The truly mature person, however (the Mort Ewings, Dick Summerses, and Ben Tates of the world), accepts the absence of clean choices, establishes his principles, and stands by them. Choices, says Ben Tate, at last, are "never clean. Take sides and you'll come to know regret or misgiving" (*Last Valley*, p. 281). Yet as Guthrie points out repeatedly, one must make those choices. Those who make them from the position of honest principle, and who stand by the consequences that ensue, are the genuine heroes of life. They meet the world on its own terms, maintaining their own integrity as human beings.

Survey of Criticism

Critical studies of Guthrie and his works are somewhat limited, for only since 1970 has he begun to attract extensive academic attention. Early studies tend to be primarily descriptive and appreciative, whereas the later accounts endeavor to reveal the nature and direction of his achievement. For the beginning investigator, the most useful studies are the longest: Thomas W. Ford's pamphlet in the Steck-Vaughn Southwest Writers Series (1968) and his more fully developed argument presented in the Twayne's United States Authors Series (1981), both of which give accounts of Guthrie's life and analyses of his work. The earlier pamphlet is made obsolescent by Ford's more recent overview, but both works contain useful insights in addition to bibliographies of Guthrie's writings and of writings about him. They should, however, be supplemented by Richard W. Etulain's "A. B. Guthrie: A Bibliography" (1969), which, though dated, lists materials not found in either of the other studies.

Several shorter studies have concentrated upon single works in the Guthrie canon. Not surprisingly, *The Big Sky* has attracted the most scholarly attention. Richard H. Cracroft, in *"The Big Sky*: A. B. Guthrie's Use of Historical Sources" (1971), identifies over a dozen primary sources used by Guthrie in the writing of the novel, including Washington Irving's *The Adventures of Captain Bonneville* (1837), George Frederick Ruxton's *Life in the Far West* (1848), and Charles Larpenteur's *Forty Years a Fur Trader* (1898), and he illustrates how Guthrie modifies his sources into a fictional narrative. In "The Man and the Book: Guthrie's 'The Big Sky' " (1971), Charles E. Hood, Jr., deals with the writing of the novel, drawing upon several interviews with the author to provide insights not available elsewhere. Richard Astro, in *"The Big Sky* and the Limits of Wilderness Fiction" (1974), acknowledges the appeal of Guthrie's writing and the historical accuracy of his detail but argues that the isolation of the mountain men prevents their full development as either human beings or as full-blown literary characters. In the most concentrated of the single-volume studies, "The Functions of Bird and Sky Imagery in Guthrie's *The Big Sky*" (1977), Donald C. Stewart traces the author's use of both images to give the novel structural and emotional unity.

Other single-work studies focus upon *The Way West* and *These Thousand Hills*. Vernon Young, in "An American Dream and Its Parody" (1950), presents *The Way West* as an archetypal "Wagons West" novel and notes that Guthrie seems consciously to be developing a commentary upon the place of humanity in the West. In "On History and Its Consequences: A. B. Guthrie's *These Thousand Hills*" (1971), David C. Stineback picks up on Young's theme and extends it to the later novel, arguing that *These Thousand Hills* deals with the nature of humanity and of history and speaks of the role of progress in destroying the mythic West. Finally, Fred Erisman, in the introduction to the Gregg Press reprint of *These Thousand Hills* (1979), points out the novel's importance as a bridge between the early West of the first two novels and the modern West of *Arfive* and *The Last Valley*.

Most of the shorter studies deal with two or more of Guthrie's novels at one time, seeking to trace the development of his ideas or to point out recurring themes and motifs in his works. The earliest of these essays, Dayton Kohler's "A. B. Guthrie, Jr., and the West" (1951), is necessarily limited to *The Big Sky* and *The Way West*; nonetheless, it makes a sound case for the importance of both books as historical records and as novelistic works of art. In chapter 3 of *The American Western Novel* (1966), James K. Folsom examines the same two novels and *These Thousand Hills*, concluding that they constitute a telling record of the human impulse to modify the world. All three novels also figure in Jackson K. Putnam's "Down to Earth: A. B. Guthrie's Quest for Moral and Historical Truth" (1971), which discusses the novels' value to cultural historians and is the first study to speak at any length of Guthrie's use of environmental determinism. Don D. Walker, writing in "The Primitivistic and the Historical in Guthrie's Fiction" (1971), also considers the place of history. Limiting himself to *The Big Sky* and *Arfive*, he suggests that Guthrie's inability to reconcile primitivism and progress creates a significant weakness in the author's fiction.

After the appearance of *Arfive*, critical attention shifted somewhat, attempting to discover and deal with the larger themes now apparent in Guthrie's works. Joe B. Hairston, in "Community in the West" (1973), initiates this movement, suggesting that the direction of the four novels is toward civilization and that in civilization (or community) rather than individualism is the promise of the human race. "A. B. Guthrie, Jr.'s Tetralogy: An American Synthesis" (1976), by Gilbert D. Coon, continues the movement toward a broader view of the works. The four novels, Coon argues, deal with a consistent—and characteristically American—character type, which, though particular goals may change as time passes, remains constant throughout the course of American settlement. The course of history is also at the heart of Donald C. Stewart's "A. B. Guthrie's Vanishing Paradise" (1976), an essay that combines description and thematic analysis to conclude that the four novels form a hymn to wilderness and an elegy for the passing of a time, a place, and a way of life.

Three somewhat related essays by Fred Erisman continue the investigation of Guthrie's themes and go on to consider his relationship to other western writers. "Western Fiction as an Ecological Parable" (1978) draws upon *The Big Sky*, *Arfive*, and *The Last Valley* to support its premise that environmental concern is inherent in the western genre. "Western Writers and the Literary Historian"

(1979) is concerned with awareness of place, putting Guthrie alongside such other authors as John Steinbeck, Frank Norris, John Graves, and Edward Abbey in an examination of how western authors deal with regional concerns. A longer treatment of the same general topic is "Western Regional Writers and the Uses of Place" (1980), which considers Guthrie (as well as Paul Horgan, Willa Cather, and others) within the framework of regional literature, its nature, and its uses.

Perhaps the broadest view of Guthrie's work and achievement is that of John R. Milton, who, in chapter 5 of *The Novel of the American West* (1980), pairs Guthrie with Frederick Manfred to develop an extended consideration of their portrayals of the mountain men, the coming of civilization, and the inevitable destruction of the wilderness. Dealing with all five of Guthrie's novels but drawing most heavily upon the first three, Milton concludes that while Guthrie may believe that civilization is a state more desirable than wildness, he is too perceptive an author to proclaim civilization a panacea. Recognizing that the course of civilization holds the seeds of its own destruction of the wilderness, Guthrie cannot help but view the linear circularity of western history with irony.

A. B. Guthrie continues to merit study; his inclusion in Milton's important examination of western literature and his being the subject of Ford's extended study are evidence enough to suggest his significance. Much, however, remains to be done. His detective novels of Jason Beard have not yet been accorded the attention they deserve, overshadowed as they properly are by the five more significant novels. Much could be written about his treatment of women in his books, from Teal Eye and Mercy McBee in the early works to Juliet Justice and Mary Jess Collingsworth in the later ones. The last word has not yet been said on his regional awareness or upon his use of autobiographical elements in his works after 1971. Of his lasting reputation, though, there is little doubt. Almost uniquely among writers of the West, he has won popular and critical acclaim, and his works stand as major contributions to the genre of western fiction.

Bibliography

Works by A. B. Guthrie

Murders at Moon Dance. New York: E. P. Dutton, 1943.
The Big Sky. New York: William Sloane Associates, 1947.
The Way West. New York: William Sloane Associates, 1949.
"The Historical Novel." *Montana Magazine of History* 4 (Fall 1954): 1-8.
These Thousand Hills. Boston: Houghton Mifflin, 1956; Boston: Gregg Press, 1979, with introduction by Fred Erisman.
The Big It and Other Stories. Boston: Houghton Mifflin, 1960; Boston: Gregg Press, 1980, with introduction by Richard W. Etulain.
The Blue Hen's Chick. New York: McGraw-Hill, 1965.
Arfive. Boston: Houghton Mifflin, 1970.
Once Upon a Pond. Missoula: Mountain Press, 1973.
Wild Pitch. Boston: Houghton Mifflin, 1973.

The Last Valley. Boston: Houghton Mifflin, 1975.
The Genuine Article. Boston: Houghton Mifflin, 1977.
No Second Wind. Boston: Houghton Mifflin, 1980.

Studies of A. B. Guthrie

Astro, Richard. "*The Big Sky* and the Limits of Wilderness Fiction." *Western American Literature* 9 (August 1974): 105-14.

Coon, Gilbert D. "A. B. Guthrie, Jr.'s Tetralogy: An American Synthesis." *North Dakota Quarterly* 44 (Spring 1976): 73-80.

Cracroft, Richard H. "*The Big Sky*: A. B. Guthrie's Use of Historical Sources." *Western American Literature* 6 (Fall 1971): 163-76.

Erisman, Fred. "Western Fiction as an Ecological Parable." *Environmental Review* 2 (Spring 1978): 15-23.

————. "Western Regional Writers and the Uses of Place." *Journal of the West* 19 (January 1980): 36-44.

————. "Western Writers and the Literary Historian." *North Dakota Quarterly* 47 (Autumn 1979): 64-69.

Etulain, Richard W. "A. B. Guthrie: A Bibliography." *Western American Literature* 4 (Summer 1969): 133-38.

Folsom, James K. *The American Western Novel*. New Haven: College & University Press, 1966, pp. 60-75.

Ford, Thomas W. *A. B. Guthrie, Jr*. SWS. Austin: Steck-Vaughn, 1968.

————. *A. B. Guthrie, Jr*. TUSAS. Boston: Twayne, 1981.

Hairston, Joe B. "Community in the West." *South Dakota Review* 11 (Spring 1973): 17-26.

Hood, Charles E., Jr. "The Man and the Book: Guthrie's 'The Big Sky.' " *Montana Journalism Review* 14 (1971): 6-15.

Kohler, Dayton. "A. B. Guthrie, Jr., and the West." *College English* 12 (February 1951): 249-56.

Milton, John R. *The Novel of the American West*. Lincoln: University of Nebraska, 1980, pp. 160-94.

Putnam, Jackson K. "Down to Earth: A. B. Guthrie's Quest for Moral and Historical Truth." *North Dakota Quarterly* 39 (Summer 1971): 47-57.

Stewart, Donald C. "A. B. Guthrie's Vanishing Paradise." *Journal of the West* 15 (July 1976): 83-96.

————. "The Functions of Bird and Sky Imagery in Guthrie's *The Big Sky*." *Critique* 19, no. 2 (1977): 53-61.

Stineback, David C. "On History and Its Consequences: A. B. Guthrie's *These Thousand Hills*." *Western American Literature* 6 (Fall 1971): 177-89.

Walker, Don D. "The Primitivistic and the Historical in Guthrie's Fiction." *The Possible Sack* 2 (June 1971): 1-5.

Young, Vernon. "An American Dream and Its Parody." *Arizona Quarterly* 6 (Summer 1950): 112-23.

Patrick D. Morrow

BRET HARTE

(1836-1902)

Today we are likely to think of Bret Harte as a short story writer who embodies the worst aspects of Victorian sentimentality and ornate diction. In college-level American literature survey courses, one day is typically spent on a Harte story for its historical value as an instructive symptom of the inadequate aesthetics and moral vision of the nineteenth century. While there is certainly a measure of truth in this judgment of Harte, he is actually a much more interesting and contradictory figure than this widespread estimate and dismissal would indicate.

However lowly regarded today, Bret Harte is understood to be the first internationally famous writer of short fiction about the American West. "The Luck of Roaring Camp," "The Outcasts of Poker Flat," and "Tennessee's Partner," published in the late 1860s, earned Harte much acclaim by the nation's popular audience and approval by Ralph Waldo Emerson, James Russell Lowell, Henry Longfellow, William Dean Howells, and other leading literary men of the day. In 1870, Harte, then editor of the San Francisco-based *Overland Monthly*, published "Plain Language from Truthful James," better known as "The Heathen Chinee." Hawked on street corners and endlessly reprinted, the poem created a sensation that made Harte a household name. Soon afterward, accepting a $10,000 contract from the *Atlantic Monthly*'s publishers, Harte took his family east.

During the next several years, his popularity declined almost as quickly as it had ascended. In 1878, following unsuccessful efforts as a magazine writer, lecturer, novel writer, and dramatist, he accepted the position of United States consul to Crefeld, Germany. After years in Crefeld and later Glasgow, Harte left the consular service and lived the rest of his life in England, an American literary expatriate. He was in poor health during this long later period but still managed to write memoirs, literary criticism, numerous letters, and an enormous amount of popular fiction about the long-gone California gold rush days. His wife and one son joined him near London in the 1890s, but the reunion was not happy. Harte felt that America had scorned, even betrayed him, and after 1878, he never set foot on United States soil. Bret Harte became an ironically justified version of one of his favorite characters—the ill-fated Phillip Nolan in Edward Everett Hale's "The Man Without a Country."

Biography

Francis Bret Harte was born on 25 August 1836 in Albany, New York. Frank, as the boy came to be called, spent considerable time indoors because of poor health, reading Emerson, Irving, Tennyson, Poe, Byron, and Dickens, besides the Bible and *Pilgrim's Progress*. In 1853, Frank's widowed mother became engaged to marry Colonel Andrew Williams, and they moved to California. By the spring of 1854, Frank, his younger sister, and the older newlyweds were settled in Oakland, only a hundred or so miles from the gold mines that had lured so many others to the West Coast. Harte almost certainly spent some time in what is now called the Bret Harte country, along Highway 49 in the Sierras. In this area he apparently taught school at LaGrange, did some mining, and met several of the picturesque models for his later stories. In 1857, he became printer's devil and editorial assistant on the newly founded weekly newspaper, the *Northern Californian* in Arcata. Harte managed to select some reprints and get some of his copy in print. Scornful of this isolated province, his editorial taste was clearly that of a lost liberal Victorian.

Run out of Arcata for a pro-Indian editorial, Harte resumed literary work in San Francisco. There he began writing for a much better paper, the *Golden Era*, contributing a long series of satirical "Bohemian" papers on subjects ranging from sensational plays to the Sacramento Fair. He also wrote his first solid piece of local-color fiction, "The Work at Red Mountain" (later entitled "M'liss"). In 1864, Harte moved on to the *Californian*, serving as coeditor and star contributor, producing a wide variety of pieces, the most famous being his literary parodies, "Condensed Novels." During these years Harte became influenced by the fiery Unitarian minister from Boston, Thomas Starr King, and contributed a number of poems to King's various abolitionist causes. In 1862, Harte married Anna Griswold, a somewhat older woman, who sang contralto in King's choir. Both families thought the match an unfortunate one, and time proved the relatives to be right. By the time Harte assumed editorship of the *Overland Monthly* (1868), he had two young sons along with a frustrated and unhappy wife.

It has been said that the *Overland Monthly* sent one editor to fame and two publishers into bankruptcy. For this periodical, Harte wrote a monthly news column, most of the generally excellent book reviews, a number of poems, and his most famous short stories. He also selected and edited copy. Harte was an editor with integrity who printed the best material available, including Henry George's famous radical criticism of progress and land development, "What the Railroad Will Bring Us." Somtimes he faced strong pressures directed against his literary taste and values, such as the incident in which a proofreader vehemently objected to "The Luck of Roaring Camp" because the story contained not only a prostitute but profanity. She almost persuaded publisher Anton Roman to omit the story, but Harte demanded that the story be printed or he would resign. He won, and with this triumph defeated the specter of Mrs. Grundy, thereby taking realism in American literature a significant step forward. With his *Overland* editorship, he was the recognized leader of a large and diverse literary movement in San Francisco, a movement that included Mark Twain, Ambrose Bierce, Charles Warren Stoddard, and Ina Coolbrith.

When Harte and his wife moved to Boston in 1871, life there started out with much excitement. The most famous literary personages of the day wined and dined them, he had several lengthy conversations with Emerson, Lowell, and Longfellow, and he was courted as a celebrity, the conquering "New Voice" from the West. Unfortunately, his eastern success and happiness turned out to be short-lived. Harte reveled in stardom so much that his social life completely eclipsed his writing career. He failed to meet the terms of his lucrative contract by not writing enough stories and poems, and the contract was not renewed.

Harte began to realize how short-lived his fame really was as the debts he and Anna accumulated became more pressing. At first he turned to lecturing, despite his fear and loathing of making a public address. With bill collectors in the wings, Harte gave well-received and profitable lectures in Boston and New York, but in the provinces, Harte fared badly as a lecturer. Despite his well-written speeches and initial success, word began to spread that a Bret Harte lecture was not all that entertaining. His last tour ended in serious financial trouble and a near nervous breakdown. Harte turned to a new literary venture—writing a novel.

Harte continued to accumulate debts and attendant scandals, but a huge advance for the promised novel, *Gabriel Conroy*, erased for a while the financial and emotional strain at the Harte household. The novel, completed in 1876, was a serious disappointment except in Germany, where it went through several printings. *Gabriel Conroy* has a few good episodes, but the novel is tedious, episodic, and confused. It contains a disturbingly large amount of writing atrocious to the point of high unintentional comedy. Small wonder that one reader, James Joyce, came to the unfortunate conclusion that all American novels were unspeakably rotten.

Having failed once again to achieve financial security, Harte turned to drama, a lifelong interest. He spent much time rewriting into a play the successful story "Two Men of Sandy Bar." This project proved a financial and artistic failure, and as a last hope Harte collaborated with Mark Twain on a play—"the swag," in Clemens's words, to be divided on an equal basis. Of course by this time the two authors' fortunes were reversed. Clemens's old mentor was down at the heels, while Mark Twain, now a literary success and married to a coal heiress, lived in the most splendid house that Hartford, Connecticut, could offer. Their play, "Ah Sin," was not only a failure but the key issue that demolished a warm and loyal friendship. Scandals about Harte's dilatory writing habits, excessive drinking, and constant debts began to appear in print during this period. The end of the road came when Harte was once again offered the editorship of a new magazine, the *Capitol*, which folded before a single issue appeared.

The nadir of Bret Harte's life came in 1877. He had failed at several literary ventures during the past half-dozen years, his health was starting to deteriorate, and his relationship with Anna was severely strained. In pursuing the chimera of recovering a lost success, he spent an increasing amount of time away from his family, which now included, besides the young boys, two little girls. Harte had become a "case," something of a national embarrassment, and his "rescue" came from an unexpected quarter. Friends in high places convinced newly inaugurated President Rutherford B. Hayes to grant Harte a consular position. After months of agony and uncertainty, Harte was offered, and quickly accepted, an appointment as commercial agent at Crefeld, Germany. He was not altogether disappointed that the position was too financially unrewarding to enable Anna and the family to go with him.

Harte began a new phase of life—on his own, but constantly fighting to find enough money to support himself and his distant family. Harte returned to fiction writing modeled on his earlier successes, and these stories sold well, especially in England. As the years wore on, he would sell stories to magazines of decreasing sophistication, then collect them on an annual basis into a separately issued volume. From 1880 until his death in 1902, Harte managed to publish a volume of short fiction almost yearly. In Europe, Harte traveled a good deal, especially to relieve his neuralgia and respiratory disorders. On 18 June 1880, he was transferred to a new consular post in Glasgow, a city he grew to detest for its foggy climate and industrial pollution and a place where he spent as little time as possible. With the inauguration of Grover Cleveland in 1885, Harte was relieved of consular duties and went to live in London with his admirers and friends, the Van de Veldes, at the invitation of Mme. Van de Velde.

Harte lived out the rest of his days in a kind of velvet-lined prison, what biographer George R. Stewart called "Grub Street De-Luxe." The letters of this period reveal an increasingly formal attitude toward Anna, along with the inevitable reminder of how much money he was sending her. After ten years, their situation, while not exactly premeditated as such, had developed into a genteel Victorian divorce, although no legal action was ever taken. Harte was comfortable but trapped, aware that he was producing not art but a salable fictional product. He continued minting nostalgic stories about a long-gone California as the literary world was turning to the realism of Henry James and William Dean Howells, the naturalism of Thomas Hardy, Stephen Crane, Frank Norris, and Emile Zola, and always the humor of Mark Twain. The spiritual depression caused by his unfulfilled artistry and life in these final years was a sad contrast to the Spanish grandees, red-flannel-shirted miners, and blushing maidens who rode the bloom of promise on the green, picturesque landscape of Harte's later romances. Doubtless a victim of the shifting taste and enthusiasms of the reading public, the final responsibility for literary failure must nevertheless rest with Harte, who made several comfortable but ultimately unwise decisions. Ill for years of throat cancer, Harte died near London on 5 May 1902.

Major Themes

In his serious poetry and fiction, Bret Harte typically wrote parables. Parables are designed to illustrate truths, reinforce an audience's expectations, or inspire an audience toward achieving ideal behavior. They are not typically critical or ironic, nor are they well-wrought, complex statements that reveal a depth of artistic consciousness. Harte recognized his debt to the parable form in the Preface to his first *Collected Works*. There he related that he "will, without claiming to be a religious man or a moralist, but simply as an artist, reverently, and humbly conform to the rules laid down by a Great Poet who created the parable of the 'Prodigal Son' and the 'Good Samaritan'" (Preface to *The Works of Bret Harte*, vol. 1, London, 1882, p. xix). Since at least the end of the last century, serious literary figures have been waging war with the parable form. As a leading practitioner of parables, Harte stood at the enemy's vanguard.

Harte's parables are typically outfitted with Christian imagery, but their primary aims are to illustrate that human beings are ultimately good, not depraved, and that a Victorian civilization always triumphs over the anarchistic wilderness. One can learn a great deal about how Harte uses the parable form by examining his "The Luck of Roaring Camp" (1868), an early story and the prototype for his volumes of parabolic fiction.

Using a mixture of picturesque and realistic details to establish an ideal setting, "The Luck of Roaring Camp" depicts the ultimate nobility of all (white) men, especially in times of crisis. The story is mythic, not realistic, and presents the age-old convention of a mysterious stranger as a rescue figure. The characters are carefully stereotyped into external villains and internal saints, a psychological trick Harte learned from Charles Dickens. Roaring Camp is an outpost, a community of self-styled renegades, and clearly these lawless types need to be saved—that is, repatriated to civilization. Cherokee Sal, of course, must succumb to the conventions of nineteenth-century melodrama, but it is surprising that in 1868, a half-breed prostitute plays an important part in a parable. Her role as perverse madonna, who brings forth in miracle and mystery the faith-giving Tommy Luck, flouts decorum and propriety. But in a striking way, she dramatizes Harte's belief that potentially everyone has some good. Complete with crèche and adoring bucolics (the miners), Tommy is born as "the pines stopped moaning, the river ceased to rush, and the fire to crackle. It seemed as if Nature had stopped to listen too" (*Writings of Harte*, 1:3). This pathetic fallacy in purple prose establishes Tommy Luck as one sent to redeem men fallen from a worthy civilization. Typically, Harte concentrates not on developing the title figure but on portraying his effect on the other characters.

Joyfully assuming their mission of collective fatherhood, the Roaring Camp miners quickly go middle class. Stumpy turns from a profane drunk into a devoted house-husband, lovingly cooing at the infant and calling him "the d——n little cuss." According to Harte's narrator (who sounds disturbingly like an *Atlantic Monthly* book reviewer), the Luck makes the camp regenerate by returning them to civilized ways. The miners take on nursery duties, tidy up their sleazy cabins, hold a christening, build new living quarters, and "produce stricter habits of personal cleanliness" (*Writings of Harte*, 1:9). Somewhat like Walt Disney's version of *Snow White and the Seven Dwarfs*, hard work and lyrical adoration create a chosen community during a halcyon summer. The luck is with them; gold claims yield enormous profits, and the "town fathers" want to move in "respectable families in the fall" (*Writings of Harte*, 1:12). At this point in the story, Harte's parable has also become an idealized microcosm of the American frontier experience.

One serious problem with the mysterious stranger story, as Roy R. Male notes in *Types of Short Fiction* (1960), is what to do with the stranger once his function is completed. If he lingers, he may move to the position of protagonist, and the story becomes something more complex, in the case of "The Luck of Roaring Camp" possibly a *Bildungsroman*. Such a complication would also change the parable form into a longer and more involved piece of fiction. What Harte does to avoid this problem and get his story back on the track of high Victorian idealism is create a disaster. Like his mother, Tommy Luck is killed by a literary convention in the guise of a flood, which also drowns several miners, including Stumpy and Kentuck. These men receive some redemption in that they die better men than they were before the Luck's arrival. But Harte's real pitch is for repatriation and is made to the audience. The story should regenerate us by providing renewed purpose, optimism, faith, and a belief in human potential. Male, and probably most contemporary readers, considers the story's ending ineptly comic bathos. But to the Victorian audience, with its very different values and expectations, the ending was tinged with high pathos. What Harte regarded as sentiment (deep, valid feelings), we would likely regard as sentimental (gratu- itous, sham feeling). Serious literature produces a theme, but parables deliver messages.

Similarly, "Tennessee's Partner" should not be dismissed as merely a mawk- ish story of implausible events and psychologically invalid characters cohabiting in a world of melodramatic conventions. "Tennessee's Partner" is a parable about the power of brotherly love. Harte treats the subject with high pathos and obscures some of the issues the story raises by plating them with his golden rhetoric. He tends here and in other stories to substitute dramatic effect for character development. The brotherly love theme fascinated Harte, and among his other treatments of the partner relationship are "Barker's Luck," "In the Tules," and "Uncle Jim and Uncle Billy." The custom of partnership was firmly rooted in mining camp folkways, as contemporary journals and historical studies have shown. Like so many of Harte's other tales, "Tennessee's Partner" has a realistic basis carefully crafted into a romantic scenario that portarys man's goodness.

Numerous other Bret Harte stories follow this parable formula. "The Outcasts of Poker Flat" shows that in a crisis, there is good in even the worst people. This tale has a fair sampling of Harte's famous colorful and picturesque characters, including the slick gambler, the whore with a heart of gold, the ingenue, and the innocent. "Outcasts" has little to do with realistic conventions such as character motivation. Rather the tale describes the conversion of several characters from evil to good when they are isolated by a blizzard in the High Sierras. "Brown of Calaveras" is a parable that demonstrates the nobility of duty over desire, a variant of the Good Samaritan parable. This tale marks the first appearance of Jack Hamlin, whose masculine objectivity and laconic stoicism Harte used in some twenty other works. "How Santa Claus Came to Simpson's Bar" is a parable with the theme of "never give up." The town's miners, a rough but chivalrous bunch, contrive to rescue a deprived boy from having a solitary and disillusioning Christmas. On the edge of despair, the boy is emotionally resurrected by Dick Bullen, who, after a tortuous mountain ride to a faraway town, returns with a present.

Harte's use of parables spanned his career, and they may be found in his children's stories and even in his few fictional works with settings other than California. But by writing formula stories, however innovatively, Harte frequently trapped himself into the role of satisfying a consumer demand for very predictable and superficial conventions. With overuse, these conventions have become hallmarks of familiar cliches: the happy ending, the sentimental tryst, the melodramatic incident, the amazing coincidence, the gentleman gambler, and the whore with a heart of gold. As he grew older, Harte increasingly became a literary reactionary, courting a younger and younger audience and rejecting opportunities for literary growth. Sometimes nothing can fail like success.

Bret Harte's talent for satire and literary criticism was too often wrongly sacrificed for the "higher purpose" of writing numerous idealized short stories. This other side of Harte finds contemporary approval among those who know of its existence. His Bohemian Papers for the *Golden Era* (early and mid-1860s) are sometimes too long, but most are also genuinely comic. For the *Golden Era* and the *Californian* during the middle and late 1860s, Harte wrote a series of "Condensed Novels," a collection of prose parodies on current novelists. These were not grumbling satires but dramatized exaggerations of the style and values of the author-victim. Probably the best example of this genre is "Muck-a-Muck," a parody of James Fenimore Cooper. In this occasionally anthologized short piece, Harte parades Cooper's grotesque diction, female characters, and Natty before the parabolic mirror. Sadly, he did not consider satire a serious enough form of literature to write very much of it.

Readers may notice in Harte's fiction the constant use of the third-person narrator, not merely as author intrusion but as authorial control. Harte, the narrator, does not so much tell a story as interpret it—giving his version, withholding or emphasizing material, unabashedly analyzing the scene, characters, and audience while at the same time relating the action. He sees the function of the narrator and literary-cultural critic as one, a joining of roles further emphasized in the narrator's frequent comments about literature. The use of a narrator who assumes the persona of a literary critic suggests his interest in this field. He did write a good deal of literary criticism in the form of essays, book reviews, letters, prefaces, and "Condensed Novels." This scattered and never systematically arranged body of criticism often points with scorn to sentimentality, unbelievable fictional characters, and prolix, affected style, curiously the very defects for which Harte the creative writer is most often cited. Harte was a professional critic for only a couple of years, while editing the *Overland Monthly*, but throughout his life he continued to write literary criticism in some form or another.

Ideologically Harte the critic was a transitional figure whose critical writings show elements of both realism and romanticism, with a preponderance of the former. While committed in his fiction, ultimately, to romanticism, Harte learned to stay clear of literary theory in his critical writing and to concentrate on a close reading of the literature. He did not try to resolve the difficult ideological problems of being both a romantic and realist by leaping to one position or the other and then expending much ink in defense of his action. Never a systematic thinker, he seldom approached literature from a perspective (formalist, moral elitist, Marxist, or whatever) but instead concentrated on writing a practical criticism, and thereby he produced some of the finest evaluations in existence of particular late nineteenth-century works and figures. Harte's success in popular fiction and poetry is not entirely an accident; he was well read in the literature of his time, knew a great deal about the craft of writing, and understood much about the taste, values, limitations, and expectations of the Victorian reading public.

Bret Harte is one of those minor writers whose widespread negative image has largely obscured his contradictory complexity. As a comparison of his serious fiction with his satire and criticism clearly shows, he was more talented and more divided than has been generally recognized. His attempt to portray the American West as a collection of losers in the wilderness who could, with luck and hard work, aspire to lofty eastern standards was no doubt wrongheaded. Instead of organically creating his western literature out of its environment, Harte imposed wholesale the Victorian liberal consciousness. In the process, however, he did make local color a viable form of writing, in addition to providing his more talented twentieth-century successors with a marvelous framework against which to rebel.

Survey of Criticism

Bret Harte's critical reputation has gone through three stages: laudatory reviews and articles from about 1869 to 1880; a polarization of overstated praise from old friends, uncritical admirers, and aficionados as opposed to severe condemnation by Mark Twain (especially in *Mark Twain in Eruption*), Twainians (such as Sydney J. Krause, *Mark Twain as Critic*), and modern critics considering Harte to be the apotheosis of sentimentality; and the 1931 publication of George R. Stewart's definitive biography, *Bret Harte: Argonaut and Exile*, beginning the modern reassessment of Harte's worth. A trend of more favorable reaction to Harte has gathered force in the last twenty-five years. Although Harte has been attacked since Stewart's book, most notably by the excoriation delivered in the Brooks and Warren text, *Understanding Fiction* (1943), the majority of critics are now turning to objectivity, and evaluating and analyzing Harte within some kind of historical context. His reputation is now low enough so that critics dismiss rather than attack him. Unless "camp" receives an unexpected resurrection, a large-scale Harte revival should not be expected in this century.

The most important contemporary scholar and critic of Harte is Margaret Duckett. She has written a substantial book comparing the lives and works of Clemens and Harte in addition to several significant articles. Her *Mark Twain and Bret Harte* (1964) must be the most important (and controversial) consideration of Harte since Stewart's 1931 biography. Duckett's study closely examines the public, private, and literary relationship between these two men, once close friends who later became somewhat bitterly estranged. The book has organizational difficulties and a bias (which Duckett clearly states) toward trying to right the reputation of a much-maligned Bret Harte. Nevertheless, many Clemens charges against Harte in *Mark Twain in Eruption* are proven false, and Twain's conduct toward Harte is shown to be scandalous, even inhuman. Duckett demonstrates Harte's considerable influence on the far superior writer, Clemens, and explores Harte as a man and writer with sensitivity, knowledge, and a careful eye for his strengths and weaknesses. *Mark Twain and Bret Harte* and Stewart's definitive biography are indispensable guides to Harte, containing much reliable information about him.

Duckett has inspired the most recent generation of Harte critics. Her student, Patrick Morrow, is the most prolific of this group. His *Bret Harte, Literary Critic* (1979) attempts to assay the nature and significance of Harte as a cultural and literary critic. Morrow has also produced several articles, a pamphlet, and several conference papers on Harte. Most of these have been concerned with Harte as a local color and popular writer, and much of this material in one form or another is included in *Bret Harte, Literary Critic*. One of Morrow's students, Linda Diz Barnett, has published *Bret Harte: A Reference Guide* (1980), an invaluable, thorough compilation of secondary sources. Jeffrey F. Thomas, who has published two articles on Harte, is the most provocative and substantial of the younger Harte critics. Another unusually imaginative Harte article is Fred E. H. Schroeder's "The Development of the Super-Ego on the American Frontier" (1974), a Freudian interpretation of "The Luck of Roaring Camp."

Finally, there has been a recent movement of limited success to make Harte's short fiction more modern than Victorian. J. R. Boggan, in "The Regeneration of 'Roaring Camp'" (1967), argues that the narrator of "The Luck of Roaring Camp" has an ironically ambiguous voice and stance. Charles E. May in a truly ingenious article ten years later, "Bret Harte's 'Tennessee's Partner,' " posits that Harte cleverly "euchres" the unwary reader of "Tennessee's Partner" by skillfully combining "sardonic humor and moral complexity." These are both cleverly inventive readings, but they do not correspond to Harte's statements and other historical facts. At his best, Bret Harte was an impressive stylist. No longer rated as a leading enemy of culture and moral values, Harte seems likely to benefit from fresh and continuing critical examination.

Bibliography

Works by Bret Harte

The Writings of Bret Harte. 20 vols. Boston: Houghton Mifflin, 1896-1914.
Kozlay, Charles M. *The Lectures of Bret Harte*. New York: Kozlay, 1909; Folcroft, Penn.: Folcroft Press, 1969.
————. *Stories and Poems and Other Uncollected Writings by Bret Harte*. Boston: Houghton Mifflin, 1914. (Now vol. 20 of *The Writings of Bret Harte*.)
Harte, Geoffrey Bret. *The Letters of Bret Harte*. Boston: Houghton Mifflin, 1926.
Sketches of the Sixties by Bret Harte and Mark Twain. Ed. John B. Howell. 2d ed. San Francisco: Howell, 1927.
Twain, Mark, and Harte, Bret. *"Ah Sin," A Dramatic Work by Mark Twain and Bret Harte*. Ed. Frederick Anderson. San Francisco: Book Club of California, 1961.

Studies of Bret Harte

Barnett, Linda Diz. *Bret Harte: A Reference Guide*. Boston: G. K. Hall, 1980.
Boggan, J. R. "The Regeneration of 'Roaring Camp.'" *Nineteenth-Century Fiction* 22 (December 1967): 271-80.
Brooks, Cleanth, and Warren, Robert Penn. *Understanding Fiction*. New York: Appleton-Century-Crofts, 1943, pp. 214-20.
Buckland, Roscoe L. "Jack Hamlin: Bret Harte's Romantic Rogue." *Western American Literature* 8 (Fall 1973): 111-22.
[Clemens, Samuel L.] *Mark Twain in Eruption*. Ed. Bernard DeVoto. New York: Harper & Bros., 1940, pp. 254-92.
Duckett, Margaret. "Bret Harte's Portrayal of Half-Breeds," *American Literature* 25 (May 1953): 193-212.
————. "The 'Crusade' of a Nineteenth Century Liberal." *Tennessee Studies in Literature* 4 (1959): 109-20.
————. *Mark Twain and Bret Harte*. Norman: University of Oklahoma Press, 1964.
Glover, Donald E. "A Reconsideration of Bret Harte's Later Work." *Western American Literature* 8 (Fall 1970): 141-51.
Krause, Sydney J. *Mark Twain as Critic*. Baltimore: Johns Hopkins Press, 1967, pp. 190-224.
Kuhlman, Susan. *Knave, Fool, and Genius: The Confidence Man as He Appears in Nineteenth Century American Fiction*. Chapel Hill: University of North Carolina Press, 1973, pp. 34-48.
May, Charles E. "Bret Harte's 'Tennessee's Partner': The Reader Euchred." *South Dakota Review* 15 (Spring 1977): 109-17.
May, Ernest R. "Bret Harte and the *Overland Monthly*." *American Literature* 22 (November 1950): 260-71.
Milton, John R. *The Novel of the American West*. Lincoln: University of Nebraska Press, 1980, pp. 12-83, passim.
Morrow, Patrick D. "Bret Harte, Popular Fiction, and the Local Color Movement." *Western American Literature* 8 (Fall 1973): 123-31.

————. *Bret Harte, Literary Critic*. Bowling Green, Ohio: Popular Press, 1979.

————. "Parody and Parable in Early Western Local Color Writing." *Journal of the West* 19 (January 1980): 9-16.

Pemberton, T. Edgar. *The Life of Bret Harte*. New York: Dodd, Mead, 1903.

Rhode, Robert D. *Setting in the American Short Story of Local Color*. The Hague: Mouton, 1975.

Schroeder, Fred E. H. "The Development of the Super-Ego on the American Frontier." *Soundings* 57 (Summer 1974): 189-205.

Stegner, Wallace. *The Sound of Mountain Water*. Garden City, N.Y.: Doubleday, 1970, pp. 223-36.

Stewart, George R. *A Bibliography of the Writings of Bret Harte in the Magazines and Newspapers of California: 1857-1871*. University of California Publications in *English* 3 (September 1933): 119-70; rpt. Norwood, Pa.: Norwood Edition, 1977.

————. *Bret Harte: Argonaut and Exile*. Boston: Houghton Mifflin, 1931; Port Washington, N.Y.: Kennikat Press, 1968.

Thomas, Jeffrey F. "Bret Harte." *American Literary Realism, 1870-1910* 8 (Summer 1975): 266-70.

————. "Bret Harte and the Power of Sex." *Western American Literature* 8 (Fall 1973): 91-109.

Walker, Franklin. *San Francisco's Literary Frontier*. New York: Alfred A. Knopf, 1939; rpt. Seattle: University of Washington Press, 1969.

Robert L. Gale

ERNEST HAYCOX
(1899-1950)

More than any other writer, Ernest Haycox was responsible for lifting western fiction about 1930 and thereafter out of the formulaic pattern inherited from Owen Wister, Zane Grey, Max Brand, and others less capable and for making it a new vehicle. Haycox first gave psychologically complex heroes rather than gun dummies, pairs of contrasting heroines, and challenging themes. Luke Short, Frank Gruber, and D. W. Newton, among many others, have acknowledged Haycox's influence and followed some of the paths he blazed.

Biography

Haycox had a "tragic childhood," in the words of his widow, Jill Marie Haycox ("Light of Other Days," p. 2). Further, he suffered an early death, of cancer at the age of fifty-one. But in between, he was happily productive. His canon of 24 novels, 254 short stories (including several novellas), and many ephemeral items (Etulain, "Literary Career," pp. 214-34) is impressive in quantity and is marked by several western classics, including the novels *Trouble Shooter* (1937), *The Border Trumpet* (1939), *Alder Gulch* (1942), *Bugles in the Afternoon* (1944), and *The Earthbreakers* (1952), and many faultless short stories. Among these was "Stage to Lordsburg," made into the movie *Stagecoach*, which brought John Wayne to fame.

Ernest James Haycox, Jr., was born 1 October 1899, in Portland, Oregon. His father was a restless "farmer, woodsman, shinglemaker, and steamboatman" (Etulain, "Literary Career," p. 33). His mother, Bertha Burghardt Haycox, was of German-Jewish heritage. Little Erny naturally accompanied his parents as they moved about. They were divorced before he was in his teens, and hit-or-miss schooling had to compete with a variety of jobs: paperboy, peanut salesboy on a train, hotel dishwasher, delivery boy, worker in a burlap factory, and bellhop. In 1915 Haycox joined the Oregon National Guard. The following summer he saw duty along the Mexican border with an infantry unit seeking Pancho Villa's followers. After graduating from high school in Portland in 1917,

Haycox served fourteen months with the United States Army in France training replacement troops, was under fire, rose to the rank of sergeant, and returned home in February 1919. He then briefly tried commercial fishing off the coast of Alaska.

Now determined to be a writer, Haycox entered Reed College, in Portland, worked on the college newspaper, transferred after his freshman year (1919-20) to the University of Oregon at Eugene, was active on collegiate publications there also, and came under the aegis of a talented professor of writing, W. F. G. Thacher, who remained a lifelong friend. Haycox spent a frustrating summer in 1922 on campus, living in a chicken coop behind a fraternity house, eating beans, writing doggedly, and papering his walls with rejection slips (Etulain, "Literary Career," pp. 45-47; Haycox, Introduction to *Border Trumpet*, p. vii). He started receiving acceptances as early as 1921, but it was not until 1924 that he began to enjoy sustained success, with seventeen publications that year in such popular pulps as *Western Story* and *Detective Story*. By then he had received the bachelor's degree in journalism from the University of Oregon (June 1923), had worked for a while on the *Portland Oregonian* as court and sports reporter, and had driven to Greenwich Village in New York City in an effort to invade the eastern publishing bastions.

Advised to concentrate on western fiction, Haycox happily returned home to work on regional narratives and then returned to New York. This time he was a passenger aboard a Union Pacific train, as was Jill Marie Chord, a native of Baker, Oregon, on her way to art school in New York. They were married on 4 March 1925 and soon headed back to Oregon—first Silverton, then Portland (*Who Was Who*, p. 382; Haycox, Introduction, p. viii; Etulain, "Literary Career," p. 78).

Richard W. Etulain, an authority on Haycox, suggests that his subject's apprenticeship in the pulps lasted until 1931, by which time he had written 105 fictional pieces, including three novels—*Free Grass* (1929), *Chaffee of Roaring Horse* (1930), and *Whispering Range* (1931). The stories are limited by their stress on plot, by too much telling and too little dramatizing, and by the primness of their heroines (Etulain, "Literary Career," pp. 80-82). With *Free Grass*, Haycox began to come into his own as an artist. It has a Dakota Territory historical background, contrasts western and eastern values, and features two different women and a melodramatic villain. *Chaffee of Roaring Horse* is a disappointment, as is *Whispering Range*, although it has a bigger set of characters, including a pair of observant sidekicks, and even contains a subplot.

Haycox soon added to his lustre when the prestigious *Collier's* accepted more than fifty of his stories and serials between 1931 and 1937. The best novel of this period is the well-researched *Trouble Shooter*, which, concerning the construction of the Union Pacific railway in 1868-69, signals its author's intention to move from formulaic to historical fiction. Haycox next announced his desire to try panoramic novels having the sweep of Victor Hugo's *Les Misérables* (Etulain, "Literary Career," pp. 122-23, 163). The first result was *The Border Trumpet*, about Apache unrest in the early 1870s. *Trail Town* (1941) is loosely patterned after Tom Smith's Abilene of 1870 (Etulain, "Literary Career," p. 143; see also Haycox's short story, "On Texas Street"), while the far better *Alder Gulch* is cast in Henry Plummer's Montana of 1863-64 and features that crooked lawman, among other actual personalities of his rambunctious era.

Etulain describes 1943 as Haycox's most satisfying year. It was then that the author saw his mediocre serial *The Wild Bunch* (1943) running in *Collier's* and also that installments of his best novel, *Bugles in the Afternoon*, his matchless Custer narrative, appeared in the *Saturday Evening Post*. The two works in serial form alone paid their author more than $50,000, and he also profited by the sale of film rights for *Bugles in the Afternoon* (Etulain, "Literary Career," pp. 145-46).

Jill Haycox comments significantly ("Light," p. 5) that her husband "was about four men rolled into one" and notes that he was a clubman, a toastmaster, a Portland Rotarian, and the like. Modesty probably prevented her from adding that he also belonged to the American Legion, was a state library board trustee and an active University of Oregon alumnus, and during World War II served as chairman of a draft board (*National Cyclopaedia of American Biography*, 39: 393; *Who Was Who*, p. 382; Ernest Haycox, Jr., Introduction, *Bugles in the Afternoon*, pp. viii-ix).

Etulain calls Haycox's final phase his "period of revolt" ("Literary Career," p. 152). During these postwar years, Haycox wrote in Hollywood briefly, grew self-critical and somewhat inconsistent, became ambitious to write an Oregon tetralogy, and was less productive. After *Canyon Passage*, which the *Post* serialized in 1945 and which was made into a stunning movie in 1946, Haycox published little short fiction of note. The best is a group of three tales telling of the Mercy family homesteading in Oregon in the early 1840s. These and a few other stories in the same vein comprise exercises for what Haycox hoped would be his masterwork: a series of panoramic novels on Oregon life from 1840 to 1900. Only *The Earthbreakers* was complete, or nearly so, when Haycox entered the hospital for surgery, which revealed incurable cancer. He died on 13 October 1950, leaving *The Adventurers* (1955), another Oregon novel, in unfinished form.

Major Themes

Haycox's plots vary greatly but turn often on revenge, range rivalries, and military duty. His main themes concern the code of the West (with contrasts to the East); the nature of individual duty in the face of clashes between community selfishness and the individualistic hero, and also between free will and fate; how women should act and be treated; and the puniness of humanity buffeted by a dynamic nature and adrift in the silent flux of time. Haycox's novels illustrate his themes best. His rather routine novellas touch on them intermittently, and although his short stories are aesthetically his most memorable form, they rarely elucidate his recurrent themes but instead develop unique ones.

The West of Haycox is composed mostly of wet mountain forests and vast, dry deserts. Both locales challenge his characters, especially his heroes. His best women seem already to have adjusted or quickly learn to do so. His villains and eastern visitors betray the code or fatally fail to learn it.

Early in *Free Grass*, Haycox has his hero define the code: "Shoulder to shoulder, fist to fist. . . . Play your own hand, ask no favors, ride straight, shoot fast. Keep all obligations." Moments later, he advises his eastern friend: "In this country, never give yourself away. Play poker with a blank face. Never tell a man anything about yourself, never ask him about himself. And no matter how you are hurt, never reveal it to a living creature" (pp. 10, 14). *Riders West* (1934) perhaps best develops the contrasts between East and West: the East has a past that is dead, is a place of fancy dances, lacks force, and is dominated by women and book lore, whereas the West is alive now, is a place to be loved, is a region where its people can do without frills, employs brutal force, and is a masculine arena with a grass-roots culture. An eastern-educated friend of the hero of *Deep West* advises an uncouth crony thus: "Don't ever regret your lack of learning, Izee. It's done nothing for me" (p. 165). The woman with the most abrasive personality in all of Haycox is Evelyn Fleming of "Secret River"; she is an eastern-bred schoolmarm, who despite her sense of superiority hungers in secret for the hero because of his western courage and even his savagery. One of Haycox's finest heroines is Martha Mercy, an Oregon homesteader from Indiana, who in "Cry Deep, Cry Still," "Call this Land Home," and "Violent Interlude" adjusts to the Northwest through trial by suffering. The cleverest aspect of "Weight of Command," one of Haycox's best stories, is the inability of the eastern newspaper correspondent to judge the military hero correctly; the smug journalist cannot penetrate cool western appearance to warm reality beneath.

Haycox often suggests that the West, contrary to popular belief, is a catalyst bringing out inherent evil traits rather than an arena offering any real second chance. Thus, we read of Boston Bill Royal, the eastern-bred villain of *The Wild Bunch*, just before his ruin: "He had come West to escape . . . , to start anew. . . . But once more the turns had been the wrong turns until he knew at last that the fault was in himself" (p. 172).

Reading Haycox helps to answer the important moral question, How should a man behave? His typical hero is a demanding but self-driving leader, more loyal to his crew than to his town, slow to anger but fierce in combat, patient and fatalistic, decent to all women, and willing to change. Dave Denver (*Whispering Range*) hopes to remain neutral in the face of demands by his town to join the vigilantes, is aware that two quite different women yearn for him, has partisan friends, and needs to protect his D Slash ranch and crew. The murder of a flawed friend propels Dave into awesome action, during which he becomes a superb but egocentric leader. The most inspiring parts of "On the Prod," probably Haycox's best novella, reveal the loyalty of hero John France's crew. France assembles them partly by example but also by summoning loyal friends from Nevada. When that bunch drops off a train in the dark, and France asks, "How many of you came?" the answer is thrilling: "You said six and six it is" (*On the Prod*, 1972, p. 116). Most town marshals and some sheriffs in Haycox are scared, inept, or, worse, hopelessly corrupt and loyal to little or nothing.

Many Haycox heroes combine self-reliant patience and monotonous fatalism. In the frequent climactic shootout, the hero wins because his adversary cannot control himself. "The Feudists," *The Silver Desert*, and *Saddle and Ride* (1940) are examples. Oddly, many villains are also loyal to the code and decline to take unfair advantage of the hero. The best example is Cash Gore, depraved killer of *Deep West* who, doomed at the end, calls out the hero's name and fights him fairly in the snowy street. The hero thinks, "Gore had had his chance for a quick surprise shot, and had refused it. It was a puzzle to which he never knew the answer" (p. 218).

Self-reliant though these heroes are, many are also fatalistic. One of the commonest images in Haycox's fiction concerns the book of fate: "All this was in the books before you and I were born. Can't change what was meant to be" (*On the Prod*, p. 148); "It was in the book" ("When You Carry the Star," in *Best Western Stories of Haycox*, p. 246); and "Long, long ago a wise man had written the fate of the transgressor in the Book of books—and Matt McQuestion had seen the inexorable sentence work out too often to doubt it" ("In Bullhide Canyon," in *Best Western Stories of Haycox*, p. 212). The most pervasive application of the notion of fatality in Haycox comes in *Bugles in the Afternoon*. In the final chapter, "It Was Written in the Book," the hero explains the Custer debacle: "Men do the best they can. . . . This thing was written in the book. The hand that writes in the book is one over which we have no control" (p. 245; see also p. 73).

Allied to the image of the book of fate are Haycox's clichés about events being in the lap of the gods and about the hero's "doin' what he's gotta do," and, better, Haycox's running metaphor of life as a poker game. Life deals one and only one hand, and the cards, which sometimes fall wrong, cannot be laid down. Play your hand well anyway, play the game out, guard your hole card, watch your chips, and never gripe. Even Haycox's villains are warned by fatal signs, but most of them merely shrug and delay mending their evil ways until it is too late. Cocky murderer Ollie Rounds in *Alder Gulch* is such an example, among many: "There were times when, in common with all fatalists, he had his strange, dark-lighted intimations of the future, and foresaw a grisly ending" (p. 104). But he misses his chances to slip away and is finally hanged. Was Ollie really born to hang?

The heroes are regularly loyal to good women, but some of these men are exasperatingly loyal to initially wrong choices. Thus, it takes Tom Gillette (*Free Grass*), Frank Peace (*Trouble Shooter*), and Adam Musick (*Long Storm*) most of their respective stories to rid themselves of clinging, shrewish females, after which they quickly find happiness. Another pattern in Haycox concerns the tired hero, who dislikes his "lonely trail" but cannot find a better one or decide to tarry a while. Jim Keene of *Rim of the Desert* (1941) finally quits drifting, settles

down with Aurora Brant, and enjoys a new life. What impels his free will to cut
the fatal trail of drifting is the sight of a hotel-wall bullet hole inscribed, "Venti-
lated by Smoky Jules from Medora. 1882," whereupon Jim determines not to be
like that unknown gunslinger—"a ghost walking the trail somewhere. All he had
to show for his life was a name on a wall" (p. 243). The heroes of "Guns of the
Tom Dee," "On Texas Street," and "Court Day" also put down roots. The very
best man for all seasons in Haycox is the minor character Jim Williams of *Alder
Gulch*. He judges all men well, is temperate and patient, and when he acts is
relentless.

Haycox's West is a man's world, but women have an important place in it, so
long as they hold themselves in check. It is wrong for a woman to try to be both
female and male (note Debbie Lunt, *Whispering Range*), to initiate amorous
activity (see spicy Annette Carvel, *Trail Smoke*), or to force her man to choose
between job and love (consider Eileen Oliver, *Trouble Shooter*). On the contrary, men in Haycox often tell their women where and when to transfer their
love (see *Border Trumpet* and *Alder Gulch*). The double standard is rampant in
Haycox (see the girl Tony Black, smitten by the hero of *Sundown Jim* but
hopeless as a wife because of her soiled reputation). The two most antifeminist
lines in all of Haycox occur in *Rim of the Desert* and "Dead Man Range." In the
former, a frustrated woman advises the heroine, "If he's not worth following
then you're not worth having" (p. 162). The latter story ends with the heroine
throwing herself and her ranch at the would-be drifting hero: "Come run Box
M—and me" (*Dead Man Range*, p. 159).

Haycox often laments the puniness of human life when compared to vast
nature and bewildering time. This is his major philosophical theme. If ever a
region ought to inspire humility in its human occupants, it should be the American West. Clay Morgan of *Saddle and Ride* loves his little patch of it—"This was
his country. He loved it with a hidden intensity few people realized....Its
spaciousness and its freedom, its smells and colors had formed most of his
thinking"—and likes "dark and silent camping" out in it. But he is well aware
that when doing so, he is "lying hard against an earth which, born of some
flaming collision, now whirled through space without destination and slowly
grew cold—carrying with it a mankind too small to matter" (pp. 48, 151, 152).
This gloomy image reappears many times, particularly in novels that Haycox
published in the 1940s. The dynamism of nature is a major if muted topic in
Haycox's best work. Lights and shadows are constantly compared to flowing,
rushing liquid. Furthermore, sounds whether natural (like those of storms) or
man-made (for example, gunfire) do not merely sound, but echo, echo. Haycox
once wrote to Professor Thacher, "I have liked...sound for its own sake frequently" (*Dear W.F.G.*, p. 8).

As for time, that puzzle and challenge to philosophers, poets, and the rest of
us, nature has plenty of it. In *The Wild Bunch*, "A thousand years of needle-fall
made a spongy surface upon which the horse's feet dropped with scarce a sound"
(p. 33). Time is linked to silence here, as it is very often in Haycox, who uses the

word *silence* perhaps more frequently than any other words but the most common: "Silence clung to the room over the lengthened moments" (*On the Prod*, p. 123); "Time stood still. His words fell flatly in the crouched, utter silence" ("Guns of Fury," in *Guns of Fury* p. 36); and, most simply. "Silence fell. Time passed" ("Lone Rider," in *Lone Rider*, p. 86).

Haycox always preferred western time to eastern time. Time is different in the West—in his West, anyway. "Out here time slid along unnoticed, unimportant. An hour was nothing, a day little more. The West lived on a long swing, measuring its tasks by seasons" (*Grim Canyon*, p. 41). This closes with a discussion of Haycox's finest symbol. The hero has been given a watch by his friends, who think he is going east to make money and hence will need a timepiece. But he stays in the West, and when he finally consults his new watch he sees that it has stopped.

Survey of Criticism

Ernest Haycox has been treated in several ways by the critics: he has been ignored, mentioned tangentially, praised briefly, and analyzed in detail.

Nameless here shall be those half-dozen or more critics who should have mentioned him in their chapters or books on the Western but who either did not do so or named him only to categorize him in a demeaning manner.

Tangential comments, often superficial, have been frequent. W. H. Hutchinson's gritty essay, "Virgins, Villains, and Varmints" (1957) links Haycox to other western craftsmen and points out that he introduced heroines in contrasting pairs. Bernard DeVoto's opinionated "Phaëthon on Gunsmoke Trail" (1954) deplores horse operas in general but commends Haycox for his narrative and scenic skills, for adding a Hamlet strain to his regrettably fatalistic heroes, and for his fine *Bugles in the Afternoon* and several splendid short stories. Kent Ladd Steckmesser handles Billy the Kid, Wild Bill Hickok, and Kit Carson as well as George Armstrong Custer in *The Western Hero in History and Legend* (1965); all the same, he brilliantly discusses Haycox's *Bugles in the Afternoon* among other treatments of Custer, concluding that it properly follows Frederic F. Van Water's iconoclastic *Glory Hunter* and "is one of the best historical Westerns ever written and probably the best novel about the Seventh Cavalry [of Custer]" (p. 228). In *The Pulp Jungle* (1967), Frank Gruber brackets Haycox and Luke Short as the "only *two* readable western novelists" (p. 151). Although devoted to a myriad of topics, Russel Nye's *The Unembarrassed Muse* (1970) accords Haycox full respect. Nye puts him in the best post-1930s company (with Henry Wilson Allen, Jack Schaefer, and A. B. Guthrie, Jr.), and praises his skill in characterization and his "strong sense of locale" (p. 303). Because Haycox did not remain a formulaic writer, John G. Cawelti only touches on him in *The Six-Gun Mystique* (1971) apart from the bibliographical entries, and neglects him even more in *Adventure, Mystery, and Romance* (1976). In an essay, "Ernest Hemingway's Grace under Pressure" (1976), Philip Durham links Hemingway, Haycox, and Raymond Chandler as exponents of the code of the West.

The following have published laudatory pieces on Haycox in the University of Oregon *Call Number*: Frederick W. Nolan (1963-64), who defines Haycox as "unique" (p. 1); Luke Short (1963-64), who praises Haycox's fictional moods, reliant heroes, personalized geography, "magical nostalgia" (p. 3), and individualized women characters; Saul David (1963-64), who comments excellently on Haycox's sense of time, well-depicted women, and unusual, "Gaelic flavored" diction (p. 30); and Thomas J. Easterwood (1963-64), who describes Haycox's personal library, presented to the University of Oregon in 1961 by his widow and now housed in the Ernest Haycox Memorial Library there.

Only five critics have written on Haycox with detailed effectiveness. In an early essay, "The West and Ernest Haycox" (1952), James Fargo describes his subject's personal appearance (small, slender, with high forehead, large nose, deep brown eyes, wide mouth, full lips), summarizes the main events of his life, and divides his production into standard, romantic Westerns, historical Westerns, and literary (not commercial) efforts. Fargo discusses Haycox's craftsmanship, accuracy to detail, and artistic integrity and proves his assertions with evidence from Haycox's best fiction. Brian Garfield in "Ernest Haycox: An Appreciation" (1973) offers the best analysis yet written of Haycox's style. Garfield especially admires *Bugles in the Afternoon* and likes *Rough Air* (for its "fascinating picture of movie people," p. 18) but much prefers his short stories; likes the adult quality of his characters; extols his "unique writing style," which features economy, warm irony, fine imagery, and "an exquisite sense of time and place" (p. 19); and approves of his effective use of subplots and land-rooted family conflicts. In three essays, D. B. Newton first considers Haycox's "decisive" influence on later writers ("Letter to a Graduate Student," 1965, p. 5), then praises his "singing prose" ("Legend of Ernest Haycox," 1973, p. 9), and finally implies that certain contemporary western authors (with their cynicism, gore, and "randy" amorality) should follow Haycox's example instead ("After Haycox," 1973, p. 6). John D. Nesbitt pairs Haycox's *Bugles in the Afternoon* and Louis L'Amour's *Hondo* in "A New Look at Two Popular Western Classics" (1980). He praises the plot of *Bugles in the Afternoon* as "an interplay between history and personal drama" but adds that "the glib style and the facile morality...will always keep it from being a good novel" (pp. 32, 35). Nesbitt especially deplores Haycox's characterizing the villain by mere invective and his rationalizing the treatment of American Indians by the United States: it was all in the name of manifest destiny.

It remains to mention Richard W. Etulain, who has done more for Haycox than any other literary critic. Etulain's dissertation, "The Literary Career of a Western Writer: Ernest Haycox, 1899-1950" (1966) is the best extended study of Haycox. It should be updated, tightened, and published, provided the Haycox family can be persuaded to release rights to the pertinent correspondence. Etulain sets Haycox in the western tradition, details the main aspects of his life (especially the early years), and provides an overview of his publishing career. Etulain's most ambitious essays on Haycox are "Ernest Haycox: The Historical Western,

1937-43" (1967) and "Ernest Haycox: Popular Novelist of the Pacific Northwest" (1979). The first concerns Haycox's discontent with formulaic writing and
his effort at historically based fiction and concentrates on *Bugles in the Afternoon*
and a few short stories about Apaches in Arizona Territory and pioneers in early
Oregon. The second describes Haycox's development through his final phase;
toward the end of his life, the novelist turned to panoramic fiction, notably with
The Earthbreakers, for which *Canyon Passage*, in Etulain's opinion, represents
preliminary work.

Bibliography

Page numbers cited in the text refer to the paperback edition, listed second
below, when one is available.

Works by Ernest Haycox

Free Grass. Garden City, N.Y.: Doubleday, Doran, 1929; New York: Popular Library,
        1958.
Chaffee of Roaring Horse. Garden City, N.Y.: Doubleday, Doran, 1930.
Whispering Range. Garden City, N.Y.: Doubleday, Doran, 1931.
Riders West. Garden City, N.Y.: Doubleday, Doran, 1934.
Rough Air. Garden City, N.Y.: Doubleday, Doran, 1934.
The Silver Desert. Garden City, N.Y.: Doubleday, Doran, 1935.
Trail Smoke. Garden City, N.Y.: Doubleday, Doran, 1936.
Trouble Shooter. Garden City, N.Y.: Doubleday, Doran, 1937.
Deep West. Boston: Little, Brown, 1937; New York: Dell, 1965.
Sundown Jim. Boston: Little, Brown, 1938.
The Border Trumpet. Boston: Little, Brown, 1939.
Saddle and Ride. Boston: Little, Brown, 1940; New York: Dell, 1963.
Rim of the Desert. Boston: Little, Brown, 1941; New York: Pocket Books, 1947.
Trail Town. Boston: Little, Brown, 1941.
Alder Gulch. Boston: Little, Brown, 1942; New York: Dell, 1957.
The Wild Bunch. Boston: Little, Brown, 1943; New York: Warner, 1972.
Bugles in the Afternoon. Boston: Little, Brown, 1944; New York: Signet, 1973.
Canyon Passage. Boston: Little, Brown, 1945.
Long Storm. Boston: Little, Brown, 1946.
By Rope and Lead. Boston: Little, Brown, 1951 (includes "Stage to Lordsburg," "Violent
        Interlude," "Weight of Command").
Dear W.F.G. [Boston]: Little, Brown, [1951].
The Earthbreakers. Boston: Little, Brown, 1952.
Pioneer Loves. Boston: Little, Brown, 1952 (includes "Call This Land Home," "Cry
        Deep, Cry Still").
Grim Canyon. New York: Popular Library, 1953 (includes "Grim Canyon").
Secret River. New York: Popular Library, 1955 (includes "Secret River").
The Adventurers. Boston: Little, Brown, 1955.
Dead Man Range. New York: Signet, 1957.
On the Prod. New York: Paperback Library, 1972.
Guns of the Tom Dee. New York: Popular Library, 1959 (includes "Guns of the Tom Dee").

Lone Rider. New York: Popular Library, 1959 (includes "Lone Rider").

The Feudists. New York: Signet, 1960.

Guns of Fury & Night Raid. New York: Tower, 1967 (includes "Guns of Fury").

The Best Western Stories of Ernest Haycox. New York: Signet: 1975 (includes "Court Day," "On Texas Street," "In Bullhide Canyon," "When You Carry the Star").

Studies of Ernest Haycox

Cawelti, John G. *Adventure, Mystery, and Romance: Formula Stories as Art and Popular Culture*. Chicago and London: University of Chicago Press, 1976.

―――. *The Six-Gun Mystique*. Bowling Green, Ohio: Bowling Green University Popular Press, [1971].

David, Saul. "The West of Haycox Westerns." *Call Number* 25 (Fall 1963-Spring 1964): 28-30.

DeVoto, Bernard. "Phaëthon on Gunsmoke Trail." *Harper's* 209 (December 1954): 10-11, 14, 16.

Durham, Philip. "Ernest Hemingway's Grace under Pressure: The Western Code." *Pacific Historical Review* 45 (August 1976): 425-32.

Easterwood, Thomas J. "The Ernest Haycox Memorial Library." *Call Number* 25 (Fall 1963-Spring 1964): 31.

Etulain, Richard W. "Ernest Haycox: The Historical Western, 1937-43." *South Dakota Review* 5 (Spring 1967): 35-54.

―――. "Ernest Haycox: Popular Novelist of the Pacific Northwest." In *Northwest Perspectives: Essays on the Culture of the Pacific Northwest*. Ed. Edwin R. Bingham and Glen A. Love. Eugene: University of Oregon, and Seattle: University of Washington Press, 1979, pp. [137]-50.

―――. "The Literary Career of a Western Writer, Ernest Haycox, 1899-1950." Ph.D. dissertation, University of Oregon, 1966.

Fargo, James. "The West and Ernest Haycox." *Prairie Schooner* 26 (Summer 1952): 177-84.

Garfield, Brian. "Ernest Haycox: An Appreciation." *WGAW News*, January 1973, pp. 18-[20]. Reprinted almost verbatim as "Ernest Haycox: A Study in Style." *Roundup* 21 (February 1973): 1-3, 5.

Gruber, Frank. *The Pulp Jungle*. Los Angeles: Sherbourne Press, 1967.

Haycox, Ernest, Jr. Introduction to Ernest Haycox, *Bugles in the Afternoon*. Boston: Gregg Press, 1978, pp. v-xi.

Haycox, Jill Marie. Introduction to Ernest Haycox, *The Border Trumpet*. Boston: Gregg Press, 1978, pp. v-viii.

―――. "The Light of Other Days." *Roundup* 21 (October 1973): 1-2, 4-6.

Haycox, Jill, and Chord, John. "Ernest Haycox Fiction—A Checklist." *Call Number* 25 (Fall 1963-Spring 1964): 4-27.

"Haycox, Ernest." *National Cyclopaedia of American Biography*, Vol. 39. New York: James T. White, 1954, pp. 392-93.

"Haycox, Ernest." *Who Was Who in America*. Vol 3: (1951-1960). Chicago: A.N. Marquis, 1960, p. 382.

Hutchinson, W. H. "Virgins, Villains, and Varmints." *The Rhodes Reader: Stories of Virgins, Villains, and Varmints*. Norman: University of Oklahoma Press, 1957, pp. vii-xxvi.

Nesbitt, John D. "A New Look at Two Popular Western Classics." *South Dakota Review* 18 (Spring 1980): 30-42.

Newton, D. B. "After Haycox: Whither Go We?" *Roundup* 21 (November 1973): 4-8.

————. "The Legend of Ernest Haycox." *Roundup* 21 (October 1973): 8-11.

————. "Letter to a Graduate Student." *Roundup* 12 (November 1965): 5-6, 17.

Nolan, Frederick W. "Ernest Haycox—Writer." *Call Number* 25 (Fall 1963-Spring 1964): [1].

Nye, Russel. *The Unembarrassed Muse: The Popular Arts in America.* New York: Dial Press, 1970.

Short, Luke. "Ernest Haycox: An Appeciation." *Call Number* 25 (Fall 1963-Spring 1964): 2-3.

Steckmesser, Kent Ladd. *The Western Hero in History and Legend.* Norman: University of Oklahoma Press, 1965.

Robert Gish

PAUL HORGAN
(1903-)

Paul Horgan's life is dedicated to art and authorship. From childhood Horgan semed destined to become an artist of some kind—painter, musician, actor, or writer—and the early years of his life amount to an exploration of that calling and a decision finally to become a writer. After that decision was made, with a few years' hiatus in the Pentagon during World War II, Horgan has been relentlessly at work, book after book. With many novels, short stories, histories, biographies, essays, plays, and poems to his name, it is important to regard him as a writer in the broadest of terms—a man of letters.

Influencing all that Horgan has accomplished as a man and an artist are two lifelong attitudes: he is a devout Catholic, a very religious man who sees his writing as a kind of devotion to the larger creative spirit that is God; and he has lived in the East and in the West, has traveled widely throughout America and Europe—is, in a word, cosmopolitan. He has won two Pulitzer Prizes and several other awards for his writing, including more than twenty honorary doctorates. His books are always reviewed in national newspapers and book reviews and enjoy large sales and multiple printings in hardcover and paperback, in American and foreign editions. He remains, however, a relatively obscure American writer, regarded inevitably (much to his puzzlement) as a regionalist, a "western" writer, and overlooked by academic critics.

Biography

Paul Horgan was born in Buffalo, New York, on 1 August 1903. His father, Edward Daniel Horgan, was Irish-American, a businessman with interests in a German newspaper (in partnership with his father-in-law) and an insurance company until he became ill of tuberculosis in 1915 and was advised to move to New Mexico for the dry climate. His mother, Rose Marie (Rohr) Horgan, was the daughter of Matthais Rohr, a German scholar, teacher, and writer who immigrated to New York, edited the *Buffalo Volksfreund*, involved himself in civic and cultural affairs, and promoted his German heritage at home and in public.

Horgan was very much influenced by the cultured life provided him in Buffalo. *Things As They Are* (1964) affords fictional insight into his New York childhood as do others of his novels and his partial memoirs, *Encounters with Stravinsky* (1972) and *Approaches to Writing* (1973). Horgan attended Miss Nardin's Academy in Buffalo, won prizes in speaking German, took violin lessons, presented his own upstairs theatricals, and generally absorbed the amenities of the city of Buffalo and his home. His father's illness changed everything, and the move to New Mexico amounted to outright culture shock.

Albuquerque was the city to which the Horgans moved. In 1915 it was a small town on the Rio Grande with no more than 20,000 population. Horgan, age twelve when he moved there, attended Highlands School and then, in his freshman year, Albuquerque High School where his English teacher was Elsie Cather, Willa Cather's sister. He made several lasting friends, notably Francis, Harvey, and Erna Fergusson, and credits the Fergussons with making his adjustment to Albuquerque easier.

In 1919 Horgan followed his brother to the New Mexico Military Institute in Roswell, located in the southeastern part of the state. He stayed at the institute through his sophomore and junior years, meeting Peter Hurd, a fellow cadet, in 1919. Horgan tells of these years with sardonic humor in *Peter Hurd: A Portrait Sketch from Life* (1965), for cadets Horgan and Hurd were not typical military school material. Luckily they were allowed to follow their artistic interests, and they thrived at their studies.

During the year 1921-22 Horgan returned to Albuquerque because of his father's worsening health and took a job as a junior reporter at the *Albuquerque Journal*. Horgan covered all kinds of events and frantically taught himself how to type. Soon he was writing literary and society articles—rather audacious in tone. Horgan's father died that year, and his mother was stricken with lethargic encephalitis. He returned to the institute in Roswell for a year in 1922-23 and combined his senior year in high school with the first year of junior college.

Encouraged to study voice by those who heard him sing, Horgan moved back to Buffalo, New York, and enrolled in the Eastman School of Music in nearby Rochester. Deciding to give up a career as a professional singer and exhausted from work and parties, he took a job as librarian at his old school, the New Mexico Military Institute, and moved back to Roswell in 1926.

Horgan remained institute librarian for sixteen years, until 1942 and World War II. During the period from 1926 until 1942 he published his first twelve books. His first published book, *Men of Arms* (1931), was a collection of character sketches of various types of soldiers throughout history. He wrote five novels before *The Fault of Angels* was published in 1933. For it he won the Harper Prize Novel Contest, which, in addition to prestige, gave him $7,000. He turned in 1935 to southwestern themes and settings with his second novel, *No Quarter Given*, refusing to repeat the basis of his first novel, which dealt satirically with artists' lives in the music and theater worlds of upper New York State. Many of Horgan's best western writings belong to this prewar period: five novels, *Main*

Line West (1936), *A Lamp on the Plains* (1937), *Far from Cibola* (1938), *The Habit of Empire* (1939) and *The Common Heart* (1942)—two volumes of short stories, *The Return of the Weed* (1936) and *Figures in a Landscape* (1940); a "suite" of character sketches forming his first "biography" of Santa Fe, *From the Royal City (1936)*; a history text, coedited with Maurice Garland Fulton, *New Mexico's Own Chronicle* (1937); and folk opera, *A Tree on the Plains* (1941). Horgan joined other writers like J. Frank Dobie and John H. McGinnis in a major phase of regional writing termed by some the "southwestern renaissance."

From 1942 until 1946 Horgan was an officer in the General Staff Corps of the army, assigned to the Pentagon in Washington, D.C. He left military service at the rank of lieutenant colonel, the recipient of the Legion of Merit. During the spring semester of 1946 he lectured in the Writers' Workshop at the University of Iowa. Flannery O'Connor was one of his students.

In 1947 Horgan received a Guggenheim fellowship to work on *Great River* (1954), a history of the Rio Grande that took him seven years to complete. *Great River* ended a twelve-year period in which Horgan published essentially nothing. The war had prevented him from writing, aside from one short story, "Old Army" (1944). But with the publication of *Great River* and its success as a Pulitzer Prize-winning history, he knew he was irrevocably a writer. In 1958 he received his second Guggenheim fellowship for work on a biography of Jean Baptiste Lamy, first bishop and archbishop of Santa Fe.

The next major postwar phase in Horgan's life began in 1960 when he became a fellow at Wesleyan University's Center for Advanced Study. That affiliation with Wesleyan has, in different capacities, lasted two decades and, although retired, Horgan at present lives on the Wesleyan campus in a converted carriage house surrounded by books and paintings. It is there that Horgan, still strong and creative at the age of seventy-eight, writes. The 1960s and 1970s were years that saw Horgan complete his semiautobiographical Richard trilogy (only the last of which, *The Thin Mountain Air* [1977], includes the Southwest in its setting), publish his biography-history, *Lamy of Santa Fe* (1975), and win another Pulitzer prize in 1976. While he was director of Wesleyan's Center for Advanced Studies, between 1962 and 1967, he published five new books, collected three early novels under the title *Mountain Standard Time* (1962), and gathered selected stories from four decades as *The Peach Stone* (1967). Before his directorship, he published two highly praised books in 1960 and 1961: one of them, *A Distant Trumpet*, a historical novel about the Apache-cavalry wars in Arizona in the 1880s and the other a biography of Lincoln's early years, *A Citizen of New Salem*. Aside from *Lamy* and *The Thin Mountain Air*, Horgan's most notable book in the 1970s with western setting and theme was *Whitewater* (1970). *Josiah Gregg* (1979) is a reworking of several earlier biographical and critical essays on the life and times of the author of *Commerce of the Prairies* (1844).

In 1973 Horgan was presented the distinguished Achievement Award by the Western Literature Association, and in 1975 he was given the Silver Spur Award

by the Western Writers of America. He has twice been honored by the Texas
Institute of Letters (1954 and 1971).

Paul Horgan is a western writer, a sophisticated one; one who lived in New
Mexico for many years and knows much about the history and people of the
Southwest; one who is aesthetically moved by its landscape and climate. But he
is fond of New York and the other mid-Atlantic states, the region where he spent
his boyhood and about which he often writes, and choosing to return to Connecticut in his maturity, he casts a decidedly eastern eye on the Southwest. And it is
in this perspective that one finds some of the major themes of his writing.

Major Themes

A major theme in Horgan's writing about the West is settlement. It is a heroic
theme told in both sweeping and limited, lyrical and prosaic, general and specific
terms, and presented in various forms: fiction, history, and biography. In this
sense, Horgan might best be regarded as a chronicler-observer in a strange and
alien land, an "uncivilized" land judged from the eastern and European assumptions of his heritage. Thus he is alone in a remote but sublime setting. Paradoxically, however, other settlers preceded him, and in their settlement is both his
and their story. Horgan speaks both biographically and autobiographically to this
point in *The Centuries of Santa Fe* (an extension of his earlier similarly designed
work, *From the Royal City*) where he identifies himself and his "settlement" as
"The Chronicler: 1915 and After" (*Centuries*, pp. 310-32). The preceding chapters follow the various phases and personages involved in settling Santa Fe, thus
making the book a biography of both persons and place. The epilogue attempts to
unite the city's past with Horgan's present by showing that history, that "frontiers," are recurrent.

Great River, an even larger historical panorama, chronicles the coming of
three cultures to the river: Indians, Spanish/Mexican-Americans, and Anglo-
Americans. With the Native American culture Horgan begins outside of time;
with the Hispanic and Anglo colonists Horgan traces their settlement across four
centuries. *The Heroic Triad* (1970), so named for these three "laminated" cultures, is an extraction of the social history in *Great River*. *Lamy of Santa Fe*
chronicles the establishment of Lamy's clerical authority over New Mexico,
Arizona, and Colorado and his struggles in reforming (and replacing) the native
Catholic clergy. *Conquistadors in North American History* (1963) follows the
battles waged by Hernando Cortés in colonizing Mexico, within the larger framework of the earlier coming of Columbus and the subsequent reconquest of New
Mexico by Diego de Vargas. *Josiah Gregg* is yet another history-biography of
western settlement. And Horgan's fiction likewise is concerned with variations
on the theme of western settlement.

Horgan's working out of this major theme of settlement and related themes can
be viewed in several ways. In one sense he seems to be following rather broadly
the frontier thesis of Frederick Jackson Turner's 1893 essay, "The Significance

of the Frontier in American History." American history is presented in the context of the winning of the wilderness, the evolution of primitive into civilized regions, and the recurrence of that process as the frontier advances wave after wave, with the "wave of the future" assumed best. Turner assumes the Americanization of the frontier as inevitable and good—and so does Horgan. Turner sees the frontier as a crucible for the formation of "composite nationality," and Horgan speaks about laminations and triads of cultures. Horgan's theme of settlement does not square in all ways with Turner's thesis (Spanish colonization is neglected in Turner's scheme), but there are several points of commonality.

In another sense, Horgan's preoccupation with the settlement theme is allegorical, symbolic of everyman's journey toward the promise of the future and the solitary struggle for that future in a wondrous but harsh land. The heroes about whom Horgan writes and with whom he seems to identify—Lamy, Gregg, Stephen Watts Kearny, Oñate, and others (real and imagined)—all face that future, that conflict. His settlement theme might also be considered biographically as the extension of his own life "myth."

When asked what he considered characteristic of the American West as a chief motivating force in fiction, Horgan said, "If there is a single pervasive theme in writing about *west*, perhaps, with all its variations, it could be identified as the theme of man, alone, against the grand immensity of nature—the nature of the land, reflected in his own soul" ("The Western Novel—A Symposium," p. 28). What brings "man alone" into conflict with "the grand immensity of nature . . . reflected in his own soul," what takes him west is settlement, the search for "home"—either for others or for self.

In the first, prewar phase of Horgan's southwest fiction, this theme occurs consistently. His first novel with a southwestern setting, *No Quarter Given*, concerns the valiant attempt of pianist and composer Edmund Abbey to find and remain true to his art—above illness, above friends, wife, and mistress. It is a long novel, which, through flashbacks, juxtaposes Abbey's past life as a student and promising musician in New York and Boston with his present life as a tuberculosis patient in Santa Fe and Albuquerque during the 1920s. Abbey incorporates the landscape and the ambiance of New Mexico, its Indian ceremonials, wind, and dust storms into the making of a triumphant symphony (in effect his autobiography), which he finishes just before his death. The West is both Abbey's self and his music—all integrally one. Abbey's patron in New Mexico, Mrs. John Mannering, significant as a pioneer who has preceded Abbey, represents "a gracious compromise between the life of the West, drawn up out of yesterday's dangers, and the life of the East or of Europe, secure in older, forgotten struggles and conquests" (*No Quarter Given*, p. 154).

Main Line West and *A Lamp on the Plains* (Horgan's third and fourth novels, respectively) are essentially companion novels (conjecturally part of an uncompleted trilogy or series that was given up for the later Richard trilogy), which follow the birth, boyhood, and adolescence of Daniel Milford Junior. As with *No Quarter Given*, though of different design, *The Common Heart*, *Whitewater*,

The Thin Mountain Air, and numerous others of Horgan's short stories and novels, these two books are maturation or initiation novels.

The first part of Danny's story, *Main Line West*, concerns Danny's father's courtship and vagabond marriage to Irma Milford, Danny's mother; his desertion of his wife and son in California at the time of World War I; and Irma's determined effort, first as the owner of a small café, and then as the Southwest's foremost female evangelist, to raise her son in the ways of love and goodness. The railroad, the "main line West," is the means and symbol of the Milfords' mobility from Kansas to Texas, New Mexico, Arizona to California, and back across the Southwest to Los Algodones, New Mexico, where Irma, preaching peace, is stoned by an overly patriotic mob. Danny helps his mother to the night train west —the conductor ironically being the one who first attacked Irma—and she dies on the train and is buried in Driscoll, Arizona. Rather than stay in Arizona, an adopted son to his mother's mortician, Danny hops a train, alone.

The second part of Danny's story, *A Lamp on the Plains*, opens with Danny in the small New Mexico plains town of Vrain, not far from Roswell, hunting like an animal for food and shelter. He is befriended by several types of people in Vrain: an ignorant but warmhearted mechanic, a minister and his wife, a cultured professor and con artist, a local rancher and his children. And he is guided on the way to manhood and uprightness by the people of the town, the books in the railroad waiting station and roadhouse, the ranch life, the military school (based on New Mexico Military Institute) where the rancher, Wade McGraw, sends him with his sons. All of these people and places represent, to varying degrees, "lamps on the plains" to Danny whose own character and moral striving make him a light of good intent as well.

Horgan's next novel, *Far from Cibola*, is one of his favorites, highly regarded by readers and one of his few prewar novels still accessible. None of Horgan's southwestern novels (except perhaps for *Whitewater*) is as satisfying aesthetically, in the conception and execution of form, as *Cibola*. As the title implies, this story too concerns a settlement journey, a quest toward and away from a fabled ideal: the seven golden cities of Cibola (Zuni Pueblo), which so long attracted and evaded Coronado and other Spanish "conquerors."

Horgan transposes the Cibola legend to a small southeastern New Mexico town in 1933, much in need of government aid in the wake of depression. Various citizens from outside town and in town converge on the courthouse at mid-morning expecting food and news of future relief plans. Individual and collective hopes are met with disappointment and hysteria. A youth is shot accidentally by the warning bullets of the sheriff trying to disperse the crowd. The lives of the people involved, from morning through the day and into night pass in parade, toward and away from the tragedy of the town shooting. The sense of humanity's folly and glory, its self-reliance and dependency, is felt on every page.

Horgan insists that *Cibola* is not a "proletarian novel." "It is," he says, "a poem with as many subjects as it has characters; but the subject underlying all others, though never stated, is human charity." ("Afterword," *Far from Cibola, Mountain Standard Time*, p. 278). Insofar as the novel's theme is charity rather than the proletarianism of man without a soul *Cibola* also portrays a town, a settlement, the common heart of the family of man.

Many of Horgan's novels advance his theme of settlement by way of community, whereby villages and towns take on a certain sense of character. In fact, all of his southwestern novels, reinforcing each other, profile the community, the locale of the Southwest in its different subregions. *The Common Heart* combines the character of its protagonist, physician, and amateur historian, Peter Rush, with the Spanish, Mexican, and Indian cultures, and the mountain, river, and mesa landscape of Albuquerque, so that place becomes a major character in the novel. It is a clear and masterful example of Horgan's pervasive west theme of the nature of the land reflected in man's soul. As Dr. Rush tells Albuquerque's visitors from the East, the author Molly Foster and her secretary, "Maybe everyone has a kind of 'early West' within himself, which has to be discovered, and pioneered, and settled" (*Common Heart*, p. 44).

Horgan's early volumes of short fiction, *The Return of the Weed* and *Figures in a Landscape*, deal with southwestern settlement in panoramic terms. The locale of *Weed* throughout the six stories is again New Mexico, from 1650 and the coming of Spanish priests as martyrs and church builders, in "The Mission," to the twentieth-century period of air transports and beacon lights in "The Star." Horgan's argument is that "we can learn from the past by thinking about its lingering walls, built by men along their way through wildernesses" (*Weed*, p. 3). No matter that the weed returns in tragic commentary to man's efforts; doing battle with nature gives man "the strange authority of daring; some whip of the spirit whose crack is a sound later men can hear" (*Weed*, p. 97).

Figures in a Landscape combines the historical settlement expositions of Horgan's essay of 1933, "About the Southwest: A Panorama of Nueva Granada," with a dozen superb stories, including "To the Mountains," "The Surgeon and the Nun," and "Tribute." The unifying theme of settlement is clear:

The land holds everything in fief, the ultimate unity. A cycle of its seasons is like a cycle of generations. . . . With the lever of memory and judgment, men lift the weight of ages and remember again and live again and predict again their own cycle: of birth, of tradition. . . , of death and decay, and of renewal. [*Figures in a Landscape*, p. 2]

The western fictions of his postwar period—*The Devil in the Desert, The Saintmaker's Christmas Eve, A Distant Trumpet, Whitewater,* and *The Thin Mountain Air*—demonstrate just how varied Horgan's talents and conceptions of design are, even within the traditional narrative form. The first two are fantasies, novellas of special miracles, of God's mysterious interventions in the lives of two ordinary though saintly Spanish priests busy in their missionary duties along the Rio Grande during the nineteenth century. *A Distant Trumpet*, like *The Habit of Empire* years before it, is a historical novel, a chronicle of more than 600 pages that must stand alone in uniting the novel of manners with the familiar tale of U.S. Cavalry in pursuit of the Apaches. Based on the exploits of General George Crook in rounding up Geronimo, the novel attempts (not always convincingly) to humanize the stereotypic Indian scout and show how Lincoln and the eastern military establishment in the Civil War affected soldiering and its image for decades to come.

Whitewater and *The Thin Mountain Air* demonstrate the truly universal and sophisticated potential that the modern western has as genre. Although the stories take place in Texas and New Mexico, respectively—the small west Texas town of Belvedere and the New Mexico of Albuquerque, Magdalena, and the San Augustin plains—both are classic accounts of growing up and self-discovery that capture the essence of a region even as they transcend it.

Survey of Criticism

Aside from numerous reviews and interviews in newspapers, popular magazines, and scholarly journals, few critical studies have been written about Paul Horgan. Reviewers generally have been kind to him and praise him above all else as a prose stylist. Even the few reviewers who find his style at times "mannered," "affected," and "sententious" acknowledge his talent for turning a phrase and his ability to re-create landscapes. Because of their variety, reviews are not considered here.

Critical studies other than reviews focus on Horgan as a southwestern writer. The best biographical account thus far is James Kraft's "No Quarter Given: An Essay on Paul Horgan" (1976). Kraft also has compiled a "Provisional Bibliography" of Horgan's work up to 1973, which was published with *Approaches to Writing*. He has, in addition, written other essays on Horgan's eastern writing and provides an almost necessary starting point for anyone interested in learning about Horgan's life and work. He believes that Horgan, somewhat like Henry James, poses the problem of relating East and West and concludes that Horgan "represents in his pattern of movement and variety a distinctly twentieth-century American phenomenon" ("No Quarter Given," p. 1). Kraft suggests through the title of his essay that Horgan, like his counterpart Edmund Abbey, devotes his entire life to his art. Many of Horgan's drawings accompany Kraft's biographical account.

After Kraft's, the most comprehensive examination of Horgan as a southwestern writer is James M. Day's pamphlet *Paul Horgan* (1967). Day says much that is essential about Horgan in a limited format of thirty-eight pages and readily admits the disadvantage of trying to assess Horgan so generally before the end of his career. Regrettably, errors of fact plague Day's study—such trifling things as calling Horgan's father "Edmond" rather than Edward; saying he was eleven when he moved to Albuquerque and not twelve; calling some of Horgan's books by the wrong title; saying Horgan was dean of Converse College when he merely gave one lecture there; saying he wrote only one historical novel, and so on. These are minor mistakes; however, they have a cumulative effect.

An even briefer account than Day's is William T. Pilkington's chapter on Horgan in *My Blood's Country* (1973). Restricting his insights to ten or so instances of Horgan's fiction (up to *A Distant Trumpet*), Pilkington considers Horgan's novels and short stories "seriatim" with control and frustration—seeing Horgan's work influenced as much by the "metaphysical bent" of Emersonian transcendentalism as by formal Christianity. Pilkington asserts this about Horgan's fiction: "He is at his best when detailing the minutiae of life; the constant flux of human relationships; the subtle strokes of destiny, the significance of which unfolds slowly and often ambiguously" (*My Blood's Country*, p. 51.) To Pilkington, Horgan conveys the power and grandeur of the Southwest "brilliantly."

In a sense, Pilkington's essay complements one written in the late 1930s by Horgan's friend and colleague, Alfred Carter. Entitled "On the Fiction of Paul Horgan" (1937), Carter's essay has the ring of prophecy to it, though little did he dream that Horgan would continue writing into the second half of the century. But early on, Carter was correct in saying of Horgan: "When he dwells upon Southwestern scenes...it is only because they help in picturing his America" ("On the Fiction of Paul Horgan," p. 209). Carter sees Horgan's regionalism as universal.

Two other critical studies that deal with groupings of Horgan's southwestern fiction are Judith Wood Lindenau's "Paul Horgan's *Mountain Standard Time*," (1964) and Jacqueline D. Hall's taped lecture, "The Works of Paul Horgan" (1976), on *Main Line West*, *A Lamp on the Plains*, *The Common Heart*, and *Whitewater*. For Lindenau:

Horgan may be classified as a Western writer because he is concerned with the effect of the land upon its inhabitants, with man's struggle to adapt to his environment, and with man's primal desire to survive. And the setting thus becomes an integral part of the action which typifies the theme of the American's primal need to become a part of the land. ["Paul Horgan's *Mountain Standard Time*," p. 60]

Hall argues that in Horgan's novels of the twentieth-century West we sense a Catholic author who has "grown up, who has substituted the past for original sin and who is searching for a way to exorcise this different devil." Hall's supporting assumption is that Horgan's sense of history is much more in sympathy with the "Spanish attitude of acceptance" than with his Anglo characters' refusal of the past. It is a provocative thesis, but its points of argument beg too many questions.

Three introductions to various editions of Horgan's fiction are valuable: D. W. Brogan's essay in *Mountain Standard Time*, Max Westbrook's in *Far from Cibola*, and W. David Laird's in *The Return of the Weed*. Brogan sees Horgan as a regional novelist but thinks his real theme is "the human dilemma, not the physical background in which his...story is set" (p. vii). Westbrook sees the theme of *Cibola* as the lure of sudden treasure couched in terms of Horgan's "own redaction of ancient myth" (p. ix). And Laird elaborates on aspects of *Weed* as Horgan's "personal statement of New Mexican realities" that advances multiple themes: "Man against Time, Man against Self and, most eternal of all, Man against Man" (pp. xv-xvi).

Robert Gish, devoting attention to a single novel, attempts in "Albuquerque as Recurrent Frontier in...*The Common Heart*" (1980) to analyze the many ways Horgan uses Albuquerque. However, aside from two dissertations in 1970 and 1971, this is more or less the extent of Horgan criticism at the present. Much more deserves and remains to be said about one of the most enduring and refined western American men of letters.

Bibliography

Works by Paul Horgan

No Quarter Given. New York: Harper, 1935.

From the Royal City. Santa Fe: Rydal Press, 1936.

The Return of the Weed. New York: Harper, 1936.

With Maurice Garland Fulton. *New Mexico's Own Chronicle*. Dallas: Banks Upshaw and Co., 1937.

The Habit of Empire. New York: Harper, 1939.

Figures in a Landscape. New York: Harper, 1940.

"A Tree on the Plains." *Southwest Review* 28 (Summer 1943): 345-76.

Great River: The Rio Grande in North American History. New York: Holt, Rinehart and Winston, 1954.

The Saintmaker's Christmas Eve. New York: Farrar, Straus and Cudahy, 1955.

A Distant Trumpet. New York: Farrar, Straus and Giroux, 1960.

Mountain Standard Time (Main Line West, Far from Cibola, the Common Heart). New York: Farrar, Straus and Cudahy, 1962.

Conquistadors in North American History. New York: Farrar, Straus and Giroux, 1963.

Things As They Are. New York: Farrar, Straus and Giroux, 1964.

Peter Hurd: A Portrait Sketch from Life. Austin: University of Texas Press for the Amon Carter Museum of Western Art, Fort Worth, 1965.

The Peach Stone. New York: Farrar, Straus and Giroux, 1967.

The Heroic Triad. New York: Holt, Rinehart and Winston, 1970.

Whitewater. New York: Farrar, Straus and Giroux, 1970.

Encounters with Stravinsky. New York: Farrar, Straus and Giroux, 1972.

Approaches to Writing (With a Bibliography of the Author's Work by James Kraft). New York: Farrar, Straus and Giroux, 1973.

"About the Southwest: A Panorama of Nueva Granada," *Southwest Review* 59 (Autumn 1974): 337-62. (Fiftieth Anniversary Issue; originally July 1933, pp. 329-59.)

Lamy of Santa Fe: His Life and Times. New York: Farrar, Straus and Giroux, 1975.

"An Amateur Librarian," *Voices from the Southwest*. Flagstaff, Ariz.: Northland Press, 1976, pp. 65-75.

The Thin Mountain Air. New York: Farrar, Straus and Giroux, 1977.

Josiah Gregg and His Vision of the Early West. New York: Farrar, Straus and Giroux, 1979.

Studies of Paul Horgan

Brogan, D. W. Introduction to Paul Horgan, *Mountain Standard Time*. New York: Farrar, Straus and Cudahy, 1962, pp. vii-x.

Carter, Alfred. "On the Fiction of Paul Horgan." *New Mexico Quarterly* 7 (August 1937): 207-16.

Day, James M. *Paul Horgan*. SWS. Austin: Steck-Vaughn, 1967.

Gish, Robert. "Albuquerque as Recurrent Frontier in . . . *The Common Heart*." *New Mexico Humanities Review* 3 (Summer 1980): 23-33.

Hall, Jacqueline D. "The Works of Paul Horgan." Western American Writers Cassette Curriculum. Deland, Fla.: Everett/Edwards, 1976.

Kraft, James. "No Quarter Given: An Essay on Paul Horgan." *Southwestern Historical Quarterly* 80 (July 1976): 1-32.

Laird, W. David. Foreword to Paul Horgan, *The Return of the Weed*. Flagstaff, Ariz.: Northland Press, 1980, pp. xi-xviii.

Lindenau, Judith Wood. "Paul Horgan's *Mountain Standard Time*." *South Dakota Review* 1 (May 1964): 57-64.

Milton, John, ed. "The Western Novel—A Symposium." *South Dakota Review* 2 (Autumn 1964): 3-36.

Pilkington, William T. *My Blood's Country: Studies in Southwestern Literature*. Fort Worth: Texas Christian University Press, 1973, pp. 51-64.

Westbrook, Max. Introduction to Paul Horgan, *Far From Cibola*. Albuquerque: University of New Mexico Press, 1974, pp. v-xiii.

Delbert E. Wylder

EMERSON HOUGH

(1857-1923)

After the publication of Emerson Hough's *Heart's Desire* in 1905, Andy Adams, a writer noted for his authentic treatment of cowboy life, wrote to Hough congratulating him on the novel: "Russell of Montana, among the artists, may continue to please a few of us old boys, but Remington, with his bad men, holds the center of the stage. The second winning of the West—for truth—is on, and I extend my hand in congratulation" (Andy Adams to Hough, 19 January 1906; this and subsequent citations to correspondence refer to the Emerson Hough Collection at the Iowa State Department of History and Archives, Des Moines, unless otherwise noted). Adams was extending a handshake welcoming Hough into the relatively small fraternity of fiction writers who insisted upon authenticity in the portrayal of the western experience. Ironically, after Hough's death in 1923, Adams wrote to Walter Prescott Webb expressing his disappointment in Hough:

> The late Emerson Hough and I were intimate friends. I happen to know that Mr. Hough never saw a trail herd of Texas cattle. Yet he could write a trail story that a publisher would want, because it qualified under the caption of "What the Public Wants." This re-hash school of writers has the field. And the funny thing is, that when these acceptable writers *lift* their material from sources of authority they are not sufficiently practical to do it intelligently. Yet it passes muster and brings home the bacon. The Saturday Evening Post paid $15,000 for the serial rights of "North of 36," the picture rights brought nearly double that amount, with handsome book values to follow. It pays to fake. [Andy Adams to Walter Prescott Webb, 21 February 1925, in Grover, "Emerson Hough and the Southwest," pp. 170-71]

According to Adams's evaluation, Hough had changed in the eighteen years between *Heart's Desire* and *North of 36* (1923) from a writer dedicated to truth about the American West to a writer of fake Westerns. There is some truth in Adams's estimate, but it is not the whole truth. During the last thirty-six years of his life as a writer of books, Emerson Hough made strong attempts to deal with the West authentically, but he was also driven by a desire for success, financial success.

Biography

Emerson Hough was forty years old when his first book, *The Story of the Cowboy*, was published in 1897. He was born 28 June 1857 to Joseph Bond Hough and Elizabeth Hough in Newton, a small farming town in central Iowa. His parents had moved from Loudoun County, Virginia, in 1852, and Joseph Bond Hough supported his family—Emerson was the fourth of six children—by schoolteaching, farming, surveying, acting as county clerk, and finally by becoming a grain and lumber merchant. Emerson remembered himself in childhood as being rather bookish but also loving to be outdoors. The most influential book of his childhood was Henry Howe's *Historical Collections of the Great West*, and he kept his copy as a source for western ideas. The most influential person in his childhood was his father, who not only taught him to hunt but instilled in him the chivalric code of the Virginia gentleman. In commenting on his father Hough made a comparison:

> My father was a great sportsman, a great mathematician, a great Christian. I myself have always been a sportsman, and have travelled much, all over this continent, in pursuit of sport. As to mathematics and Christianity, I do not say so much. [Hough to Edward J. O'Brien, 28 October 1918]

Although Hough did not become a mathematician and his religious beliefs deviated certainly from the Quaker-oriented beliefs of his father into a strange amalgamation of religion, the ethical principles implicit in the code of the Virginia gentleman, and the sportsman's creed, and a type of nature worship, his father's influence carried beyond the love of hunting and fishing. Emerson Hough co ued through high school and graduated with three other students at a time when young people, and particularly boys, were not required to complete a high school education. He tried to teach school for a year but, according to his own estimates, failed miserably. Then he went on to the university at Iowa City, where he played football, edited the newspaper for a time, and majored in modern languages.

After he had graduated with the bachelor's degree in philosophy, he returned to Newton to work as a surveyor. That position proved unsatisfactory, and Hough, with the encouragement of his father, read law with the Honorable H. S. Winslow of Newton and was admitted to the bar in 1882. That year saw the publication of his first article, "Far from the Madding Crowd," published in *Forest and Stream*. It was the first of many articles written for magazines devoted to outdoor sports. Hough received an invitation from a friend, Eli H. Chandler, to join him in his law office in White Oaks, New Mexico. Because of a "misunderstanding," Hough's fiancée, whom he had met at the State University of Iowa, broke their engagement, and Hough had little to keep him in Newton. He made arrangements with *American Field*, another outdoor magazine, to pay his way to the West in return for writing some sketches for them on the Southwest. Hough took a train and then a wagon to White Oaks, a town of fewer than a thousand people in its boom-town days. Gold had been discovered in Baxter Mountain, just northwest of the town. The area was also cattle country, and some of the Lincoln County war had spilled over into the little valley where White Oaks was situated. Although Hough lived in White Oaks for fewer than two years, it was a time he would remember with nostalgia for the rest of his life.

In White Oaks, he practiced the law sporadically, wrote for a local newspaper, the *Golden Era*, and continued to send articles and sketches to *American Field*. He also did some hunting. His mother became ill, and Hough returned to Iowa, only to find that his father's business had failed. Hough tried newspaper work in order to make some money, working in Des Moines, Sandusky, Ohio, and finally in Chicago, and making extra money by writing humorous stories for the McClure-Phillips syndicate. Finally, he teamed with an artist friend in writing and illustrating county and city histories. When their partnership ended, Hough bought a half-interest in a newspaper in Wichita, Kansas. However, his partner in the newspaper absconded with all of the funds, and Hough thought himself ruined. He returned to Iowa to tell the bad news to his reconciled fiancée. Gathering together his resources, he saved the newspaper and, just as he was prepared to enjoy his success, his fiancée once more ended the engagement. Hough was heartbroken.

He left for Chicago determined to find his livelihood by writing; he had learned, in New Mexico, to hate the practice of the law. Because of his experiences in the West, he was employed as the western editor of *Forest and Stream*. His duties were to manage the office, edit the "Chicago and the West" column, and solicit advertising. Except for the last task, the job was perfect for Hough. His employer, George Bird Grinnell, was more than one thousand miles away. Hough was able to spend much of his extra time in writing for newspapers and writing articles for magazines, and he was able to travel in the West to gather information. He also wrote a four-act drama, *Madre D'Oro (1889)*, and a children's book, *The Singing Mouse Stories* (1895). But his "career of crime," as he called it, did not really begin until the publication of *The Story of the Cowboy* in 1897. That was also the year that he married Charlotte Amelia Cheesebro.

Reactions to *The Story of the Cowboy* were so positive, including a congratulatory letter from Theodore Roosevelt, that Hough began a novel. Newly wedded and at the age of forty, Hough wrote the novel between the hours of ten at night and three or four in the morning while maintaining his work load at his office. His first novel, *The Girl at the Halfway House*, was published in 1900. Although it was not a financial success and the reviews were not too encouraging, Hough received congratulations from a number of westerners. He once again embarked on an all-night writing project. The result was *The Mississippi Bubble*, a novel published in 1902 and Hough's first best-seller. With the exception of 1920, Hough produced at least one book a year, and sometimes two, for the rest of his life; in 1916 and 1918 three Emerson Hough books appeared. Two novels were left in manuscript when he died and were published posthumously. He also wrote

more than 200 articles and short stories for such popular magazines as *Century,*
Frank Leslie's Popular Monthly, Outing, The Saturday Evening Post, and *Har-*
per's Weekly, and he maintained his position as western editor for *Forest and*
Stream until 1903. Then he moved to *Field and Stream* for two years before
devoting full time to writing.

Hough, a man of amazing energy, was of Scotch-Irish ancestry, short, approx-
imately five feet nine inches tall, with a rather stocky, muscular build. He was a
nervous, often irritable man who, as publishers often noted, was not easy to work
with. His nervous temperament, which he believed he had inherited from his
mother, often caused him distress, and in his correspondence he refers to "the old
nervous breakdown," or to his "nervousness and irritability."

Indeed, Hough's life was not easy, and he worked long and diligently in an
attempt to make his writing financially successful. Between *The Mississippi*
Bubble in 1902 and *54-40 or Fight* in 1909, none of his books was a best-seller,
and none of them made much money. *Heart's Desire*, his most successful novel
artistically, did not make enough money in royalties to pay back the money he
had been advanced and he characteristically offered to repay the publisher,
Macmillan. Sometimes he blamed the publishers, and he switched from Bobbs-
Merrill to the Outing Publishing Company to Macmillan, and then back to
Bobbs-Merrill. Hough kept himself solvent by writing articles and short stories.

Between books, Hough made trips to hunt and to fish and to gather information to use in his articles and stories. As he grew older and saw the changes
occurring in American society, especially after World War I, Hough's thoughts
turned more and more to his younger days in the Old West. He brought some
of these memories back to mind when he wrote his autobiography, *Getting a*
Wrong Start, published anonymously in 1915. His historical novel of the Lewis
and Clark expedition, *The Magnificent Adventure* (1916), allowed him to reflect
on the Northwest, and in *The Man Next Door* (1917), he brought two western
characters to the city in a humorous novel of contrasts. But when he had the
opportunity to rethink the western experience and his ideas about it for a book in
the Chronicle of America Series, he was convinced that he should concentrate on
novels of the West. *The Sagebrusher*, published in 1919, was only moderately
successful, but he sold it to the movies. *The Covered Wagon* was published in
1922 and was made into a very successful film which Hough saw only a few
weeks before his death. His novel, *North of 36*, the cattle trail novel that Andy
Adams considered "faking," was appearing in *Saturday Evening Post* when he
died, and he had managed to sell the serial rights, the book rights, and the film
rights, as well as to sign other contracts for shorter materials. He believed that he
had finally become a success. He died on 30 April 1923 from heart and respiratory complications following surgery.

Major Themes

Although he may have hoped, Emerson Hough never believed that he would
be remembered; thus, being remembered was not one of his criteria for success.

He wanted, first, to be financially successful. In some ways more important, however, was his desire to record two great migrations, one a continuation of the other. One of his major themes was the dominance of the Anglo-Saxon race, particularly the role of the Anglo-Saxons in the discovery and the settlement of the American West. His first novel included an entire chapter on the subject, and his third novel, *The Law of the Land*, presented his case for the intellectual and physical superiority of the Anglo-Saxon over the Negro. Part of that superiority lay in the aggressiveness of the Anglo-Saxon. He made roughly the same claims in *The Covered Wagon*, only this time in comparison to the American Indian. After driving off a Sioux attack and then holding a successful buffalo hunt, the members of the wagon train hold a feast. The narrator describes the celebration and concludes, "The Americans, most terrible and most successful of all savages in history" (*The Covered Wagon*, p. 164).

Hough's Anglo(Saxon)philia stemmed not only from his awe of their aggressiveness or even from the fact that one of Hough's ancestors came to America with William Penn, but also from his belief in the superior legal codes and concepts of human rights in English society and from his reading in English literature. His favorite poem he once identified to an inquiring reader as Tennyson's *Idylls of the King*. For Hough, the best of the English influences survived in the South, where his "old Virginia daddy" had come from. Finally, he believed in the southerner as the major force in the winning of the West. He wrote to Laurance Chambers that "it is singularly true that most of our gain in territory came through Southern men and that most of our dramatic leaders came from the South" (Hough to Laurance Chambers, 23 January 1909). He wrote of Thomas Jefferson in *The Magnificent Adventure*, and John Calhoun was one of the heroes of *54-40 or Fight*. Most of Hough's cowboy characters come from south of the Mason-Dixon line, and the cowboy heroes, as well as the protagonists of all his other novels, either come from the South or have adopted the southern code of chivalry as their own. But it is important to note that the words that preceded his comments on the South in the letter to Chambers were, "I do not want my book to be thought Southern, and do want it to be thought American."

Another strong theme in Hough's writing was Americanism. This was as true of his nonfiction as it was of his fiction. One of his early works was *The Way to the West, and the Lives of Three Early Americans, Boone, Crockett, Carson* (1903). Many of his historical novels are about the sweep and movement of the settling of the West and about the American spirit. *The Covered Wagon* is, in effect, a hymn to the settlers who moved along the Oregon Trail. Having lived in the West and having returned to it time and again on hunting expeditions, he found his vision of England diminishing significantly. After his only trip abroad, he concluded that everything in England seemed on such a small scale compared to the West.

But Hough also saw changes in the American scene, and much of his writing in his last years became either attacks on contemporary mores or expressions of nostalgia for the "good old days." In 1919, he wrote a broadside, "The One

Hundred Per Cent American," in which he attacked the concept of hyphenated Americanism. He believed that it took several generations to become an American and that people should give up their heritage and declare undivided loyalty to America. *The Sagebrusher* is a novel that attacks bolsheviks and Jews, and *The Web* (1919) is his history of the American Protective League, a citizen's investigative organization that operated during World War I. In his posthumous novel, *The Ship of Souls* (1925), Hough attacked many of the things he disliked about the new morality: women smoking, drinking, wearing scanty bathing suits, getting divorces; men being disloyal, unmanly. But in his most successful novels of the West, *The Covered Wagon* and *North of 36*, he could write of earlier times when men were self-sufficient, and at least the good ones operated from a code of honor that was traditional and rigid. He wrote of the western migration as a model and an inspiration to his readers. As he once explained:

> As I grow older—I am sixty-one years of age now—I take even more interest than ever in the Old West and in early America, and I am sure that if ever I am remembered at all—most of us are not—it will be because of what little I have done to learn about the West and about early America, and to tell about them the best I knew how. [Hough to the Editors, *Youth's Companion* 10 December 1917]

His love of America and of nature led him to espouse conservation even before the conservation movement began. He was credited with saving the buffalo herd in Yellowstone Park by exposing the poaching that was going on within the park limits. Many of his articles for popular magazines expressed his views on the destruction of trees and of animals. When he agreed to write a column called "Out of Doors" for *Saturday Evening Post*, he wrote frequently about the wasteful practices of American industry and American hunters. He even wrote a series of books for adolescents, *The Young Alaskans* and several sequels, in which one of the major themes was conservation. On this subject, too, Hough felt that he had been rather successful.

In one area of writing, however, Hough did not feel a success. In his correspondence, there are infrequent references to his desire for time—time to write a novel, and evidently time to write a novel that would be considered literary. He had great hopes for *Heart's Desire*. He had written a number of stories for *Saturday Evening Post*, many of them featuring a cowboy named Curly, but other stories as well, all set in the town of White Oaks, New Mexico, called Heart's Desire in the stories. Hough worked closely with Herbert P. Williams, his editor at Macmillan, and also hired Harris Dickson, another popular novelist, to help him put together the short stories into a novel that would be unified and coherent. The dominant mood of the novel, like the individual short stories, was humorous, although there is a serious theme beneath the surface. The story, symbolically, is about the destruction of the frontier West—a West of freedom and irresponsibility— by the introduction of civilization in the form of a cultured, well-educated woman. She is Eve brought into the Garden of Eden. As one of the characters explains to this Eve,

A man's a right funny thing, ma'am. He's all the time hankerin' to git into some country out at the end of the world, where there ain't a woman within a thousand miles; and then as quick as he gets there, he begins to holler for some woman to come out and save him. [*Heart's Desire*, p. 156]

It is not, however, only the woman, Constance Ellsworth, who will destroy Eden; her father represents eastern capital and the railroads, and his entrance into the quiet little valley brings greed, ambition, envy, and competition to the surface in the little community. These qualities have always been there, as many of the short stories illustrate, but never on such an uncontrollable scale. Fortunately, the protagonist, Dan Anderson, recognizes that he is selling out his friends because of his love for Constance, and he destroys the plot of the easterners. The love affair is saved by some mock-heroic antics, and the novel ends happily for two young lovers. Williams believed that the novel was superior to Owen Wister's *The Virginian*, but it did not prove successful in the bookstores. Ironically, it remains Hough's only novel now in print and has long been considered a classic of southwestern literature.

The financial failure of the novel caused Hough to move back to the formula historical novel. Furthermore, he had always liked the epic. He had thought of the cowboy as resembling a reincarnation of the medieval knight, but an unassuming one. As he described the cowboy in his first book:

From the half-tropic to the half-arctic country he has ridden, his type, his costume, his characteristics practically unchanged, one of the most dominant and self-sufficient figures in the history of the land. He never dreamed he was a hero, therefore perhaps he was one. [*Story of the Cowboy*, p. viii]

It is this concept of the cowboy and a fairly similar one of the wagon train boss that led Hough to his greatest financial successes in the novels *The Covered Wagon* and *North of 36*. Both were made into films and were extremely successful on the screen. *The Covered Wagon* (1923) had a longer run than *Birth of a Nation* (1915). Its director, James Cruze, took advantage of the epic quality of the westward movement, and his photography highlighted the vastness and grandeur of the American West in contrast to the puny but steady progress of the wagon train. The film was hailed as a major achievement, despite the unfortunate love story, and *The Covered Wagon* has served as the model for generations of films about the overland trails.

To a certain degree, the same is true of *North of 36*, the first successful trail drive film. Film critics found it less appealing than *The Covered Wagon*, though greater efforts were made toward authenticity in this film. Two other films were made of *North of 36* with different titles, but neither could quite overcome the love story that intruded into the action even more than that in *The Covered Wagon*.

In some ways, Andy Adams was correct in accusing Hough of fakery in *North of 36*. Hough had learned that the love affair in the popular historical novel sold books. Over a period of years, he had adapted his writing to what would sell, and he could not break the habit when he worked on *North of 36*. Ironically, however, Hough became ill when writing it, and he called on Andy Adams to help him finish, primarily because he thought Adams was the only writer who could handle the subject with authenticity. Hough recovered temporarily and managed to finish without Adams's help. Hough tried for authenticity, and most of his cowboy characters were treated realistically, but the protagonist and the romantic plot were unbelievable. Hough had, however, in his lifetime, developed a reputation for western writing. Some of his novels were published in several languages, and *The Covered Wagon* was still in print in the 1950s.

Survey of Criticism

Hough was largely forgotten by the critics until the 1960s, when the formation of the Western Literature Association inspired considerable research on many western writers. There are few significant articles on Hough between Lee Alexander Stone's *Emerson Hough: His Place in American Letters* (1925) and W. H. Hutchinson's "Grassfire on the Great Plains" (1956) an essay concerned with the literary controversy arising from Stuart Henry's ill-timed attack on *North of 36*, and then Delbert E. Wylder's essay, "Emerson Hough's *Heart's Desire*," in the first issue of *Western American Literature* (1966).

Since 1966, however, a good deal of research has been conducted on the life and works of Emerson Hough. The most impressive work of scholarship on his western writing is a dissertation by Carole McCool Johnson, "Emerson Hough and the American West: A Biographical and Critical Study" (1975). It includes biographical material but is an analysis, primarily, of Hough's western fiction and nonfiction. Johnson has also collected into a volume the "Curly" stories not included in *Heart's Desire*, as Hough once thought of doing. Hough decided against the project, thinking that a collection of short stories would be difficult to publish; Johnson's collection has not found a publisher.

Delbert E. Wylder has authored the Steck-Vaughn pamphlet *Emerson Hough* (1969) and the Twayne volume *Emerson Hough* (1981). Wylder includes biographical information and critical analysis in both works, and the Twayne volume begins with two long chapters (almost half the book) on Hough's life. Thus, it is the most detailed biography yet available. Other chapters discuss Hough's influence as a conservationist, a western writer, and a historical novelist, as well as the influence that Hough's novels have had on western film-making, with special attention to *The Covered Wagon*. Wylder concludes that, though definitely a minor writer, Hough should be remembered for his work as western writer and conservationist.

W. H. Hutchinson includes some material on Hough in his biography, *A Bar Cross Man: The Life and Writings of Eugene Manlove Rhodes* (1956). There is still a great deal of work left to do in biographical studies despite Johnson's and Wylder's works. The largest collection of documents is in the Iowa State Deaprtment of History and Archives in Des Moines, a collection ordered and catalogued by Ellen E. Spaulding. The Lilly Library and the University of Indiana Library in Bloomington include material from the files of Bobbs-Merrill. The University of Iowa Libraries, Iowa City, also have a collection of correspondence, manuscripts, and first editions.

There has been little textual criticism on Hough's work, and no complete bibliography has been published. The most complete listing appears in Carole McCool Johnson's dissertation, but bibliographical work has also been published by Frank Paluka, *Iowa Authors: A Bio-Bibliography of Sixty Native Writers*, and Richard W. Etulain, *Western American Literature: A Bibliography of Interpretive Books and Articles*, as well as Wylder's *Emerson Hough* Twayne volume.

Little has been done in the study of Hough's nonwestern novels, nor has there been a study of Hough as a humorist, although he was most effective as a comic writer. The establishment of the Popular Culture Association has not resulted in significant research on Hough as a popular novelist or on the films made from his novels. There is material available, for Hough's novels were easily adaptable. *The Covered Wagon*, a tremendous success, was one of the first movies to use a musical score sound track, *North of 36* was adapted several times under a variety of titles, and *The Way of a Man* was one of the first novels made into a feature and a serial production.

Hough's southwestern classic, *Heart's Desire*, which has only been available in the first edition, is being reprinted by the University of Nebraska Press, with an introduction by Peter White. Thus, it may be that Emerson Hough will be remembered, after all, for the novel that is most deserving, the one that led Andy Adams, cowboy turned writer, to write him a letter of congratulation.

Bibliography

Works by Emerson Hough

"Southwestern Sketches." *American Field* 19-21 (2 July 1883-10 July 1886).
The Story of the Cowboy. New York: D. Appleton, 1897.
The Girl at the Halfway House. New York: D. Appleton, 1900.
"Sheriff." *Frank Leslie's Popular Monthly* 52 (June 1901): 118-27.
The Mississippi Bubble. Indianapolis: Bobbs-Merrill, 1902.
The Way to the West, and the Lives of Three Early Americans, Boone, Crockett, Carson. Indianapolis: Bobbs-Merrill, 1903.
"The Wasteful West: Timber." *Saturday Evening Post*, 23 December 1905, pp. 6-7ff.
Heart's Desire. New York: Macmillan, 1905; Lincoln: University of Nebraska Press, 1981. Introduction by Peter White.
The Story of the Outlaw. New York: Outing, 1907.
The Way of a Man. New York: Outing, 1907.
"Slaughter of the Trees." *Everybody's* 18 (May 1908): 578-92.

54-40 or Fight. Indianapolis: Bobbs-Merrill, 1909.
The Purchase Price. Indianapolis: Bobbs-Merrill, 1910.
The Magnificent Adventure. New York: D. Appleton, 1916.
The Man Next Door. New York: D. Appleton, 1917.
The Sagebrusher. New York: D. Appleton, 1919.
The Covered Wagon. New York: D. Appleton, 1922.
North of 36. New York: D. Appleton, 1923.
Mother of Gold. New York: D. Appleton, 1924.
The Ship of Souls. New York: D. Appleton, 1925.

Studies of Emerson Hough

Downey, Linda K. "Woman on the Trail: Hough's *North of 36*." *Western American Literature* 14 (Fall 1979): 217-20.

Gray, Richard H. "A Dedication to the Memory of Emerson Hough, 1857-1923." *Arizona and the West* 17 (Spring 1975): 19-29.

Grover, Dorys C. "Emerson Hough and J. Frank Dobie: A Study of Influences." *Southwestern American Literature* 5 (1975): 100-110.

———. "Emerson Hough and the Southwest: Selected Letters." Unpublished manuscript.

———. "W. H. D. Koerner and Emerson Hough: A Western Collaboration." *Montana: The Magazine of Western History* 29 (April 1979): 2-15.

Hutchinson, W. H. "Grassfire on the Great Plains." *Southwest Review* 41 (Spring 1956): 181-85.

Johnson, Carole M. "Emerson Hough and the American West: A Biographical and Critical Study." Ph.D. dissertation, University of Texas, 1975.

———. "Emerson Hough's American West." *Books at Iowa* 21 (November 1974): 26-42.

———. "Emerson Hough's *The Story of the Outlaw*: A Critique and a Judgment." *Arizona and the West* 17 (Winter 1975): 309-26.

Miller, John H. "Emerson Hough: Merry Christmas. Sued You Today." *Indiana University Bookman* 8 (March 1967): 23-35.

Stone, Lee Alexander. *Emerson Hough: His Place in American Letters*. Chicago: n.p. 1925.

Wylder, Delbert E. *Emerson Hough*. SWS. Austin: Steck-Vaughn, 1969.

———. *Emerson Hough*. TUSAS. Boston: Twayne, 1981.

———. "Emerson Hough and the Popular Novel." *Southwestern American Literature* 2 (Fall 1972): 83-89; reprinted in William T. Pilkington, ed., *Critical Essays on the Western American Novel*. Boston: G. K. Hall Company, 1980, pp. 111-17.

———. "Emerson Hough as Conservationist and Muckraker." *Western American Literature* 11 (August 1977): 93-109.

———. "Emerson Hough's *Heart's Desire*." *Western American Literature* 1 (Spring 1966): 44-54.

Robert Brophy

ROBINSON JEFFERS
(1887-1962)

Robinson Jeffers's distinctive voice belongs to primordial time. His poems are mythic; they deal with elemental passions and primal forces. The strength of his poetic line forces his readers to confront what is most abhorrent: pain, tragedy, an indifferent universe, death. But it also moves them to appreciate beauty.

Jeffers has often been characterized as the grim pessimist in his western tower muttering oracles of doom, a man without joy, or hope, or love, a nihilist. The words are interesting. Pessimism is a relative concept. Jeffers certainly was not pessimistic about the universe; he saw its future as glorious and assured. About the solar system he was scientifically realistic: he knew it was fast burning out. About man he was also realistic, knowing man's penchant for self-destruction ("Science"). He was grim; he would rather say "earnest," which was a quality of beauty ("Boats in a Fog"). Although at times he praised annihilation and pictured the darkness of uncreation as holy, he was hardly a nihilist; he clearly had his values; he was a celebrator, not a denier. Joy, for him, was too superficial and immediate an emotion, unless it was turned toward God, imbibing the beauty of things. *Hope* was a word he used ironically ("Hope Is Not for the Wise"); it sounded too much like wish-fulfillment and unreality. Love, especially philanthropic love, was a trap; the best men dissipated their energies in useless forms of it. Jeffers would say: "Love the wild swan of the world"; "The divine beauty of the universe. Love that, but not man apart from that" ("The Answer").

Biography

Robinson Jeffers was born on 10 January 1887. His father, an austere man, was professor of Old Testament literature and exegesis and of biblical and ecclesiastical history at Western Theological Seminary (Presbyterian) near Pittsburgh, Pennsylvania. His mother, an orphan, had been raised by wealthy relatives. She was twenty-five, Dr. Jeffers almost forty-seven, when they married in April 1885. The difference in their ages and temperaments has given rise to various conjectures as to the family dynamics and their effect on the son who was born almost two years later. Dr. Jeffers was a tall, homely man, a hypochondriac and blatantly antisocial. In Robinson's early years, the father seems to have found the boy a threat to his life of secluded and scholarly intensity. He was very hard on his son, demanding Latin from him at the age of seven, closing him off from normal contact with other children, and eventually driving him into a pattern of headaches.

The father's unhappiness with "Robin's" schooling is given as the reason behind the decision in 1898 to send the boy to European schools. Annie, his mother, spent the next four years in Switzerland with her two sons (Hamilton was seven years his junior), Dr. Jeffers joining his family only during the summers and then seemingly with the primary intent of moving Robinson to yet another school. Stern teachers, an awesome landscape, some perversion among his classmates, separation from family, and repeated relocation took their toll. He became an introverted young man, known as the "little Spartan" by his teachers and classmates. In 1902 the family moved back to America where Robin entered the University of Western Pennsylvania, now the University of Pittsburgh.

In 1913, ostensibly for health reasons, Dr. Jeffers decided to move west, taking his family first to Long Beach and then to Highland Park, Los Angeles. Here Robin was enrolled in a small Presbyterian college, Occidental, as a junior. For the first time he was able to establish solid friendships and take part in a variety of sports. He studied biblical literature, economics, geology, history, Greek, rhetoric, and astronomy, a discipline that featured frequent field trips to Mount Wilson and Echo Mountain observatories. Here he began writing verse and publishing it in the school's literary magazine, of which he became editor in his senior year.

Graduating in an intimate class of eleven in 1905, he entered the graduate school of the University of Southern California (USC) as a student of literature. Here he met his future wife, Una, who was then married to a successful young lawyer. After another family sojourn in Europe where Robinson studied philosophy, Old English, French, Italian, and Spanish literature at the University of Zurich, he entered USC's medical school—not to become a doctor but to learn more about the mysterious workings of the human body. Meanwhile he had begun a clandestine affair with Una Kuster that was to extend agonizingly over the next seven years, ending finally in their marriage 2 August 1913 in Washington state where he had gone to study forestry.

The war in Europe cut short their plans for settling in England and, after a short stay in La Jolla, north of San Diego, they took an exploratory trip to Carmel on the recommendation of a friend. They were overwhelmed by the stark beauty of the rock, cypress, sand, and sea. To Jeffers it was the "inevitable place," by now a cliché in Jeffers lore but no less true. Their life there was simple, almost primitive: a rented log cabin, walks in the woods and along the beaches, much reading, few friends. They had lost both their first child, Maeve, and Jeffers's father in 1914; in 1916 twin boys were born to them, Donnan and Garth. The war years were particularly painful for Robinson, torn between an idealism that led him, abortively, to enlist in the balloon corps and a gathering disillusionment that would eventually make him a pacifist.

In 1919 Robinson and Una managed to buy a knoll overlooking Carmel Bay facing Point Lobos. There on 15 August, apprenticed to a stonemason, Jeffers began work on the structures that some see as his greatest poems, first Tor House, then the forty-foot Hawk Tower from which he could brood over the mind-subduing Pacific.

During his early adult years Jeffers had been writing poetry, publishing books of imitative verse in 1912 and 1916. Sometime in the decade between his advent in Carmel and his book *Tamar* (1924), he experienced a dramatic conversion from the tentative hedonism of his postgraduate days to a devout pantheism, from predictable romantic lyrics to powerful turbulent verse that measured itself by the seasons, the tides, and the course of the stars. *Tamar*, his first book embodying this verse, was hardly noticed, and Jeffers seems to have settled back to write, whether he had an audience or not. But obscurity was not to be his fate. James Rorty, an eastern critic and editor of *New Masses*, having been given *Tamar*, was so enthralled that he convinced Mark Van Doren and Babette Deutsch to join him in appreciative reviews. As a result, the prestigious publishing house of Boni and Liveright reissued *Tamar* together with a new selection of verse in *Roan Stallion, Tamar and Other Poems* (1925). Jeffers enjoyed almost instant notoriety because of the uncommon power of his verse and the sensational quality of his themes—incest, murder, holocaust, and bestiality.

Jeffers's biography from this point on could easily become a list of yearly publications. There were few dramatic moments in his life. He became a poet-stonemason, working on his poems in the mornings, usually in the loft of his home, in the afternoons fermenting his ideas while releasing inner tensions and violences in stonework or in planting thousands of eucalyptus and cypress seedlings. Evenings brought a simple meal and reading aloud to his wife and sons from classic authors to the light of a kerosene lamp (the family resisted electricity until 1949). Over the years there were three trips to Ireland (1929, 1937, 1948) instigated by Una, a change of publishers (Liveright to Random House in 1933), and yearly summer trips to Taos, New Mexico, again at Una's urging. Their twin sons grew up, leaving for the University of California, Berkeley, in 1936. Recognition came only sporadically with a doctor of literature from his alma mater, Occidental, in 1937, an honorary Phi Beta Kappa from USC in 1940, and election to the National Academy of Arts and Letters in 1945. Jeffers's one public appearance, a reading tour in 1941 to inaugurate a poetry series at the Library of Congress, was forced upon him, ironically, by a sewer-tax of $1600 assessed on his thirty-six lots—for development of Carmel Point, an intrusion of the humanity that he had methodically shunned.

If there was a central theme to Jeffers's life-concern in the 1930s it was the new great war preparing in Europe. Jeffers believed with Spengler in the inevitability of the grand processes of history, but there was an anguish within him that made him protest in poem after poem the stupidity and arrogance of warmakers.

As early as 1933 he was writing antiwar poems. Each book he published became stronger and more strident in its opposition. The postwar volume *The Double Axe* (1948) brought this stage of his career to disaster. His bitter judgments on the motives of his nation's leaders led to widespread rejection and sharp denunciation of his poetry and person.

It was during these years that Jeffers earned his reputation as the hermit of the Pacific. Though there was a family car, there was surprisingly little travel. Jeffers wanted to go nowhere and see no one. Celebrities did come to visit, among them Edgar Lee Masters, Louis Adamic, Edna St. Vincent Millay, George Sterling, Lincoln Steffens, Charlie Chaplin, Liam O'Flaherty, Krishnamurti, George Gershwin, Bennett Cerf, Thornton Wilder, Langston Hughes, William Rose Benét, William Saroyan, Aldous Huxley, Arturo Toscanini, and Salvador Dali. But most often they found themselves talking to the bright and witty Una, with Jeffers only reluctantly being drawn into the conversations. Visitors found a charming but austere household—a low-ceilinged, dark-stained living room with a family bulldog by the hearth, a stone-floored dining room with rough-hewn table and benches, a tiny kitchen, a colorful garden, and of course the legendary tower. If they were lucky enough to be housed overnight, visitors slept in the guest room celebrated in "The Bed by the Window."

In 1948, after the triumph of Judith Anderson in the Broadway production of his *Medea*, Jeffers went to Ireland with Una and almost died there of pleurisy. Then in 1950 the unthinkable happened: after a prolonged battle, which took her at one point to the University of California Hospital in San Francisco for desperate, experimental treatments, his beloved wife died of cancer. Jeffers's devastation is poignantly recorded in "Hungerfield" and in the lyric "Whom Shall I Write For." Una had been more than half his life; she had been his bridge to reality. She had kept the family fed, clothed, and joyous, had planned trips, arranged what social life they enjoyed. More than all this she had been his companion. There was a hollowness in his soul when she left. Though he lived another twelve years (because he had long before formally rejected suicide), he lived as a ghostly figure, while his son Donnan and daughter-in-law Lee and their children carried on the life of the house. He died on 20 January 1962; residents of Carmel awoke that morning to a startling mantle of snow that seemed meant to mark his departure.

Major Themes

Jeffers's themes are, not surprisingly, identical with his overview of life; they are consistent from the writing of *Tamar* through his final, posthumous volume, *The Beginning and the End* (1963). Jeffers believes that God is the evolving universe, a self-torturing god who discovers himself in the violent change that is at the center of being's dynamism ("At the Birth of an Age"). One need not go far in Jeffers's work to discover that all of his images are reductively cyclic. The cycle is the truth of the stars, the life of the planet, the fate of nations and of man, insect, and flower. The cycle moves through birth, growth, fulness, decay, and death ("Shine, Perishing Republic"). The rituals Jeffers celebrates are rituals of nature: sacrifice (fragmentation, decay, and death as in "Salmon-Fishing") and sacrament (reintegration and rebirth as in the ending to "Tamar").

For Jeffers there is only matter and energy; there is no spirit or soul or immortality; these merely reflect man's desire to escape the reality of the cycle. God endures forever; the 82 billion year cycles of the oscillating universe are as though his heartbeat ("The Great Explosion"). Man is a temporary phenomenon, something of a misfit in the universe because of his megalomania, which turns him from God and from the whole. Yet this "bad experiment" of evolution is one of God's sense organs ("The Beginning and the End"). Death ends the individual existence; the material from the body is reassembled in earth, air, and water ("Hungerfield"). The world in its myriad cycles is determined. Universes form and dissolve, oceans condense and evaporate, mountains and civilizations rise and fall, nations emerge and grow old. All is determined en masse, but the individual may choose, to some extent at least, whether to be caught in the process or to stand apart and contemplate it ("Shine, Perishing Republic"). One may avoid what men call evil, but actually there is no evil; it is but a dark chip in the mosaic of beauty, a downward turn of the cycle ("The Answer").

Jeffers believes the "good life" consists in detachment from desire, in a calculated indifference. He thinks men should live miles apart and look on the crises of life as though from a mountain in Asia or from a far star ("Tamar" VI). The "good person" avoids the trap of saviorism. As it assuredly would be self-delusion, if not insane arrogance, for a swimmer to put up his hand thinking he could stop a wave, so also for the savior trying to prevent the evils he abhors. Instead, the good person loves God and praises him in all the world's life. Even Tamar for all her perversions and melodramatic fatal acts was able to see this and thus live on two levels, one at war and the other at peace.

Although it has proved a stumbling block to some, Jeffers's prosody is relatively simple. By "Tamar" he had put aside rhyme and meter for the more ancient rhythms of Hebrew and Anglo-Saxon verse, which utilize vowel quantity and the natural fall of the voice for stress rhythms. His narratives use a ten-beat line with variations. The lyrics, which can be divided into short poems and long philosophical meditations, work with five and even three beats per line.

Jeffers's diction is very precise; he spent hours at his unabridged dictionary sorting out possibilities. His imagery is taken from his coast—hawks, herons, wild swans, pelicans, cormorants, mount lions, deer and cattle, redwood, cypress, grass, wildflowers, rock, ocean, headlands, clouds, sky, stars, and planets.

Hawks are his totem birds, expressing what is noble, fierce, independent, and farsighted. Lion and deer are predators and their victims, metaphors for all victimhood. Fauna and flora almost always fulfill a twofold function in Jeffers's narratives. They are part of the realistic backdrop; they also foreshadow the imminent tragedy, recalling the feral surrogates of the year gods and the sacrificial flowers that sprang from the gods' spilled blood. Rock is consistently a

divine image or an example of stoic endurance. The sea is a mind-stretching
expanse, a moat suggesting passage up and out rather than across; it is the source
of life ("Continent's End") and an apocalyptic end to it ("November Surf").
Mountain and headland are the measure of the heavens and a reminder of human
life's precariousness, even though their life too is brief in the relativity of time
("The Treasure"). Sky and stars are the universe beckoning; the galaxies are
swirling pinwheels of God's glory. Although Jeffers uses stars mythically, as in
his references to the constellations Orion and Scorpio in "Tamar," he more often
views them through the sobering science of astronomy where they are the atomic
fusion furnaces whose life span predicts the fate of our sun and solar system
("Nova"). The universe of stars and galaxies is the ultimate actor in Jeffers's
ultimate metaphor, the expanding and contracting universe, his god discovering
himself.

Elsewhere I have called Jeffers the "metaphysician of the West" (*Robinson
Jeffers* [WWS], p. 44). Metaphysics is that part of philosophy that studies Being
itself; it deals with all that exists; it delves into the nature of all processes—the
whirlings and interactions of the cosmos and atom. "Of the West" suggests not
only writing in the West or from its point of view or using it as a setting. Jeffers
does all of these, but his peculiar genius is his use of the West, the continent's
end on which he raised his stone tower, to explore the nature of Being, the
relevance of the human race, and the bridge between man and the cosmos.

The Pacific landscape is re-created exactly in Jeffers's poems—that section
stretching from Point Pinos in the north to Point Sur in the south. This fifty miles
of precipitous headlands, storm-scoured points, wind-twisted trees, and white,
churning surf was known to him intimately. The place names of his stories and
lyrics fall as from a survey map: Point Pinos and Joe, Carmel Beach and River,
Point Lobos, Mal Paso Creek, Palo Colorado Canyon, Sovranes Reef, Notley's
Landing, Rocky Point, Bixby's Landing, Mill Creek, Little Sur River, Point
Sur. The beaches, weather, flowers, and animals are all part of the daily scene.

His characters are authentic also, rising as they do from the violent legends of
this forbidding and isolating terrain. There is a local understanding in Big Sur
that something in its dynamism either produces or attracts madness, the grotesque, the macabre. Jeffers's characters are the remote ranch owners, self-exiled
hermits in shacks, wandering Indian cowboys from a previous era, mystic vi-
sionaries, and passion-entrapped isolates.

Writing as a westerner, Jeffers perceives his land and his conscience as scarred
with the vestiges of westward expansion. Jeffers's double, the self-stigmatizing
hermit in "A Redeemer," sums it up:

> . . . Not as a people
> takes a land to love it and be fed,
> A little, according to need and love, and again a little; sparing
> the country tribes, mixing
> Their blood with theirs, their minds with all the rocks and rivers,
> their flesh with the soil: no, without hunger

Wasting the world and your own labor, without love possessing,
    not even your hands to the dirt but plows
Like blades of knives; heartless machines; houses of steel: using
    and despising the patient earth. . .
Oh, as a rich man eats a forest for profit and a field for vanity,
    so you came west and raped
The continent and brushed its people to death. Without need,
    the weak skirmishing hunters, and without mercy.

On the knoll by Jeffers's house a spade might turn over the remains of a tribal feast, abalone and clam shells and charcoal from a fire. All around him are the ghosts of Indians who fell easy victims to the white man's ambitions and diseases. He imagines the Carmel River's mouth as a funnel to oblivion, in the center of the final coast, for the migrations that began millennia ago, crossing Asia, Europe, the Atlantic, and finally the North American continent ("Tamar" V, "Loving Shepherdess" VII).

Jeffers is not a regionalist in the usual sense of the word—one who writes intimately of his geographic section, reflecting its genius and foibles, relating its topographic and climatic peculiarities, echoing its idiom and its folk philosophy. The California coast, to him, is not a region; it is a final statement, a metaphysical study. Therein is confronted all of humanity's hopes and illusions and indirections, all of America's violence, rape of land, betrayal of Indians, and pillaging of resources.

Before concluding a discussion of Jeffers, one must come to grips with some of the objections to his writing—not to excuse his failures but to clarify his intent and establish his genre so that criticism may be more justly made. With regard to his narratives, one can merely repeat what has already been said: Jeffers is a tragedian; his intent was to write parables; his goal was to move readers beyond their limits. His stories are structured on a Dionysian process, a life-death ritual. Jeffers's men tend to be Apollonian, stoic, cerebral, presumptuous of their power and plans. His women tend to be Dionysian, sudden, intuitive, destructive—divine agents of change. Readers must be cautioned not to identify Jeffers with his characters; their attitudes and statements rarely or never coincide with his. He has no heroes or heroines, only maimed, stammering "idols." One should also remember the Jeffers warning that his true protagonists are the mountains; his characters are only symbolic interpreters of landscape that itself translates the "outer magnificence" ("My Loved Subject").

As to his lyrics, several additional precautions are in order. Jeffers has many voices, the most prominent of which is that of prophet. A prophet is one obsessed with truth, which he must communicate whatever the bitter consequences. He has a vision of what reality should be, a vision of the holiness in things that people desecrate. He deals in hyperbole. As Flannery O'Connor declares, for those who are almost blind the prophet must write in huge letters; for those who are marginally deaf he must shout. The prophet by definition must shock to communicate. But just as Isaiah did not rant and excoriate all of the time but also cajoled, admonished, comforted, and extolled, so Jeffers has other voices and messages. At times he is pure mystic, praying to his god in the solitude of his tower as in "Night." At other times he is teacher, reasoning and unfolding, suggesting how to live, as in "Signpost" or "The Answer." He can be a discerning philosopher, as in "Theory of Truth." He can even be autobiographic, as in "To His Father," "Ante Mortem," or "The Bed by the Window." He could assume a sort of priesthood over the rituals of nature and celebrate their holiness and rhythms, as in "Salmon-Fishing" and "To the House." He could turn himself inward to purify his art and sharpen his focus, always questioning the validity of his message and examining his poetic talents from the perspective of the stars, as in "Self-Criticism in February" or "Soliloquy." Often his tones take on the gravity of the ecologist, lamenting the imbalance and guilts perpetrated by his nation, or the apocalyptist judging cities the ultimate idolatry and forecasting global purgation.

Jeffers is to be approached with some patience and informed understanding. He cannot be summed up in one poem, nor is he heard well until he has been listened to in several voices. He has often been dismissed by critics and the general reader as a misanthropist, pessimist, or nihilist. Isaiah might fall under the same charges. As one rightly balances the vitriolic rhetoric of the Old Testament prophet's first chapters with his Book of Comfort (Isaiah 40ff.) or his suffering servant songs, so one needs to balance Jeffers's heavier poems like "Summer Holiday" or "Original Sin" with lighter and more positive statements as in "The Excesses of God" or the conclusion of "The Beginning and the End."

Deep within, Jeffers carries a self-contradiction that gives tension to his poetry. On the one hand he espouses an Eastern passivity and inner peace, proclaiming that nothing can be done. War, betrayal, social and political corruption are variations on a natural process of decay that inevitably follows the cresting of a nation's vitality and idealism. He can pronounce this process "not blameworthy" as in "Shine, Perishing Republic." On the other hand he can, and most often does, deal with these facts of life with a heavy prophetic hand. Although he rejects the savior syndrome, he acts in many ways as the redeemer whom he parodies in the narrative of that title, "here on the mountain making/ Antitoxin for all the happy towns and farms, the lovely blameless children, the terrible/ Arrogant cities."

At times he seems to reject not only American life but the life of the race as well. Yet he cannot escape his roots; he is ever paying his "birth-dues" uncovering wisdom for his people. The westering experience is the exemplar of all journeys. Western motifs, and he uses them all, give him vehicles for a larger philosophizing. The continent's end provides a yardstick to measure the divine cosmos.

Survey of Criticism

The initial critical response to Jeffers was awe at his strength and at the headlong quality of his stories. His verse was recognized as original and as an excellent vehicle for his themes. The themes themselves were mostly misunderstood. In "Tamar" Jeffers was doing in some ways what T. S. Eliot accomplished in "The Waste Land"—a myth-ritual reflection on his times. Jeffers, however, provided no footnotes, and his work was judged according to holdover criteria from nineteenth-century realism and naturalism. To readers and critics "Tamar" was a revolting but fascinating story of incest, and "Roan Stallion" was the tale of a woman in love with a horse.

Alex Vardamis's annotated checklist of reviews, articles, and books, *The Critical Reputation of Robinson Jeffers* (1972), re-creates the critical situation rather well. Through the late 1920s and the 1930s Jeffers was mostly praised for the wrong reasons and condemned for equally wrong ones. His admirers saw him as the ultimate in romanticism. Benjamin De Casseres's *The Superman in America* (1926) is typical. Jeffers was the greatest American literary genius since Whitman and compared favorably with Shakespeare, Dante, Aeschylus, and other giants. He received special handling in booklet essays by George Sterling (*Robinson Jeffers*, 1926) and Louis Adamic (*Robinson Jeffers*, 1929).

But by 1932 Jeffers's critical reputation had reached its zenith. Surprise was gone. The grimness of his view of the world began to pall. Early enthusiasms, like seeds fallen on shallow ground, flourished only briefly. By then mainline critics had begun to cool their accolades and withdraw their support, even their interest. The decade was a time of social unrest and of a politically conscious public. Jeffers was attacked for his general pessimism and for his lack of social involvement. At the extreme he was condemned by those with Marxist leanings as an example of the effete leisure class, living off money not his own and betraying a decadent lust for cruelty and a propensity for fascism. New humanists found him revolting, maudlin, and lacking in any value structure. New critics ignored him as cloddish, below notice. The religious press rejected what they saw as vulgar, obscene, and pagan. And so it went.

In 1932 Lawrence Clark Powell published a doctoral dissertation that he reedited as the first substantial and balanced introduction to the poet, *Robinson Jeffers, The Man and His Work* (1934). S. S. Alberts's *A Bibliography of the Works of Robinson Jeffers*, a comprehensive and precise compilation of publication data and primary resource material, followed in 1933. These beginnings in Jeffers scholarship were followed by a vacuum. Between Powell's 1934 edition and Radcliffe Squires's *The Loyalties of Robinson Jeffers* (1956), nothing of note appeared. The poet had all but disappeared from serious critical view. Indeed there were three books on Jeffers in this twelve-year hiatus, but they were slight—Rudolph Gilbert's absurdly lyrical tribute, *Shine, Perishing Republic* (1936); Melba Bennett's amateur attempt at psychology and criticism, *Robinson Jeffers and the Sea* (1936); and William Van Wyck's very slight encomium, *Robinson Jeffers* (1938). Jeffers's unpopularity meanwhile had been compounded by a new element in his stern vision. In the early 1930s Jeffers felt the groundswell of a new general war that fast became his obsession. His pained and caustic poetic outcries were always several leaps ahead of the reading public's comprehension of political realities, and Jeffers's work was judged pessimistic ranting. The crushing blow to his career came with his postwar publication of *The Double Age* (1948). America had won the war, had developed the atomic bomb and dropped it, and stood ready to police the globe. Jeffers condemned the war as a pointless tragedy, refused to rejoice in victory, and stridently warned of the folly of the new big brotherism. He was universally condemned.

Squires's *The Loyalties of Robinson Jeffers* (1956) represents the first in-depth analysis of Jeffers's philosophical and cultural wellsprings—the relation of his poetry to his temperament, to philosophy and science, and to the work of other writers. This book was followed by another thoughtful study of Jeffers's philosophical context, Mercedes Monjian's *Robinson Jeffers: A Study in Inhumanism* (1958). Again there followed a ten-year gap. Frederic Carpenter's *Robinson Jeffers* (1962) was a superior effort of consolidation and analysis, but its purpose was more like Powell's—an introduction to Jeffers's life and times, philosophy, and literary genres.

The decade 1968-78 was a rich one for Jeffers scholarship. William Everson, then the Dominican Brother Antoninus, brought Jungian insights to Jeffers's work in a somewhat tortured but fresh and insightful way in his *Robinson Jeffers: Fragments of an Older Fury* (1968). The year 1968 also marked a change in the *Robinson Jeffers Newsletter* (Occidental College, 1962—) toward a more academic format. It was to become not only a clearinghouse for "news and notes" but a vehicle for serious articles, memoirs, explications, reviews, bibliographical studies, and a series of Una Jeffers's letters. In 1969 the public was reintroduced to the poet through the paperback edition of *Not Man Apart*, a stunning photobook by the Sierra Club using Jeffers's poetry. *Jeffers Country* with photos by Horace Lyon and lyrics by Jeffers followed two years later. Arthur Coffin's *Robinson Jeffers: Poet of Inhumanism* (1970) completed and expanded upon what Squires had done, relating the poet rather strikingly with Nietzsche, Schopenhauer, and Lucretius. Robert Brophy's *Robinson Jeffers: Myth, Ritual, and Symbol* (1973) explored the mythic dimensions to the narratives and Jeffers's use of sacrificial and sacramental rituals. In 1975 came two Everett/Edwards cassette studies and three books. William Hotchkiss's *Robinson Jeffers: The Sivaistic Vision* (1975) reassessed the objections of Jeffers's major critics, examined Jeffers's philosophy and mysticism, and gave selected poems a close reading. Brophy's pamphlet *Robinson Jeffers* (1975), in the meantime, tried to set Jeffers in focus as a western writer, and Kenneth White's *The Coast Opposite Humanity* (1975) analyzed the California writer from a contemporary English poet's vantage point.

These works were followed by two more substantive books. Marlan Beilke's rather eccentric but thorough volume, *Shining Clarity* (1977), reviewed Jeffers's entire canon to point up his religious themes and philosophical development, while William Nolte's strongly reasoned and lucid *Rock and Hawk* (1978) reexamined and carefully redefined Jeffers's romanticism.

Although there is not yet a standard collected edition of Robinson Jeffers even in preparation, editing of Jeffers has gone apace with the later criticism. William

Everson has been a pioneer in this area, ferreting out manuscripts at Yale and the University of Texas and, with close detective reasoning, presenting thesis after thesis as to influences and patterns of development, especially for the crucial years between *Flagons and Apples* and *Tamar*. His introductions have been particularly enlightening—in the New Directions *Cawdor/Medea*, and in his Cayucos editions of *Californians*, *The Alpine Christ*, and *Brides of the South Wind*, and also in his reedition of *The Double Axe* (Liveright, 1977). His treatment of Jeffers as a pivotal figure in California literary history in "Archetype West" is also seminal and influential.

Bibliographic studies abound. Although the scholar's world still awaits an updating of Alberts's *Bibliography* (1933), stop-gap descriptive checklists are available. Covington Rodgers's Jeffers section of *First Printings of American Authors* (1978) brings Jeffers's book publication up to 1978, as does the slightly flawed but useful *The First Editions of Robinson Jeffers* (1978) by Robert Harmon. Checklists by Brophy (1976) and Rodgers (1977) in the *Robinson Jeffers Newsletter* have identified Jeffers's prose and poetry, a project that Robb Kafka's "Robinson Jeffers' Published Writings, 1903-1911" (1979) completes. The *Robinson Jeffers Newsletter* is currently running a series, "Jeffers Scholarly Resources," which itemizes and describes, library by library, holdings in Jeffers manuscripts and other source materials. From this listing will come shortly a directory to his manuscripts.

Bibliography

Works by Robinson Jeffers

Flagons and Apples. Los Angeles: Grafton, 1912
Californians. New York: Macmillan, 1916.
Tamar and Other Poems. New York: Peter G. Boyle, 1924.
Roan Stallion, Tamar and Other Poems. New York: Boni and Liveright, 1925.
The Women at Point Sur. New York: Boni and Liveright, 1927.
Cawdor and Other Poems. New York: Liveright, 1928.
Dear Judas and Other Poems. New York: Liveright, 1929.
Descent to the Dead. New York: Random House, 1931.
Thurso's Landing and Other Poems. New York: Liveright, 1932.
Give Your Heart to the Hawks and Other Poems. New York: Random House, 1933.
Solstice and Other Poems. New York: Random House, 1935.
Such Counsels You Gave to Me and Other Poems. New York: Random House, 1937.
The Selected Poetry of Robinson Jeffers. New York: Random House, 1938.
Be Angry at the Sun. New York: Random House, 1941.
Medea. New York: Random House, 1946.
The Double Axe and Other Poems. New York: Random House, 1948.
Poetry, Gongorism and a Thousand Years. Los Angeles: Ward Ritchie, 1949.
Hungerfield and Other Poems. New York: Random House, 1954.
Themes in My Poems. San Francisco: Book Club of California, 1956.
The Beginning and the End and Other Poems. New York: Random House, 1963.

Robinson Jeffers: Selected Poems. New York: Vintage, Random House, 1965.
The Selected Letters of Robinson Jeffers. Ed. Ann N. Ridgeway. Baltimore: Johns Hopkins, 1968.
The Alpine Christ and Other Poems. N.p.: Cayucos Books, 1974.
Brides of the South Wind: Poems 1917-1922. N.p.: Cayucos Books, 1974.
In This Wild Water: The Suppressed Poems of Robinson Jeffers. Ed. with extensive commentary by James Shebl. Los Angeles: Ward Ritchie, 1976.
What Odd Expedients and Other Poems. Hamden, Conn.: Shoestring, 1981.

Studies of Robinson Jeffers

Adamic, Louis. *Robinson Jeffers: A Portrait*. Seattle: University of Washington Bookstore, 1929.
Alberts, Sydney S. *A Bibliography of the Works of Robinson Jeffers*. New York: Random House, 1933.
Beilke, Marlan. *Shining Clarity: God and Man in the Works of Robinson Jeffers*. Amador City, Calif.: Quintessence, 1977.
Bennett, Melba. *Robinson Jeffers and the Sea*. San Francisco: Gelber, 1936.
––––––. *The Stone Mason of Tor House*. Los Angeles: Ward Ritchie, 1966.
Brophy, Robert J. "The Prose of Robinson Jeffers: An Annotated Checklist." *Robinson Jeffers Newsletter* 46 (September 1976): 14-36.
––––––. *Robinson Jeffers*. WWS. Boise, Idaho: Boise State University, 1975.
––––––. *Robinson Jeffers: Myth, Ritual and Symbol in His Narrative Poems*. Cleveland: Case Western Reserve, 1973.
Carpenter, Frederic I. *Robinson Jeffers*. New York: Twayne, 1962.
Coffin, Arthur. *Robinson Jeffers: Poet of Inhumanism*. Madison: University of Wisconsin, 1971.
DeCasseres, Benjamin. *The Superman in America*. Seattle: University of Washington Bookstore, 1926.
Everson, William [Brother Antoninus]. "Archetype West." *Regional Perspectives*. Ed. John G. Burke. Chicago: American Library Association, 1973.
––––––. *Robinson Jeffers: Fragments of an Older Fury*. Berkeley: Oyez, 1968.
Gilbert, Rudolph. *Shine, Perishing Republic: Robinson Jeffers and the Tragic Sense in Modern Poetry*. Boston: Humphries, 1936.
Harmon, Robert. *The First Editions of Robinson Jeffers*. Los Altos, Calif.: Hermes, 1978.
Hotchkiss, William. *Robinson Jeffers: The Sivaistic Vision*. Auburn, Calif.: Blue Oak, 1975.
Kafka, Robb. "Robinson Jeffers' Published Writings, 1903-1911." *Robinson Jeffers Newsletter* 53 (June 1979): 47-68.
Monjian, Mercedes. *Robinson Jeffers: A Study in Inhumanism*. Pittsburgh: University of Pittsburgh, 1958.
Nolte, William. *Rock and Hawk: Robinson Jeffers and the Romantic Agony*. Athens: University of Georgia, 1978.
Powell, Lawrence Clark. *Robinson Jeffers: The Man and His Work*. Los Angeles: Primavera, 1934.
Rodgers, Covington. "A Checklist of Robinson Jeffers' Poetical Writings since 1934." *Robinson Jeffers Newsletter* (March 1977): 11-24.
––––––, and Brophy, Robert. "Robinson Jeffers." *First Printings of American Authors*. Ed. Richard Layman. Detroit: Gale, 1978.

Squires, James Radcliffe. *The Loyalties of Robinson Jeffers*. Ann Arbor: University of
    Michigan, 1956.
Sterling, George. *Robinson Jeffers: The Man and the Artist*. New York: Boni and Liveright,
    1926.
Van Wyck, William. *Robinson Jeffers*. Los Angeles: Ward Ritchie, 1938.
Vardamis, Alex. *The Critical Reputation of Robinson Jeffers*. Hamden, Conn.: Archon,
    1972.
White, Kenneth. *The Coast Opposite Humanity*. Dyfed, Wales: Unicorn, 1975.

Judy Alter

DOROTHY M. JOHNSON
(1905-)

Biography

Dorothy Johnson once told an interviewer, "Anytime I write anything that isn't the West of the 19th Century, I'm sort of off my trail" (Smith, "The Years, the Wind and the Rain," p. 139). Although the bulk of her work is firmly rooted in the American West, particularly her home state of Montana, she is not quite a native westerner. Born in Iowa on 19 December 1905, Dorothy Marie Johnson moved to Montana early enough to absorb its culture and traditions. Home was Whitefish, a railroad town some forty miles south of the Canadian border in heavily timbered mountains, where Johnson lived from the time she was six until she went to college. She has never claimed her Whitefish childhood as background for her writing, pointing out that the old-timers in Whitefish never told Indian stories but always talked about railroad wrecks and that the traditional attitude toward Indians was that they were all bad (Arthur, "Straight Talk," p. 5). Still, one suspects that she developed there her western attitude toward character, her admiration of courage, strength, and friendliness.

Although Johnson recalls giving up writing after one or two attempts, marred by spelling difficulties, when she was very young, she did write in high school, publishing poetry in the yearbook and, with a friend, writing a farce, "The Lively Life of Leon," with a popular classmate as the hero. At the University of Montana, she majored in English and turned her attention seriously to writing. Her education was interrupted briefly by illness, but she graduated with a record of several poems and short stories published in the campus magazine, the *Frontier*. During her college years, her attention turned from poetry to prose: "I suddenly became *not* a poet. I began to think differently. I began to think in terms of short stories. It all had to do with the emotions or the expression of emotion. Somehow, the channeling of my emotion changed to short stories" (Smith, "The Years," p. 59). Her biographer, Stephen Smith, suggests that her interest also focused on western subjects during this time because of the influence of Professor Harold G. Merriam, who edited the *Frontier* and was strongly

interested in regional literature (Smith, "The Years," pp. 58-59). Johnson dedicated her first collection of short stories, *Indian Country* (1953), to Merriam.

After college, Johnson's achievement as a writer is due perhaps equally to
perseverance and talent. Through a variety of jobs in Washington, Wisconsin,
and New York, she kept writing, without the reward of publication. Finally in
1930 a short story, "Bonnie George Campbell," was accepted by the *Saturday
Evening Post*. She was paid $400, a large sum at the time, for a story that brings
together the lines from an English ballad and Johnson's impression of a rodeo she
had attended on an Indian reservation.

Publication of "Bonnie George Campbell" seemed to assure her future, or so
Johnson thought at age twenty-four; she had no way of knowing that it would be
eleven years before she sold another story. Meantime she took another job as a
secretary, this time to the advertising manager of a paper-converting company in
Wisconsin, writing direct mail copy about waxed paper and butter cartons. A
move to New York followed in 1935, when she accepted a position with Gregg
Publishing Company. For the next fifteen years, New York was her home. She
advanced to advertising manager at Gregg, then became managing editor of the
Woman, a digest magazine for which she wrote countless articles under a variety
of pseudonyms.

Johnson loved New York City and used all of its opportunities to advantage.
In its museums and libraries, she spent hours learning the facts about the West
she knew by intuition. She has said that the accuracy of her portrayal of the life
of the Plains Indians came from this intensive study. But she did not love the
people of New York. She found they "just did not act like the kind of human
beings I was raised among in Montana" (Smith, "The Years," p. 142). Johnson
devoted most of her free time to writing. She tried a novel to prove to herself
she could write at length. The 90,000-word manuscript was never published, and
her fiction career seemed likely to end with one major publication.

Then in 1940 she wrote four stories about a meddling spinster schoolteacher in
an imaginary little town in Washington. The *Saturday Evening Post* bought
them all, and this time her career was indeed launched. She wrote several more
stories about Beulah Bunny, and, in 1942, a collection of those stories became her
first book, *Beulah Bunny Tells All*. Within a brief time, she was established as a
short story author. Her production was high, and her work was published in the
Post, Seventeen, Argosy, Collier's, Cosmopolitan, and others. In the early 1950s,
she left New York, returning briefly to Whitefish as a reporter and photographer
for the local paper, then moving to Missoula as secretary of the Montana Press
Association and assistant professor of journalism. She continued to write short
stories.

But by the late 1950s, the short story market was dying. After some hesitation,
Johnson turned to the juvenile field. Over the next sixteen years, she published
nine books for young readers, most on western subjects but three devoted to
Greece, a land she had come to love during several trips there. Ill health forced
her to slow her pace in the late 1960s. Faced with the choice of resigning her

position with the press association or giving up writing, she quit her job. "I couldn't quit writing," she has explained. "That was what I was working for" (Smith, "The Years," p. 298).

Two novels, both published in the late 1970s, mark her latest book publications to date, although in 1980 she is at work on a non-Western novel, *The Unbombed*, based on her experiences as an air raid warden in New York City during World War II.

Major Themes

Selecting Johnson's most significant works is complicated by the wide range of her writing. Her publications, sixteen books and numerous articles and short stories, include fiction and nonfiction, history and biography, much set in the West but enough based in Greece, New York, and other locales to blur her distinction as a western writer. Still, many consider her the dean of women writers of western fiction, and her literary reputation, which outstrips her popularity in the marketplace, rests solidly on the western works. Any judgment is subjective, but her most important works appear to be the two collections of previously published short stories, *Indian Country* and *The Hanging Tree* (1957), and two later novels, *Buffalo Woman* (1977) and *All The Buffalo Returning* (1979).

Three of the stories from the two collections were made into movies, and two of those, "A Man Called Horse," and "The Hanging Tree," illustrate the basic themes found in both collections. Johnson wrote "A Man Called Horse" after reading Robert Lowie's *The Crow Indians*. The Crow way of life became so real to her that she felt that she could have lived in a Crow camp; then she wondered how someone would have survived without reading the book (Arthur, "Straight Talk," p. 6). The story places a neurotic tenderfoot, totally ignorant of Indian ways, as a captive in an Indian camp and follows his growing self-confidence as he builds himself an honored place within the camp.

Johnson insists that the hero did not find character in his experience as a captive. "You can only get acquainted with what's in yourself if you have something to begin with" (Arthur, "Straight Talk," p. 7). Of a book with a similar plot in which a man makes a grueling journey to find himself and returns unsatisfied, she wrote: "I cannot pity this empty man. He exasperates me...his world is blank. I cannot accept such heresy. Nobody's world is that bad" ("A Fruitless Search for the Meaning of Life," *New York Herald Tribune Book Review*, 24 April 1960, p. 11). Johnson likes strong people, those who can survive hardship, and she tests them against the challenges of frontier life—a hostile landscape and a bitter clash between two cultures. She believes in such virtues as courage, honor, and integrity, and she brings these values to life in characters like Horse. Her impatience with those who have a weak character perhaps in part explains her fascination with the West of the last century: she admires the people who survived there. An interviewer once suggested that she writes of people with "no obvious claim to distinction." She was quick to reply that her people "have no claim to distinction except that they all have strength" (Arthur, "Straight Talk," p. 1). For Dorothy Johnson, the West is not only a geographical area and a special time, but more importantly, a state of mind.

Another of Johnson's themes, the clash between two cultures, is defined in "A Man Called Horse" by the captive's inability to understand Indian ways. In this instance, that clash is overcome by his gradual adaptation to Indian life. In some stories, that adaptation is never accomplished. In "Lost Sister," a story based on the recapture of Cynthia Ann Parker, or in "Journey to the Fort," a captivity story, characters, most of them white people, remain locked into their way of life, with no understanding of the other culture. Johnson develops an ability to see the world through Indian eyes, and she often makes the point strongly that the Indian world was a civilization with an order and pattern to its existence, even though most whites are unable to appreciate it. Clash between the two is inevitable in Johnson's work, given the circumstances of the frontier, but there is never an assumption on her part that one culture was superior to the other.

"A Man Called Horse" is distinguished, as are all Johnson's western works, by accuracy of detail. Her years of research in New York are evident in the reality she brings to the frontier world. One reviewer, writing of this short story, makes the point clear:

Miss Johnson treats her subject with the respect it deserves, and the rest takes care of itself. When she tells you that a Crow Indian brave wouldn't think of talking to his mother-in-law, you believe her. You get the full odor of the plains; the good smells and the foul smells...and best of all, the Indians...become beings of flesh and blood. [Johnson to Judy Alter, 16 March 1979].

Her characteristic brevity of style is also evident in "A Man Called Horse." Noted for economy of treatment and concentration of dramatic effect, Johnson has an incisive way of condensing an entire story into a paragraph, then spinning out the story behind that paragraph. Witness this early passage from "A Man Called Horse," describing the easterner who went west in search of his equals: "On a day in June, he learned what it was to have no status at all. He became a captive of a small raiding party of Crow Indians" (p. 181). In his foreword to *Indian Country*, the western novelist Jack Schaefer wrote, "The stories move, flow forward with swift, at times almost racing, vigor, and then, like a nugget in the rewarding ore, comes the sudden singing sentence that implies more than it says and gives depth and meaning to the whole."

The same brevity of style characterizes "The Hanging Tree," although Johnson moves from the clash of cultures to a psychological study of the strengths and weaknesses of individuals. This novelette is probably her most complex work. The story involves a strange triangle: Doc Joe Frail, an embittered, cynical, and almost desperate physician, playing the role of a dangerous gambler but, in truth, incapable of firing his pistol; Rune, a young would-be robber indebted to Frail for his life but bitterly resentful of his savior; and Elizabeth, an eastern girl who survives a stagecoach robbery (in which her father is killed) and exposure to the desert only to develop a phobic fear of open spaces. When a religious fanatic incites the mining town of Skull Creek against Elizabeth, Frail, who has come to love her, shoots the appropriately named Grubb and faces the hanging tree at the hands of an unruly mob of miners. Elizabeth, held prisoner in her cabin for months by her fears, finds the strength to leave and walk to the hanging scene, where she scatters gold nuggets for the miners who forget all about hanging Frail as they scramble for the treasure.

Arthur suggests that both characters here learn "that the essential for contented survival is acceptance of the need for mutual dependence" (*Hanging Tree*, p. xi). The bonds between people are more important than individual needs, and the strength of Johnson's characters is never diminished by their need for each other but, instead, enhanced by the sacrifices they make. The same phenomenon is seen in "A Man Called Horse" when Horse postpones his chance at freedom because it would mean abandoning his Indian mother-in-law to poverty and homelessness. This theme of sacrifice is important in many of Johnson's stories because, as she herself has said, she admires people capable of sacrifice and change (Mathews and Healy, "Winning of the Western Market," p. 161).

"The Hanging Tree" also illustrates a plot device that Johnson uses frequently. She calls it "the switch," defining it as turning a situation around and looking at it from another angle. Sometimes referring to this as "iffing," she asks herself "What if. . . ?" and arrives, for instance, at "What if it were a woman stranded in the desert instead of a man?" Johnson, who has said she cannot build a story but has to find one, found the base for "The Hanging Tree" in two movies she saw of men stranded in the desert. She began to wonder about a woman in such a situation, and the pity she felt for this imaginary woman gave rise to "The Hanging Tree" (Arthur, "Straight Talk," p. 7).

The same brevity of style characterizes the two later novels, *Buffalo Woman* and *All The Buffalo Returning*, but these works have a straightforward story line without the twist of the short stories. *Buffalo Woman* follows the life of a Lakota woman from childhood to her death of old age and starvation on the long foot journey north to a Canadian haven. Buffalo Woman is an ideal Indian woman, strong with courage and ability, skilled at the tasks performed by women, proud of her culture and community. As a child, she is a member of a prosperous family and lives a comfortable life; in her final days, she is part of a ragged and homeless band. Her final act is one of courage and strength: she starves herself to death, giving her food and life and strength to her hungry people.

All The Buffalo Returning, the sequel, begins with the Lakotas miserably settled in Canada for a brief period before they return to this country and life on a reservation. The focus of the book is Stormy, Buffalo Woman's grandson, who is educated at an Indian school in the East and inevitably is caught between two cultures, comfortable neither in the white world nor the Indian one. Stormy finally recovers his faith and his sense of himself as an Indian when he travels to Pine Ridge with his family for Wovoka's Ghost Dance. The book ends with the massacre at Wounded Knee, where Stormy and his family are killed. Dying, Stormy realizes he will be with Buffalo Woman and the others in the Land of Many Lodges. Both books end with defeat and death, but that death equals spiritual renewal for the characters. Like all of Johnson's other work, these two novels are affirmative. They tell of strong people who meet with pride and dignity the challenges life throws at them. Both books illustrate Johnson's facility for seeing the Indian world as a developed civilization and for presenting the Indian view of the white world. And, finally, both novels are firmly grounded in an accurate historical picture of the disintegration of Indian culture in the last quarter of the nineteenth century. Johnson creates a sense of the inevitable passing of time toward a foreordained conclusion so that Buffalo Woman is not only distinctive as an individual but is seen as part of a larger pattern.

Buffalo Woman demonstrates another aspect of Johnson's work that has been praised by reviewers: the presentation of women on the western frontier. Western literature is so often male oriented that woman characters tend to be underdeveloped and, frequently, uninteresting. Johnson's women, like Buffalo Woman, are strong and determined, fully developed fictional characters. Her economical style enables her to bring them into full relief with a sentence or a detail that gives them life. There are memorable women throughout the short stories: Mrs. Foster in "Journey to the Fort," who survives Indian captivity, all the time uncertain of the fate of her daughter; Mary Amanda in "Flame on the Frontier," who chooses to remain with her Indian husband and son when the long-awaited chance for freedom comes; Bessie, the reluctantly recaptured woman in "Lost Sister," who finds her white family alien and who, in the end, sacrifices herself for her Indian son. The list could go on and on. One of Johnson's juvenile anthologies, *Some Went West* (1967), is devoted to stories of real women on the frontier, both the famous and the obscure.

The elements of these few works—brevity of style, accuracy of historical background, and, most of all, a positive affirmation of the strength of ordinary men and women and of the bonds between them—characterize all of Johnson's work in one way or another. They are strong in her biography of Sitting Bull and her collection of the lives of famous lawmen; they appear, by negative implication, in her account of the lives of famous badmen.

Finally, there is in much of Johnson's work a strong thread of humor, although it is least evident in the western short stories and later novels. At its most outrageous in a collection, *The Bedside Book of Bastards* (1973), it appears subtly in juvenile works: "Flat irons are sometimes called sad irons. You can figure out why" (*Some Went West*, p. 159). It is almost outright laughter in the Beulah Bunny stories, emerging in Miss Bunny's unorthodox approach to life: "I'm free to poke into other people's business whenever my conscience will allow and my conscience is pretty elastic in that respect" (*Beulah Bunny Tells All*, p. 4). And it is often an integral part of the nonfiction.

The use of prose rhythms to create not only humor but a variety of emotions is one of Johnson's major stylistic devices. In the opening of "The Last Boast," a short story, she uses it to create tension: "When the time came for them to die, Pete Gossard cursed and Knife Hilton cried, but Wolfer Joe Kennedy yawned in the face of the hangman" (*The Hanging Tree*, p. 24). In "Flame on the Frontier," prose rhythms emphasize the horror of a massacre:

On Sunday morning, wearing white man's sober clothing, a Sioux chief named Little Crow attended the church service at the Lower Agency and afterward shook hands with the preacher. On Sunday afternoon, Little Crow's painted and feathered Santee Sioux swooped down on the settlers in bloody massacre. There was no warning. [*Indian Country*, p. 1]

Invariably, her use of rhythm and sound in the language gives impact to the opening of a story, as the first lines of "A Time of Greatness" illustrate: "I was ten years old the summer I worked for old Cal Crawford. For years afterward I remembered it as a time of terror. I had grown up before I understood it had been a time of greatness, too" (*The Hanging Tree*, p. 71).

Survey of Criticism

Critical studies on Johnson's work are relatively scarce. She has recently been included in the Boise Western Writers Series, published by Boise State University in Idaho, in a sixty-page pamphlet by Judy Alter, *Dorothy M. Johnson* (1980), that presents a critical survey of her career, a brief biographical description, and a short summary of critical material available.

A study of major themes in Johnson's work, "A Thematic Analysis of Dorothy Johnson's Fiction" (1971), was written as a master's thesis by Elizabeth Ann James. James limits her study to the collected western short stories, in which she finds three basic themes: a clash between two cultures, one man's search, and an affirmation of humanity. However, Johnson, who dislikes attributing symbolism to an author who did not intend it in the story, is in disagreement with the interpretations of James, who writes "an author's intentions are not a valid guide for the interpretation of what he has said in a written work" ("A Thematic Analysis," p. 87). James's work is of value for her insight into such stylistic matters as Johnson's compressed style and her appreciation of Johnson's high value for the links between people.

Both James's work and the only biography of Johnson are limited by date. Written in the late 1960s, both omit more than ten productive years of her career. Nonetheless, Stephen Smith's biography, "The Years, the Wind and the Rain" (1969), is the most useful and interesting study yet available on the author. A detailed and lengthy work of over three hundred typewritten pages, Smith's biography relies heavily on interviews with Johnson, and also reprints, in their entirety, several major book reviews. Although there is some attempt at critical appraisal of the work, Smith's purpose clearly is biographical, and his greatest achievement is in presenting Dorothy Johnson as an individual and as an author with a definite approach to the craft of fiction.

Probably the best critical work to date on Johnson is that done by Anthony Arthur. Two of Arthur's studies were presented to meetings of the Western Literature Association and are, as yet, unpublished; however, most of the material on *The Hanging Tree* is found in his introduction to the Gregg Press edition (1980) of that collection. His analysis of the title story touches briefly on Johnson's earlier career and employs several other stories to argue that she is a storyteller more than a historian. According to Arthur, "The Hanging Tree" most fully develops the twin themes of isolation and community which he finds basic to the western stories. Arthur's 1978 paper, "Straight Talk in Missoula" is an interview in which Johnson reveals her creative methods and, most interestingly, her personality.

Western novelist Jack Schaefer wrote an appreciative introduction to the 1953 edition of *Indian Country* (and Johnson, in turn, wrote the introduction to the 1967 collection, *The Short Novels of Jack Schaefer*). Alter's introduction to the 1979 Gregg Press edition of *Indian Country* attempts a more critical analysis of the themes and successes of that collection. Johnson claims to have found the new introduction thought provoking, though her comments echo her reaction to James's study. She wrote, "It startles me, because what a scholar sees in a literary work is naturally illuminating to the author who had other things in mind when he wrote the stories" (personal letter, Johnson to Judy Alter, 25 April 1979).

Finally, there is an interview by Sue Mathews and James Healy, done in 1977 and published in 1979, "The Winning of the Western Fiction Market," that repeats many of Johnson's artistic theories found elsewhere but adds new insight on her view of the relationship between the western and women.

More thorough critical study of her work will surely come in the future, demanded by Johnson's strength as a regional writer. In that category, she is important because she joins the slim but strong tradition of women who have written about the West: Mary Hallock Foote, Helen Hunt Jackson, Willa Cather, and a few others. As a western writer, she ranks with contemporaries such as Schaefer and A. B. Guthrie, Jr., both of whom she counts as literary friends and whose work she admires. Most of all she must be considered one of today's major regional writers because of the dignity she brings to the western through her affirmative belief in the strength of ordinary people. Johnson's characters, because of their strength, give us once again the ideal that the frontier can symbolize, an ideal of individuality and honor too often missing or blurred in the contemporary western novel.

Bibliography

Works by Dorothy M. Johnson

Beulah Bunny Tells All. New York: William Morrow, 1942.

Indian Country. New York: Ballantine, 1953; Boston: Gregg Press, 1979, with introduction by Judy Alter.

The Hanging Tree. New York: Ballantine, 1957; Boston: Gregg Press, 1980, with intro-
   duction by Anthony Arthur.
Famous Lawmen of the Old West. New York: Dodd, Mead, 1963.
Farewell to Troy. Boston: Houghton Mifflin, 1964.
Greece: Wonderland of the Past and Present. New York: Dodd, Mead, 1964.
Flame on the Frontier. New York: Dodd, Mead, 1967.
Some Went West. New York: Dodd, Mead, 1967.
Witch Princess. Boston: Houghton Mifflin, 1967.
Sitting Bull: Warrior for a Lost Nation. New York: Westminster Press, 1969.
Western Badmen. New York: Dodd, Mead, 1970.
With T. R. Turner. *The Bedside Book of Bastards*. New York: McGraw-Hill, 1973.
The Bloody Bozeman. New York: Dodd, Mead, 1977.
Buffalo Woman, New York: Dodd, Mead, 1977.
Montana. New York: Coward-McCann, 1977.
All the Buffalo Returning. New York: Dodd, Mead, 1979.

Studies of Dorothy M. Johnson

Alter, Judy. *Dorothy M. Johnson*. WWS. Boise: Boise State University, 1980.
Arthur, Anthony. "Straight Talk in Missoula." Paper presented to the Western Literature
   Association, 1978.
James, Elizabeth. "A Thematic Analysis of Dorothy Johnson's Fiction." Master's thesis,
   Colorado State University, 1971.
Mathews, Sue, and Healy, James W., "The Winning of the Western Fiction Market."
   Prairie Schooner 53 (Summer 1979): 158-67.
Schaefer, Jack. Introduction to *Indian Country*. New York: Ballantine, 1953.
Smith, Stephen. "The Years, the Wind and the Rain: A Biography of Dorothy M.
   Johnson." Master's thesis, University of Montana, 1969.

Dorys C. Grover

ELMER KELTON
(1926-)

Biography

It may be somewhat surprising that the child of a cowboy should be artistically inclined and grow up to be a significant western writer, yet that is true of Elmer Kelton. He was born on the Scharbauer Cattle Company's Five Wells Ranch in Andrews County, Texas, on 29 April 1926, where his father R. W. ("Buck") Kelton was a working cowboy. Kelton's mother had been a schoolteacher at the little town of Faskin before she married. In 1929 the family moved to the McElroy Ranch near Crane, where Kelton grew up. His father went to work as a cowboy, became foreman in 1931, and later was general manager of the McElroy Company. When the company was sold and liquidated in 1965, his parents bought a small ranch in Brown County, Texas.

Kelton attended Crane High School where he was an avid reader and where his journalism teacher, Paul Patterson, encouraged him to write. His attendance at the University of Texas, Austin, from 1942 to 1944 was interrupted by two years of army service. While on duty in Austria, he met his wife, Anna; they have three children. He returned to Austin in 1946 and graduated in January 1948 with the bachelor of science degree in journalism. He went to San Angelo as farm and ranch reporter for the *San Angelo Standard Times*, became the agricultural editor, and remained on the staff fifteen years. He spent five years as editor of the *Sheep & Goat Raiser Magazine* in San Angelo and in 1968 joined *West Texas Livestock Weekly* as associate editor, the position he now holds.

Kelton began writing western stories while at the university and during his final semester sold his first story to *Ranch Romances*. He continued to write magazine fiction until the mid-1950s when the short fiction market began to die. At the urging of his New York agent, he began working on a novel, and in 1955 Ballantine Books published *Hot Iron* about a great cattle empire in Texas. By 1974 Ballantine had published paperback editions of sixteen of his novels. He has also written *Shotgun Settlement* (1969) under a house pseudonym, Alex Hawk, for Paperback Library. *Joe Pepper* (1975) and *Long Way to Texas* (1976) were issued under the pseudonym Lee McElroy. Talley Press of San Angelo published *Looking Back West* (1972), a collection of his historical prose written for the *Pioneer News-Observer*, and Doubleday has issued four other novels.

As a youngster, Kelton learned about ranching from firsthand experience, and his works are careful studies of the background, manners, speech, and stories of the settlers who gradually penetrated the Llano Estacado and other parts of Texas. His family, long established in west Texas, gave him an important cultural heritage that he has supplemented by reading history, studying old newspapers, diaries, and journals, and listening to the tales of the old cowboys. His grandfather grew up as a cowboy in Callahan County near Baird, and his great-grandfather had come to west Texas from east Texas in 1875 with a wife, a wagon, and a string of horses.

Kelton says he was never a cowboy, never was good at horseback work, and when he had to ride always took along a book. While managing the McElroy Ranch, his father leased the Lea Ranch in the same area and ran his own cattle. Kelton spent two summers there taking care of his father's cattle, and when he later needed a pseudonym, he chose Lea McElroy. His publisher changed Lea to Lee, fearing Lea might be misread as "Leah." Kelton personally knew many of the drifter type of cowboy, and he had heard his father and others tell stories about old cowboys whose names were household words with his family.

Perhaps a major influence upon Kelton, along with growing up on a ranch among cowboys, was his father, now deceased. Buck Kelton's West was not fictional, for Elmer Kelton says he never read novels or went to movies. Buck Kelton's West was a reality. He had a good memory for detail, Kelton says, and could tell what day of a month of a year something happened, what horse he was riding, who was with him and what horse *he* was riding, including the markings, color, and temperament of the horses and of the men. Kelton says his father was always more interested in characters than in incidents. When Kelton translates his father's tales into fiction, he tries to entertain as well as give some history and insight into the people and their times. In this sense Kelton writes about the kind of people who are his roots, and he has a deep respect for those who settled the country and endured the hardships in that era of frontier settlement.

Besides his father and Paul Patterson, Kelton was largely influenced by his study of folklore under Mody Boatright at the University of Texas and depends considerably upon folklore to add to his stories. He purposely avoids the standard hero-versus-villain plot and centers on the working rancher and the working cowboy in portraying his characters. There are no "walk-downs" in his stories, nor do his main characters ride off into the sunset to a happy future. Unlike Owen Wister or Zane Grey, he does not see the West as a land that purges man of the superficiality and corruption of eastern overcivilization. His West is real, and his characters are worried by the heat, insects, drought, nesters, Indians, cattle rustlers, stray longhorns, and other matters that make life difficult on the cattle frontier. What his characters experience—on the ranches and hardscrabble farms, or in the historic battles of Texas—are plausible incidents. He draws upon Texas and southwestern history to tell about people who might have participated in the famous battles of Goliad, San Jacinto, or the Alamo, and who could have settled in west Texas.

Major Themes

Kelton's basic themes center on the courage and integrity of the cowboy and settler; the ordeals, losses, and successes of his people; the authenticity of his locales; the effect of change upon people and how they meet the challenge of change. In his most recent works, Kelton concentrates on delineation of character. Charlie Flagg, the main character in *The Time It Never Rained* (1973), is a proud and strong man who has a determination to stay on the land. Hugh Hitchcock in *The Day the Cowboys Quit* (1971) is an honest cowboy who feels a man proves himself by his horsemanship and his independence. Hewey Calloway in *The Good Old Boys* (1978) is one of the last of his breed and a true drifter of his time.

Kelton's most recent novel, *The Wolf and the Buffalo* (1980), is a departure from his other westerns. The story is about the black cavalry in Comanche Indian territory on the Texas plains and concerns Gray Horse Running and Gideon Ledbetter, whose lives and destinies cross during the late 1870s. Not many other western writers have given so warm and human a portrayal of blacks, Indians, and Mexicans as Kelton has in his novels.

The cited novels are Kelton's best works. They point to the artistry western American literature can achieve and how, at its best, it concerns a realistic, if painful, depiction of the events, forces, and predicaments human beings are caught in by the often overwhelming forces of western life. Such forces complicate the life of Charlie Flagg, the hard-headed, old-fashioned, proud cow rancher in *The Time It Never Rained*, when a seven-year drought almost ruins him. Set in west Texas in the 1950s, the novel deals with a changing way of ranch life when cattlemen were forced off their land by drought and economic conditions. Old Charlie Flagg refuses to accept government help when everyone else is getting it. He clings to the "man-earns-his-dollar" heritage and is confused by those who declare he is wrong. He is a good, strong man, and Kelton admits there is some of Buck Kelton in the characterization of Charlie Flagg (Lee, "Elmer Kelton: A *PQ* Interview," p. 29).

The landscape is especially important, and for Charlie Flagg, "It was a comforting sight, this country. It was an ageless land where the past was still a living thing and old voices still whispered" and "where a few of the old dreams were not yet dark with tarnish" (*The Time It Never Rained*, p. 9). Charlie often lives in the past, recalling events and incidents that make the country meaningful to him. He calls his ranch Brushy Top after the brushy Concho divide, which runs along the edge of it, and though he does not consider the ranch a large spread, he has fifteen sections of rangeland, some deeded and the rest under lease. Detailed descriptions of horses, cows, people, windmills, sheep, goats, and land are seen through Charlie's mind. He watches a roadrunner and gives the reader a lesson on the bird.

The real villain in the story is the drought. Its persistence year after year forces many of Charlie's neighbors into bankruptcy. Charlie also has family troubles, including a conflict with Tom, his only son. It is in his sympathetic treatment of the Mexicans who work for him that one sees the humanity of Charlie. The novel closes when one morning "the smell of rain brought Charlie suddenly awake" (*Time It Never Rained*, p. 365). Then he remembers the goats have just been sheared. "Let's save these goats," he says (p. 367); but, as is true for most ranchers and farmers, if the elements are not against them, insects, animals, people, and all manner of things cause grief. Charlie loses the goats because when the rain comes, it is a deluge.

The Day the Cowboys Quit concerns the Canadian River cowboy strike of 1883 and relates the grievances of rugged, proud men. One man in particular, Hugh Hitchcock, is torn between his affection and respect for his employer and sympathy and responsibility toward those who look to him for leadership. The novel centers on a bitter, little-known episode in America's past. Everything the cowboy stands for—open space, trust, and freedom—is being challenged and threatened by eastern money and Yankee ways, which have come to the plains spreading suspicion, new rules, and restrictions. Cowboys were proud of their independence and this, Hitchcock feels, started the cowboy strike. Yet "old cowboys in later years argued no end over the causes of the strike, and the starting of it. To each it began in a different place and in a different way" (*The Day the Cowboys Quit*, p. 2). The outcome had great consequences for the Old West.

Many of the episodes in *The Good Old Boys* come from Kelton's reminiscences of his boyhood on the McElroy Ranch, where he heard stories about the 2560-acre homesteads of the first years of the twentieth century. The McElroy Ranch had gradually acquired many of the homesteads, incorporating them into its holdings. Kelton recalls that the pastures and many of the windmills still bore the names of the people who had homesteaded the various parcels of land: Mayfield, Dawson, Porter, and Lodd. His family lived for more than a year on the Mayfield place in a house that had been three or four homestead shacks, hauled there on a wagon, and nailed together to make one fair-sized house. The novel is a semihumorous story about a footloose cowboy, Hewey Calloway, who in 1906, is one of the last of "the good old boys." Set in Upton City, San Angelo, and Midland, Texas, its background is of the homesteader days in which the state of Texas "was betting a man a piddlin parcel of land against three good years of his life, and the odds were against the man" (*The Good Old Boys*, p. 25).

Calloway's brother, Walter, is a farmer in the area. He and his wife, Eve, a strong-minded and capable woman and one of Kelton's best female characters, urge Calloway to give up his wandering way of life and settle down. Calloway owns only what he can pack on his horse, Biscuit, and he has drifted for most of his thirty-eight years. He struggles to find an answer for himself in a new era in the West.

Calloway does not like farming and thinks, "They ought not to allow a plow within a hundred miles of here,. . . unless it was passing through on a freight train with the doors sealed" (*Good Old Boys*, p. 56). There had always been a shortage of rainfall in the region and a lack of water, and Calloway tells his nephew, Cotton, that "the homestead law. . . I say it's wrong to make a man plow out a field to hold his claim. He ought not to rip up land that God has already planted to grass and handed to him as a gift" (p. 57). Events occur that give him a brief interlude of farming after he and a friend, Snort Yarnell, lasso a 1906 automobile, having failed to win a team roping event. In the ensuing action his brother is injured, and Calloway, an honorable man, stays on the farm to complete the cultivation, harvesting, and sale of a crop of hegari, thus saving his brother from losing the homestead. The brief term of farming is apparently enough for Calloway, and though he does leave for old Mexico with Snort Yarnell, time is his persistent enemy.

The major emphasis in the novel is on Calloway's unsuccessful attempt to change. He cannot give up his freedom for a settled life although he knows that most of the good old boys are gone and that his time is changing. This is particularly evident in the characterization of the old-time cowboy drifter, Boy Rasmussen, who drops dead while opening a pasture gate. He is not buried as the pauper he really is; his funeral is paid for by the cowboys of Upton City who donate more to the memory of the old way of life represented by Rasmussen than to the man himself. This realistic view has a quality of nostalgia that infects many who rue the passing of the Old West and its people.

Kelton says he spent two years researching and writing his most recent historical western, *The Wolf and the Buffalo*. The setting is early day Fort Concho, Saint Angela (San Angelo), and the Texas plains stretching from the Concho River to the upper reaches of the Panhandle. It is the period immediately following the Civil War when black troops were sent west to help control the Indians. The novel opens in Comanche country, where eighteen-year-old Gray Horse Running is going through a warrior's initiation, seeking his spiritual power for the life of a man of his tribe, the Comanches, or "the People." Unsuccessful on past trips, this time he returns with the spiritual medicine of the wolf and decorates his war shield with a white lightning streak and a buffalo tail.

Gideon Ledbetter, a freed slave who is a teenager, has faced the handicaps of illiteracy, racial discrimination, and a lifetime of conditioning that has discouraged self-reliance. Forced to leave his home in Louisiana when carpetbaggers take over the old Hayworth plantation during Reconstruction, Ledbetter, accompanied by Jimbo, another ex-slave, starts westward. They encounter a unit of cavalry, and when Jimbo demonstrates his talents as a horse handler, they are persuaded to join the cavalry and are sent to Texas. The Indians call the black troopers "buffalo soldiers" because of "the darkness of their faces and the short, kinky hair that somehow brought to mind the topknot of the buffalo" (*The Wolf and the Buffalo*, p. 43). The story is told principally from the viewpoints of these two characters. The first encounter between Gray Horse and Ledbetter ends in glory for both, although Ledbetter is praised for his cool nerve when actually his horse ran away in the wrong direction.

On two other occasions, Ledbetter fights off the Indians and saves the lives of his friends. Things also go well for Gray Horse so long as he listens to the wolf, but soon the animal seems to turn against him. The two men are alike in many ways, for the black and the Indian had a great deal in common in those days, though few of them seem to have realized it at the time. Kelton, however, puts this thought in Ledbetter's mind.

The battle at Adobe Walls on the Texas high plains, told in bloody detail from the Indian's point of view, results in a major defeat of the Plains Indians who were attempting to drive out the ever-increasing hide hunters, killing off the buffalo. There are several minor themes in the novel, but the author concentrates on the changing frontier and the changing life for the Plains Indians. The story is also one of survival for the black troopers, many of whom die, as do their horses, while they are on an eighty-six-hour patrol without water under a baking July sun.

The black soldiers are looked upon with disdain by the Saint Angela residents, who take their money in gambling dens, saloons, and brothels but who despise them because of their color, although the troopers are charged with protecting them from Indian raids. The bigotry of the townspeople, the hatred of the Indians, and the dislike by white personnel in the higher echelons of the military as well as at the fort, cause many conflicts. It appears that the buffalo soldiers lose even when they win because of their color.

There are several strong minor characters in the story, including Limping Boy, Gray Horse's faithful cousin; Jimbo, Ledbetter's trusted friend; Esau Nettles, a sergeant who recognizes Ledbetter's potential and tries to help him; Hollander, the white officer in charge of the patrols; and Hannah York, a post laundress. Once again Kelton develops a strong female character, as he did with Eve Calloway, who is a determined, strong-minded, and high-tempered woman in *The Good Old Boys*. Hannah York is an attractive and desirable black woman dominated by her old granny. Ledbetter's relationship with Hannah is disappointing to him, but it does make him a more mature person. He attends the post chaplain's school where he learns to read and write, assumes more responsibility, and proves to be a first-rate trooper. The confrontation between Gray Horse and Ledbetter is inevitable, and the proud Comanche demonstrates his courage to his death.

The Wolf and the Buffalo is Kelton's best novel. It re-creates a tumultuous period of history in areas of now heavily populated west Texas that once were known only to the Indians and a few white men. The story revises Hollywood's view of the Indian, who was a truly heroic figure. Kelton neither condemns nor condones the violence and inhumanity of the Indian, black, or white. He simply tells the story and lets the readers judge. He places the officers and their families in living conditions only a little better than those of the black troopers, who face privation and loneliness, and live always on the edge of poverty. The single common suggestion running through the novel is the effect of change upon people and how people meet the challenge of change.

Other novels of significance include *Buffalo Wagons* (1956), which brought Kelton his first Spur Award in 1957 from Western Writers of America, and the Buckalew tetralogy: *Massacre at Goliad* (1965), *After the Bugles* (1967), *Bowie's Mine* (1971), and *Long Way to Texas*. *Buffalo Wagons* concerns the hide hunter Gage Jameson who in 1873 ventures across the Cimarron River in pursuit of the last great buffalo herd. Jameson and his men justify their business in the belief they are advancing civilization by making room for the cowman and the settler.

The Buckalew tetralogy recounts events in Texas history and opens with *Massacre at Goliad*. Joshua Buckalew is moving from Tennessee to Texas by wagon with his brother, Thomas, and Muley Dodd. They settle on a claim on the Colorado River southwest of present-day Austin. The story closes after the massacre at Goliad and the fall of the Alamo. Joshua and Muley are among the surviviors of San Jacinto in the second novel, *After the Bugles*, and with Ramon Hernandez they begin the long ride back to their home on the Colorado River.

Daniel Provost, a minor youthful character in *After the Bugles*, appears as the main character in *Bowie's Mine*. Daniel is helping his father on a Colorado River farm. One day Milo Seldom rides to the farm leading a string of pack mules loaded with contraband tobacco, which he plans to sell across the Mexican border. Proceeds from the sale are to finance Seldom's trip to find Jim Bowie's silver mine in the Indian country. Kelton draws upon old legends and folklore about the lost mines on the San Sabá where the Spaniards had built their mission and fort. The legend is that Jim Bowie found the mine, then lost it, and many have searched for it since. Daniel joins Seldom, finds adventure but not the mine, and leaves the legend to others.

In *Long Way to Texas*, the hero, Lieutenant David Buckalew, son of Joshua, finds himself in the territory of New Mexico in 1862, fighting a Union cavalry unit and the Indians in an attempt to transport to the Confederate troops a Union ammunition supply train he has commandeered. The fact he finally must admit is that it is too far to Texas.

Along with many other western writers, including Eugene Manlove Rhodes, Willa Cather, Conrad Richter, Harvey Fergusson, and Mary Austin, Kelton is selective in the handling of his story. Although life in his novels is far from pleasant and the ranching and military atmosphere is often bleak, there is little violence for violence's sake. Bitter adversaries shoot each other over land and cattle and horses but rarely over women.

There are those who seem to believe that all western novels are sensational, gun-slinging shoot-outs, assuming they are little more than formula good guy versus bad guy versions of the same stories their parents and grandparents read years ago. Kelton's stories have the flavor and drama of the West without the melodrama and sentiment, and their authenticity warrants closer inspection. The qualities that set his stories apart from the two-gun epics of the pulp magazines are restraint, selectiveness, use of history and folklore, an attention to surface details, and a close narrative structure that gives these details a texture of style. Kelton enlivens and reshapes his stories of the West by his treatment of pride, loyalty, endurance, and courage.

Many of his characters who face ordeals and challenges fail. In fact, many of the worthy fall by the way, yet these people are ennobled for at least facing the challenge, whether or not they eventually win. Hardship, too, is a fact of life in the West, and it is usually overcome through hard work. The Buckalews, Provosts, Flaggs, and Calloways all undergo what today is considered extreme hardship, although they probably did not think of it as that at the time. Essential too is the character who must overcome his enemies—human, animal, or nature— by his efforts and courage; otherwise he is not a true western man or a self-made man.

Kelton's characters, rather than undergoing a westernizing process, are already natives; their locales are ordinary places, and their history is being made by men and women who have come to build the land. These people live and die in a land that is at once hostile and marvelous to them.

Survey of Criticism

Many realistic and worthy books about the West have been ignored by critics who take conventions and clichés of the western story for granted. Writers of real talent such as Eugene Manlove Rhodes and Mary Austin have passed almost unnoticed, as has Kelton. A few recent studies of Kelton's work deserve mention. The first complete survey is that of Dorys C. Grover, "Elmer Kelton and the Popular Western Novel" (1978), who finds Kelton's three most recent novels, *The Time It Never Rained, The Day the Cowboys Quit,* and *The Good Old Boys,* to be his best. Grover also notes that the Buckalew tetralogy is significant for its relating of a family to the major historical events of Texas, and the novel, *Manhunters* (1974), receives attention because of Kelton's sympathetic treatment of the Mexicans. The story is based on an actual event that occurred in Karnes County, Texas, and illustrates how frontier justice is enforced by the Texas Rangers.

In "The End of the West Motif in the Work of Edward Abbey, Jane Kramer, and Elmer Kelton" (1979), Lawrence Clayton has briefly compared Kelton's *The Good Old Boys* with novels by Edward Abbey and Jane Kramer, finding the work a departure from the formula Western in that Kelton's characters represent the "transition to more contemporary modes of life and thought" (p. 15). A journalistic account is that of Carlton Stowers, "Tale of a Typewriter Cowboy" (1974), who finds that Kelton ignores myths in favor of a fictionalized history. The article briefly surveys Kelton's life and selected novels and concludes that his fiction departs from stereotyped Westerns.

Kelton has received a number of honors and awards. In 1977 he received the Golden Saddleman trophy at the Western Writers of America convention in Oklahoma City, an award that recognizes an author's complete work. Besides

Buffalo Wagons, two other novels have won him Spur awards: *The Day the Cowboys Quit* in 1973 (which in 1972 was named the Best Southwest Novel of the Year by the Border Regional Library Association), and *The Time It Never Rained* in 1974. The latter novel and *The Good Old Boys* are winners of the Western Heritage Award from the National Cowboy Hall of Fame. Kelton is the only western writer to win the Western Heritage Award for two best novels of the year.

Bibliography

Works by Elmer Kelton

Hot Iron. New York: Ballantine, 1955.
Buffalo Wagons. New York: Ballantine, 1956.
Massacre at Goliad. New York: Ballantine, 1965.
After the Bugles. New York: Ballantine, 1967.
Shotgun Settlement. New York: Paperback Library, 1969. [Written under the pseudonym Alex Hawk.]
Bowie's Mine. New York: Ballantine, 1971.
The Day the Cowboys Quit. Garden City, N.Y.: Doubleday, 1971.
Looking Back West. San Angelo, Texas: Talley Press, 1972.
The Time It Never Rained. Garden City, N.Y.: Doubleday, 1973.
Manhunters. New York: Ballantine, 1974.
Joe Pepper. Garden City, N.Y.: Doubleday, 1975. [Written under the pseudonym Lee McElroy.]
Long Way to Texas. Garden City, N.Y.: Doubleday, 1976.
The Good Old Boys. Garden City, N.Y.: Doubleday, 1978.
The Wolf and the Buffalo. Garden City, N.Y.: Doubleday, 1980.

Studies of Elmer Kelton

Clayton, Lawrence. "The End of the West Motif in the Work of Edward Abbey, Jane Kramer, and Elmer Kelton." *RE: Artes Liberales* 6 (Fall 1979): 11-18.
Grover, Dorys C. "Elmer Kelton and the Popular Western Novel." *Southwest Heritage* 8 (Summer 1978): 8-19.
Lee, Billy C. "Elmer Kelton: A *PQ* Interview." *Paperback Quarterly* 1 (Summer 1978): 16-30.
Stowers, Carlton, "Tale of a Typewriter Cowboy." *Dallas Morning News Scene Magazine* 5 (12 May 1974): 6-8, 10, 12.

KEN KESEY
(1935-)

Biography

At times Ken Kesey's life has received as much attention as his novels, especially after the publication in 1968 of *Electric Kool-Aid Acid Test* by Tom Wolfe, in which Kesey appeared a character as large as the heroes in his novels *One Flew over the Cuckoo's Nest* (1962) and *Sometimes a Great Notion* (1964).

Ken Kesey was born 17 September 1935 in La Junta, Colorado. After his father left the navy, Kesey's family moved to Oregon, where Kesey, Sr., was mainly responsible for the development of a marketing cooperative for dairy farmers, the Eugene Farmer's Cooperative. Voted "most likely to succeed" by his classmates at Springfield High in Oregon, Kesey went to the University of Oregon, where he was a wrestling champion, actor, and budding writer of plays, poetry, stories, and an unpublished novel about college athletics titled "End of Autumn."

Starting in 1958, he attended Stanford University for several years on fellowships. He studied with Wallace Stegner, Malcolm Cowley, Richard Scowcroft, and Frank O'Connor. Classmates included Larry McMurtry and Peter S. Beagle. During his Stanford years, Kesey worked on an unpublished book about San Francisco's North Beach, called "Zoo," and on *Cuckoo's Nest*. A published fragment of "Zoo" describes the valiant efforts of Big White (he foreshadows the scrappers in Kesey's fiction) in a cock fight; the pride of a character named Hoover, he is a fighter that "don't run from nothin" (Strelow, *Kesey*, p. 183). Chapters of *Cuckoo's Nest* were read aloud in class to a generally receptive audience that included Malcolm Cowley, who remembers "that hallucinated but everyday style, smelling of motor oil, was something new in fiction" (Strelow, *Kesey*, p. 3).

When Frank O'Connor, who was less sympathetic to Kesey's writing, took over the advanced writing course Kesey spent less time in class and more at Perry Lane, Stanford's bohemian quarter at the time, where he invited members of the class to join other writers he had met and learned from: Ken Babbs, Wendell

Berry, Gurney Norman, and Bob Stone. At one of these gatherings, Malcolm Cowley recalls "a huge bowl of green punch from which clouds of mist or steam kept rising" (Strelow, *Kesey*, p. 4). Vic Lovell, to whom *Cuckoo's Nest* is dedicated, had told Kesey about government drug experiments run by the Veterans Hospital in Menlo Park. Kesey volunteered and tried a range of drugs, including LSD, which he introduced to his circle of friends on Perry Lane, starting the psychedelic movement on the West Coast.

During a job as night attendant on the psychiatric ward, Kesey continued work on *Cuckoo's Nest*, which he finished in June 1961, and then he returned for a while to Oregon and gathered materials on the coast for his next novel. After the publication of *Cuckoo's Nest* in February 1962, Kesey returned to Perry Lane and began writing *Great Notion*. When the Perry Lane cottages were bulldozed by developers, he moved to a home he purchased in nearby La Honda, California. After finishing revisions, Kesey and others planned a trip to New York for the publication in July of *Great Notion*. With Neal Cassady at the wheel, an old school bus, a sign on the front reading "Furthur" [*sic*] and one at the back reading "Caution: Weird Load," carried Kesey and the Merry Pranksters to New York. On the way they hoped by tweaking its nose to awaken the world outside the bus to new social possibilities. On the bus and in Kesey's new community, everyone would relate to everyone else in an open way, possessions would be shared, competition would be eliminated, and the acid experience would be an exploration into the possibilities of group consciousness. Believing the written word was inadequate to express this new experience, the Pranksters turned to film to record their trip.

During much of the fall of 1964 and into the spring of 1965, Kesey and the Pranksters worked at cutting "The Movie," the color film shot on the bus trip. On 23 April 1965, there was a raid on La Honda, and Kesey was charged with possession of marijuana. That fall he was invited by members of the Vietnam Day Committee to address an antiwar rally in Berkeley on the University of California campus. To the organizers' dismay, Kesey told 15,000 people that marching was not going to stop the war, generally deflating their mood. Later in the year the first Acid Test, people gathering to take drugs together in a search for total experience, was held. Mixed media entertainment, acid rock, and psychedelic poster art came straight out of these Acid Tests. Further tests were held in California, Oregon, and Mexico, culminating in the Trips Festival, 21-23 January 1966, at the Longshoreman's Hall in San Francisco.

On 17 January 1966, Kesey was found guilty on the marijuana charge; arrested a second time for possession two days later, he fled for Mexico. In October he was in San Francisco; it was rumored that he had returned to announce that it was time to go beyond acid. After appearing as a guest on a television newscast, Kesey was spotted and arrested. Beginning in June he served concurrently two brief sentences and was released in November. Later, using his jail journals, Kesey wrote and illustrated an unpublished book, "Cut the Motherfuckers Loose."

In 1968 Kesey moved to a small farm in Pleasant Hill, Oregon. Tom Wolfe's Day-Glo re-creation of the Pranksters' antics was published in August. In the same year, Kesey published letters and short pieces in various underground publications. From March to June 1969 Kesey lived in London and did some work for *Apple*, the Beatles' recording company. *Atlantis Rising*, an unreleased children's movie, was filmed in the spring of 1970, and work continued on "The Movie." Plans were also made for a mixed media news service and production company called Intrepid Trips that put out in 1976 two issues of a magazine titled *Spit in the Ocean* and jointly produced with the Viking Press *Kesey's Garage Sale*, including "Over the Border," in which Deboree (Kesey) is the test pilot in various kinds of flights across borders geographical, emotional, imaginative, and spiritual.

A screen version of *Great Notion* was filmed by the Newman-Foreman Company on the Oregon Coast during the summer of 1970 and was released by Universal late in 1971. In the spring Kesey coedited with Paul Krassner *The Last Supplement to the Whole Earth Catalogue*.

Kesey and Ken Babbs were the main organizers of a Media Referendum on Political Issues called The Bend in the River Council, 4, 5, 6 July 1974. Hoping to pioneer revolutionary social legislation, the council planned to open new channels of communication, using newspapers and television coverage to involve people in a public discussion and vote on issues such as transportation, land use, health, consciousness, and communication.

Accompanied by Charlie Percy, one of the magazine's associate editors, Ken Kesey, looking for the occult pyramid known to the followers of Edgar Cayce as the Hall of Records, headed the *Rolling Stone* Expedition in Search of the Secret Pyramid; he sent back five dispatches, published in *Rolling Stone* between 21 November 1974 and 13 February 1975.

The movie version of *Cuckoo's Nest* was released in December 1975 and became a box-office hit, winning five Academy Awards. Several months after its release, Kesey charged the owners, producers, and distributors with breaking the contract that entitled him to 5 percent of the film's gross receipts. Kesey was especially upset that no writer was mentioned at the Academy Awards, comparing those receiving awards to pump salesmen who sell the virtue of their pumps without realizing that it is the well that provides the water. At the end of 1976, an out-of-court settlement was reached, reportedly giving Kesey 2.5 percent of the net profits.

Kesey and his wife, Faye Haxby, and their children live on a small farm in Pleasant Hill, Oregon. For the last several years, after having apparently given it up, Kesey is again writing fiction. Living on his land has provided the material for his two fictional memoirs published in *Esquire*, "Abdul and Ebenezer" (1976) and "Day after Superman Died; A Story" (1979). He continues to write about strength, struggles against fear and death, and the promise of the revolution. Although there are more novels he wants to write, "one about vanity, and then one about attachment" ("Novelist Ken Kesey Says He's Come Back to His

Land," p. 15), he wonders about American novelists' not improving on their first novel and whether he will improve on *Cuckoo's Nest*.

Major Themes

"I wrote about fear in 'Cuckoo's Nest' and despair in 'Notion' " (Allen, "Novelist Ken Kesey," p. 15), Kesey said of his novels. This statement is a helpful introduction to a brief discussion of the major concerns of Kesey's two published novels.

Bromden, the half-Indian narrator of *Cuckoo's Nest*, wakes in the ward of a mental institution to a world of fear in the persons of the black aides, hired for their hatred of whites and their own color by Big Nurse, a representative of the Combine. His paranoia makes visible emotional, moral, and political realities. He experiences a world that is completely mechanized; walls hum and whiz, and human beings are robots, tuned and repaired by the staff at the asylum, with the Nurses' Station as Control Central. Big Nurse, Miss Ratched (ratchet), makes men wretched by controlling them for the Combine, an organization that adjusts men's lives in the ward and outside. She plays on the weaknessess of the Hardings and the Bibbits and their willingness to participate in her therapeutic sessions (pecking parties) to control them. Pretended kindness and considerateness mask hatred and fear of disruptions.

There is a continuity in Bromden's experience of the Combine, from government men treating him when young as if he were deaf and dumb, to the sight of black girls in a cotton mill in California tied together by white lines, to the mechanized, totalitarian world of the ward. Bromden notices everything and sorrows but feels powerless and believes that he must be cagey so as not to be vulnerable. Whenever he wants to hide, his fear generates a fog that protects and isolates him. Before the arrival of McMurphy he is in a fog of retreat to the point that he is willing to accept his death, as are most other men on the ward.

Randall Patrick McMurphy (RPM), smelling of dust, sweat, and work—unlike the doll-like and antiseptic Miss Ratched—rides onto the ward and challenges Harding, president of the Patient's Council, to a showdown before sunset. A brawling drifter, "No one to *care* about, which is what makes him free enough to be a good con man" (Pratt, p. 89), McMurphy is the energy that challenges the deathlike power of the Combine. Introduced to pecking parties, electroshock therapy, and other ills of the ward, McMurphy quickly has to learn the rules the inmates and staff play by. He introduces men to different games, including monopoly, the game of the Combine. McMurphy hopes that by learning to beat him at games, the men will learn to beat Miss Ratched at her game. The hands that the men are dealt in cards reflect the hands dealt them by life.

When McMurphy finds out that he is dependent on Big Nurse for his release, he has to choose between knuckling under or bucking the system. Haunted by the faces of the inmates, he is not able to resist their need. Forcing him on, they conjure up heroes out of their television, film, and cartoon past. When the Big

Nurse, for example, announces her intention to punish them for their unruly behavior by taking away the privilege of using the tub room for their card games, the inmates—the townspeople—look to McMurphy for help: "He was the logger again, the swaggering gambler, the big redheaded brawling Irishman, the cowboy on the TV set, walking down the middle of the street to meet a dare" (Pratt, p. 189), Seen as a savior by the inmates, he takes twelve men with him on a fishing trip, where they fish for their own power and sexuality. During the trip McMurphy's infectious laughter ripples out, is joined by others, and rolls inland to threaten the power of the Combine.

McMurphy, as Bromden recognizes, "signed on for the whole game" (Pratt, p. 296) in the never-ending battle for existence. After ripping open the starched uniform of Big Nurse and exposing her fulsome breasts, McMurphy is lobotomized; he has bet his life that the men would win their humanity, their lives. Bromden suffocates him so that Miss Ratched will not have a constant reminder on the ward of the consequences of bucking the system, escapes the ward, and lights out for the territory of his memories, a natural world different from the totalitarian, mechanical world of the Combine.

In *Sometimes a Great Notion* we turn from a cuckoo's nest to an ancient wood-frame house on the banks of the Wakonda Auga River, "like a two-story bird with split-shake feathers, sitting fierce in its tangled nest" (*Notion*, p. 1). The only house on the bank for twenty miles before the sea, it has "surrendered seldom a scant inch" (*Notion*, p. 4), the shorings and pilings reflecting a century of struggle against the river. The incessant rain gathering drop by drop, threatening to destroy or tranquilize to numbness, the angry townspeople, the union members—the forces of despair and death are pitted against the will to resist and insist in the Stampers.

Great Notion begins at the end. The union president, Jonathan Bailey Draeger, pulls up across from Stamper's house to find union members angrily yelling out "Hank Stamper," outraged that he has inexplicably changed his mind about breaking his contract to deliver logs to Wakonda Pacific. The rest of the novel demonstrates the inevitability of Hank's decision not to give an inch and to float his booms down the river, with his father's severed arm twisting above the river from a pole hanging out the window, its middle finger defiantly signaling Hank's answer to union demands. "*So the book is on the surface a long exploration of the arm. And why someone would hang such a symbol of defiance,*" Kesey wrote in his notes (Strelow, *Kesey*, p. 51).

The narrative courses along, fed by different points of view and time, returning to the past for reasons for Hank's decision—to 1898, for example, the year Jonas Armand Stamper struck out from Kansas for new frontiers in Oregon, one in a line of iron-willed "stubborn west-walkers" (*Notion*, p. 16). After struggling for three years against a lush nature that strives to take back all labors, he abandoned his family, driving Henry Sr., one of his sons, to forge an iron-clad commandment: "NEVER GIVE AN INCH!" (*Notion*, p. 31), an attitude taken up by Hank, Jr. In defying the union, Hank continues to swim upstream, as he had when training for high school swimming meets. He learned early about the relentless danger of the river. When a youngster he lost three caged bobcats to the river when it sliced away part of the bank during a downpour, after which he shared with his father the duties of compulsively shoring up the house, fighting the river for things that belonged to the Stampers. Joe Ben Stamper, a cousin, realized that Hank is the stoic cowboy and diehard mountain man who is constantly pressed to prove himself and that Hank's lot is to fight bullies, unions, vine maple, the river, the ocean, and death.

In the battle for life, Hank is on one side and Lee, his brother, on the other. Lee has to ask himself, Why fight to live? Why not jump into the river? At the same moment that the mailman is delivering the postcard calling him back to Oregon, he is trying to kill himself. He flirts with the notion of giving in to the sea and returning to the mother whom he never had. Despising his brother's macho strength, Lee plots to cut Hank down by sleeping with Viv, Hank's wife.

After Joe Ben drowns in the river—realizing that all his struggles could not save Joe Ben from death or himself the hurt of finding Lee in bed with Viv, succumbing to Lee's arguments pointing out the futility of strength, and tired of being the villain in the community—Hank's resistance is eroded, and he momentarily abandons hope of filling the Wakonda Pacific contracts. The sweet milk of victory, however, curdles in the stomach of all those who want to whittle Hank down to size; Evenwrite, Teddy, and Big Newton are dissatisfied, vaguely recognizing that Hank represents the strength in the community that they admire and hate. If Hank has toppled, nothing is firm.

The brothers' struggle culminates in a brutal fight, an embrace of "Hate and Hurt and Love" (*Notion*, pp. 613-14). Lee resists the voice in him that urgently shouts for him to give up and run; he fights not to beat Hank but for his life. And Hank realizes that he is not fighting to beat Lee but to revive his spirit. After the fight they sail the logs down the river, an act that can be read as a triumphant assertion of will or a despairing gesture of defiance.

Hank needed someone to support him; Lee needed someone who responded to his need. Viv, scarred by the battle between the divided brothers, had given up her life to others. She is trying to be what Hank calls an "Informed Female" (*Notion*, p. 129). Caught in a man's world and wanting to flee, she turns her back on the woman who responded to the needs of others and chooses her own life by leaving Wakonda. Viv by leaving and Jenny by calling herself by her Indian name, Leahnoomish, have the last word in the novel.

In an interview Kesey said, "Women's Lib was the real issue in *Notion*. I didn't know this when I wrote it, but think about it. It's about men matching egos and wills on the battle of Vivian's unconsulted hide. When she leaves at the end of the book, she chooses to leave the only people she loves for a bleak and uncertain but at least *equal* future" (*Garage Sale*, p. 218).

The most fully developed character in Kesey's fiction since *Great Notion* is Grandma Whittier, an eighty-six-year-old woman, who has appeared in the first two of "Seven Prayers by Grandma Whittier," a new novel, called by Kesey "form in transit" (Strelow, *Kesey*, p. 99).

Kesey's writings are his "arms against a sea of troubles" (*Notion*, p. 65), his resolve not to give in to meaninglessness. His hand, aroused by his vision of need, creates words that are to rouse us.

Survey of Criticism

Noting similarities in Kesey's fiction to works such as Clarke's *Childhood's End*, Hesse's *Journey to the East*, and Heinlein's *Stranger in a Strange Land*, Tony Tanner in "Edge City" (1971) concludes that Kesey is a pioneering figure in American literature and society in the late 1960s, "a figure who has to be understood and, it seems to me, respected" (p. 392).

Antiestablishment fiction, black humor, absurd laughter, apocalyptic novel, and nihilistic picaresque are terms applied to a group of writers that includes Joseph Heller, John Barth, Kurt Vonnegut, Terry Southern, Bruce Jay Friedman, and Ken Kesey. These are writers who often resort to the metaphor of insanity for comprehending reality in a world frequently seen as chaotic and absurd, "the West of Madness," in Fiedler's phrase (Pratt, p. 379). James F. Miller (Pratt, pp. 397-400), Joseph J. Waldmeir in "Only an Occasional Rutabaga" (1969), and others see Kesey affirming the authentic self against the pressure to conform and insisting on life and energy in the face of apathy and a nightmare world of doomsday visions. W. D. Sherman, "The Novels of Ken Kesey" (1971), suggests that Kesey's novels be read as metaphors for psychedelic experiences of psychic liberation, describing a pattern of the disintegration, death, "and ultimate rebirth of the ego which lies at the heart of the LSD 'trip' " (p. 185).

In a review of trends in American fiction since 1945, Waldmeir adds Kesey to a list of writers of quest such as Saul Bellow, Norman Mailer, Bernard Malamud, Flannery O'Connor, and J. D. Salinger, who react to issues of the time and seek new bases of order and value. The attempts of McMurphy and the inmates to organize are compared to political organizations of the 1960s such as SNCC and CORE: loose, basically unpolitical, organizations of collective individualism, committed to individual rights and dignities. Or as John Wilson Foster says in "Hustling to Some Purpose" (1974), McMurphy can be seen as a bustling entrepreneur who initially believes that all things are "secular, comprehensible, and exploitable" (p. 115) but who out of a spirit of sacrificing fellowship "is converted to the cause of the disfranchised" (p. 123) in the tradition of revolutionary mythology.

James Knapp, "Tangled in the Language of the Past" (1977), too, reads Kesey's novels in the context of the critiques of a technological, efficient society, but he is troubled by the contradictions in the novels between self-sacrificing brotherhood and aggressive individualism. Just as the Pranksters moved through a world of nonpeople, he argues, Kesey's fiction describes characters—Big Nurse, charter boat captains, and union men—for whom we feel no sympathy. Although there is concern in his books for the problems of forging some kind of community in the face of an alienating world, "for all the 'anti-Establishment' cast of its surface appearance, Kesey's work actually conveys the most traditional of messages: it is the right and destiny of strong individuals to shape the world to their wills" (p. 408). Addison Bross is also disturbed by Kesey's apparent indifference to presenting believable fictional characters and is dismayed by his doctrinaire dependence upon an ideology that insists the reader accept the view that "a repressive Establishment is in command in our world" (L & S, p. 60).

Peter Beidler, however, partially attributes the appeal of *Cuckoo's Nest* to Kesey's development of themes that "modern American audiences respond to: the modern world as divorced from nature, modern society as repressive, modern establishment leaders as mechanical and destructive, modern man as victim of rational but loveless forces beyond his control, and modern man as rabbit" (L & S, p. 56).

Nicolaus Mills, "Ken Kesey and the Politics of Laughter" (1972), and Stephen Tanner, "Salvation through Laughter" (1973), see the responses to mechanization, manipulation, and matriarchy in laughter and the willingness of Kesey's characters to act, demonstrating that their laughter and actions were "not intended to eliminate death and failure but to show that death and failure need not prevent them from acting" (Mills, "Ken Kesey," p. 90).

Disagreeing with those who argue that the fisher king myth informs *Cuckoo's Nest*, Carol Pearson in "The Cowboy Saint and the Indian Poet" (1974), argues that the romantic myth of the king, the hero, and the fool shapes the novel, with Big Nurse (the king) as representative of moral seriousness, conformity, and efficiency, and McMurphy as the fool who is associated with individuality, natural sexuality, humor, and mystic religion. Bromden, who tells the story, is the hero: "As McMurphy has done justice to the whole of life through laughter, Bromden does justice to it through art" (p. 98).

Kesey's interest in folk materials, comic book superheroes, television cowboys, and science fiction has received considerable critical attention. Kingsley Widmer, in "The Post-Modernist Art of Protest" (1975), summarizes the many folklorish characteristics of McMurphy discussed by critics: "brawling and lecherous red-haired Irishman, 'giant from the sky' to the Indian, con-man and gambler, Wild West two-fisted tough-guy, heel-slamming logger and high-tailing hobo, swaggering hyberbolic comic and bravado parodist, but also manly scapegoat and compassionate martyr" (p. 129). Richard Blessing, "The Moving Target" (1971), traces the change in McMurphy from confidence man to a father figure who leads his sons to maturity, his death thrusting Bromden into manhood. Focusing on Bromden's Indian heritage, Don Kunz, "Mechanistic and Totemistic Symbolism in Kesey's *One Flew over the Cuckoo's Nest*" (1975), believes Kesey is drawing on the symbolic representations available in native totemism. The bird totem is held before readers in references to the inmates as different kinds of birds; their recovery is associated with animal imagery as well. A regenerative fertility god, "McMurphy, then, is the Indian's mythical guardian spirit that resides in the animals of air, land, and sea" (p. 77). Peter Beidler (L & S, pp. 18-22) focuses on Kesey's use of familiar stereotypes in portraying Chief Bromden as Tonto, the Indian sidekick (see too Leslie Fiedler's *The Return of the Vanishing American*), America's first ecologist, and the child to the Great White Father.

Terry Sherwood (Pratt, pp. 382-96) points out the relationship between Kesey's aesthetic, informed by comic strip principles, and his moral vision, embodying clear-cut oppositions between good and evil, but resulting in a somewhat sentimentalized oversimplication of moral problems. Referring to the cybernetic models described in E. H. Forster, Aldous Huxley, and Harlan Ellison, Edward Gallagher (L & S, pp. 46-50) describes the ward in *Cuckoo's Nest* as a nightmarish vision of the triumph of technology, serving all men's needs at the expense of their freedoms.

Parallels in the plot between McMurphy's actions and the life of Christ have been set out by John W. Foster, "Hustling to Some Purpose" (1974), and Bruce E. Wallis, "Christ in the Cuckoo's Nest" (1972). McMurphy's story is told by a disciple, the son of an Indian fisherman, and is about a man who is crucified on a cross-shaped table. There is a fishing expedition with twelve inmates, the hero's friendship with prostitutes, Taber as the voice in the wilderness, and a doctor who washes his hands of the whole thing. McMurphy's actions suggest a pattern for redemptive action.

Wallis, however, questions the comparison to Christ, since he believes that Kesey neglects the conception of original sin and mistakenly believes that man is naturally benevolent. In attacking institutions, Kesey is attacking symptoms instead of the disease.

Other readers are disturbed by what they consider Kesey's stereotypical depictions of men and women. According to Robert Forrey, "Ken Kesey's Psychopathic Savior" (1975), Kesey depicts McMurphy as "a masculine Christ whom the conspiring world of weak-kneed men and bitchy women try to emasculate" (p. 223). McMurphy is a sexist savior, Forrey continues, who on the fishing trip gives real men what they want: "fishing, drinking, smoking, swearing, and whoring" (p. 237).

Although she acknowledges the strengths of *Cuckoo's Nest*, Leslie Horst (L & S, pp. 14-18), too, cautions readers to pay attention to the demeaning depictions of women and men. Women are presented as castrators (Big Nurse) and quintessential bitches (Harding's wife) or as the vulnerable and available prostitutes from Portland. For the most part, the men are eunuchs except for macho-man McMurphy. Annette Benert (L & S, pp. 22-26) reminds us that we read the novel through the eyes of Bromden and argues that Bromden's perception of white women, blacks, and machines is not the total truth. She calls our attention to the kindnesses to the inmates of the Japanese nurse and Mr. Turkle, a black aide, Bromden's beloved grandmother, and the liberating boat ride. Kingsley Widmer also suggests that readers should not dismiss *Cuckoo's Nest* for its forcing of the picaro-to-saint pattern and its male chauvinism, but he believes that they weaken Kesey's profound perception of totalitarian institutions.

In spite of the popularity of the film version, reviewers' disappointments (they described it as an elephantine, pretentious, disappointing sequel to *Cuckoo's Nest*) appear to have established the pattern for the critical reception of *Great Notion*, since relatively little attention has been paid to the novel. Those who have singled it out for comment have noted the continuity of Kesey's concerns. As James Knapp, "Tangled in the Language of the Past" (1977) points out, Hank Stamper is in a line of heroes who struggle against "a world of stultifying, institutional conformity—whether Combine and hospital, or company suburb, or manipulative union" (p. 402). Kesey is preoccupied, writes Bruce Carnes in *Ken Kesey* (1974), "with investigating the possibility (if not the necessity) of heroism in the midst of an apocalyptic state of human affairs in this country" (pp. 4-5). Carnes's pamphlet is the most extensive commentary on Kesey and is a useful summary of other discussions of Kesey's novel." The relationship between Hank and Lee is central to W.D. Sherman's discussion of *Great Notion* in "The Novels of Ken Kesey" (1971). Hank shows Lee how to live life to the full and not give in to nature or the union, and Lee teaches Hank the necessity of submitting oneself to those forces. "The kind of affirmation which arises from Kesey's novels," Sherman continues, "is an anarchic 'yes' to life, which, despite its joyousness, leaves a man prey to unbearable isolation" (p. 196).

Bibliography

Articles about Kesey reprinted in *One Flew over the Cuckoo's Nest: Text and Criticism*, edited by John C. Pratt, New York: Viking Press, the Viking Critical Library, 1973, and in the issue of *Lex et Scientia: The International Journal of Law and Science* devoted to discussion of *Cuckoo's Nest*, vol. 13, nos. 1-2, 1976, are not listed in the bibliography. References in the text to *Cuckoo's Nest* and to articles in the Viking Critical Library edition will be given as Pratt; references to articles in *Lex et Scientia* will be given as L & S. References to *Sometimes a Great Notion* are to the Compass Books edition, New York: Viking Press, 1971, given as *Notion*.

Works by Ken Kesey

One Flew over the Cuckoo's Nest. New York: Viking Press, 1962.

Sometimes a Great Notion. New York: Viking Press, 1964.

Kesey's Garage Sale. New York: Viking Press, 1973. Gathers many of Kesey's short pieces published elsewhere.

"Seven Prayers by Grandma Whittier." In *Spit in the Ocean* 1-2, a magazine © 1976 by Ken Kesey. Pleasant Hill, Oregon: Intrepid Trips Information Service. Reprinted in *Kesey*. Ed. Michael Strelow. Eugene, Oregon: Northwest Review Books, 1977, pp. 96-166.

"Abdul and Ebenezer." *Esquire* 85 (March 1976): 55-59.

"Day After Superman Died; A Story." *Esquire* 92 (October 1979): 42:54.

Studies of Ken Kesey

Allen, Henry. "Novelist Ken Kesey Says He's Come Back to His Land." *Sunday Oregonian*, 7 July 1974, sec. 2, p. 15.

Blessing, Richard. "The Moving Target: Ken Kesey's Evolving Hero." *Journal of Popular Culture* 4 (Winter 1971): 615-27.

Carnes, Bruce. *Ken Kesey*. WWS. Boise, Idaho: Boise State University, 1974.

Fiedler, Leslie A. *The Return of the Vanishing American*. New York: Stein & Day, 1968, pp. 179-85.

Forrey, Robert. "Ken Kesey's Pschopathic Savior: A Rejoinder." *Modern Fiction Studies* 21 (Summer 1975): 222-30.

Foster, John Wilson. "Hustling to Some Purpose: Kesey's *One Flew over the Cuckoo's Nest*." *Western American Literature* 9 (Summer 1974): 115-29.

Knapp, James F. "Tangled in the Language of the Past: Ken Kesey and Cultural Revolution." *Midwest Quarterly: A Journal of Contemporary Thought* 19 (Summer 1977): 398-412.

Kunz, Don R. "Mechanistic and Totemistic Symbolism in Kesey's *One Flew over the Cuckoo's Nest*." *Studies in American Fiction* 3 (Spring 1975): 65-82.

Mills, Nicolaus. "Ken Kesey and the Politics of Laughter." *Centennial Review* 16 (Winter 1972): 82-90.

Pearson, Carol. "The Cowboy Saint and the Indian Poet: The Comic Hero in Kesey's *One Flew over the Cuckoo's Nest*." *Studies in American Humor* 1 (October 1974): 91-98.

Sherman, W. D. "The Novels of Ken Kesey." *Journal of American Studies* 5 (August 1971): 185-96.

Strelow, Michael, ed. *Kesey. Northwest Review* 16, no. 1, 2. Eugene, Oregon: Northwest Review Books, 1977. Contains notes, drafts, short pieces, and poems by Kesey.

Sullivan, Ruth. "Big Mama, Big Papa, and Little Sons in Ken Kesey's *One Flew over the Cuckoo's Nest*." *Literature and Psychology* 25 (November 1975): 34-44.

Tanner, Stephen L. "Salvation through Laugher: Ken Kesey and the Cuckoo's Nest." *Southwest Review* 58 (Spring 1973): 125-37.

Tanner, Tony. "Edge City." In *City of Words: American Fiction 1950-70*. New York: Harper & Row, 1971, pp. 372-92.

Waldmeir, Joseph J. "Only an Occasional Rutabaga: American Fiction since 1945." *Modern Fiction Studies* 15 (Winter 1969): 467-81.

Wallis, Bruce E. "Christ in the Cuckoo's Nest: Or, the Gospel according to Ken Kesey." *Cithara* 12 (November 1972): 52-58.

Widmer, Kingsley. "The Post-Modernist Art of Protest: Kesey and Mailer as American Expressions of Rebellion." *Centennial Review* 19 (Summer 1975): 121-35.

Weixlmann, Joseph. "Ken Kesey: A Bibliography." *Western American Literature* 10 (Fall 1975): 219-31.

Wolfe, Tom. *The Electric Kool-Aid Acid Test*. New York: Farrar, Strauss & Giroux, 1968.

Michael T. Marsden

LOUIS L'AMOUR
(1908-)

Bantam Books is quite proud and pleased that their author is "the World's Bestselling Frontier Storyteller," an appellation that Louis L'Amour enjoys and deserves as the chronicler of the endless western frontier of the American imagination. His most recent book, *Buckskin Run* (1981), is his seventy-ninth and by no means his final volume, for his plans call for an additional forty or fifty titles, which, if they are not in the typewriter, are certainly in mind.

To celebrate the publication of his one hundred millionth book in the summer of 1980, Louis L'Amour embarked on a book-signing bus tour through the heart of the country that embraces his fiction to meet and talk with his readers. Sixty-five of his books have sold over a million copies, his books have been published in ten foreign languages, and thirty-three of his stories have been purchased for films or television programs. Yet his feeling for the American landscape and its people is as deep and sincere as it was when he traveled its real landscape in search of himself, his roots, and his place in America's present. His stated goal is to chronicle a three-hundred-year history of the settling and taming of America utilizing the primary vehicle of a three-family saga, the specific details of which are just beginning to take on a more definite form with the publication of his seventy-seventh (*Lonely on the Mountain*, 1980) and seventy-eighth volumes (*Milo Talon*, 1981).

Readers and reviewers recognize that he is a compelling storyteller. He is not a literary giant in traditional terms. Rather, he is a giant at the loom of the American imagination, on which he weaves his popular yarns with the threads of the history, geography, and geology of the western landscape, developing in the process a national consciousness about the country's past as it was and as it should have been. His readers send him handwritten diaries that have been in their families for generations, work tirelessly to have a Congressional gold medallion struck in his honor, and scan the paperback racks each week for the appearance of one of his new titles.

Biography

Louis L'Amour was born 22 March 1908 in Jamestown, North Dakota, to Louis Charles and Emily (Dearborn) LaMoore. After enjoying a pleasant boyhood in North Dakota, Louis took to the road at the age of fifteen to be less of a burden to his financially troubled family. His father, a country veterinarian, farm machinery salesman, and deputy sheriff, was the victim of an economic collapse in that rural farm community in the early 1920s. For almost twenty years Louis wandered the world, a part of his life he is just beginning to pay tribute to, as in a recent collection of a number of his earlier stories entitled, appropriately, *Yondering* (1980).

The details about those twenty years remain somewhat vague, despite frequent narratives spun about them by newspaper and magazine writers as well as by L'Amour himself. He worked as a longshoreman, lumberjack, dead cattle skinner, gold prospector, elephant handler, hay shocker, flume builder, and fruit picker in this period of "yondering" across the United States. During these early travels he met and listened to old outlaws recount the Lincoln County wars, old mountain men tell about the opening and settling of the West, and a variety of other personifications of archetypes tell their stories. Like many other American writers before him, L'Amour took to the sea and journeyed to the West Indies, Europe, and Asia. During the 1930s he found himself making a living as a professional boxer in Oklahoma. During this period of his life he began to pursue the writing career that he says was always in his mind:

I remember in the first grade once I was asked by a teacher what I intended to be when I grew up. I said scientist, but that wasn't what I was thinking about. Actually, had I been able to phrase it, I probably would have said a philosopher. What I was really thinking about was writing about people. I was twelve years old when I first tried to write....I'd grown up on stories. My grandfather had fought Indians and he was around home when I was a little boy....He told me all sorts of stories about Indian fighting and the fighting of the Civil War. I was fascinated by military tactics, so when I was a little boy, he used to talk to me about them and used to draw diagrams on the blackboard....So I got tuned into listening to older people and then when I started knocking around and began meeting them, I'd listen and constantly picked up an awful lot. [Marsden, "A Conversation with Louis L'Amour," pp. 646-48]

During the 1930s he was not as successful at his literary pursuits as he had hoped. He did, however, publish a number of stories in the popular magazines of the period. And after World War II he began to place his stories in the more prestigious popular magazines, such as *Argosy* and *Saturday Evening Post*. In 1939 he published a volume of poetry, *Smoke from This Altar*.

After a four-year career as an officer in World War II, he returned to the United States determined to make a living by writing. His first novel, *Westward the Tide* (1950), was published in England. (This novel was reprinted under its original title in paperback by Bantam in 1977.) The publication of *Yondering*, a collection of his work from 1939 to 1977, helps bring together a variety of his stories that span those important, formative years in his writing career. By the time of his marriage to Katherine Elizabeth Adams in 1956, he was firmly established as an important writer of Westerns.

Learning to write in the popular marketplace of the 1930s and 1940s, L'Amour developed the ability to write fast and well in a single draft, and he continues to write an average of three and four books a year. The major lesson he learned in those early years of his writing career was to respect the reader, to tell the reader the truth: "the West was wilder than any man can write it, but my facts, my terrain, my guns, my Indians are real. I've ridden and hunted the country. When I write about a spring, that spring is there, and the water is good to drink." (This statement can be found in the front of a number of his Westerns.)

This respect for his audience has won him their admiration and remarkable book sales. The physical reality of his West is quite tangible for his readers, and the more spiritual West he writes about continues to engage them in volume after volume of his continuing saga. In a sense his biographical details are vague because all of the information readers need to know about him can be found in the pages of his novels. His novels are biographical in that they are a record of his mental projections of himself and his family back in time to the fenlands of England and then forward to the nineteenth-century West that exists in eternalized time in the American imagination. The following, almost random quotation from one of his recent novels, *The Warrior's Path*, while ostensibly discussing the wandering Jubal Sackett, is a clear identification of the L'Amour hero with the author himself:

He was ever the lonely wanderer, ever the remote one, loving us all and being loved, yet a solitary man who loved the wild lands more. He had gone westward, and he had returned from time to time with tales of a great river out there, greater than any we knew, and of wide, fertile lands where there was much game. And then he had come no more. [P. 200]

Major Themes

The importance of the past is a crucial theme in L'Amour's fiction, for in his landscape nothing is really ever new or being done for the first time. His characters, especially in his more recent novels, have developed a deep sense of their personal past as well as of their familiar past. In *The Warrior's Path*, Kin Ring Sackett meets John Tully, who knew Kin's father, Barnabas, and the following recollection-prediction follows:

Ah, you are your father's son! He looked to the westward too! To his far blue mountains. But was it the mountains? Or was it that something beyond? We need such men, lad, men who can look to the beyond, to ever strive for something out there beyond the stars. It is man's destiny, I think, to go forward, ever forward. We are of the breed, you and I, the breed who venture always toward what lies out there—westward, onward, everward. [P. 163]

This sense of the past is most visible in the landscape, for the geology and the geography are no mere backdrop but an active force in his fiction. Their role is important because they underscore the necessity of reflecting upon the past in building the present and the future, as L'Amour would have his readers understand:

I do not view the American frontier as isolated in time, but as a piece of the ages; the people in my stories come from everywhere, and often return; nor are they only the un-lettered, but the younger sons of noble families, soldiers, the adventurous and the desperate, having one thing in common: the courage to sever old ties and enter a vast new world they must change with their hands and their minds. I write of people who live with awareness, with perspective, and who are a part of all they have met, and will meet. [Letter to Charles Campbell, Oklahoma Department of Libraries, 24 March 1973, re-printed in *Surging Seventies*, p. 64]

The concept of the family is perhaps the central theme in his fiction, one that to a large degree defines all the values in his fiction. He has created three fictional families who embrace the cast of characters for his new saga of the American West. The Sacketts, of Welsh and English ancestry, are his best-known and most fully developed family. They are divided into three major branches: the Smoky Mountain Sacketts, the Cumberland Gap Sacketts, and the Clinch Moun-tain Sacketts. While each of the branches of the Sackett dynasty is significantly different from the others, they all respond to a call for help from any other Sackett. The Smoky Mountain Sacketts include L'Amour's Abraham Lincoln of the western landscape, William Tell Sackett, who, while socially backward, is graceful and efficient under fire. In novel after novel he searches for his family and is concerned about maintaining family traditions. The Cumberland Gap Sacketts have produced less notable offspring, but they are generally honorable and trustworthy. The Clinch Mountain Sacketts, however, tend toward meanness and have produced notable gunfighters, such as the brothers Logan and Nolan. Fam-ily ties eclipse all other ties and obligations as Tell Sackett succinctly notes: "We Sacketts never had much. Mostly we wanted land that we could crop and graze, land where we could rear a family. We set store by kinfolk, and where trouble showed we usually stood against it as a family" (*Sackett*, p. 19).

The Sacketts are the pioneers, the trailblazers, and the Indian fighters who opened the West for settlement. The other two family groupings in L'Amour's fiction are the Talons and the Chantrys. The Talons, who came from France, are the settlers, the builders, the ones who complete the land after the Sacketts have tamed it. They tend to be talented with their hands and plant themselves as well as their crops in the land. Completing the familial triad are the Chantrys, who come from Ireland and who are the conceptualizers. Because of their more recent immigration to the New World, they have sufficient distance from the western landscape to comprehend the significance of the relationships that have been established among people, landscape, and the forces of nature. The Chantrys move west because they find the old ways morally deficient. As representatives of the third stage of national development, the Chantrys are the least rounded of the three L'Amour families, but they represent nineteenth-century wilderness becoming twentieth-century civilization.

While this familial triad provides a formal structure within which L'Amour is able to frame many of his stories, there are also less formal family structures that reinforce a whole series of beliefs, attitudes, and values characteristic of his fiction. The concept of the family is the thread that determines the texture of his fiction and can be divided into four broad segments: the male principle, the female principle, the hearth or the focused family, and the family unit or the extended family. The male principle in L'Amour's fiction is generally consistent with that of traditional western formula fiction in which the hero is self-reliant, somewhat homely, but always honorable and certainly courageous. The female principle is important in his fiction because of the scarcity and influence of women in the American West. There is no greater sin on the L'Amour landscape than molesting a woman, and his characters frequently preach the gospel of the proper treatment of women: "One thing a man didn't do on the frontier was molest a woman, even an all-out bad woman. Women were scarce, and were valued accordingly. Even some pretty mean outlaws had been known to kill a man for jostling a woman on the street" (*The Sackett Brand*, p. 18). A good woman in a L'Amour novel will walk beside a man, not behind him. She forms a partnership with her husband: "Carpenter was a solid looking citizen, and his wife had the firm, quiet face of a woman who knew how to build a home and had courage enough to build it anywhere" (*Kilkenny*, p. 38).

L'Amour's handling of women in his fiction can be quite sensitive, as in *The Californios* (1974), but it can also be inconsistent, which may be due to the various social and cultural pressures surrounding the depiction of women in the popular arts in general in recent decades. The third part of the concept of the family comes into play when the female principle merges with the male principle to produce the hearth, or the focused family:

Like himself, they had come to this wild land bringing the potential of home, and homes demanded order and consideration for the rights of others, a recognition of the necessities of regulations and law. Their women folk came with them or followed after, bringing their own desires, among them the need for church and school, for human association. [*The Key-Lock Man*, p. 5]

L'Amour is here, of course, being quite consistent with the Western formula, which demands a resolution of the tension between wilderness and civilization. Progress and society triumph because of the marked intervention of the woman, of the civilizing influence, of the human qualities necessary to sustain a civilization. The hearth is the mediator between individualism and society, between the forces of nature and the forces of civilization. The L'Amour hero neither leaves his family behind as he heads west nor forgets the necessity of founding his new family out there when time and circumstances are right. It is from the hearth that the hero's concerns radiate to the extended family that encompasses all of the civilized West. The hero, then, becomes a parent to the fledgling society evolving in the western landscape and applies to that newborn world the lessons he has learned from the male principle, the female principle, and the hearth of the focused family. It is in the founding of a new order, a new society, that these principles coalesce and come to fruition in the form of an extended family.

There is also a strong ecological theme in L'Amour's fiction, especially his more recent fiction. While such an ecological concern is not surprising in western fiction, L'Amour's heroes articulate a responsibility for preserving the land: "There was something her father had said. 'We do not own the land, Angie. We hold it in trust for tomorrow. We take our living from it, but we must leave it rich for your son and for his sons and for all of those who shall follow' " (*Hondo*, p. 59). This ecological theme has been continued in a number of L'Amour's novels since the publication of *Hondo* in 1953.

The theme of violence is commonplace in the popular Western, and L'Amour's work is no exception. The essential conflict in traditional western stories from dime novels to the present is resolved by a cleansing action through violence. A new order can be established only after the old order has been physically purged. L'Amour's fiction, while containing its share of brutal violence, does not focus on dehumanized violence. The hero and the villain struggle physically to work out a moral conflict, as seen in *The Warrior's Path* (1980). Kin Ring Sackett has his final confrontation with Max Bauer, one of the masterminds of a white slave trade, and is aided by his courageous wife, Diana Macklin, in destroying his opponent physically and spiritually:

For a long time I simply stood there, staring at his fallen body, hands hanging empty at my sides. There was no more fighting. Our Catawbas had scattered into the woods, and I knew there would be no stragglers reaching the coast, not even to report what had happened. I could only stand, exhausted and empty, staring at the man who had brought so much trouble to so many. That he was dead I had no doubt, for my knife must have severed his spine, and it had been thrown hard. [*Warrior's Path*, p. 225]

L'Amour's treatment of the American Indian is worthy of special notice. His early fiction deviated from the purely formulaic treatment of the Indian as a malevolent force of nature, and his later works presented a fairly complex and balanced view. Barnabas Sackett, the grand sire of the Sacketts, articulates the Sackett policy toward the American Indian quite well in *Sackett's Land*:

Dealing with Indians I found them of shrewd intelligence, quick to detect the false, quick to appreciate quality, quick to resent contempt and to appreciate bravery. So much of the Indian's life was predicated upon courage that he respected it above all else. He needed courage in the hunt, and in warfare, and to achieve success with the tribe he needed both courage and wit. [Pp. 152-53]

There is no stoical or noble "savage" for L'Amour. He chooses instead to remind us that the Indian had a fine sense of humor, enjoyed a good fight, and yet could rise to the level of statesman and prophet, all qualities exemplified by one of his Indian spokesmen:

The white man is not fitted to survive, for he knows not content. He knows not peace. Wars and more wars and bitter famine and pestilence shall end his pride. He cannot learn. Wherever he goes there is war. The Indian fought, but his battles were short and soon over, and the Indian returned to his hunting and his lodge and his squaw. But the white man lives in violence. Where he goes there is fury, and he will die, tearing at the agony of his wounds, crushed and bloody and wondering because in all his hurry and his doing he has never understood his world nor what he does. [*Westward the Tide* (1977), p. 156]

L'Amour's perspective on the American Indian is a balanced one, which examines strengths and weaknesses, and one that balances them in turn against the strengths and weaknesses of the whites. But the Indian in L'Amour's fiction does come to the inevitable truth that the white man's familial bonds will prove stronger than the Indian's, at least initially. An Indian named Powder-Face proclaims in *Treasure Mountain* (1972):

"I know," he said simply. "We killed them and killed them and killed them, and still they came. It was not the horse soldiers that whipped us, it was not the death of the buffalo, nor the white man's cows. It was the people. It was the families.

"The rest we might conquer, but the people kept coming and they built their lodges where no Indian could live. They brought children and women, they brought the knife that cuts the earth. They built their lodges of trees, of sod cut from the earth, of boards, of whatever they could find.

"We burned them out, we killed them, we drove off their horses, and we rode away. When we came back others were there as if grown from the ground—and others, and others, and others." [P.130]

The American Indian is humanized in L'Amour's fiction, but despite the Indian's cultural complexity, he still must surrender to the more willful white man who kept coming and coming because he did not know how to quit and go home.

L'Amour's readers credit him with a high degree of factual accuracy, and he has developed a form of fiction Irving Wallace refers to as "faction." He provides his readers with popular historical treatments of western events from the Custer disaster to basic information about the reading habits of frontiersmen. Included in one of his novels might be a discussion of the Dutch influence on house design in Albany, New York (*Rivers West* [1975]), the origins of words like *Dixie Land* (*Treasure Mountain*), or a discussion of the nature of Indian-white conflicts (*Westward the Tide*). In one novel, *Lando* (1962), L'Amour gives his readers polite lessons on the historical and cultural importance of Madeira wine, the nature of longhorn cattle, the great hurricane of 1844, and the several cultural functions of a nineteenth-century western saloon, all the while entertaining them with a good story. L'Amour takes the classical mandate for a writer seriously: to enlighten as well as to entertain. As he says, this is an important mission: "The average guy is kind of confined in his job and is limited as to how much he can learn. Even the average university professor has become too specialized in this age of specialization. So I see myself as a kind of funnel through which a lot of knowledge is flowing to other people" (Nuwer, "Louis L'Amour: Range Writer," p. 100).

In recent years there has been a clear new direction in L'Amour's fiction. It is important to remember that while he became famous for his virile, formula Westerns with single-name titles such as *Hondo, Kilkenny*, and *Lando*, his first published novel, *Westward the Tide* (1950), was a frontier epic. The 1960s saw the emergence of the Sacketts and their family dynasty. In the 1970s, while one can find a mixture of forms and developments, the family saga predominates. Toward the end of the 1970s L'Amour wrote larger epic romances, such as *Fair Blows the Wind* (1978) and *Bendigo Shafter* (1979), which are more like his first novel in form and style than those his popular reputation was based upon. *Bendigo Shafter* and his other epic frontier novels reach outward from the western experience to the more universal experience of the epic adventure romance while insisting upon the uniqueness and special significance of the westward American migration. L'Amour's unparalleled popular success as a western writer has allowed him to follow the path of the frontier epic and then the epic adventure romance carefully but freely. As he creates new depth and breadth in his fiction, he must frequently make sure the audience is still with him. For he and they have shared a special relationship that should continue to grow and develop as it is nurtured by both parties.

L'Amour considers himself to be more in the tradition of the oral storyteller than of the scribe. If he were an early American storyteller, he would be using the campfire instead of the hand-fitting form of the paperback to communicate with his audience. In the tradition of the epic romance, his fiction is just as much about the West as it ought to have been as it is about the West as it was. Despite the reality of seventy-nine titles in print, L'Amour is telling one long tale with many parts.

His success in the field of the popular Western exceeds that of any of his predecessors or his contemporaries and would seem to suggest the existence of a special relationship with his audience. This relationship appears to take the form of a fellow family member telling tales that reveal the significance of the American past and present in a highly personalized manner. His fiction, thus, forms an organic whole that helps his readers define who they are by examining where they have been, or at least should have been.

Survey of Criticism

Given the noteworthy success of L'Amour's fiction in the popular marketplace, the lack of a concomitant emphasis on it in the academic marketplace is somewhat surprising. Only recently have journals such as *Western American Literature* and *South Dakota Review* devoted significant space to studies of his work. About a half-dozen convention papers dealing with aspects of his fiction have been delivered at meetings of the Western Literature Association and the Popular Culture Association. While the popular press is replete with interviews and articles about Louis L'Amour and his fiction (which are generally concerned with helping to promote one of his new books), serious, scholarly analysis of his work has just commenced.

Michael Marsden has published several articles dealing with L'Amour's fiction as cultural artifact and analyzing the concept of the family as an organizing theme in many of his works. He argues in "The Concept of the Family in the Fiction of Louis L'Amour" (1978), "The Modern Western" (1980), and "The Popular Western Novel as Cultural Artifact" (1980), that L'Amour's fiction, like that of many other popular writers, reflects the attitudes and values of the audience who enjoys his fiction. The popular Western becomes, then, an important cultural index for understanding the significance of the American West.

In "The Frontier Novels of Louis L'Amour" (1978), Candace Klaschus traces several key themes in his work, which include the centrality of the family, the taming and developing of the West as a society, his use of history and mythology, and his writing style. Included in her wide-ranging analysis are biographical discussions based on extensive interviews with L'Amour.

In "Change of Purpose in the Novels of Louis L'Amour" (1978), "A New Look at Two Popular Western Classics" (1980), and "Louis L'Amour's Pseudonymous Works" (1980), John Nesbitt has monitored changes in L'Amour's fiction from his early writings in popular magazines to present-day trends. His research is particularly useful in providing background material for an understanding of L'Amour's development as a writer. In "Mexican and Mexican-American Images in the Western Novels of Louis L'Amour" (1977), Harold Hinds, Jr., provides an overview of one of L'Amour's major innovations as a writer of popular Westerns: his significant and often sensitive treatment of Mexicans and Mexican-Americans in his fiction. Hinds suggests that an analysis of L'Amour's treatment of Mexicans and Mexican-Americans may well serve as a model for similar studies of the theme in the works of other popular writers.

Certainly John Cawelti's two major works dealing with the formula Western, *Six-Gun Mystique* (1971) and *Adventure, Mystery, and Romance* (1976) remain necessary background material for a serious study of any popular western writer, especially Louis L'Amour. Also needed is the openness of scholars such as Don Walker who has, in his occasional publication *Possible Sack*, devoted serious if not always favorable attention to L'Amour's work.

While these critical efforts mark a beginning of meaningful scholarship on popular Westerns, they are only glimpses of the in-depth and detailed work that is needed. It is unfortunately still accurate to say that in the case of major popular western writers such as Louis L'Amour, there is little scholarly mediation between the author and his audience.

Bibliography

Works by Louis L'Amour

Westward the Tide. London: World Works, 1950; New York: Bantam, 1977.
Hondo. Greenwich, Conn.: Fawcett, 1953.
Kilkenny. New York: Ace Books, 1954.
Sackett. New York: Bantam, 1961.
Lando. New York: Bantam, 1962.
Shalako. New York: Bantam, 1962.
Mojave Crossing. New York: Bantam, 1964.
The Key-Lock Man. New York: Bantam, 1965.
The Sackett Brand. New York: Bantam, 1965.
Galloway. New York: Bantam, 1970.
North to the Rails. New York: Bantam, 1971.
Tucker. New York: Bantam, 1971.
Ride the Dark Trail. New York: Bantam, 1972.
Treasure Mountain. New York: Bantam, 1972.
The Ferguson Rifle. New York: Bantam, 1973.
The Californios. New York: E. P. Dutton, 1974.
Sackett's Land. New York: Bantam, 1974.
The Man from the Broken Hills. New York: Bantam, 1975.
Rivers West. New York: Bantam, 1975.
War Party. New York: Bantam, 1975.
The Rider of Lost Creek. New York: Bantam, 1976.
Where the Long Grass Blows. New York: Bantam, 1976.
Borden Chantry. New York: Bantam, 1977.
To the Far Blue Mountains. New York: Bantam, 1977.
Fair Blows the Wind. New York: Bantam, 1978.
Bendigo Shafter. New York: Bantam, 1979.
The Strong Shall Live. New York: Bantam, 1980.
The Warrior's Path. New York: Bantam, 1980.
Yondering. New York: Bantam, 1980.
Lonely on the Mountain. New York: Bantam, 1980.
Milo Talon. New York: Bantam, 1981.
Buckskin Run. New York: Bantam, 1981.

Studies of Louis L'Amour

Cawelti, John. *Adventure, Mystery, and Romance: Formula Stories as Art and Popular Culture*. Chicago: University of Chicago Press, 1976.
————. *The Six-Gun Mystique*. Bowling Green, Ohio: Popular Press, 1971.
Hinds, Harold E. "Mexican and Mexican-American Images in the Western Novels of Louis L'Amour." *Latin American Literary Review* 5 (Spring-Summer 1977): 129-41.
Klaschus, Candace. "The Frontier Novels of Louis L'Amour." Master's thesis, San Francisco State University, 1978.
Marsden, Michael T. "The Concept of the Family in the Fiction of Louis L'Amour." *North Dakota Quarterly* 46 (Summer 1978): 12-21.

————. "A Conversation with Louis L'Amour." *Journal of American Culture* 2 (Winter 1980): 646-58.

————. Introduction to *Hondo* by Louis L'Amour. Boston: Gregg Press, 1978, pp. v-x.

————. "The Modern Western." *Journal of the West* 19 (January 1980): 54-61. Reprinted in *The American Literary West*. Ed. Richard W. Etulain. Manhattan, Kans.: Sunflower University Press, 1980.

————. "The Popular Western Novel as Cultural Artifact." *Arizona and the West* 20 (Autumn 1980): 203-14.

Nesbitt, John D. "Change of Purpose in the Novels of Louis L'Amour." *Western American Literature* 13 (Spring 1978): 65-81.

————. "A New Look at Two Popular Western Classics." *South Dakota Review* 18 (Spring 1980): 30-42.

————. "Louis L'Amour's Pseudonymous Works." *Paperback Quarterly* 3 (Fall 1980): 3-6.

Nuwer, Hank. "Louis L'Amour: Range Writer." *Country Gentleman* 130 (Spring 1979): 99-100, 102.

Surging Seventies: "Oklahoma Writers, Published in 1970-71-72-73." Arranged by Charles Campbell. Oklahoma Department of Libraries, 1973.

Walker, Don W. "Notes on the Popular Western." *Possible Sack* 3 (November 1971): 11-13.

JACK LONDON
(1876-1916)

"This great, incoherent, amorphous West! Who could grip the spirit and the essence of it, the luster and the wonder, and bind it all, definitely and sanely, within the covers of a printed book?" wrote Jack London, praising Frank Norris's *The Octopus* in the June 1901 issue of *Impressions*. If Norris had succeeded in grasping the spirit and the luster of the West in his great epic novel, as London attested, Jack himself managed to capture them in his legendary career. "I am a Westerner, despite my English name," he declared; and no other writer better epitomized the "coarseness and strength combined with acuteness and inquisitiveness," the "restless nervous energy," the "dominant individualism," the "buoyancy and exuberance" delineated by Frederick Jackson Turner as the essential characteristics of the frontier spirit.

Through his daring personal escapades and his equally bold literary ventures, Jack London completely captivated the public imagination during America's strenuous age, producing in less than twenty years more than fifty books on such varied subjects as adventure, agronomy, astral projection, atavism, boating, boxing, bullfighting, business-buccaneering, gold hunting, hoboing, penal reform, political corruption, racial exploitation, social apocalypse, warfare, and the wilderness. His best-known works—among them, "Love of Life," "To Build a Fire," *The Call of the Wild, White Fang,* and *The Sea-Wolf*—have become popular classics, and while U.S. critics have neglected him until recently, his mastery of the art of storytelling has won London worldwide recognition as an author of major importance.

Biography

The only son of spiritualist Flora Wellman, then common-law wife of astrologer William Henry Chaney, was born in San Francisco on 12 January 1876 and named John Griffith Chaney. Chaney had denied his paternity and deserted his wife when he learned of her pregnancy; the majority of London's biographers suggest, nevertheless, that Chaney was Jack's father. On 7 September 1876,

Flora married John London, a Civil War veteran and widower, who gave the child his name and treated him as his own son.

The loneliness and drudgery of Jack's early years, which he later recalled as a time of near poverty and deprivation, instilled in him a lifelong yearning to escape; this escapism may have been the genesis of London's writing career. At first he escaped into the worlds of the imagination and literature, reading such romantic books as *The Voyages of Captain James Cook*, Washington Irving's *The Alhambra*, and Ouida's *Signa* (the inspirational tale of a peasant girl's illegitimate son who rises to fame as a great Italian composer). One of the most important discoveries of his life occurred in 1885 when his family moved back to the city from the farm and Jack found that the Oakland Public Library would lend him books as fast as he could read them: "It was this world of books, now accessible, that practically gave me the basis of my education," he later wrote (*Letters from Jack London*, p. 439).

Other, coarser worlds also played significant roles in young London's education and were afterward incorporated into his writings: the worlds of the slum, the gutter, and the factory; and of the saloon, the sea, and the road, the last three becoming modes of escape from the world of the "work beast," as London depicted the former in such autobiographical works as "The Apostate" (1906) and *John Barleycorn* (1913). Forced early in his life to start working to help support his family, he asserted that "from my ninth year, with the exception of the hours spent in school (and I earned them by hard labor), my life has been one of toil" (*Letters*, p. 86). Repelled by such toil, at the age of fifteen he joined the oyster pirates on San Francisco Bay; the next year he switched to the side of the law as a member of the Fish Patrol; and one week following his seventeenth birthday, he signed as an ablebodied seaman aboard the *Sophia Sutherland*, a sealing schooner bound for Japan and the Bering Sea. This voyage not only provided many of the experiences that would later be fictionalized in *The Sea-Wolf* (1904); it also gave Jack the material for his first successful literary venture, "Story of a Typhoon off the Coast of Japan," which won first prize in a writing contest sponsored by the *San Francisco Morning Call* in November 1893.

Although he tried repeatedly after this initial success to break into print again, it was not until late 1898, after his return from a year in the Klondike, that he was able to sell any of his literary efforts. In the intervening years his education had been further enriched by more toil, by his tramping experiences (recounted in *The Road* [1907]), and by a thirty-day term for vagrancy in the Erie County (N.Y.) Penitentiary. This last was a crucial experience, motivating him to resume his formal education in order to escape the world of "the submerged tenth." Jack returned to Oakland in the fall of 1894, after six months on the road, and enrolled in Oakland High School at the beginning of the next year. There he published several items in the *High School Aegis*, and during this period he began meeting other young intellectuals in the Henry Clay Club and in the Socialist party with whom he could discuss his new-found ideas from such writers as Kant, Darwin, Marx, and Herbert Spencer. In August 1896, after three terms in high school, he managed, through intensive cramming, to pass the entrance examinations for the University of California. The following spring, needing money and impatient to get ahead, he quit school to try his hand at writing. In a feverish flurry lasting several weeks, he typed, sometimes for fifteen hours a day, writings ranging from jokes and triolets and short stories to ponderous essays on science and philosophy. For these efforts he got nothing but blistered fingers, an aching back, and a discouraging pile of rejection slips—an ordeal later fictionalized in *Martin Eden* (1909). Again, to survive, he returned to the world of toil— until 25 July 1897, when with the financial help of his brother-in-law, Captain James H. Shepard, he sailed aboard the S.S. *Umatilla* for Juneau, Alaska, as one of the early argonauts in the great Klondike gold rush.

This was the making of London the writer: "It was in the Klondike that I found myself," he later observed. "There you get your perspective. I got mine" (*Jack London by Himself* [New York: Macmillan, n.d.]). Although he brought back less than five dollars in gold when a severe case of scurvy forced him to return home next summer, he had mined untold riches in human drama, which he would transmute into literary art. He set himself again to writing, with renewed perspective, in the fall of 1898. By the end of that year he had sold the first of several Klondike stories to the *Overland Monthly*; by the next July his "Odyssey of the North" had been accepted by the *Atlantic*; and by the spring of 1900 his first book, *The Son of the Wolf*, had been published by the distinguished Boston firm, Houghton Mifflin. Reviewers immediately recognized in London's work a freshness and narrative power missing in the sentimental romances so popular at the turn of the century, and this new "Kipling of the Klondike" became something of a celebrity almost overnight.

Attempting to settle into a sensible domestic routine, in 1900 London married Bessie Maddern, who bore two daughters: Joan (1901) and Becky (1902). But before the birth of the second child, he became passionately attracted to a brilliant young Stanford student and socialist, Anna Strunsky, with whom he coauthored a dialogue on scientific versus romantic love titled *The Kempton-Wace Letters* (1903). Frustrated in this affair, he subsequently fell in love with Charmian Kittredge, whom he married when his divorce decree became final in November 1905.

In the meantime he had spent the summer of 1902 living in the East End of London, one of the world's worst slums, gathering material for his *People of the Abyss* (1903). He spent several months in Japan and Korea in 1904 reporting the Russo-Japanese War for the Hearst Syndicate. He was also an active crusader for the socialist cause during these years, running for mayor of Oakland on the Socialist ballot in 1901 and 1905, and being elected first president of the Intercollegiate Socialist Society in 1905. In the fall of the same year he went on the lecture circuit through the Midwest and East, including stops at Harvard and Yale, preaching the gospel of revolution, the text of which is found in *War of the Classes* (1905), *The Iron Heel* (1908), and *Revolution and Other Essays* (1910).

In the spring of 1905, after moving from Oakland to the hamlet of Glen Ellen in the heart of the Sonoma Valley, London had been inspired with the idea of sailing his own ship on a seven-year cruise around the world. On 23 April 1907, despite the multifarious problems caused by the San Francisco earthquake the year before, London and his mate-woman Charmian sailed the *Snark* with a crew of five out of San Francisco Bay for Honolulu. The next two years were spent sailing the South Seas until a combination of tropical ailments forced London to abandon his cruise and return to California in the spring of 1909. Although a disaster both physically and fiscally, the *Snark* voyage nevertheless provided London with materials for such important books as *The Cruise of the Snark* (1911), *South Sea Tales* (1911), and *The House of Pride and Other Tales of Hawaii* (1912).

From 1910 until his death, London's primary interest was the development of his famous "Beauty Ranch." From 130 acres in 1905 he had enlarged this model farm to nearly 1500 acres by 1916, employing the latest methods in scientific agriculture and stockbreeding. Although he still traveled frequently—on a four-horse journey into northern California and Oregon in 1911, a six-month voyage around Cape Horn in 1912, to Mexico as a war correspondent for *Collier's* in 1914, and several months in Hawaii in 1915 and 1916—his heart now lay in the Valley of the Moon, and much of his serious writing during these years dealt with his agrarian vision. Examples are *Burning Daylight* (1910), *The Valley of the Moon* (1913), *The Acorn-Planter: A California Forest Play* (1916), and *The Little Lady of the Big House* (1916). At the same time, his socialist fervor was waning; and on 7 March 1916, he resigned from the party "because of its lack of fire and fight, and its loss of emphasis on the class struggle" (*Letters*, p. 467). Shortly afterward he discovered still another new world: the world of archetypes and racial memory as set forth in the recently translated work of C. G. Jung. During the last six months of his life it was this world that fascinated London and permeated such stories as "Like Argus of the Ancient Times" (1917), "The Red One" (1918), and the Hawaiian tales in *On the Makaloa Mat* (1919).

His health, particularly his kidneys, which had been seriously damaged by the tropical fevers contracted on the *Snark* voyage, began to fail at least two years before his death. His physician prescribed a regimen of strict diet, adequate rest, proper exercise, and no alcohol; but, characteristically, London refused to follow this advice, and his condition worsened. He was sent home from Mexico in 1914 after a near-fatal attack of dysentery. By the next year he was suffering chronically from edema, calculi, rheumatism, and the other symptoms of nephritis. Still he kept on, overworking and refusing to heed the ominous signs. On 22 November 1916 he died from an acute attack of "gastro-intestinal type of uremia." His passing was front-page news around the globe, and as friends and fans mourned worldwide, his ashes were buried beneath a large red-lava boulder on the ranch he had worked so lovingly to build.

Major Themes

The pattern of London's writings, like that of his life, is extraordinarily complex, distinguished by contrariety and paradox. Primitivism, Darwinism, environmental determinism, naturalistic nihilism, scientific meliorism, Anglo-Saxonism, rugged individualism, socialism, Christian humanism, pastoralism—all these thematic motifs, apparently conflicting in many instances, are interwoven into his works. Still, there is a discernible pattern in those works, central to which are two recurring questions and an underlying thematic antithesis: What is man's relationship to the natural world? and What is the individual's relationship to his fellow human beings? The thematic antithesis, from which derives the essential creative tension for his literary artistry, is the opposition of materialism versus spiritualism—that is, the tension between the logical and the scientific on one hand and the irrational and the mystical on the other. London persistently denied the latter, professing throughout his life that he was a materialistic monist; but his art betrays him, time and again revealing him to be, in fact, a philosophical dualist and a mythopoeic genius who often wrote better than he knew.

The tension between these contrasting thematic elements is apparent from the outset in London's Northland fiction. At first glance, the stories of the Klondike saga would seem to be standard naturalistic fare: puny man pitted against the inexorable forces of a hostile universe, nature's dice loaded against the individual, who is doomed to extinction, violently and pitilessly. Yet London's presentation is scarcely that of the coldly scientific observer. As was sometimes the case with other naturalists like Frank Norris and Theodore Dreiser, there is a pervading sense of mystical awe toward the cosmic unknown. This mysticism is revealed in "The White Silence," the first story in his first book:

Nature has many tricks wherewith she convinces man of his finity,—the ceaseless flow of the tides, the fury of the storm, the shock of the earthquake, the long roll of heaven's artillery,—but the most tremendous, the most stupefying of all, is the passive phase of the White Silence. All movement ceases, the sky clears, the heavens are as brass; the slightest whisper seems sacrilege, and man becomes timid, affrighted at the sound of his own voice. Sole speck of life journeying across the ghostly wastes of a dead world, he trembles at his audacity, realizes that his is a maggot's life, nothing more. Strange thoughts arise unsummoned, and the mystery of all things strives for utterance. And the fear of death, of God, of the universe, comes over him,—the hope of the Resurrection and the Life, the yearning for immortality, the vain striving of the imprisoned essence,—it is then, if ever, man walks alone with God. [Son of the Wolf, p. 7]

In the face of this awesome natural force, only the fittest stand a chance of survival, and the key to survival is adaptability. Ostensibly this theme appears to be Darwinian; however, London's Northland code demands not only physical but spiritual and moral adaptability, and the greatest "strength of the strong" (as he would preach in his socialist writings) is communal rather than individual. As he stresses in his exemplum "In a Far Country," the real pinch comes not so much in changing one's material habits to meet the rigors of the Northland as in adjusting one's attitude toward one's fellow man: "For the courtesies of ordinary life, he must substitute unselfishness, forbearance, and tolerance. Thus, and thus only, can he gain that pearl of great price,—true comradeship" (Son of the Wolf,

p. 70). Even London's canine protagonists are not entirely exempt from this higher ethic. For instance, Buck, before finally succumbing to "the Call of the Wild," undergoes a spiritual transformation through his selfless devotion to his master, John Thornton, and at the end of the novel he has completely transcended his naturalistic milieu to become the legendary "Ghost Dog" of the Northland. White Fang, in his transformation from killer wolf to household pet, is similarly redeemed by the loving ministry of Weedon Scott: "Human kindness was like a sun shining upon him, and he flourished like a flower planted in good soil" (*White Fang*, p. 305).

The inevitable failure of the ego-centered, loveless individualist is London's major theme in both *The Sea-Wolf* and the autobiographical *Bildungsroman*, *Martin Eden*. "I believe that life is a mess," declares Wolf Larsen; "the strong eat the weak that they may retain their strength. The lucky eat the most and move the longest, that is all" (*Sea-Wolf*, p. 50). One of the strongest characters in American literature, Larsen is nevertheless bound to fail because he is inflexible in his ruthless materialism and because he is incapable of loving the fellow creatures of this earth. Martin Eden, though a more sympathetic character, is likewise doomed: "Being an Individualist, being unaware of the needs of others, of the whole human collective need, Martin Eden lived only for himself, fought only for himself, and, if you please, died for himself," explained London; "[he] failed and died, in my parable. . . because of his lack of faith in man" (*Letters*, p. 307).

Unlike Martin, London himself was redeemed from his own "long sickness" of pessimistic disillusionment because he lived and fought for something besides himself. As he confessed in *John Barleycorn*, "Love, socialism, the PEOPLE . . . were the things that cured and saved me" (p. 257). A humanitarian compassion and a humanistic faith in man, coupled with a righteous resentment of social injustice and of a political system that condoned the economic victimization of the working classes, constituted the basis for London's socialist convictions. His compassion was poignantly articulated in *The People of the Abyss*. And his humanistic faith was clearly proclaimed in the *War of the Classes*:

The capitalist must be taught that socialism deals with. . . the warm human, fallible and frail, sordid and petty, absurd and contradictory, even grotesque, and yet, withal, shot through with flashes and glimmerings of something finer and God-like, with here and there sweetnesses of service and unselfishness, desires for goodness, for renunciation and sacrifice, and with conscience, stern and awful, at times blazingly imperious, demanding the right,—the right, nothing more nor less than the right. [Pp. xvi-xvii]

His socialistic fervor reached its greatest artistic intensity in *The Iron Heel*. Ernest Everhard, the hero, is a composite of Walt Whitman, Eugene V. Debs, Jesus Christ, and London. "He was a poet. A singer in deeds," rhapsodizes his widow and biographer Avis. "And all his life he sang the song of man. And he did it out of sheer love of man, and for man he gave his life and was crucified" (*Iron Heel*, p. 182). Ironically, however, the universal "Brotherhood of Man," for which Everhard has sacrificed his life, must be postponed while the proletariat endures several more centuries under the "Iron Heel" of capitalist oppression.

The waning of London's socialist enthusiasm during the last decade of his life is evident in the shift of major thematic emphasis in his writings, first toward pastoralism and then toward spiritualism, notably Jungian psychology.

Pastoralism is the main theme of London's three Sonoma novels—*Burning Daylight*, *The Valley of the Moon*, and *The Little Lady of the Big House*—and of his last play, *The Acorn-Planter*. In the first of these, the hero, a Klondike bonanza king turned robber baron, is redeemed by the love of a woman who persuades him to renounce the savage world of big business for the arcadian world of ranch life in the Valley of the Moon. In the second, a young working-class couple whose lives have been blighted in the strike-torn city undertake an odyssey that ultimately leads them into the Edenic valley. *The Little Lady of the Big House* dramatizes the agrarian dream on a grander scale but, by contrast, ends in tragedy because the hero, Dick Forrest, becomes totally obsessed with scientific ranching and efficiency. He degenerates into a sterile clockwork character—a successful breeder of stock but a failure as a husband. His wife Paula, childless and frustrated, falls in love with his best friend, and then commits suicide. To be genuinely fruitful, London implies, science must be tempered by the warmer human affections, head balanced by heart. This theme is explicit in his California forest play, which concludes with "the celebration of the death of war and the triumph of the acorn-planters," who with loving hands plant for "life more abundant" as "The New Day dawns, / The day of brotherhood, / The day of man!" (*Acorn-Planter*, p. 84).

The tempering of London's tough-minded scientism is evident in the growing inclination toward spiritualism in his later writings; significantly, this proclivity seems to have been fostered by his agrarian dream. Return to the Edenic valley and the restoration of nature's abundance: these become symbols for spiritual restoration and rebirth. For example, Darrell Standing, the protagonist of *The Star Rover* (1915), is a professor of agronomics sentenced to life imprisonment for killing a colleague in a fit of passion. While in San Quentin, he masters the art of astral projection, or "soul flight," which enables him to move freely in time and space. He dreams of being a peaceful farmer in his next life and at the end of the novel philosophizes: "Spirit alone endures and continues to built upon itself through successive and endless incarnations as it works upward toward the light" (*Star Rover*, p. 329).

London's fascination with the spiritual, which he had rejected dogmatically in his earlier years, culminated with his discovery of Carl Jung's ideas in the late spring of 1916. "I tell you I am standing on the edge of a world so new, so terrible, so wonderful, that I am almost afraid to look over into it," he exclaimed to Charmian that summer (*Book of Jack London*, 2:323). He was not afraid, however, to incorporate this brave new world into his fiction. The stories he produced during the few months before his death were filled with Jungian archetypes.

"The Water Baby," the last story he wrote, is exemplary. Cast in the form of a dialogue between an ancient Hawaiian native who claims the sea as his mother and a younger man named John Lakana (Jack's own Hawaiian name) who claims such mythic stuff is nonsense, the tale clearly dramatizes the interior debate between the author's two conflicting selves: the materialistic monist and the myth-making idealist. London was loath to forgo his scientific skepticism—"But listen, O Young Wise One, to my elderly wisdom," admonishes the old Hawaiian—

This I know: as I grow old I seek less for the truth from without me, and find more of the truth from within me. Why have I thought this thought of my return to my mother and my rebirth from my mother into the sun? You do not know. I do not know, save that, without whisper of man's voice or printed word, without prompting from otherwhere, this thought has arisen from within me, from the deeps of me that are as deep as the sea. [*On the Makaloa Mat*, pp. 150-51]

Strangely enough, and evidently without London's own full awareness, it had been this truth from the deeps within him (this "primordial vision" as Jung called it) that had from the beginning given his best work its great universal and lasting appeal.

Survey of Criticism

Of all the major figures in American literature, London has perhaps received the least critical attention. The reasons are several: traditionally our critical establishment has been eastern and elitist; London was western and popular. While other western writers had won the acceptance of the establishment, including Mark Twain, Hamlin Garland, and Frank Norris, they had done so by moving east; moreover, these three had received the personal approbation of the leading convert to eastern gentility, William Dean Howells. Unlike them, London openly scorned both the East and the establishment. It is worth noting that in all of Howells's hundreds of reviews, London—the most widely publicized literary figure of the age—is nowhere mentioned. Of course, London scarcely helped his own case with his blatant materialism and art-be-damned attitude. Consequently he was dismissed as a "barbarian" and "the traveling salesman of literature" by academic critics like Philo M. Buck, Jr., and Lewis Mumford.

Regardless, a handful of noteworthy critical essays had begun to appear by the 1950s. Maxwell Geismar's "Jack London: The Short Cut," in *Rebels and Ancestors* (1953), though disparaging London's capitulation to the marketplace, brilliantly illuminated the psychological depths of his fiction. Kenneth Lynn's "Jack London: The Brain Merchant," in *The Dream of Success* (1955), suggested that Horatio Alger was a more important influence on London's work than Karl Marx and that *Martin Eden* dramatized a rejection of both the success myth and socialism. Sam Baskett's "Jack London on the Oakland Waterfront" (1955) and "Jack London's Heart of Darkness" (1958), appearing in leading scholarly journals, provided a new credibility for London studies, a credibility further enhanced by Gordon Mills's "Jack London's Quest for Salvation" (1955) and "The Symbolic Wilderness: James Fenimore Cooper and Jack London" (1959).

The academic awakening was clearly in evidence during the next decade, which witnessed the publication not only of an increasing number of critical essays on London but also of three books of seminal importance: *Letters from Jack London*, edited by King Hendricks and Irving Shepard (1965); *Jack London: a Bibliography*, compiled by Hensley Woodbridge et al. (1966); and Franklin Walker's *Jack London and the Klondike* (1966). The *Letters* and *Bibliography*, though not works of criticism themselves, were invaluable tools for the critic. Walker's book combined, for the first time, responsible scholarship and critical assessment in a definitive treatment of the first major phase of London's career, demonstrating that this popular writer was worthy of serious attention. Moreover, there emerged from the graduate schools during this decade a new generation of young scholars willing to dedicate their critical energies to London's works: Alfred S. Shivers, "The Demoniacs in Jack London" (1961) and "Jack London's Mate-Women" (1964); Earle Labor, "Jack London's Symbolic Wilderness: Four Versions" (1962) and "Paradise Almost Regained" (1965); James Giles, "Beneficial Atavism in Frank Norris and Jack London" (1969) and "Jack London 'Down and Out' in England: The Relevance of the Sociological Study *People of the Abyss* to London's Fiction" (1969); and Earl J. Wilcox, "Jack London's Naturalism: The Example of *The Call of the Wild*" (1969).

London criticism came of age in the 1970s. A harbinger was James McClintock's pioneering study, "Jack London's Use of Carl Jung's *Psychology of the Unconscious*" (1970). Two years later *The Fiction of Jack London: A Chronological Bibliography*, compiled by Dale L. Walker and James E. Sisson, provided London scholars with another precise, indispensable tool, including brief critical observations along with publication data. In 1974 appeared the first book-length critical survey of London's career, Earle Labor's *Jack London*. Demonstrating that London, contrary to received academic opinion, was not only a dedicated professional craftsman but also a mythopoeic genius who often wrote better than he knew, Labor concluded that the recognition of London as a major figure in American literature was long overdue. James McClintock's *White Logic* (1975) was a perceptive in-depth critical analysis of London's short fiction, which indicated that the enduring, universal appeal of this fiction was due not so much to "a robust celebration of turn of the century popular values" as to "London's ability to use his craft to capture the struggle between the most fundamentally human desire for salvation and the most fundamentally human fear of damnation" (p. 174).

Nineteen seventy-six was distinguished by celebrations of the one-hundredth anniversary of Jack London's birth, as well as the nation's bicentennial. The Pacific Center for Western Historical Studies sponsored the International Jack London Centennial Symposium. Three scholarly journals—*Modern Fiction Studies*, *Western American Literature*, and *Pacific Historian*—published special Jack

London numbers, which revealed the extraordinary range of this writer's literary achievement. London studies at last had achieved academic respectability. Two more important books appeared in 1977. Joan Sherman's *Jack London: A Reference Guide* handily complemented the Woodbridge and Walker/Sisson bibliographies. Andrew Sinclair's *Jack*, while overplaying the pathological aspects of London's life, nonetheless proved useful to the critics in debunking the myths and misconceptions of such fictionalized biographies as Irving Stone's *Sailor on Horseback* (1938). Further evidence that London had indeed arrived as a serious literary artist was Ray Ownbey's *Jack London: Essays in Criticism* (1978), a collection of essays by nine academic critics, which would have been virtually impossible to assemble a decade earlier. Three more basic tools for the London scholar became available in 1979. Dale Walker's *No Mentor But Myself*, the first collection of London's extensive but heretofore scattered comments on the craft of writing, conclusively proved London to be a thoroughgoing professional who took his trade far more seriously than he had usually admitted in his public voice. Richard Etulain's *Jack London on the Road*, a gathering of hobo writings, was, in the same tradition with Walker's *Jack London and the Klondike*, a first-rate scholarly work that shed definitive light on another crucial phase of London's career. Finally, in 1979, Russ Kingman's *A Pictorial Life of Jack London* gave the critics an unpretentious, reliable source of biographical information, sympathetic but without the exaggerations that had marred previous popular studies of London's life.

The 1980s promise to secure London's reputation with forthcoming biographical and critical studies by such scholars as Howard Lachtman, Susan Ward, and Charles Watson; the inclusion of London's best works, edited by Donald Pizer, in the Literary Classics of the United States series; and the publication by the Stanford University Press of a new three-volume edition of London's correspondence, edited by Earle Labor, Robert Leitz, and Milo Shepard.

Bibliography

Works by Jack London

The Son of the Wolf. Boston: Houghton, Mifflin, 1900.
A Daughter of the Snows. Philadelphia: J. B. Lippincott, 1902.
Children of the Frost. New York: Macmillan, 1902.
The Call of the Wild. New York: Macmillan, 1903.
The People of the Abyss. New York: Macmillan, 1903.
The Sea-Wolf. New York: Macmillan, 1904.
War of the Classes. New York: Macmillan, 1905.
White Fang. New York: Macmillan, 1906.
The Road. New York: Macmillan, 1907.
The Iron Heel. New York: Macmillan, 1908.
Martin Eden. New York: Macmillan, 1909.
Revolution and Other Essays. New York: Macmillan, 1910.

Burning Daylight. New York: Macmillan, 1910.

The Cruise of the Snark. New York: Macmillan, 1911.

John Barleycorn. New York: Century, 1913.

The Valley of the Moon. New York: Macmillan, 1913.

The Star Rover. New York: Macmillan, 1915.

The Acorn-Planter: A California Forest Play. New York: Macmillan, 1916.

The Little Lady of the Big House. New York: Macmillan, 1916.

The Red One. New York: Macmillan, 1918.

On the Makaloa Mat. New York: Macmillan, 1919.

Letters from Jack London. Ed. King Hendricks and Irving Shepard. New York: Odyssey, 1965.

Curious Fragments: Jack London's Tales of Fantasy Fiction. Ed. Dale L. Walker. Preface by Philip José Farmer. Port Washington, N.Y.: Kennikat, 1975.

No Mentor But Myself: A Collection of Articles, Essays, Reviews and Letters by Jack London, on Writing and Writers. Ed. Dale L. Walker. Foreword by Howard Lachtman. Port Washington, N.Y.: Kennikat, 1979.

Jack London on the Road: The Tramp Diary and Other Hobo Writings. Ed. Richard W. Etulain. Logan: Utah State University, 1979.

Studies of Jack London

Baskett, Sam S. "Jack London on the Oakland Waterfront." *American Literature* 27 (November 1955): 363-71.

————. "Jack London's Heart of Darkness." *American Quarterly* 10 (September 1958): 66-77.

————. "*Martin Eden*: Jack London's 'Splendid Dream.' " *Western American Literature* 12 (Fall 1977): 199-214.

Campbell, Jeanne. "Falling Stars: Myth in 'The Red One.' " *Jack London Newsletter* 11 (May-December 1978): 86-96.

Etulain, Richard. "The Lives of Jack London." *Western American Literature* 11 (Summer 1976): 149-64.

Geismar, Maxwell. *Rebels and Ancestors: The American Novel, 1890-1915*. Boston: Houghton Mifflin, 1953, pp. 139-216.

Giles, James R. "Beneficial Atavism in Frank Norris and Jack London." *Western American Literature* 4 (Spring 1969): 15-27.

————. "Jack London Down and Out in England: The Relevance of the Sociological Study *People of the Abyss* to London's Fiction." *Jack London Newsletter* 2 (September-December 1969): 79-83.

Kingman, Russ. *A Pictorial Life of Jack London*. New York: Crown, 1979.

Labor, Earle. "From 'All Gold Canyon' to *The Acorn Planter*: Jack London's Agrarian Vision." *Western American Literature* 11 (Summer 1976): 83-101.

————. *Jack London*. TUSAS. New York: Twayne, 1974.

————. "Jack London's Symbolic Wilderness: Four Versions." *Nineteenth-Century Fiction* 17 (Summer 1962): 149-61.

————. "Paradise Almost Regained." *Saturday Review*, 3 April 1965, pp. 43-44.

Lachtman, Howard. "Revisiting Jack London's Valley of the Moon." *Pacific Historian* 24 (Summer 1980): 141-56.

London, Charmian Kittredge. *The Book of Jack London*. 2 vols. New York: Century, 1921.

London, Joan. *Jack London and His Times: An Unconventional Biography*. New York: Doubleday, Doran, 1939; Seattle: University of Washington, 1968, with a new introduction by the author.

Lynn, Kenneth S. *The Dream of Success: A Study of the Modern American Imagination*. Boston: Little, Brown, 1955, pp. 75-118.

McClintock, James I. "Jack London's Use of Carl Jung's *Psychology of the Unconscious*." *American Literature* 42 (November 1970): 336-47.

———. *White Logic: Jack London's Short Stories*. Grand Rapids, Mich.: Wolf House Books, 1975.

Mills, Gordon. "Jack London's Quest for Salvation." *American Quarterly* 7 (Spring 1955): 3-14.

———. "The Symbolic Wilderness: James Fenimore Cooper and Jack London." *Nineteenth-Century Fiction* 13 (March 1959): 329-40.

———. "The Transformation of Material in a Mimetic Fiction." *Modern Fiction Studies* 22 (Spring 1976): 9-22.

Ownbey, Ray Wilson, ed. *Jack London: Essays in Criticism*. Santa Barbara, Calif.: Peregrine Smith, 1978.

Peterson, Clell T. "Jack London's Sonoma Novels." *American Book Collector* 9 (October 1958): 15-20.

Sherman, Joan R. *Jack London: A Reference Guide*. Boston: G. K. Hall, 1977.

Shivers, Alfred S. "The Demoniacs in Jack London." *American Book Collector* 12 (September 1961): 11-14.

———. "Jack London's Mate-Women." *American Book Collector* 15 (October 1964): 17-21.

Sinclair, Andrew. *Jack: A Biography of Jack London*. New York: Harper and Row, 1977.

Stasz, Clarice. "Androgyny in the Novels of Jack London." *Western American Literature* 11 (Summer 1976): 121-33.

———. "The Social Construction of Biography: The Case of Jack London." *Modern Fiction Studies* 22 (Spring 1976): 51-71.

Stone, Irving. *Sailor on Horseback: The Biography of Jack London*. Boston: Houghton Mifflin, 1938; rpt. as *Jack London, Sailor on Horseback: A Biographical Novel*. New York: New American Library, 1969, and as *Irving Stone's Jack London and Twenty-Eight Selected Jack London Stories*. Garden City, N.Y.: Doubleday, 1977.

Walker, Dale L., and Sisson, James E., III, comps. *The Fiction of Jack London: A Chronological Bibliography*. El Paso: Texas Western, 1972.

Walker, Franklin. *Jack London and the Klondike*. San Marino, Calif.: Huntington Library, 1966.

Wilcox, Earl J. "Jack London's Naturalism: The Example of *The Call of the Wild*." *Jack London Newsletter* 2 (May-August 1969): 91-101.

Woodbridge, Hensley C. "Jack London's Current Reputation Abroad." *Pacific Historian* 21 (Summer 1977): 166-77.

———; London, John; and Tweney, George H. comps. *Jack London: A Bibliography*. Georgetown, Calif.: Talisman, 1966; enlarged ed., Millwood, N.Y.: Kraus, 1973.

Kerry Ahearn

LARRY McMURTRY
(1936-)

I once asked a friend interested in western writers if he had read Larry McMurtry, and he replied, "Which one?" He was facetious and not. McMurtry, native of the Texas plains, son and grandson of cattlemen, began as a writer of his region and has continued to make place very important in his fiction, but he has sought to leave Texas behind. He has reenacted the story—Willa Cather, Wright Morris, and others have gone before—of the talented youth who must leave the small midwestern town to search for challenge and complexity. He completed three novels, *Horseman, Pass By* (1961), *Leaving Cheyenne* (1963), and *The Last Picture Show* (1966), while still in his twenties, when he had spent little time outside his home state and had seen, he admitted, little inside it; those novels occupy themselves with Texas rural and small-town life. In his thirties, after moving to the Washington, D.C., area, he published three more novels—*Moving On* (1970), *All My Friends Are Going to Be Strangers* (1972), and *Terms of Endearment* (1975)—each of which moves for its major statement more beyond the rural and Texas than the one before. His most recent novel, *Somebody's Darling* (1978), concerns itself with Hollywood and allows Texas only a minor role.

Early in his career, McMurtry wore a sweatshirt inscribed *MINOR REGIONAL NOVELIST*; he too was being facetious and not. From his first published work, his ambivalent attitude toward Texas has been clear. Although one can rightfully refer to him as a western writer, it should be with the understanding that he is struggling to escape "regional," a term far more pejorative (as it has been used on him) than "minor." He complained in 1968, "We [Texans] aren't thought of as quaintly vulgar anymore. Some may find us *dangerously* vulgar, but the majority just find us boring" (*In a Narrow Grave*, p. xiii). Seven years later he added, "I was halfway through my sixth Texas novel when I suddenly began to notice that where place was concerned, I was sucking air" ("The Texas Moon and Elsewhere," p. 29). The connection between outsiders' views and his difficulties with Texas material can only be guessed at, but a thoughtful reading of his novels shows that disenchantment with the possibilities of Texas began long before

Terms of Endearment to influence seriously the shape and content of his fiction, and not always for the better. Escape was overdue.

Biography

Perhaps the child is father of the man, but McMurtry's adulthood is more significant than his early years, and his art is more important than his life. Yet since he has written in intimate detail about his home country, biography is of some literary as well as voyeuristic interest.

Larry McMurtry was born in Wichita Falls, Texas, on 3 June 1936, spent his first eighteen years in or near Archer City, and graduated at age twenty-two from North Texas State University. From the outside, his young life seems a not atypical plains-Texas rearing: high school letterman in basketball and baseball, 4-H Club officer, band member, school newspaper editor, student actor. Only from the college years do a few short stories, some bad poetry, an insightful piece of criticism on the Beat Generation, and the McMurtry-founded, renegade *Coexistence Review* (an updated title might be *Détente Digest*) suggest that the mild-mannered fellow from Archer City would cast a cold eye on his native place and seek to become its literary interpreter.

Speaking recently about his Texas background, he predicted "I think it will gradually fade out of my future. I think I've written most of what interests me about [it]" (Schmidt, *Unredeemed Dreams*, p. 3). His novels, taken in order, show his movement, physical and spiritual, away from home. Though the fiction has portrayed an attachment to wild and impulsive action, McMurtry has broken gradually from his high plains heritage, and to know just how places his novels in an interesting perspective.

Directly from secondary school, he enrolled at Rice University in Houston but moved back after a semester to the congenial plains and North Texas State, where he claims to have written fifty-two stories—he later committed them to the flames—before deciding that his links with ranch life might serve his fiction. Out of this decision came *Horseman, Pass By*, much of the first draft written in the summer of 1958 before McMurtry began work toward the master's degree in English at Rice.

Success came with startling speed: a Wallace Stegner Fellowship to Stanford in 1960, the publication of his first novel the next year, work begun by Paramount on *Hud* in 1962, his second novel out the following year, a Guggenheim Award for creative writing in 1964. As his experience outside rural Texas grew, so did his willingness to express disdain for the parochialism of the home place, culminating in the frantic satire of *The Last Picture Show*.

During this time, McMurtry had been composing essays, collected as *In a Narrow Grave* (1968), that show that his maverick dissatisfactions gradually extended beyond the small town to Texas of cities and suburbs. He announced in the Preface: "Pussyfooting is a vice I have been concerned to avoid." Homer Bannon would have said it with more salt, but it is true that McMurtry shares with him a no-nonsense view of oil-Texas's vulgar shows. His Introduction, for example, judged that the force or passion of Texas is "part ridiculous and part tragic." In "Love, Death, & the Astrodome," he described the decade's greatest symbol for urban oneupsmanship and conspicuous consumption. "A Handful of Roses" generalized further: all cities of Texas are like Houston, tainted by "wheelerdealerism...an extension of the frontier ethos" and too young to be generally urbane. He adorns his account with such eccentrics as "a very wealthy sixtyish lady [who ordered] her chauffeur to pull her Cadillac alongside an acquaintance's Chrysler, so she could be sure her car was longer" (p. 125). One finds little pussyfooting here but also little weight—his satire nips at the heels rather than going for the vitals.

McMurtry focuses most of his attention on rural Texas, which he categorizes by the divisions of his growing up: "I think of my childhood as country; and my youth as small town" (Peavy, *Larry McMurtry*, p. 26). The difference, as he explains it, lay in social complexity, and his description of that index is instructive: in the country "you work things out in terms of your family and neighbors," while life in the towns "tends to be generally confusing. It often contains more unsatisfactory elements—things that embarrass you, or humiliate you, or challenge you" (Peavy, *McMurtry*, p. 26). For a man to recall his adolescence as "generally confusing" does not seem unusual, but to attribute the unpleasant memories largely to a social place, and specifically people outside the family, provides an interesting lead. The comparison seems more appropriate between innocent childhood and turbulent adolescence (inevitable "passages") than between country and town. No one can speak so well for McMurtry's case, of course, as he can, but a reader does well to remember this hint of bias against social complexity and to look for its influence on McMurtry's fiction.

McMurtry's eagerness to belittle his native state, small town and large, does not by itself make him either interesting or reprehensible; his volume of essays, though the best biographical source available, would bear no more than mentioning if the final piece, "Take My Saddle from the Wall: A Valediction," were not of such a remarkably different tenor from the rest of the collection. To examine this difference is to understand a basic fact about McMurtry's creative temperament— that negative reactions (not merely ambiguous ones) set him to write those novels that he is still pleased publicly to call his own—and another fact about his perception of himself as a regional writer—that whereas a safe course lay in treating the "simple" (the country Texas of his childhood, the now-dead magic of the working cowboy's life), to write honestly of Texas meant dealing with the complexities of small town (as in *The Last Picture Show*) and then urban life (as in *Moving On* and subsequent novels). His sympathetic impulse was monopolized in the beginning by a vanished Texas and has since been transferred to sensitive women and confused, artistic men; to write about modern Texas in general reduced sympathy and increased the incidence of caricature and black humor in his fiction.

In "Take My Saddle from the Wall," McMurtry writes of his family and the west Texas land where in the 1880s they bought a half-section for three dollars an acre. He was born there recently enough to have known the cattleman's "heroic concept of life." He writes: "Riding out at sunup with a group of cowboys, I have often felt the power of that myth myself" ("Take My Saddle," p. 148). Even so, he recognizes that to partake of the myth risks mental and emotional gelding: cowboy manhood excludes women, promotes stoicism, substitutes aphorisms for hard thinking, and turns away from the present toward a simplified view of the past. As an example of the condition, McMurtry quotes his Uncle Jeff, who wrote a week after his wife died in an automobile accident, "Yes it was an awful tragedy to have Mint crushed in the smashup, my car was a total loss too" ("Take My Saddle," p. 152).

"Take My Saddle" distinguishes itself from all the others by its indulgent tone, and that seems a result not simply of family but also of place. Although the clan ascended to Cadillacs and big ranches, he does not picture them as part of the vogue: "When I saw the McMurtrys, I saw them on the ground that had always held them, the great ring of the plains, with the deep sky and the brown ridges and the restless grass being shaken by the wind as it passed on its long journey from the Rockies south" ("Take My Saddle," p. 157). In those images lies the strength of Texas in McMurtry's imagination, but such a force counts for little in the world of the novel, that social and middle-class art form.

McMurtry understands and has sought to make a new life and out of it a new expression. "The East," he says, "encourages one to think hard and subtly, the West prompts one to imagine. . . . The value of the East is . . . above all, social" ("Sky Hunger," p. 76). The limitations of his Texas background (as distinct from the millions of other Texas lives) are not difficult to perceive. They cluster around the word *social*; he has written about Archer County's lack of books and its stultifying uniformity of thought. But most important, McMurtry the novelist has been left with a past that does not "mesh [with his] present" ("Sky Hunger," p. 40), and one almost irrelevant now to his creative temperament.

Major Themes

In a Narrow Grave defends Texas as a rich ground for the novelist because it is in transition from rural to urban: "As the cowboys leave the range and learn to accommodate themselves to the suburbs, defeats that are tragic in quality must occur and may be recorded" (p. xv). Thus the most persistent themes in McMurtry's early fiction concern social change, the death of old traditions, and the plight of young men and women trying to make their way without guidance. Again and again, McMurtry indicts the parents of the new suburban class or those of parental age, sometimes by means of cynical portraits such as Lois Farrow, Hud, Professor Duffin, and Godwin Lloyd-Jones, sometimes by the conspicuous absence of all parental figures. But the best theme to begin with is the land itself. In the early fiction, the relationship between the protagonist and the place was paramount, with most other themes defined by it. Homer Bannon, Sam the Lion, Gideon Fry's Dad, Roger Waggoner—all have lived knowing life's best contentment because of their connection with the land. They are also anachronisms. The young protagonists who must make their way in the towns elicit from McMurtry more sympathy than any other characters in the early novels.

The land defines conflict in *Horseman, Pass By,* and so completely do it and its representative Homer Bannon monopolize positive values that McMurtry has subsequently rejected the novel as slight and sentimental. But McMurtry admits he has not reread his work, and his story of Homer, Lonnie, and Hud is better than he remembers, a sparer, more honest tale than the film Paramount made of it.

The opening words of Lonnie's prologue establish a reverence in retrospect for the uncomplicated country life he knew on Homer's ranch:

I remember how green the early oat fields were, that year, and how the plains looked in April, after the mesquite leafed out.... When I rode out with him on Saturdays, Grandad would sometimes get down from his horse, to show me how the grass was shooting runners over the droughty ground; and he told me that nature would always work her own cures, if people would be patient. [*Horseman, Pass By,* p. 5]

Homer represents a yeoman ethic, for he is in harmony with the land. His eyes are "clear," and "the plains lay clear"; his hair is "sandy," like the "droughty ground." His patterns and sense of time are formed by the natural world, and as such he cannot respond to the exploitative ethic represented by his stepson Hud, who wants to convert the ranch into an oil field. Hud's villainy reveals itself in a host of ways: his lazy walk, his sour moods, his flashy clothes, the way his "cattle-caller" horn and loud engine blast the evening stillness. Utterly indifferent to the land, he becomes an amoral force in the novel, destroying Homer and supplanting his ethic. The grass runners knit the world together, but the oilmen's roads will tear up the turf and let the wind blow the land away.

Horseman, Pass By—the phrase from Yeats's poetry and gravestone—is an elegy, as concerned with myth as Yeats was, and speaking from the heart as it does, embodies the kind of wisdom found in the purest fairy tales. Yet to read the novel only on this level is to give less than its due; McMurtry also portrays a reality of a different sort, and that too begins in the prologue when Lonnie climbs the windmill at night to dream, as he puts it, "of all the important things...my honors, my worries, my ambitions.... When it was clear enough I could see the airplane beacons from the airport in Wichita Falls" (*Horseman, Pass By,* p. 7). The plains are empty, and life, outside the moments of conflict, can be ineffably boring. Lonnie can appreciate the endurance of his grandfather and the hired hand Jesse, but he romanticizes the honkytonk life of the towns over that of the ranch. Homer's life has taken on a kind of purity because, as he admits, his wild days are past. Hud and Lonnie live in a land of temptation. McMurtry's narrative hints that temptations of money and machines pervade the world as never before. The land is losing its magic power, even for those who still live on it.

McMurtry has in his own life moved toward the city and its complexities and confusions, and his essays and articles recounting subsequent visits to the plains

West show his lack of interest now in the simplicity of the country. His fictional protagonists reenact that movement; once exposed to towns and cities, they cannot regress, even though they fear the complexity. When Sonny Crawford tries to flee into the country at the end of *The Last Picture Show*, he sees only emptiness and returns to town. In *Moving On*, when Patsy Carpenter's life in Houston begins to fall apart, she finds solitude at her uncle-in-law Roger Waggoner's ranch but no answers; later she violates the sanctuary by taking her lover there. When Danny Deck, victim-hero of *All My Friends Are Going to Be Strangers*, returns to Texas after a year in California, he is at first exultant at seeing the huge Texas sky but becomes increasingly depressed when he lowers his eyes to see the dirty towns, vicious and ignorant Texas Rangers, and especially his own Uncle L of the Hacienda of the Bitter Waters, a bitter parody of Homer Bannon—finally, Danny admits, a "sonofabitch." By the third novel of the Houston trilogy, *Terms of Endearment*, the plains seem no longer worth mentioning; the cowboy figure has metamorphosed into man-boy Vernon Dalhart, Aurora Greenway's toy, who lives in his Lincoln Continental atop a twenty-story parking garage, and who in his most serious conversation characterizes himself by saying, "It's just ignorance. That's my trouble" (*Terms*, p. 231).

In truth, the limitations of the landscape themes become apparent in the second novel, *Leaving Cheyenne*, a story exclusively rural. This description of a lifelong love triangle stands as a curious regression for McMurtry; his first-person narrators seem true but, like his Uncle Jeff, cannot articulate much more than garrulousness or respond with any depth or self-awareness to their setting or situation. McMurtry learned that the rural Texas milieu had no magic except what he brought to it, that the man-on-the-range myth becomes powerful only in retrospect and from another point of reference. Little wonder that in subsequent novels the land plays its thematic role only by indirection, if at all. It is a power McMurtry still feels, but on a recent trip west he noted, "for that. . .two days is enough" ("Sky Hunger," p. 76). Like love, the magic of the land cannot be excited in any reader who does not already know its feel. McMurtry's fiction after *Leaving Cheyenne* seeks other sources of strength.

Numerous critics have noted that McMurtry's Texas fiction focuses upon initiation; the transition from adolescence to adulthood is the dominant theme in the first three novels, and initiations of other sorts are central to the last three. Like most other writers dealing with the theme, McMurtry emphasizes loss as a part of the initiation process, usually the loss of innocence. Thus Lonnie finds himself without family and security as Hud seizes control. In *Moving On* Jim and Patsy Carpenter find that their leisure and dilettantish ways cannot insulate them from a harsh world. Danny Deck strays into California and marriage only to be mangled by both and returns to Texas but finds no balm. Emma Horton, McMurtry's most sympathetic recent characterization, learns that life is most efficiently lived if one becomes truly intimate with no one; she refuses to accept that initiation, and her death becomes a thematic necessity—cancer arrives to provide a means. Her mother Aurora lives efficiently on.

The distinctive role initiation plays in revealing McMurtry's vision involves another turn of the screw: initiation and loss can be equated. The loss his characters experience is not, as in the archetypal initiation, the abandonment of an inferior state for a better one. What McMurtry's characters will lose is hope; their situations are always worse than before. Lonnie is too young to recognize this plight, and the trio in *Leaving Cheyenne* is exempted from self-knowledge, but that does not alter the essential McMurtry statement. Danny Deck's success as a novelist takes him to San Francisco, where he has all his dreams: sufficient money, time to write, a wife, the excitement of awaiting their child's birth. Strange forces beyond his control, the "complexities" McMurtry ascribes to life outside the ranch, bring Danny down with the rapid absurdity of Greek drama. Emma Horton, born under the same star, suffers a similar fate. Patsy Carpenter pursues hope to the end of *Moving On*, seems to have found a good California life in *Terms of Endearment*, but in the recent *Somebody's Darling* we learn that she has again divorced and has "moved north."

The progression from innocence to unhappiness is most clearly shaped in *The Last Picture Show* and was well dramatized in the Hollywood film. Orphan Sonny Crawford's coming of age in a Texas town very much like McMurtry's Archer City presents a bitterness at the adult world's betrayals that is barely disguised by slapstick humor.

The basic statement of *The Last Picture Show*—that there is nowhere for Sonny to hide and nothing for him to seek—shapes every chapter. The "good" people can offer a passive concern, while the others are filled with a passionate intensity. Love has no power. In this survey of human existence, three aspects stand out as representative of life's demeaning futility: human sexuality, the absence of community and family, and the illusory nature of friendship.

For the first time in his fiction, McMurtry frankly portrays the sexual; he gives, in fact, a complete catalog of bestialities and infidelities. The young men of Sonny's age seem demonic, and the attractive women, Lois and Jacy Farrow, are cynical and exploitative. Sonny's affair with the lonely wife of his football coach produces no joyous intimacy or communication. As Ruth admits, he is just a boy; ironically, she proves herself no more stable. At the end, when he returns to her by default, she longs to give him "something it had taken her forty years to learn, something wise or brave or beautiful that she could finally say. . .just what Sonny needed to know about life," but the rush of desire makes her forget (*Last Picture Show*, p. 219).

The absence of family and community is more than just an index of small-town boredom. There is a suggestion that once life offered more; in Sam the Lion's youth, the town created a different kind of energy, but now men like Abilene and Coach Popper seem the best male specimens. Oil money has brought only boredom to the Farrows, and the decline of cattle ranching has brought the town to its last breath (the only cattle in the novel arrive in a stranger's truck, which kills the mute sweeper Billy). Sonny is a Lonnie with self-consciousness;

in the novel's opening sentence we learn that he is special, sensitive, and feels a loneliness close to anguish.

Without traditions or a secure social order, the young men have little but sex and sports to occupy them, and McMurtry creates a host of ironies by intersecting the two and playing with notions of teamwork and competitive individualism, comradeship and sexual competition. Thus Sonny sleeps with his coach's wife. The gang victimizes Billy at the drive-in, demeaning him with the pretended gift of sexual initiation. McMurtry gives best expression to this theme of illusory friendship when he pits Sonny against Duane, his best pal, for the favors of Jacy (Sonny should have known better, for he played in the line, with Duane in the backfield), who will tease them both but save the ultimate for the fraternity boys in Dallas.

Even a quick reading of *The Last Picture Show* yields many such examples of social satire, yet an equally effective way of examining the darkness of Sonny's initiation is to consider the positive forces in the novel. Sam the Lion, like Ruth Popper, gives warmth and a kind of authority for Sonny but counts no more in the end than the mute Billy, whose brotherly affection is also removed by death. McMurtry chooses for this tale the same pattern of personal losses found in his first two novels: losing makes these stories move. Sonny loses everyone, and as his creator said later, he "is never going to get beyond the view of manhood that the town offers him. . . the prowess of a high school athlete" (Peavy, *McMurtry*, p. 95). Some readers might find such a conclusion imposed rather than earned, for Ruth and Sam and the cafe waitress Genevieve attempt to make Sonny something more, and he, uniquely, has a sense of being "the only human creature in the town" (*Last Picture Show*, p. 1). To limit him to the views of the caricatured society is to ignore the "invisible man" theme or suggest that the novel does not take it seriously. That might be the most convincing evidence of the darkness.

Loss as the inevitable outcome of initiation is not a theme left behind when McMurtry focuses on older characters in his final three Texas novels. The great exploration for such postadolescent characters as Jim and Patsy Carpenter, Flap and Emma Horton, and Danny Deck is sex and marriage. In every case, holy matrimony is wholly miserable, incompatible with the basic human (usually masculine, usually sexual) desire to exploit.

Those who make their way through *Terms of Endearment* and emerge puzzled as to what organizes and directs the novel might well think of marriage as the major theme and widow Aurora Greenway the aging prophetess. Like *Leaving Cheyenne*, this novel presents not a vision of life as it is lived but a fantasy antidote: men's savage and possessive love is somehow lulled by a strong woman who charms them so completely that she occupies the center, loved by all but controlled by none. At this trick, Molly is but a rough country cousin to Houston's Aurora, who controls an ex-general, a retired opera singer, a jet-setting yachtsman, a bank executive, and Vernon the doll-hearted cowboy-oilman. McMurtry remarks that *Leaving Cheyenne* depended on a "what-if" premise, so "little wonder people adored it" (Peavy, *McMurtry*, p. 34). *Terms of Endearment* tries to tickle the same way.

Although the novel never really touches ground, it has an internal logic of its own relative to the subject of marriage. Aurora swings counterpoint to everyone else, and so she is, the novel tries to convince us, happy. While her maid Rosie and her daughter Emma bring themselves anguish trying to take marriage and life seriously, she operates by the philosophy that the highest goal in life is to be charming, an "inestimable delight." She avoids remarrying because the world has taught her that strength and compassion do not go together in men; "the nicer [suitors] seem to be the hopeless ones" (*Terms of Endearment*, p. 153). As final confirmation, the novel's last chapter details the breakdown of Emma's marriage and her life, coterminously. Her mother and Patsy Carpenter stand over her grave, like monuments of How To.

The philosophy of taking nothing seriously seems to guide even McMurtry, who creates superficial characters only to condescend to them. Yet *Terms of Endearment* is good evidence that he cannot think positively of any truly intimate relationship between a man and a woman. The suitors in Aurora's section represent various sorts of confused aggression and aggressive confusion, none of which she acknowledges, but none of them shows the destructiveness of Emma's husband Flap, who makes her life as bleak as the Nebraska town his career finally leads them to. Aurora's men receive McMurtry's condescending humor, and Flap his contempt. Intimacy means exploitation of the most cancerous kind, and loss rules this novel too.

McMurtry the novelist is now in a period of conflicting tendencies. *Somebody's Darling* continues the theme of skepticism about marriage, and its preoccupation is with loss and the inevitable victimization of sensitive and kind human beings. Yet the novel also shows McMurtry's eagerness to escape the Texas mythos, though Owen Oarson—ex-tractor-salesman from Lubbock and a double-zero whoreson—provides much of the sexual predation in the Hollywood setting. The focus on a non-Texas milieu seems to ease McMurtry away from the stereotypes, punning, and facile black humor of the previous four novels and toward a more subtle and sensitive use of character. He has lately spoken of a return to writing about Texas, and it will be interesting to read and consider the results. Texas might be the first Wild West state to outgrow its stereotypes, and a mature McMurtry might render that.

Survey of Criticism

McMurtry's last three novels have not received strongly favorable reviews, and he is still introduced by *Holiday* as the "well-known author of *Hud*, [and] *Last Picture Show*." As yet, a large body of criticism and commentary has not appeared; what has focuses upon his early Texas writing.

The major assessment of his work, from college poems through *Terms of Endearment*, is Charles D. Peavy's *Larry McMurtry* (1977), a well-researched and generally laudatory but not uncritical book, including much biographical information and commentary on all the Texas novels. He incorporates his three previous articles in *Western American Literature*, personal interviews, and his reading in the McMurtry manuscripts at the University of Houston. Two monographs worth consulting are Thomas Landess's *Larry McMurtry* (1969), an intelligent study of the first three novels plus *In a Narrow Grave*, and R. L. Neinstein's *The Ghost Country* (1976), which focuses on the weight of Texas past.

A number of good journal articles have appeared on specific aspects of McMurtry's fiction. Raymond C. Phillips, Jr., "The Ranch as Place and Symbol in the Novels of Larry McMurtry" (1975), and Janis P. Stout, "Journeying as a Metaphor for Cultural Loss in the Novels of Larry McMurtry" (1976), consider the novels to and including *All My Friends*. Kerry Ahearn's "More d'Urban: The Texas Novels of Larry McMurtry" (1976) charts his "decline to success."

Those interested in McMurtry and film should read E. Pauline Degenfelder's "McMurtry and the Movies: *Hud* and *The Last Picture Show*" (1975), James K. Folsom's "*Shane* and *Hud*: Two Stories in Search of a Medium" (1970), and Pauline Kael's chapter on *Hud* in *I Lost It at the Movies* (1965), though she barely mentions the novel.

Fitting no category but worth reading are Naomi Lindstrom's "The Novel in Texas: How Big a Patrimony?" (1978) and William T. Pilkington's "The Dirt Farmer and the Cowboy: Notes on Two Texas Essayists" (1969). Both would interest students of southwestern literature.

Bibliography

Works by Larry McMurtry

Horseman, Pass By. New York: Harper, 1961.
Leaving Cheyenne. New York: Harper and Row, 1963.
The Last Picture Show. New York: Dial Press, 1966.
"Cowboys, Movies, Myths, and Cadillacs: Realism in the Western." In *Man and the Movies*. Ed. W. R. Robinson. Baton Rouge: Louisiana State University Press, 1967, pp. 46-52.
In a Narrow Grave: Essays on Texas. Austin: Encino Press, 1968.
Moving On. New York: Simon and Schuster, 1970.
All My Friends Are Going to Be Strangers. New York: Simon and Schuster, 1972.
Terms of Endearment. New York: Simon and Schuster, 1975.
"The Texas Moon, and Elsewhere." *Atlantic Monthly* 235 (March 1975): 29-36.
"Sky Hunger." *Holiday* 58 (April 1977): 38-41.
Somebody's Darling. New York: Simon and Schuster, 1978.

Studies of Larry McMurtry

Ahearn, Kerry. "More d'Urban: The Texas Novels of Larry McMurtry." *Texas Quarterly* 19 (Autumn 1976): 109-29.

Davis, Kenneth W. "The Themes of Initiation in the Works of Larry McMurtry and Tom Mayer." *Arlington Quarterly* 2 (Winter 1969-1970): 29-43.

Degenfelder, E. Pauline. "McMurtry and the Movies: *Hud* and *The Last Picture Show*." *Western Humanities Review* 29 (Winter 1975): 81- 91.

Folsom, James K. "*Shane* and *Hud*: Two Stories in Search of a Medium." *Western Humanities Review* 24 (Autumn 1970): 359-72.

Kael, Pauline. "*Hud*, Deep in the Divided Heart of Hollywood." In *I Lost It at the Movies*. Boston: Little, Brown, 1965, pp. 78-94.

King, Larry. "Leavin' McMurtry." *Texas Monthly* (March 1974): 70-76.

Landess, Thomas. *Larry McMurtry*. SWS. Austin: Steck-Vaughn, 1969.

Lindstrom, Naomi. "The Novel in Texas: How Big a Patrimony?" *Texas Quarterly* 21 (Summer 1978): 73-83.

Neinstein, R. L. *The Ghost Country: A Study of the Novels of Larry McMurtry*. Modern Authors Monograph Series, No. 1. Berkeley: Creative Arts Book, 1976.

Peavy, Charles D. *Larry McMurtry*. TUSAS. Boston: Twayne, 1977.

Phillips, Raymond C. "The Ranch as Place and Symbol in the Novels of Larry McMurtry." *South Dakota Review* 13 (Summer 1975): 27-47.

Pilkington, William T. "The Dirt Farmer and the Cowboy: Notes on Two Texas Essayists." *RE: Arts and Letters* 3 (Fall 1969): 42-54.

Schmidt, Dorey, ed. *Larry McMurtry: Unredeemed Dreams*. Edinburg, Texas: Pan American University Press, 1978.

Stout, Janis P. "Journeying as a Metaphor for Cultural Loss in the Novels of Larry McMurtry." *Western American Literature* 11 (May 1976): 37-50.

Dick Harrison

FREDERICK MANFRED
(1912-)

The writings of Frederick Manfred cannot easily be considered in isolation from the man, with his giant 6 foot 9 inch frame and his compelling personality. As Wallace Stegner has said, "He is not a writer in the usual sense. He is a natural force, related to hurricanes, deluges, volcanic eruptions, and the ponderous formation of continents" (Foreword to *Conversations with Frederick Manfred*, p. xi).

Biography

Born Frederick Feikema on a farm near Doon, Iowa, 6 January 1912, he seemed destined for anything but a literary career. Books were not common in the Feikema household; the father could not read, and Frederick could often indulge his appetite for books only by hiding them in his shirt and reading as he rode a cultivator behind a team of horses. Manfred recalls having felt like an orphan, intellectually, and further isolated by being a conspicuously gawky youth and a Frisian, which placed him in a minority among the Dutch minority in America. After a conventionally nonliterary education at a high school run by the Christian Reformed church in Hull, Iowa, Frederick went on in 1930 to the church's Calvin College in Grand Rapids, Michigan, where he failed freshman English. A less robust literary spirit would have taken all this as discouragement, but Manfred, characteristically, took it as provocation. He began writing seriously, contributing sketches and poems to campus publications. His unliterary Iowa childhood, for its part, later provided the authentic fiber for at least ten of his realistic novels and "rumes," the latter a semiautobiographic form of fiction developed by Manfred himself.

Manfred's years at Calvin College, later fictionalized in *The Primitive* (1949), gave him a chance to develop, less through the classes he took than through dating, playing college basketball, reading, and debating in the philosophy club. One outcome of his intellectual development, his rejection of the church's fundamentalism, opened the way for the more individualistic tenets of faith that were to inform his fiction.

Graduating in the middle of the depression, Manfred set aside the teaching certificate he had earned and spent from 1934 to 1937 hitchhiking from coast to coast, sometimes in search of work but always in search of America. He now says quite simply, "Couldn't get jobs" (*Conversations*, p. 24), but he can also be seen to have undertaken the typical literary preparation of a romantic young American of that era. While he wrote only occasionally, his wanderings were filling the well from which he would draw his later fiction. His first trip to Yellowstone Park in 1934, for example, provided the framework for his first novel, *The Golden Bowl* (1944). More generally, his broadened experience of American society helped him to find his place in it and fix his character as westerner, maverick, individualist. Like the hero of his *Wanderlust* trilogy, Thurs, who pronounces New York a "glorified warehouse of the world," Manfred set himself against the East.

While working as a reporter for the *Minneapolis Journal* in 1937, Manfred evinced his thorough commitment to the writing of fiction. After a party at which he found his tales of hitchhiking across America could hold an audience, he worked all night at what was to become the first of seven drafts of *The Golden Bowl*. Two years later he left the *Journal* to devote himself entirely to finishing the manuscript but contracted tuberculosis. As Joseph Flora says in *Frederick Manfred* (1974), "The wandering giant, weakened from chain smoking and improper food, overwork and disappointment, entered the Glen Lake Sanitorium in Oak Terrace, Minnesota, in April of 1940 to fight for his life as well as to ponder the course it should take" (p. 7). The making of Frederick Manfred, novelist, took determination and sacrifice, but even the months spent in the sanitorium yielded their contribution. There he met another patient, Maryanna Shorba, who later became his wife; the experience of recovery inspired his first rume, *Boy Almighty* (1945).

The publication of *The Golden Bowl* in 1944 marked the beginning of Manfred's prolific publishing career, or at least that phase of it conducted under the pen name Feike Feikema. Manfred was now married, living by his pen and by a long series of fellowships, grants, and awards from regional and national organizations recognizing his talent, and publishing almost a book a year. Two more rural novels, *This Is the Year* (1947) and *The Chokecherry Tree* (1948), developed his fictional region of Siouxland—roughly the area where South Dakota, Minnesota, Iowa, and Nebraska meet. He also published two rumes, *Boy Almighty* (1945) and *World's Wanderer*, a trilogy that ended the Feikema phase of his career. The three volumes, *The Primitive* (1949), *The Brother* (1950), and *The Giant* (1951), drew upon Manfred's experiences in college, his travels east, and his life in the Minneapolis area. Under pressure from the publisher, Doubleday, Manfred allowed the volumes to be published separately before he had finished the trilogy. The effect was what publisher Alan Swallow later described as a "first draft," a condition Manfred was able to correct when he rewrote the work, compressing it from 1280 pages to 727 and having it republished in 1962 by Swallow as *Wanderlust*. But the damage had been done to the book's reputation and to Feikema's.

Manfred again acted with determination. He changed his publishing name from Feike Feikema to Frederick Manfred in 1952, choosing an almost literal translation of the Frisian name, "free man." He also began the first of the Buckskin Man tales, which celebrate the nineteenth-century past of his Siouxland region and which have brought him his greatest critical recognition, popular acclaim, and financial success. *Lord Grizzly* (1954), the story of mountain man Hugh Glass, was followed by *Riders of Judgment* (1957), about the Johnson County range wars; *Conquering Horse* (1959), a pre-white era Indian tale; *Scarlet Plume* (1964), about the Sioux uprising in Minnesota; and *King of Spades* (1966), about the Black Hills gold rush.

In this same period, Manfred moved to Luverne, Minnesota, in the heart of his Siouxland, and continued to write his Siouxland novels, including *The Man Who Looked Like the Prince of Wales* (1965) and *Eden Prairie* (1968); other novels such as *Morning Red* (1956) and *Milk of Wolves* (1976); another tale, *The Manly-Hearted Woman* (1976), a collection of poems, *Winter Count* (1966) and collections of stories to be found in *Arrow of Love* (1961) and *Apples of Paradise* (1968). He has also published another rume that may represent a kind of culmination of that form. In *Green Earth* (1977), Manfred returns to his personal Siouxland heritage to explore the meaning of his family through his formative years.

Even this crowded list of Manfred's major publications does not do justice to the monumental energy of the man, who continues to write essays and reviews, to take active part in literary meetings, and to teach creative writing at the University of South Dakota.

Major Themes

The major themes of Frederick Manfred's fiction vary with the genre in which he is working. In the Siouxland novels, he develops many of the themes traditional in rural midwest fiction from Hamlin Garland to the present. The Thors of *The Golden Bowl*, for example, represent the endurance of the pioneer spirit through the devastating drought of the 1930s, a stubborn faith in the land (which defies reason), and a sustaining family love. Maury, the drifter, represents skepticism and selfishness. He refuses to join the family until he has traveled enough to learn the value of the human family, the necessity of place and of the bond with the mother earth that is the cosmic extension of family. As spare, economical, and unsentimental as the Dakota plains, the novel has been described as a *Grapes of Wrath* in which the Okies stay home. In the end there is promise because the family is completed, and Kirsten Thor is pregnant by Maury, but the characters stand, literally, in the eye of a tornado.

In *This Is the Year*, perhaps the strongest of the Siouxland novels, Manfred carries the themes of land and family a step further. His giant protagonist, Pier Frixen (with possible echoes of Piers the Plowman or Rölvaag's Per Hansa), is a man of the soil, capable of heroic efforts to make his farm prosper. He consciously identifies the fertility of his land with the fertility of his wife, significantly named Nertha. The bonds of blood and soil would seem to be complete, but Pier ultimately fails because he violates both bonds. He callously drives his parents from the farm, fails to give love to his wife and child, and stubbornly refuses to practice the conservation measures that would save his land. Clearly, to love the land or family is insufficient unless that love is expressed with intelligence, understanding, and unselfishness.

Because Pier is part of a Frisian community, the novel develops another prominent theme of the Siouxland novels and rumes, the ethnic distinctiveness of Manfred's people. The Frisians express the attendant immigrant themes of attachment to the new land and to the hereditary culture, yet they seem quintessential midwesterners: proud, stubborn people, devoted to each other and to quarreling with each other, capable and enduring yet often childlike in their absolute convictions.

Later Siouxland novels and stories give progressively less emphasis to the land and more to marriage and the family, exploring the complexities and moral ambiguities of familial and erotic love. In *Eden Prairie*, for example, themes of the darker extensions of family love emerge, especially in the characters of Kon and Brant, the intensity of whose brotherly love is in some degree both homosexual and incestuous. These and other less prominent themes engage readers because of the minute fidelity with which Manfred recreates the daily life of his Siouxland. As Wallace Stegner says, "Few writers ever achieve so sure a sense of place, and of how human beings are shaped by it" (*Conversations*, p. xv).

With the Buckskin Man tales, Manfred moves from the prosaic present to the heroic past. Although three of the five tales take place mainly in the same Siouxland territory, their historical setting and Manfred's approach to his material produce a shift from the Midwest to the classic themes of the West and from the actual and realistic to the legendary and mythic. The bond with the land, for example, becomes not merely an elemental need but, in Max Westbrook's terms, put forth in "*Riders of Judgment*" (1977), a primal reality, a source of contact with those spiritual energies that have an absolute authority over man's moral nature.

Western, as opposed to midwestern, American literature typically concerns the frontiersman, the heroic individualist caught between the freedom of wild nature and the attractions and responsibilities of civilized order, reluctantly helping to create a new and just civilization out of the virgin wilderness. It offers a rough paradigm for the creation of America, and its themes are usually those of the individual's adaptation to nature and to society. The Buckskin Man tales as a group cover the range of these themes, and like all other serious western American literature, they question the easy solutions to the frontier dilemma that typify the popular Western. The best of the tales—*Conquering Horse, Lord Grizzly*, and *Riders of Judgment*—define the stages of the white man's adaptation to the West.

Conquering Horse, set in pre-white Siouxland around 1800, is Manfred's search for spiritual ancestors and for the original, unsullied genius of the place. Its hero, No Name—like Manfred's middle America—approaches maturity and must find his name, which is to say his place in the human, natural, and spiritual orders. No Name's vision and quest are fraught with moral ambiguities in that his true father must die before he can succeed to manhood, and the white stallion he conquers to earn his name destroys itself rather than accept servitude. But No Name becomes Conquering Horse because he can see the ultimate unity beyond life and death and the contradictions of the actual: "Life is a circle. All things try to be round. Life is all one. It begins in one place, it flows for a time, it returns to one place. The earth is all that lasts" (*Conquering Horse*, Signet ed., p. 226). For the white immigrants to Siouxland, of course, Conquering Horse's natural religion of merging with the eternal flow is unattainable, but it remains as one polarity of their nature.

Hugh Glass in *Lord Grizzly* occupies the point of original contact between the natural and the civilized and, like any other traditional mountain man, is caught between two worlds. Yet it should be recognized that both worlds are necessary to his development. By rejecting what little society is afforded by the fur trading expedition, Glass puts himself in a position to be struck down by the grizzly. In his crawl to civilization, as John R. Milton explains in *The Novel of the American West* (1980), Glass must act out a process of evolution, crawling on his belly, on all fours, and finally walking like a man. The imagery provides a rough analogy to his spiritual development from a primitive, Old Testament motive of revenge upon the young men who left him for dead, to a civilized, Christian spirit of forgiveness. Glass's final position is his highest spiritual state, but it could not have been reached without the original descent to his basic animal nature, without the rebirth given him by the female grizzly in the forest. It is also significant that he reaches only a tentative reconciliation with society before shambling back off into nature. The assumption of much western American fiction is that nature's is the easier bond to sustain.

The final stage of the civilizing process is represented in *Riders of Judgment*, based on the Johnson County range wars of Wyoming at the end of the nineteenth century. The Indian is no longer in evidence; the remnant forces of nature must descend from the mountains in the person of Cain Hammett. The question is one of sustaining natural justice in a world where the individual must face the political and economic power generated by an established society. As Cain sacrifices himself to hold off the cattle barons until the small ranchers can organize, the tale might be a simple dramatization of the struggle for individualism in the West, but here, as in Manfred's other tales, the moral world is more problematic. Cain, as his name suggests, is not innocent, and the ambivalence of his standing in the brotherhood of man is reflected in the Hammett family relationships. The love of the three brothers for their first cousin carries overtones of incest and fratricide, which change the significance of Cain's sacrifice. The semisavage individual, lacking balance in his nature, brings on his own destruction. Yet the ideal of individualism is preserved in the face of civilization with the suggestion that Cain goes from death straight into legend.

Robert Wright, in *Frederick Manfred* (1979), examines the Buckskin Man tales in a chapter entitled "Searching for an American Self," and the dilemma of civilization and nature Manfred confronts does certainly go back in the American consciousness as far as James Fenimore Cooper's New York State. Ostensibly the resolutions to the dilemma that Manfred's tales achieve imply a belief in balance, yet like so much other western American fiction, they tilt the balance toward nature. The assumption may be that a balance must be redressed, an Old World influence thrown off, as suggested in the less successful tales, *King of Spades* and *Scarlet Plume*. At a deeper level, the object may be to balance the conscious with the unconscious. John R. Milton speculates that the tales may show "American man before and during the process of having his 'blood-consciousness sapped by a parasitic mental or ideal consciousness' " (*The Novel*, p. 188).

Manfred's rumes, the most directly autobiographical of his fictions, are also the most explicitly personal in their themes. The essence of the rume, as Manfred explains, is that it utters a cry of either distress or joy from the heart; the private materials are merely a "point of departure" (*Conversations*, p. 33). The form therefore extends to a variety of themes but concentrates on the growth of the individual, his search for identity or for a self-definition in terms of his unfolding nature and the society of which he must be a part. In the rumes, as in romances such as *Morning Red*, the process of self-definition is hampered by an artistic temperament. The artist is inevitably an outsider, ill suited to living in the world and cursed with a more complex and fragile inner nature to unfold. In the three volumes of *Wanderlust*, for example, Thurs Wraldson explores religion, Marxism, and science as ways of giving intelligible form to the world, finally rejecting them all in favor of art. At the same time, the implicit theme of family remains as strong in this genre as in the others. For Thurs, the supposed orphan, it is the discovery of his dying father that signals his maturity and releases his artistic powers.

The overt, public themes of Manfred's fiction suggest its range and relevance to western American consciousness. To appreciate his work as a coherent body of fiction, it is necessary to consider the more private, implicit themes, often existing only as recurrent motifs, which unify the reader's experience of the novels and condition Manfred's treatment of the overt themes. In *Riders of Judgment*, for example, the public themes have to do with justice. Westbrook, in "*Riders of Judgment*," identifies an implicit theme that accounts for the handling of the overt theme and for the Freudian family entanglements: "The central theme of the novel, in fact, is failure in maturity, an inability to unite the wild energies of youth with the legal and moral restraints of the adult world" (p. 48). The inability results in a selfish assertion of ego to the detriment of ultimate good. Once identified, the problem of maturity can be seen in the other tales: as the explicit theme of *Conquering Horse*, the source of oedipal conflicts in *King of Spades*, as one explanation of the behavior of "old" Hugh Glass, or of the temporary transsexual behavior in the later tale, *The Manly-Hearted Woman*.

The theme is prevalent in the novels but especially prominent in the rumes. Eric, in *Boy Almighty*, pits himself against a malignant deity called "the Whipper," who is identified with his authoritarian father. Thurs, in *Wanderlust*, dreams that he is spurning the advances of a girl named "Hero" who had jilted him in college: " 'Rain on you, Hero,' he thought to himself. 'Now it's me that's top dog, not you' " (p. 530). If this were not embarrassing enough evidence of immaturity for a man in his mid-twenties, Thurs wakes to find he has wet the bed. The theme obtrudes itself because of such grotesque variations upon it, and Manfred explores many of its aspects. Both Eric and Thurs, for example, are giants, suggesting the incongruities between physical and emotional growth. For both characters, maturity involves balancing the ego, though certainly not subduing it. As Manfred has said to John R. Milton, "the whole trick of education, of having a family, everything, is to raise egos. There is no harm in the word 'ego.' To raise egotists that other people will tolerate" (*Conversations*, p. 113).

The maturity theme, then, might be restated as the struggle of the individual to reach a degree of maturity at which the raw imperatives of the ego can be balanced against the demands of moral law and social responsibility. It stands at the center of a cluster of related themes that help to unify Manfred's fiction across generic divisions. Manfred's ubiquitous themes of family grow out of it because the family is at once the metaphor for a successful achievement of that maturity and the microcosm in which it can be worked out. Most of the tales move toward a theme of family, including *Lord Grizzly*, in which Old Hugh is reminded of his betrayal of the universal family by "them haunt sons" he deserted when he escaped to the freedom of the wilderness. Maury's mature self-realization is signaled by his joining the Thor family; Elof, the comic hero of *The Choke-cherry Tree*, achieves a comic marriage. The best, most autobiographical rume, *Green Earth*, is devoted openly and explicitly to family. In Manfred's fiction the family is not always a symbol of resolution. Failures to achieve maturity are expressed in failures or distortions of family bonds; hatred of fathers and oedipal urges, for example, reflect arrested development in *Boy Almighty, Morning Red, King of Spades*, and elsewhere. Incest is a dark possibility hovering over family themes in most of Manfred's fiction, suggesting the perils of maturity and love. At times it is the merest implication, as when Maury replaces Pa Thor's lost son and seduces the daughter, Kirsten. At other times it is explicit, as in *Morning Red, Eden Prairie*, and *King of Spades*. Minor themes of impotence and homosexuality are not unrelated.

The family metaphor can expand to reflect the individual's relationship not only to society but to the mother earth, as it does in *The Golden Bowl* and *Conquering Horse*. Pier Frixen's failure with his family and his land are suggestively linked, and again the problem is ego and maturity. When, at the end of the novel, Pier declares that his heart is still "green," the expression can be taken in two ways, for he has remained a great, egotistical child.

Beyond the complex use of family motifs, the ego-maturity tension is equally basic to the western themes of individualism, naturalism, justice, and violence expressed in the tales. If we are to believe John Cawelti in *The Six-Gun Mystique* (1971), it lies at the heart of the American condition, which is something Manfred explores tirelessly. The ego-maturity tension can be seen not merely as a theme but as a nexus in Manfred's fiction, a source of energy out of which many of his themes are generated. Nor is it surprising that Manfred should return continually to that tension surrounded by its few basic archetypes of ego, maturity, sex, family, and earth. It is consistent with his belief in individualism and in the "Old Lizard," that wise primate nature within us all that is being wiped out by civilization.

Survey of Criticism

Although first published in St. Paul, Manfred's work attracted immediate, favorable attention from eastern reviewers, and essays by major western critics such as John R. Milton appeared as early as 1957. Important contributions can be found in the essays. In Milton's "Voice from Siouxland" (1957), Manfred's earlier work is bathed in that pure light that characterizes the dawning of recognition of a new talent: "He has been compared with Rölvaag, Wolfe, Steinbeck, Dos Passos, and Faulkner, and it is not altogether presumptuous to say that he combines the best of those men with his own unique talents, while also sharing some of their weaknesses" (p. 104). In his later writings Milton would never be quite as unrestrained in his praise for Manfred. The substance of his other essays has been incorporated into *Conversations* and *The Novel of the American West*. Alan Swallow, in his "The Mavericks" (1959), commends Manfred as a neglected writer "of prodigious labour and prodigious ability," while acknowledging that he "must learn a somewhat better style" (p. 90). James C. Austin's "Legend, Myth and Symbol" (1963-64) is a careful tracing of references and allusions in *Lord Grizzly* to demonstrate how Manfred has assimilated ancient, and especially biblical, archetypes of an heroic age to serve the American need for origins expressed in literary prototypes. Austin praises Manfred's design of re-creating Hugh Glass as America's "first father."

The special issue of *South Dakota Review* of 1969-70, devoted to Manfred and Sinclair Lewis, brings together a valuable set of critical essays. Even the order in which editor John Milton has arranged them is expressive. Don Bebeau, in "A Search for Voice, A Sense of Place in *The Golden Bowl*" (1969-70), is concerned mainly with demonstrating Manfred's accomplishment as a regional writer in that larger sense in which "the universal is both contained and revealed in the particular" (p. 85). Russell Roth's "The Inception of a Saga" (1969-70) moves on to the Buckskin Man series and outward to relate Manfred to the mainstream of American intellectual life. He identifies the Buckskin Man as "the new essential American," engaged in what D. H. Lawrence called "that 'great and cruel sloughing' of 'the old European consciousness' " (p. 89). He goes on to an extensive comparison of Manfred with Faulkner as creator of "a mythical kingdom...complete and living in all its details" (p. 96). Delbert Wylder's "Manfred's Indian Novel" (1969-70) is both more particular and more universal in its implications. Concentrating on *Conquering Horse*, he traces the mythic, romantic, and realistic elements that relate Manfred's art to the timeless traditions of literary form. He also attests to Manfred's success in harmonizing the broad range of formal elements: "It is a tribute to Manfred's art that the symbolism is so much a part of the pattern of structure and character that it does not call attention to itself as device" (p. 106).

The first monograph on Manfred was Joseph M. Flora's *Frederick Manfred* (1974). Despite restrictions of size and format, Flora provides a good summary treatment of Manfred's writing, looking at each major work with clarity, directness, and balanced critical judgment. Without underestimating the value of either Manfred's contemporary or historical fiction, Flora can acknowledge, for example, that *Morning Red* suffers from diffuseness ("The reader gets too much detail about characters who do not matter," p. 21) and that the character of Judith in *Scarlet Plume* is sometimes less than plausible: "Judith is never convincing as a mother in grief; she too soon views the Yanktons with a kind of intellectual detachment" (p. 33). Flora also identifies certain root themes common to the range of Manfred's fiction, such as the search for fathers, antagonism between fathers and sons, and the related themes of incest. He finally concludes that Manfred "has achieved a place in American literature" (p. 46), based primarily on *Lord Grizzly, Conquering Horse, Riders of Judgment* and *This Is the Year*.

The most ambitious commentary on Manfred to date is Robert C. Wright's *Frederick Manfred* (1979). Wright examines Manfred's work in three groupings, which correspond roughly to the author's own: the Siouxland novels, the Buckskin Man tales, and the rumes, romances, stories, and poems. For each major work, Wright does an extensive exploration of themes, with some attention to form and technique. In addition, he devotes a chapter to a thematic overview. Such thematic groupings as "Spirit of Place" and "Useable Past" are informative, but in the section "Bonding," Wright becomes involved with some theorists of group behavior (with the unlikely names of Lionel Tiger and Robin Fox) who lure him away from Manfred's fiction.

Wright includes an impartial sampling of favorable and unfavorable critical reaction to each novel yet in his commentary seems to shy away from critical judgments, particularly negative ones. It is therefore ironic that he should single out Wallace Stegner's Foreword to *Conversations with Frederick Manfred* as the best evaluation of Manfred's work, when Stegner is unrestrained in both his praise and his criticism of Manfred.

The most authoritative and concrete analysis of Manfred's achievement can be found in John R. Milton's *The Novel of the American West*. Milton confines his attention to the Buckskin Man tales, but he expands the critical dialogue by showing the limited usefulness of merely thematic approaches to Manfred and by assessing Manfred's place in the development of the western novel as form. He analyzes the structure of *Lord Grizzly* in some detail, including its structure of meaning, which involves a rhythmic movement among naturalistic, psychological, and symbolic levels. The meaning, he explains, emerges not from detachable themes but from the rhythmic alternations between these levels. Such structural rhythm Milton identifies as the distinguishing formal quality of the western novel: "the western regional novel is constantly in a state of rhythm, an ebb and flow between the brutal and the beautiful, between the painfully real and the ideal" (*Novel*, p. 174).

In a less detailed analysis of the other tales, Milton credits the design of the Buckskin Man series while criticizing *Scarlet Plume* and *King of Spades* as inferior to the other three in thematic significance and technical skill. He also acknowledges some general weaknesses in Manfred's control of language, symbol, and plausibility of incident.

Despite its brevity, Wallace Stegner's Foreword to *Conversations with Frederick Manfred* deserves separate attention as a germinal work in Manfred criticism. Outspoken, exuberant, not always gentle, it has a refreshingly western openness to it that seems appropriate to its subject. The vitality of the figurative language with which Stegner describes Manfred and his work breeds a wealth of provocative implications to be explored by less poetic critics. For example:

Reality is too small for him, language is sometimes too arthritic for his needs, and his efforts to loosen and enlarge them are not uniformly successful. He is a very tall man who can never learn to duck to the doors of habitual humans and keeps cracking his head. [P. xiii]

A kind of boisterous western humor keeps breaking out of the metaphors, and Stegner is equally vivid in describing the rough spots in Manfred's style: "He wrenches and shoves at his verbs, forcing them into a kind of locoed vigor that in the end defeats his purpose by calling attention to itself" (Foreword to *Conversations*, p. xii).

Stegner, as fellow novelist and westerner, can voice his opinions about Manfred's strengths and weaknesses freely. He is equally unstinting in his praise, saying that after reading or talking with Manfred, he has the feeling "that I have been somewhere, in a real presence, blown around and tossed by an elemental force" (Foreword to *Conversations*, p. xvi).

For a comprehensive listing of secondary sources, readers should consult George Kellogg's "Frederick Manfred: A Bibliography" (1965), the selected bibliography in Flora's monograph, and the annotated bibliography in Wright's *Frederick Manfred*.

Bibliography

Works of Frederick Manfred

The Golden Bowl. St. Paul: Webb, 1944.
Boy Almighty. St. Paul: Webb, 1945.
This Is the Year. Garden City, N.Y.: Doubleday, 1947.
The Chokecherry Tree. Garden City, N.Y.: Doubleday, 1948.
The Primitive. Garden City, N.Y.: Doubleday, 1949.

The Brother. Garden City, N.Y.: Doubleday, 1950.

The Giant. Garden City, N.Y.: Doubleday, 1951.

Lord Grizzly. New York: McGraw-Hill, 1954.

Morning Red. Denver: Alan Swallow, 1956.

Riders of Judgment. New York: Random House, 1957.

Conquering Horse. New York: McDowell, Obolensky, 1959; New York: Signet, 1965.

Arrow of Love. Denver: Alan Swallow, 1961.

Wanderlust. Denver: Alan Swallow, 1962.

Scarlet Plume. New York: Trident, 1964.

The Man Who Looked Like the Prince of Wales. New York: Trident, 1965; rpt. as *The Secret Place*, New York: Pocket Books, 1967.

King of Spades. New York: Trident, 1966.

Winter Count. Minneapolis: James D. Thueson, 1966.

Eden Prairie. New York: Trident, 1968.

Apples of Paradise. New York: Trident, 1968.

Conversations with Frederick Manfred. Moderated by John R. Milton, with Foreword by Wallace Stegner. Salt Lake City: University of Utah Press, 1974.

The Manly-Hearted Woman. New York: Crown, 1976.

Milk of Wolves. Boston: Avenue Victor Hugo, 1976.

Green Earth. New York: Crown, 1977.

The Wind Blows Free. Sioux Falls, S. Dak.: Center for Western Studies, 1979.

Sons of Adam. New York: Crown, 1980.

Studies of Frederick Manfred

Austin, James C. "Legend, Myth and Symbol in Frederick Manfred's *Lord Grizzly*." *Critique* 6 (Winter 1963-64): 122-30.

Bebeau, Donald. "A Search for Voice, A Sense of Place in *The Golden Bowl*." *South Dakota Review* 7 (Winter 1969-70): 79-87.

Cawelti, John. *The Six-Gun Mystique*. Bowling Green: Bowling Green University Popular Press, [1971].

Flora, Joseph M. *Frederick Manfred*. WWS. Boise, Idaho: Boise State University, 1974.

Kellogg, George. "Frederick Manfred: A Bibliography." *Twentieth Century Literature* 11 (April 1965): 30-35.

Meldrum, Barbara. "The Agrarian versus Frontiersman in Midwestern Fiction." *Heritage of Kansas* 11 (Summer 1978): 3-18.

Meyer, Roy W. *The Middle Western Farm Novel in the Twentieth Century*. Lincoln: University of Nebraska Press, 1965.

Milton, John R. "Frederick Feikema Manfred." *Western Review* 22 (Spring 1958): 181-96.

———. "Interview with Frederick Manfred." *South Dakota Review* 7 (Winter 1969-70): 110-31.

———. "*Lord Grizzly*: Rhythm, Form and Meaning in the Western Novel." *Western American Literature* 1 (Spring 1966): 6-14.

———. *The Novel of the American West*. Lincoln: University of Nebraska Press, 1980.

———. "Voice from Siouxland; Frederick Feikema Manfred." *College English* 19 (December 1957): 104-11.

Roth, Russell. "The Inception of a Saga: Frederick Manfred's 'Buckskin Man.'" *South Dakota Review* 7 (Winter 1969-70): 87-100.

Swallow, Alan. "The Mavericks." *Critique* 2 (Winter 1959): 74-92.
Westbrook, Max. *"Riders of Judgment*: An Exercise in Ontological Criticism." *Western American Literature* 12 (May 1977): 41-51.
Wright, Robert C. *Frederick Manfred*. TUSAS. Boston: Twayne, 1979.
Wylder, D. E. "Manfred's Indian Novel." *South Dakota Review* 7 (Winter 1969-70): 100-110.

Alan Rosenus

JOAQUIN MILLER
(1837-1913)

Biography

Though called recently "the inceptor of the Western Archetype" (Everson, *Archetype West*, p. 27) as much for his prose as for his poetry, Joaquin Miller has nevertheless been known since 1871 as the Poet of the Sierras and was celebrated as western America's first real poet. He was born Cincinnatus Hiner Miller in Liberty, Indiana, on 8 September 1837, to Hulings and Margaret DeWitt Miller and grew up under the tutelage of an extremely tolerant, nonviolent Quaker father who traded with the Indians of the region for some of his needs and taught his children not to value money overmuch. In 1852 the family emigrated to the Willamette Valley in Oregon, and two years later, at the age of seventeen, Miller went to the mines of California. The following ten years established the basis of most of his important work. He was drawn into two Indian conflicts, the battle of Castle Crags (1855), in which he was wounded, and the Pitt River war (1857). By late 1856 he was living with an Indian woman of the McCloud tribe, Sutatot, who was later known to Californians as Amanda Brock. They had a daughter, Cali-Shasta.

His *California Diary* (1936) provides an interesting record of his activities following the recovery from the wound he received in the battle of Castle Crags and refers to important events in northern California for the years 1855-57. The early poetry of the *Diary* consists of comic doggerel and sentimental evocations of camp life. The prose, though crude, reveals the curious detail and the relaxed, humorous elements that would characterize some of his more polished writing. The lengthy accounts of hunting expeditions show Miller groping for a precise language with which to describe the imagery of the terrain, indicating that California was already suggesting ultimate terms.

An argument with Bill Hurst, a belligerent mining operator in Siskiyou County, caused Miller to be cited on two criminal counts, and in 1860 he left northern California. After working as a gold carrier in Idaho, he bought a newspaper in Eugene, Oregon, and asked his readers if Oregon ought not "to be the very heart of song and poetry in America" (*Eugene City Review*, 29 November 1862). As editor his ambivalent feelings on racial matters were very much in evidence: one of his published verses pictured native Americans and whites sitting down to the same table in a pastoral setting (more hopeful than prophetic for the future of Oregon); but during the same period Miller's newspaper editorials made him seem like a caricature of humorist David Ross Locke's Nasby at the Confederate Crossroads.

By 1863 he had published several verses, including "Cape Blanco," in the *San Francisco Golden Era*, and the same year he began the practice of law in Canyon City, Oregon. In 1866 he was elected first judge of Grant County. His admiration for Orpheus C. Kerr and Artemus Ward could be seen in the aggressive sallies he made against some of his fellow residents of the region, published in a series called "Canyon City Pickles" in *The Dalles Daily Mountaineer*. His first book of poems, *Specimens*, appeared in 1868, and was followed by *Joaquin et al.* (1869), which received praise from Bret Harte in the *Overland Monthly*.

Miller's divorce from his second wife, Theresa Dyer (whom he had married in 1862), preceded his famous trip to London. Here in the English capital, his self-published *Pacific Poems* (1870) gained for him an audience of distinguished English and Irish readers. The volume was expanded into *Songs of the Sierras* (1871), and overnight Miller became the creator of a new mythology. His past experiences enabled him to epitomize the western man as no other writer of the period had been qualified to do, and it is probably true that this type, as it was later broadcast to the world, was framed in Miller's image. Sometimes dressed in correct English attire but more often in the colorful outfits he had worn on the frontier, Miller was celebrated by the great social and literary figures of England, including Gladstone, Lord Houghton, Browning, Rossetti, Swinburne, Tennyson— even the queen. At home the writers who continued to admire his work were Walt Whitman, James Whitcomb Riley, Hamlin Garland, and Charles Warren Stoddard.

In 1873 *Life Amongst the Modocs: Unwritten History* was published in England and appeared a year later in America as *Unwritten History*. It was recognized as being "superior to his poetry" and was called a "contribution to the knowledge of human nature in some of its most peculiar conditions" (*Spectator*, 9 August 1873, p. 1016). Although England was quick to understand its significance as a protest novel detailing the abuses suffered by native Americans at the hands of the settlers and the Indian Bureau, the press at home did its best to ignore the work.

After traveling throughout Europe, Miller returned to the United States, settling first on the East Coast. He continued to produce novels, poems, and plays in prolific style, and from 1885 until his death he lived in the group of small buildings called The Hights in the hills of Oakland, California. He contributed to numerous periodicals, including the *Century*, the *Arena*, the *New York Independent*, and *Lippincott's*. In 1886 he established Arbor Day in California. The Bear Edition of his poems with important commentary by him appeared in 1909, and he died four years later on 17 February 1913.

Major Themes

As an author, Miller's primary concerns were with the limitless space, beauty, and promise of the frontier. His vilification of the city as a destroyer of democratic hope was another, but no less significant theme, and he continued to lament the swift changes that were transforming the region. He frequently turned his attention to the dream of utopia—aware, however, that the greed of the newcomers to the West would cause them to turn their backs on an unprecedented chance for renewal.

His two early books, *Specimens* (1868) and *Joaquin et al.* (1869), were comparatively austere and illustrated his inability to deal with himself. He had confronted emptiness and the vast promises of the frontier, but reflecting back from the land was a deep sense of isolation. In the long poems of the *Songs of the Sierras* he developed a more decorative and picturesque verse, creating a series of heroic figures designed to match the immensity of the frontier, but these heroes were not altogether successful as imaginative creations. The Tall Alcalde, Kit Carson, William Walker, and the Arizonian were, however, exciting characters to the generation then growing up. The book was praised for its virile force, narrative qualities, and faithful depiction of America's youthful myths. The English were quick to point out that the women in Miller's poetry too often resembled Byronic lay figures "transported to the mountains and the prairies" (*Spectator*, 8 July 1871, p. 833). Certain stanzas in later poems such as "Dawn at San Diego," "A Ship on Fire," and "With Love to You and Yours," show how completely Miller could surrender to an image. These passages are still beautiful and exotic today. A considerable number of his short poems are highly accomplished, including "The Bravest Battle," which celebrates the inconspicuous heroism of women; "To Juanita," a charming lyric to his daughter; "A Shasta Tale of Love," in which a coyote brings the unwanted gift of love to the white man; "Don't Stop at the Station Despair," "Lo! On the Plains of Bethel," and the confessional "Adios." The religious poems that precede the prose chapters of *The Building of the City Beautiful* (1892) are also among his most effective.

Miller probably will be admired most by today's readers and by readers in the future for his fine prose evocations of primitive California and Oregon. The best of his stories and novels present the dramatic conflict between preservers and despoilers, a conflict absent from his verse. Only John Muir could be more precise in describing natural phenomena, but Muir's range was more limited than Miller's in recording the human dimension of the frontier.

Miller portrays the West as a place of cataclysmic changes where whole traditions and peoples could vanish overnight. As he watched the floods of new arrivals pouring into the region on highways and railroads, "paving their way with gold where we came long ago with toil and peril," he knew that "even these will be levelled, as our graves are levelled, and give place to others" (*Selected Writings*, p. 90). The newcomers were invariably callous toward the people already there. Miller realized it would be only a matter of time before he too would represent a type that would be scorned by the immigrants. Two of his most poignant descriptions of himself have to do with being an unwanted person: first in the *California Diary* (*Selected Writings*, p. 158) and again in the journal of his trip from New York to London (*Selected Writings*, p. 5).

Rough and uncouth looking as the West's older inhabitants might be, they were reliable in times of hardship. "An Old Oregonian in the Snow" celebrates Joe Meek, who is able to save some haughty Californians from a flood caused by a Chinook wind. Throughout the tale, however, the Californians hold him in contempt. Appearances are deceptive in "Rough Times in Idaho," too, but are treated as part of the larger concern of moral ambiguity. Here a road agent, Dave English, turns out to be the benefactor—rather than the robber—of some travelers he intends to relieve of their gold, when suddenly they must endure a fierce blizzard together. By killing their horses and forcing them to lie down inside the protective warmth of the dead animals, he saves their lives. A character in the story points out that a brave robber "may be better than many legal thieves who infested the land" and that there is so much good in what the world calls evil and so much evil in what the world calls good that it is sometimes impossible to draw the line "where God has not" (*Selected Writings*, p. 108).

In *Unwritten History: Life Amongst the Modocs*, the most lowly people are the native Americans who have "suffered nearly four hundred years of wrong, and never yet had an advocate" (p. 5). From them, the invading settlers might have learned how to make reasonable demands on the land. But like the people in eastern cities who have believed the lies newspapers have been telling them about the native Americans, the miners are not aware of the truth of the situation. They never show gratitude and, unable to see the real wealth on hand, they choose gold. The fragile California Eden will be destroyed as the biblical garden was. The hapless preservers—the land's first people—cannot even articulate their rage, for the Indians are "poets without the gift of expression" (p. 6). In what is surely Miller's most ambitious book, he attempts to represent an inward and outward transgression that is simultaneous. Outwardly, the settlers' greed dooms the Shasta region, but the source of the land's betrayal can also be found within the dream of innocence itself—in the idealistic heart of a well-meaning white youth who is unaware of the undermining, self-destructive side of his nature. Compounding the settlers' blindness is the boy's inability to acknowledge the voice of his hidden white identity or to understand that despite his laudable idealism, he has very real capacities for evil. The book addresses itself to the universal problem of self-knowledge, bringing the youth from passive inactivity to more advanced stages of maturity and then revealing that he is his own enemy. He becomes prone to self-destructive "accidents" and in the Pitt River war "enters into the spirit of the war against my allies" (p. 285). As the narrator blackens himself with guilt, Miller succeeds in creating a novel of expiation. The reader feels shock and disgust for the boy as he turns from hero to demon; vicariously, Miller takes upon himself the guilt of the white man's crimes against the Indian. In a sense, the novel is an apology from one culture to another, and

since the massacre as described in *Unwritten History* is darker than anything
Miller was guilty of in real life, and the reader's opinion of the narrator never
quite recovers from the shock of the disgraceful confession, it is plain that Miller
was not trying to enhance the boy's popular appeal but was trying to reveal a
more complete picture of his ambivalent inner self than a purely factual narration
could have rendered.

A second type of preserver appears in the book. This is the Prince, James
Thomas, who assumes responsibility for two Indian children whose parents have
been killed in a massacre. This type of noble individual, who survives as an alien
among his kind, is seen again in the character of Walton in *The Destruction of
Gotham* (1886) and in Forty-Nine in the *Shadows of Shasta* (1881). In each case
he becomes the protector of unwanted children. At the center of Miller's social
ethic is a child, vulnerable and often abused, who must be shielded from the
world's brutality.

In a rhythmic prose that has a peculiar spatial beauty to it and an unusual
clarity of diction as well, Miller had found the right language for conveying the
indigenous land spirit and, simultaneously, an inner landscape. The moon "cold
and crooked overhead," the frozen streams, the surf of the dawn "breaking over
the wall of the Sierra" (*Unwritten History*, pp. 196, 344), are the outward
correlatives of the boy's inner nature—his purity and unknown regions of darkness, his passion and flawed idealism.

Regarding the strange reception *Unwritten History* received in America,
a set of circumstances came together about the time of its publication that has
continued to affect opinion on Miller until this day. Bret Harte, who was jealous
of Miller and his spectacular fame, had been telling other editors that nothing
Miller wrote was true. This was hardly the case. Miller's understanding that the
poet and Indian sympathizer were types not wanted on the frontier came from a
series of unfortunate experiences in northern California. While living on the
McCloud River with his Indian wife, Sutatot, he was captured by a road-building
pioneer named Sam Lockhart and was accused of complicity with the Pitt River
Indians in the murder of Sam's brother, Harry, and other white settlers along the
Pitt River. The moment of psychological and spiritual crucifixion at the hands of
Lockhart is used in the novel as a hub around which the other incidents in the
book are made to turn. While the order of chronology is often changed to suit the
novel's structure and development, there is considerable historical fidelity in those
sections dealing with Bill Hurst, Judge Rosborough, Sam Lockhart, Lockhart's
employees, Fowler and Whitney, the battle of Castle Crags, the Idaho and
eastern Oregon sequences, and events leading up to the Pitt River war. The
remainder of the book, though not based on fact, is brilliantly imagined.

The *Alta California*'s remarks were typical of the few American reviews that
did appear: "How much is true we do not know and do not much care" (30
November 1874). William Dean Howells had already said, "It is rather a ruinous
thing to be a phenomenon" (*Atlantic Monthly*, December 1871, p. 770), and
though the English press had rightly praised the book and declared, "It is well

that the red men have at last found a witness to speak for them" (*Spectator*, 9 August 1873, p. 1017), *Unwritten History* was set aside in America.

Few of Miller's other productions were as strong. In *First Fam'lies of the Sierras* (1875) (from which the successful play, *The Danites of the Sierras*, was developed), he did not consistently rely on his own voice; this fault was seen in the play as well. His next two novels, *The One Fair Woman* (1876) and *Shadows of Shasta*, failed to receive the extensive editing they required. Of greater interest is *The Destruction of Gotham*, an abrasive attack on the rich. In an essay of 1880, "Utopia," Miller observed the contradiction between the "one hard, dominating idea of Yankee character" (*Selected Writings of Joaquin Miller*, p. 234), money getting, and the need for a more equitable distribution of wealth. With his anger highly charged, he developed this theme in his only urban novel, describing a world that was not worth saving. In some respects the book prefigures Stephen Crane's *Maggie* and the fiction of Frank Norris. One of its ironies is that the upper economic world is really a lower world, for the millionaires' emotions are less refined than animals'. Friends to no one—certainly not to the quiet journalist, Walton, or to Dottie, who has unwisely attached her affections to a financial schemer—the wealthy of New York are of no help to the arts either, and their homes are vulgar, yet America has seen fit to worship them. Although the narrative and its development are naive compared with the novels of Gertrude Atherton or Stewart Edward White, Miller was obeying the spontaneous impulse to take action with his work and wanted to attack New York's obvious injustices, which, in fact, he did not exaggerate. Based on his personal observations, he could see that individual hoarders of wealth like Jay Gould, not blind economic forces, were causing most of the city's misery.

Walton states that if he possessed all the millions of dollars going to waste in New York, he would build a new kind of city—out on new ground. But for Dottie and her daughter it is already too late and their fates are described with naturalistic harshness: the mother dies in a room full of rats, and the little girl, long before the age of ten, looks old and shriveled. Here, in the destroyed child, is the ultimate consequence of greed and cultural self-betrayal.

We will probably never know if Miller would have written *The Destruction of Gotham* with exactly the same venom if he had not been swindled out of a large sum of money by Jay Gould, but we must look for different motives behind *The Building of the City Beautiful*. Miller once confessed with undisguised candor, "I get drunk on abnegation, recite my own poems, and dance a two-step inspired by self-sacrifice. I am touched with madness, but sane enough to know it. I have a good time on nothing" (Hubbard, *So Here Then Is a Little Journey*, p. 13). Humor was an antidote to Miller's sense of personal failure and to his clear realization of the West's inevitable deterioration. *The Building of the City Beautiful*, which is essentially lacking in humor, indicates that Miller tended to rely on philosophical consolation as well. The novel approaches the same question on a timeless scale that *Unwritten History* had asked in the specific historical milieu of Mount Shasta: how does man deal with his self-destructiveness? "Sorrow, suicide, despair. Man stood staring before him, even in the most civilized places and under the most favorable conditions, and kept asking, 'Is life worth living?' " (*Building of the City Beautiful*, p. 24).

In this, his most personal novel, Miller's identity as autobiographical hero has been stripped down to that of evolutionary soul and initiate. His source of renewal is Miriam, a Jewish woman of superhuman wisdom who educates him. Her faith transcends all creeds, and she builds a genuine utopia on the ruins of an ancient Indian civilization in Mexico. Under her guidance he becomes a scorned idealist and, like the Prince, a protector of the battered and helpless of the world—himself a child in the body of her belief.

A high symbolic plane is reached in the novel's seventh chapter, which takes place in the Egyptian desert. Here, all of pre-Christian time as well as the present age are blended into a single night inhabited by a fearful yellow moon. Through the columns of a temple comes a lion with a head that is manlike, and he seems to pose the question of violence. The City-builder is saved from the gigantic sphinx as Miriam—who has intuition greater than his—stands naked facing the beast. The surreal landscape with its pure symbols exists in a golden light that signifies objective truth. Despite lapses into forms of realism that are antagonistic to the book's symbolic texture, Miller succeeds in rendering the surreal landscapes of the desert and the idealistic cloudland which the City-builder establishes above San Francisco Bay as the novel's method turns to parable. The utopia Miriam creates is reached by traveling past the "porch of heaven...pavilioned with stars, propped with fearful arches formed of uncompleted worlds" (*Building of the City Beautiful*, p. 169). Like the ill-fated Indian republic of Mount Shasta, the utopia resembles the hub of a wheel and is built on the remains of a city made by the lowly Indians, the world's "most perfect communists." All the buildings, streets, and vehicles have been fashioned from despised desert sand. It is the ideal home for humanity's progeny, the child "that comes laughing down out of heaven to us, clapping its tiny hands with delight all day in the open fields" (*Building of the City Beautiful*, p. 172).

The book, like *Unwritten History*, is expiatory, confessional, and ultimately a self-judgment. Its main flaw perhaps is excessive earnestness. This might have been offset had Miller been willing to reveal in his writings his great capacity for physical self-indulgence. A sexual complement to the ethereal Miriam would have added to the fiction of his day an unprecedented level of honesty.

By the time Miller completed the chapters that became *Overland in a Covered Wagon* (published posthumously in 1930) the papered windows of American frontier dwellings had either disappeared or been replaced with glass, but the autobiography engaged Miller on a high artistic level, and the scenes he sought to remember from the 1850s mirrored a world he still trusted. Almost seventy years old, he remained a superb local colorist, writing precisely of the things he knew best and loved most.

As writer and individual Miller knew he was an affront to pretentious, genteel America. He was an entirely original product of his philosophy and environment, his sensitivity, shrewdness, and childishness. He developed an intimate prose style and an original life-style as well—one in which feeling, bathos, and comedy predominated. His stance toward mass society was basically defensive, and his combative attitude toward the press prefigured strategies used by writers of more recent times. Few of his works are perfect, nor do they need to be: Miller's failings, and his attitude toward failure, are part of the reason we read him.

Survey of Criticism

Of real encouragement to the student of Miller is O. W. Frost's *Joaquin Miller* (1967). Frost's book quotes accurately and is scrupulous regarding dates. He cites court records and other documents in detail, providing the kind of reliable information that has been lacking for decades. Unfortunately, the prosaic style of the biography disguises many of its virtues, and Frost's literary judgments are not always easy to follow.

More valuable from the critical standpoint is William Everson's attempt to grapple with Miller from the inside as a creator—and with many of the perplexing questions regarding his participation in myth—as well as his place in California writing. Although Everson had not completed his background research on Miller when *Archetype West* (1976) was published, the book raises issues that will continue to be a challenge to Miller's readers.

A. H. Rosenus suggests one approach to an understanding of Miller's personal psychology, as well as to some of the underlying conflicts of *Unwritten History: Life Amongst the Modocs*, in the article, "Joaquin Miller and His 'Shadow' " (1976).

Of the early biographies, still best is *Joaquin Miller and His Other Self* (1929) by Harr Wagner, publisher, novelist, and Miller's friend. Many of its anecdotes are faithful to Miller's personality, and the remarks, letters, and criticisms by other writers make the book highly valuable.

Stuart Sherman's perceptions in his Introduction to the *Poetical Works of Joaquin Miller* (1923) and in *Americans* (1923) are keen enough to deserve study. He was hampered by not having the *California Diary* at his disposal, and his reliance on some of the apocryphal stories Miller told the press led him to write some embarrassing passages. Nevertheless Sherman, along with Charles Warren Stoddard, was one of the first to observe that Miller's prose in *Memorie and Rime* (1884) and in *Unwritten History* was superior to anything he had done in poetry.

Martin Peterson's *Joaquin Miller: Literary Frontiersman* (1937) is neither insightful from the critical standpoint nor accurate on historical matters; the book's bibliography and notes are far more valuable than the text.

Perhaps the best known and most destructive of Miller's biographers is M. M. Marberry, who wrote *Splendid Poseur* (1953). Composed as a piece of journalistic libel, it is not always the well-researched book it pretends to be and contains numerous factual errors. A single passage on page twenty-one reveals four errors in one group; two are deliberate falsifications designed to prove Miller did not take part in the battle of Castle Crags. In order to do this, Marberry had to discredit all pioneer accounts and a contemporary newspaper report as well, so he alluded to a secret diary to suggest Miller was elsewhere during the battle. The secret diary, however, does not exist. Nor was Marberry faithful on peripheral matters, such as the whereabouts of Bret Harte or the character of Mrs. Frank Leslie. Although it can be relied upon only somewhat less than half the time, Marberry's work has carried on what has already been described by some critics as a tradition of prejudice against Miller—an interesting phenomenon, impossible to overlook once the critical works on him have been considered. Biographers of Twain, for instance, most often characterize the relationship between Twain and Miller by referring to DeVoto's *Mark Twain in Eruption* (1940), which describes a London dinner in a recollection twenty years old when it was written. Twain's far more spontaneous remarks about Miller from the same period—given in *Mark Twain to Mrs. Fairbanks* (1949)—are seldom cited. Similarly, if a careful search of Ambrose Bierce's correspondence is made, the conclusion has to be reached that Miller was a rarity among contemporary literary figures in enjoying Bierce's affection until the end of his career.

A thoroughgoing evaluation of the English response to Miller's work is offered by Benjamin S. Lawson, Jr., in his "Joaquin Miller in England" (1974-75). Since many of the English articles are still perceptive, Lawson's bibliography is indispensable.

A detailed account of Miller's relationship with Ina Coolbrith and other San Francisco literary figures can be found in *Ina Coolbrith* (1973) by Josephine Rhodehamel and Raymund Wood.

Bibliography

Works by Joaquin Miller

Specimens. Portland: Carter Hines, 1868.
Joaquin et al. Portland: S. J. McCormick, 1869.
Songs of the Sierras. London: Longman, Green, Reader and Dyer, 1871; Boston: Roberts Bros., 1871
Life Amongst the Modocs: Unwritten History. London: Richard Bentley & Son, 1873; revised and published as *Unwritten History: Life Amongst the Modocs*. Hartford: American Publishing Co., 1874; ed. with intro. by Alan Rosenus. Reprint of 1873 edition, Eugene, Oreg.: Urion Press, 1972.
First Fam'lies of the Sierras. London: G. Routledge, 1875.
The One Fair Woman. London: Chapman and Hall, 1876.
The Danites in the Sierras. Chicago: Jansen, McClurg, 1881.
Shadows of Shasta. Chicago: Jansen, McClurg, 1881.
Memorie and Rime. New York: Funk and Wagnalls, 1884.
The Destruction of Gotham. New York: Funk and Wagnalls, 1886.
The Building of the City Beautiful. Chicago: Stone & Kimball, 1892.

True Bear Stories. With introductory notes by David Starr Jordan. Chicago: Rand, Mc-
Nally, 1900.
The Building of the City Beautiful. New edition. Trenton, N.J.: A. Brandt, 1905.
Joaquin Miller's Poems. Bear Edition. 6 vols. San Francisco: Whitaker and Ray, 1909-10.
The Poetical Works of Joaquin Miller. Ed. Stuart P. Sherman. New York: G. P. Putnam,
1923.
Overland in a Covered Wagon: An Autobiography. Ed. Sidney G. Firman. New York and
London: D. Appleton, 1930.
Joaquin Miller: His California Diary. Ed. John S. Richards. Seattle: F. McCaffrey at his
Dogwood Press, 1936.
Selected Writings of Joaquin Miller. Ed. Alan Rosenus. Eugene, Oreg.: Urion Press,
1976.

Studies of Joaquin Miller

Clemens, Samuel. *Mark Twain to Mrs. Fairbanks*. Ed. Dixon Wecter. San Marino,
Calif.: Huntington Library, 1949.
Everson, William. *Archetype West*. Berkeley: Oyez, 1976.
Frost, O. W. *Joaquin Miller*. TUSAS. New York: Twayne, 1967.
Howells, William Dean. "Review of *Songs of the Sierras*." *Atlantic Monthly* 28 (Decem-
ber 1871): 771.
Hubbard, Elbert. *So Here Then Is a Little Journey to the Home of Joaquin Miller*. East
Aurora, N.Y.: Roycrofters, 1903.
Lawson, Benjamin S., Jr. "Joaquin Miller in England." *South Dakota Review* 12 (Winter
1974-75): 89-101.
Longtin, Ray C. *Three Writers of the Far West: A Reference Guide*. Boston: G.K. Hall,
1980.
Marberry, M. M. *Splendid Poseur*. New York: Thomas Y. Crowell, 1953.
Peterson, M. S. *Joaquin Miller: Literary Frontiersman*. Stanford University, Calif.:
Stanford University Press, 1937.
Rhodehamel, Josephine DeWitt, and Wood, Raymund Francis. *Ina Coolbrith*. Provo,
Utah: Brigham Young University Press, 1973.
Rosenus, A. H. "Joaquin Miller and His 'Shadow.' " *Western American Literature* 11
(May 1976): 51-59.
Sherman, Stuart. *Americans*. New York: Scribners, 1923.
Wagner, Harr. *Joaquin Miller and His Other Self*. San Francisco: Harr Wagner, 1929.

N. SCOTT MOMADAY
(1934-)

Biography

"N. Scott Momaday...is twenty-five, unmarried, unpublished, and largely unconcerned," the *New Mexico Quarterly* noted in its 1959 summer issue (p. 237) as first publisher of a Momaday poem, "Earth and I Gave You Turquoise." Now, at the beginning of the new decade of the 1980s, twice married and auspiciously published, N. Scott Momaday is largely concerned with the native American—the principal focus of his writing, his lectures and service to America, and his beliefs and themes. Momaday, "one of the best novelists of any sort in America today" (Velie, *American Indian Literature*, p. 245), is also poet, memoirist, epicist, essayist, autobiographer, and lecturer. Not narrowly a western or, in popular terminology, a Kiowa writer, he presents, with imagery, symbolism, and sensitivity, subject matter traditionally considered intrinsic to the western states.

His work comprises *House Made of Dawn* (1968), 1969 Pulitzer Prize-winning novel; *The Way to Rainy Mountain* (1969), poetic prose epic of the Kiowa people; *The Gourd Dancer* (1976), his collected poems incorporating his earlier *Angle of Geese* (1974); and *The Names* (1976), his prebirth through postpubescence autobiography. A campus lecturer and a participant in humanities forums, creative writing conferences, and dedications of native American centers, he leaves a trail of video/audio tapes across the United States. He serves as proponent for the native American in milieus as diverse as the First Convocation of Indian Scholars in 1970 and current meetings of the board, of which he is a member, of the American Indian Museum in New York City. A fellow poet credits him for helping usher in a decade of creativity that will become a lasting body of literature by native American writers (Ortiz, "Literature," p. 32).

Distinct influences on Momaday's literary and personal development prevail: his formal graduate education, parental dedication to his early intellectual enrichment, and childhood cultural assimilation in all its manifestations. With a 1958 bachelor's degree from the University of New Mexico, Momaday entered

Stanford as a Creative Writing Fellow in 1959, receiving the master's degree in 1960 and the Ph.D. degree in 1963. This four-year period served as catalyst for all that he had studied, learned, and perceived.

Yvor Winters, called by Momaday "one of the truly great men of his time" (*Viva*, 2 September 1973), exerted a singular influence on Momaday's writing as professor and friend. Edmund Wilson not only first led Momaday to Frederick Goddard Tuckerman, the subject of his doctoral dissertation, but was responsible for its publication in 1965. Studying Tuckerman and a growing admiration of other writers—Emily Dickinson, Karen Blixen (Isak Dinesen), James Joyce, William Faulkner, and Herman Melville—further influenced Momaday's intellectual integrity, his sensitivity for imagery, and his narrative art. Momaday identified easily with the isolation revealed in Tuckerman's poems and his resistance to mainstream nineteenth-century American romanticism. From the writers of narrative, Momaday reached a conviction that "the storyteller's attitude" ("A Conversation," p. 21) is similar in both the oral and written traditions. His introduction of a course in the American Indian oral tradition, first at Berkeley and then at Stanford, and the writing in his *Viva* column on subjects as diverse as Sir Francis Drake, Georgia O'Keeffe, Quincy Tomaha, and five pieces on Billy the Kid, indicated the dual direction of his career. When Momaday left for the Soviet Union in 1974, where he lectured and traveled, he had completed a manuscript on Billy the Kid, which Charles Woodard read as part of a longer manuscript and discusses at length in his dissertation, "The Concept of the Creative Word in the Writings of N. Scott Momaday" (1975). From the catalytic magic of formal education evolved a new alchemy in the crucible that is N. Scott Momaday, writer, professor, humanist.

Parental dedication to his early intellectual enrichment becomes evident throughout *The Names*. Momaday's parents, Alfred Morris Momaday, artist, and Natachee Scott Momaday, writer, each well educated, highly literate, and talented, were initially teachers. His mother he credits for her concern that English be his "native" language. From her sharing her "love of books," he was able to see "Grendel's shadow on the walls of Canyon de Chelly" (*The Names*, p. 60). The artistic influence of his father, illustrator for *The Way to Rainy Mountain*, surfaces on the title page of *The Gourd Dancer*. From Momaday's early days at Shiprock and Hobbs, New Mexico, his mother read to him and his father told Kiowa stories. Although he lacked interest in schools, he terms the school at Jemez Pueblo, where his parents taught for a quarter of a century, "the last, best home of my childhood" (p. 117). These years not only prepared him for what he encountered at Stanford but fostered his inclination for literature, language, and learning.

The fortuity of Momaday's birth endures as the constant influence on his life and writing. Born 27 February 1934 near the old Anadarko Agency, Lawton, Oklahoma, Momaday possesses a government document certifying him as "of ⅛ degree Indian blood as shown on the Kiowa Indian Census roll opposite Number 2035" (*The Names*, p. 42); his paternal lineage is Kiowa, his maternal

Cherokee and French. His father changed *Mammedaty*, "Sky-walker," to *Momaday*. Even though Momaday has consistently used the initial *N.* in his name, confusion has arisen that he has appropriated the name of his mother, *Natachee*. Researchers should be alerted to a recent Library of Congress card mistakenly imprinted with *Natachee* as Momaday's first name.

Tricultural throughout his childhood and "at home in the English language" (*The Names*, p. 127), Momaday earlier than most other children became aware of the importance of language and the significance of the word. Traveling between Oklahoma and the Southwest from the first year of his life, he lived *in* languages, traditions, and rites, not only in Kiowa country but on southwestern reservations and at Jemez Pueblo; he was, moreover, no stranger to Catholic liturgy. He answered to two Kiowa names, *Tsoai-talee*, "Rock-Tree Boy," and *Tsotohah*, "Red Bluff"; traveled Francisco's and Abel's old road to San Ysidro; saw the eyes of one of the fallen geese while hunting with his father; learned the words of his grandmother, Aho; and lived instinctively in the oral tradition unaware of the impact of these years on his future.

Few other writers are in the enviable position of Momaday, American scholar, able to retrace one's own heritage; to create through excellence of command of the written word the essence of oral and ritual traditions as manifestations and potential multiplicity of lingual, cultural, and ecological-environmental wholeness; and to obscure if not completely obliterate the centuries-old stereotype non-natives have had of native Americans on this continent.

Major Themes

Momaday, as those who explore the abstrusity of his creative expression and literary achievements begin to understand, writes and speaks from a fundamental faith that the native American is a universal being possessing attributes from a long, rich heritage. The substantiality of character of his heritage, he believes, posits for him an identification for which Americans who have no such source of identity feel a need. With his faith as postulate, Momaday develops three major themes: a sense of the earth (place) or landscape, imagination, and its reciprocal quality, appropriateness; the word and oral tradition, language, and, ultimately, the author's craft as evidence of man's being; and self-knowledge. Recurrent throughout his work, these themes invite attention to Momaday's singular facility in fusing belief with control of and versatility in genre, subject matter, and style.

The first theme, tripartite and remarkably inclusive albeit unified as Indian belief, Momaday expresses both symbolically and explicitly. Aware that few people understand how the native American sees himself with respect to the land, Momaday emphasizes that the land is, like Tai-me, the Kiowa spiritual being, a source of power, a "repository of heritage" (Abbott, "An Interview with N. Scott Momaday," p. 22). He also suggests that the greater the remove from one's heritage, the greater the risk of loss of heritage. That the land is also sacred he believes developed early in man's mind, giving the self a sense of the sacred. Momaday can see the Garden of the Gods in Colorado "as surely the work of the old obscure deities" (*Colorado*, p. 34). "We Americans," he writes, "must come again to a moral comprehension of the earth and air. . . [and]. . . live according to the principle of a land ethic" ("An American," p. 11). The passage following, "Once in his life a man ought to concentrate his mind upon the remembered earth" (*Way to Rainy Mountain*, p. 113; "An American," p. 10), subsumes all that earth means to the native American. Taking possession of a landscape means begin-ning to be a part of the physical world as Abel begins his eighth day home, almost at peace in the canyon, wishing he could sing a "creation song," aware of the "consuming earth" (*House Made of Dawn*, pp. 57, 58). Momaday freely employs earth images, metaphors of all the living things of earth. In *The Names* he confesses that he existed in, as an indivisible part of, the landscape at Jemez.

Imagination, outgrowth of this interrelationship between man and earth, en-gendering, as it does, power, the numinous, and holism, enables a person to envision the imponderable into possible, "for at the most fundamental level we are what we imagine ourselves to be" ("Native American," p. 80). Ko-Sahn's appearing before him as he is completing *The Way to Rainy Mountain* is a unique personal example of the power of imagination; she assures him that her having existence in his imagination may well be the best kind of existence. Abel grad-ually begins to imagine himself as whole. Billy the Kid leans his back against the wall of Momaday's lecture hall, rides with Momaday and his horse Pecos in "The Pear-Shaped Legend / A Figment of the [Momaday's] Imagination." The epilogue of *The Names* brings the reader very close to the gossamer between imagination and reality. Few others in the modern world fully comprehend capsulated imagination as creation and creativity so completely as do the native Americans or as Momaday challenges his readers to understand it, proceeding as it does from "racial memory" (Abbott, "Interview," pp. 80-81).

Appropriateness, reciprocal extension of imagination, embraces the natural, moral rightness of existence. It helps the Indian to "understand malice" though he cannot understand white America's inclination toward ambivalence in attitude and ambiguity in morals and ideas ("The Morality of Indian Hating," p. 31). Abel's discarding his uniform for prewar attire, finally, on his fifth day home and preparing Francisco for burial at book's end are examples of appropriateness, as are Momaday's own retracing of the Kiowa trek and the boy's giving the black horse to Mammedaty in the titular prose-poem, "The Gourd Dancer" (*Gourd Dancer*, p. 37). Appropriateness as inherence tends to escape non-native readers.

The potential for detecting themes in Momaday appears to be limitless. Only as a reader understands this first theme do motifs or lesser themes appear to be manifestations of a moral, spiritual, or metaphysical purport, sufficiently inter-dependent to confound a critic. Especially do abstractions beg to be treated singly: alienation, hating, evil, order, belief/faith/religion, transcendence, myth, psychology, time, power, death, and vision, for example. Concrete phraseology— or what appears concrete—implies singleness of theme until a reader becomes aware that Momaday's metaphorical, symbolic use of language subtly shifts sense of, for example, the following: pollen, house made of dawn, bear, eagle, horse, fish, geese, spider. The first theme affords an insight to the range and behavior and belief—a way of life—of the native American for comprehensive interpretation.

The first theme, however, is of little value without weighing the dimensions to which it is relayed by the second theme. That "the word is sacred" (*Way to Rainy Mountain*, p. 42; "A Note," p. xx) Momaday makes clear by iteration and exemplification. Tosomah preaches the word; Aho believes in and uses the word. "The first word gives origin to the second, the first and second...to the third...a chain of becoming" (*The Names*, p. 154). Momaday's emphasis on and his command in written English of the oral tradition support the word and language as a second theme. He sees man embodied of an idea through language; "we are all made of words" ("The Man," p. 49). Inarticulation—Abel's in the novel and, by implication, the world's—he views as tragic. The arrowmaker he particularizes as a man of words. Attributes of patience and time serve the arrowmaker to craft the best arrows. Momaday's description of the shoes Josie gave Abel is an apt summary of his craft: "finely crafted and therefore admirable" (*House Made of Dawn*, p. 98). Too reticent or modest to speak of his superior craftsmanship, Momaday exemplifies it.

Total writer-reader concord discloses a third theme threading through his work with haunting reverberations of the Delphic "Know thyself," or overtones of Carlyle's reinterpretation of knowing what one can do. This knowledge of self goes beyond imagination to cognition of capabilities and action. Venturing this theme proves fruitful. A first clue is one word: "they had dared," he writes of the Kiowas, "to imagine and *determine* who they were" (*Way to Rainy Mountain*, p. 2). Momaday's finding the Tai-me bundle after learning during his 1963 visit that his grandmother knew where it was and his setting out to retrace the Kiowa path go beyond imagination to determination and action. In "The Delight Song of Tsoai-talee," the *am* as the finite form of the verb implies self-knowledge (*Gourd Dancer*, p. 27). Elsewhere he speaks of "aesthetic perspective" and "an idea of humanity" ("I Am Alive," p. 26), as western concepts. Momaday may not realize how close to Descartes' *Cogito, ergo sum*, his ideas are and the extent to which the history, literature, philosophy, and metaphysics of the Western world imbue his beliefs. He is a unique blend of two western worlds; but which is old, which is new? He writes what he is; he is what he writes. Momaday, beyond imagination, knows who he is and what he can share with the world, as carrier of his own dream wheel.

Survey of Criticism

What started as generally slight initial evaluation of Momaday (Trimble, *N. Scott Momaday* [1973], pp. 19-20), possibly due to unfamiliarity with the tribal tradition, is yielding progressively to a solid core of serious criticism. Fewer

critics treat *House Made of Dawn*, for example, narrowly as a limited, sociological Indian-white or a stock Abel-antagonist conflict. The generally favorable
interpretation by the scholarly community reveals a growing awareness of Momaday's
intent of reciprocal acculturation and of his literary and creative accomplishment.
His multigenre treatment in four principal publications not only establishes him
in an anomalous self-competition but provides critics a wide range for exegesis.

House Made of Dawn evokes the bulk of critical work. Two books attest to the
divergence of criticism of the novel. In *In Time and Place* (1977), Floyd C.
Watkins discusses it as one of eight American classics, each portraying a different culture and revealing the degree of knowledgeability and creativity of the
author. Perceptive and thorough, Watkins, explicating carefully, tracing possible
sources for characters and setting, and quoting Momaday, contributes valuable
insight to the novel. He lauds Momaday for his authenticity and his precise
adaptation of the traditions to culture. Suggesting the occult as a theme, he sees
the book as showing man's loss of qualities, including meaning, that tie him to
his heritage. Of all books written on Indian culture, he calls *House Made of
Dawn* "the fullest and best representation" (*Time and Place*, p. 170).

In *American Indian Fiction* (1978), on the other hand, Charles R. Larson
terms the novel "radically experimental," "the most complex and . . . obscure
novel written by an American Indian" (p.78). As one of sixteen works in a
history of fiction by native American writers, it is, he states, "the most searing
indictment of the white world by a Native American novelist" (p. 87). He sees
bitterness in Momaday and faults him for "fascination with structure" (p. 78). As
Wayne Ude aptly observes in a review of *American Indian Fiction*, Larson
"seems not to have immersed himself sufficiently in Indian metaphysics" to read
the book well (Review [1979], p. 75). Another critic, Roger Dickinson-Brown,
who lauds Momaday for his abilities and reputation and gives an excellent
appraisal of "Angle of Geese," calls the novel "a memorable failure" in "The Art
and Importance of N. Scott Momaday" (1978, p. 30).

Kenneth Rosen, "American Indian Literature" (1979), gauges the novel as "a
work that will stand up under a great deal more careful scrutiny" (p. 58). In a
very good essay he acknowledges both Momaday's novel and the resolution of
the National Council of Teachers of English for supplementary study of native
American literature in the schools for eliciting interest and serious work in the
field. He questions why research, of a less literary nature, he admits, cannot
uncover the movie, with Larry Byrd of Circle Films playing Abel, of *House
Made of Dawn* that he saw in a private showing. He explains well why Momaday's
book "opened some heretofore closed doors" (p. 58).

Cuts from the film, by courtesy of New Line Cinema, serve as illustrations for
an illuminating essay in 1978 of Abel by Alan R. Velie ("Cain and Abel . . .").
Velie, building upon the biblical allusion, although Momaday disavows anything
more "than a composite Abel" (p. 56), counters students' judgment of the white
victimization of Abel by pointing out that Abel's brother Indians are his antagonists. The Cains in the novel are Tosomah, by ridicule; the Albino, by humilia-

tion; and the policeman Martinez, an Indian with a Spanish surname, by assault. Abel's entering the race signifies his survival from his tormentors, his terrors. Velie suggests a comparison between Momaday and Melville, between Abel and Moby Dick. The ending, he concedes "is as happy . . . as the novel will allow" (p. 62).

The chronological framework of the novel, each chapter headed by a date, leads H. S. McAllister in "Incarnate Grace and the Paths of Salvation in *House Made of Dawn*" (1975) to a singular, perceptive essay. Working from the premise that Angela, if mere stereotype, is a flaw in a well-structured novel, McAllister presents an exquisitely refined exploration of salvation and suggests the novel is a Christian morality play. His drawing parallels between Angela and the Virgin Mary and between the given dates and those in the Catholic holy year lead his reader carefully through his interpretation. He identifies details of given saints and explicates clearly to prepare for his conclusion: that Angela assumes the role of Abel's spiritual redeemer serving as his motive for the run at dawn. The run, McAllister concludes, is not a resurrection but the "beginning of forty days of penance" (p. 12).

Two other critics treat the sacred vein in the work. For Vernon E. Lattin, "The Quest for Mystic Vision in Contemporary Native American and Chicano Fiction" (1979), who reads the theme of the novel as the mythic vision as today's alternative to the failure of Christianity, Abel's finding himself in the universe fulfills the sacred vision. Baine Kerr, "The Novel as Sacred Text" (1978), who calls the novel "a brave book" (p. 173) and Momaday "a preserver of holiness" (p. 179), suggests that the modern novel may be Momaday's way of presenting a sacred text. Extremely perceptive in his judgments, he sees the book as profound in its metaphysical implications and gives creation schemata for support as a creation myth. He interprets Angela as mythmaker, transcending culture to preserve what is holy in Abel.

Date control of content is, in Joseph F. Trimmer's "Native Americans and the American Mix" (1975), no more than a seven-year sequence important to Abel's maturation; time and vision he interprets as the novel's major motifs. Perceiving distinct cultural contrasts in the American and native American cultures, he credits the Pulitzer committee for the "appropriateness" (p. 89) of its selection. Viewing Abel's relationship with Angela as unproductive, he considers Abel reborn as he runs for his new cultural role.

McAllister in another, more provocative essay, "Be a Man, Be a Woman" (1975), finds three manifestations of the characteristic of evil in Father Nicolás, the witch Nicolás, and the Albino, a concept Velie calls "far-fetched" ("Cain and Abel," p. 58). Opening with the most succinct plot summary available, McAllister defines the term *androgyny*, "reproduces" the priest's journal, and details moral complexity in his development of the thematic function of Father Nicolás.

Four more critics warrant mention. Norma Baker Barry, "The Bear's Son Folk Tale in *When the Legends Die* and *House Made of Dawn*" (1978), establishing criteria for European and Asiatic folktales of the Bear's Son type, develops

Momaday's interweaving the tale into his context for Abel to emerge as "hero." She very ably shows how he emerges both a universal hero and a hero of the imagination, with "Beowulfian" echoes evident in Abel's killing the Albino and an optimistic (healing) outcome of the struggle within himself.

Peter G. Beidler, "Animals and Human Development in the Contemporary American Indian Novel" (1979), skillfully traces the use of animals in Momaday: those with tenure in (belonging to) the land and those without tenure—the invaders. Using the analogies of animals, Momaday, as Beidler shows, takes Abel from blindness to sight, making the theme of vision central to the novel. David Espey, "Endings in Contemporary American Indian Fiction" (1978), interprets Abel's running as overcoming the fear of death experienced earlier. Responding to his grandfather's death, then, becomes "an act of union" (p. 138) with his ancestral past. Charles Woodard in "Momaday's *House Made of Dawn*" (1978) views Abel at the height of his powers of imagination in the race, thereby making the reader not reader only but participant in the race as well.

Engrossment with the enigmatic possibilities of *House Made of Dawn* suggests that a definitive reading is a prospect for a somewhat distant future, especially since critics tend to dismiss the word and language as a theme and to slight Momaday's other genres. Jack L. Davis, however, in "The Whorf Hypothesis and Native American Literature" (1976), points out that Momaday, cognizant of the white man's loss of relationship with words, takes care to distinguish, for example, nonverbal perception from nonperception. Basing his essay upon Benjamin Lee Whorf's theory that language structure determines a people's perception of the world, Davis makes clear the superior skill Momaday possesses in understanding deep structure, particularly to cross linguistic-cultural barriers. Two critics give perceptive treatment to the word as theme. Laurence J. Evers, "Word and Place" (1977), carefully explicates how Abel's lack of words separates him from his community just as finding words serves to aid in his reemergence. Charles Woodard's dissertation, fully deserving of publication, is a careful examination and exemplification of the "humanization of language . . . Momaday's central concern" (p. 19). He treats Momaday's works as a progression in language, giving considerable insight to the word and language as controlling Momaday's "angles of vision" (p. 113).

The likeliest vehicle for sensing language as a theme is *The Way to Rainy Mountain*, in which, Simon Ortiz claims in "Literature" (1980), Momaday rendered the oral literature into a mythic narrative of epic proportions" (p. 33). Passages of Kiowa concern for language appear on a fifth of the pages of the book. Although a few critics very early recognized *the word* in the prose-epic, Robert L. Berner, "N. Scott Momaday" (1979), cognizant of Momaday's belief that the word is sacred, suggests allegorical intent in his perceptive argument that the subject of the book is language, "its origins, its power, its inevitable collapse, and finally, its rebirth as art" (p. 57). "Defying generic description" (p. 57), the book gives, in Berner's eyes, the soul, body, and (through the author's mind) mind of the Kiowa people. He explicates each part carefully, with a graphic representation of the Kiowa religious vision, development of the author's discovery of himself as a Kiowa, and advancement of "the grandmother principle" (p. 66), the influence of Aho, Momaday's grandmother, as the unifying force of the book. Berner aptly observes that all people are "on the way to Rainy Mountain" (p. 64). Charles Nicholas, in another perceptive essay, *"The Way to Rainy Mountain"* (1975-76), details how Momaday dramatizes the process by which traditional myth becomes the creative myth, both acts of the imagination. Woodard calls the book "a triumph in language" ("The Concept," p. 113).

To Barbara Strelke, "N. Scott Momaday" (1975), both the novel and the "multi-genre" (p. 348) prose-epic operate on two levels: one the response native Americans make to their "racial memory," their background, their being Indian, and the other Momaday's revealing these native responses through his belief in the word as sacred and creative to the personal and universal levels. Her analogy of the fine craftsmanship of Indian weaving or silversmithing explains the art of his structure. Momaday's dependence upon western literature and philosophy she recognizes as combining with his intimate knowledge of native American belief. Her comprehensive appraisal and good explication bring both Abel and Momaday to the same "destination," rarely arrived at in western literature—and she does not mean of the American West—for the person needs "to call upon the power of the spirit" (p. 357) for affirmation of existence.

The Names has yet to receive the full interpretation that its stream of consciousness and unique personal revelation warrant. William Bloodworth perceptively discusses it, however, with *The Way to Rainy Mountain* in his "Neihardt, Momaday, and the Art of Indian Autobiography" (1978); by contrasting Neihardt's emphasis upon vision and Momaday's emphasis on the oral tradition, Bloodworth shows the two directions of Indian autobiography, concerned that discrepancy between "cultural content and...literary form" (p. 154) be reconciled.

Largely ignored in America is foreign research on Momaday. Thekla Zachrau, research assistant, Ruhr-Universität, Bochum, in an essay printed simultaneously in the *Dutch Quarterly Review* and *American Indian Culture and Research Journal*, "N. Scott Momaday" (1979), reads *The Names* and the other two prose works, all three oddly termed *novels*, as a progression in a search for identity. Careful reading and detailed explication serve to support his interpretation. He questions, with distinct Rousseauistic overtones, whether Momaday's suggesting the native American way of life for white man is the solution to any identity-quest.

Momaday's poetry richly deserves a separate discussion elsewhere, for as the publishers observe on the book jacket of *The Gourd Dancer*, "Momaday is drawing on a rich body of traditions and influences that produce a poetry quite outside contemporary trends in American verse." Teachers write of their success in using the poetry for its precise western imagery and a first acquaintance with the oral tradition as an initial, apt step to reading all of Momaday. In "A Note on Contemporary Native American Poetry," Momaday addresses the spirit of the indefinable term *poetry*, useful for establishing criteria by which to judge him.

Although occasional perceptive critiques of the poems have appeared, Kenneth C. Mason's five-part essay on *The Gourd Dancer*, "The Poetry of N. Scott Momaday" (1980), is the most comprehensive appraisal to date. He discusses the poetic progression of Momaday from the metaphysical poems exploring the "elusive nature of reality" (p. 64) in part I and the beauty of the oral tradition in part II, "Carriers of the Dream Wheel" identified as defining the oral tradition, to his final maturity in part III, which manifests the originality and rhetorical skill evidenced in his prose works to mark the work as distinctly his own. Mason is perceptive and clear.

The potential for continued scholarship is good, the theses and dissertations available through interlibrary loans indicative of careful research and judicious criticism. A discussion of the poetry should include, for example, the dissertations of Norma Jean Wilson and Charles Woodard; space limitations here, however, preclude all that the unpublished work and the earlier criticism merit. As critical interpretation of Momaday's four-genre art increases and improves, a growing respect for and an understanding of Momaday evolve. Critics recognize him for the fusion of his superior craftsmanship and his Kiowa heritage as an established creative voice in the West, assessing reacculturation and the metaphysical aspects of existence.

Bibliography

Works by N. Scott Momaday

Page numbers in the text refer to the paperback edition, when one is available. In the case of two paperback editions, the starred edition has been consulted.

"The Morality of Indian Hating." *Ramparts* 3 (Summer 1964): 30-40.

The Complete Poems of Frederick Goddard Tuckerman. Edited with an introduction by N. Scott Momaday and with a critical foreword by Yvor Winters. New York: Oxford University Press, 1965.

House Made of Dawn. New York: Harper & Row, 1968; New York: Signet, 1969*; New York: Perennial, 1977.

The Way to Rainy Mountain. Albuquerque: University of New Mexico Press, 1969; New York: Ballantine, 1969.

"The Man Made of Words," Assembly Presentation. *Indian Voices*. First Convocation of American Indian Scholars. San Francisco: Indian Historian Press, American Indian Educational Publisher, 1970, pp. 49-84.

"An American Land Ethic." *Sierra Club Bulletin* 55 (February 1970): 8-11.

Viva, Sunday supplement, *Santa Fe New Mexican*. Contributor of a column from 16 April 1972 through 9 December 1973.

Colorado—Summer/Fall/Winter/Spring. Photography by David Muench. New York: Rand McNally, 1973.

Angle of Geese and Other Poems. Boston: David R. Godine, 1974.

"I Am Alive." *The World of the American Indian*. Washington, D. C.: National Geographic Society, 1974, pp. 11-26.

"A Note on Contemporary Native American Poetry." *Carriers of the Dream Wheel*. Ed.
    Duane Niatum. New York: Harper & Row, 1975, pp. xix-xx.
"The Pear-Shaped Legend." *Stanford Magazine* 3 (Spring-Summer 1975): 46-48.
The Gourd Dancer. New York: Harper & Row, 1976.
The Names. New York: Harper & Row, 1976.
"Native American Attitudes to the Environment." *Seeing with a Native Eye: Essays on
    Native American Religion*. Ed. Walter H. Capps. New York: Harper & Row,
    1976, pp. 79-85.

Studies of N. Scott Momaday

Abbott, Lee. "An Interview with N. Scott Momaday." *Puerto del Sol* 12 (1973): 21-38.
Barry, Norma Baker. "The Bear's Son Folk Tale in *When the Legends Die* and *House
    Made of Dawn*." *Western American Literature* 12 (Winter 1978): 275-87.
Beidler, Peter G. "Animals and Human Development in the Contemporary American
    Indian Novel." *Western American Literature* 14 (Summer 1979): 133-48.
Berner, Robert L. "N. Scott Momaday: Beyond Rainy Mountain." *American Indian
    Culture and Research Journal* 3 (1979): 57-67.
Bloodworth, William. "Neihardt, Momaday, and the Art of Indian Autobiography."
    Where the West Begins. Eds. Arthur R. Huseboe and William Geyer. Sioux Falls,
    S. Dak.: Center for Western Studies, 1978, pp. 152-60.
"A Conversation with N. Scott Momaday." *Sun Tracks: An Indian Literary Magazine* 2
    (1976): 18-21.
Davis, Jack L. "The Whorf Hypothesis and Native American Literature." *South Dakota
    Review* 14 (Summer 1976): 59-72.
Dickinson-Brown, Roger. "The Art and Importance of N. Scott Momaday." *Southern
    Review* 14 (January 1978): 30-45.
Espey, David. "Endings in Contemporary American Indian Fiction." *Western American
    Literature* 13 (Summer 1978): 133-39.
Evers, Laurence J. "Words and Place: A Reading of *House Made of Dawn*." *Western
    American Literature* 11 (Winter 1977): 297-320.
Kerr, Baine. "The Novel as Sacred Text: N. Scott Momaday's Myth-Making Ethic."
    Southwest Review 63 (Spring 1978): 172-79.
Larson, Charles R. *American Indian Fiction*. Albuquerque: University of New Mexico
    Press, 1978, pp. 78-93.
Lattin, Vernon E. "The Quest for Mythic Vision in Contemporary Native American and
    Chicano Fiction." *American Literature* 50 (January 1979): 625-40.
McAllister, Harold S. "Be a Man, Be a Woman: Androgyny in *House Made of Dawn*."
    American Indian Quarterly 2 (Spring 1975): 14-22.
————. "Incarnate Grace and the Paths of Salvation in *House Made of Dawn*." *South
    Dakota Review* 12 (Winter 1974-75): 115-25.
Mason, Kenneth C. "Beautyway: The Poetry of N. Scott Momaday." *South Dakota Review*
    18 (Summer 1980): 61-83.
Nicholas, Charles A. "*The Way to Rainy Mountain*: N. Scott Momaday's Hard Journey
    Back." *South Dakota Review* 13 (Winter 1975-76): 149-58.
Ortiz, Simon J. "Literature." *American Indian Journal* 6 (January 1980): 32-33.
"Poets in this Issue." *New Mexico Quarterly* 29 (Summer 1959): 237.
Rosen, Kenneth. "American Indian Literature: Current Condition and Suggested Re-
    search." *American Indian Culture and Research Journal* 3 (1979): 57-66.

Strelke, Barbara. "N. Scott Momaday: Racial Memory and Individual Imagination."
    Literature of the American Indians: Views and Interpretations. Ed. Abraham
    Chapman. New York: New American Library, 1975, pp. 348-57.
Trimble, Martha Scott. *N. Scott Momaday*. WWS. Boise, Idaho: Boise State College,
    1973.
Trimmer, Joseph F. "Native Americans and the American Mix: N. Scott Momaday's
    House Made of Dawn." *Indiana Social Studies Quarterly* 28 (Fall 1975): 75-91.
Ude, Wayne. Review of *American Indian Fiction* by Charles R. Larson. *Western American
    Literature* 14 (Spring 1979): 74-75.
Velie, Alan R. "Cain and Abel in N. Scott Momaday's *House Made of Dawn*." *Journal of
    the West* 17 (April 1978): 55-62.
————, ed. *American Indian Literature*. Norman: University of Oklahoma Press, 1979,
    pp. 245-46, 282-83, 336.
Watkins, Floyd C. *In Time and Place*. Athens: University of Georgia Press, 1977.
Wilson, Norma Jean. "The Spirit of Place in Contemporary American Indian Poetry."
    Ph.D. dissertation, University of Oklahoma, 1978.
Woodard, Charles Lowell. "The Concept of the Creative Word in the Writings of N.
    Scott Momaday." Ph.D. dissertation, University of Oklahoma, 1975.
————. "Momaday's *House Made of Dawn*." *Explicator* 36 (Winter 1978): 27-28.
Zachrau, Thekla. "N. Scott Momaday: Towards an Indian Identity." *American Indian
    Culture and Research Journal* 3 (1979): 39-56.

WRIGHT MORRIS
(1910-)

Biography

In 1958, Wright Morris noted, "Before coming of age...I had led...half a dozen separate lives. Each life had its own scene, its own milieu...the only connecting tissue being the narrow thread of my *self*" (*The Territory Ahead*, p. 15). Morris was born on 6 January 1910 in Central City, Nebraska, and in spite of the varied scenes he speaks of, is widely identified with the Nebraska plains, the setting for many of his novels. His mother died shortly after his birth, and he was brought up by his father and various relatives. After leaving Central City at age nine, he moved on to Omaha and eventually Norfolk, Nebraska; Chicago; and rural Texas. He attended Pomona College in Claremont, California (1930-33), and spent 1933-34 touring Europe before returning to California in 1934 determined to become a writer.

Morris's early work is shaped by an "infatuation" with the past (both the historical past of the pioneer tradition and the personal past of his plains boyhood), a "conviction that the past was real and desirable, and should be the way life is" (Bleufarb, "Point of View," p. 45). This infatuation contributes to the failure of his first two novels. *My Uncle Dudley* (1942) deals with a cross-country trip like several Morris had taken with his father between 1927 and 1929, and one section of *The Man Who Was There* (1945) concerns an artist's return to his Nebraska home place in an attempt to recapture and thereby understand his past. In these books, the author has not yet attained the emotional detachment necessary to understand the meaning of the personal experiences that inspired them. As a result, he merely describes the experiences, expecting them to speak for themselves. Morris's infatuation is further evident in his celebration of the pioneer tradition, about which he was later to express doubts.

In the mid-1930s, Morris turned to photography as a medium through which the past could be recovered with an immediacy greater than was possible through words. About the time he moved to the Philadelphia suburbs (where he lived and taught from 1944 to 1956), his work with photography earned him Guggenheim

Fellowships in 1942 and 1946 and led to two books combining his photos and text: *The Inhabitants* (1946) and *The Home Place* (1948). His stark, largely unpeopled photographs of decaying American artifacts and dwellings neither condemn social injustice nor document deprivation. To Morris, the well-worn objects suggest not material poverty but spiritual richness, for the owner has "inhabited" the objects, placing his signature on them in years of use. The objects in turn have inhabited the owner in making up part of the world of which he has been conscious. In this way, photographs of objects thus imbued with moral and psychological significance become time capsules preserving the essence of the past.

In the autobiographical novella that forms the text of *The Home Place*, Morris begins to examine the limitations of the pioneer tradition. To make clear that he was primarily a writer, Morris dropped the photos from the sequel, *The World in the Attic* (1949), and the autobiographical novel makes a sharp break with the past as the hero's nostalgia for small-town Nebraska life turns to "nausea" at the emotional and cultural sterility that is the modern legacy of the pioneer tradition. Morris's new perspective on the past is only one sign of his growing self-consciousness about the meaning of his materials. In the later 1940s and early 1950s, three important books contributed to this enlarged self-consciousness. F. Scott Fitzgerald's *The Great Gatsby* helped to teach Morris the meaning of the West and the importance of the American dream in our national life. Henry James's *The American Scene* emphasized to him the American male's abdication of his role in the family and the resulting ascendancy of the female in social relations. D. H. Lawrence's *Studies in Classic American Literature* contributed to his picture of the American experience as a conflict between the desire to get away from the past, to discover the new, and the longing to retreat into the past out of fear of the new.

The novels Morris was now to publish serve notice that his protracted apprenticeship was ended. *Man and Boy* (1951), *The Works of Love* (1952), and *The Deep Sleep* (1953) demonstrate how emotional reserve and sexual stereotypes fostered by the protestant ethic of the pioneers led to the failure of love in the modern family. *Man and Boy* gives a comic view of the dominating mother, the ineffectual husband, and their alienated son in suburban Philadelphia. Set on the plains and loosely based on the life of the author's father, *The Works of Love* is regarded by some critics as one of Morris's major novels. *The Deep Sleep* returns to the setting and subject of *Man and Boy*, but its treatment of them is more satisfying because, in the later novel, Morris's use of five centers of narrative consciousness, each of which has a special psychological perspective on the action, allows him to depict more truly the ambiguity and complexity of relationships in real life. Morris's fiction had always focused on consciousness, but in *War Games* (published in 1972 but written in 1951-52) he widened that focus to include questions about the relation of consciousness to objective reality. Paul Kopfman transforms his vision of himself and his world: in his imagination, he is a woman; in reality, a man. After *War Games*, consciousness and transforming vision emerge as major Morris subjects; a significant step in that emergence is the narrative structure in *The Deep Sleep*. This novel, one of the works on which Morris's reputation will stand, is thus also important because it employs for the first time the structure of multiple narrators that is so well suited to his subject, consciousness, and that he was to use again with variations in some of his best fiction, including *The Field of Vision* (1956), *Ceremony in Lone Tree* (1960), *One Day* (1965), and *In Orbit* (1967).

In *The Huge Season* (1954), Morris experiments with a structure contrasting first- and third-person narratives. The first-person sections, set in the 1920s, emphasize action, while the third-person sections, set in the 1950s, emphasize consciousness. With this structure, the author portrays the imaginatively crippling effects that the art and life of the past can have on the present. The concept of creative evolution introduced in the novel and Morris's growing interest in physical nature were influenced by his friendship, during his Philadelphia days, with the essayist and biologist Loren Eiseley. *The Huge Season*, Morris's most intellectually ambitious work, is evidence of his growing interest in using fiction as a medium for ideas. The year it was published, he received his third Guggenheim Fellowship. From 1956 to 1963, he traveled widely to Mexico and Europe before finally settling in California to teach at San Francisco State.

With the books he published between 1956 and 1960, Morris's writing reaches full maturity. *The Field of Vision*, which won a National Book Award in 1957, analyzes a wide range of obstacles to creative living, including nostalgia for a mythic historical past or a personal past, refusal to accept the world's limits, sexual repression, failure of emotion and imagination, overreliance on outworn clichés of experience, and excessive distortion of reality by vision. As an alternative, it argues for existential engagement with the present, acceptance of finitude, and recognition of man's ties to nature and his place in evolution. The comic novel *Love Among the Cannibals* (1957) portrays spontaneous sexuality as a way of becoming attuned to nature. *Ceremony in Lone Tree*, a sequel to *The Field of Vision*, registers Morris's reaction to the growing violence in America as typified by the Starkweather murders in Nebraska. *The Territory Ahead* argues that American authors have tended to misuse the past and rely on the raw material of personal experience at the expense of imagination and technique.

By 1960, the major concerns of Morris's writing had made their appearance, and his subsequent works fill in, with refinement and variation, the general outlines already established. *What a Way to Go* (1962) and *Cause for Wonder* (1963) are set in Europe and reexamine themes from previous books. One of Morris's best later works, *One Day*, uses the Kennedy assassination to focus on man's frustration at his finite condition and at the materialistic culture of contemporary America (the latter is also the subject of the essays in *A Bill of Rites, A Bill of Wrongs, A Bill of Goods* [1968]). The somberness of *One Day* does not prevail in subsequent novels. *In Orbit, Fire Sermon* (1971), and *A Life* (1973) celebrate the power of life as a whole to survive the destruction of individuals, expressing an almost mystical acceptance of life as a process involving both destruction and creation, death and continuity.

Since his retirement in 1975, Morris has lived in Mill Valley, California, except for time spent as visiting lecturer at several universities. In recent years, he has published two photo-text books, *God's Country and My People* (1968) and *Love Affair: A Venetian Journal* (1972); a collection of stories, *Real Losses, Imaginary Gains* (1976); two critical books, *About Fiction* (1975) and *Earthly Delights, Unearthly Adornments* (1978); and two novels, *The Fork River Space Project* (1977) and *Plains Song* (1980), winner of an American Book Award in 1981.

Major Themes

The volume of Morris's writing is matched by the number and variety of his themes. After he breaks the spell of the past in *The World in the Attic*, his intellectual and artistic development comes not through any change of attitude about his subjects but through additions, clarifications, and elaborations. What Morris wrote of Henry James is true of himself: he possesses a "ceaselessly expanding consciousness" in which "one thing always leads to another, [and] that in turn to another...like ripples lapping on a pond" (*Territory Ahead*, p. 97). A single datum of experience will come to have more than one level of application—taking on first social and then aesthetic, metaphysical, or epistemological significance.

Since Morris's thought originates with the dichotomy between the present he lives in and the past he longs to recapture, an important subject in his fiction is the effects of the past on the present. Morris eventually realized that in his case, one effect had been to cloud his sense of what he was doing in his early fiction. For instance, the title character of *My Uncle Dudley* practices a combination of Whitman's democracy and Emerson's self-reliance intended to exemplify what it means to live creatively in the present, but his final act in the novel, spitting in the eye of a corrupt policeman, is more appropriate to the frontier past where difficulties were often dealt with through violent physical confrontations.

A second effect is to poison the emotional life of the modern family. In *The Home Place*, Morris defines the pioneer heritage as a protestant ethic emphasizing hardihood, courage, austerity, and moral sobriety—qualities necessary for the taming of the wilderness but destructive in a settled land where domestic virtues of love and understanding are required. In *The Works of Love*, the protestant myth of the pure and sexless woman makes it impossible for the hero Will Brady to love women both sexually and spiritually, a problem compounded by the rule of the plains to leave feelings unstated. Extending from the Nebraska prairie in the 1880s to Chicago in the 1920s, Brady's life epitomizes how emotional reserve in the wilderness becomes the death of love in the modern wasteland. In *Man and Boy* and *The Deep Sleep*, the same protestant myth clothes Mrs. Ormsby and Mrs. Porter in a false mantle of moral authority, making them both wives and exacting mothers to their weak and immature husbands. Emotional aridity within marriage is linked to sexual repression in the frigid Lois McKee of *The Field of Vision* and *Ceremony in Lone Tree*. In the former novel, she is almost sexually awakened by the artist Boyd, who relishes shattering small-town decorum by expressing his feelings openly, but she marries the prosaic McKee, who never delves beneath the surface of emotions. The pioneer heroine of *Plains Song*, Cora Atkins, finds sexual contact as traumatic as she had been taught to expect and justified only by her duty to bear a child. Although Morris suggests in *Plains Song* that a life devoid of sexual pleasure can be more satisfying than we might think, the reserve between Cora and her husband means their life is not completely fulfilled.

Just as the protestant ethic shapes emotional life within the modern family, the form of heroism characteristic of the pioneers encourages a destructive response to the frustration at failure to make emotional connection. Virgil Ormsby, the "boy" of *Man and Boy*, rebels against his domineering mother by emulating a romanticized archetype of male heroism, an archetype of which the frontiersman-cowboy was an important expression. Like Natty Bumppo, Virgil becomes a hunter at one with nature and, like Robert Jordan, a soldier killed in combat. Morris depicts such physical heroism as a childish escape from the intimidating present embodied in the maternal female and civilization. Virgil is like Huck Finn on the run from Aunt Sally, and his destination, his "territory ahead," is really the territory behind, the womanless wilderness of the past where problems could be resolved with guts and a gun. Since life can be truly lived only in the present, Virgil's getaway to the past expresses a fear of life and leads inexorably to death. Nevertheless, Morris recognizes that the hero archetype has great imaginative power. In *The Field of Vision*, for instance, the bullfighter courts death in the ring, the aged Scanlon shuns life for his dream of mythic passage across the West by wagon train, and five-year-old Gordon risks injury by dashing around the ring firing his cap pistol. Destructive and childish though such behavior is, the bullfight kindles liberating insights in the spectators, Scanlon's dream is the most powerful writing in Morris's work, and Gordon's romp helps free Boyd from his bondage to childhood. On the other hand, Morris treats the hero archetype as unambiguously destructive in *Ceremony in Lone Tree*, where the cowboy image is associated with feelings of male sexual inadequacy leading to violence and murder.

As Scanlon's case illustrates, Morris sees admiration for the hero archetype as part of a general nostalgia for the adventure of western expansion, a nostalgia that forms one pole of the American character. Because of their special place in American history, the plains are the ideal stage on which to dramatize the contradictions of that character. American culture has long combined pragmatism with optimism about the future, reflecting a deeper faith in life's potential to delight and satisfy, but material success and technological progress proved easier to attain than genuine delight, and great expectations have been followed by disenchantment. In the nineteenth century, the plains stood for a future in which the promise of the American dream could be realized; in the twentieth century, the plains became small-town wastelands as the dream turned to nostalgic longing for a western past when the dream still seemed possible. Once up and coming, Morris's dying prairie villages of Junction and Lone Tree faced west as a vote of confidence in the future, but when the future became the present, the villages became the past that younger inhabitants deserted for a new future in the big cities of the East and the new West of California. Only Scanlon is left. In reality a member of the farming generation that followed the pioneers to Nebraska, he still gazes west at an illusory dream of mythic adventure.

If nostalgia prevents one from living, so too do the technological advances achieved by American pragmatism. *The Huge Season* and *One Day* are set in New York City and California, respectively, locales in Morris's moral geography (along with Chicago and Philadelphia) representing the materialistic and spiritually impoverished present. In both, an appetite for more and more things drives out feeling and imagination; moral growth fails to keep pace with technological progress, and the atomic bomb is the result. Space flight, on the other hand, once more expresses the American impulses to dream and to get away.

Morris's photography suggests metaphysical and epistemological themes that complement these social themes. At the start of the 1940s, his Nebraska past was inexorably slipping away, but photographs, he believed, could arrest the motion of time and could preserve moments of the past in the timeless stasis of the snapshot. The dichotomy between motion in space-time and timeless stasis thereafter forms the metaphysical heart of his work. For instance, nostalgia, the tendency to dream, and the reversion to the hero archetype and covert longing for death are cultural manifestations of a desire for stasis or "transcendence." When Morris thinks of consciousness as a product of mind (rather than a process of arriving at insights) and when he thinks of such elements of consciousness as memory and imagination, he tends to regard them as "immaterial" and transcendent. He often uses the emptiness of the plains as a symbol of transcendent consciousness (just as crowded cities are symbols of the fullness of material, time-bound reality). Morris also presents transcendence as a state that characters sometimes achieve. As Will Brady fails in various personal relations, his "works of love" become progressively more abstract and impersonal, culminating in an attempt at pity for all of suffering humanity. This final love, however, is so mystical and its object so disembodied that it leads, in a favorite Morris phrase, "out of this world" to complete transcendence and death. Lawrence, of *The Huge Season*, seeks not universal love but an impossible perfection of heroic gesture that will transcend the "bullshit" of ordinary life. But since perfection is not possible in this imperfect world, his quest, like Brady's, ends in death.

The concept of transcendence has aesthetic implications that appear as themes in Morris's fiction. For him, all art has an inviolable, transcendent status; its beauty survives forever in a "platonic" realm even if the artifact itself is destroyed. Morris's ambivalence about the hero archetype arises from this paradox: the inevitable end for transcendent heroes is death and thus destructive, yet their gestures are like inviolable works of art and thus immortal and creative. In another sense, however, transcendence in art is destructive. Boyd, in *The Field of Vision*, carries Lawrence's hunger for impossible perfection over into aesthetics. The myth of unlimited possibilities in life has fostered a parallel myth in American writing that the greatest art must try the impossible in order to capture the impossible greatness of America. Great art is therefore necessarily characterized by failure since it is only by failing that one knows he has tried the impossible. Boyd's long career courts failure as the one infallible test of success.

In his critical books, Morris consistently argues that the truly creative act lies in devotion to the present and to what can be realized in the world. This judgment, in both its moral and aesthetic applications, is also dramatized in his fiction. For instance, in *The Field of Vision*, the moment when the action of the bullfighter's cape brings the bull to a standstill signifies that man has the power of transcendence, the power to transform brute reality "into a frieze of permanence" (*Field of Vision*, p. 111), a work of art, but the bullfighter is heroic precisely because he remains in time and in the finite world (as his subsequent goring attests). His gesture, his essence, is complete in the past and transcendent; the man himself, his existence, remains in the present, where all actions must occur. The bullfight is one instance of Morris's treatment of "immanence," the state of being in motion through time-space that complements transcendence. The journeys he often uses in his plots are emblems of immanence. Immanence is variously identified with all time-bound creativity, with commitment to the possible and to love and communication, with existence as opposed to essence, with creative process as opposed to creative product, and with consciousness considered as process of thought. In *The Field of Vision* and *One Day*, immanence is depicted as something similar to existential acceptance of responsibility for one's selfhood in the contingent world of time, accident, and death. In *Fire Sermon* and *A Life*, it involves simple acceptance of time and change as parts of the natural order.

Morris associates immanence with the physical side of man's nature. It is implicit in the notion (appearing in books from *The Man Who Was There* to *Plains Song*) of physical life passed on from one generation to the next and also in the concept of creative evolution. As represented in the Lehman sections of *The Field of Vision* and elsewhere, creative evolution entails both unpredictability and freedom, for no one can say at one moment what life form may evolve in the next moment, and what cannot be predicted cannot be determined. Full creativity in the individual requires that he retain his ties with nature and the evolutionary past. In *Love Among the Cannibals*, immanence is embodied in the heroine, whose healthy enjoyment of life and sex reflects wholeness within the self, natural harmony with the living universe, and dependence on instinct in personal relationships.

The themes of immanence and transcendence come together in Morris's mature aesthetic theory. His work with photography demonstrates that reality has an objective existence apart from man's apprehension of it, but each person knows reality only through his transforming vision of it. Both of these principles are implied in Morris's use of multiple centers of narrative consciousness. Human vision continuously evolves so that nature might better understand itself. Morris further holds that the art of the past shapes the vision of the present and in so doing creates the world in which man perceives himself to be. As Morris summarizes it, "If man is nature self-conscious. . .art is his expanding consciousness, and the creative act, in the deepest sense, is his expanding universe" (*Territory Ahead*, p. 229). The changing character of life requires an originality in art equivalent to the freedom in action. A problem of the contemporary artist is that the world has been overprocessed, so that he finds it hard to see the world in a new way rather than through clichés, the tired visions of his predecessors.

Survey of Criticism

Considering the quality and quantity of his work, Morris has received little critical attention and is generally thought of as a neglected writer. In a 1957 essay, "The Two Worlds in the Fiction of Wright Morris," Wayne Booth laid the groundwork for what criticism there is. There are two worlds in Morris's fiction, Booth argues: the impermanent world of material reality and a permanent world outside of time and real in a platonic sense. Morris's characters seek the higher reality through "moments" or "getting 'out of this world' " ("The Two Worlds," p. 377), and in their search, three bridges are open to them: heroism, imagination, and love. Booth's distinction between the two worlds is fundamental to an understanding of Morris, but his bridge metaphor leads Booth to equate the character's transcendence or self-transformation with his transformation of the world and obscures the degree to which Morris sees a character's transcendence as a problem. As a result, Booth does not distinguish clearly enough between figures (like Brady) who permanently transcend the world and those (like the bullfighter) whose acts are transcendent but who remain immanent themselves.

In an essay, "The Great Plains in the Novels of Wright Morris" (1961-62), David Madden discusses the role of the plains in Morris's work; in a second essay, "The Hero and the Witness in Wright Morris' Field of Vision" (1960), he argues that the heart of the fiction is a relationship between a hero who has transcended the world through "audacity," "improvisation," and "transformation," and a witness who observes the hero and picks up his imaginative charge. In his book on Morris, Madden systematically applies the concepts from these essays to Morris's works through *Cause for Wonder*. In addition to explications of the novels, the study contains chapters on Morris's character types and on his style and technique, including such topics as his disruption of chronology, his punning on verbal clichés, and his focus on consciousness. Madden also suggests that in the first five books and *The Works of Love* Morris is concerned chiefly with the meaning of the past and in the rest with what it means to live in the present. The study is somewhat out of date, and the author is more at home with nostalgia, transcendence, the timeless photograph, and the mystical properties of consciousness than with creative evolution, existential engagement, and the social aspects of Morris's fiction. Nevertheless, Madden's hero-witness concept is important, and his explications are sound.

In an essay surveying Morris's novels through *Cause for Wonder*, "Wright Morris" (1964), Marcus Klein argues that they began as a fictional quest for the real in Booth's sense. This quest culminated in *The Works of Love*, where Morris learned that such a reality can be attained only through death. Thereafter, his work is marked by a deliberate tentativeness and ambiguity as he chooses accommodation to the nature of things rather than the search for ultimate solutions. Even when his characters seek solutions, Morris is distanced from the search by his use of multiple narrators. Although Klein's comments on Morris's early development are astute, his essay is designed to support a larger thesis that postwar fiction in general is characterized by accommodation, and this leads him to dismiss elements such as the theme of immanence that do not fit his thesis. A more reliable overview (of the works through *A Bill of Rites, A Bill of Wrongs, A Bill of Goods*) is Leon Howard's pamphlet, *Wright Morris* (1968). Howard's stress on Morris's characters as fallen individuals inhabiting a finite position in time and space, on his comedy, and on his social themes is a healthy corrective to the platonic Morris of previous critics.

An issue of *Critique* (1961-62) devoted to Morris contains one of Madden's essays, an essay on the development of Morris's multiple-point-of-view structure by Alan Trachtenberg ("The Craft of Vision"), an essay on nostalgia by Arthur E. Waterman ("The Novels of Wright Morris"), and an explication of *Ceremony in Lone Tree* by Jonathan Baumbach ("Wake before Bomb"). A later issue includes "The Journey Back" (1962), a discussion of the early books by John Hunt. All are excellent. *Conversations with Wright Morris*, edited by Robert E. Knoll (1977), contains essays by several critics coupled with interviews between each critic and Morris, an essay by Morris, and a thorough primary and secondary bibliography through 1975. The interviews are superb. Among the essays, Wayne Booth's discussion of *The Works of Love* is the best study of that novel, and Peter C. Bunnell's essay is especially helpful to literary critics because it deals with Morris's photography.

The Novels of Wright Morris, by G. B. Crump (1978), the second book-length study of Morris, focuses on the novels through *A Life* with some discussion of the photo-text and critical books. The study argues that Morris's world view is more Bergsonian than platonic, that he emphasizes the life-denying elements of transcendence, and that from his earliest fiction, he looks for forms of creative activity that can remain in time. The book also explores Morris's debts to Lawrence and James and distinguishes two structures in his novels: the still-point structure, focusing on consciousness at a moment in time, and the open-road structure, focusing on character growth taking place through movement in time and space. Recent as Crump's study is, Morris has published several books since its appearance, illustrating once again that he is a protean and gifted writer worthy of more critical attention than he has received.

Bibliography

Works by Wright Morris

My Uncle Dudley. New York: Harcourt, Brace, 1942.

The Inhabitants. New York: Charles Scribner's Sons, 1946.

The Home Place. New York: Charles Scribner's Sons, 1948.

The World in the Attic. New York: Charles Scribner's Sons, 1949.

Man and Boy. New York: Alfred A. Knopf, 1951.

"Privacy as a Subject for Photography." *Magazine of Art* 44 (February 1951): 51-55.

The Works of Love. New York: Alfred A. Knopf, 1952.

The Deep Sleep. New York: Charles Scribner's Sons, 1953.

The Huge Season. New York: Viking Press, 1954.

The Field of Vision. New York: Harcourt, Brace, 1956.

Love Among the Cannibals. New York: Harcourt, Brace, 1957.

The Territory Ahead. New York: Harcourt, Brace, 1958.

"Nature since Darwin." *Esquire* 52 (November 1959): 64-70.

Ceremony in Lone Tree. New York: Atheneum, 1960.

"Made in U.S.A." *American Scholar* 29 (Autumn 1960): 483-94.

"Letter to a Young Critic." *Massachusetts Review* 6 (Autumn-Winter 1964-65): 93-100.

One Day. New York: Atheneum, 1965.

"The Origin of a Species, 1942-1957." *Massachusetts Review* 7 (Winter 1966): 121-35.

In Orbit. New York: New American Library, 1967.

Fire Sermon. New York: Harper & Row, 1971.

A Life. New York: Harper & Row, 1973.

About Fiction: Reverent Reflections on the Nature of Fiction with Irreverent Observations on Writers, Readers, & Other Abuses. New York: Harper & Row, 1975.

Plains Song. New York: Harper & Row, 1980.

Studies of Wright Morris

Baumbach, Jonathan. "Wake before Bomb: *Ceremony in Lone Tree*." *Critique* 4 (Winter 1961-62): 56-71.

Bleufarb, Sam. "Point of View: An Interview with Wright Morris, July 1958." *Accent* 19 (Winter 1959): 34-46.

Booth, Wayne C. "The Two Worlds in the Fiction of Wright Morris." *Sewanee Review* 65 (Summer 1957): 375-99.

Crump, G. B. *The Novels of Wright Morris: A Critical Interpretation*. Lincoln: University of Nebraska Press, 1978.

Howard, Leon. *Wright Morris*. UMPAW. Minneapolis: University of Minnesota Press, 1968.

Hunt, John W., Jr. "The Journey Back: The Early Novels of Wright Morris." *Critique* 5 (Spring-Summer 1962): 41-60.

Klein, Marcus. "Wright Morris: The American Territory." *After Alienation: American Novels in Mid-Century*. Cleveland: World Publishers, 1964, pp. 196-246.

Knoll, Robert E., ed. *Conversations with Wright Morris: Critical Views and Responses*. Lincoln: University of Nebraska Press, 1977.

Madden, David. "The Great Plains in the Novels of Wright Morris." *Critique* 4 (Winter 1961-62): 5-23.

———. "The Hero and the Witness in Wright Morris' Field of Vision." *Prairie Schooner* 34 (Fall 1960): 263-78.

———. *Wright Morris*. TUSAS. New York: Twayne, 1964.

Miller, Ralph N. "The Fiction of Wright Morris: The Sense of Ending." *MidAmerica III: The Yearbook of the Society for the Study of Midwestern Literature* (1976), pp. 56-76.

Trachtenberg, Alan. "The Craft of Vision." *Critique* 4 (Winter 1961-62): 41-55.

Waterman, Arthur E. "The Novels of Wright Morris: An Escape from Nostalgia." *Critique* 4 (Winter 1961-62): 24-40.

Lucile F. Aly

JOHN G. NEIHARDT
(1881-1973)

Biography

John G. Neihardt set his goals early and at ninety could reflect that he had done what he set out to do. Born 8 January 1881 in Illinois of German-Irish parentage, descendants of pioneers, he differed from most of his literary contemporaries by remaining in the Midwest away from publishing centers where writers tend to collect. He disliked city life, and his writings reveal his affinity for the Nebraska prairies, western mountains, and rivers. From childhood, when he listened to the tales of old settlers in Kansas and stared at the Missouri River from a bluff, he felt the power and magnitude of the West and formed his determination to write about its heroes. From his father, who wanted him to be a poet, he learned a love of the outdoors and an awareness of events in the world around him. His mother, Alice Culler Neihardt, was the dominant influence in his early life; her indomitable spirit and brisk attack on the problems of surviving poverty with some degree of dignity set him a vigorous example. He learned to respect work and made himself strong in spite of his short stature—he was five feet tall—by a strict regimen of swimming, walking, and wrestling. His mother taught him to appreciate beauty and encouraged his avid reading. She had great hopes for her son.

Neihardt's sketchy education included three years at Nebraska Normal College in Wayne, which deepened his already formed taste for classical literature, especially epics. He read Virgil and Ovid in Latin and devoured the romantic poets, as well as Tennyson and, to a lesser degree, Whitman. His real education came from his compulsive reading. His critical views were strongly affected by Hippolyte Taine, and he absorbed Taine's theory that relates historical currents to the movement of ideas. Later he was influenced by George Edward Woodberry, Paul Elmer More, Irving Babbitt, F. W. H. Myers, and particularly Henri Bergson.

Neihardt's life seems to fall into clearly marked periods, in which his writing followed distinct lines. In the youthful period he concentrated on lyrics and short stories. From the age of eleven, when a fever dream of flying, impelled by a strong mystic force, convinced him that poetry was his mission, he thought of himself as a poet. He crystallized the force in a lyric, "The Ghostly Brother," as a spirit compelling him to write. Later the force became "Otherness," a source he could tap by making himself receptive. His short stories, or any other prose, did not derive from "Otherness" and might therefore be regarded as a source of income; it helped to support him, but poetry was his mission.

His lyric period (1901-12) covers the years of his schooling, his early jobs as country schoolteacher, assistant to a land agent for the Omaha Reservation at Bancroft, Nebraska, where Neihardt began his long and fruitful association with Indians, and his brief editorship of the town paper. In these years he wrote all but five of his lyrics, for he believed that at thirty a poet should renounce subjective poetry for work that expressed a wider view of the world. All but one of his short stories were written in this period, when he was testing themes, structures, and techniques in both prose and poetry. He tried free verse before the New Poetry movement began and abandoned it for the greater possibilities in disciplined meter, rhythm, and rhyme. His first long poem, *The Divine Enchantment* (1900), was inspired by his interest in Hindu philosophy aroused by the *Upanishads*, Max Müller's book on the Vedanta Scriptures, and Louis Jacolliot's *The Bible in India*.

Neihardt's first volume of lyrics, *A Bundle of Myrrh* (1907), brought him critical acclaim and, more important, the approval of Mona Martinsen, a sculptor and a student of Rodin in Paris. Her appreciative letter to Neihardt opened a correspondence that culminated six months later in their marriage. Neihardt's wife was a sustaining force in his life. He respected her abilities, took her advice, and counted himself fortunate. Although she subordinated her own career, she modeled excellent busts of her husband, including the one in the Nebraska Hall of Fame. Two more volumes of lyrics appeared— *Man-Song* (1909) and *Stranger at the Gate* (1911)—and in 1919 a collection, *The Quest*, from these volumes.

Along with lyrics Neihardt wrote some thirty short stories about fur trappers and the Omaha Indians. His respect for the Omaha culture and his unusual rapport with the people prepared him for his later association with Black Elk and the Sioux. Another work, *The River and I* (1910), is an account of his exuberant journey down the Missouri River in a custom-built boat, which familiarized him with the scenes of the epic he was already projecting.

In the period of writing the epic (1912-41), Neihardt produced both poetry and prose and followed three simultaneous careers. His need for money prodded him into the literary editorship of three papers: the *Minneapolis Journal* from 1912 to 1920, the *Kansas City Journal-Post* for six months in 1926, and the *St. Louis Post Dispatch* from 1926 to 1938. In these positions he turned out a sizable body of criticism and advanced the epic whenever he could find time. A second career of lecture-recital tours increased his solvency but also delayed the epic. Traveling over most of the country acquainted him with the western areas, and reading his poetry to diverse audiences enabled him to test its reception. Two critical books written in this period—*The Laureate Address* (1921), delivered in Lincoln when he received official notice of his legislative appointment as poet laureate, and

Poetic Values: Their Reality and Our Need of Them (1925), presented at the University of Nebraska—constitute major documents of his poetics.

His third career was the writing of the five-part epic, *A Cycle of the West* (1949), which he considered his master work. He followed Jane Harrison's theory that epic periods were times of dislocation of civilizations. Neihardt began the epic in 1913, delayed his progress in 1919 to write a prose biography of Jed Smith that prepared for the epic segment on Smith, and also alerted historians to the importance of a neglected figure. He delayed a second time in 1930 to collect material about the Messiah movement among Indians. At Pine Ridge Reservation he met Black Elk, the Sioux holy man, whom Neihardt considered the greatest influence on his life and work. The power vision Black Elk disclosed to him became the subject of *Black Elk Speaks* (1932), Neihardt's most widely known book. The writing of the epic extended over twenty-eight years, in alternating periods of intensive writing and frustrating concentration on earning a living.

Neihardt's working methods were adapted to his mysticism. He began each session by rereading the manuscript and thinking himself into the mood, making himself receptive to his "Otherness." He wrote only a few lines a day, perfecting each before he left it. The *Songs* were based on extensive research in western history, not only in books, documents, journals, and letters, but also in interviews with old-timers, Indians, and old army men who had fought in the Indian wars. The *Songs* appeared singly: *The Song of Hugh Glass* in 1915; *The Song of Three Friends* in 1919; *The Song of the Indian Wars* in 1925; *The Song of the Messiah* in 1935; and *The Song of Jed Smith* in 1941. In 1949 they were published in a single volume, *A Cycle of the West*. Reviews were complimentary, and Neihardt considered his lifework completed.

During World War II Neihardt served as director of information in the Office of Indian Affairs in Chicago. Through this position he met the Sioux Eagle Elk and gained material for his last major work, *When the Tree Flowered* (1952), a novel about Sioux life. In 1948 he accepted an appointment as lecturer in English at the University of Missouri, taught popular courses in epic literature, and made television appearances in Missouri and Nebraska. In his eighties he wrote the first volume of his autobiography, *All Is But a Beginning* (1972), and was at work on the second volume, *Patterns and Coincidences*, when he died in 1973. The latter was published posthumously in 1978.

Neihardt won many honors in his lifetime. He held three honorary doctorates, won numerous awards, and was a member of the National Institute of Arts and Letters. The state of Nebraska honors him with an annual Neihardt Day in Bancroft and helps to fund the Neihardt Foundation. Neihardt was the first person to have his bust placed in the Nebraska Hall of Fame while he was still alive.

Major Themes

Neihardt's major themes accord with his critical theory that writers should not make life seem "a bad business" or present people as essentially worthless or wicked; the true function of literature is to teach us to "live together decently on this planet." The themes he thought proper concern man's place in the cosmos and the values he should live by. His first work, *The Divine Enchantment*, forecasts his major themes dealing with an integrated universe infused with wonder and miracle, and of man, not a chance creation but a being in a universe governed by an ordering principle and able to rise through reason and love to godly height. The overruling theme is the necessity of distinguishing reality from unreality.

The lyric poems record Neihardt's search for reality as he responds to the world of nature and wrestles with doubts and fears, seeking values that will not corrode. The love lyrics trace his search for enduring love from its exotic beginnings through the struggle to free himself from a mistaken passion to reach at last the spiritually satisfying love. A following sequence in *Man-Song* reveals the progress of love to the marriage night, and a third volume, *Stranger at the Gate*, pictures the parents awaiting a child in cosmic unity with all mothers; this segment brings full circle the cyclic fruition that runs through Neihardt's work. Some few lyrics, prophetic of the epic, express Neihardt's sense of confinement and his longing for the "ancient bigness" and "feasts of larger men"; others use Plato's cave metaphor of the philosopher who emerges into the light to point the way to reality. A few of the lyrics reveal Neihardt's sense of alienation, sometimes his defiance of despair in a reassertion of courage, as in *"Battle Cry."* A set of poems, written when Neihardt was contemplating a drama based on the French Revolution, deals with social issues, antimaterialism, and the doom of exploiters.

The short stories of Neihardt's experimental period deal with such themes as the artist in an unsympathetic world, the ruthless struggle for power, either of medicine men or fur trappers; heroism in crises by red men or white, now and then a woman; and the struggle to survive in the wilderness. Two poignant stories, "Vylin" and "The Last Thunder Song," suggest the inability of two cultures to understand each other; and two or three center on the psychic phenomena of expanded awareness that always intrigued Neihardt. "The Alien," one of his two best stories, develops the theme that the values of civilization cannot be transferred to the savage world; the other, "The Discarded Fetish," combines humor and pathos in the wistful romance of a widow and an unlikely hero. All of the Omaha stories sound a wistful note, even when they present selfless heroism for the tribe, and "The Last Thunder Song" in tone and mood seems to underscore the prayer of Black Elk on Harney Peak. Several stories may have been trial runs for later work. "The Brutal Fact" is the Carpenter-Fink story with different names, for example, and the prairie fire in "Nemesis of the Deuces" forecasts the same *Song* even in some of its wordings.

The search-for-self theme in Neihardt's early work is strong in *The River and I*, which is not a travel book, although its structure is the course of the river. It makes explicit Neihardt's theme of the epic West; he names the trappers who are to be his heroes and conveys the exaltation he drew from the wild, unspoiled world. In his stories and in the epic he repeatedly emphasizes the evil, and the danger, of violating the environment.

The themes of Neihardt's poetic theory are most clearly stated in his Laureate Address, presented at ceremonies for his appointment as poet laureate of Nebraska in 1920, and in the Poetic Values lectures at the University of Nebraska. In both he pursues the theme that poetry is essential to make men "citizens of all time and of all countries." The poet brings wider vision, and hence a quickening of human perceptions and sympathies, to his readers. He argues for the wider dimensions of awareness described by Jung, as well as P. D. Ouspensky, F. W. H. Myers, and George Edward Woodberry, among others. He adds a dimension to the defense of poetry by advocating not more poetry but more regard for the poetic *experience*—the state of mind in which poetry is written by the poet and appreciated by the reader. The heightened receptivity to the insights and human understanding that poetry gives leads to wiser, more humane decisions. Neihardt urges further that poetry should be written for everyone, not for a privileged group, and that a jaundiced view of humanity distorts the truth.

In the Indian books Neihardt pictures a society in many respects more enlightened than the white man's because it is based in a religion of reverence for the land as well as for the Great Spirit. *Black Elk Speaks* blends several themes amenable to Neihardt's philosophy: the interwoven cycles of nature and man from seed to bloom to death to rebirth, and the Grandfather's gifts to Black Elk, particularly the healing herb of understanding. In *When the Tree Flowered* Neihardt elaborates some of the Sioux myths and legends that explain the power of spirit force and deals extensively with the Sioux ethos, the admirable social system that required integrity in its chosen leaders, took care of its poor, and rewarded generosity with status.

Neihardt's epic cycle gathers most of his major themes. He said he intended it to preserve a great race mood of courage to convince Americans that they had the stuff of heroes in them. The *Songs* build a value scale to incorporate lower and higher values without confusing their levels. The first *Song*, the story of the shooting of Carpenter by his friend Fink, uses the betrayal theme to say that physical courage, although essential, is not sufficient to solve a moral problem. The *Song* of Hugh Glass's hundred-mile crawl across the desert raises the level to magnanimity in the betrayal theme, when Hugh accepts the human frailty that explains Jamie's desertion, and forgives him. In the third *Song* about Jed Smith, Neihardt shows that a man powered by spiritual faith can operate successfully in a harsh world and that such a man sustains and strengthens his fellows. The *Song* about the Indian wars develops the Virgilian social ideal of sacrifice for the general good, for both white men and Indians fight for the survival of their society, with the bravery and devotion that ought to draw them together instead of setting them murderously against each other. Neihardt refines this theme by distinguishing the genuine sacrifice from the Lilith-lure of personal glory. In the final *Song* about the Messiah movement, although Wovoka is not the real Messiah, Neihardt stresses the validity of the Christ principle as seen finally by

Sitanka in his last moments. Through all five *Songs* runs the basic theme that all men strive for essentially the same ends, whatever their race; that understanding and compassion are the keys to men's security; and that the cycles of the universe demonstrate the interrelation of spirit and matter, and therefore the security of man, in the cosmos.

The masculinity of Neihardt's writing has been noted by many reviewers; his poetry is not heavily peopled by women. The lyrics deal freely with the romantic vision of woman, the sensual yearnings of a youth in search of love, and the commitment of spiritual love. Neihardt tends to divide women into two categories— Eves and Liliths—with a clear personal preference for the Eve, who represents fulfillment and is associated always with procreation. The mother image recurs frequently in the epics, usually in the thoughts of the men, but she is an old mother, "haloed like a saint" (*Song of Hugh Glass* in *A Cycle of the West*, p. 207) who represents the security and comfort people recall in moments of duress. Neihardt suggests his own picture of women as tenders of the hearth and partisans of their husbands in such scenes as the vignettes of Sitting Bull's old wife berating the Indian police who arrest her husband, the old lady shaking her fist at Carrington, and the "thrifty wives" searching the ruins of Crazy Horse's village for anything usable.

Minor themes weaving through the epic include the operation of chance that reminds of the uncertainty of human affairs and the joy of accomplishment that is greater in the progress than in the arriving, for a "goading purpose/And a creeping gait" (*Song of Hugh Glass*, p. 185) teach the striver that "what matters is the light upon the back" (*Song of Jed Smith*, p. 56). The struggle of the artist appears as a motif in *The Song of Hugh Glass* and in the lyrics—the artist as sufferer in lonely hardship but compensated by the glory of his vision. A collateral motif of the cathartic value of art appears in Hugh's discovery that telling his story, making it into art, has dissolved his bitterness.

Survey of Criticism

Major critics of Neihardt's time ignored his work; only recently has scholarly examination of his writings begun to burgeon. Few midwestern writers attract critical attention unless they migrate to the East; moreover, Neihardt, as he recognized, was "out of the time mood" in both subject matter and style. Epic was considered a dead genre, and his verse form was unpalatable to the New Critics. H. L. Mencken in 1910 and Harriet Monroe in 1912 praised Neihardt's lyrics, but Monroe withdrew her approval after a quarrel with Neihardt in 1913.

Despite generally good reviews of Neihardt's books, very few scholarly articles appeared before the mid 1960s. Roger Segel predicted in a review (1916) that *Hugh Glass* would "belong to world literature"; Katharine Lee Bates dubbed Neihardt the "Walter Scott of Nebraska" (1925). Frank Luther Mott's article, "John G. Neihardt and His Work" (1922), emphasized the innovative achievement— in any literature—of a democratic epic, wherein a reader "imagines himself the hero of every tale" (p. 316). He noted also the effects of joining blank verse rhythms by rhyme that unifies sentences, paragraphs, and cantos. Another article in the 1920s by Nelson F. Adkins (1928) establishes that *The Song of Three Friends* meets the requirements of epic and analyzes the necessary alterations of character and events as valid for epic purposes.

The first doctoral dissertations on Neihardt's work were written in the 1950s. George Paul Grant's study, "The Poetic Development of John G. Neihardt" (1957), presents a thorough analysis of Neihardt's prosody, from the experimental lyric period to the refinement of meter and sound combinations in the epic. This dissertation also includes the full text of *The Divine Enchantment* and the Preface to *Hugh Glass* that Mrs. Neihardt dissuaded her husband from publishing with the *Song*. Lucile Aly's dissertation, "John G. Neihardt as Speaker and Reader" (1959), examines the rhetoric of his occasional speeches and literary lectures and the techniques of oral interpretation in the poetry recitals. Two of the best dissertations to date are Billie Wahlstrom's "Transforming Fact: The Poetics of History in John G. Neihardt's *Cycle of the West*" (1975), a perceptive, in-depth analysis of Neihardt's fusion of poetry and history in the *Cycle* to adjust historical facts to the needs of epic, and Diane de Pisa's "All Life That is Holy" (1978), a teleological study of the working of language and symbol in Black Elk's religion. Her focus on the word *wakan* allows a new illumination of Black Elk's vision and its implications. Linda DeLowry's intelligent discussion of Neihardt's themes and patterns, "Dynamic Patterns" (1975), contains a highly competent chapter on the short stories.

Three biographies of Neihardt have been published, the first by Neihardt's close friend and admirer, Julius T. House, entitled *John G. Neihardt, Man and Poet* (1920). The book is indispensable, even though it is not documented and presents the critical view of a total enthusiast, for House preserved in it valuable information about Neihardt's life, working methods, and attitudes that would otherwise have been lost. Most of the documents and letters of that period were destroyed in a moving van fire. House was a devoted biographer, and his often astute observations are given in gratifying detail. Because the book was published in 1920, it covers only the early years.

Blair Whitney's biography, *John G. Neihardt* (1976), was intended, as the writer said, to be a first step in a critical reappraisal of Neihardt's work. Despite some minor factual errors, Whitney draws a clear picture of Neihardt's life and presents a competent analysis of his works. The book is well structured, and the summary chapter is excellent. The book should have the intended effect of helping to alter perspective on Neihardt's work. Lucile Aly's biography, *John G. Neihardt: A Critical Biography* (1977), is based largely on documents and letters and a long acquaintance with the Neihardt family. It is intended as a rhetorical study of his purposes and his ways of fulfilling them.

In the last ten years, with the growth of interest in western literature, Neihardt's work has begun to receive additional attention from scholars. *Black Elk Speaks*, his best-known work, received its initial notice from Jung, who made it known in

Europe as mystic and visionary literature. Neihardt's appearance on the Dick Cavett show made him famous overnight; *Black Elk Speaks* is now in print in more than twelve languages. In 1962 Mott noted with great approval a "resurgence" of Neihardt ("Resurgence of Neihardt"), and scholarly articles are now proliferating rapidly.

Outstanding among the current essays are Paul Olson's study, "*Black Elk Speaks* as Epic and as Ritual Attempt to Reverse History" (1980). His analysis of symbolism in ceremonies and in the vision itself is both informative and provocative. Robert F. Sayre's "Vision and Experience in *Black Elk Speaks*" (1971) explains the vision as social and tribal and describes the functions of visions in the culture and the attitude of Indians toward them. Lynne O'Brien, *Plains Indian Autobiographies* (1973), presents Black Elk as a tragic hero given a great mission he was too weak to use, a vision doomed by a difference in cultures.

Sally McCluskey, in an article based on interviews with Neihardt, "Black Elk Speaks and So Does John Neihardt" (1972), notes that the merits of *Black Elk Speaks* as psychology, anthropology, sociology, religion, and history have overshadowed in current criticism its merits as literature. She deals with the confusion about actual authorship of the book, occasioned partly by the subtitle, "As Told to John G. Neihardt"; the assumption that Neihardt functioned simply as recorder has given rise to some misconceptions about the real authorship. McCluskey makes clear that Neihardt's was the "shaping intelligence and lyric voice" (p.231) of the book. She provides further a stylistic comparison of *Black Elk Speaks* with Joseph Epes Brown's book on Black Elk.

Articles about the *Cycle* follow discernible patterns. Some probe the question whether it qualifies as the American epic, an American epic, or an epic at all. Edgeley Todd, "The Frontier Epic" (1959), measures the *Cycle* against Frank Norris's ideal of an American epic and judges it a genuine attempt but perhaps not a complete fulfillment. Kenneth Rothwell, "In Search of a Western Epic" (1970), considers the *Cycle* a compelling account, possibly an Astoriad, but flawed in style, too diverse in plot, and overpopulated with heroes. He concludes that the *Cycle* is a "memorable document in the unfinished search for an American epic" (p.59). Aly's "John G. Neihardt and the American Epic" (1979) evaluates Neihardt's qualifications as an epic poet and the extent to which he succeeds in the *Cycle*, with the reminder that epics are too often judged by standards proper for short lyrics and that time is the arbiter. John T. Flanagan, "John G. Neihardt, Chronicler of the West" (1965), calls the *Cycle* a noble effort, successful in telling a vigorous story with unconventional heroes, and convincingly portraying the "vast panorama" of the West. In his analysis of individual *Songs* he deplores the style as well as the use of more than one hero and concludes that Neihardt's prose may prove more enduring than his poetry.

The harshest criticism comes from Lucy Lockwood Hazard in *The Frontier in American Literature* (1927), who objects to Neihardt's "indecisiveness" in refusing to take sides in *The Song of the Indian Wars*, to *Hugh Glass* and other *Songs* for meter, Homeric metaphor, and general style. She protests particularly the distorting of frontier material "merely to furnish a problem of the individual soul" (p.134). The Hugh Glass story attracted various critics, frequently for comparison with Manfred's *Lord Grizzly*. Anthony Arthur's "Manfred, Neihardt, and Hugh Glass" (1978) presents Manfred's version as superior in point of view and style, faults Neihardt for imposing an alien form on American experience with his pentameters and metaphors, and using the environment as an enemy to Hugh, not a means. This criticism suggests a prevailing confusion about the purposes and methods of epic and their differences from those of the novel.

W. E. Black's study of *The Divine Enchantment* in "Ethic and Metaphysic" (1967) draws Neihardt's work into a concerted whole, for Black recognizes that the state of expanded awareness in Devanaguy's vision in which the "meek souls" saw that "all is one" recurs in *The Song of the Messiah* and "motivates the ethic" when the creatures, kneeling together, see the world illuminated from within. The focus has shifted from an awaking of the universe to an awaking of the individual in the person of Sitanka, and in the vision recounted by Wovoka.

In noting the resurgence of interest in Neihardt, Mott commented that it was encouraging to see a renewal occur without the critical support of a "claque of critics." By isolating himself from the publishing centers where critics and writers come together, Neihardt inevitably lost the kind of support close acquaintance brings, and he suffered some critical eclipse because his subject matter was not in the popular vein at a time when poetry tended to be urban and addressed chiefly to a small, highly sophisticated audience. And yet he held an audience, even when all his books were out of print.

Bibliography

Works by John G. Neihardt

The Divine Enchantment. New York: James T. White, 1900.
A Bundle of Myrrh. New York: Outing, 1907.
The Lonesome Trail. New York: John Lane, 1907.
Man-Song. New York: Mitchell Kennerley, 1909.
The River and I. New York: G. P. Putnam's Sons, 1910.
The Stranger at the Gate. New York: Mitchell Kennerley, 1912.
The Song of Hugh Glass. New York: Macmillan, 1915.
The Song of Three Friends. New York: Macmillan, 1919.
The Splendid Wayfaring. New York: Macmillan, 1920.
Laureate Address of John G. Neihardt. Chicago: Bookfellows, 1921.
The Song of the Indian Wars. New York: Macmillan, 1925.
Poetic Values: Their Reality and Our Need of Them. New York: Macmillan, 1925.
Black Elk Speaks. New York: William Morrow, 1932.
The Song of the Messiah. New York: Macmillan, 1935.
The Song of Jed Smith. New York: Macmillan, 1941.
A Cycle of the West. New York: Macmillan, 1949.
When the Tree Flowered. New York: Macmillan, 1952.

All Is But a Beginning. New York: Harcourt Brace Jovanovich, 1972.
Patterns and Coincidences. Columbia & London: University of Missouri Press, 1978.

Studies of John G. Neihardt

Adkins, Nelson F. "A Study of John G. Neihardt's *A Song of Three Friends*." *American Speech* 3 (April 1928): 276-90.

Aly, Lucile F. "John G. Neihardt and the American Epic." *Western American Literature* 13 (February 1979): 309-25..

———. *John G. Neihardt: A Critical Biography*. Amsterdam: Rodopi, 1977.

———. "John G. Neihardt as Speaker and Reader." Ph.D. dissertation, University of Missouri, 1959.

Arthur, Anthony. "Manfred, Neihardt, and Hugh Glass." *Where the West Begins*. Eds. Arthur R. Huseboe and William Geyer. Sioux Falls, S.Dak.: Center for Western Studies, 1978, pp. 99-109.

Bates, Katharine Lee. "John G. Neihardt Called 'Walter Scott of Nebraska.' " *New York Evening Post Literary Review*, 3 October 1925.

Black, William E. "Ethic and Metaphysic: A Study of John G. Neihardt." *Western American Literature* 2 (Fall 1967): 205-12.

Bloodworth, William. "Neihardt, Momaday, and the Art of Indian Autobiography." *Where the West Begins*, pp. 152-60.

DeLowry, Linda, "Dynamic Patterns: A Thematic Study of the Works of John G. Neihardt." Ph.D. dissertation, University of Pittsburgh, 1975.

De Pisa, Diane. "All Life That Is Holy: The Religion of *Black Elk Speaks*." Ph.D. dissertation, University of California, Berkeley, 1973.

Flanagan, John T. "John G. Neihardt, Chronicler of the West." *Arizona Quarterly* 21 (Spring 1965): 7-20.

Grant, George Paul, "The Poetic Development of John G. Neihardt," Ph.D. dissertation, University of Pittsburgh, 1957.

Hazard, Lucy Lockwood. *The Frontier in American Literature*. New York: Thomas Y. Crowell, 1927.

House, Julius T. *John G. Neihardt, Man and Poet*. Wayne, Neb.: F. H. Jones and Son, 1920.

Kay, Arthur Murray. "The Epic Intent and the American Dream: The Westering Theme in American Narrative Poetry." Ph.D. dissertation, Columbia University, 1961.

Lee, Fred M. "John G. Neihardt: The Man and His Western Writings: The Bancroft Years, 1900-1921." *Trail Guide* 17 (September-December 1973): 3-35.

McCluskey, Sally. "Black Elk Speaks and So Does John Neihardt." *Western American Literature* 6 (Winter 1972): 231-42.

———. "Image and Idea in the Poetry of John G. Neihardt." Ph.D. dissertation, Northern Illinois University, 1974.

Mott, Frank Luther. "John G. Neihardt and His Work." *Midland* 8 (November 1922): 315-24.

———. "Resurgence of Neihardt." *Quarterly Journal of Speech* 48 (April 1962): 198-201.

O'Brien, Lynne Woods. *Plains Indian Autobiographies*. WWS. Boise, Idaho: Boise State College, 1973.

Olson, Paul. "*Black Elk Speaks* as Epic and as Ritual Attempt to Reverse History." Paper presented at the Western Literature Association, 1980.

Rothwell, Kenneth. "In Search of a Western Epic: Neihardt, Sandburg, and Jaffe, as Regionalists and 'Astoriadists.' " *Kansas Quarterly* 2 (Spring 1970): 53-63.

Sayre, Robert F. "Vision and Experience in *Black Elk Speaks*." *College English* 32 (February 1971): 509-35.

Segel, Roger. Review of *The Song of Hugh Glass*. *Midland* 2 (January 1916): 25-28.

Todd, Edgeley W. "The Frontier Epic: Frank Norris and John G. Neihardt." *Western Humanities Review* 13 (Winter 1959): 40-45.

Wahlstrom, Billie Joyce. "Transforming Fact: The Poetics of History in John G. Neihardt's *Cycle of the West*." Ph.D. dissertation, University of Michigan, 1975.

Walker, Don. "The Mountain Man as Literary Hero." *Western American Literature* 1 (Spring 1966): 15-33.

Whitney, Blair. *John G. Neihardt*. TUSAS. Boston: Twayne, 1976.

Warren French

FRANK NORRIS
(1870-1902)

Biography

Benjamin Franklin Norris, Jr., was born in Chicago on 5 March 1870. Appropriately for the apocalyptic writer that Norris was to become in *The Octopus* (1901), one of the first traumatic events of his life was the great Chicago fire in October 1871, which destroyed the offices of his father, a flourishing wholesale jeweler. Recovery came fast, however, for this self-made Victorian businessman and when Frank, Jr., was only eight the family took a grand tour of Europe. Two surviving brothers, Lester and Charles, were born in 1878 and 1881, respectively. Then in 1882, the family moved into a Michigan Avenue mansion. When the elder Norris's hip ailment was aggravated by Chicago's raw climate, the family moved to California in 1884—first to Oakland and then to the Henry Scott house on Sacramento Street in San Francisco, a few blocks from the setting of *McTeague* on Polk Street.

Young Frank's education was erratic, as he was never a good scholar. After breaking an arm playing football, he dropped out of first an exclusive preparatory school and then the city's Boys' High School, enrolling at last in the San Francisco Art Association because he intended to become an artist. From San Francisco, he progressed with his family to Europe, where, finding London schools unsatisfactory, he enrolled at last in the fashionable Bouguereau studio of the Julien Atelier in Paris, and then he proceeded also to study in Italy.

As a painter, however, he proved a dilettante. By the time he was eighteen, he was writing more than he was sketching. Discouraged by the failure of his attempts to create a huge canvas of the Battle of Crecy, he returned home to enter the University of California as a special student. He disliked his English teachers but he responded enthusiastically to the lectures of a science instructor, Dr. Joseph LeConte, who sought to reconcile evolution with Christian doctrine. Norris also entered enthusiastically into the activities of Phi Gamma Delta fraternity. For Christmas 1891, his mother subsidized his first publication, *Yvernelle*, a long ballad, in a lavishly illustrated edition.

In 1892, Norris's parents divorced, and Frank moved with his mother and brother Charles (Lester had died in 1887) to Harvard to study creative writing in a pioneering program under Lewis Gates. Here he submitted as themes preliminary versions of material subsequently used in *Vandover and the Brute* (1914), *McTeague* (1899), and *Blix* (1899). In 1895 he was assigned by the *San Francisco Chronicle* to submit reports of a daring trip across Africa from Cape Town to Cairo but a severe case of South African fever, contracted soon after his arrival, cut short the junket and marked the beginning of a series of health problems that led to his early death.

Back in San Francisco, he took his first real job in 1896 as assistant to the editor of the *Wave*, a promotional journal for the fashionable Del Monte resort hotel and an outlet for major regional writers. He made about 100 contributions to the paper in two years, even though he took a leave in 1897 to complete *McTeague*. In the issue for 8 January 1898, he began to serialize his first published novel, the still unfinished *Moran of the Lady Letty*, an improbable tale about the shanghaiing of a San Francisco society man. After reading an early installment, S. S. McClure, New York publisher of the popular *McClure's Magazine*, offered Norris an editorial job that would leave him half the day free for writing. Shortly before his twenty-eighth birthday in February 1898, Norris arrived, virtually unknown, in the eastern capital of the publishing business.

He soon met and was encouraged by William Dean Howells, the then acknowledged Dean of American letters. He also met Stephen Crane, though the two writers had little use for each other during a Caribbean cruise reporting the Spanish-American War. (Norris much more admired then popular novelist Richard Harding Davis.) War work led to another bout of ill health, a case of malarial fever, which forced Norris back to San Francisco to recuperate. In September 1898, *Moran of the Lady Letty* was published, followed by *McTeague* in February 1899, just three years before the author's death. *Blix* appeared later in 1899 and *A Man's Woman* in 1900.

Norris retired to Gaston Ashe's ranch near Hollister, California, to gather material for *The Octopus*, the first volume of a projected "Trilogy of the Wheat," based in part on the notorious Mussel Slough confrontation between the Southern Pacific railroad and local ranchers in 1880. He returned to New York to accept a position as a reader for Frank Doubleday that provided Norris with an adequate income to marry Jeannette Black on 12 January 1900. In this position, he insisted upon the publication of Theodore Dreiser's first novel, *Sister Carrie*.

On 15 December 1900, he finished his most ambitious novel, *The Octopus*. It was published in April 1901 and enjoyed the largest sale of any of his works during his lifetime. Meanwhile he had moved to Chicago to collect material for *The Pit*, second volume of the projected trilogy about an effort to corner the wheat futures market. In 1902, shortly after the birth of his only child, Jeannette, Jr., on 9 February, he finished what was to prove his last novel. Out of patience with life in New York, he decided to leave, planning, after returning to San Francisco, a trip around the world on a tramp steamer to collect material for "The

Wolf," the planned third volume of his trilogy. He also began to think about
another trilogy, each volume of which would be devoted to one day of the Battle
of Gettysburg.

He began hunting for a country home in the Santa Cruz Mountains, but he was
never to settle there, for on 25 October 1902, while his wife was recovering from
an appendicitis operation, he himself died suddenly of a neglected abdominal
pain that led to a perforated appendix and peritonitis. *The Pit* appeared posthumously in 1903, along with a collection of short stories and *The Responsibilities
of a Novelist*, a gathering of his critical essays.

In 1914 the novel he had not been able to publish during his lifetime, *Vandover
and the Brute*, was edited by his brother Charles (himself later a successful social
novelist) with an introduction and some additions. The most famous adaptation
of a Norris work, director Erich Von Stroheim's film *Greed*, based on *McTeague*,
was released amid a storm of controversy in 1924, after having been filmed on
location in the San Francisco Bay region. Norris's wife long outlived him and
remarried but continued to help in efforts to bring together his scattered books
and papers.

Major Themes

So much criticism of Frank Norris has been devoted to speculation about the
influence of the French naturalist Emile Zola, other writers, college teachers, and
contemporary events upon him that the artist's preoccupation with the themes
that provided the motivating force for his still powerful works has been long
neglected and his aims often misconstrued. Encouraged by the episodic structure
of Norris's rapidly written works, critics have too often treated his novels as
dramatized guidebooks to fin-de-siècle notions rather than as impassioned em-
bodiments of a grim and often unpalatable vision of the materialistic civilization
of his time.

Coming to terms with Norris has been especially and unnecessarily complicated by the fascination of many critics with the novelist's possible relationship
to naturalism, a term that may not have any literary utility except as a description
for the viewpoint underlying Zola's panoramic Rougon-Macquart novels about
the influence of hereditary factors on French society. Indeed Edwin H. Cady
appears justified when he writes in *The Light of Common Day* (1971) that "there
really are no naturalists in American literature" and no work of fiction "which
will stand adequately and consistently for the naturalistic sensibility," which
Cady defines as a position that reduces man "to the merest organism fighting
meaninglessly, at the mercy of chance and force, to foredoomed loss" (pp. 45,
51, 47). Whether Cady's extreme position is acceptable or not, most recent
critics have agreed that Norris was certainly no textbook naturalist. The problem
about tagging any writer other than those whose theories and works give rise to a
categorical label with one like naturalism is that the oversimplification reduces a
work of fiction (which Richard Poirier has most aptly described as "a world

elsewhere," an alternative reality that serves as an escape from or criticism of our own) to a classroom chalk sketch of philosophical or scientific principles. (Some novels are indeed nothing more, but they are rarely much read.) It is at best misleading to treat an unsystematic, frenetically enthusiastic, and easily confused thinker like Norris as one of the apostles of some scheme for ordering the universe. But if the approach to Norris through naturalism proves more harmful than helpful, where may we turn?

The most sustained effort to isolate and illustrate the tangled themes in Norris's major works—*Vandover and the Brute*, *McTeague*, *The Octopus* and *The Pit*—is William B. Dillingham's *Frank Norris: Instinct and Art* (1969). In three central chapters, Dillingham establishes as Norris's major themes his infatuation with "the mystery of instinct" and his phobic concern with human degeneration and "the nightmare of emasculation." Dillingham argues that in dealing with instinct, Norris follows the theories of Hippolyte Taine and Friedrich Nietzsche and is particularly concerned (like Jack London, despite the lack of any proved relationships between the men and their works) with the rousing of primitive emotions that still lie very close to man's surface, obscured only by a thin veneer of civilized restraints, by a brutal act that triggers a chain reaction culminating in disaster (like Marcus Schouler's encounter with McTeague in the bar room that leads at last to death in the desert). Dillingham sums up his view by illustrating how in *The Octopus* Norris uses the three main characters (whom the critic believes to be Presley, Annixter, and Vanamee) to show "the depth and primacy of feeling as opposed to the superficial and *often erring* intellect" (p. 64, italics added).

Dillingham parallels Norris's concern with degeneration with the theories advanced in Max Nordau's once sensationally popular *Degeneration* (translated into English in 1895), based on Cesare Lombroso's theories that criminals are a distinct type of people exhibiting tendencies based on race and atavism. The critic further argues that in *Vandover and the Brute* Norris deals with the viewpoint more effectively than any other novelist in any other novel. Finally Dillingham considers the way in which Norris was disturbed that "masculine seriousness and genuine virility" (once displayed by the Anglo-Saxons following their course of empire) had been superseded by "triviality and the ghosts of true passion" in the fashionable society depicted in the San Francisco scenes of *Moran and the Lady Letty* and *The Octopus* (p. 100).

Useful as these strictures are as a guide to the obsessions driving Norris's pen, Dillingham's book, like most other Norris criticism, fails to provide any synthesis (as indeed the novelist himself failed, except in the still disturbing conclusion to *The Octopus*, which proclaims that though men die, nature proceeds resistlessly on its course). The three themes that he discusses are really not so much separate or even complementary ideas as manifestations of an underlying rejection of nineteenth-century progressive civilization that equals that voiced at the end of an American classic with which Norris's work has rarely been compared, Mark Twain's *The Adventures of Huckleberry Finn*, when Huck rejects efforts to "civilize" him because he's been there before. Although Twain never succeeded in portraying Huck escaping to "the territory" for which he lit out, one fictional character that made it there is Norris's Vanamee.

Part of the trouble in seeing Norris clearly has been that until recently it has been impossible to place his fiction before *The Pit* in its proper context. Norris has most frequently been associated by literary historians with Stephen Crane because they seem meteors who lighted the sky simultaneously only soon to burn out. Actually, however, Crane and Norris had little more in common as writers than they did as individuals who were not at all impressed with each other during their one encounter. Crane, as recent studies like Frank Bergon's *Stephen Crane's Artistry* (1975) are beginning to make clear, was no naturalist at all but an apostle of light, an early limner of what Jerry H. Bryant in *The Open Decision* (1970) calls "the drama of consciousness," pioneering the increasing internalization of the artist's vision in the twentieth century. Norris, quite to the contrary, had no use at all for what Dillingham calls "the often erring intellect" until in *The Pit* he turns backward to come out finally for the maintenance of the traditional set of values defended by William Dean Howells.

Norris has been classified as naturalistic, however, because historians lacked anyone to compare him with except Zola, Crane, and Dreiser, even if such an approach meant patronizing *The Pit*, his most tightly constructed and intellectually consistent work, as a disappointment.

In recent years, however, the successive discoveries of Harold Frederic's *The Damnation of Theron Ware* (1896), Kate Chopin's *The Awakening* (1899), and George Cabot Lodge's long unpublished *The Genius of the Commonplace*, along with probably still other unrecovered works of the period, have provided a new context for *Vandover*, *McTeague*, and *The Octopus*.

"What our awareness at last of this body of work illuminates," Warren French has argued in an introduction to a recent edition of *Vandover and the Brute*, "is the existence during the dying years of the nineteenth century of an American 'decadent' literature, comparable to that of the *Yellow Book* period in England" (p. xi). The particular characteristic of these works as illustrated especially by astonishing similarities between the behavior of Norris's Vandover and Edna Pontellier in *The Awakening* (and one should add also Jack London's Martin Eden) is that, to quote a reference in the *Vandover* preface to an argument of Joseph McElrath's, these characters lack "the energy to meet the demands placed on the individual by a society that measures worth in terms of one's adherence to meaningless but exhausting conventions" (p. xiii). (Even Howells acknowledges the problem in *The Rise of Silas Lapham* when he observes that "it is certain that our manners and customs go for more in life than our qualities," but he finally found it prudent to stay on the side of "manners," since "the price we pay for civilization is the fine yet impassable differentiation of these.") Norris in his early work was unwilling to see this price paid.

To return from this analysis to Dillingham's outline of Norris's themes, one can argue that the three he cites are reflections of the youthful Norris's often hysterical observation that his society was decayed because of its addiction to the kind of artificial rituals that meant so much to Edna's husband in *The Awakening*, to the San Francisco socialites in *The Octopus*, and to the political temptations that at last demoralize the Derrick family in that novel. Instinct, Norris felt most of his life, is far more powerful than the thin hold of unnatural conventions on human beings, so that the least violation of a contrived routine (Trina's winning the lottery in *McTeague*, the shipwreck in *Vandover*, Ross's kidnapping in *Moran*, the railroad's deceitful practices in *The Octopus*) can destroy a thin and incompletely assimilated training and plunge naive individuals back into instinctively defensive and ultimately self-destructive courses of behavior. Perhaps the comment that penetrates most deeply into the martyrdoms of Norris's innocents is Don Graham's in his analysis of *Vandover and the Brute* as "a history of a poorly trained sensibility" (*The Fiction of Frank Norris*, p. 21).

Graham fails, however, to follow up his remarkable insight, so that he does not confront the vital question of how Norris conceives a sensibility might be properly "trained"—certainly not in the ateliers of Paris or the drawing rooms of San Francisco. Graham's observation leads to the perception that whatever we may think of the improbabilities of the Vanamee subplot in *The Octopus*, it remains, as many recent critics have perceived, Norris's most affirmative answer to the malaise of decadence and degeneration before *The Pit*. (The exceptions, of course, are those like the sophistical railroad president Shelgrim and the opportunistic Lyman Derrick in *The Octopus*, who have, like Theron Ware, sold out; but Norris is interested in such figures only as passing butts for his contempt.)

The drift of Norris's thought should have been apparent from the time of the publication of *McTeague*; the principal characters in this novel and *Vandover* are hopelessly doomed because they have neither the intellect nor the training to deal with even moderate affluence. (Of course, in *McTeague* the romance between Old Grannis and Miss Baker provides a contrast with the fate of the principals, but I fail to find any critic impressed with Norris's sentimental effort to balance the scales.) Even the three pot-boiling novels are important because of their comments on the decadence of affluent San Francisco society. In *Blix*, Norris hints at what he will spell out in *The Octopus* when he says of the lovers, "They were all for the immediate sensation; they did not think—they felt" (*Complete Edition*, 3:123). Vanamee in *The Octopus* has turned his back on his college education to develop some kind of telepathic and hypnotic abilities that are apparently available to those who have not lost touch with the rhythms of nature, with the resistless forces that keep the wheat growing while greedy, "civilized" men, "motes in the sunshine," lose touch with their instinctive gifts and perish.

As most recent critics have acknowledged, Norris is in no sense, like the muckrakers with whom he is sometimes associated, a social reformer; "society," by virtue of its very dependence on artificially prescribed forms of behavior that encourage charlatans and thwart honest innocence, is doomed to decay, so the decent individual's only recourse is to save himself by anarchical behavior like Vanamee's. Yet neither could Norris be considered a revolutionary, for he harbors no illusions that others may profit by Vanamee's example. Most of his characters are irrevocably set on self-destructive courses and the implication of the concluding meditation in *The Octopus* is that things may be better that way so that nature is not too much impeded in its cyclical process by too many sterile intellectuals. Vanamee triumphs because he gets back in rhythm with nature, but Shelgrim also triumphs because he rejects all responsibility and skims the profits off nature's resistless march.

What finally gives Norris's work a special power that enables it to triumph over its undeniable excesses and confusions is the quality that makes it especially *western*. In the passage already quoted from *Blix*, Norris concludes: "The day was young, the country was young, and the civilization to which they belonged, teeming there upon the green, Western fringe of the continent, was young and heady and tumultuous with the boisterous, red blood of a new race" (*Complete Edition*, 3:123). Norris was very conscious—as Whitman had been earlier when writing "Facing West from California's Shore" and Steinbeck would be later in "The Leader of the People"—that the Pacific coast of the United States represented the terminal point for the realization of an as yet unfulfilled dream. There is an especially poignant contrast between the promising setting and the decadent action in most of Norris's California novels, but he did not share Whitman's and Steinbeck's misgivings because he finally placed the impersonal forces of nature above the dreams of men.

This antihumanistic position leads us to the question that Don Graham poses several times about why one would write at all if life is better than literature. At one point, Graham quotes Vanamee, saying to Presley in *The Octopus*, "But why write? Why not *live* in it?" (*Complete Edition*, 1:39).

For an answer, we must turn to *The Pit*, despite the uneasiness many critics have felt about its inconsistency with Norris's other work. In this novel the principal characters learn at last to curb their greedy ambitions and survive without simply going back to nature as Vanamee does in *The Octopus*. That Norris did continue writing and refused to become an early version of the organization man suggests that he had been moving in this conservative direction since he had begun to write and that—after giving vent to his early excesses—he had worked out at last a credible, if traditional, individual solution to problems of survival. Critics in comparing *The Pit* with Norris's other works to its detriment have failed to notice that it is in many ways an updated version of *The Rise of Silas Lapham*. While speculation about unwritten books is useless, one cannot suppress the feeling shared by Joseph McElrath (in "Frank Norris: A Biographical Essay") that had Norris lived, his views would have become steadily more conventional as he moved from adolescent enthusiasm to sober maturity, nor the feeling that he would still have been most valued for his youthful excesses.

Survey of Criticism

Criticism of Norris was for three decades after his death largely determined by William Dean Howells's essay, "Frank Norris" (1902), which stressed Norris's reliance on Zola and limited his work worthy of consideration to the "epical" *McTeague* and *The Octopus*. Although many regarded the later novel as the mythical "great American novel," Norris received minimal critical attention until the appearance in 1932 of Franklin Walker's detailed and carefully documented biography, *Frank Norris*.

Serious criticism of his work did not, however, really begin until 1940 when H. Willard Reninger's "Norris Explains *The Octopus*" explained that the "alleged inconsistencies" in the novel are reconciled in the all-embracing philosophy expressed in the final conversation between Presley and Vanamee. The article was followed by the first book-length critical study of Norris, Ernest Marchand's *Frank Norris, A Study* (1942), which was concerned almost entirely with influences of various other authors, a process continued in the only significant foreign study of Norris, Lars Ahnebrink's *The Beginnings of Naturalism in American Fiction* (1950).

The most productive period in Norris scholarship began in 1956 with the appearance of Franklin Walker's invaluable collection of Norris's letters. The year before, Donald Pizer had begun his distinguished studies of Norris with "Another Look at *The Octopus*," stressing the relationship of the novel to transcendentalism and reconciling the inconsistencies in Presley's developing philosophy.

Charles Walcutt's *American Literary Naturalism* (1956) attempted to write off Norris by establishing the philosophical weaknesses of his thought, but by this time critics were looking at the novelist as something other than a naturalist. Warren French's *Frank Norris* (1962) considers also the transcendental aspects of Norris's work, his "romantic anarchism" and pervasive anti-intellectualism, though without the benefit of the insights afforded by the other "decadent" novels discussed in this essay.

The landmark work in Norris studies is Donald Pizer's *The Novels of Frank Norris* (1966), which brings together the author's long studies of the influence upon Norris of Professor Joseph LeConte and his theories of evolutionary ethical dualism. Since then emphasis has begun to shift to the design of the novels themselves. William B. Dillingham's *Frank Norris: Instinct and Art* (1969) is the starting point for any consideration of Norris's themes. It also contains chapters on the style and form of the novels.

After the publication of Dillingham's book, Norris criticism was largely confined to trivial and highly specialized matters until the appearance of Richard A. Davison's brilliant "Frank Norris's *The Octopus*: Some Observations on Vanamee, Shelgrim and St. Paul" (1975), which surveys much previous criticism of the novel to provide background for stressing that "Vanamee is a much more reliable philosophical frame of reference for the author than is usually granted" (p. 193).

Joseph R. McElrath, Jr., also began his outstanding work on Norris by correcting what he considers another misreading of an important novel in "Frank Norris's *Vandover and the Brute*: Narrative Technique and Socio-Critical Viewpoint" (1976), in which he treats the novel not as a moralistic tale and an attack on Vandover's self-indulgence but rather as an attack upon "nineteenth-century popular morality and the archaic life-vision of a world of fixed certainties which informed it" (p. 42). McElrath followed up this article with not only bibliographical works but also his important "Frank Norris: A Biographical Essay" (1978), which discusses the difference between what the author's works reveal of his personality and the very different personality that emerges from early posthumous criticism by friends and admirers. McElrath stresses Norris's stable family life and the possible strength of his Episcopalian faith in speculating about the "change of perspective and life-style" (p. 230) that the author seemed to be developing after his marriage, which suggests a disappearance of his adolescent enthusiasm and a surrender to "the more enduring pleasures of the American middle-class" (p. 230). McElrath has also published many of the documents upon which his analysis is based in "Frank Norris: Early Posthumous Responses" (1979).

Surprisingly little has been written about Norris as a western writer, but some important speculations are advanced in Glen A. Love's "Frank Norris's Western Metropolitans" (1976), which points out that the study of western literature has usually concerned "the solitary individual set against a wilderness landscape" (p. 3), but that Norris attempted to portray the primitive qualities of western life as they were manifested in urban society. The essay is an important reminder that the West includes not just Monument Valley and the Big Sky country but San Francisco (and regrettably Los Angeles) and that Norris was the first important writer to suggest the dramatic significance of this landscape.

A truly fresh approach to Norris's work has also been opened by Don Graham's *The Fiction of Frank Norris: The Aesthetic Context* (1978), which provides "aesthetic documentation" for Norris's novels, by which Graham means "extensive references to all manners of art in Norris's fiction, including paintings, interior decor, drama, literature, sculpture, music, landscapes" (p. 3).

Bibliography

Works by Frank Norris

Complete Edition of the Writings of Frank Norris. 10 volumes. Garden City, N.Y.: Doubleday, Doran, 1928. Facsimile reprint: Port Washington, N.Y.: Kennikat Press, 1967. Vols. 1-2: *The Octopus* (1901); vol. 3: *Blix* (1899) and *Moran of the Lady Letty* (1898); vol. 4: *The Third Circle* [short stories] (1909) and *A Deal in Wheat and Other Stories of the New and Old West* (1903); vol. 5: *Vandover and the Brute* (1914); vol. 6: *A Man's Woman* (1900) and *Yvernelle* (1891); vol. 7: *The Responsibilities of the Novelist* [critical essays] (1903); vol. 8: *McTeague* (1899); vol. 9: *The Pit* (1903); vol. 10: *Collected Writings Hitherto Unpublished in Book Form*.

Frank Norris of "The Wave." Foreword by Charles Norris. San Francisco: Westgate Press, 1931.

The Letters of Frank Norris. Ed. Franklin Walker. San Francisco: Book Club of California, 1956.

The Literary Criticism of Frank Norris. Ed. Donald Pizer. Austin: University of Texas Press, 1964.

A Novelist in the Making: *A Collection of Student Themes and the Novels* Blix *and* Vandover and the Brute. Ed. James Hart. Cambridge: Harvard University Press, 1970.

Studies of Frank Norris

Ahnebrink, Lars. *The Beginnings of Naturalism in American Fiction.* Upsala, Sweden, and Cambridge, Mass.: Lundequistska Bokhandeln, 1950.

Cady, Edwin H. *The Light of Common Day*: *Realism in American Fiction.* Bloomington and London: Indiana University Press, 1971.

Crisler, Jesse E., and McElrath, Joseph R., Jr., eds. *Frank Norris*: *A Reference Guide.* Boston: G. K. Hall, 1974.

Davison, Richard A. "Frank Norris's *The Octopus*: Some Observations on Vanamee, Shelgrim and St. Paul." *Literature and Ideas in America*: *Essays in Memory of Harry Hayden Clark.* Ed. Robert Falk. Athens: Ohio University Press, 1975, pp. 182-203.

————. "A Reading of Frank Norris's The Pit." *The Stoic Strain in American Literature: Essays in Honour of Marston LaFrance.* Toronto: University of Toronto Press, 1979, pp. 77-94.

Dillingham, William B. *Frank Norris*: *Instinct and Art.* Lincoln: University of Nebraska Press, 1969.

French, Warren. *Frank Norris.* TUSAS. New York: Twayne, 1962.

Graham, Don. *The Fiction of Frank Norris*: *The Aesthetic Context.* Columbia and London: University of Missouri Press, 1978.

————, ed. *Frank Norris*: *Critical Essays.* Boston: G. K. Hall, 1980.

Howells, William Dean. "Frank Norris." *North American Review* 175 (December 1902): 769-78.

Love, Glen A. "Frank Norris's Western Metropolitans." *Western American Literature* 11 (Spring 1976): 3-22.

Marchand, Ernest LeRoy. *Frank Norris*: *A Study.* Palo Alto, Calif.: Stanford University Press, 1942.

McElrath, Joseph R., Jr. "Frank Norris: A Biographical Essay." *American Literary Realism 1870-1910* 11 (Autumn 1978): 219-34.

————. "Frank Norris: Early Posthumous Responses." *American Literary Realism 1870-1910* 12 (Spring 1979): 1-76.

————. "Frank Norris's *Vandover and the Brute*: Narrative Techniques and Socio-Critical Viewpoint." *Studies in American Fiction* 4 (Spring 1976): 27-43.

————, ed. *Frank Norris*: *The Critical Reception.* New York: Burt Franklin, 1979.

Meyer, George Wilbur. "A New Interpretation of *The Octopus*." *College English* 4 (March 1943): 351-59.

Pizer, Donald. "Another Look at *The Octopus*." *Nineteenth-Century Literature* 10 (December 1955): 217-24.

————. *The Novels of Frank Norris.* Bloomington: Indiana University Press, 1966.

————. *Realism and Naturalism in Nineteenth-Century American Literature.* Carbondale and Edwardsville: Southern Illinois University Press, 1967.

Reninger, H. Willard. "Norris Explains *The Octopus*: A Correlation of His Theory and Practice." *American Literature* 13 (May 1940): 218-27.

Walcutt, Charles Child. *American Literary Naturalism, A Divided Stream*. Minneapolis: University of Minnesota Press, 1956.

Walker, Franklin. *Frank Norris: A Biography*. Garden City, N.Y.: Doubleday, Doran, 1932.

FREDERIC REMINGTON
(1861-1909)

Biography

Frederic Remington was born at Canton, New York, on 4 October 1861. He died forty-eight years later, on 26 December 1909. During his relatively brief lifetime, he was illustrator, painter, sculptor, journalist, novelist, and writer of short fiction. The works he produced in each of these several careers—which he pursued more or less concurrently—bear the stamp of his complicated personality. He was often at cross purposes with his audience, even when he was most widely admired and acclaimed.

Seth Pierre Remington married Clara Sackrider, the daughter of a Canton hardware merchant, in January 1861. When Frederic was born in October, his father had already begun his preparations to leave for active duty as a Union officer in the Civil War, not to return until Frederic was nearing his sixth birthday. The first five years of Remington's life were difficult and influential. When Seth returned to Canton, he resumed his newspaper work, but without much success. His offices and presses were destroyed by fire in 1869 and again in 1870. He then moved his family to nearby Ogdensburg, where he worked as a customs officer at the port and began a partnership with a friend who trained trotting horses. Frederic, who was about thirteen when the move to Ogdensburg became permanent, thus encountered early several of the concerns he would later treat in his painting, writing, and sculpting.

Young Remington's reading centered on tales of adventure, such as Cooper's Leatherstocking Tales, and on accounts of western travel, such as those he found in the journals of Lewis and Clark. At Highland Military Academy in Worcester, Massachusetts, where he was sent to prepare for college in 1876, he continued his enthusiasm for the wandering loners he characterized as "villains," "toughs," and the like, drawing them mostly as cowboys, Indians, and soldiers. He entered Yale in 1878, but refused to pursue the business curriculum his parents advised. He took art courses and played football instead. In 1879, his father, who was to die early the next year, became suddenly ill; Remington returned home before the end of the fall term, leaving academic life behind for good. He soon left home as well, but not for the usual reasons, embarking on a solitary pilgrimage to Little Big Horn Creek in Montana, where Custer had made his last stand five years earlier.

Remington dated the beginning of his career as a serious artist from his 1881 trip, where, he said, he suddenly realized that the West he had imagined, read about, and sketched since childhood was about to be replaced by a more prosaic region of farms and small towns. For the present, however, he returned to Ogdensburg and worked at odd jobs until coming into his patrimony at age twenty-one. Early in 1883, he bought a quarter-section of land near Peabody, Kansas, where he planned to start a ranch. The experiment proving a failure, he managed to sell his property in 1884 and immediately set out for the Southwest to try his hand at supporting himself with his art. He sold a few paintings in Kansas City and invested what remained of his inheritance in dubious business ventures, where he promptly lost it all.

However hard Remington tried to succeed, he was tripped up by his own unruly imagination. This was the lesson he began to learn during the winter of 1886, when, having married Eva Caten, a New York girl he had courted since 1880, he returned to Kansas City and tried to make his way as a freelance illustrator for New York periodicals. After less than half a year of marriage, Eva left for an extended visit with her parents. Remington rode off in the other direction, to Arizona, where he sketched soldiers and native subjects in and around the San Carlos Indian reservation, the same place where Mexican and U.S. troops were hunting for Geronimo. Although Remington found no hostile Indians to draw, he did carry a portfolio of lively sketches away with him in the fall of 1885. This time, he took them to New York personally, where he hoped to sell them to the journals. He had little success until he encountered Poultney Bigelow, a former classmate at Yale and editor of a sportsman's magazine, *Outing*. The military operations against Geronimo were just then being stepped up, and *Outing* had begun a series of articles on the subject. The sudden newsworthiness of the Apache war launched Remington as an illustrator.

Remington's popularity grew quickly after 1886. In 1888, nearly two hundred of his pictures were printed in various periodicals, and he made illustrations of considerably more distinction for Theodore Roosevelt's *Ranch Life and the Hunting Trail*. He also launched himself as a journalist with a series of Indian articles in *Century*. By the end of the decade, he had risen from obscurity to become one of America's foremost illustrators and artists.

Although Remington's skeptical turn of mind continued to serve him after he had achieved prominence, his success was a mixed blessing. It supplied him with money, a comfortable residence in suburban New Rochelle, New York, and some appeasement for his considerable ego. It also put him in the false position of being obliged to satisfy "genteel" tastes he never ceased to despise. When he went to South Dakota in 1890 to cover the Sioux uprising for *Harper's Weekly*, he did so as a servant of the establishment. The infamous massacre of Big Foot's band of Minneconjou Sioux at Wounded Knee was an event he very nearly witnessed but which was also too horrible for him to parody and about which he could not express his outrage. As a celebrity, he could no longer afford the outspoken irreverence he had enjoyed as an outsider.

Significantly, the artist turned away from the West in 1892, making a trip to North Africa, Germany, and Russia with his old friend, Poultney Bigelow. He returned in September, disgusted with diplomatic red tape and convinced that he needed a new American type for his work. This he found in the cowpuncher, to whom he turned his interest early in 1893.

Remington's enthusiasm for the cowpunchers he encountered in Mexico and the American Southwest was doubtless influenced by his disgust with Europe and by the growing dismay he felt concerning domestic affairs in the United States. These complex feelings inform his first bronze, the *Bronco Buster*, which he finished in 1895 and displayed in a successful one-man show held in New York late in the year. About a year later, near the end of 1896, Remington went to Cuba with Richard Harding Davis as a correspondent for William Randolph Hearst's *New York Journal*. There he drew pictures to accompany Davis's often inflammatory articles about the Cuban revolt against Spain.

When the United States declared war on Spain in 1898, Remington was already at Tampa. From there, he embarked aboard the battleship *Iowa* in April, to report on the naval blockade of Havana. He also became one of the press contingent aboard the flagship *Segueranca* when the U.S. invasion force sailed for Cuba on 15 June. When he was taken back to Tampa aboard a hospital ship in July, a victim of malaria, he began almost at once to cultivate the finish he had been too busy to worry about before. His bronzes became more polished and harmonious, his paintings more subtly impressionistic. He largely gave up illustrating, except for projects that allowed him a free hand, as did the Great Explorers series he undertook for *Collier's* in 1903. He turned away from journalism and reporting and toward the writing of serious fiction.

Remington's retrospective orientation after the Cuban war did not signal a diminution of his vitality. Indeed, he held shows with increasing frequency and success. After seeing the favorable critical response to his 1908 exhibition in New York, he jubilantly wrote to a friend that "I am no longer an illustrator." The large house and studio he built near Ridgefield, Connecticut, were completed in the spring of 1909. His last show, which opened in New York on 29 November 1909, was his most successful to date. Shortly after the show closed in December, he became ill but delayed consulting a physician. On the day after Christmas, following an appendectomy, he died.

That Remington was almost universally eulogized as a chronicler of the West and as a celebrator of mainstream American values is not surprising. The generous array of paintings, drawings, and statues he left suggests the copiousness as well as the continuity of history, and the geopolitical theme he called "that old cleaning up of the West" had, by 1909, been fully assimilated into the American mythos. Remington, however, was neither historian nor patriot, although he played at both roles from time to time. From beginning to end, he was fundamentally a skeptic and a rebel. His greatest personal success was that he left the stamp of his iconoclastic intelligence firmly imprinted on the American imagination.

Major Themes

Although Remington is often hailed as a historian of western themes, he is rarely considered an important writer of either history or fiction. The chief reason probably lies in the overwhelming visual impact of his pictures and bronzes, works that often tell stories (or suggest historic circumstances) without resorting to words. Even the letters he wrote to friends and associates are peppered with sketches that show, rather than tell, what he had on his mind. Yet to argue that Remington preferred to express himself in visual forms rather than in language would not be correct. He was a voracious reader and a writer of surprising skill and complexity.

Remington's earliest notable publication was an essay on horses printed by the *Century* in 1889. This piece grew directly out of his work, as an illustrator, on Theodore Roosevelt's *Ranch Life and the Hunting Trail*, which had just finished serial publication in the same journal. It is a lively, informative account of the various equine types that developed from the European horses left to go wild on the American plains. Next, came three more considerable essays on Indian reservation life, also published by the *Century*. The first of these treats the San Carlos reservation in Arizona, where Remington had sojourned some three years earlier, looking for Geronimo; the second essay focuses on Comanches and the third on Cheyennes, both of whom had been transplanted to reservations near Fort Sill, in Oklahoma. All three essays testify to Remington's outrage at the degradation he found among the captive peoples he believed were "made of soldier stuff." His characteristically romantic solution—which he proposed without believing that it would be credited—was to train the Indians as soldiers.

During the summer of 1889 while his Indian essays were appearing in the *Century*, Remington was showing his large oil, "The Last Stand," at the Paris Exhibition, where it won a silver medal. The painting, which depicts George Custer's ill-fated troopers surrounded by Sitting Bull's Sioux cavalry in Montana, shows just how double-edged the proposal was that Remington made in the essays. History even then was corroborating the demonstration in South Dakota, where the U.S. government was pressuring Sitting Bull and his fellow Sioux to sell the most valuable part of their reservation. Remington chronicled the ensuing conflict as a war correspondent for *Harper's Weekly*. He covered General Nelson Miles's November 1890 tour of the area, noting both the rebellious Sioux, who were by then performing the "Ghost Dance," and the crack squads of military "Indian police" he saw at nearby Fort Keough. In one of his several articles, he admired the Fort Keough scouts, who were Cheyennes; in another, he predicted "the biggest Indian war since 1758." After Sitting Bull was killed on 15 December, Remington returned west. He narrowly missed being present at the Wounded

Knee massacre, where the scouts he had admired at Fort Keough participated in killing some of the Sioux he had seen performing the Ghost Dance. As though to drive home the grim irony of the situation, the leader of the Fort Keough scouts, a white lieutenant with whom Remington had become friends, was also killed.

Remington's chronicle of the Sioux uprising is interesting chiefly for the way in which it acts as a counterpoint to his early *Century* essays. The accounts of reservation life vividly state Remington's dismay in terms that seem to have a strong humanitarian grounding. The dispatches from South Dakota reveal the historically and personally catastrophic possibilities of Remington's fundamentally romantic vision. Remington responded bitterly and confusedly, rejecting humanitarian impulses because, it seemed to him, they brought catastrophe. This is nowhere more evident than in his first published attempt at fiction, a short narrative called "The Affair of the —th of July," where he tried to imagine what might have occurred if the 1894 Chicago Pullman riots had escalated into full-scale civil war. The subject was not without interest, but Remington could wring only gratuitous violence from it. The compassion he had felt for the reservation Indians in Arizona and Oklahoma had not survived Wounded Knee. In consequence, the rioters and government troops who butcher each other in "The Affair of the —th of July" are not convincing.

The most interesting of the stories Remington wrote before the Cuban war is probably "Joshua Goodenough's Old Letter," first published in the November 1897 *Harper's Monthly*. The title character addresses his son from New York in 1798, recording his participation in various American military conflicts from the siege of Fort Ticonderoga in 1758 to the battle of Bunker Hill some twenty years later. He has not, according to his account, distinguished himself as a soldier, but he has survived. As he puts it at the close, "I served faithfully in what I had to do." Questions concerning why he has had to fight or to whom he has been faithful never come up. Through Goodenough—whose name fits almost too well—Remington presented the colonization of America and the rise of the republic as events that not only came about through fighting but required curiously faceless citizen-soldiers. He justified printing the "letter" on the ground that Goodenough seemed one of "those humble beings who builded so well for us the institutions which we now enjoy in this country."

After Cuba, Remington abruptly dropped the pretenses he tried to perpetuate in works like Goodenough's "letter." War lost its awesomeness; institutions no longer required veneration; "humble" builders and makers acquired faces, voices, and other individual characteristics. In "With the Fifth Corps," his 1898 account of the Cuban experience, Remington even examined the faces of the Spanish dead, finding in them evidence that "life never runs so high in a man" as it does "on the field of battle." Four new stories about Sun Down Leflare, the "half-breed" hero he had created in 1897, express this complex awareness—a growing conviction that defeat is more expressive than victory.

The first story, "How Order No. 6 Went Through," concerns Sun Down's successful execution of a military order some twenty years earlier, near the time

of the fight at Little Big Horn. Sun Down, regarded as an Indian in the story, has
taken on most of the characteristics of a white man by the time of its narration.
In "Sun Down Leflare's Money," the second story, the hero's conversion to
artificial currencies is traced. Real values, Sun Down says, are (or were) expressed by real things—ponies, pelts, women—but card sharps, prostitutes, and
other representatives of European civilization have brought to the plains mone-
tary systems in which fake values are substituted for real ones. Paper currency,
decks of playing cards, flexible credit, and the like, he maintains, are "bad, all
bad." Accordingly, "Sun Down Leflare's Warm Spot," the penultimate tale,
chronicles Sun Down's corruption at another level, beginning with an account of
how he twenty years before acquired a Gros Ventre woman by trading twenty-
five ponies for her and ending with an account of his currently reduced circumstances. His most recent woman, a white prostitute who conducts her business
in cash, has left him with a baby boy he must pay to have cared for at a nearby
fort. "Sun Down's Higher Self," the last of the tales, constitutes a bitter indictment of the white values Sun Down has adopted over the years. Still he cannot
reject these values. He vows that when his son is older he will take him east to
grow up among the genteel influences that gradually brought about his own
change from Indian to European habits of mind and conduct. In the East, at least,
the European habits will be less recognizable as perversions. Finally, then, Sun
Down emerges as a truly pathetic figure—a man who still remembers the heroic
roles he once played but who has been enfeebled by the very institutions he
serves.

"When a Document Is Official" is the best short story Remington wrote
utilizing his newly discovered pathetic hero. This tale, set in the American
Southwest, sees a thirty-year-old cavalry sergeant named William Burling sacrifice himself for the sake of symbols generated by the settlement process. Burling
is about to be commissioned a second lieutenant, after having studied all the
necessary regulations. However, while his commission is still on its way from
Washington, Burling undertakes to deliver another official document to a field
commander and is killed by Indians in the attempt. More important, his actions,
which may be traced by means of tracks and other signs, constitute a document
that may be read by those who know the language. Written messages, signed by
the proper authorities and sent through legally constituted channels, are neither
more nor less official than the marks in the snow that tell Burling's story.
Language, Remington maintained, involves the interpretation of all meaningful
signs. On the other hand, conquest and settlement of the West by whites substitutes one set of signs for another, with a consequent loss of real literacy. For
Burling to become literate in the manner of army regulations is therefore for him
to become pathetic much as Sun Down Leflare does. In both cases, something
false takes the place of something real.

While others wrote about winning the West in history, Remington addressed a
darker and less spectacular subject, albeit one that had a special urgency for him:
that of losing the West in the mind. His two novels, published in 1902 and 1906

respectively, explore the moral consequences of this loss. In *John Ermine of the Yellowstone*, a young white man who has been reared as an Indian attempts to reconcile white values with those he has learned from his Crow foster parents. In *The Way of an Indian*, a Cheyenne brave, who views the world as mythic and spiritual, struggles to comprehend the fragmented physical universe he glimpses as a result of his contact with white traders, trappers, and soldiers. Both books are set in the Rockies and Great Plains, but the common focus they most importantly share is even broader: what happens when the mysterious region Remington called a "silent country" can no longer compel belief?

Remington's first answer to this question was also the title of the final chapter in *John Ermine*—"The End of All Things." Ermine, born at about the same time as Remington, has been taken in by the Crows as an infant and grows up under the name of White Weasel. When he has reached young manhood, however, his foster parents reluctantly surrender him to a white hermit who goes by the name of Crooked Bear. Crooked Bear renames him, reeducates him, and sends him to join General George Crook in pursuit of the Sioux and Cheyenne following the Little Big Horn Massacre of 1876. Even though Ermine outwardly becomes a good soldier, Crooked Bear's teachings fail him when he falls in love with Catherine Searles, the flirtatious daughter of a veteran officer. Ermine wants to take the girl, Indian fashion, and cannot accept the fact that she regards him as socially unacceptable. Finding a photograph of her on the prairie, he comes to confuse it with talismans he knew as "medicine" while growing up. Matters become more difficult still when he has an altercation with the young officer to whom Catherine is engaged and gives him a superficial gunshot wound. He then flees to Crooked Bear's lodge in the mountains, where he is told that he must live by the white laws, even though he cannot understand them. He returns to the fort, where he is shot to death by a jealous Crow. In losing the West as a viable myth, Ermine loses everything else as well, including his life.

This is not the case in *The Way of an Indian*, Remington's second and final novel, where a more skillfully managed sense of irony saves the conclusion from despair as an aged Cheyenne warrior, Fire Eater, carries the corpse of his infant son into the mountains, with Crook's troops in pursuit. Reared in a Cheyenne village as White Otter until puberty, when he became the Bat, Fire Eater has acquired his present name by charging a group of white frontiersmen who defend themselves by exploding kegs of dynamite. However, the act of seeming bravery occurred when the warrior was still young and actually resulted from his ignorance about whites. Later, he leads an attack against an outpost of traders but is astonished when all the attackers except himself are killed. Rather than return to his own village in disgrace, he joins a band of Shoshones, with whom he lives for years.

Meanwhile, the white presence becomes more and more visible as trappers, drifters, and soldiers come west in ever larger numbers. Fire Eater returns to the Cheyenne village in 1875, presenting himself as his own reincarnation. He marries and fathers a son. When Crook's troops attack the village in the summer of 1876, but are driven away, Fire Eater attributes the victory to his potent "medicine"—a dried bat skin he has carried with him since youth. It does not occur to him that the troops will return, as they do that winter. This time, Fire Eater forgets to bring his bat skin with him into battle and watches helplessly as the whites destroy the village. Retreating with a handful of survivors, he discovers that his son has turned cold and stiff. He then calls on the "Bad Gods" to come for him as well. Although Fire Eater will surely lose his life—and although the book shows that his belief in "medicine" has been misplaced from the first, for that matter—the mystery of the West remains mysterious. For Fire Eater to lose the West is therefore for him to retain it, albeit as something different from what he has come to suppose: something real has taken the place of something false.

Remington's work as a writer helps explain the optical and affective darkness of his work as a painter and a sculptor. Falling riders like the *Bronco Buster* and soldiers about to be killed, like those in "The Last Stand," represent the moment of crisis that is examined in prospect and retrospect by works like *John Ermine* and *The Way of an Indian*. This instant, argues Remington, is reality itself. To read it well, with courage and insight, is the artist's sole task.

Survey of Criticism

Remington achieved popular renown during his lifetime, but his subsequent recognition as a serious artist has been slow in coming. Ironically this is probably because he recorded his vision with such vividness and on such a copious scale that its complexity and intensity have tended to be obscured by the numerous types it contains—cowboys, Indians, and soldiers vigorously rendered as evocations of the truly mystical region too often dismissed as merely the wild West. Scholars attempting to write about Remington have therefore been faced with a peculiarly difficult task: the artist's recorded vision is so overwhelming that many people resist regarding it as art.

Harold McCracken has served as curator of two major Remington collections: the Frederic Remington Art Memorial at Ogdensburg, New York, and the Buffalo Bill Historical Center at Cody, Wyoming. His groundbreaking *Frederic Remington: Artist of the Old West* (1947) was the first important book about Remington. McCracken's other books on Remington include *Frederic Remington's Own West (1960)* and *The Frederic Remington Book: A Pictorial History of the West* (1966). As the titles suggest, McCracken treats Remington chiefly as a painter and a sculptor and concentrates on his interpretation of western subjects. The approach is basically biographical but tends to ignore the darker, more complicated aspects of Remington's personality. Consequently, one gets the sense of Remington as an engaging but not quite credible anachronism—a man of great energy, strong convictions, considerable talent, and very little mind. Nobody who contradicted himself as much as Remington did could be as simple as McCracken makes him out to be. Yet McCracken's work, although sometimes misleading, is very valuable. It treats Remington as an artist rather than merely as a character; it begins to explore the relationships between the artist and his subject; and it establishes an authoritative canon of paintings, drawings, sculptures, essays, short fiction, and novels.

Atwood Manley's *Frederic Remington in the Land of His Youth* (1961) is an attempt to broaden the canon McCracken established in 1947. It has as its focus not Remington's associations with the West but his associations with upper New York State, where he was born and reared and where he spent a good deal of his leisure time hunting, fishing, and painting. This brief book reveals a folksy side of the artist that tends to be ignored by McCracken. Manley—a lifelong resident of the region and a retired publisher of the newspaper Remington's father started— argues that Remington was a man as well as an artist. There is a humanizing thrust here that deserves attention. The maker of myths is shown to have had interests and impulses that do not at first appear to be related to the myths he made. However, closer scrutiny suggests that these interests and impulses contribute in rather complicated ways to the artist's vision. Unpretentious though it is, Manley's book thus makes a considerable contribution to Remington scholarship.

Robin McKown's *Painter of the Wild West: Frederic Remington* (1959), Douglas Allen's *Frederic Remington and the Spanish-American War* (1971), and LaVerne Anderson's *Frederic Remington: Artist on Horseback* (1971) follow the leads left by McCracken but without the authority McCracken brings to the enterprise. Each of the three books makes a contribution, but none takes very seriously the implications of Manley's study. In them, Remington remains largely a cult hero for western buffs.

Quite another situation obtains in G. Edward White's *The Eastern Establishment and the Western Experience: The West of Frederic Remington, Theodore Roosevelt, and Owen Wister* (1968). White, a professional historian, attempts to consider Remington's career as typical in some ways of American experience in the later nineteenth century, when technocratic easterners who had been born around the time of the Civil War and had grown up reading works such as James Fenimore Cooper's Leatherstocking Tales tried to act out as adults the various fantasies of the West they had formulated for themselves as adolescents. The book, the first to examine closely the sociopolitical implications of Remington's work, is well done. White's thesis is that Remington, Roosevelt, and Wister regarded the West as a complex symbol of youthfulness and that each found ways of giving his perception powerful cultural meaning. The thesis fits Remington at least as well as it does Roosevelt or Wister. White's application of the thesis to Remington lacks force, however, mainly because White does not seem to take Remington very seriously as an artist. Besides offering penetrating insights into questions of motivation and context, White raises the question of whether Remington's several conflicting roles can ever be adequately reconciled. Indeed, he even suggests that what holds these roles together is a typically American disharmony: "reluctance on the part of Americans to wholly embrace an urban and industrial society without positing alternatives to it" (p. 202).

The impulse White identifies as "reluctance" is also examined by Ben Merchant Vorpahl in *My Dear Wister: The Frederic Remington-Owen Wister Letters* (1972) and *Frederic Remington and the West: With the Eye of the Mind* (1978). The first book centers on Remington's uneven friendship with Owen Wister, which began in 1893 and lasted until about the end of the century. The second studies some of the ways in which Remington tried to hold on to his autonomy as a human being while under pressure to conform to genteel standards. The letters Remington wrote to Wister, many of them illustrated with sketches, reveal the artist as abrasive, humorous, and eccentric. These qualities, Vorpahl argues, inform Remington's work, as well. Vorpahl finds in Remington's early illustrations for popular journals such as *Harper's Weekly* a strong tendency to parody the texts with which the illustrations were printed. Similarly, he finds evidence in the artist's more mature work of a tendency to rediscover and re-form the assumptions upon which the earlier works were founded—a very serious variety of self-parody. Vorpahl maintains that Remington was a major artist whose work as a whole expresses an intensely personal continuity of self. The difficulty, as Vorpahl acknowledges, is that Remington produced so much and in so many different media. It therefore becomes necessary to replace the continuity McCracken began by calling "of the Old West" in 1947 with one Vorpahl wants to call "of the mind."

Interestingly, Peter Hassrick's *Frederic Remington* (1973), which reproduces in color and black and white ninety-four of the Remington works housed in the Amon Carter Museum at Fort Worth, seems a step in the latter direction. Hassrick's work is far more than a picture book. Although most of the scenes depicted in it are western ones, its emphasis is on Remington and his interactions with those around him. Hassrick's detailed introduction to the volume is helpful, but even more impressive are his extensive and authoritative commentaries on each of the works reproduced.

Studies of Remington as writer are few, limited, perhaps, by the inaccessibility of his published works until 1960 and after. All of his extant writings are now available in *The Collected Writings of Frederic Remington* (1979), edited and with a useful introduction and bibliography by Peggy Samuels and Harold Samuels. The only long work to examine Remington as writer is Fred Erisman's pamphlet, *Frederic Remington* (1975), which makes good use of the Western Writers Series format to consider Remington's artistic and intellectual development; a detailed bibliography accompanies the work. Two shorter pieces are Judith Alter's "Frederic Remington's Major Novel: *John Ermine*" (1972), which examines Remington's first sustained piece of fiction as an outgrowth of his vision of the West, and "Frederic Remington: The Artist as Local Colorist" (1974-75), by Fred Erisman, which argues that Remington's fiction in many ways adheres to the pattern of local color writing pioneered by Hamlin Garland and others.

Recent interest in Remington seems to be of quite a different kind from that which made the artist into a celebrity during his lifetime or that which revived the popularity of his work in the middle twentieth century. Hassrick, for instance, carefully calls Remington a "student," and Vorpahl speaks of his career as "resonant" with echoes from Thoreau and Melville. A key to this new interest may be a willingness to study what White calls "reluctance" as an element of the author's work. What seems to be emerging is a picture of Remington as a reluctant romantic, but the last word is yet to be said.

Bibliography

Works by Frederic Remington

Pony Tracks. New York: Harper, 1895; Norman: University of Oklahoma Press, 1961.
Crooked Trails. New York: Harper, 1898; Freeport, N.Y.: Books for Libraries Press, 1969.
Stories of Peace and War. New York: Harper, 1899; Freeport, N.Y.: Books for Libraries Press, 1970.
Sun Down Leflare. New York: Harper, 1899.
Men With the Bark On. New York: Harper, 1900.
Done in the Open. New York: Russell, 1902.
John Ermine of the Yellowstone. New York: Macmillan, 1902; Boston: Gregg Press, 1968.
The Way of an Indian. New York: Fox Duffield, 1906.
The Collected Writings of Frederic Remington. Ed. Peggy Samuels and Harold Samuels. Garden City, N.Y.: Doubleday, 1979

Studies of Frederic Remington

Allen, Douglas. *Frederic Remington and the Spanish-American War*. New York: Crown, 1971.
Alter, Judith. "Frederic Remington's Major Novel: *John Ermine*." *Southwestern American Literature* 2 (Spring 1972): 42-46.
Anderson, LaVerne. *Frederic Remington: Artist on Horseback*. Champaign, Ill.: Garrard, 1971.
Erisman, Fred. *Frederic Remington*. WWS. Boise, Idaho: Boise State University, 1975.
———. "Frederic Remington: The Artist as Local Colorist." *South Dakota Review* 12 (Winter 1974-75): 76-88.
Hassrick, Peter. *Frederic Remington*. New York: Abrams, 1973.
McCracken, Harold. *Frederic Remington: Artist of the Old West*. Philadelphia: Lippincott, 1947.
———. *The Frederic Remington Book*. Garden City, N.Y.: Doubleday, 1966.
———. *Frederic Remington's Own West*. New York: Dial, 1960.
McKown, Robin. *Painter of the Wild West: Frederic Remington*. New York: Messner, 1959.
Manley, Atwood. *Frederic Remington in the Land of His Youth*. Canton, N.Y.: Privately printed, 1961.
Vorpahl, Ben Merchant. *My Dear Wister: The Frederic Remington-Owen Wister Letters*. Palo Alto, Calif.: American West, 1972.
———. *Frederic Remington and the West: With the Eye of the Mind*. Austin: University of Texas, 1978.
White, G. Edward. *The Eastern Establishment and the Western Experience: The West of Frederic Remington, Theodore Roosevelt, and Owen Wister*. New Haven, Conn.: Yale University Press, 1968.

Edwin W. Gaston, Jr.

EUGENE MANLOVE RHODES
(1869-1934)

Strange enough is a destiny that leads a frontier New Mexican horse wrangler reluctantly but voluntarily into exile along the banks of the Susquehanna in New York and finally on the shores of the Pacific in California. That strangeness becomes capriciousness when that destiny touches the exile with the compulsion to mix faithful realism and naive romance in writing about the land his person left but his spirit never departed. The heir of such a destiny was Eugene Manlove Rhodes, fictionist, poet, and essayist.

Biography

Like most other Anglo-Americans writing about the early Southwest, Rhodes was born outside the region on 19 January 1869 in Tecumseh, Nebraska. His father, Hinman Rhodes, a veteran of the Mexican and Civil wars and a participant in the California gold rush, enjoyed the reputation of raconteur and practical joker. Eugene inherited both tendencies. His mother, Julia Manlove, instilled in her son a fondness for books. By the age of ten, in fact, Eugene had completed most of his formal education and thereafter depended upon independent reading and abbreviated attendance of college. His reading tastes gravitated to romantic writers later influential upon his own works: Burns, Byron, Cooper, Dickens, Holmes, Longfellow, Poe, Scott, and Whittier. Shakespeare, Milton, Tennyson, Twain, Stevenson, and Kipling also interested him.

In 1881, Hinman Rhodes moved his family to the Tularosa basin in New Mexico, a hard land 150 miles long and 50 miles wide and bounded on the west by the White Sands and the San Andrés range and on the east by the Sacramentos. The area became the setting for many of Eugene's novels and stories.

When he was nineteen, in 1888, Eugene Rhodes entered the University of the Pacific at Stockton, California. Financial distress, however, compelled him to withdraw after two years and to return to New Mexico, where he engaged in a variety of odd jobs that eventually provided backgrounds for his writing: mining, wagon freighting, road building, dishwashing, and schoolteaching. His longest continuous employment was as a horse wrangler on the famed Bar Cross Ranch, an experience that later enabled him to start his own modest horse ranch. Hired man or rancher, Rhodes excelled as a horseman but never as a cowboy.

Only five feet eight inches tall but weighing a firm 150 pounds, the horse-wrangling Rhodes nevertheless managed to move so easily that he first impressed the woman he would marry as being "quick as greased lightning" (Powell, *Southwest Classics*, p. 164). His mouse-colored blond hair and mustache deepened the blue of his eyes, and his high-pitched voice filtered through a cleft palate that helped prompt him to create the fictional character "Lithpin' Tham" (Lisping Sam) Clark. Rhodes's compact physique and combative nature inspired J. Frank Dobie to compare him to Cyrano de Bergerac and embroiled him as often as Cyrano in fights. From one such encounter he emerged with a permanently bent nose. Some of his more notable fights occurred in bar rooms even though Rhodes never drank liquor, believing it responsible for most frontier killings, including the thirteen he actually witnessed. Frequenting saloons instead to gamble (his "The Come On" is a classic poker tale) and to play pool, Rhodes once threw billiard balls at an adversary who had slurred the reputation of a woman. He later drew on the incident in two of his novels.

Rhodes said that, from earliest recollection, he had felt that he could write if ever given the chance. The chance came slowly even though he probably began to try his hand at writing as early as his college student days. Not until he was twenty-seven did his first published work, the poem "Charlie Graham," appear in the April 1896 issue of C. F. Lummis's *Land of Sunshine* magazine in Los Angeles. Lummis became a lifelong friend and candid literary adviser. Rhodes's first publication, nevertheless, did not mean instant success. As he frequently confessed, he always wrote laboriously. And he published only a few more poems between 1896 and 1901, the year that his presumed first story in print, "The Professor's Experiment," appeared in the December issue of Munsey's *Argosy*.

Meanwhile, on 9 August 1899, Rhodes married the woman who first appraised him as being "hard as nails," May Davison Purple, of Apalachin, New York. He had met the widow, with two small sons, through protracted literary correspondence. For two years after 1900, he and his ready-made family resided in Tularosa, New Mexico, twenty-five miles from his San Andrés horse ranch that provides background for his novel *Stepsons of Light* (1921). His own son Alan, named for Alan Breck in Stevenson's *Kidnapped*, was born 12 June 1901 in Tularosa. A daughter, born in 1909 in New York, died in infancy.

Rhodes's continuous financial hardship, her resentment of the frontier, and her parents' declining health prompted May Rhodes in 1902 to return with the children to her family farm on the Susquehanna River in New York. Rhodes himself reluctantly followed four years later; he never cared much for the East, claiming that he did not live there but rather was snowed in for twenty years.

Joining his wife and children in Apalachin, Rhodes helped his father-in-law in farming and devoted what little spare time he had left to writing. His first novel, *Good Men and True* (1910), was published in hardcover after it had been serial-

ized in the 8 and 15 January 1910 issues of the *Saturday Evening Post*. It established the publishing pattern for his succeeding novels and novelettes, all except
one of which, *West Is West* (1917), appeared in magazines before in book form.
During his two decades in New York, Rhodes either published or began most of
his novels, novelettes, and stories, about half of his essays, and a scattering of his
poems. He also collaborated with Henry Wallace Phillips in several tailored-for-
the-trade novels published in Phillips's name by McClure and Bobbs-Merrill.
Finally, Rhodes began selling motion picture rights to his works.

What is remarkable about the flowering of Rhodes's literary career in alien soil
is that most of his works were set not in New York but in New Mexico and
elsewhere in the Southwest. The achievement required a photographic memory.
And, indeed, Rhodes once said that, in his New Mexican youth, his mind had
been a "fresh, blank page," absorbing everything he saw, each "rock, canyon,
peak, spring" (Powell, *Southwest Classics*, p. 166).

Suffering an influenza attack in 1919 that permanently weakened his heart,
Rhodes moved alone to Los Angeles in search of a better climate. He also hoped
to sell additional motion picture rights in Hollywood. The climate proved kinder
(if not curative) to his health, however, than Hollywood did to his bank balance.
Only six of his novels ever were produced as motion pictures, three of them with
the aid of and starring Rhodes's friend, the veteran actor Harry Carey: *Bransford
in Arcadia*, in 1914, and *The Desire of the Moth*, in 1917 (remade in 1921 as *The
Wallop*), both sold before Rhodes journeyed to Hollywood; *West is West*, in
1920, *Good Men and True*, in 1922, *Stepsons of Light*, in 1923; and *Pasó Por
Aquí* (as *Four Faces West*), posthumously in 1948.

Returning to New York in 1922, Rhodes remained until 1926 when he and his
wife sold her family farm and moved to Sante Fe, New Mexico. In 1931, they
took up final residence in Pacific Beach, California, again in search of a more
congenial climate for the husband, now old and physically broken. Each place
afforded Rhodes an opportunity not readily available in rural New York, the
chance to associate with other writers. His literary friends in Santa Fe included
the poet Alice Corbin Henderson and the novelist-folklorist Mary Austin. In
Pacific Beach and environs, Rhodes associated with C. F. Lummis, his first
publisher; Will Rogers, the humorist; and W. L. Comfort, H. H. Knibbs, Stewart Lake, Alan Le May, and Charles Russell, all fiction writers. Knibbs especially looked to Rhodes for advice about writing and even used his mentor as the
model for one or more of his fictional characters. On 27 June 1934, Rhodes died
in Pacific Beach. His widow, in response to his wish, took his body for burial to
the remote San Andrés mountains in which he had grown up and ranched. His
grave is marked by a large boulder on which a bronze plaque bears the epitaph:
Pasó Por Aquí ("He passed this way").

Major Themes

Although he published in virtually every literary genre except drama, Rhodes
left as his chief legacy stories and novels. His essays and letters, however,

provide insights into his life and thought to be found nowhere else, and his poetry serves as the first and essentially last medium in which he published. Those lesser forms thus provide a convenient starting point for an analysis of his writing.

Of nearly fifty essays that Rhodes published, six provide a representative view. In content, they reveal his interests to be extensive, ranging from the past to the present. "Peñalosa" (1917) honors the memory of Don Diego Dionisio de Peñalosa Briceño, Spanish governor of New Mexico from 1661 to 1665, for defending Apache Indians against the inquisitorial domination by the Spanish church and state; and "In Defense of Pat Garrett" (1927) repudiates Walter Noble Burns's depiction of the outlaw Billy the Kid (William H. Bonney) as a western Robin Hood and defends Sheriff Pat Garrett, who killed the Kid in 1881. Of Rhodes's essays concerning contemporary events, one, "The Barred Door" (1911), criticizes Congress for delaying New Mexican statehood; and two others—an essayical digression in the novel *Stepsons of Light* (1920) and "The West That Was" (1922)—rebuke eastern literary critics for their neglect of western American authors. Similarly, *Say Now Shibboleth* (1921) chastises eastern arbiters of American English, asserting sarcastically that, to them, anything is provincial that does not conform to the New England usage.

In theme, Rhodes's essays show his inherent humanity, democracy, and distaste for credulity and affectation, positions for which he can hardly be faulted. Neither can his sprightly literary style, enlivened by southwestern idiom, except for the fact that his use of figurative language often obscures the point he is attempting to make. The author's tendency to digress, however, detracts from the unity of his thought, and his quarrel with what he called the eastern "literary establishment" may be questioned at least so far as it is conducted defensively and predicated on a provincial assumption. Like his Texas friends, Dobie and Walter Prescott Webb, Rhodes tended to prize fidelity to the actualities of western American life above universality.

Rhodes's letters, including those published by his widow in *The Hired Man on Horseback* (1938) and by W. H. Hutchinson in *A Bar Cross Man* (1956), provide clues to his character and his attitudes toward his writing. Letters to his brother-in-law George Davison exhibit Rhodes's indomitable spirit in the face of continuous financial adversity. Letters to the southwestern writer Agnes Morley Cleaveland, who elicited advice for Rhodes from the Munsey editor Robert Hobart Davis, reveal Rhodes's early naiveté about getting his writing published. Then, once he became nationally known, Rhodes's letters reflect his deep sense of obligation to his readers. In fact, the author spent hours painstakingly answering in longhand almost every fan letter he received. When the burden became impossibly heavy, he devised a humorous form letter that enabled him to check standard answers. Finally, his letters to Webb and other writers stress his determination to be realistic in writing; and still other letters betray Rhodes's deep resentment of having to write for a living rather than for personal satisfaction.

Qualitatively, poetry stands in the middle of Rhodes's works, superior to his essays and letters but inferior to his fiction. His nearly fifty poems may be classified as elegies, love, nature, protest, religious, and miscellaneous. Because the poems revolve around essentially the same themes as his essays and fiction, though, the variety indicates topical breadth more so than intellectual diversity. A sampling illustrates the point.

Of the elegies, "Charlie Graham" (1896) memorializes an old-timer for whom Rhodes once worked, and "The Last L'Envoi" (1931) amounts to Rhodes's personal epitaph, something of a private elegy modeled after Kipling's. Marginally elegiac, "Night Message" (1930) longs for the West that was. Those poems illustrate a characteristic peculiar to American elegiac writing. Whether Mark Twain's *Life on the Mississippi* or Whitman's "When Lilacs Last in the Dooryard Bloom'd," the American elegy has tended to transcend the writer's personal grief over the death of a friend or a place and to become a nation's or a region's lament for the death of the way of life symbolized by the subject.

Among Rhodes's love poems, perhaps his weakest, "White Fingers" (1910), likens love to hands playing on a mandolin. His nature poems celebrate familiar regional landscapes and natural creatures: the yucca plant ("A Blossom of Barren Lands," 1899), the primrose ("With An Evening Primrose," 1902), the hills ("A Ballade of Gray Hills," 1900), and bees ("A Ballade of Wild Bees," 1902). Curiously, the foregoing two poems that Rhodes calls ballads actually are lyrics.

Rhodes's protest poems joust with a variety of adversaries: "Te Deum Laudamus" (1901), with proponents of American imperialism in the Philippines; "Pegasus at the Plow" (1920), with civilization's incursion into man's natural freedom; "Nineteen Thirty-one" (1931), a populistic imitation of Kipling's "Danny Deever," with lending agencies charging farmers high interest rates; "The Hired Man on Horseback" (1928), perhaps Rhodes's best poem, with contemporary journalistic detractors of the cowboy; and "Fire Song" (1932), with modern muckrakers for their criticism of Benjamin Franklin and other Founding Fathers. Of Rhodes's religious poems, "A Song of Harvest" (1932) offers a prayer that the speaker may accept his "row" or life as it has been. Ranging from whimsical to serious, Rhodes's miscellaneous poems often prove to be his best. Among those in a lighter vein, "Relativity for Ladies" (1931) facetiously insists that a woman's age, unlike a man's, does not change, and "Little Next Door" (1916) dwells on the innocence of childhood. Of the more serious miscellaneous poems, "Important—Einstein's Universe" (1931) reflects upon the scientist's revisions of his opinion of the universe.

Except for the protest poems, Rhodes's poetry is naively romantic in content. Nearly all of it is conventional in structure, employing traditional stanzaic patterns and such familiar forms as the ballad and lyric. Unlike such contemporary poetry as Edwin Arlington Robinson's, it reveals no experimental impulses. The imagery, for example, is more abstract than concrete. Mostly end rhymed, the poems often suffer from irregular meter that obviously is not calculated and contributes no unique effects. Were it not for the fact that the poet's unquenchable spirit and humor survive the limitations of the other aspects of his poesy,

Rhodes's poems would be no better than those of the popularizers Edgar A. Guest and Eugene Field, the latter to whom Rhodes alludes in his works and whose poetry inferentially he admired. Finally, however, his poems surpass those of Guest and Field but still fall far short of those of Robert Frost, whom Rhodes respected and who, in turn, liked Rhodes's prose works.

Most of Rhodes's writing consists of novels and stories. Many of the stories, however, ultimately became incorporated into the novels, and those that did not ordinarily contribute only detail to an understanding of the fiction. For those reasons, analysis may be confined to the novels.

Rhodes works with materials inherently realistic but builds naively romantic plot structures. His basic plot pattern pits evil, with an initial advantage, against good that finally triumphs. *Good Men and True*, Rhodes's first novel, for example, concerns a sinister politician who attempts to discredit and murder a Texas Ranger. Although the antagonist initially succeeds in casting suspicion on the ranger, ultimately he is thwarted by the protagonist, a cowboy named Jeff Bransford, and his "good men and true."

Similarly, the novelette *Hit the Line Hard* (1915) concerns a corrupt politician. The antagonist (a lawyer) and four accomplices (including a banker) steal both from the estate of a deceased rancher and then from each other. Their villainy is detected by the rancher's nephew, an eastern college man, and a cunning native old-timer.

Bransford in Arcadia, or the Little Eohippus (1914), retitled *Bransford of Rainbow Range* in the collected novels *Romances of Navaho Land* (1920), features a banker who burglarizes his own bank. His crime is exposed by Jeff Bransford (also of *Good Men and True*), who carries as a good-luck piece a turquoise replica of an eohippus.

Another example of a corrupt lawyer is found in *Copper Streak Trail* (1922). The lawyer, Oscar Mitchell, is a rival of his cousin Stanley for their aging uncle's wealth. Both Oscar and the uncle reside in New York, but Stanley has come west to mine. When Oscar conspires with a rival miner to frame Stanley with a crime committed by another, Stanley's fiancée, his mining partner, and even the uncle join forces to disrupt the conspiracy. *Once in the Saddle* (1927) also turns on a corrupt miner, who denies his workers decent housing and compels them to shop at his company store. His strongman, however, is even more villainous: he robs a paymaster but ultimately suffers detection by two canny well diggers.

In three of Rhodes's novels, law enforcement officers are the villains. *The Desire of the Moth* (1916) depicts a corrupt sheriff who attempts to ruin his political adversary, a young rancher. The rancher's fiancée enlists the aid of John Wesley Pringle (also of *Good Men and True*) to foil the scheme. In *Stepsons of Light*, a deputy sheriff murders a miner and blames a cowboy, Johnny Dines (from *The Desire of the Moth*). The cowboy's friends reveal the actual criminal, in the process dispersing an intended lynch mob with billiard balls thrown about in a manner reminiscent of an actual bar room brawl in which Rhodes once

engaged. *Beyond the Desert* (1934) concerns the abortive effort of another deputy sheriff and a businessman to steal a rancher's land. The rancher's friends,
including "Lithpin' Tham" Clark, save the land and its water rights in which a
railroad is interested.

About the only one of Rhodes's novels with a decent official is *The Proud
Sheriff* (1935), his last and published posthumously. The sheriff proves the
innocence of a youth in a murder committed by another man having a love affair
with the victim's wife.

But if persons of high station frequently are corrupt in Rhodes's novels, many
of low station paradoxically are noble. In *West Is West*, a killer dies in the act of
saving a girl from a mock marriage with his villainous employer; and a gambler
rescues a virtuous young woman on the verge of being tricked into service in a
brothel. Another novel, *Pasó Por Aquí* (1927) is about a bank robber. Fleeing
from his robbery, the protagonist halts his escape to render aid to a Mexican
family stricken with diphtheria. His act of nobility enables the sheriff to capture
him, but it also convinces the officer that the outlaw should be allowed to escape
again. Finally, *The Trusty Knaves* (1934) employs a real-life outlaw, Bill Doolin.
Using an alias, he appears in town concurrently with a series of robberies in the
region. When the robbers attempt to enlist his services in other crimes, however,
Doolin becomes a "trusty knave" and turns them over to the law.

Beyond the incipiently romantic nature of their plots, Rhodes's novels are
often weakly motivated and episodic. They digress at the expense of narrative flow. Chapter 3 of *The Desire of the Moth*, for example, provides an
informative but intrusive history of the Chihuahuan desert, the *Jornado del
Muerto*.

Rhodes peoples his novels with stereotyped characters, among the protagonists the quick, tough cowboy or miner; the slightly older and hence less physically agile but more sharp-witted compatriot; the garrulous, shrewd old westerner
whose abundant speech contains rich veins of wisdom; the young newcomer,
eager companion of the old-timer, who proves himself a man; and the loyal
friend who risks fortune or life, or both, to do a favor. Rhodes proves incapable of
depicting believable women unless they have reached middle age. Betraying his
lifelong addiction to the chivalric code, his younger women are hopelessly romantic. Finally, like Shakespeare's Iago but much less credibly, the antagonists
evidence self-conscious villainy. They are one-dimensionally evil, usually reflecting no redeeming features.

Part of the problem of characterization is that Rhodes borrows freely from
actual life for his fictional personages and even neglects often to change their real
names in the transferral. William Beebe and Jeff Bransford (*Good Men and
True*), Johnny Dines (*Stepsons of Light*), and Emil James (*West Is West*) are but a
few examples. Apparently because he knew his fictional models so well, Rhodes
fails to provide detail enough to enable the reader to understand the characters'
motivations. Moreover, like Sinclair Lewis, Rhodes employs characters promis-
cuously, assigning a name to every person appearing on the range or the street

whether the character really does anything in the story. Such extravagance detracts from the full development of major characters.

Somewhat offsetting the failures of plot and characterization, the themes of Rhodes's novels adhere faithfully to the realities of time and place. Their dominant concern is corruption in high places and the reverse corollary: decency among lawbreakers. The cupidity of supposedly upright citizens, of course, was not peculiar to the frontier West except that there (more so perhaps than in settled areas) the badge—as Rhodes employs it in *Beyond the Desert*—often became a convenient refuge in one place for the fugitive from another place. On the other hand, the nobility of the outlaw, as Walter Campbell and others have shown, was something of a frontier phenomenon. The criminal both in Indian and white frontier communities, unless mentally disturbed, was neither antisocial nor intentionally destructive of community mores. Moreover, the eastern laws imposed upon western conditions did not always prove appropriate. One of Rhodes's characters has that in mind when he says that a man who "keeps a foolish law is only a fool—but a man who doesn't break a wicked law is a knave and a coward, or both, and fool besides" (*West Is West*, quoted in Gaston, *Eugene Manlove Rhodes*, p. 33).

Further offsetting weaknesses of plot and characterization, Rhodes's rendition of place proves masterful. The key is his power of language and observation. No detail is too trivial, no sound or action too insignificant, no quality of nature too unimportant. As De Maupassant insisted a writer must, Rhodes sees something unique in the commonplace, and as Ford Madox Ford said of Hemingway, Rhodes uses ordinary words in an extraordinary way to express his vision. Witness the richly evocative description of a prominent landmark in *The Desire of the Moth*:

> Organ Mountain flung up a fantasy of spires, needle-sharp and bare and golden. The long straight range—saw-toothed limestone save for this twenty-mile sheer upheaval of the Organ—stretched away to north and south against the unclouded sky, till distance turned the barren gray to blue-black, to blue, to misty haze; till the sharp, square-angled masses rounded to hillocks—to a blur—a wavy line—nothing. [*The Best Novels and Stories of Eugene Manlove Rhodes*, p. 301]

Next to landscapes, Rhodes's dialogue stands as the hallmark of his art. Bernard DeVoto insisted that in his handling of dialogue Rhodes rivals Twain, and he was reasonably correct. The language that Rhodes attributes to his characters is natural and fresh, liberally punctuated with unusual figures of speech, and spirited. Above all perhaps, it is ironically humorous, as in the warning one character issues another in *The Trusty Knaves*: "When you ride up to that camp, you ride a-whistlin' real loud and pleasant. That Charlie Bird, he's half Cherokee and half white, and them's two bad breeds" (*Best Novels and Stories of Eugene Manlove Rhodes*, p. 269).

If Rhodes's paramount failure is his paradoxical blending of naive romance and faithful realism, his mixed proclivities can be understood in part because he usually wrote for the *Saturday Evening Post* and other popular magazines promoting Victorian virtues. A better explanation, however, is that long after incipient romance departed the American eastern seaboard, it thrived southwest of the Mississippi because of a persistent cultural lag characteristic of all frontiers. Neither Rhodes nor any other southwestern writer contemporary with him escaped its contagion.

Survey of Criticism

His romantic excesses notwithstanding, Rhodes was one of the first southwestern writers to make a sincere attempt to be faithful to the realities of the place. In trail-driving terms, he is thus something of the "point" in the slow transition from naive to mature regional expression. Because of his pioneering efforts, he has commanded more attention from scholars than a minor writer might otherwise have received. The scholarship, however, has been more descriptive than analytical. W. H. Hutchinson, for example, has devoted most of a lifetime to extending the biographical work of Rhodes's widow in her *The Hired Man on Horseback* (1938). His *A Bar Cross Man* (1956) and *A Bar Cross Liar* (1959) contribute biographical and publishing detail, as well as exhaustive bibliographical information. With his more recent articles, Hutchinson's books establish him as the premier authority on Rhodes. Nevertheless, Hutchinson's purpose has not been to provide extensive critical analysis. An early attempt at criticism was Edwin W. Gaston's *Eugene Manlove Rhodes: Cowboy Chronicler* (1967), a study abbreviated by the editorial limitations of the Southwest Writers Series of which it is a part. Subsequent critical analyses of even shorter compass have been Lawrence Clark Powell's typically perceptive chapter on Rhodes in his *Southwest Classics* (1975) and discerning individual essays by Mark Busby, Jim L. Fife, James K. Folsom, and Richard Skillman and Jerry C. Hoke.

Whether Rhodes deserves a full-scale critical examination is debatable. Now, nearly a half century after his death, he is mainly of historical interest. Certainly he hardly deserves the same consideration as such notable successors as Conrad Richter, Paul Horgan, Frank Waters, and Walter Van Tilburg Clark. But those successors might not have sung so well had they stood with Rhodes in the forefront of the literary transition that now has brought respectability to regional letters. Richter, indeed, said as much. And if those successors have brought uniformly high art to their writing, they have succeeded no better than Rhodes in their depiction of place and in their use of native language. Quite likely they would agree that, for the trail drive to southwestern literary maturity, Eugene Manlove Rhodes would be a good man to ride the river with.

Bibliography

Works by Eugene Manlove Rhodes

Good Men and True. New York: Henry Holt, 1910.
Bransford in Arcadia, or The Little Eohippus. New York: Henry Holt, 1914.

The Desire of the Moth. New York: Henry Holt, 1916.

West Is West. New York: H. K. Fly, 1917.

Romances of Navaho Land [includes *Good Men and True*, *Bransford in Arcadia* changed
    to *Bransford of Rainbow Range*, *The Desire of the Moth*, *West Is West*, *Hit the
    Line Hard*, and *The Come On*]. New York: Grosset and Dunlap, 1920.

Stepsons of Light. Boston: Houghton Mifflin, 1921.

Say Now Shibboleth. Chicago: Bookfellows, 1921.

Copper Streak Trail. Boston: Houghton Mifflin, 1922.

Once in the Saddle and *Pasó Por Aquí*. Boston: Houghton Mifflin, 1927.

The Trusty Knaves. Boston: Houghton Mifflin, 1934.

Beyond the Desert. Boston: Houghton Mifflin, 1934.

Peñalosa. Santa Fe: Rydal Press, 1934.

The Proud Sheriff. Boston: Houghton Mifflin, 1935.

The Little World Waddies. Chico, Calif.: W. H. Hutchinson, 1946.

The Best Novels and Stories of Eugene Manlove Rhodes. Ed. Frank V. Dearing. Boston:
    Houghton Mifflin, 1949.

The Rhodes Reader: Stories of Virgins, Villains, and Varmints. Ed. W. H. Hutchinson.
    Norman: University of Oklahoma Press, 1957.

The Line of Least Resistance. Ed. W. H. Hutchinson. Chico, Calif.: Hurst and Yount,
    1958.

Studies of Eugene Manlove Rhodes

Busby, Mark. "Eugene Manlove Rhodes: Kesey Passed by Here." *Western American
    Literature* 15 (Summer 1980): 83-92.

Dobie, J. Frank. "Gene Rhodes, Cowboy Novelist." *Atlantic Monthly* 183 (June 1949): 75-77.

Fife, Jim L. "Two Views of the American West." *Western American Literature* 1 (Spring
    1966): 34-43.

Folsom, James K. "A Dedication to the Memory of Eugene Manlove Rhodes: 1869-1934."
    Arizona and the West 2 (Winter 1969): 310-14.

Gaston, Edwin W., Jr. *Eugene Manlove Rhodes: Cowboy Chronicler*. SWS. Austin:
    Steck-Vaughn, 1967.

Hutchinson, W. H. *A Bar Cross Liar*. Stillwater: Redlands Press, 1959.

――――. *A Bar Cross Man: The Life and Personal Writings of Eugene Manlove Rhodes*.
    Norman: University of Oklahoma Press, 1956.

――――. "I Pay for What I Break." *Western American Literature* 1 (Summer 1966):
    91-96.

――――. "New Mexico Incident: An Episode in the Life of Western Writer Eugene
    Manlove Rhodes." *American West* 14 (November-December 1977): 4-7.

――――. "The West of Eugene Manlove Rhodes." *Arizona and the West* 9 (Autumn 1967):
    211-18.

Powell, Lawrence Clark. *Southwest Classics*. Pasadena, Calif.: Ward Ritchie Press, 1975.

Rhodes, May Davison. *The Hired Man on Horseback: My Story of Eugene Manlove
    Rhodes*. Boston: Houghton Mifflin, 1938.

Skillman, Richard, and Hoke, Jerry C. "The Portrait of the New Mexican in the Fiction of
    Eugene Manlove Rhodes." *Western Review* 6 (Spring 1969): 26-36.

William T. Pilkington

CONRAD RICHTER
(1890-1968)

One of the few critics to offer an assessment of Conrad Richter's work, John T. Flanagan, has dubbed Richter a "romancer of the Southwest." The not-so-subtle taint conveyed by the word *romancer*—a "romancer," after all, deals in the melodramatic and the shallowly improbable—perhaps explains why the author has been more or less neglected by critics of western American literature. To be sure, Richter began his fiction-writing career by cranking out stories for such mass-circulation periodicals as *Saturday Evening Post* and *Ladies' Home Journal*. His fiction, however, was always better than the company it kept; the literary quality of even the meanest of his tales is several cuts above that of the usual *Saturday Evening Post* formula story. Unlike the kind of writer the term *romancer* connotes, Richter was a careful researcher and a conscientious craftsman— in short, a serious artist. His southwestern fiction, while not flawless, deserves more attention and analysis than it has to this point attracted.

Biography

Conrad Richter was born and reared in precincts far from the magical Southwest that he eventually was to exploit so skillfully. Richter's father was a Lutheran minister who was assigned to pastorates in a number of small towns in eastern Pennsylvania. The author was born 13 October 1890 in the village of Pine Grove in Schuylkill County, about seventy-five miles northwest of Philadelphia. He completed high school in 1906 in the not-much larger community of Tremont, Pennsylvania. Instead of proceeding on to college, as his family hoped he would (plans called for him to become a clergyman, as his father and grandfather had been), Richter worked for several years at a wide variety of jobs; teamster, farm laborer, bank clerk, and logger were among the often physically demanding tasks by which the young Richter made a living. After a few years of such labor he acquired a position as reporter for the *Johnstown Journal*, thus obtaining his first writing-related job. For the next decade and a half Richter worked for various Pennsylvania newspapers. Like so many other American writers of the late nineteenth and early twentieth centuries, however, he used journalism merely as an entry to more serious kinds of writing. In 1913 he began to compose and publish short fiction, in time making enough money to consider his fiction writing as a supplemental occupation. In 1924 a dozen of his early stories were collected in *Brothers of No Kin*. Also in the 1920s he published *Human Vibration* (1926) and *Principles in Bio-Physics* (1927), treatises that are indicative of the author's lifelong, if rather amateurish, interest in philosophical discourse.

In 1915 Richter married Harvena Achenbach. The Richters' only child, a daughter, Harvena, was born in 1917. His wife's declining health was a major factor in prompting Richter in 1928 to liquidate his Pennsylvania assets and move his family to the Southwest. Settled in Albuquerque, the author, who had already read a good deal about the region, quickly began to indulge his imaginative curiosity in what had always seemed to him a lovely, exotic land. He traveled throughout New Mexico and adjacent states, listened to tales told by the region's old-timers, and dug through back issues of newspapers and into manuscript collections. The results of his probings filled several thick notebooks. The notebooks, in turn, supplied background materials for a series of memorable and authentic stories and novels set in New Mexico and the Southwest.

Richter lived in the Southwest for more than two decades, from 1928 to 1950. In 1950 he returned to his native town of Pine Grove where he resided until his death on 30 October 1968. During his career he published more than a score of books, only about a fourth of which are set in the West (that is, the trans-Mississippi West). Some critics believe that Richter's finest work is *The Awakening Land* (1966), his fictional trilogy of the Ohio frontier—the individual titles being *The Trees* (1940), *The Fields* (1946), and *The Town* (1950). Certainly these novels attain a high level of historical accuracy and literary polish, and they brought to Richter much-deserved praise and recognition when *The Town* was awarded a Pulitzer Prize in 1951. Other of his important works not set in the Southwest include *Always Young and Fair* (1947), *The Light in the Forest* (1953), *The Waters of Kronos* (1960, winner of a National Book Award in the same year), *A Simple Honorable Man* (1962), *The Grandfathers* (1964), and *A Country of Strangers* (1966).

The entire body of Richter's writing is characterized by its high literary quality. This having been acknowledged, remarks here will focus on the author's southwestern fiction, since that fiction is responsible for his reputation as a western writer. His southwestern books are *Early Americana* (1936), a collection of stories; *The Sea of Grass* (1937), *Tacey Cromwell* (1942), and *The Lady* (1957), all novels; and a curious work that is part fiction, part philosophy, entitled *The Mountain on the Desert* (1955). A posthumous collection, *The Rawhide Knot and Other Stories* (1978), reprints several short narratives that first appeared in *Early Americana* and adds two stories of the Pennsylvania frontier and a couple of previously uncollected, and rather mediocre, southwestern tales.

Major Themes

The general excellence of Richter's southwestern fiction has many sources. The author's mastery of language (for example, his uncanny ability to say—to suggest—much in few words) is truly remarkable. In her introduction to *The Rawhide Knot and Other Stories*, Richter's daughter, Harvena, speaks of the "swift pictures" that her father often employed "to compress the times and spaces of a country into tight mythic structures" (pp. vii-viii). This indeed was one of Richter's favorite literary devices, and when it succeeds, as it often does in his stories, even a brief passage may unfold a suggestive complexity that works at once on the intellectual, imaginative, and mythic levels of awareness.

Perhaps the most important factor in Richter's literary artistry, however, is the extraordinary richness of his thematic concerns. The author's themes, in a general way, spring from his philosophy of life. Like a number of American writers from the late nineteenth and early twentieth centuries (Mark Twain and Harvey Fergusson are two that come to mind), Richter considered himself as much a philosopher as a litterateur. Today the author's "philosophy" seems decidedly amateurish and even confused. As it relates to his writing, however, the significance of the philosophy is that it gave him a code to live by and a consistent perspective from which to view the characters who people his fiction.

In *Human Vibration, Principles of Bio-Physics*, and *The Mountain on the Desert*, the author develops what he calls "the theory of psycho-energics." This theory evolved out of Richter's concern about the clash between science and religion in turn-of-the-century America, as well as out of his painful rejection of orthodox Christianity (painful primarily because of his family's commitment, over several generations, to the Lutheran church and its theology). Richter wished to formulate a philosophy that answered to the claims of science—for example, the new concept of humankind supplied by Darwinian theory, the growing knowledge of the chemical and biological foundations of life provided by the physical sciences, and the insights into the workings of the mind that came out of the beginnings of clinical psychology—while retaining a strong reverence for the metaphysical. For Richter psycho-energics accomplished this difficult task.

Psycho-energics translates into Richter's fiction mainly through his characters. The writer's basic assumptions concerning character formation, for instance, seem to be a variation on the Darwinian idea of the survival of the fittest. In Richter's fiction suffering and hardship usually assist self-discipline and growth, while luxury and ease lead to weakness and death. For Richter true strength of character is formed only in the crucible of conflict and struggle. Thus the author seems particularly to admire women, presumably for their superior powers of endurance and of overcoming adversity. (Each of the three southwestern novels is told from the point of view of a young man who is enthralled and influenced by a strong and resourceful woman.)

Given this view of character development, it is easy to understand why Richter preferred writing about the past to writing about the present. The qualities he believed to be necessary for growth of character—courage, dedication, persistence, individualism—flourished in frontier America; they have not, seemingly, flourished in modern-day America. The celebration of the past, therefore—the mythic as well as the historical past—is an important theme in the writer's works. Certainly Richter is adept at instilling in his fiction a strong sense of the past. He does this, by his account, by weaving a "pattern of. . .endless, small authenticities" through which the social and historical fabric of a distant time and place becomes manifest in words (*Early Americana*, p. vi).

Although it was his fourth published book, *Early Americana*, according to one critic, marked for Richter "the real beginning of a lengthy and distinguished career as a writer of stories and novels about American backgrounds" (Edwards, *Conrad Richter's Ohio Trilogy*, p. 9). Moreover, the stories collected in the volume, all set in west Texas and New Mexico, introduce many of the themes and techniques that he elaborated and developed in later works. Six of the nine tales, for example—"New Home," "Long Drouth," "Frontier Woman," "Buckskin Vacation," "The Square Piano," and "Early Marriage"—focus on the trials and tribulations of pioneer women in the nineteenth-century Southwest. In each of these stories a frontier woman faces alone a difficult and usually dangerous situation; by overcoming the difficulty with fortitude and dignity, the woman proves herself and grows as an individual. The predominance of women protagonists in the *Early Americana* stories may be dismissed simply as a reflection of the fact that several of the tales were first published in *Ladies' Home Journal* and were consciously aimed at a female reading audience. Surely, though, the predominance also derives from Richter's genuine admiration for that special strength of character that he believed to be unique in the female of the species.

Judged by purely literary standards, the most accomplished story in the collection is "Smoke over the Prairie." The central character of the tale, Frank Gant, is owner of a "rude empire. . .a land as feudal as old England, larger than the British Isles, with lords and freemen, savages and peons" (*Early Americana*, p. 38). Most of Gant's fortune is tied up in a hundred thousand sheep that dot the New Mexico landscape. In order to preserve his feudal kingdom, Gant attempts to prevent the intrusion onto his property of the railroad as it moves westward. The climactic event of the story is an impromptu race between the sheep baron, with buggy and team, and a newly arrived train. Gant wins but is killed as he tries to cross the track in front of the engine. His death suggests the tenacity of the old order and also the inevitability of the changes that were sweeping across the West in the late nineteenth century. The oppositions established in the story are familiar ones in western literature: West versus East, pastoral stability versus technological change. In the context of Richter's writing, "Smoke Over the Prairie" is notable because it introduces a point of view that the author uses effectively in a number of later works: the tale is narrated by an older man— Frank Gant's son, Johnnie—who is recalling the exciting events of his youth. This point of view, with its implicit contrast between past and present, youth and age, seems especially appropriate to the exploration of one of Richter's most important themes: the formation and development of character.

The Sea of Grass, first published in 1937, is Richter's best-known southwestern book (perhaps because it was the only one of his regional stories to be made into a motion picture). A widespread misconception about the novel is that it is the story of a Texas cattle king (paperback editions of the work have even advertised it as such). Actually the novel is laid in west central New Mexico; the mistaken assumptions about setting no doubt derive from an early reference in the book to Jim Brewton's "fabulous herds of Texas cattle sprinkled like grains of cinnamon across the horizons" (*Sea of Grass*, p. 4). Setting is certainly not unimportant in the novel. Much of the beauty and nostalgic tone of the narrative spring from the metaphor suggested in the title. Time and again the prairie grasslands are described as, for example, "vast, brown, empty plain, dipping and pitching endlessly like a parched sea" (p. 13).

Historically and mythically *The Sea of Grass* concerns the nineteenth-century conflict between cattleman and nester, or more generally between the Old West and the new West. In terms of story the conflict is shown dramatically as a personal triangle: the cattleman Jim Brewton, his wife Lutie, and the district attorney Brice Chamberlain, who champions the nesters' cause. Interestingly the triangle extends into the next generation, the Brewton children: Jimmy is a replica of his father; Sarah Beth closely resembles her mother; and Brock looks and acts like Brice Chamberlain (whose son he is). The narrative spans about two decades, during which wrenching changes occur. At first the cattleman rides tall in the saddle. Gradually, however, the nesters gain control of the land, plowing under the native grasses to put in their crops. Extended drought eventually proves that dryland farming in the area is not feasible, blows away much of the top soil, and drives out the nesters, thus returning the land, without its precious grass, to Brewton. The character in the book who arouses the most sympathy in the reader is Jim Brewton, a circumstance that suggests that Richter's loyalties are clearly with the old order, though the author cannot deny the historical reality of progress and change. However arrogant and privileged he seems at the beginning of the novel, Brewton ultimately shows himself to be a responsible and compassionate human being, much more so than the self-serving and politically motivated Brice Chamberlain.

The Sea of Grass is narrated by Brewton's nephew, Hal, who visits the ranch a number of times as a youth and then returns, as an adult, to a nearby town to practice medicine. In Hal's imagination his uncle is always a larger-than-life figure; it is the mystery and complexity of Lutie, however, that endlessly fascinate Hal. Lutie never adjusts to life on the plains. She is too civilized and refined to accept the raw country or her husband's ways. Her discontent, presumably, leads her to infidelity to and separation from Jim Brewton. At the close of the novel, following the death of Brock, Lutie and Jim are reunited. Lutie compromises, a compromise that occurs ironically only after her husband's defeat: his beloved grasslands have been destroyed, his "son" slain. Hal observes the fate of his aunt and uncle, and it is Lutie who seems to teach him the most. Lutie, in her beauty, manners, and self-assured charm, appears to represent the world of civilized values, and it is in that world that Hal must live. His uncle's world, however lamentably, is dead; Hal may seek to emulate Jim Brewton's more admirable character traits, but it is Lutie who provides the model for a necessary reconciliation of East and West, old and new.

If the moral implications of the character of Lutie seem somewhat ambiguous, such implications regarding the title character of *Tacey Cromwell* (1942) are more clear-cut. The story is told from the point of view of "Nugget" Oldaker, who as a middle-aged man reminisces about the events and personalities that, for him, were the bridge between childhood and adulthood. As an eight-year-old boy Nugget runs away from his home in eastern Kansas in search of his half-brother, Gaye. He goes first to New Mexico, then to the mining town of Bisbee, Arizona. There he finds Gaye, and he also finds Tacey Cromwell, who (unofficially) adopts him, along with Seely Dowden, another Bisbee urchin. The crux of the story is Tacey's continuing struggle to hold together her "family."

As the beginning of the novel Tacey is a bawdy-house madam who rather abruptly shifts roles to become a "mother" and respectable businesswoman. Her motivation for making this drastic change is never altogether clear. Probably, however, Richter was attempting to dramatize in Tacey a historical fact: that most of the prostitutes and dance-hall girls of the old West eventually went legitimate, became wives and mothers, often happy and successful ones. In explaining Tacey's success as "mother," Richter once wrote an acquaintance that "more intelligence in bringing up children is found in the once sporting house woman than in the soft loving mother" who has been educated in more normal circumstances (Edwards, *Ohio Trilogy*, p. 104). Tacey's discipline, self-reliance, and self-effacing loyalty to her family are truly heroic—and perhaps not completely believable. Still, without such qualities she could never have psychologically survived the Bisbee ladies' puritanical ire; without them surely she could never have won her sizable, if largely private, victory over an inert public morality that would have crushed a lesser person.

Nugget observes with growing admiration Tacey's unyielding struggle, and in the end she bestows on him the most bountiful gift a parent can give a child: a model for character building. For some of the people in the book things come too easily, and as a result they remain weak and indulgent. Tacey suffers and endures, becomes a source of strength, a refuge, and a returning point for her "family." The narration ends with the family circle closed. Nugget comments that, in the beginning, "it had been Tacey and Seely and Gaye and I. Now here were the four of us again" (*Tacey Cromwell*, p. 208). This reunion seems the necessary conclusion to Richter's characterization of Tacey, for her indomitable courage and determination are the elastic and unseen bonds that have drawn the family back together.

The Lady, serialized in the *Saturday Evening Post* in early 1957 and brought out in book form later the same year, is Richter's final fictional attempt to come to terms with southwestern materials. Clearly the novel is based, if only loosely, on an unsolved historical mystery: the disappearance in 1896 of Judge Albert J. Fountain and his nine-year-old son somewhere between Lincoln and Las Cruces, New Mexico. The story is told (once again) from the vantage point of an orphan lad, Jud, who is taken into the home of Judge Albert Sessions and his wife, Doña Ellen. From this perspective Jud witnesses the destructive effects of a vengeful feud in which the Sessions family is involved, a feud that pits family against family, cattleman against sheepman, Anglo against Mexican-American. The feud accounts, apparently, for the eventual disappearance of Judge Sessions and his son, Willy; true to the historical event, the mystery of the fictional disappearance is never solved.

The focus of the narrative, however, is not so much on the mysterious disappearance as on the character of Doña Ellen. Ellen comes from an old established Hispanic family, the Johnson y Campos. As the title of the novel indicates, she is, in every sense of the term, a lady. She smoothly handles the class distinctions inherent in the feudal society of late nineteenth-century New Mexico. Indeed she seems most at home in situations in which she must deal with those below her on the social scale. Ellen is truly compassionate, taking seriously the responsibilities of noblesse oblige. Courageously (though unsuccessfully) she attempts to run the family sheep ranch after the disappearance of her husband. Like other Richter narrators before him, Jud gradually but definitely learns valuable human lessons in his relationship with this graceful and strong-willed woman.

With *The Lady*, Richter must have concluded, probably accurately, that his formula—young, impressionable narrator fascinated by strong older woman—was wearing thin; he never used the situation again. *The Lady* was published in 1957, seven years after the author had left New Mexico to return to Pennsylvania. In later books Richter did not again employ the Southwest as the setting for his fiction. *The Mountain on the Desert*, published two years before *The Lady*, had used a background ostensibly southwestern, but that work can scarcely be called a novel or even regional literature. The frame story of *The Mountain on the Desert*—an eastern engineer retires to the Sandia Mountains of New Mexico to become a rug weaver and to hold court before a group of eager college students— is but a transparent device to provide coherence for the book's real subject: the author's philosophical speculations. The best of Richter's western fiction is *The Sea of Grass* and *Tacey Cromwell*, along with three or four of the *Early Americana* stories. In quantity that does not add up to an overwhelming achievement. In quality, however—in subtlety of style, depth of characterization, and richness of theme—Richter's output will stand comparison with that of any of the more celebrated western writers.

Survey of Criticism

That Richter has not been celebrated to the degree that some other western authors have been is a statement that can hardly be questioned. Only a few critics of western American literature have examined Richter's works in any detail. On the broad ground of western fiction, Richter appears to have staked only a very small claim. James K. Folsom's *The American Western Novel* (1966) adjudges *The Sea of Grass* to be a "brilliant novel" (p. 94) but takes no notice of any other of Richter's works. A more recent survey of western fiction, John R. Milton's *The Novel of the American West* (1980), finds even less to praise in the Richter canon than does Folsom's book. Milton devotes less than two pages to Richter, and much of that space is given over to a generally negative comparison of Richter with Willa Cather. (The apparent similarities between Richter's and Cather's western novels have been remarked by a number of critics.)

The earliest critical evaluations of Richter's fiction, aside from reviews of individual books, were a batch of journal articles published in the 1940s and 1950s. Bruce Sutherland's "Conrad Richter's Americana" (1945), for example, champions Richter as the author of superior historical fiction. Sutherland concludes that Richter's "restrained realism...combined with an understanding of people, a feeling for historical things which transcends mere knowledge, and the ability to think and write in terms of his characters and their environment places him among the chosen few who have made the past of America come alive" (p. 422). Dayton Kohler's "Conrad Richter: Early Americana" (1947) discusses the author's books published during the 1930s. Kohler believes that Richter's historical novels "belong to the eager nationalism of the depression thirties, when writers as divergent as Van Wyck Brooks and Kenneth Roberts tried to find in the certainties of a recovered past an answer to the problems of the present"; however, unlike many other explorers into the fictional past, Richter, Kohler says, is nothing less than "an artist in prose" (pp. 221-22).

Frederic I. Carpenter's "Conrad Richter's Pioneers: Reality and Myth" (1950) remains the most acutely perceptive analysis, short or long, that has yet been performed on Richter's work. Carpenter praises Richter's realism but claims the real power of the author's fiction lies in its penetration into the caverns of its characters' unconscious.

Sailing the sea of grass in their prairie schooners or plunging beneath the surface of a sea of leaves into the dark wilderness of Ohio, his pioneers live not only as actual adventurers but also as explorers of the primeval past and the racial unconscious. While they cut down the trees and plow the fields and build the new town, they also remember something of the mythical wisdom of the race—and suggest its continuing value for our times. [P. 83]

Despite his unfortunate choice of the term *romancer*, John T. Flanagan, in "Conrad Richter: Romancer of the Southwest" (1958), offers a laudatory survey of the writer's southwestern books. Flanagan defines *romance* in the general way in which Hawthorne used the word: "the novel," says the critic, "aimed at minute fidelity.... The romance, on the other hand, permitted considerable latitude, and while it did not encourage a false picture of the human heart it nevertheless allowed the writer to mellow, deepen, enrich the atmosphere in any way which would contribute to the desired goal." Richter, Flanagan contends, chose the latter approach in his southwestern fiction, which is "atmospheric, dramatic, and episodic" in the best sense of those terms (p. 189).

Edwin W. Gaston's *Conrad Richter* (1965), in Twayne's United States Authors Series, is the first of several book-length critical examinations of Richter's work. While the Twayne format is often unduly confining, Gaston makes advantageous use of series requirements by providing the most helpful biography of the writer yet published, as well as the most extensive bibliography. Perhaps Gaston's basic contention is that Richter's fiction "reflects temporal and spiritual values that constitute, as it were, a paean to goodness," but that the author avoids for the most part the obvious pitfalls of sentimentalism and didacticism that often weaken the literary affirmation of such values (p. 7). Robert J. Barnes's *Conrad Richter* (1968), a pamphlet in the Southwest Writers Series, is Gaston's book in miniature. Barnes offers few new insights but does supply a useful and concise survey of the southwestern works.

A substantial segment (pp. 62-95) of Clifford D. Edwards's *Conrad Richter's Ohio Trilogy: Its Ideas, Themes and Relationships to Literary Tradition* (1970) deals with the writer's southwestern books. Those books, however, are treated primarily as background to a consideration of the trilogy. Edwards asserts that the Ohio trilogy is undeniably Richter's "finest achievement." It weaves together, he continues, all "the epic strands of the American experience: the nomadic penetration into the primeval wilderness, the cultivation of the fields, the growth of community from the soil, and the emergence of an industrial civilization and mode of life which threaten to destroy something vital and noble in the human spirit"; further, the trilogy is said to be notable for its dramatization of "the cosmic necessity in the historical process, of the inevitability of suffering, and of the emasculating effects of time" (p. 10).

Marvin J. LaHood's *Conrad Richter's America* (1975) is a rather impressionistic but often helpful critical study. About one-fifth of LaHood's book focuses on Richter's southwestern works. LaHood's thesis is that Richter's best fiction reflects "the glory of a nation in its vigorous youth," an America in which "thrift, hard work, perseverance, manliness, courage, honesty and...integrity" were virtues held in common by most of its citizens (p. 12).

During his lifetime Conrad Richter earned a number of prestigious literary awards. A half-dozen honorary doctorates, from schools ranging from the University of New Mexico to Temple University, were conferred upon him. His works have been translated into twenty-six languages, in dozens of different editions. The continuing popularity and universal appeal of those works are beyond question. A just critical consensus on the author's literary accomplishment, however, has not yet emerged. Although a handful of critics has provided analyses of the fiction, Richter's ranking within the fraternity of western authors— or American authors generally—remains, at best, disputed. Clearly a more searching critical examination of Richter's literary artistry is a desideratum for future western literary scholarship to supply.

Bibliography

Works by Conrad Richter

Brothers of No Kin and Other Stories. New York: Hinds, Hayden, and Eldredge, 1924.
Human Vibration. New York: Dodd, Mead, 1926.
Principles of Bio-Physics. Harrisburg, Pa.: Good Books Corporation, 1927.
Early Americana. New York: Alfred A. Knopf, 1936.
The Sea of Grass. New York: Alfred A. Knopf, 1937.
The Trees. New York: Alfred A. Knopf, 1940.
Tacey Cromwell. New York: Alfred A. Knopf, 1942.
The Free Man. New York: Alfred A. Knopf, 1943.
The Fields. New York: Alfred A. Knopf, 1946.
Always Young and Fair. New York: Alfred A. Knopf, 1947.
The Town. New York: Alfred A. Knopf, 1950.
The Light in the Forest. New York: Alfred A. Knopf, 1953.
The Mountain on the Desert. New York: Alfred A. Knopf, 1955.
The Lady. New York: Alfred A. Knopf, 1957.
The Waters of Kronos. New York: Alfred A. Knopf, 1960.
A Simple Honorable Man. New York: Alfred A. Knopf, 1962.
The Grandfathers. New York: Alfred A. Knopf, 1964.
A Country of Strangers. New York: Alfred A. Knopf, 1966.
Over the Blue Mountain. New York: Alfred A. Knopf, 1967.
The Aristocrat. New York: Alfred A. Knopf, 1968.
The Rawhide Knot and Other Stories. New York: Alfred A. Knopf, 1978.

Studies of Conrad Richter

Barnes, Robert J. *Conrad Richter*. SWS. Austin, Tex.: Steck-Vaughn, 1968.
Carpenter, Frederic I. "Conrad Richter's Pioneers: Reality and Myth." *College English* 12 (November 1950): 77-83.
Edwards, Clifford D. *Conrad Richter's Ohio Trilogy: Its Ideas, Themes and Relationships to Literary Tradition*. The Hague and Paris: Mouton, 1970.
Flanagan, John T. "Conrad Richter: Romancer of the Southwest." *Southwest Review* 43 (Summer 1958): 189-96.
Folsom, James K. *The American Western Novel*. New Haven, Conn.: College and University Press, 1966.
Gaston, Edwin W. *Conrad Richter*. TUSAS. New York: Twayne, 1965.
Kohler, Dayton. "Conrad Richter: Early Americana." *College English* 8 (February 1947): 221-28.
LaHood, Marvin J. *Conrad Richter's America*. The Hague and Paris: Mouton, 1975.
Milton, John R. *The Novel of the American West*. Lincoln: University of Nebraska Press, 1980.
Pearce, T. M. "Conrad Richter." *New Mexico Quarterly* 20 (Autumn 1950): 371-73.
Sutherland, Bruce. "Conrad Richter's Americana." *New Mexico Quarterly* 15 (Winter 1945): 413-22.

THEODORE ROETHKE
(1908-1963)

As a poet Theodore Roethke was a late starter. He published his first book *Open House* (1941), a stylized and competent work, at the age of thirty-three and his first major volume, *The Lost Son and Other Poems* (1948), at forty. His friend and biographer Allan Seager was to say, "Ted started out as a phony and became genuine, like Yeats. . . . I had no idea that he'd end up as fine a poet as he did. No one knew in the early days, Ted least of all" (James Dickey, "Greatest American Poet," p. 54). Today Roethke is counted a major writer in whose work American poetry finds another center of coherence.

Much of the satisfaction in reading Roethke's collected poems comes from witnessing his struggle for articulation. There is an underground note of poignancy that echoes through the poetry, as though he fought continually against barriers keeping him from a purity, both aesthetic and visionary, that he could imagine yet rarely sustain. Few would have attempted such a battle, yet Roethke produced a poetry that is both original and evocative. His particular gift was his remarkably sensitive response to the natural world. "There is no poetry anywhere," as James Dickey writes, "that is so valuably conscious of the human body . . . no poetry that can place the body in an environment—wind, seascape, greenhouse, forest, desert, mountainside, among animals or insects or stones—so vividly and evocatively, waking unheard of exchanges between the place and human responsiveness at its most creative. He more than any other is a poet of pure being" (*Babel to Byzantium*, p. 148).

Biography

Roethke was born in Saginaw, Michigan, on 25 May 1908. His parents were of German extraction. His father, in partnership with his uncle, had inherited the family business, an extensive greenhouse establishment. As the poet described it, "When the firm was at its height, it took up twenty-five acres within the city of Saginaw with a quarter of a million feet under glass" (Seager, *The Glass House*, p. 12). As a child, Roethke worked alongside his father, cultivating the flowers and then delivering them by hand to customers. He spoke of the greenhouses as "several worlds, which, even as a child, one worried about, and struggled to keep alive" (*On the Poet and His Craft*, p. 9). No young poet could ask for a more perfect image since in the imagination the greenhouse could become a primitive microcosm with its eschatology of heaven and hell, a moist artificial womb of growth and a place of death with the father-gardener, all powerful, all ordering, at its center. It seems to have been such to Roethke, his "symbol for the whole of life, a womb, a heaven-on-earth" (*Poet and His Craft*, p. 39), since he came into his own as a poet when he was able to recover the image in his sequence of greenhouse poems published in *The Lost Son*.

When Roethke was fifteen, his father died of cancer. With a sensitive adolescent, the complex of fear and guilt caused by the early death of a father can be profound and destructive throughout a lifetime. Many of Roethke's poems are a kind of ritual exorcism dealing with this theme. For whatever psychological and physiological reasons rooted in his particular history, he was to be plagued by periodic mental breakdowns from the age of twenty-seven. Resisting easy diagnosis, he once wrote, "If I have a complex, it's a full-life complex" (Seager, *Glass House*, p. 94). With a writer's resilience he was able to turn these to the service of his art. From his notebooks it can be concluded that the experience of psychic disorder convinced him of the existence of other forms of consciousness apart from the rational, and the need to explore these forms became the obsessive preoccupation of his poetry. Few other poets have so thoroughly sounded the extremes of consciousness, from the blind inchoate longings of the subliminal mind in states of terror to ecstatic oracular moments of mystical identification with the natural world.

Roethke began writing poetry as a student at the University of Pennsylvania and Harvard and committed his life to teaching and writing with a singular dedication that is remembered by his many students. He taught at Lafayette, Michigan State, Penn State, Bennington, and the University of Washington where, from 1947 to 1963, he helped to inspire a new generation of West Coast writers.

His life as teacher and poet was a relatively private one. He published his first book in 1941 and completed nine volumes in his lifetime. In 1953 he married Beatrice O'Connell. He began to travel, visiting Europe on his honeymoon. In 1955, he received a Fulbright grant and traveled to Ireland, Spain, and Italy. Surprisingly little of this experience enters the poetry. Roethke achieved considerable public recognition, including the Pulitzer Prize in 1953 and the National Book Award in 1959. While he continually struggled with illness, his dedication to teaching and writing remained the center of his life. He died on 1 August 1963 of a heart attack. The drama of his life had been entirely interior but was lived on a heroic scale. Perhaps for this reason he has often been eulogized by his contemporaries in poems: John Berryman's "A Strut for Roethke"; Robert Lowell's "For Theodore Roethke 1908-1963"; Richard Murphy's "The Poet on the Island."

Major Themes

In his first volume of poetry, *Open House*, Roethke identifies the self—not the private but the generic self—as the major concern of his poetry. The title poem is the first primitive statement of this obsession: "Myself is what I wear" (*Collected Poems*, p. 3). The book is a workshop of experiments in verse forms. Of it, he said: "It took me ten years to complete one little book, and now some of the things in it seem to creak" (*Poet and His Craft*, p. 16). He always felt that he began slowly as a consequence of his isolation as a midwestern poet in an environment where serious intellectual interest was conspicuously absent and artistic ambition scarcely tolerated. In his notebooks he wrote, "I think no one has ever spoken about the peculiar, the absolute—can I say—cultural loneliness of the American provincial creative intellectual" (*Straw for the Fire*, p. 228).

He found his voice as a poet when he began to write his greenhouse poems between 1944 and 1946. Kenneth Burke, a colleague and friend at Bennington where Roethke was teaching, has called this period "the cult of the breakthrough" ("Cult of the *Breakthrough* [review of *Selected Letters*]," *New Republic*, 21 September 1968, pp. 25-26). The poems are remarkable in their simplicity and in their power of sympathetic apprehension, whereby the poet seems to enter intuitively into the subliminal organic world of plant life he contemplates. As Roethke remarked, "In those first poems I had begun, like the child, with small things and had tried to make plain words do the trick" (*Poet and His Craft*, p. 10). Instead of external descriptions of flowers, the poems are focused on growth, on the willful, tenacious struggle of life. It is as if the poet were seeking to penetrate to the root sources of life in order to achieve his own resurrection.

> I can hear, underground, that sucking and sobbing,
> In my veins, in my bones I feel it,—
> The small waters seeping upward,
> The tight grains parting at last.
> When sprouts break out,
> Slippery as fish,
> I quail, lean to beginnings, sheath-wet.
> [*Collected Poems*, p. 37]

Roethke's strategy is obvious: intensely seen, image becomes symbol, and the plants in their artificial womb live in a violent and humiliating inferno of creation.

> Nothing would sleep in that cellar, dank as a ditch,
> Bulbs broke out of boxes hunting for chinks in the dark,
> Shoots dangled and drooped,
> Lolling obscenely from mildewed crates. [*Collected Poems*, p. 38]

Life, the sheer tenacious impulse to live, is terrifying and perverse. Throughout his life Roethke sought to understand the bond between human nature and the vegetal realm, to integrate himself to what he called that "rhythm, old and of vast importance" (*Collected Poems*, p. 40), the creative unidirectional impulse of life. For this reason his poetry can be understood only as a struggle against death or, more precisely, a struggle to accommodate death as part of natural processes. The fear of death as an arbitrary and ubiquitous force threatening the frail "I" had to be continually challenged by explorations into the nature of identity itself. "The human problem," he wrote, "is to find out what one really is: whether one exists, whether existence is possible. But how? 'Am I but nothing leaning toward a thing?' " (*Poet and His Craft*, p. 20).

After the greenhouse poems Roethke was able to write his first major autobiographical sequence, *The Lost Son Poems*. Clearly by cultivating his past in the greenhouses of childhood, he was able to explore some of the mental tangles of his youth. Of these poems he wrote, "I have tried to transmute and purify my 'life,' the sense of being defiled by it, in...poems which try in their rhythms to catch the very movement of the mind itself " (*Poet and His Craft*, p. 20). The poems are allegorical journeys; struggles "out of the slime; part of a slow spiritual progress; an effort to be born, and later, to become something more" (*Poet and His Craft*, p. 37). Roethke was a perceptive reader and probably learned how to manipulate the archetypal patterns of the poems through his intense reading of Maud Bodkin's *Archetypal Patterns in Poetry*, a study of the recurrent theme of rebirth in literature. For these are rebirth poems in which intense experiences of spiritual introversion are focused through womb, cave, and grave images, and the dynamic of the poem is the struggle for interior reconciliation. At first sight the poems appear to be surrealistic, but their strategy quickly becomes obvious. Roethke uses juxtapositions of nursery rhymes, riddles, songs, and chants to convey the mind in a state of extremity. His intention is to force language to carry the rush and thrust of primitive emotions, to make language instinctive.

"The Lost Son," the best and most representative poem of the cycle, begins with the lost son at Woodlawn where his father lies buried. The persona takes an archetypal journey to the "quick waters" in the valley of the psyche where he confronts "Mother Mildew," the root source of all life. This journey into complete self-absorption, "crawling into your hole and pulling your hole in after you," is terrifying, but a return is achieved through a healing memory from the past—in this case, of the father as the benevolent and ordering principle of the greenhouse world. It is worth commenting on the method of this poem because it is symptomatic of Roethke's quasi-allegorical mode whereby the personal psychological adventure is made the symbol for a spiritual journey. The fourth section of the poem ends with the protagonist back in the greenhouse of childhood.

> Scurry of warm over small plants.
> Ordnung! ordnung!
> Papa is coming!
>> A fine haze moved off the leaves;
>> Frost melted on far panes;

> The rose, the chrysanthemum turned toward the light.
> Even the hushed forms, the bent yellowy weeds
> Moved in a slow up-sway. [*Collected Poems*, p. 57]

Both plants and child respond to the father-sun in a primitive striving toward the light as the mere presence of the paternal principle brings order and assurance to the greenhouse world. It is as though, through the father's cry of order, the redirective will to self-discipline, self-attention, had been discovered, and terror of dissolution arrested. On the personal level, fear and the torment of remorse, raised almost to a mythological level in the childish mind, have been expelled by a recovery of an intimate and benevolent memory of the father. But as Hilton Kramer was the first to insist, in "The Poetry of Theodore Roethke" (1954), there is a further ramification to the image of homecoming: a tension, never stated explicitly, between this image as a private reconciliation with the father and as an "objective dramatization of a certain situation of the soul." What is described is a "Return" in final terms to a "spiritual solidarity," captured in the image of the flowers "giving themselves to the light. . . after their nocturnal drowse" (p. 140). The old notion of "Father Fear" is abandoned as life itself is seen to be creative. The poem ends in a winter purgatorial world, the "beautiful surviving boncs" of weeds swinging in the wind. In a moment of light and silence, the poet experiences an intense communion with the natural world, and this profound sense of interior reconciliation is something Roethke sought throughout his life to understand.

In 1951, Roethke published *Praise to the End!* a sequence of nine poems written in the same surrealistic fashion as the earlier pieces. He wrote, "If intensity has compressed the language so it seems, on early reading, obscure, this obscurity should break open suddenly for the serious reader who can hear the language: the 'meaning' itself should come as a dramatic revelation, an excitement. The clues will be scattered richly—as life scatters them" (*Poet and His Craft*, p. 42). Roethke was a master craftsman. These poems are experiments recording the welter of psychic processes at the level of fantastic logic that psychologists call primary thinking and that is reached by the mind on the extreme edge of psychic distress. The poems speak the "coarse shorthand of the subliminal depths" (*Collected Poems*, p. 170).

The sequence can be thought of as an imitation of Wordsworth's *Prelude*, more psychological and less philosophical than its model, that seeks to record the gestation and evolution of the mind of a child. The first poem, "Where Knock Is Open Wide," describes a prelapsarian world of innocence tragically shattered by the death of the father. The rest of the sequence describes the child's struggle through fears and guilts and onanistic withdrawal to achieve a mature and stable sense of self. The poems are more than the rehearsal of private anxieties and self-disgust; they are night journeys into the subliminal mind.

> I was far back, farther than anybody else.
> On the jackpine plains I hunted the bird nobody knows;
> Fishing, I caught myself behind the ears. [*Collected Poems*, pp. 89-90]

In Roethke's work, minnows are part of the minimal life still on the threshold of beginnings, the extremity of instinct that corresponds to the darting multitudinous life of the mind beneath the rational. Salvation depends upon contact with this part of the self. The implication is that the unconscious, if it harbors desperate fears and guilts, nevertheless will unleash natural, redirective impulses to life. It should not surprise that penetration to the unconscious recovers the transcendental powers of the self. Roethke, following Jung, would insist unequivocally that the psyche, in its deepest reaches, participates in a form of existence beyond space and time. Nature is now discovered to be symbolic.

> Sing, sing, you symbols! All simple creatures,
> All small shapes, willow-shy.
> In the obscure haze, sing! [*Collected Poems*, p. 90]

Roethke regarded nature as sacramental. In moments of intensity, natural objects could sound deep responses within the individual, convincing of a co-inherence of interior being and exterior world in a relation that he called worshipful. In one instance he wrote: "If the dead can come to our aid in a quest for identity, so can the living...including the sub-human. This is not so much a naive as a primitive attitude: animalistic maybe....Everything that lives is holy" (*Poet and His Craft*, p. 24). Roethke's description of nature as symbolic is less a philosophical conception than an animistic belief in a single, creative, propulsive energy, the soul of things, animating all living matter, including the human and subhuman in its embrace. In the stanza in question, he is asking, simply, delicately, whether the directive instinct at the core of his being, which is one with the impulse that moves all nature, is a cry for the father, the ultimate transcendent father as creative progenitor. When he writes, "At first the visible obscures:/Go where light is," it is because "the eye perishes in the small vision." A greater comprehensive vision can bring life to a cosmic unity: "Speak to the stones, and the stars answer." In this directive lies a program of recovery: "I'll seek my own meekness./What grace I have is enough" (*Collected Poems*, p. 91).

In 1952, after what he described as a dry period, Roethke embarked on a new direction in his poetry. "Going to school at Yeats," as he put it, he began to write love poems. The poems, published in *Words for the Wind* (1958) and *The Waking* (1953), are sheer epithalamium to the beloved, rampantly, triumphantly sexual. The beloved is a green elemental creature "easy as a beast," yet like Rilke's lover, she carries immemorial sap in her veins.

> I met her as a blossom on a stem
> Before she ever breathed, and in that dream
> The mind remembers from a deeper sleep. [*Collected Poems*, p. 119]

Love, as one might expect, is sought as a principle of order. It must prove itself a mystical channel to the spirit and a bulwark against an obsessive preoccupation with death.

> Incomprehensible gaiety and dread
> Attended what we did. Behind, before,
> Lay all the lonely pastures of the dead;
> The spirit and the flesh cried out for more.
> We two, together, on a darkening day
> Took arms against our own obscurity. [*Collected Poems*, p. 106]

In *The Lost Son* and *Praise to the End* volumes, Roethke regressed to a language of sheer intuition in his researches into the subliminal mind. In the love poems, his intention seems to have been to include a broader symbolical dimension that could include the metaphysical. Kenneth Burke has analyzed Roethke's early language in his essay, "The Vegetal Radicalism of Theodore Roethke" (1950), where he contrasts his vocabulary with T. S. Eliot's in *The Four Quarters* to show that Roethke deliberately tried to avoid abstraction by such devices as a continual application of communicative verbs to inanimate objects or by replacing eschatological concerns with the concrete notions of womb heaven and primeval slime. Here Roethke tries to incorporate the realm of abstractions within his own aesthetic, without abandoning the spontaneous immediacy that is his greatest strength. His solution is to turn to the lessons of the metaphysical poets: to yoke the abstract to the concrete image. Yet what stays longest with the reader is Roethke's empathic grace.

> Love, love, a lily's my care,
> She's sweeter than a tree.
> Loving, I use the air
> Most lovingly: I breathe. [*Collected Poems*, p. 123]

It is as if the beloved were a manifestation of elemental beauty and Roethke embraces her with the timidity of one submitting to nature: "Nature's too much to know" (*Collected Poems*, p. 123).

Roethke's greatest and final achievement was his North American Sequence published posthumously in *The Far Field* in 1964. There was always an intimate connection between Roethke's life and his art. Arnold Stein, a close friend, says that he lacked the common talents for sustaining himself at the ordinary level of living. "One had the frequent sense that the whole range of wit, knowledge, imagination, and sensitivity hung in the balance; that if the poetry stopped...the whole personality would lose its recognizable shape" (*Theodore Roethke*, p. xiii).

Allan Seager indicated that at this period of Roethke's life, a profound impulse toward wholeness and unity was movingly apparent. These were years of exhilaration and a new sense of freedom discernible in the poetry's impulsive drive for harmony and resolution. Yet these were also times of suffering and illness: "I have left the body of the whale, but the mouth of the dark is still wide" (*Collected Poems*, p. 188). The poems read like final poems, attempts to bring his vision to a synthesis. A poem of age and parting, the sequence expresses the need to find a way to accommodate the fact of death within an acceptable view of life. It is also the fulfillment of a long-standing ambition to come to terms with the western American landscape.

The sequence, with its loose-limbed structure and Whitmanesque cadence, is a meditation on landscape wherein the poet seeks to identify with the natural world, yet he is cut off from complete identification by the spectre of his own death.

> I long for the imperishable quiet at the heart of form;
> I would be a stream, winding between great striated rocks in late summer;
> A leaf, I would love the leaves, delighting in the redolent disorder of this mortal life,
> This ambush, this silence. [*Collected Poems*, p. 188]

The poet would celebrate life as redolent disorder, even as ambush and silence (accepting the potentialities of life and death in its manifold activities), if he could begin to discover a principle of order within contingency. Reality is ordered into form exactly to the degree to which it satisfied thought. Order, in that sense, is the mind finding itself again in things. For Roethke, the perception of order in nature comes not through rational investigation but suddenly in moments of stillness, at-one-ment. He can discover the "imperishable quiet" only through what William Meredith has called a "wise and attentive passiveness" before nature until order is revealed within it, not imposed, but discovered intuitively in embrace (Stein, *Roethke*, p. 41). Any attempt to impose order on nature, and that includes the mechanical order of cause and effect (the terrifying vision of the industrial landscape), as well as abstract idealistic systems of thought (the exclusiveness of ascetic orthodoxy), is anathema to Roethke's sensibility.

The paradox of his attitude toward form is clear in his use of water, the symbol of process and formlessness, to integrate his sequence in its quest for form. The metaphorical burden of the sequence is to reconcile the poet with the element of life as water, with its advance and retreat, its havoc, until finally he can experience these fluctuating orders without threat. But to accept the fluidity of experience, he needs a still center, a "point outside the glittering current" of experience. How, then, to find this order? The North American Sequence is an attempt to recover attachment to place by immersion, almost a kind of baptism, in primal waters. The process will be one of unlearning: "I would unlearn the lingo of exasperation, all the distortions of malice and hatred" (*Collected Poems*, p. 188). His solution is to reject civilized mentality with its egocentric emphasis—"O pride, thou art a plume upon whose head?" (*Collected Poems*, p. 188) and its alienation from nature and to begin to feel his way backward toward a more primitive mode of consciousness that might enter wholly and finally into nature. The solution is one of self-effacement before reality. In a later poem he will ask to be "a simple thing / Time cannot overwhelm" (*Collected Poems*, p. 240). Here, as James McMichael points out so well, he seeks intuitive communion with those mindless things, "at once more transient and more permanent than the concepts with which we try to structure our responses to them" since they are representative of the natural process that subsumes us all ("The Poetry of Theodore Roethke," p. 21).

Symbolic topography is crucial to this theme. The sequence begins at the Pacific, yet Roethke often reminisces back through the interior continent to the Saginaw, Michigan, landscape of youth and childhood, a movement that reproduces the interior journey into the deeper reaches of the self. It is through this regression and subsequent integration of past and present that the poet recovers the attitude of mind that will allow him finally to merge with the dark and oncoming waters. This process is one of de-creation. The mind trapped by its memories roves backward in search of purification until a new category of memory—almost a racial memory—is discovered in the child's celebration of nature: "Once I was something like this, mindless, / Or perhaps with another mind, less peculiar" (*Collected Poems*, p. 200). It is a radical metaphor of belief that asks for commitment to the natural world, trusting that it can accommodate the soul even as it annihilates the accepted categories of self.

As he was writing the North American Sequence, Roethke was also working on individual lyrics in the style of the love poems, which he gathered under the title *Sequence, Sometimes Metaphysical* (1964). These are religious poems, reaching toward "God." Few other major twentieth-century poets have been willing to risk the double heresies of God and of salvation. Eliot, Auden, Yeats, and perhaps Rilke are among the exceptions. Without Eliot's willingness to submit to traditional theological dogma, or Yeats's capacity to construct his own elaborate spiritual system, Roethke found himself in Rilke's position. Emotionally and imaginatively he still felt a strong need for the name of God, yet he was unable to commit himself to any final system of belief. The idea of God becomes in his poetry an emotional hypothesis built out of the sheerest force of will, an act of faith that must be constantly renewed. His poems become assertions of longing, of desperate faith, and also momentary assertions of despair. They are lyric poems. Roethke speaks of them continually as songs: "In purest song one plays the constant fool"; "I'll make a broken music, or I'll die." One is reminded of an earlier line: "O to be delivered from the rational into the realm of pure song" (*Collected Poems*, pp. 244, 240, 172). The belief is that if only one can get beyond cerebration one can begin to attend on final things.

Describing the order of these poems, Roethke wrote: "They begin at the abyss, at the edge of being, and descend into a more human, more realizable condition. They turn away from loneliness to shared love" (*Straw for the Fire*, p. 191). "The Motion" is representative.

Who but the loved know love's a faring-forth?
Who's old enough to live?—a thing of earth
Knowing how all things alter in the seed
Until they reach this final certitude,
This reach beyond this death, this act of love
In which all creatures share, and thereby live. [*Collected Poems*, p. 243]

It is a moving and primitive act of faith in creative love as the propulsive force, the motion of life. In the greenhouse world, child and plant responded to the sun-father in a primitive striving toward the light. In "The Abyss," the tendrils with their eyeless seeking toward the light were the poet's image for his own longing. What the images have in common is the notion of a generative principle of energy or, as the poet would have it, of love, attractive and propulsive, acting from within and from without, that orders the whole of life. This is a common form of mystical belief but one that Roethke has made imaginatively his by his inclusion of the fearful small within its schema.

The last three poems of *Sequence, Sometimes Metaphysical*, "The Restored," "The Right Thing," and "Once More, the Round," are the final note by which Roethke wished to be remembered. He wrote: "In spite of all the muck and welter, the dark, the dreck of these poems, I count myself among the happy poets: 'I proclaim, once more, a condition of joy' " (*Poet and His Craft*, p. 40). In his notebook he wrote: "Poetry comes out of a moral fierceness. There is nothing more disconcerting than when a rich nature thins into despair" (*Straw*, pp. 13, 186).

For him despair comes with the mind's searchings after assurances, but the mind can gain no access to the mystery of being that we incarnate, the only theme that ultimately concerned him. Instead he calls for rage and wailing and the divine madness of the dance as the only appropriate response to life lived in final terms. Celebrating in his figure of the happy man the capacity to rest in mystery without feeling the need to reach after certainties, he rejects the self-destructive and in so doing purges a deep impulse in himself. Few other poets have known so deeply the capacity for self-destructive probing: "The loneliest thing I know / Is my own mind at play" (*Collected Poems*, p. 215). His last poem in the *Collected Poems* is an affirmation of life, a proclamation in the manner of Yeats and Blake. Its power seems to come from its profound assertion of the will to love. For Roethke the greatest power of the poet was the capacity to face up to genuine mystery and celebrate. The book indeed descends as he put it, into a more human, more realizable condition, moving from loneliness to shared love.

Now I adore my life
With the Bird, the abiding Leaf,
With the Fish, the questing Snail,
And the Eye altering all;
And I dance with William Blake
For love, for Love's sake;

And everything comes to one,
As we dance on, dance on, dance on. [*Collected Poems*, p. 251]

Survey of Criticism

There has been much excellent writing on Roethke's work. To date there are six full-length critical studies, two collections of essays, hundreds of articles, and the complementary apparatus of scholarship: biography, letters, edited notebooks, concordances, annotated bibliographies. Roethke was a poet's poet; his triumph over the anguish of his life and his dedication to the craft of poetry were exemplary. Stanley Kunitz's essay, "Roethke: Poet of Transformations," remains one of the most perceptive portraits of Roethke, describing him as a "shape shifter" struggling against the greatest odds to submit to the shapes of his poetic landscape. He inspired many poems, among the best Berryman's "A Strut for Roethke"; Lowell's "For Theodore Roethke 1908-1963"; and Richard Murphy's "The Poet on the Island."

Critical commentaries provide a wide variety of responses to his work. Kenneth Burke's "Vegetal Radicalism," though written in 1950, is still valuable in defining the kind of linguistic virtuosity the reader must bring to Roethke's work. One of the best recent books on Roethke's technique is Richard Blessing's *Theodore Roethke's Dynamic Vision* (1974), an account of Roethke's style as poet and teacher: "In his poems Roethke's 'meaning' —never mind the ostensible subject—is always a celebration of the dance of being, the energy of life" (p. 5). Blessing studies the artistic evolution of Roethke's strategies—of rhythm, theme, diction, imagery, and structural devices—always with a view to seeing how he was driven to record the "terrible and beautiful" dynamism of life.

One of the recurring attacks on Roethke's poetry is against its alleged imitativeness. He was a poet who made continued use of poetic tradition and seemed to have had a personal need to come to terms with the modern masters—Whitman, Yeats, Eliot—so that their cadences were often the starting point for experiments in his work. But this strategy has led to allegations of dependency and lack of originality. The issue is a serious one and discussed at length by Jenijoy La Belle in *The Echoing Wood* (1976), which studies sources and demonstrates how, by "continually referring the reader to a heritage of poetry that at once defines the cultural ambiance in which the work must be understood and aids the poet in moving beyond 'solitary experience' to the creation of transpersonal experience" (p. 4), Roethke is in fact following Eliot's advice in "Tradition and the Individual Talent" to the young writer who would learn from his predecessors.

Finally, Jay Parini's *Theodore Roethke: An American Romantic* (1979) in a collaborative dialogue with previous critical commentaries, places Roethke firmly in the context of American romanticism traced back to its root in Emerson. The autobiographical myth of the greenhouse, "from first to last his primary subject" (p. 4), is explored as the personal variation he played on that great romantic vision, the quest for total immersion in nature. In Parini's hands, Roethke becomes a poet of the "egotistical sublime" in the high romantic mode, and his poetry is traced through its evolutionary development from self-discovery to self-transcendence. In this critical encounter Roethke's place in the American poetic tradition is firmly established.

No doubt there will be many more studies of Roethke's work as readers continue to respond to its challenges. As Parini puts it in his Introduction, "Just as each new generation of poets modifies the views of the previous one, so critics participate in an ongoing critical act." What has been demonstrated to date is that Roethke is indeed one of those rare voices through whom American poetry finds a new center of coherence.

Bibliography

Works by Theodore Roethke

Open House. New York: Knopf, 1941.
The Lost Son and Other Poems. Garden City, N.Y.: Doubleday, 1948.
Praise to the End! Garden City, N.Y.: Doubleday, 1951.
The Waking: Poems 1933-1953. Garden City, N.Y.: Doubleday, 1953.
Words for the Wind: The Collected Verse of Theodore Roethke. Garden City, N.Y.: Doubleday, 1958.
Sequence, Sometimes Metaphysical. Iowa City: Stonewall Press, 1964.
The Far Field. Garden City, N.Y.: Doubleday, 1964.
The Collected Poems of Theodore Roethke. Garden City, N.Y.: Doubleday, 1966.
On the Poet and His Craft: Selected Prose of Theodore Roethke. Ed. Ralph J. Mills, Jr. Seattle: University of Washington Press, 1965.
Straw for the Fire: From the Notebooks of Theodore Roethke 1943-1963. Ed. David Wagoner. Garden City, N.Y.: Doubleday, 1972.

Studies of Theodore Roethke

Blessing, Richard A. *Theodore Roethke's Dynamic Vision*. Bloomington: Indiana University Press, 1974.
Burke, Kenneth. "The Vegetal Radicalism of Theodore Roethke." *Sewanee Review* 58 (Winter 1950): 68-108. Reprinted in *Language as Symbolic Action*. Berkeley and Los Angeles: University of California Press, 1968.
Dickey, James. *Babel to Byzantium: Poets and Poetry Now*. New York: Farrar, Straus, and Giroux, 1968, pp. 147-52.
————. "The Greatest American Poet." *Atlantic* 222 (November 1968): 53-58. Reprinted in *Sorties*. Garden City, N.Y.: Doubleday, 1971.
Kramer, Hilton. "The Poetry of Theodore Roethke." *Western Review* 18 (Winter 1954): 131-46.
Kunitz, Stanley. "Roethke: Poet of Transformations." *New Republic* 152 (23 January 1965): 23-29.
La Belle, Jenijoy. *The Echoing Wood of Theodore Roethke*. Princeton, N.J. Princeton University Press, 1976.
McMichael, James. "The Poetry of Theodore Roethke." *Southern Review* 5 (Winter 1969): 4-25.

Malkoff, Karl. *Theodore Roethke: An Introduction to the Poetry*. New York: Columbia University Press, 1966.

Martz, William J. *The Achievement of Theodore Roethke*. Glenview, Ill.: Scott, Foresman, 1966.

Mills, Ralph J., Jr. *Theodore Roethke*. UMPAW. Minneapolis: University of Minnesota Press, 1963.

Parini, Jay. *Theodore Roethke: An American Romantic*. Amherst: University of Massachusetts Press, 1979.

Scott, Nathan A., Jr. *The Wild Prayer of Longing: Poetry and the Sacred*. New Haven, Conn.: Yale University Press, 1971.

Seager, Allan. *The Glass House: The Life of Theodore Roethke*. New York: McGraw-Hill, 1968.

Stein, Arnold, ed. *Theodore Roethke: Essays on the Poetry*. Seattle: University of Washington Press, 1965.

Sullivan, Rosemary. *The Garden Master*. Seattle: University of Washington Press, 1975.

Barbara Howard Meldrum

O. E. RØLVAAG
(1876-1931)

Biography

Ole Edvart Rølvaag was born 22 April 1876 on the island of Dønna, Norway, just south of the Arctic Circle, in an ancient timber cottage that had been the family home for six generations. The sea and the mountains exerted a strong formative influence. The Seven Sisters, jagged peaks along the eastern horizon, were troll maidens to be feared; during long summer nights, cloud formations between the peaks became a castle more real than anything else to young Rølvaag. As Jehovah was to the Israelites, so *"The Sea Was"* to this boy and his family who depended upon the sea for sustenance. "The sea was kind and beneficent, treacherous and terrible, all depending on his mood," wrote Rølvaag in his autobiographical fragment, "The Romance of a Life." "Upon the sea I lived, most of the time; about it my dream-life was woven; for the sea was at one and the same time the most vital reality and the unfathomable mystery.... The sea was full of the supernatural." The crashing of gigantic breakers echoed in Rølvaag's ears; the tales of fishermen impressed him deeply. "To me the periodic crashes sounded like the detonations of some infernal explosions. No wonder that living in such surroundings should cast shadows on receptive minds." Yet "my natural cheerfulness overcame the awe." Rølvaag asserted that "during my entire childhood I lived in battle with the North Sea.... There was no fear in any of us [Rølvaag boys]." (Jorgenson and Solum, *Ole Edvart Rølvaag*, pp. 2-5). The sea presented a constant challenge; Rølvaag's earliest ambition was to kill a whale. Rølvaag's complex portrayal of nature in his fiction and the psychology of his characters in their interaction with nature surely derive from his early years along the Helgeland coast.

Closely linked to the influence of nature was that of folklore and the Norse sagas, acquired through oral traditions and extensive reading. As a boy, Rølvaag and his friends sometimes read selections aloud and discussed their meaning; Søren Kierkegaard's *Either-Or* was one of their favorites. During this period Rølvaag first became acquainted with Ibsen's works, an interest that continued throughout his life; in later years his course in Ibsen was a favorite for both Rølvaag and his students. The pietism of the Norwegian Lutheran church also influenced young Rølvaag, through his warmhearted mother and his more dogmatic, doctrinally contentious father. These early influences contributed to the special character of his fiction, leading many to conclude that he was more nearly a Norwegian than an American author. For Rølvaag, however, his Norwegian background and American experience were inextricably and dynamically interrelated. He believed the principal factors in American development were the westward movement and immigration; the Norwegians who pioneered in the Midwest were modern-day Vikings responding to the same romantic spirit. Rølvaag's psychological, cultural, and literary roots were undoubtedly Norwegian, but the fact of his emigration together with his New World experience made him Norwegian-American, which to Rølvaag meant being most fully and productively American.

Rølvaag felt the westward pull, which he expressed in more general (nondirectional) terms in *The Boat of Longing* (1921) as a quest for the castle of Soria Moria. Although he loved Norway and his people, he felt frustrated, unfulfilled. A fierce storm, which he barely survived on a fishing voyage, made him aware of the futility of his life and prompted him to write to an uncle, who had emigrated to South Dakota, for a ticket to the New World. It arrived several years later; but Rølvaag's choice was made more difficult when his fishing master offered him a new boat. This material enticement, though tempting, was not enough to answer the longings within, so the twenty-year-old Rølvaag made his way to his uncle at Elk Point, South Dakota. Undoubtedly Rølvaag was torn within by this choice, unable to understand fully the motivation that led him to spurn certain success for an unknown future and to break deep family ties. The sense of loss, even of guilt, later found poignant expression in *The Boat of Longing*.

Three years of farming in South Dakota brought more frustration than fulfillment to Rølvaag. Here, though, he became acquainted with the prairie setting he used in his famous trilogy; here too he perceived the impoverishment of soul that afflicted those immigrants who severed their cultural ties with the homeland and succumbed to a materialistic vision of the good life. Here were the beginnings of his sense of mission: to be a prophet to his people through teaching and writing.

Convinced that he could not fulfill himself without further education and a better command of English, he enrolled at Augustana Academy in Canton, South Dakota, supporting himself by summer work as a traveling salesman and farmhand. He next attended St. Olaf College, graduating in 1905. Then followed a year of graduate study at the University of Christiania (Oslo), where he finished at the head of his class. He had written his first novel, "Nils and Astri," while a student at St. Olaf; attempts to place it with a Norwegian publisher failed, and this early novel was never published. Following a family reunion at Dønna, Rølvaag returned to St. Olaf to teach Norwegian language and literature and to marry Jennie Berdahl, whom he had met during his student years at Augustana.

Throughout his career at St. Olaf, Rølvaag sought earnestly to teach his students about life through the study of literature and to confirm and expand their cultural heritage through the study of Norwegian language and literature. He believed the most difficult, and most dangerous, transition an immigrant had to make was the acquisition of a new language. A people's ways of thinking, even of feeling, are locked within their language; to learn another is an expansion of self, but to repudiate one's native language is to cut oneself off from one's roots. Those who do so are lost souls. His commitment to the continuation of Norwegian heritage in America led him into many activities, including numerous speaking engagements, a term as president of the Nordland Society of America (1919-22), founding membership and service as secretary (1925-31) of the Norwegian-American Historical Association, and the writing of textbooks and a volume of essays, *Concerning Our Heritage* (*Omkring Fedrearven*, 1922). He wrote his fiction in Norwegian but worked closely with his English translators so that the translations published during his lifetime were joint efforts. His strong espousal of the Norwegian language was not anti-English; he did his best to promote careful English composition in his students and his daughter. Because American culture itself provided ample inducements to learn English, he took on the role of prophet for the heritage of his people.

Rølvaag's career as a writer can be dated from his emigration when he kept a diary that later became the basis for his first published book, *Letters from America* (*Amerika-Breve*, 1912). This epistolary account of a young immigrant's first impressions of America, his problems of adjustment, and his efforts to obtain an education was so strongly autobiographical that Rølvaag published under the pen name of Paal Morck. He used the same pseudonym for *On Forgotten Paths* (*Paa Glemte Veie*, 1914), a novel that foreshadows *Pure Gold* (1930) and *Giants in the Earth* (1927) in depicting the loss of soul through a materialistic quest of the Norwegian immigrant, Chris Larsen. Unlike the later novels, the spiritual drama unfolds in doctrinally religious terms, culminating in the deathbed conversion of the protagonist. No English translation of this novel has been published. Rølvaag's next work reflects his anguish during World War I when antiforeign (especially anti-German) Americanism led to an ever stronger repudiation of the cultural heritage of immigrants. *Pure Gold* (*To Tullinger* [Two fools], 1920) portrays the marriage of two children of immigrants, Lizzie and Louis Houglum, who gradually become so obsessed with the pleasures of accumulating money that they sever ties with family, heritage, community, and God, finally dying, individually and alone, of freezing and starvation, actual and symbolic. When the novel was translated for publication in 1930, Rølvaag substantially revised and expanded his text. In 1921 he published the novel closest to his own soul, *The Boat of Longing* (*Laengselens Baat*). Nils Vaag's story begins in Norway, continues in America with his youthful immigration to an alien culture that threatens to drown his sensitive soul, and concludes in Norway where Nils's aging parents suffer their loss of hope through their son.

These novels were all published in Norwegian by Augsburg Publishing House in Minneapolis. Rølvaag was reaching at least a portion of his potential Norwegian-American audience. When he learned that the Norwegian novelist Johan Bojer was coming to America to prepare to write a novel about the role of Norwegian immigrants in settling America, Rølvaag reacted personally because he believed himself best qualified to write such a work. Taking a year's leave of absence from his professorship at St. Olaf, he worked steadily at the novel that was to gain him an international reputation. Besides his own experience, he drew upon information from his father-in-law, Andrew Berdahl, who could provide first-hand reminiscences of the pioneering period. Rølvaag completed his novel in Oslo, where he successfully negotiated Norwegian publication in two volumes (1924, 1925). Norwegian reviewers immediately acclaimed his work; he had reached his second audience, the Norwegians of his homeland. When Lincoln Colcord learned of Rølvaag's work, he became interested in the possibilities of English translation. Thus developed the cooperative translating efforts of these two men, assisted by others, which culminated in a free, idiomatic translation published by Harpers in 1927. Soon named a Book of the Month Club selection, *Giants in the Earth* earned Rølvaag a permanent place in American letters.

Rølvaag continued the saga of Norwegian-American pioneering experience into the next generation through his last two novels, *Peder Victorious* (*Peder Seier*, 1928) and *Their Fathers' God* (*Den Signede Dag* [The Blessed Day], 1931). Although Beret continues as a principal character in these works, they are primarily about son Peder's quest for fulfillment, his rejection of religious and literary heritage, and his gradual recognition of the importance of maintaining cultural ties to the land of his racial roots.

Rølvaag was never physically robust, though he admired strength and drew upon the fabled exploits of his uncles while writing *Giants*. From the time of his graduate student days in Oslo (1905) he was plagued by illness. His biographer, Theodore Jorgenson, believes his illness "colored his moods; it served to intensify his inner life; it gave to his days a rhythmic wave motion" (Jorgenson, "Main Factors," p. 142). Although he worked with seemingly tireless energy, his heart failed him, and he did not live to write the sequels he had planned for Peder and for Nils.

A complex person of many moods, he was both Per Hansa and Beret; the ambiguities sensed by his readers stem in part from the conflicts within himself. Moreover, though Rølvaag's message may at times have seemed overly conservative and reactionary, he grew beyond dogmatism, especially in his religious views. He was strongly affected by the accidental drowning of his five-year-old son, Paul Gunnar, in 1920: "I think it changed my entire view of life." His earlier concept of a logical God who planned and willed all things gave way to a recognition that "much of what takes place is due to chance and to lawbound nature" (Jorgenson and Solum, *Rølvaag*, p. 252). After visiting his father in 1924, he concluded that "religion has served to disturb the natural development of many people" (Jorgenson and Solum, *Rølvaag*, p. 341). Some members of his church severely condemned his trilogy for his use of profanity and sexuality and his often negative portrayals of ministers. Moreover, his own religious views were not obvious because of the detached point of view he adopted. Nonetheless, there is ample evidence that Rølvaag remained a strongly committed Christian; any who doubt this should read his essay, "Christian Doctrine in Ibsen's 'Peer Gynt,' " written in 1930, only a year before his death. Rølvaag's Christian vision became broadly humanistic, as reflected in this advice he gave to a friend: "Be good to all life about you. That I think is the sum and substance of all religion" (Haugen, "O. E. Rølvaag," p. 72). Undoubtedly Rølvaag was well aware of the grim, even pessimistic endings of each volume in his trilogy; the dark vision of Beret's brooding religion seems to prevail. Nonetheless, he chose to identify himself with the hope of Per Hansa's vision. Shortly before his death on 5 November 1931, he chose a burial plot with a westward view.

Major Themes

Rølvaag agreed with historians who named immigration and the westward movement as the two principal distinguishing traits in American historical development. His works embody both of these traits as major themes, though Rølvaag focused more directly and consistently on immigration. The title chosen by Rølvaag's translators (his daughter and granddaughter) for his first published novel—*The Third Life of Per Smevik* (1971 [*Amerika-Breve*, 1912])—dramatizes the immigrant theme, for the protagonist, newly arrived in America, calls his "first life" his years in Norway, his "second life" the journey to America (brief in time but momentous in its psychological significance), and his "third life" his new one in America (p. 1). Most of the narrative focuses on material, external matters (difficulties in learning English, adjustments to farm life and to the landlocked prairie). Rølvaag suggests some of the psychological problems: homesickness, infrequent communication with family, and misunderstandings that arise because of different environments. When Per's father and brother consider emigrating, he does not advise them to come; instead he quotes a Fourth of July speech he has heard that outlines the gains and losses of immigration and concludes that the losses outweigh the gains. This view persists in Rølvaag's novels.

Per Smevik sadly learns that his fellow Norwegian immigrants are too often more concerned with material goals than with spiritual or intellectual values. Rølvaag's subsequent novels continue this theme, usually as a subordinate motif, but in *Pure Gold* it is the principal theme. In an address delivered in 1906 Rølvaag says: "Neither the Yankee nor the Norwegian American has been able to determine the proper relation between earning money and using it in the interest of human wellbeing" (Jorgenson and Solum, *Rølvaag*, p. 100). *Pure Gold* demonstrates the Norwegian-American side of this statement with a vengeance. Extreme materialism coincides with rootlessness. Louis and Lizzie Houglum, descendants of immigrants, have neither direct memories of Norwegian culture nor a dynamic relationship to American culture. In this spiritual wasteland they sever what ties they have to their Norwegian past, partly to become more American (Lizzie insists on changing Lars's name to Louis), partly to save more money (Lizzie wants to economize by cancelling their subscription to *Skandinaven*). What begins as a reasonable desire for financial security and achievement becomes an obsession for both Louis and Lizzie, whose sexual and parental instincts perversely center on their lust for gold. Their psychological deterioration may seem exaggerated, but Rølvaag is careful to show that they are not alone in using money as the measure of value. A Norwegian-American confidence man gets Lizzie to invest in a fraudulent land scheme, and the Lutheran minister seems more intent upon collecting money from his parishioners than upon promoting their spiritual welfare.

Boat of Longing is Rølvaag's only novel that dramatizes scenes in Norway. Even more evocatively than in *Giants in the Earth* he uses Norwegian folklore to suggest theme: the cost of emigration, both to the immigrant and to loved ones left behind. Like Rølvaag, young Nils Vaag responds to a restless yearning for fulfillment by seeking a new life in America. Unlike Rølvaag, however, Nils remains adrift and unfulfilled, a wandering soul who neither maintains essential ties with his fatherland nor pursues his artistic goals with the self-discipline essential to any artist. Rølvaag here explores the theme of the artist. Nils is a violinist who creates music; he is befriended in Minneapolis by an older Norwegian immigrant who is a poet. The poet lacks a cultural milieu that can encourage and give life to his work; he escapes through drinking. Nils's musical talent first emerges in Norway and is closely associated with the yearnings of his soul, which lead him to emigrate. Although he is encouraged by the poet and by another immigrant (an older woman), he does not find an appropriate place for his music. When we last see him, he is standing at a busy street corner, searching; the violin—his gift from Norway—is conspicuously not mentioned. Undoubtedly much of the dynamic vision of Rølvaag's own art came from his immigrant experience. That he was well aware of the perils facing the artist—or any other immigrant with sensitive soul—is poignantly and faithfully expressed in Nils's sad fate.

Giants in the Earth, Rølvaag's acknowledged masterpiece, successfully fuses the two major concerns of his fiction: immigration and the westward movement. Rølvaag emphasizes the human cost of these endeavors: directly, for Beret, who suffers from the loss of cultural ties to her homeland and from the barrenness and privation of pioneering; indirectly, for Per Hansa, who ages before his time and is forced into a fatal snowstorm through a complex of psychological factors that stem from their culturally uprooted condition and their pioneering experience. To Beret, the westward movement is the result of "the west-fever," which is a "plague" (*Giants*, p. 227). To her, the act of pioneering denies the past and its values and exalts instead a materialistic goal that leads to earth's victory over the human soul. Per Hansa, however, responds to the romantic spirit of the age and plays his part in a process Rølvaag describes as "incomparable" in human history: these Nordic pioneering immigrants sought "to do mighty deeds and build for a greater human happiness" ("Vikings of the Middle West," p. 46). Rølvaag praises the accomplishments but recognizes that the pioneer was often "a tragic figure" ("Vikings," p. 86). His view of the westward movement is embodied in the dynamics of Beret's and Per Hansa's contrasting perspectives and in the dynamics of their relationship to each other and to the land. Neither is wholly right or wrong; each represents a point of view that virtually equals the other, so that Rølvaag's art embodies a paradox that can rarely be tolerated in life itself.

After the era of the conquering pioneer comes the era of adjustment and growth. *Peder Victorious* continues Rølvaag's trilogy from the time of Per Hansa's death to Peder's marriage. Central to this novel is the division between first- and second-generation immigrants: a tale of youth growing up is complicated by the immigrant theme, for Peder must wrestle with choices of language and religion that arise because of the immigrant context. The novel seems to end on a fairly positive note (unlike most of Rølvaag's other works), for Beret recognizes the inevitability of Peder's match with Susie, the Irish-Catholic girl, and blesses their union instead of opposing it. However, this novel is part of a two-volume sequel to *Giants*, no more a self-contained work than is the first volume of *Giants* ("The Land-Taking"). The seeds of future discord ripen quickly in *Their Fathers' God* as both Peder and Susie discover painfully that their racial-cultural backgrounds are more important to them than they had realized. The differences are enough to separate them, in spite of an initially strong physical bond. *Peder Victorious* is a novel of youth's rebellion; *Their Fathers' God* is a novel of discord through disunity of the self. At the end, all seems to be lost, but there is at least the recognition that the direction to wholeness and fulfillment lies in fidelity to one's roots. "There is an intimate kinship between the soul and the soil," Rølvaag once wrote. "It's a long process to build a Fatherland" ("Contemporary Writers and Their Works," p. 84).

Rølvaag's fiction explores the major themes of immigration and the westward movement through an intense focus on the psychology of his characters. Subsidiary themes also developed through his psychological approach are marriage and masculine-feminine contrasts, materialism (its effect on the soul and on human relationships), nature (nearly always seen as it affects human beings), and contrasting values (integrity-compromise, change-tradition, Old World-New World, romance-realism, good-evil, youth-age). Several of the novels (especially the trilogy) can be called farm novels: realistic depictions of midwestern farm life. Rølvaag also looks closely at two basic cultural institutions of his immigrant people: the school and the church. Both often become battlegrounds for conflicting attitudes toward the role of Norwegian cultural traditions in American life. All too often, those who should provide wise and charitable guidance for the people are weighed and found wanting. Rølvaag does, however, present a few positive portraits: for instance, the minister in *Giants* and Reverend Kaldahl in *Their Fathers' God* (whose dinner speech in section four of the novel is pure Rølvaag doctrine). Rølvaag's views on the themes he develops are fairly self-evident in the pre-*Giants* novels. His trilogy, however, achieves a remarkable objectivity of tone, especially where major characters are concerned. Although his own views provide the direction of his narratives, he tries to stay true to the psychology of the characters he creates. Because of this, his works are much more than period pieces. They embody the universal dilemmas of the human spirit.

Survey of Criticism

Ole Edvart Rølvaag: A Biography (1939), by Theodore Jorgenson and Nora Solum, remains the basic source for Rølvaag's biography. Liberal quotations from primary sources enhance the value of the book. The authors have utilized the voluminous resources of the Rølvaag collection at St. Olaf College and have drawn upon their personal acquaintance with the author. They include critical commentary on the fiction, especially as such comments derive from their knowledge of Rølvaag's intentions. Essays by various writers contribute biographical perspectives. Lincoln Colcord, "Rølvaag the Fisherman Shook His Fist at Fate" (1928), provides a lively, brief account of Rølvaag's life and the circumstances surrounding the writing and publication of *Giants in the Earth*. John Heitmann, a lifelong friend of Rølvaag, sheds light on the Norwegian roots of Rølvaag's career in "Ole Edvart Rølvaag" (1941). Rølvaag's daughter, Ella Valborg Rølvaag Tweet, draws upon her memories in several essays. Einar I. Haugen, a former student of Rølvaag, utilizes personal knowledge and biographical sources in "O. E. Rølvaag" (1933) but extends his approach to analysis of theme and characterization in the novels; his essay remains a useful introduction to the man and his work.

Paul Reigstad's *Rølvaag: His Life and Art* (1972) is the only book-length study in English of Rølvaag the novelist. The book is heavily biographical, presenting much of the earlier Jorgenson-Solum account in abbreviated form and drawing also upon interviews and correspondence with Rølvaag's widow. Especially valuable is Reigstad's summary and discussion of *On Forgotten Paths*, which is not available in English translation. Analyses of the novels reveal Rølvaag's sources and the literary influences upon him.

Several recent studies have focused on the effect of sources and literary influences on Rølvaag's work. Owen Jordahl, "Folkloristic Influences upon Rølvaag's Youth" (1975), connects Rølvaag's skill as a storyteller to oral tradition as well as to literary folkloristic influences. Kristoffer Paulson, "Berdahl Family History and Rølvaag's Immigrant Trilogy" (1977), illuminates Rølvaag's creative process by demonstrating the realistic basis for incidents in the trilogy. Neil T. Eckstein, "*Giants in the Earth* as Saga" (in Huseboe and Geyer, pp. 34-41), stresses formative literary influences, especially the Icelandic sagas, as a means of explaining the presence and treatment of particular themes, characterization, and description. Steve Hahn, "Vision and Reality in *Giants in the Earth*" (1979), approaches *Giants* through consideration of parallels to the Icelandic sagas, Ibsen, and Kierkegaard. Harold Simonson, "Rølvaag and Kierkegaard" (1977), and Kristoffer F. Paulson, "What Was Lost" (1980), both use the Kierkegaard influence as a means of analyzing Rølvaag's themes and the psychology of his characters. Curtis D. Ruud, "Rølvaag, the Ash Lad, and New and Old World Values" (in Huseboe), emphasizes the role of Norwegian folklore, especially the Askeladd tales and the quest for Soria Moria. Many critics recognize Ibsen's influence; the most useful discussions are by Erling Dittmann, "The Immigrant Mind" (1952), Paulson (in Thorson), Simonson, and Hahn.

Rølvaag's portrayal of immigrant experience has prompted various critical approaches. Theodore Blegen, *Grass Roots History* (1947), and Dorothy Skårdal, *The Divided Heart* (1974), use fictional accounts as sources for the social history of immigration. Nicholas J. Karolides uses fiction for similar purposes in his *The Pioneer in the American Novel, 1900-1950* (1967). Charles Boewe, "Rølvaag's America" (1957), relates Rølvaag's nonfiction statements to an analysis of his fictional portrayal of the immigrant experience. (Lloyd Hustvedt, "Values in Rølvaag's Trilogy" [in Huseboe], uses a similar approach but focuses on value analysis and characterization rather than the immigrant theme.) Several critics stress the problems of cultural loss and the generation gap: Dittmann, Wayne F. Mortenson, Paulson (in Thorson), and S. K. Winther.

Criticism of Rølvaag's portrayal of the westward movement and the pioneering experience has shifted in emphasis in keeping with our changing national views on these subjects. Early critics, especially Henry S. Commager and Vernon L. Parrington, praised Rølvaag for revealing so well the psychological side of pioneering, the human cost, even the futility in individual terms. Nonetheless, Per Hansa was praised as a noble pioneer; Beret was not equal to the challenge (see especially Joseph E. Baker, "Western Man against Nature" [1942], and Robert Steensma, "Rølvaag and Turner's Frontier Thesis" [1959]). Recent critics have taken a more positive view of Beret and a more negative view of Per Hansa's relationship both to Beret and to the land: Robert Scholes, "The Fictional Heart of the Country: From Rølvaag to Gass" (in Thorson, pp. 1-13), Barbara Meldrum, "Agrarian versus Frontiersman in Midwestern Fiction" (1982), and Paulson, "Ole Rølvaag, Herbert Krause, and the Frontier Thesis of Frederick Jackson Turner" (in Huseboe and Geyer, pp. 24-33).

Discussion of the western theme or of nature often leads to a study of the psychology of Rølvaag's characters. Both Ann Moseley, "The Land as Metaphor in Two Scandinavian Immigrant Novels" (1978), and Curtis Ruud, "Beret and the Prairie in *Giants in the Earth*" (1979), see the prairie in *Giants* as "a sexually competitive force" that seduces Per Hansa away from Beret (Ruud, "Beret," p. 219); Ruud's essay demonstrates the possibilities of a close reading of the text. Maynard Fox, "The Bearded Face Set toward the Sun" (1961), is one of the first critics to point out that Per Hansa's failure to understand Beret and meet her needs contributes to his death. He calls Per Hansa "the archetypal masculine in the exploitation of nature," but apparently without passing negative judgment; rather, death, using Beret as agent, is "evil . . . clothed in the mantle of Christianity" (Fox, "Bearded Face," p. 64). Sylvia Grider, "Madness and Personification in *Giants in the Earth*" (1979), concludes that since Beret's recovery from madness leads to the "demonic Plain['s]" triumph over Per Hansa, "she is demon-possessed at last" (p. 117). Sidney Goldstein, "The Death of Per Hansa" (1967), calls Per's death a suicide brought on by Beret's lack of appreciation for his achievements, his best friend's impending death, and his sense that his household "no longer needs him" (p. 466). Meldrum, "Fate, Sex, and Naturalism in Rølvaag's Trilogy" (in Thorson, pp. 41-49), examines the marital relationships of Per and Beret, Peder and Susie as self-determining psychological and physical factors that underlie the stated philosophies of the characters.

Two studies review Rølvaag's novels in terms of single, unifying themes. Raychel Haugrud, "Rølvaag's Search for Soria Moria" (1974), examines Rølvaag's personal search for Soria Moria (happiness or personal fulfillment) and then traces the quests of his protagonists. Erling Larsen, "The Art of O. E. Rølvaag" (1972), defines the essential tragedy in Rølvaag's works as "the spiritual soul destroyed by a material environment" (p. 19). "Spirit" is closely associated with national heritage. Larsen's analyses carefully highlight the ambiguities of Rølvaag's fiction and note structural parallels that give clues to interpretation.

As might be expected, most of the criticism has focused on *Giants in the Earth*, with some critics extending discussion to the other two volumes of the trilogy. A few scholars have touched on all or most of the novels in single essays. Paul Reigstad approaches each novel separately in his *Rølvaag* (1972); only occasionally have essays been devoted to single works (apart from *Giants*). Paulson, "What Was Lost" (1980), and Raychel Haugrud Reiff, "Nils Vaag: Human Soul in Search of the Perfect" (in Thorson, pp. 33-40), analyze *Boat of Longing*, Paulson focusing on the immigrant theme and Reiff stressing the universal quest for the ideal. Robert L. Stevens, "*Pure Gold*: An Appreciation" (in Thorson, pp. 25-31), examines the materialism theme in *Pure Gold*: Lizzie and Louis are extreme manifestations of a pervasive social condition. Addison Hibbard, in "Analysis of O. E. Rølvaag's *Pure Gold*" (1930), analyzes Rølvaag's realistic method in writing a farm novel, which is also a study of degradation of character.

In addition to the studies noted here, many brief discussions or passing references to Rølvaag (especially to *Giants*) appear in countless studies of American literature and culture. The list of doctoral dissertations and master's theses on Rølvaag is growing. Rølvaag continues to receive considerable attention from critics. After the initial enthusiastic reception of *Giants*, however, most of the critical response has come from those of Scandinavian descent and has appeared in midwestern or Scandinavian-American publications. *Giants* may rightly be called a classic of American literature, but to date the author has not received the widespread critical attention he deserves.

Bibliography

Works by O. E. Rølvaag

[Paal Morck.] *Paa Glemte Veie* [On Forgotten Paths]. Minneapolis: Augsburg Publishing House, 1914.

Giants in the Earth. Introduction by Lincoln Colcord. New York: Harper and Brothers Publishers, 1927. English version of *I de Dage* [In those days], 2 vols., 1924, 1925.

"Contemporary Writers and Their Works: *Giants in the Earth*, by O. E. Rølvaag." *Editor*, 6 August 1927, pp. 81-85.

Peder Victorious. Trans. O. E. Rølvaag and Nora Solum. New York: Harper and Brothers Publishers, 1929. English version of *Peder Seier*, 1928.

"The Vikings of the Middle West." *American Magazine* 108 (October 1929): 44-47, 83, 86.

Pure Gold. Trans. Sivert Erdahl and O. E. Rølvaag. New York: Harper and Brothers Publishers, 1930. English version (revised and expanded) of *To Tullinger* [Two fools], 1920.

Their Fathers' God. Trans. Trygve M. Ager. New York: Harper and Brothers Publishers, 1931. English version of *Den Signede Dag* [The blessed day], 1931.

"Christian Doctrine in Ibsen's 'Peer Gynt.' " *Religion in Life* 1 (1932): 70-89.

The Boat of Longing. Trans. Nora Solum. New York: Harper and Brothers Publishers, 1933. English version of *Laengselens Baat*, 1921.

The Third Life of Per Smevik. Trans. Ella Valborg Tweet and Solveig Tweet Zempel. Introduction by Ella Valborg Tweet. Minneapolis: Dillon Press, 1971. English version of *Amerika-Breve* [Letters from America], 1912.

Studies of O. E. Rølvaag

Baker, Joseph E. "Western Man against Nature: *Giants in the Earth*." *College English* 4 (October 1942): 19-26.

Blegen, Theodore C. *Grass Roots History*. Minneapolis: University of Minnesota Press, 1947.

Boewe, Charles. "Rølvaag's America: An Immigrant Novelist's Views." *Western Humanities Review* 11 (Winter 1957): 3-12.

Colcord, Lincoln. "Rølvaag the Fisherman Shook His Fist at Fate." *American Magazine* 105 (March 1928): 37, 188, 190, 192.

Commager, Henry Steele. "The Literature of the Pioneer West." *Minnesota History* 8 (December 1927): 319-28.

Dittmann, Erling. "The Immigrant Mind: A Study of Rølvaag." *Christian Liberty* 1 (October 1952): 7-47.

Eckstein, Neil T. "The Social Criticism of Ole Edvart Rølvaag." *Norwegian-American Studies* 24 (1970): 112-36.

Fox, Maynard. "The Bearded Face Set toward the Sun." *Ball State Teachers College Forum* 1 (Winter 1961): 62-64.

Goldstein, Sidney. "The Death of Per Hansa." *English Journal* 56 (March 1967): 464-66.

Grider, Sylvia. "Madness and Personification in *Giants in the Earth*." *Women, Women Writers, and the West*. Ed. L. L. Lee and Merrill Lewis. Troy, N.Y.: Whitston Publishing Co., 1979, pp. 111-17.

Hahn, Steve. "Vision and Reality in *Giants in the Earth*." *South Dakota Review* 17 (Spring 1979): 85-100.

Haugen, Einar I. "O.E. Rølvaag: Norwegian-American." *Norwegian-American Studies and Records* 7 (1933): 53-73.

Haugrud, Raychel A. "Rølvaag's Search for Soria Moria." *Norwegian-American Studies* 26 (1974): 103-17.

Heitmann, John. "Ole Edvart Rølvaag." *Norwegian-American Studies and Records* 12 (1941): 144-66.

Hibbard, Addison. "Analysis of O. E. Rølvaag's *Pure Gold*." *Creative Reading* 4 (15 February 1930): 153-69.

Huseboe, Arthur R., ed. *Big Sioux Pioneers: Essays about the Settlement of the Dakota Prairie Frontier*. Sioux Falls, S. Dak.: Nordland Heritage Foundation, Augustana College, 1980.

————, and Geyer, William, eds. *Where the West Begins: Essays on Middle Border and Siouxland Writing, in Honor of Herbert Krause*. Sioux Falls, S. Dak.: Center for Western Studies Press, Augustana College, 1978.

Jordahl, Owen. "Folkloristic Influences upon Rølvaag's Youth." *Western Folklore* 34 (January 1975): 1-15.

Jorgenson, Theodore. "The Main Factors in Rølvaag's Authorship." *Norwegian-American Studies and Records* 10 (1938): 135-51.

————, and Solum, Nora. *Ole Edvart Rølvaag: A Biography*. New York: Harper and Brothers, Publishers, 1939.

Karolides, Nicholas J. *The Pioneer in the American Novel, 1900-1950*. Norman: University of Oklahoma Press, 1967.

Larsen, Erling. "The Art of O. E. Rølvaag." *Minnesota English Journal* 8 (Winter 1972): 17-29.

Meldrum, Barbara. "Agrarian versus Frontiersman in Midwestern Fiction." In *Vision and Refuge: Essays on the Literature of the Great Plains*. Ed. Virginia Faulkner and Frederick C. Luebke. Lincoln: University of Nebraska Press for the Center for Great Plains Studies, 1982, pp. 44-63.

Mortensen, Wayne F. "The Problem of the Loss of Culture in Rølvaag's *Giants in the Earth*, *Peder Victorious*, and *Their Fathers' God*." *Minnesota English Journal* 8 (Winter 1972): 42-50.

Moseley, Ann. "The Land as Metaphor in Two Scandinavian Immigrant Novels." *MELUS* 5 (Summer 1978): 33-38.

Parrington, Vernon Louis. *Main Currents in American Thought: The Beginnings of Critical Realism in America: 1860-1920*. New York: Harcourt, Brace, 1930, pp. 387-96.

Paulson, Kristoffer F. "Berdahl Family History and Rølvaag's Immigrant Trilogy." *Norwegian-American Studies* 27 (1977): 55-76.

————. "What Was Lost: Ole Rølvaag's *The Boat of Longing*." *MELUS* 7 (Spring 1980): 51-60.

Reigstad, Paul. *Rølvaag: His Life and Art*. Lincoln: University of Nebraska Press, 1972.

Rølvaag, Ella Valborg. "My Father." *American Prefaces* 1 (April 1936): 105-8.

Ruud, Curtis D. "Beret and the Prairie in *Giants in the Earth*." *Norwegian-American Studies* 28 (1979): 217-44.

Simonson, Harold P. "Rølvaag and Kierkegaard." *Scandinavian Studies* 49 (Winter 1977): 67-80.

Skårdal, Dorothy Burton. *The Divided Heart: Scandinavian Immigrant Experience through Literary Sources*. Lincoln: University of Nebraska Press, 1974.

Steensma, Robert. "Rølvaag and Turner's Frontier Thesis." *North Dakota Quarterly* 27 (August 1959): 100-104.

Thorson, Gerald, ed. *Ole Rølvaag: Artist and Cultural Leader*. Northfield, Minn.: St. Olaf College Press, 1975.

Tweet, Ella Valborg. "Recollections of My Father, O. E. Rølvaag." *Minnesota English Journal* 8 (Winter 1972): 4-16.

Winther, Sophus K. "The Emigrant Theme." *Arizona Quarterly* 34 (Spring 1978): 31-43.

Helen Stauffer

MARI SANDOZ
(1896-1966)

Mari Sandoz is noted as a writer, teacher, historian, and authority on Great Plains Indians. Her first book, *Old Jules* (1935), is the biography of her father, but it is also in many and subtle ways a biography of the early years of the author herself. Indeed all twenty-one of her books reflect in some way her early life as the child of immigrant homesteaders on one of the last frontiers in America, and on her ten years as a struggling writer in Lincoln, Nebraska.

Biography

Mari was born on 11 May 1896 to Jules and Mary Fehr Sandoz, Swiss immigrants to northwestern Nebraska. The oldest of six children, she grew up in a volatile, impoverished household, dominated by her father's violent temper. Because of Jules's erratic behavior and their poverty, the family was held in low regard in the new community, but Mari later realized that she was extremely fortunate in being Jules's daughter and in growing up in that place at that time. The family lived beside an old Indian and trapper crossing on the Niobrara River, not far from two Indian reservations. Often friends of her father—Indians, trappers, traders, settlers, old prospectors—would stop to exchange yarns with him, and Mari grew up learning the history of her area, and also the art of storytelling, from these visitors. The little girl also saw, or heard her parents tell of, the disappearance of the Indians' way of life and the settlers coming to establish their "new" civilization.

Her physical environment also held places of importance to her. Flowing by their homestead, the Niobrara River, known as the Running Water to the Indians, attracted her interest because of its historical aspects, and perhaps even more because of its geographical and geological characteristics. The high, soft limestone cliffs along the bank of the swift-flowing river were repositories of fossils. Jules shared his interest and knowledge of these prehistoric remains with his children. Mari early recognized the ongoing cycles of life and her ties to the ancient past.

Some distance east of the house was Indian Hill, another spot of great significance to the little girl. When she was small the hill, overlooking the Niobrara, still was strewn with ashes from Indian camp and signal fires; the children hunted there for Indian artifacts. This was for her a place for solitude and musing. When she learned that the great Oglala Sioux chief Crazy Horse had lived in this area, had been perhaps on this very hill, it became doubly important to her.

At the foot of the hill, tepees were often set up. Indian friends of Old Jules, coming down from the nearby reservations for visits or hunting, would set their tepees there or across the road from the house. Mari, restricted from leaving the farmstead by her stern father, was allowed to visit and play with the Indian children, as she describes in *These Were the Sioux* (1961). Old Cheyenne Woman, later a major source for her *Cheyenne Autumn* (1953), was one of those who visited frequently. In her early years of writing, Mari evidently failed to realize the importance of the knowledge she gained from her Indian acquaintances, but later she drew heavily on these experiences.

In 1910, when Mari was fourteen, the family moved from the Niobrara place twenty-five miles southeast into the sandhills. The original homestead had been on hard-land table, marginal farmland, west of the hills. Now the Sandozes moved into an area considered even less suitable for farming. It was a harsher physical world. The hills seemed desolate to many: blazing hot in summer, bitterly cold in winter, constantly wind blown, and treeless. Mari soon came to terms with the sandhills, learning details of the landscape, the flora and fauna. They both frightened and fascinated her; it was the Sandoz ranch in the hills that she always considered home. Both the Niobrara place and the sandhills were settings for her writing.

After graduating from the eighth grade, Mari taught in a nearby country school. Two weeks after her eighteenth birthday she married a neighboring rancher, Wray Macumber. She continued to teach intermittently during the next five years. In 1919, Mari divorced her husband and thereafter completely expunged any reference to him or her marriage from all her correspondence and eventually, it seems, from her memory. One of her early stories, "The Vine" *(Prairie Schooner,* Winter 1927), may be based on an incident of the marriage, but no other published work seems to refer to that experience.

In the fall of 1919, Mari left the sandhills for Lincoln, 450 miles across the state. She attended business college, taught again in a western country school, and then in 1922, managed to get admitted to the University of Nebraska at Lincoln as an adult special student; she did not have the required high school credits for regular admission. During the next thirteen years she worked at various jobs, attended the university when she could, and wrote constantly, concentrating on the short story.

During most of those years, Mari eked out a precarious living, preferring to spend her time on the education she knew she needed and on her writing rather than holding a secure job. She worked whenever she could fit it into her other priorities. Diligently she wrote and sent out story after story, but with almost no success. She wrote a novel, also rejected, and, after the death of her father in 1928, wrote his biography. It, too, was rejected time after time.

In 1930, Mari and her friend Eleanor Hinman took a 3000-mile trip to the Rosebud and Pine Ridge reservations in South Dakota, the Custer battlefield in Montana, and sites of other important Indian battles. On the Pine Ridge, they interviewed several Indian veterans of the wars, friends and relatives of Crazy Horse, learning much about the chief whom white historians had never known. Until that time Mari had concentrated her writing on white settlers or protagonists, but after this trip she began to experiment with Indian stories, told from the Indian point of view. None of these was accepted either.

Her poverty and lack of recognition eventually brought on acute depression and ill health. Extremely thin and malnourished, she gave up writing and retired to the sandhills in 1933, but with a job promised her at the Nebraska State Historical Society, she was back in Lincoln within three months, *Slogum House*, her third long work, already started.

In June 1935, fellow employees at the Nebraska State Historical Society heard Mari's rather high-pitched voice exclaiming, on an even higher note than usual: "I don't believe it!" She had received a telegram from the *Atlantic*, announcing that *Old Jules* had won their 1935 nonfiction contest; the prize was $5000. *Old Jules* had been sent to thirteen previous editors, rejected, and completely rewritten thirteen times before *Atlantic* took it.

From that time on, Mari's life was devoted primarily to research and writing. Her battles were no longer with poverty and lack of recognition; instead she began the skirmishes that really never ceased with eastern publishers and editors who wanted to standardize her language or modify her story. She almost always won.

In 1940 the author moved from Lincoln to Denver, ostensibly because of better research facilities for her book on Crazy Horse, but also to escape criticism and harassment by Lincolnites incensed by her 1939 novel about a midwestern state capital, *Capital City*. She asserted it was fiction and allegorical, but local citizens were sure her mythical capital city of Franklin was really Lincoln and that the book's unattractive characters were based on actual people there. When *Crazy Horse* (1942) was finished, she moved to Greenwich Village in New York, temporarily, she said. She had learned that much important western research material had been collected in eastern repositories; she also now acknowledged that a writer needed to be near publishers and editors to work effectively with them. New York, she claimed, was never home to her; she always planned to move back west, and she spent many months of every year in the West, lecturing, promoting her books, and exploring the scenes described in her work, but she died in New York on 10 March 1966. At her request she was buried on a hill on the Sandoz ranch in the sandhills, overlooking the homestead, the hay meadows, and the orchards planted by Old Jules.

Major Themes

Mari Sandoz's major work is her six-volume Great Plains Series, a study of men and women on the plains from the stone age to the present. Three of her finest books, her biographies *Old Jules, Crazy Horse*, and *Cheyenne Autumn*, are included. Her themes, developed throughout the series, indicate her concern for minorities overwhelmed by a majority greedy for their possessions; man's inhumanity to man; nostalgia for lost civilizations of the past; detestation and fear of excessive individual power; admiration for individuals who met their fate with dignity; and the beauty of nature. As is true with most other western writers, Sandoz's work is closely tied to nature. She had a remarkably intimate knowledge of the land on which she grew up—a legacy from her father—and all her works are based on her close association with the natural world. *Old Jules*, for instance, includes in its list of characters, "The Region: The Upper Niobrara country—the hard-land table, the river and the hills." Her paramount interest is the relationship between humans and the land.

Jules Sandoz dominated Mari's life as a youngster and long after she left home, as is clear in her book elucidating his experiences as a settler in a yet untamed country. But her book, once titled *Thunder on the Running Water*, is the biography of a community as well as of her father, the community of the upper Niobrara river country. She researched the subject and the area for years before she began to write, through newspapers, books, letters, and interviews. Even though she had participated in some of the events, she did not trust her memory.

Old Jules has few rivals. With rare skill, Sandoz portrays the strengths and weaknesses of a remarkable man while re-creating the background as it must have been, both the life of the family and of the larger community.

Crazy Horse is also a biography, but in structure, style, and purpose it differs a great deal from *Old Jules*. Whereas *Old Jules* is a string of anecdotes with considerable rising and falling action, *Crazy Horse* is carefully plotted, everything pointing to the inevitable betrayal and death of the hero at the end. Sandoz had a closer sense of identity with this hero, a greater sense of sympathy for him than for any other of her protagonists. Crazy Horse was a successful and charismatic Indian leader and war chief, but it was his mysticism to which the author responded. She also recognized that the life of the Sioux war chief who fought successfully against Generals Crook and Custer before he was killed by treachery had in it the archetypal elements of the Greek classical heroes and that the defeat of this man and his tribe had universal implications beyond those of a tribal chief defeated in the Indian wars of the nineteenth century.

For this book Sandoz developed a language form and point of view compatible with her subject, the Plains Indians. The narrative voice is Indian; the metaphors and similes are Indian terms. While the use of Indian language patterns and points of reference limited her audience, it has the great advantage of giving readers a sense of authenticity concerning Indian tribal life.

Sandoz continued to stress her themes of human greed, as well as the dignity and courage of the oppressed, in *Cheyenne Autumn*. This is the story of the trek of a small band of Cheyennes who fled their hated Oklahoma reservation and attempted to return to their homeland in Montana in the winter of 1878-79, a year after the death of Crazy Horse. Her belief that the United States had destroyed much of its potential greatness because of its treatment of the Indians, its attempts at genocide, is also implied.

Here, too, Sandoz re-creates an Indian culture in minute detail, telling the story from their point of view, using Indian figures of speech. As in *Crazy Horse*, readers know only what the Indians know; thus they are sympathetic to Indians' reactions to the situation. Sandoz stresses the heroism of the fleeing Cheyennes, their idealism, their strong sense of the religious, and their way of life that was almost destroyed by the United States government. The description of the attempted escape of Dull Knife's band from Fort Robinson, Nebraska, and the pursuit and slaughter, is particularly graphic. This book, too, reflects many aspects of the classic epic.

In the other three books of the series—*The Buffalo Hunters* (1954), *The Cattlemen* (1958) and *The Beaver Men* (1964)—the author traces western history using animals as the focus. Particularly in *The Buffalo Hunters* and *The Beaver Men* she develops the theme that human greed destroyed these important animals, upset the ecology, and contributed directly to the destruction of the plains Indians' way of life. In these books, as well as in *Love Song to the Plains* (1961), she emphasizes her contention that eastern financiers used the West as a colonial region, despoiling it in order to bring its riches back to the East.

The three books using an animal as hero and *Love Song* cover long periods of time—*Love Song* begins with prehistoric ages—and very wide landscapes. All are based on Sandoz's prodigious research but are told in an anecdotal style, including vignettes, often direct dialogue, and occasional wry humor, a literary mode clearly drawing from her early recollections of the storytellers in her mother's kitchen during her childhood. The books are well written and interesting, but because they lack a protagonist and contain so much material, they are weaker in structure than the biographies. Readers may have difficulty remembering important details or the characters that race across the pages.

From her first book to her last, Sandoz's ideas and themes are consistent. *The Battle of the Little Bighorn* (1966), published after her death, continues to show her views on American history. She spends relatively little time on Custer (a man she detested), more on the survivors—Benteen, Reno, and others, and on the victors, the Indians. Because of her close association with both Sioux and Cheyenne, she had information about the battle given from their point of view that others lacked. Her sympathy is with the Indians. The irony implicit in their victory that led directly to their defeat is not lost on the author or her readers.

In many ways Sandoz's fiction was experimental and not always successful as far as her reading public was concerned. Her three most successful works, all novellas, are the most conservative in form. *Winter Thunder* (1954), using the severe 1949 blizzard in Nebraska as its focus, relates the adventures of a sandhills country schoolteacher and her pupils, stranded in an isolated pasture for nine days. It was based on an incident in which her niece and pupils were isolated for twenty-three days (fortunately they found a line shack, provisioned). *The Horsecatcher* (1957) and *The Story Catcher* (1963), each tracing the growth of a young Indian boy as he attempts to integrate his personal life with that of his tribe, are replete with intimate details of Indian village life in the 1800s on the plains and use Indian points of view and Indian figures of speech. All three, depicting the reactions of young people to their environments, project the author's ideas of self-reliance, self-restraint, and courage. Her theory that one can become a responsible adult only by meeting and passing a series of tests, and that one can reach maturity only by cutting the apron strings—the sooner the better— is clearly developed in all three stories.

Most of Sandoz's longer fiction is generally considered to be less effective, but it is interesting as it reflects the ideas and goals of the author. *Slogum House* (1937) is her most successful novel. Although the locale is the Niobrara region, the setting is on a mythical bend of the river and in two mythical counties nearby. On the surface the story is of a struggle for land and power in the West. Gulla Slogum, the protagonist, surely one of the most reprehensible and memorable villains in American literature, is a ruthless, will-to-power woman who uses her sons as outlaws and her daughters as prostitutes in her roadhouse to extend her power. On its second level, Sandoz intends the story to be an allegorical study of a will-to-power nation using force and guile to overcome those with good intentions but lacking the will or strength to fight back. Sandoz had read Hitler's *Mein Kampf* and was concerned that too many Americans were attracted to fascist ideas. She feared the possibility that Hitler would one day reach the United States.

Her second long work of fiction, *Capital City* (1939), is more easily recognized as allegory and less interesting as a novel. The third in her allegorical trilogy, *The Tom-Walker* (1947), tracing effects of the Civil War, World War I, and World War II, on one family, suffers from similar problems. The characters in both are flat, the plots obvious and contrived, and the machinery almost visible. Both are prophetic of world events, however, and *Capital City* is interesting as an experiment in the author's attempt to make the city itself, rather than an individual, the protagonist.

Son of the Gamblin' Man (1960) gave the author more trouble and is perhaps the least satisfactory of her novels. In attempting to re-create the life of the famous American artist Robert Henri, she determined that she would incorporate only those facts about his family she could verify. Because Henri, who lived as a youngster in the Nebraska town named for his father, John Cozad, had deliberately obscured much of his early life, Sandoz was at a disadvantage in refusing to speculate on or invent pertinent scenes. She had set herself an almost impossible, and some thought unnecessarily rigid, standard. Her intent was to illustrate the remarkable development of Henri's artistic talent in a family, time, and place from which such development was unusual and unexpected. Again, the result is a flawed novel, but an interesting experiment for the writer. Here, as in all her other work, the theme is the relationship of the man and the land. The man shaped the land, but the land, in turn, shaped the man, and she was interested in both facets.

Sandoz never attempted to write on a subject for which she did not feel emotional ties, but she combines her sympathy for her heroes with solid historical research, much of it in primary material, some never used by other historians. She quarrels with the histories and the historians who perpetuated incorrect information. Something of a mystic, she shares with most other western writers the classical view of myth and tragedy, and is attracted to the use of myth, image, and symbol. The concrete images of childhood include the guns of her father and the cattlemen he opposed; the smoky kitchen of her home; Indian Hill, the Niobrara, and the sandhills. Later she includes the image of the magnificent Nebraska State Capitol. There is also her constant awareness of all aspects of nature, the physical environment.

Survey of Criticism

Sandoz's work has until recently been largely ignored by major critics. The difficulty in placing her nonfiction in a recognized literary category to some extent may account for the lack of critical attention in American literature. That in her nonfiction she uses the research techniques of the historian but writes in the narrative voice causes a problem for those who prefer a recognized model by which to judge a book. Sandoz's work is known to most western writers and authorities; they use it for reference but seldom have discussed it as literature.

Within recent years, interest in the author and her work has increased. Published articles evaluating her literary techniques are appearing, such as Pam Doher's "The Idioms and Figures of *Cheyenne Autumn*" (1977), which examines Sandoz's use of figures of speech to picture the world of the Cheyennes. Selections from Sandoz's longer works are now in several anthologies, and dissertations and theses are in progress. At a recent Western Literature Association meeting, the number of papers relating to her work was second only to those on Willa Cather. Her name and work are appearing more frequently in collections of biographies of American writers. Among unpublished sources, Kathleen O'Donnell Walton's "Mari Sandoz: An Initial Critical Appraisal" (1970) covers all Sandoz's major works, and Helen Winter Stauffer's "Mari Sandoz: A Study of the Artist as Biographer" (1974) is concerned with the writing of *Old Jules*, *Crazy Horse*, and *Cheyenne Autumn*.

Most studies to date tend to dismiss Sandoz's fiction as inferior, pointing out the weaknesses of her work rather than the experimental aspects or the author's intent and goals. However, Helen Struble Meldrum's "Great Plains Women, Fact and Fiction, with Examples Chiefly from the Writing of Mari Sandoz" (1962) is a thoughtful consideration of several of the novels. Beatrice Morton applies feminist criticism in "A Critical Appraisal of Mari Sandoz' *Miss Morissa*: Modern Woman on the Western Frontier" (1977); Scott Greenwell discusses authorial intent in two of Sandoz's early proletarian works in "Fascists in Fiction: Two Early Novels of Mari Sandoz" (1977). Rosemary Whitaker compares the author's attitude and responsibility toward her material in "Violence in *Old Jules* and *Slogum House*" (1981). Other studies of individual novels are underway.

Since Sandoz's death in 1966, memoirs or recollections of the author have appeared in several journals and magazines, but there is no definitive book-length study of the writer, her life, and work, although Helen Winter Stauffer's *Mari Sandoz: Story Catcher of the Plains* will be published in 1982 by the University of Nebraska Press. Biographical articles, such as Dorothy Nott Switzer's "Mari Sandoz's Lincoln Years" (1971) and Bruce Nicoll's "Mari Sandoz: Nebraska Loner" (1965), both relating to Sandoz's years in Lincoln, are interesting but are based on personal recollections rather than on research. Caroline Sandoz Pifer's *Making of an Author* (1972) is a useful account by the author's sister.

All of Sandoz's books are still in print. Some are praised and in some cases considered definitive works by historians, anthropologists, sociologists, geographers, and students of women's writing. Her nonfiction is used as texts in schools, more often studied, I suspect, as history or social science than as literature. The interest her books generate in other fields does not denigrate their worth as literature; serious literature, after all, often embraces other areas as it expresses the writer's world view.

Bibliography

Works by Mari Sandoz

Old Jules. Boston: Little, Brown, 1935.
Slogum House. Boston: Little, Brown, 1937.
Crazy Horse: The Strange Man of the Oglalas. New York: Alfred A. Knopf, 1942.
Cheyenne Autumn. New York: McGraw-Hill, 1953.
The Buffalo Hunters: The Story of the Hide Men. New York: Hastings House, 1954.
Miss Morissa: Doctor of the Gold Trail. New York: McGraw-Hill, 1955.
The Horsecatcher. Philadelphia: Westminster Press, 1957.
The Cattlemen: From the Rio Grande Across the Far Marias. New York: Hastings House, 1958.
Hostiles and Friendlies: Selected Short Writings of Mari Sandoz. Ed. Virginia Faulkner. Lincoln: University of Nebraska Press, 1959.
Love Song to the Plains. New York: Harper and Row, 1961.
The Beaver Men: Spearheads of Empire. New York: Hastings House, 1964.
The Battle of the Little Bighorn. Philadelphia: J. B. Lippincott, 1966.
Introduction to Helen Blish and Amos Bad Heart Bull. *A Pictographic History of the Oglala Sioux*. Lincoln: University of Nebraska Press, 1967.
Sandhill Sundays. Lincoln: University of Nebraska Press, 1970.

Studies of Mari Sandoz

Doher, Pam. "The Idioms and Figures of *Cheyenne Autumn*." *Platte Valley Review* 5 (April 1977): 119-30.
Greenwell, Scott. "Fascists in Fiction: Two Early Novels of Mari Sandoz." *Western American Literature* 12 (August 1977): 133-43.

MacCampbell, Donald. "Mari Sandoz Discusses Writing." *Writer* 48 (November 1935): 405-6.

McDonald, Judith L. "Anteus of the Running Water: A Biographical Study of the Western Nebraska Years of Mari Sandoz, 1896-1922." Research paper, University of Denver, 1972.

Meldrum, Helen Struble. "Great Plains Women, Fact and Fiction, with Examples Chiefly from the Writings of Mari Sandoz." Master's thesis, University of Wyoming, 1962.

Moon, Myra Jo, and Whitaker, Rosemary. "A Bibliography of Works by and about Mari Sandoz." *Bulletin of Bibliography* 38 (April-June 1981).

Morton, Beatrice K. "A Critical Appraisal of Mari Sandoz' *Miss Morissa*: Modern Woman on the Western Frontier." *Heritage of Kansas* 10 (Fall 1977): 37-45.

Nicoll, Bruce H. "Mari Sandoz: Nebraska Loner." *American West* 2 (Spring 1965): 32-36.

Pifer, Caroline Sandoz. *Making of an Author: From the Mementoes of Mari Sandoz*. Gordon, Nebraska: *Gordon Journal* Press, 1972.

Stauffer, Helen Winter. *Mari Sandoz, Story Catcher of the Plains*. Lincoln: University of Nebraska Press, 1982.

———. "Mari Sandoz: A Study of the Artist as Biographer." Ph.D. dissertation, University of Nebraska, 1974.

———. "Two Authors and a Hero: Neihardt, Sandoz, and Crazy Horse." *Great Plains Quarterly* 1 (January 1981): 54-66.

Switzer, Dorothy Nott. "Mari Sandoz's Lincoln Years." *Prairie Schooner* 45 (Summer 1971): 107-15.

Walton, Kathleen O'Donnell. "Mari Sandoz: An Initial Critical Appraisal." Ph.D. dissertation, University of Delaware, 1970.

Whitaker, Rosemary. "Violence in *Old Jules* and *Slogum House*." *Western American Literature* 16 (Fall 1981): 217-24.

JACK SCHAEFER
(1907-)

Biography

Jack Schaefer's career is marked by a versatility of interests that reflects a restless determination to chart new courses, to examine new insights. Born in Cleveland, Ohio, on 19 November 1907, he was not a Westerner by birth or inclination. His father, a lawyer, was greatly interested in Abraham Lincoln, and likely this encouraged Schaefer's abiding interest in history. Earning the bachelor of arts degree from Oberlin College in 1929, his concentration was in Greek and Latin classics, as well as creative writing (Haslam, *Jack Schaefer*, p. 6). Upon graduation, he spent a year in graduate studies (English literature) at Columbia University, but when he tried to pursue a new interest for his thesis— the development of motion pictures—he was refused. No doubt this experience with academia helps explain his comment that "nothing that I took in college ever helped me with my work. I'd say that the value of a college education is that it teaches us *how* to learn" (Nuwer, "An Interview with Jack Schaefer," pp. 48-49).

Leaving Columbia in 1930, Schaefer turned to a career in journalism, beginning as a United Press reporter. He held a number of editorial positions on newspapers in Connecticut, Maryland, and Virginia; from 1931 to 1938 he combined journalism with a stint as assistant director of education at the Connecticut State Reformatory. Somewhat surprisingly, Schaefer declines to espouse journalism as a learning ground for aspiring writers. It was a worthwhile apprenticeship for him only because "it was editorial work and on papers that still regarded editorial pages as more important than comics and sports and insisted on reasonable competence with knowledge and study and thought behind it" ("Autobiographically Speaking," *Adolphe Francis Bandelier*, p. 22). His own misgivings aside, it is this very "knowledge and study and thought behind it" that critics so frequently identify as his greatest contributions to western fiction.

Although he was clearly successful at journalism, it did not fully satisfy him. In 1945 he was acting editor of a paper in Norfolk, Virginia. As a means of relaxation, he started to write fiction in the evenings. Most of his reading had been in history, and unaware of what he terms "the tremendous amount of bad Western writing that was flooding the market" (Nuwer, "Interview," p. 50), he began a short story about a legend of the West; it grew into a novella, which he submitted to *Argosy*. An editor brought the manuscript home by mistake, read it, and accepted it. It was published as a three-part serial in July, September, and October 1946, with the title, *Rider from Nowhere* (Marsden, "*Shane*," p. 60). By 1948, Schaefer had gone to New York to find a publisher for a revised version, now titled *Shane*, and in 1949 Houghton Mifflin published the novel.

With the success of *Shane*, Schaefer was encouraged to pursue writing fiction full time. Two novels, *The Canyon* and *First Blood*, were published in 1953, and two collections of short stories appeared about the same time. Yet though he had four books of western writing in print, Schaefer had never been west of the Mississippi. At the invitation of *Holiday* magazine, he traveled through the West, writing a series of articles. He was soon won over, and two weeks after his return, he was on his way back. Originally headed for Colorado, he was detoured to New Mexico, where he still resides (Nuwer, "Interview," p. 54).

Major Themes

Although any discussion of Jack Schaefer's career need not end with *Shane*, it would be fruitless not to begin with it. Everyone knows Shane. It may not be the most famous western novel; it is arguable that titles such as *The Last of the Mohicans*, *The Virginian*, or *Riders of the Purple Sage* are more recognizable. But *Shane* is a book people have read—and continue to do so. By 1978 over 4 million copies were in print in more than seventy editions in thirty-one languages (Marsden, "*Shane*," p. 60). More recently, a committee of British readers selected it as one of the hundred best novels of the twentieth century.

Everyone knows *Shane*. Young readers love it: it is short; it has action; it has a young narrator who has the good fortune to know a hero who has the power and wisdom—and yes, toughness—to enforce justice singlehandedly. Teachers like to teach it because it has literary merits commonly absent in popular literature: the natural symbolism of the masculine stump-pulling scene and the feminine baking scenes; the elegant, quicksilver prose perfectly suited to its subject; characters who are at once recognizable yet unique; the themes of sacrifice, loyalty, honor, courage; and even a tasteful treatment of a love triangle. And scholars compete to uncover multiple layers of its "meaning": epic, Freudian, Judeo-Christian, mythic, archetypal.

From a perspective of over thirty-one years, it is safe to say that *Shane* has the staying power characteristic of quality literature. But the brilliant magnitude of its success should not blind readers to the luster of Schaefer's other works, for it is a tribute to his artistic integrity that having written *Shane*, he was not content to rewrite it in thinly disguised imitations. Schaefer's enduring accomplishment as a western writer is his versatility of subject, tone, and themes. He is the author of several novels, three collections of short stories, and a number of nonfiction works. *Old Ramon* (1960) and *Stubby Pringle's Christmas* (1964) have been labeled juvenile novels, although they may as easily be read as allegories. *Monte Walsh* (1963) is his longest, most ambitious, and in some ways, best effort. *Company of Cowards* (1957) describes the rehabilitation of Civil War deserters and only in the last pages is it recognizably "western." He has also edited a collection of short stories by other writers, written nonfiction, and most recently addressed environmental and philosophical concerns in *An American Bestiary* (1975) and *Conversations with a Pocket Gopher* (1978).

The best of these works—and there are many—evidence the same skilled craftsmanship, historical veracity, and sharp insight into character so evident in *Shane*. Yet his short and long fiction stand apart from the familiar formulas. There are nature stories, animal stories, Indian stories, tall tales, pioneer stories, cavalry stories, to name a few. Within this broad range are several themes that form the core of his work. One is maturation, the individual's attempts to reconcile personal desires with the demands of society. The other is common to all other western writers: an attempt to determine the effects of western expansion on the land and those who went there.

In *Shane*, the theme of maturation is filtered through the observations of the young narrator, Bob Starrett. To be sure, the novel embodies the mythical aura that Schaefer intended to create, a mysterious, self-sufficient hero who comes from nowhere to resolve the familiar conflict between good and evil. But in many important ways, the novel is the account of how a boy comes to terms with the difficult and dangerous problems of a hostile world he is only beginning to understand. For although Shane's physical prowess with fists and guns stands out so prominently, beneath it are manifestations of deeper values: loyalty, self-sacrifice, compassion. These are the qualities that Bob finds on a human scale in his father, and the confluence of his two role models allows Bob to "stay clean inside through the muddied, dirty years of growing up" (*Shane*, p. 202). This merging of Shane as avenging god and symbol of human potential is evident in the last pages of the novel. The retrospective narration of an adult Bob shows us that his story of Shane offers more than the familiar deus ex machina resolution of the traditional gunfighter story. For Shane has not left entirely; he is in the rock-solid corral post he set on the Starrett farm and in the abiding example of decency and courage he set for Bob.

On a smaller scale, the short story "Jacob" also examines the way in which heroic role models, even those glimpsed for an instant, shape the values of one's later life. But in almost all other ways, this story is the opposite of *Shane*. Jacob (Mountain Elk) is a defeated Nez Percé chief being transported by train to a reservation; his nobility is not found in victory but in his coming to terms with defeat. Like the other boys anxious to see the fierce Indians passing through town, the narrator is disappointed at the frailness and smallness he finds. But this perception changes when he witnesses a scene at the back of the train. Insulted and manhandled by a boorish soldier, Jacob heaves him off the train with the effortless ease of a Shane. The boy is struck not so much by Mountain Elk's physical prowess but his unfaltering courage as he quietly faces the soldier's gun, unflinching, waiting for the bullet. The narrator then understands that his surrender was not due to fear of death but for the salvation of his people. And in that moment the storyteller comes to understand that humiliation can come only from within. The story concludes with the boy's remark, "Remembering that has helped me sometimes in tough spots" (*Collected Stories*, p. 229).

First Blood is a novel that also presents a young protagonist with differing role models who force him to define his values. But it also expands upon the theme of growing up through its consideration of the individual's responsibility to society. Jess Harker is a freight driver drawn to the bravado, skill, and quick action of Race Crim. Tom Davisson is a stolid sheriff who stands for a legal system reliant on due process for the protection of all. In the end, Jess reluctantly upholds responsibility to the community good by killing the vengeful Race. But there is no easy resolution of his competing instincts, and his decision is not made without reservations about the pain of growing up: "Things were so much easier when I was young and living was simple...without the endless shading gradations.... *If this is being a man...I don't like it. But I can't change it*" (*First Blood*, p. 105).

The Canyon also examines the growing-up process by opposing personal desires to community good. Little Bear, a Cheyenne, cannot condone his culture's commitment to war and the pain it brings to all involved. After stumbling into a canyon, he comes to prefer the isolation of nature. He then rejoins his tribe, marries, and returns to the canyon, where his son is born. But when his son becomes ill and dies, Little Bear learns with difficulty the futility of cutting off oneself from society: it has cost him the medical knowledge and cumulative experience of others that might have saved the child. Little Bear's epiphany is an eloquent expression of fundamental humanism:

A man comes into a canyon and makes it his own. With the cunning of his mind and the courage of his heart he makes it his own.... But he has not done this alone.... In his hand is a knife that was made far away by another man, a knife that was given to him by an old one, a great one. In his mind is the knowledge to make fire and weapons and clothing and to find food and to provide shelter, knowledge given to him by those who taught him when he was a boy and those who showed him by their own doing.... By himself he is nothing. Only the courage is his alone. All of those others are with him, even in his canyon, and he cannot ever be free of them for what they have given is with him and is part of him and without them he could not have made the canyon his own. [*The Canyon*, pp. 118-19]

On the personal level, then, many of Schaefer's protagonists are able to grow up satisfactorily, accommodating the demands of society and their personal integrity. When Schaefer confronts the broader theme of western growth and settlement, however, his vision is more unsettling. The transformation of the frontier that he chronicles is a steadily declining world for which man is responsible. The coming of civilization to the West is permeated by its own corruption, and nothing escapes that corruption— not nature and not the emerging society.

"Something Lost" is an allegory of the harmful effects of civilization. It is a simple story with two major characters, a man and a bear. The man is the first human in the valley. For some time the two coexist, for the bear has no prior experience of man and the man has no desire to confront or exploit the bear. But the man's presence inevitably attracts other, lesser men—two failed miners out to steal the man's prospected gold. About to be tortured, he tells them that it is hidden in a cave he knows the bear inhabits. The bear kills the surprised thieves but is wounded in the fight. The balance of man and nature has been upset, however, and the man is later forced to kill the injured bear. Knowing his own guilt in destroying the harmony of primeval nature, the man leaves the valley, "unbelievably small in the vastness...with...a new sense of loneliness and a sense of something lost" ("Something Lost," *Collected Stories*, p. 198).

The theme of man's responsibility for his actions against nature is again evident in "Enos Carr," a story about an old hunting guide in the modern West. Enos states that only through a sense of humility will man be sensitive to the rights and problems of "lesser" animals. This humility is dramatized in "Stalemate" when a cocky mountain man goes after a grizzly for the $500 reward. But the man's cockiness gives way to respect when the bear has the opportunity to kill him but does not. In an act of symbolic retribution, the man tracks the bear with great effort and skill, captures it in the sights of his high-powered rifle— then spares it.

Another theme involving the effects of western settlement is that of the changing role of the individual in society. In *Shane, First Blood, The Canyon, Stubby Pringle's Christmas*, and other works, the society of the nineteenth-century West appears to move forward not unerringly but hopefully. But still other works address the results of progress with less hopeful conclusions. *Monte Walsh* dramatizes the diminution of individual freedom as the world becomes denser and more relentlessly technological. It is a sprawling account, covering Monte's early cowboy days from 1872 to his death in 1913. The early years teach him the value of loyalty, friendship, and an honest day's work. One of the best achievements of the novel is its depiction of the routine, gritty life of the cowboy who did "the hard rough work that stiffened the spines of the men and made them proud they could do it" (*Monte Walsh*, p. 122).

The novel also deals with the concept of loyalty on a number of levels: to oneself, to friends, to the outfit, to a way of life. But the world is in flux and eventually passes Monte by. Open range gives way to barbed wire, independent owners are bought out by syndicates, the horse gives way to the automobile. By the close of the novel, Monte is an eccentric holdover stubbornly maintaining his way of life in increasingly remote regions. It is Monte's quixotic resistance to a spiritless world that reveals Schaefer's regret for the values lost in the wake of progress.

The Kean Land (1959) and *Mavericks* (1967) echo this sense of regret with an edge of bitterness. Their protagonists are locked in by encroaching cities, suburbs, and factories. In *Mavericks*, old Jake Hanlon comes to realize, despairingly, that he has inadvertently helped to destroy the wildness and freedom of the mustangs he loves so well. He sees the highway as "the symbol. . . of the relentless onrush of what was called progress, of inevitable indifferent power driving forward regardless of what might be in its path. . . , taking over the whole world" (*Mavericks*, p. 169). Schaefer's "conversations" with animals offer a final rebuke to all who blindly march down the wrong trail. Recently he has pointed out that it is not civilization that he blames: "It is the *kind* of civilization we humans have been pursuing and developing in modern times, initiated in the industrializing nations and now spreading everywhere else. There have been and there could be other types of civilization. We have simply opted for the wrong kind" (letter to the author).

Nevertheless, it would be a mistake to hold Schaefer accountable for a pessimism that many would agree is an essentially accurate assessment of American history. For however reliable the historical basis of his work, it is only the backdrop for characters who occupy center stage. And these characters (with the exception of Shane) are not symbols or manifestations of a national consciousness. They are individuals, and regardless of the historical patterns stretching behind and before them, they must be measured on individual merit.

Judging by the successes many of his characters achieve, it is plain that Schaefer refuses to adopt the guise of knowing cynic. His works are full of the victories that bring meaning and value to the lives of his people. Foremost among these qualities is the commitment to honest effort honestly given. His characters, he has said, are "more dedicated to wringing some meaning out of their 'ordinary' jobs and lives than in performing glamorous heroics" (letter to the author). For Tom Davisson, it is a dedication to duty independent of the approval of others: "It's got to do with doing my job and what a man believes in" (*First Blood*, p. 49). For the title character of "Hugo Kertchak, Builder," it is a stubborn refusal to compromise quality with the shortcuts of technology. For Monte Walsh, it is the knowledge that a man is measured in "seasoning. . . absorbing the skills of a trade, of a way of life" (*Monte Walsh*, p. 31). In "Salt of the Earth," it is Clyde Foskins's inability to accept retirement when there is work to be done and the will to do it. In *Old Ramon*, it is an unwavering dedication to the welfare of the flock.

In the end, perhaps, the quality that underlies all of Schaefer's characters and themes is endurance. Not survival, merely, for that suggests compromise at any cost, a trait notably absent in his people. By facing the challenges of fears gnawing within and dangers threatening without, his characters rise to meet these perils on their own terms, and they endure.

Survey of Criticism

Robert Mikkelsen's "The Western Writer: Jack Schaefer's Use of the Western Frontier" (1954) is the first attempt to analyze Schaefer's success in breaking from stereotyped versions of the Western. Mikkelsen outlines the two central elements that subsequent critics develop: the use of the frontier to reveal the individualism of characters and a fresh description of the environment. Mikkelsen contends that *First Blood* is a representative novel that depicts the individual's need to make decisions after examining the values of others. Through an immediacy of description that gives the West a tangible reality, Schaefer creates situations that demand both moral and physical action based upon senses of justice and decency.

Gerald Haslam expands many of these observations in "Jack Schaefer's Frontier: The West as Human Testing Ground" (1967). Haslam contends that because Schaefer avoids the formulaic plots and easy sentimentality of the popular Western, he is more accurately described as a writer of a sectional literature that combines realism and romance. Haslam observes that *Shane* describes the competing value systems inherent in the early frontier and the growing civilization that is changing it. Citing Schaefer's admission that he attempted to create an American version of the knight-errant, Haslam concludes that the author's concern, "like that of ancient tale-tellers, is man and man's endless struggle to prevail in a world he can scarcely understand" ("Schaefer's Frontier," p. 71).

The theme of individual maturation is extended to encompass national maturation in Fred Erisman's "Growing Up with the American West: Fiction of Jack Schaefer" (1974). Using *Shane, First Blood, Company of Cowards,* and *The Canyon* for illustration, Erisman traces the four major characteristics of nationhood proposed by Clinton Rossiter. He concludes that Schaefer is optimistic regarding American potential; if the nation recognizes its strengths and limitations, it "will endure, growing up, like its people, with serenity, dignity, and worth" (Erisman, "Growing Up," p. 73). This study illuminates the fact that Schaefer's West is no unchanging twilight world but one that evolves through the actions of the individuals who confront it.

The theme of national development is also the focus of Michael Cleary's "Jack Schaefer: The Evolution of Pessimism" (1979), which disputes the optimistic conclusion of Erisman. The article measures the effects of civilization on the West by charting the six stages of frontier development defined by Frederick Jackson Turner. Examining the effects of settlement in *Shane, First Blood, The Kean Land, Monte Walsh,* and *Mavericks,* Cleary finds a gradual shift of perception from the initial optimism of *Shane* to the pessimism of *Mavericks,* and he concludes that the beginning of Schaefer's career is marked by preconceived notions, which inspired the elegiac *Shane.* But as he followed his theme through historical developments of the twentieth century, "he was disenchanted by the negative influences of civilization: the reality of the present did not measure up to the promise of the romantic past" (Cleary, "Jack Schaefer," pp. 46-47).

James C. Work also views Schaefer's work as a mirror to history. "Settlement Waves and Coordinate Forces in *Shane*" (1979) traces the three settlement waves that John Mason Peck theorized. Work states that *Shane* is a manifestation of what happens when there is a collision of two waves of civilization: that of the pioneer opportunist and the civilizing agriculturist. The author finds that the resolution of the novel hinges on the coordination between the primitive characteristics of the first wave (Shane) and the civilized force of the third wave (the Starretts).

Gerald Haslam's pamphlet, *Jack Schaefer* (1975), is the most comprehensive treatment of Schaefer to date. Building on the themes of the individual in society and the historic development of the West outlined in his earlier article, Haslam provides a thorough and insightful analysis of biographical information, themes, style, and Schaefer's place in western fiction. *Shane* is viewed as mythic and symbolic. Haslam discusses a number of the short stories, suggesting their versatility and merit. There is also a solid appraisal of the film version of *Shane* weighed against the strengths of the novel. He also offers thoughtful commentary on works infrequently discussed, such as *Company of Cowards*, *Old Ramon*, and *Monte Walsh*.

In addition to Haslam's pamphlet, two articles offer a good view of Schaefer's personal and professional background, the initiation of his writing career, publishing history, and his comments about western writing. Henry Joseph Nuwer's "An Interview with Jack Schaefer" (1973) provides insight into Schaefer's upbringing and writing interests. Michael T. Marsden's "*Shane*: From Magazine Serial to American Classic" (1977-78) covers the novel's origins, its redivisions and additions (including the famous stump-pulling scene), and the manner in which the dark vision of *Mavericks*, Schaefer's last novel, serves as ironic counterpoint to the hope and positivism of *Shane*.

Although primarily concerned with the film treatment of the novel, James K. Folsom's "*Shane* and *Hud*: Two Stories in Search of a Medium" (1970) enables readers to understand better the merits of the written version. Discussing the inherent differences between the two art forms, Folsom points out the book's more complex vision engendered by the retrospective point of view and deliberate ambiguity of physical descriptions. Harry Schein's "The Olympian Cowboy" (1955) only tangentially deals with the film ("an imperfect attempt") but is notable for its perception of the film Western as a ritualistic embodiment of American mythology, encompassing the three elements of the genre: symbolic, psychological, and moral.

Two quite different articles attempt to define Schaefer's view of societal responsibility. In "Jack Schaefer: The Writer as Ecologist" (1978), Fred Erisman discusses how Schaefer's apparently recent concentration on ecological issues is rooted in his fictional treatment of man and the environment and the whole man. Citing both short stories and novels, he shows a long-standing view of the balanced world of nature and the imbalance resulting from the actions of men in it. Erisman concludes that only by accepting his role in the natural scheme can man escape destroying it. Gerald Haslam's "Sacred Sources in *The Canyon*" (1979) also illustrates the theme of man's responsibility to nature and society. The novel implies that only through understanding the interdependence of nature is man able to come to terms with the cultural bonding of society.

Bibliography

Works by Jack Schaefer

All page citations to *The Canyon* and *First Blood* given in the text refer to the paperback edition (Bantam).

Shane. Boston: Houghton Mifflin, 1949.

The Big Range. Boston: Houghton Mifflin, 1953.

The Canyon. Boston: Houghton Mifflin, 1953; New York: Bantam, 1968.

First Blood. Boston: Houghton Mifflin, 1953: New York: Bantam, 1961.

The Pioneers. Boston: Houghton Mifflin, 1954.

Out West: An Anthology of Stories. Boston: Houghton Mifflin, 1955.

Company of Cowards. Boston: Houghton Mifflin, 1957.

The Kean Land and Other Stories. Boston: Houghton Mifflin, 1959.

Old Ramon. Boston: Houghton Mifflin, 1960.

The Great Endurance Horse Race: 600 Miles on a Single Mount, 1908, from Evanston, Wyoming, to Denver. Santa Fe: Stagecoach Press, 1963.

Monte Walsh. Boston: Houghton Mifflin, 1963.

The Plainsmen. Boston: Houghton Mifflin, 1963.

Stubby Pringle's Christmas. Boston: Houghton Mifflin 1964.

Heroes Without Glory: Some Goodmen of the Old West. Boston: Houghton Mifflin, 1965.

Adolphe Francis Bandelier. Santa Fe: Press of the Territorian, 1966.

The Collected Stories of Jack Schaefer. Boston: Houghton Mifflin, 1966.

Mavericks. Boston: Houghton Mifflin, 1967.

New Mexico. States of the Nation Series. New York: Coward-McCann, 1967

The Short Novels of Jack Schaefer. Boston: Houghton Mifflin, 1967.

An American Bestiary. Boston: Houghton Mifflin, 1975.

"A New Direction." *Western American Literature* 10 (Winter 1976): 265-72.

Conversations with a Pocket Gopher. Santa Barbara, Calif.: Capra Press, 1978

Studies of Jack Schaefer

Cleary, Michael. "Jack Schaefer: The Evolution of Pessimism." *Western American Literature* 14 (Spring 1979): 33-47.

Corder, Jim W. "Efficient Ethos in *Shane*, with a Proposal for Discriminating Among Kinds of Ethos." *Communications Quarterly* 25 (Fall 1977): 28-31.

Dieter, Lynn. "Behavioral Objectives in the English Classroom: A Model." *English Journal* 59 (December 1970): 1258-62, 1271.

Durham, Philip. "The Cowboy and the Myth Makers." *Journal of Popular Culture* 1 (Summer 1967): 58-62.

Erisman, Fred. "Growing Up with the American West: Fiction of Jack Schaefer." *The Popular Western*. Ed. Richard W. Etulain and Michael T. Marsden. Bowling Green, Ohio: Bowling Green University Popular Press, 1974, pp. 68-74.

―――. "Jack Schaefer: The Writer as Ecologist." *Western American Literature* 13 (Spring 1978): 3-13.

Folsom, James K. "*Shane* and *Hud*: Two Stories in Search of a Medium." *Western Humanities Review* 24 (Autumn 1970): 359-72.

Gleason, G. Dale. "Attitudes Toward Law and Order in the American Western." Ph.D. dissertation, Washington State University, 1978.

Haslam, Gerald. *Jack Schaefer*. WWS. Boise, Idaho: Boise State University Press, 1975.

————. "Jack Schaefer's Frontier: The West as Human Testing Ground." *Rocky Mountain Review* 4 (1967): 59-71.

————. "Sacred Sources in *The Canyon*." *Western American Literature* 14 (Spring 1979): 49-55.

Marsden, Michael T. "*Shane*: From Magazine Serial to American Classic." *South Dakota Review* 15 (Winter 1977-78): 59-69.

Mikkelsen, Robert. "The Western Writer: Jack Schaefer's Use of the Western Frontier." *Western Humanities Review* 8 (Spring 1954): 151-55.

Nuwer, Henry Joseph. "An Interview with Jack Schaefer." *South Dakota Review* 11 (Spring 1973): 48-58.

Oliva, Leo E. "The American Indian in Recent Historical Fiction: A Review Essay." *Prairie Scout* 1 (1973): 95-120.

Schein, Harry. "The Olympian Cowboy." *American Scholar* 24 (Summer 1955): 309-20.

Work, James C. "Settlement Waves and Coordinate Forces in *Shane*." *Western American Literature* 14 (Fall 1979): 191-200.

Richard W. Etulain

LUKE SHORT (Frederick D. Glidden)
(1908-1975)

Frederick Glidden, better known by his pen name Luke Short, belongs among the dozen or so authors of the twentieth century who have produced a large number of significant popular Westerns. If the group were limited to those writing since 1940, Short should be included with Ernest Haycox, Louis L'Amour, and perhaps Alan LeMay and Henry Wilson Allen (Will Henry and Clay Fisher) as the most notable recent writers of popular Westerns. Although not as polished a craftsman as Haycox or as prolific as L'Amour, he is a notable writer of Westerns known for their readability and compact plots. The irony of his life is that he is remembered for his many works in a genre he came to dislike.

Biography

Frederick Dilley Glidden was born 19 November 1908 in Kewanee, Illinois, the son of Wallace D. Glidden, a clerical worker, and Fannie M. Glidden, a high school teacher. One year younger than his brother Jonathan "Jon" (1907-57), who also became a writer of Westerns under the name Peter Dawson, Glidden spent his early years in Kewanee. While in high school, Glidden did well academically, took part in social activities, and played basketball and football. Following his graduation in 1926, he attended the University of Illinois for two years. Then, deciding he wanted to write for a living, he transferred to the University of Missouri in Columbia, from which he graduated with a major in journalism in 1930.

As Robert L. Gale points out in his admirable study (*Luke Short*, 1981), for the next few years Glidden was something of a fiddlefoot. At first he worked as a reporter for several newspapers in the Midwest, but as the depression deepened, he found newspaper jobs difficult to land. Many years later he wrote of his early frustrations with journalism: "I've read or heard that all newspapermen are disappointed writers, but in me you behold a writer who is a disappointed newspaperman. I've been fired from more newspapers than I like to remember, even if I could" (*Contemporary Authors*, p. 209). Unsure of his future in journalism, Glidden turned to trapping in Canada, but that too played out. He then moved to northern New Mexico, married Florence Elder of Grand Junction, Colorado, and began to try his hand at fiction.

When his first literary efforts were rejected, Glidden decided in 1935 to secure an agent. Acting on the recommendation of another writer, he wrote to Marguerite Harper of New York City. She agreed to represent Glidden, beginning a mutually satisfactory association that lasted until her death in the mid-1960s. In the first few months of their association, they hit upon Luke Short as a nom de plume (Glidden seems to have suggested the name), and Harper sold a story to one of the Street and Smith pulp magazines.

During the next few years Short quickly made his mark as a writer of Westerns. By the end of 1940, five years after he sold his first story, Short had placed numerous short stories and serials with a variety of pulp magazines and had hit the big time with stories and serials in *Collier's* and *Saturday Evening Post*. He had moved up the ladder much more quickly than Ernest Haycox, the writer with whom he most wanted to compete. In fact, he hit the *Post* earlier, ten years younger, and with nearly fifteen years less experience than Haycox. Moreover, Glidden achieved these goals while the magazine markets were in the tight grip of the depression.

Once Short's first novel (*The Feud at Single Shot*) was serialized in 1935 and published in book form in 1936, he began a routine of producing an average of three or four serials each year. Short's routine paid off; by 1940 he was averaging more than $1000 a month from his writing.

The next decade may have been the most successful period of Short's career. Not only did he continue writing at a rapid pace (fourteen novels appeared in the 1940s, nine of which ran in *Saturday Evening Post*), he was able to abandon the pulps. In addition, Short spent several months in Hollywood working on scripts for Westerns. Although not many of his scripts were filmed, some of his novels were made into movies. In 1947, *Ramrod* was released, starring Joel McCrea. The following year four of his Westerns appeared as films: *Dead Freight for Piute* as *Albuquerque*, *Gunman's Chance* as *Blood on the Moon*, *Coroner Creek*, and *Station West*. If Short dreamed of making millions from the filming of his Westerns, he was disappointed. Although the movie rights to *Ramrod* totaled $25,000, he was unable to follow with continued large royalties.

Meanwhile, other responsibilities weighed on Short. His family grew with the birth of three children in the early 1940s, and in 1947 the family decided to move to Aspen, Colorado, where they resided, off and on, until his death. Short also spent one year (1943-44) working in Washington, D.C., for the Office of Strategic Services.

After World War II Short capitalized on a new development in popular fiction, selling paperback rights of his Westerns to such publishers as Bantam and Dell. Thus, just as it seemed that serial markets might shrink, he was able to take advantage of new paperback markets. In the 1940s Short was paid between $10,000 and $20,000 for his *Post* serials, but none of the hardback books published from those serials sold very well. Once paperback markets were available, however, they provided Short and Harper another opportunity for sales should serial outlets vanish or hardback returns diminish.

Although the 1940s were a productive decade, Short seemed to tire of writing Westerns in the 1950s. His output rapidly dwindled. During the Eisenhower era he published but six Westerns, fewer than half the number he produced in the 1940s, and nearly every letter from his agent encouraged, urged—even browbeat—him to write more. But Short seemed satisfied with his income and weary of writing Westerns. He frequently threatened to abandon the Western field and to turn to other kinds of fiction, but he never carried out his threats, despite a few halfhearted attempts to write popular fiction with a nonwestern setting.

Short did, however, take on other activities to diversify his interests. In 1952 he and a friend wrote the lyrics and music for a domestic comedy, *I've Had It*. Although the show enjoyed some success in Aspen and Denver, it never appeared elsewhere despite the high hopes of Short and his partner. In 1955, he tried to work out an agreement with Desi Arnaz and Lucille Ball to write scripts for a series of television Westerns, but the relationship was never consummated.

Although Short was frustrated in these ventures, his Westerns continued to sell. Despite his growing aversion to writing popular fiction about the West, his ties to the paperback houses proved profitable. Bantam reported that his paperbacks were selling steadily, and his impressive sales were such that, with the help of the indefatigable Harper, he was able to wrangle ever larger royalties from Bantam. And in 1959 Short's original paperback, *Summer of the Smoke*, appeared under a Bantam imprint, the first of several books written for paperback publication.

Some of the same discontents and disappointments characterized Short's career in the 1960s. Although he continued to dream of freeing himself from writing Westerns, his one attempt at writing contemporary fiction, a novel ("Pearly") about a wino, remained unpublished, notwithstanding Short's confidence in the work. Even his reputation as the best-known writer of Westerns, a position he gained after the death of Ernest Haycox in 1950, was being challenged. By the late 1960s, Louis L'Amour, who had begun publishing Westerns in the 1950s, was threatening to surpass Short's impressive sales records.

For Short the 1960s were marked by tragedy. In 1960 his son James, a student at Princeton, drowned in the university swimming pool. Six years later his lifelong friend, confidante, and agent Marguerite Harper died, and with her death Short lost his closest contact to the publishing world.

Although Short averaged a novel a year between 1965 and 1975, physical problems began to take their toll. In 1969, his eyes, already congenitally weak, demanded corrective surgery for a worsened cataract. The operation and another a bit later were not successful, and Short was forced to dictate his work or to write while in continual discomfort. But even worse difficulties were soon apparent: he was discovered to have throat cancer. Radiation and other treatments could not arrest the problem, and Short died on 18 August 1975 at the age of sixty-six.

Major Themes

Like most other writers of popular fiction, Luke Short worried more about pleasing his editors, markets, and readers than he fretted about the development of themes in his Westerns. Although he did not place major stress on ideas, he did use his heroes and heroines to express opinions on a variety of topics. Some of these appeared in Short's earliest Westerns and recurred in his works throughout his forty-year career.

One such theme is the relationship of law and lawlessness. In his first novel, *The Feud at Single Shot* (1936), Short portrays a well-meaning but slow-witted lawman who opposes Dave Turner because he thinks Turner deserves the prison sentence he received as a result of a frame-up. In this case the sheriff is ineffectual because he is obtuse and cannot recognize villainy. Other sheriffs are crooked (*First Claim*, 1960), and still others are unwilling to buck the bad guys (*The Man on the Blue*, 1937). Whatever the cause, the lack of adequate law enforcement on the frontier allows most of Short's heroes to appeal to a higher law and to declare war on evil persons who lurk on the edge of society or control it, untouched by authorized law.

Short's treatment of this theme is similar to that of many other writers of Westerns. Most of these authors seem to agree with the hero of Owen Wister's *The Virginian* (1902): the frontier is lawless, and if lawmen are unable to quell unlawful forces, individualistic frontiersmen (the most typical hero in the Western) must assert their leadership and finish off the villains even if, in the short run, laws are broken in bringing peace to a community. How much this theme was a strongly held conviction among writers of western fiction and how much it was a convenient device for introducing fictional heroes is difficult to discern, but Short retained the idea throughout his career.

If Short often tied his heroes to the need for more lawful communities, he frequently characterized his heroines by their reactions to the protagonist's attempts to establish law and order. Several of his women are so repelled by violence that they sermonize against it. In *King Colt* (1937) and *Bold Rider* (1936) women question the necessity of violence in opposing villainy, although they desire law-abiding communities. What is true of Wister's *The Virginian* is also true of several of Short's Westerns: the early parts of these books are powered by the conflict between heroes who are convinced that violence is necessary to handle the "hardcases" and heroines who are persuaded that violence is unnecessary. (Wallace Stegner, the noted western novelist, expands this theme even more when he argues that the notion of the heroine as civilizer and community maker is a major theme in all western fiction.)

A second theme is the changing roles of women and minorities. In many of his novels, Short reflects the tendency of many writers of Westerns to allow their heroines little more identity than that arising from their relationship with the hero. But not all of his women are cut from this restrictive cloth. In one of his early Westerns, *Hard Money* (1940), Short proves that he is capable of creating three noteworthy heroines.

Two of these heroines illustrate a familiar conflict. One, Sharon Bonal, the daughter of a hard bitten mine owner, is a selfish, arrogant shrew in need of taming. The product of new wealth in a frontier mining town, she has to be taught by the hero to comprehend the ways of working people. Her initiation into understanding underscores Short's interest in social classes in this Western. The other, Vannie Shore, is a warm, erotic woman who has lived unmarried with a now-deceased mine owner. Although she is an appealing woman, her tarnished background keeps her from being a suitable partner for the hero. Short uses the differences between Sharon and Vannie, and the reactions of the community to the two women, for his most extended commentary on the sense of community— or the lack of it—in the mining hamlet. Clearly, Sharon, once she has been "tamed," is a suitable woman on which to build the community, but Vannie is destined to live on the edge of society, desirable but not acceptable.

The third woman, Mazie Comber, represents another part of the mining town. Although rich and living in a castle-like home, she wears frumpy clothes and cares little about the social graces expected of her. Middle-aged and ma- tronly, she acts as confidante of the other women and adviser to several men. Removed from a romantic role in the novel, she can serve as the commentator on and the preserver of the community. In his characterizations of these three women, Short proves that he can move beyond the narrow restrictions often placed on women's roles in the Western and that he can use his characters to symbolize ideas beyond their actions.

Later in his career Short becomes even more creative with his heroines. In *Paper Sheriff* (1966), Callie Hoad Branham, whom the hero has gotten pregnant and married before the novel begins, is a bitchy woman tied more to her Hoad clan than to her husband. She accuses him of wanting to sleep with Jen Truro, a lawyer and the other leading woman of the novel. Although Callie is the "bad" woman and accidentally killed late in the novel, she is probably the most fully realized character in the book. Callie's forthright talk of sex is unusual for a genre so conservative as the Western. Conversations about the subject are even more explicit in *The Outrider* (1972) and *The Stalkers* (1973), where a prostitute lives openly with a man and a hapless hooker, on a bet, runs naked down the main street of the town.

Much more significant than these suggestions of an increasingly liberal atti- tude toward sex in Short's Westerns is his positive treatment of a Hispanic woman in *Trouble Country* (1976). While not explicitly racist in most of his early Westerns, Short showed little sympathy for minority characters, and he, like most other writers of popular fiction before the 1960s, did not allow minority figures to play leading roles in his novels. This is not true in *Trouble Country*. In this book Sam Dana throws his "hardcase" brother off the Bar D because he learns that Walt is a rustler. When Walt flees the ranch, he abandons his Mexican wife, Rita, and she is barely able to survive. Learning of his brother's mistreat- ment of Rita, Sam becomes her protector. But his interest moves beyond her protection, and before Walt is killed near the end of the novel, Sam finds Rita more attractive than Sistie Cable, the sheriff's daughter, a more typical western heroine. Despite Sistie's being the "appropriate" match for Sam and despite Rita's being a Mexican widow, it is Rita whom Sam will marry. The differing treatment of heroines in *Hard Money* and *Trouble Country* indicates that Short's ideas changed a great deal from 1939 to 1975.

A third and final theme, as a recent commentator on popular culture, John Cawelti (*The Six-Gun Mystique* and *Adventure, Mystery, and Romance*) suggests, is that of the involvements between individuals and communities. Some of Short's characters reflect this conflict, but on other occasions, he is explicit in his portrayal of individual-community relationships. In *Ride the Man Down* (1942), one of the heroines will never be a satisfactory mate for the hero because she is too selfish, too isolated from the goals of a community that mean little to her. Kate Miles faces a similar problem in *First Claim* (1960) until her boss, the editor of the local newspaper, shows her that he will stake his reputation and life on an issue benefiting the community, even though the issue may ruin his business. After a good deal of mental turmoil, Kate realizes that she too must support an act that will help the town and countryside.

In other novels the sheriff replaces the newspaper editor as the caretaker of society. Reese Branham plays this role in *Paper Sheriff*, one of Short's best Westerns. Torn between his wish to shield his unheroic wife, Callie, and protect his reputation and his desire to keep a group of Callie's evil relatives from dominating his community, he resolves to carry out measures protecting the town rather than ones bearing on his personal concerns. Toward the end of his career, Short seemed increasingly interested in forces that sustained a community, and he often voted, as he did in *Paper Sheriff*, for group needs over individualistic interests.

In his extended study, *Luke Short*, Robert Gale catalogs several other themes in Short's Westerns. Arguing that obtaining justice, demonstrating loyalty, and protecting women are Short's most obvious motifs, Gale also lists the power of the past, self-examination and reform, and discovering joy without seeking it directly as other notable ideas in Short's works. Finally, Gale notes comparisons of East and West, the use of pragmatic means for worthy ends, and the victory of rugged individuals over mob action as notable minor themes. Yet after discussing these themes, Gale rightly concludes that Short emphasized action most of all, that he was "limited in thematic range and ingenuity" (*Luke Short*, p. 100).

Survey of Criticism

The scholarship on Luke Short and his writings is similar to that on many other writers of Westerns, comprising a few general essays and books on western writing and the American West that mention Short and his novels and one or two essayists dealing specifically with his Westerns. But unlike Max Brand, Haycox, LeMay, and L'Amour (and like Zane Grey), Short has received book-length attention. Robert Gale's volume is the beginning place for information on Short, although room still exists for further study of his career, particularly from the perspectives of literary historians and students of popular culture.

The best brief overview of the Western is that in Russel Nye's *The Unembarrassed Muse* (1970). In about twenty-five fact-studded pages, Nye provides a useful summary of the Western and notes that Short produced "tightly-written, controlled action" (p. 299). Nye asserts that Short is, in fact, "the best of action-Western writers" (p. 302) but is artistically inferior to Jack Schaefer, Henry Wilson Allen, A. B. Guthrie, and Haycox.

In a comparative study of cinematic and historical treatments of the American West, *There Must Be a Lone Ranger* (1974), Jenni Calder, an English critic, deals with a few novels by Short. Centering on western myths, her book treats the subject topically and utilizes the works of Short to illustrate her generalizations about western legends. She considers Short one of the "readable mainstream writers" who have produced "solid Westerns" (p. 233). This study is uneven, curious in its judgments, and too often mistaken on dates and facts to be entirely satisfactory, and none of her comments on Short adds a great deal to an understanding of his art or career.

In his abbreviated summary of the rise of the Western, "The Historical Development of the Western," Richard W. Etulain places Short in the third period of a three-part division of the genre's history in the twentieth century. He sees Short as an author whose stories appeal to many readers but a writer who did not tinker much with the ingredients of the traditional Western, a view also argued in Etulain's "The Western," *Handbook of American Culture* (1978).

The best of the essays to deal specifically with Short is Phillip D. Thomas's "The Paperback West of Luke Short" (1974). For several years the only available overview of Short's Westerns, this summary provides a brief biographical introduction and then lists the major ingredients of Short's novels. Thomas notes that Short drew on his experiences in and knowledge of the West for his Westerns but that he rarely dealt with historical persons. While Short's books are action packed, he avoids emphasizing guns or dramatic gunfights.

Thomas suggests that Short is particularly intrigued with life in frontier towns. Like feudal societies, towns in Short's Westerns are dominated by money and power; crooked businessmen, greedy landowners, and weak lawmen tend to rule these communities. Citizens survive by understanding their places on the social and economic ladders. Short's characters, Thomas adds, are not difficult to recognize early in his novels, for their dress and initial actions reveal whether they belong among the white or black hats. Occasionally his heroes have a flawed past, but most often their direct, simple action proves they are on God's side. Thomas believes that Short's popularity rests in large part on his ability to produce action novels, believable characters, and suspenseful plots. In addition, his heroes provide cathartic resolution by solving their problems. To illustrate these useful generalizations, Thomas utilizes several long quotations from about a dozen of Short's Westerns.

By far the most important source on Short is Gale's volume in the Twayne series, *Luke Short*. Gale begins his study with a general section on western fiction and a brief overview of Short's career, and then he provides summaries of all of Short's more than fifty Westerns. He devotes single chapters to Short's sense of place, characterizations, plots, and themes and two chapters to his literary artistry. A brief summary and a helpful bibliography complete the book. By devoting separate chapters to Short's settings, characters, and plots—as well as providing plot summaries of each of Short's Westerns—Gale includes a great deal of factual material in his book. Not only do readers gain overviews of the major ingredients of Short's novels, but they are also given comparisons between Short and other American writers.

Above all, Gale's monograph is a study of Short the literary artist. Unlike many other interpreters of the Western, Gale presents extended evaluations of Short's writings. Noting Short's stylistic, grammatical, and dialogic idiosyncrasies, he also examines his subject's humor, points of view, structures, and his attempts at unity and his verisimilitude. Throughout these well-documented discussions and in other sections of his book, he provides close readings of Short's Westerns and commentary on his extensive correspondence with Marguerite Harper. No one could argue that Gale has overlooked any of Short's writings, published or manuscript, in this exhaustive study.

Gale has given such perceptive and full coverage of the plots, characterizations, and literary artistry of Short's Westerns that this material will not have to be covered again. But there are other ways to discuss these ingredients, and there are other subjects Gale does not treat. During the last three decades, interest has mounted in scrutinizing popular fiction as a reflection of its times. Since the publication of Henry Nash Smith's *Virgin Land* in 1950, historians and critics have given increasing attention to the relationship between the Western and its milieu. More recently John Cawelti has urged scholars to study carefully the changing ideas, plots, and character types in Westerns to see if these changes are closely related to shifting currents in American culture. The Westerns of Short have yet to be subjected to this kind of scrutiny.

The stages of Short's career are also in need of further study. Short wrote Westerns for forty years, and during those four decades his career overlapped those of such well-known writers of Westerns as Grey, Brand, Haycox, LeMay, and L'Amour. Comparative studies are needed to show the differences and similarities among the works of these authors, for inadequate comparative work is one of the major limitations of current interpretations of the Western.

Finally, no one has yet studied the impact of market shifts on Short's career. His first novels appeared serially in pulp magazines before hardback publication. By the early 1940s his serials were appearing in *Collier's*, *Saturday Evening Post*, and other slick magazines. Within the next decade, he enjoyed the financial rewards of paperback reprints, and by the 1960s, though serial markets had vanished, his original paperbacks took up much of the slack. In sum, Short's career embraced several important changes in market conditions, and changes in his writings suggest that editors and readers played significant roles in influencing his work. In his earliest pulp serials and his last paperback originals, Short's heroes are more violent than most of his protagonists in the serials for *Collier's* and *Saturday Evening Post*. Additional study of Short's correspondence with his agent and editors and comparisons between his serial and book publications may demonstrate other such changes in his Westerns. This topic, and others, indicate that several aspects of Luke Short's career and his Westerns merit additional research.

Bibliography

For a complete listing of Short's Westerns, see the bibliography in Robert Gale's *Luke Short*.

Works by Luke Short

The Feud at Single Shot. New York: Rinehart, 1936; New York: Bantam, 1950.
The Man on the Blue. Serial, 1936-37. New York: Dell, 1978.
Bold Rider. Serial, 1936. New York: Dell, 1975.
King Colt. Serial, 1937; New York: Bantam, 1963.
Hard Money. Garden City, N.Y.: Doubleday, 1940; New York: Bantam, 1978.
Ride the Man Down. Garden City, N.Y.: Doubleday, 1942; New York: Bantam, 1961.
Ramrod. New York: Macmillan, 1943; New York: Bantam, 1977.
And the Wind Blows Free. New York: Macmillan, 1945; New York: Bantam, 1955.
Station West. Boston: Houghton Mifflin, 1947; New York: Bantam, 1976.
Vengeance Valley. Boston: Houghton Mifflin, 1950; New York: Bantam, 1972.
Saddle by Starlight. Boston: Houghton Mifflin, 1952; New York: Bantam, 1959.
Rimrock. New York: Random House, 1955; New York: Bantam, 1974.
First Claim. New York: Bantam, 1960.
First Campaign. New York: Bantam, 1965.
Paper Sheriff. New York: Bantam, 1966.
The Outrider. New York: Bantam, 1972.
The Stalkers. New York: Bantam, 1973.
Trouble Country. New York: Bantam, 1976.
A Man Could Get Killed. New York: Jove Publications, 1980. Primarily a reprint of *The Primrose Try*. New York: Bantam, 1967.

Studies of Luke Short

Calder, Jenni. *There Must Be a Lone Ranger: The American West in Myth and Reality*. New York: Taplinger Publishing Company, 1974.
Cawelti, John G. *Adventure, Mystery, and Romance: Formula Stories as Art and Popular Culture*. Chicago: University of Chicago Press, 1976.
————. *The Six-Gun Mystique*. Bowling Green, Ohio: Bowling Green University Popular Press [1971].
Etulain, Richard W. "The Historical Development of the Western." *The Popular Western: Essays Toward a Definition*. Eds. Richard W. Etulain and Michael T. Marsden. Bowling Green, Ohio: Bowling Green University Popular Press, 1974, pp. 75-84.
————. Introduction to Luke Short, *Hard Money*. Boston: Gregg Press, forthcoming.

————. "The Western." *Handbook of American Popular Culture*. Vol. 1. Ed. M. Thomas Inge. Westport, Conn.: Greenwood Press, 1978, pp. 355-76.

Frazee, Steve. "Meet Fred Glidden." *Roundup* 3 (October 1955): 3-4.

Gale, Robert. *Luke Short*. TUSAS. Boston: Twayne, 1981.

Garfield, Brian. "The Fiddlefoot From Kewanee." *Roundup* 23 (November 1975): 6-7,11.

"Glidden, Frederick D(illey) 1908-1975 (Luke Short)." *Contemporary Authors: Permanent Series*. Vol. 2. Detroit: Gale Research Company, 1978, pp. 215-16.

Nye, Russel. "Sixshooter Country." *The Unembarrassed Muse: The Popular Arts in America*. New York: Dial Press, 1970, pp. 280-304.

Olsen, T. V. "Luke Short, Writer's Writer." *Roundup* 21 (March 1973): 10-11, 13.

Smith, Henry Nash. *Virgin Land: The American West as Symbol and Myth*. Cambridge: Harvard University Press, 1950.

Thomas, Phillip D. "The Paperback West of Luke Short," *The Popular Western: Essays Toward a Definition*. Bowling Green, Ohio: Bowling Green University Popular Press, 1974, pp. 59-66.

GARY SNYDER
(1930-)

Biography

Appropriately enough for a writer associated with the San Francisco renais-sance of the 1950s, Gary Snyder was born in that city on 8 May 1930 but grew up on a farm near Seattle with the woods, and logging, not far away. As a boy, Snyder was fond of Ernest Thompson Seton's writings on scouting and Indian woodcraft, and a love of the wilderness and an eagerness to learn from the American Indian are two forces permeating all of Snyder's work in poetry and prose.

Snyder's family moved to Portland when he was twelve, and before he was out of high school he had become virtually self-supporting after the break-up of his parents' marriage. He attended Reed College from 1947 to 1951. Reed offers intellectual rigor but encourages innovative approaches, so Snyder was able to pursue a combined major in anthropology and literature. Just how much he learned is clear from his bachelor's thesis, recently published as *He Who Hunted Birds in His Father's Village* (1979). The Haida myth of the title is subjected to a number of approaches: social, literary, psychological, and even metaphysical analysis. The thesis foreshadows Snyder's later use of allusions and quotations from primitive literature in poems like *Myths & Texts* (1960). In the thesis, as in the poetry, Snyder is concerned with the authentic use of the material; he knows that it represents part of a world view, and he introduces myths and songs into his poems to represent that world view. At the same time, he knows that the meaning of the material is relevant to our own culture. For example, Coyote is an Indian trickster figure, but he can also serve symbolic functions for the wider American culture. Indeed a trickster element is at the core of technological society. In his recent work, Snyder is more likely to create his own animistic myths and songs than to quote from ethnological collections.

While at Reed, Snyder married Alison Gass in 1950, a union dissolved in 1952. After a semester of graduate work in linguistics at Indiana University in 1951, Snyder returned west and worked at manual jobs for several years: he was a logger, a fire lookout, a trail crew worker in Yosemite National Park, and a seaman. He also spent much of the time from 1953 to 1956 studying Oriental languages at Berkeley. He had been writing poetry since his undergraduate days, and he wanted to commit himself to poetry. The manual labor and the study of Chinese and Japanese furthered this ambition. Much of Snyder's work is set in the wilderness; sometimes it deals with contemplation, sometimes with labor, and sometimes with contemplation after work. His style is influenced by the terseness and imagistic qualities of Oriental poetry, especially the lyric poems of the T'ang dynasty poets like Han-shan, whose work he has translated as *Cold Mountain Poems*.

There were other writers in the Bay Area while Snyder was at Berkeley: Robert Duncan, whose interest in myth and symbol appealed to Snyder, and Kenneth Rexroth, whose fine poems display both wilderness settings and a deep knowledge of Oriental literature and religion. Jack Kerouac and Allen Ginsberg brought a nascent Beat movement with them from New York. The ingredients for a West Coast literary explosion were present, and the celebrated poetry reading at the Six Gallery in 1955 was the fuse. Kenneth Rexroth presided, and Snyder read along with his friends, Michael McClure and Philip Whalen, but the real detonation was Ginsberg's *Howl*. There was soon talk of a San Francisco renaissance, and Snyder became known as a Beat poet.

But before the smoke could clear, Snyder was in Kyoto, Japan, studying Zen Buddhism. Jack Kerouac's novel, *The Dharma Bums*, made him a celebrity as "Japhy Ryder," but Snyder was not around to enjoy or suffer from the notoriety. The exuberant Ryder of the novel talks a great deal about Zen, while Snyder knew that Zen is a matter of practice rather than talk. He had decided in 1953 that Zen offered a living spiritual tradition that he could learn from, and it became a motive for his study of Oriental languages. Zen extols work, and its meditative practices clarify the perceptions; further, it has a long tradition of profound feeling for nature that has nourished the arts in China and Japan. Snyder's teacher was Oda Sesso Roshi, chief abbot of Daitoku-ji Monastery. Sesso died in 1966, and Snyder returned to the United States to live in 1968, bringing with him his third wife, Masa Uehara, and their first son, Kai. (Snyder's second wife, the poet Joanne Kyger, was married to him from 1960 until 1965.)

Snyder returned to the United States during the social upheavals of the late 1960s and quickly became a spokesman for the ecology movement and an elder statesman (before his fortieth birthday) for the hippies. His "Smokey the Bear Sutra" was circulated anonymously for the ecology movement, while the anonymous "Four Changes" encouraged social reform on the model of the Industrial Workers of the World—the Wobblies of an earlier western America—"Building the New Society within the shell of the Old." Snyder and his family were even the centerfold for an ecology issue of *Look Magazine*. After several years of work for ecology, Snyder began to live a quiet life in the foothills of the Sierras at Kitkitdizze, a home named for a local plant. The Japanese-style house has no telephone, so when Snyder won the Pulitzer Prize for *Turtle Island* in 1975, a neighbor had to bring him the news. He does not, however, see his life as isolated. He is part of an influential minority shaping public attitudes toward the environment and government. He was appointed to the California Arts Council by Governor Jerry Brown; his poetry reading tours take him all over the United States, and he is a best-seller among poets. He has attained considerable fame for a man who considers television "bad medicine."

Major Themes

At the heart of Snyder's work is an image of the shaman, the poet-prophet-healer of many primitive societies. A shaman's visions usually involve a deep communion with nature, often through the magical aid of a totem animal, and the result of the vision may be a healing song revealed in trance or some kind of knowledge needed to deal with a problem of the tribe. In an interview Snyder has said that shamanism "has at its very center a teaching from the nonhuman" (*The Real Work*, p. 156). His own poetry is a communion with the nonhuman, a dialogue with nature and living beings. Snyder's admiration for primitive societies is tied up with their closeness to nature. He wants to offer healing visions and insights to his own society, which he feels is dangerously alienated from nature and a menace to ecological stability.

A communion with the nonhuman, then, is Snyder's fundamental theme. His poems fall into lyrical and mythopoeic modes, and each has its characteristic way of dealing with nature. In the lyrical, the poet's perceptions are the vehicle for a teaching received through the direct experience of nature, while in the mythical mode the insights are usually conveyed through symbolic figures like Coyote and Raven, or through equivalents from the myths and spiritual teachings of the Orient. His first collection, *Riprap* (1959), is predominantly lyrical, evoking nature through concise language and strong images. The book is named for a rough cobble laid down by trail crews in the wilderness, and work is a major theme in the poems. Labor is one way to come to terms with external reality, and many of Snyder's best poems are about the pleasures and pains of work. Zen teaches respect for work, but Snyder shows an interest in work that is not merely theoretical. The theme of labor runs through all of his writing, and a destructive kind of labor is the subject of the opening section of *Myths & Texts*, his major mythopoeic collection to date.

That book reveals the full range of his learning and sensibility. The first section, "Logging," deals with the greed that leads people to cut down forests, while "Hunting" dramatizes the contrasting primitive attitude of reverence for nature, and the "Burning" section presents the Buddhist critique of human egotism. The work is an extended vision quest on behalf of his society, and some of it is written as shaman songs. The lore is often exotic, but Snyder's allusions to Oriental and American Indian materials have served as a precedent for a generation of western American poets. In his new preface to the work, Snyder says that it has become more accessible over the years: "The references to gods, peoples, and places sound less exotic, which is right; the Buddha, Seami, the Great Bear are not exotica but part of our whole planetary heritage" (p. vii). The reader who is a little mystified by such references in the poem might consult Howard McCord's *Some Notes to Gary Snyder's Myths & Texts* (1971) for helpful glosses.

Since the mid-1950s Snyder has been working on a long poem, *Mountains and Rivers Without End*, which is modeled on Zen landscape paintings and will deal with a panoramic journey through space, time, and the unconscious. Along with the sweep of Zen painting, in which human travelers are tiny figures in a vast setting, Snyder has spoken of the Japanese Noh drama as another model for the poem. He apparently means the Noh situation in which a pilgrim or ghost visits a special place that triggers a profound experience or memory. It is difficult to judge a work in progress, especially when only a few sections have been published. Clearly the poem will be Snyder's most ambitious mythopoeic project.

Travel is a recurring theme in Snyder's third full collection, *The Back Country* (1968), which brings together poems about work in western America and journeys in the Far East. The book contains some of his best poems, but the style and subjects are familiar. The most distinctive poems are the ones about his trip to India in 1962, where he saw great misery and at the same time learned something of the theory of Tantra, a radical tendency in both Hinduism and Buddhism. The Tantric practitioner strives for involvement in the world of the senses. The full influence of the Tantric attitude becomes apparent in *Regarding Wave* (1970).

A real transition occurs in that book. Snyder shows new trends in style and theme. The influence of Tantra and his stay at the Banyan Ashram on Suwa-no-Se Island led to a deepening of his nature poetry. Tantra encouraged a view of the interdependence of all things and a sense of the intricacies of physical process. Life in a commune on a small island between Okinawa and Japan demonstrated that these attitudes need not be merely theoretical. Interdependence is a key to the book: the related theme of the beauty and harmony of physical processes is another. And mind itself is part of the entwining wave-form dance of reality. The title of *Regarding Wave* is important: *regarding* here means "involvement." Style expresses involvement through the inventiveness of a free typography that represents the dance of mind among things and the dance of things themselves. The images present more than scenes or landscapes: they number the streaks of the tulip, the streaks in clamshells and tree bark.

The poems dealing with communal life and the family represent new themes for Snyder. His poetry had often dealt with solitary contemplation, but *Regarding Wave* celebrates the life of a tiny but real community. His marriage to Masa Uehara on Suwa-no-Se Island and the birth of his son Kai resulted in some fine poems that foreshadow the familial warmth of poems like "The Bath" in *Turtle Island* (1974). His two earlier marriages left few traces in his poetry, but his sons, Kai and Gen, are now familiar figures in Snyder's work.

In *Regarding Wave* the poet also deals with his return to America in 1968. Snyder wanted to get in touch with the local nature spirits, as he likes to put it, and the book often records his encounters with places and creatures in western

America. The best poems in the book are probably the songs in Part II, in which Snyder creates shamanistic lore instead of echoing it. Snyder returned during a period of social upheaval, and poems like "Poke Hole Fishing after the March" and "Revolution in the Revolution in the Revolution" take up some of the issues controversial in the 1960s. There is a strong current of protest against civilization itself, not just against some of the problems of American society. The mechanisms of industrial civilization oppress and alienate, in Snyder's view. In the concluding poem, "Civilization," he says, echoing Blake, "Fetch me my feathers and amber." His utopia would not be a Jerusalem but a hunting ground. And in place of the state, he would propose a society on the tribal model.

The protest against civilization runs through Snyder's prose. In *Earth House Hold* (1969) he suggests that an alternative culture, which he calls the Great Subculture, surfaces from time to time, and that the hippie or counterculture movement of the 1960s was such an emergence. Snyder shared, and helped create, the interest in communal living and a return to the land that so concerned that decade. The primitive for him is not a barbaric way of life but one of grace and full development of human capacities. He does not wish to eliminate technology, but he wants to put it in its place, a fairly subordinate one. The tribe is a more humane nexus than the cities that distinguish civilization. The tone of the essays is sometimes utopian, but the interviews collected in *The Real Work* (1980) make clear that Snyder can work out the details of his return to the land with practicality and patience.

In *Earth House Hold* Snyder collected a variety of writings: journals, book reviews, a Zen text in translation, an account of life on Suwa-no-Se Island, a rich harvest of work in several prose genres. The writing is clear and crisp. A more recent book, *The Old Ways* (1977), brings together essays and talks that are more uneven in style. The high points are "The Yogin and the Philosopher," a brief piece on the persistence of the human craving to commune with nature, and "The Incredible Survival of Coyote," a lecture on the ways in which contemporary poets have communed with one particular being. Coyote is a trickster, buffoon, and deity as well as a wily animal and appears often in the poems. The essay "Re-inhabitation" expresses Snyder's perception that Americans need to settle their country all over again, but in a loving and responsible way. Perhaps the most ranging and revealing prose collection of all is *The Real Work*, a gathering of Snyder's most important interviews, along with several talks. Here and there the interviews have been abridged from their original printed versions, which means that scholars will have to check the original sources.

The most recent collection of poems (with a prose appendix), *Turtle Island*, is itself a work of "re-inhabitation." Snyder wants to recapture the original America, to find the physical and spiritual reality beneath the asphalt and the suburban lots. That means repudiating the very name *America*, a cartographer's error—hence "Turtle Island," an aboriginal name for the continent, representing an Indian perspective that sees beyond the imaginary lines that divide up the landscape and the very real cities that cover much of it. Some of the poems are familiar enough: celebrations of family, of nature, of wild animals. Others, like "What Happened Here Before" and "Toward Climax," deal with great sweeps of time to provide a perspective on this relatively new phenomenon, civilization. "What Happened Here Before" makes clear that the New World is not very new after all: it began 300 million years ago. And "Toward Climax" presents the war in Vietnam as the culmination of a development that began with the rise of city states and kings.

The note of ecological anger is strong in the book, stronger than in Snyder's earlier poetry. In *Myths & Texts* he wrote as one of the loggers, a regretful one to be sure, but in *Turtle Island* he wants to draw battle lines. The war is a mental fight, however. He puts it this way in "Four Changes," a prose piece from the 1960s:

Since it doesn't seem practical or even desirable to think that direct bloody force will achieve much, it would be best to consider this a continuing "revolution of consciousness" which will be won not by guns but by seizing the key images, myths, archetypes, eschatologies, and ecstasies so that life won't seem worth living unless one's on the transforming side. [*Turtle Island*, p.100]

The wilderness poems are ways of indicating that the ecstasies and key images lie not with industrial civilization but in an imaginative dialogue with nature. In *Turtle Island* Snyder truly seeks the shaman's role: to find the visions that bring healing and sanity to a battered continent. The real energy crisis, he believes, is spiritual. The culture that he wishes to warn wants to find new sources of energy to do the same wasteful, destructive things it has done with the conventional sources. In several essays included in the "Plain Talk" section, Snyder suggests that we pursue different kinds of growth: intelligent stewardship of renewable resources is a more valuable enterprise than new techniques of strip-mining. "Electricity for Los Angeles is not energy. As Blake said: 'Energy is Eternal Delight' " (*Turtle Island*, p. 105). Snyder is a prophet who wants to lead his people not out of the wilderness but into it.

Survey of Criticism

Snyder has had a number of sympathetic critics. For an understanding of his development, Robert Ian Scott's "The Early Uncollected Poetry of Gary Snyder" (1977) is a good place to start, along with the early prose journals from *Earth House Hold*. Scott reprints ten poems that Snyder published while a student at Reed College. The poems are apprentice work, but they show an interesting apprenticeship. Ezra Pound, T.S. Eliot, and Robert Graves were among the apparent influences, and Scott shows what Snyder learned from Graves about the primitive, the muse, and the earth goddess. The early poems make clear that Snyder's interest in Buddhism was strong by 1951.

Two early articles still serve as excellent introductions to Snyder's writing. In "The Work of Gary Snyder" (1962), a pseudonymous article by James Wright, some important observations are made. Wright notes the western American ethos of Snyder's work, the dignity of the human beings who appear in it, his sympathy for nonhuman life, his meditative power and "privacy," and his ability to "express the inner life without resorting to the worn-out abstractions which often nullify the public discussions of spiritual matters ("Work of Snyder," p. 29). Wright distinguishes Snyder's work from the other so-called beat poets by pointing to his seriousness and intelligence, an intelligence that manifests itself in "myths of the senses" ("Work of Snyder," p. 36). He also notes the importance of the Oriental influence on Snyder and compares him to Whitman, another poet who celebrated work and the wilderness.

Thomas Parkinson's "The Poetry of Gary Snyder" (1968) is a fine and intimate introduction to the man and the writing. Snyder's engaging personality is described, and his achievement in creating a culture out of such western American interests as Zen, the Wobblies, Indian lore, and the wilderness mystique is praised. Parkinson describes Snyder's technical traits in the early poems sympathetically but critically. Parkinson notes that Snyder's "spiritual influence" on younger poets is strong but dangerous: he deplores "a certain mechanical quality" in the Gary Snyder Poem, a derivative poem written by apprentices ("Poetry," p. 618).

Other overviews are provided by Bob Steuding, Abraham Rothberg, Sherman Paul and Bert Almon. Steuding's *Gary Snyder* (1976) is the only book-length treatment. He offers a full but concise discussion of Snyder's eclectic intellectual framework—those for whom Snyder has not created a culture will find his book a valuable guide. It has an excellent bibliography. His readings of individual poems are helpful, though his praise tends to be hyperbolic and his handling of chronology in discussing Snyder's style is careless. Rothberg's "A Passage to More Than India" (1976) fails to advance on Parkinson's similar introduction. Sherman Paul's long chapter on Snyder in *Repossessing and Renewing* (1976) uses the prose in *Earth House Hold* to discuss Snyder's development, and the relation of Snyder to Thoreau is made clear. Bert Almon's pamphlet, *Gary Snyder* (1976), deals with Snyder's work in a brief survey that pays some attention to the esoteric sources.

More specialized studies have begun to appear. Thomas J. Lyon's "Gary Snyder, A Western Poet" (1968) and "The Ecological Vision of Gary Snyder" (1970) consider two important dimensions of the poetry. Yao-Fu Lin's " 'The Mountains Are Your Mind': Orientalism in the Poetry of Gary Snyder" (1975-76) is the most comprehensive discussion of the Zen background and the Chinese influences and never fails to illuminate. Bert Almon's "Buddhism and Energy in the Recent Poetry of Gary Snyder" (1977) examines Snyder's more recent interest in Tantric Buddhism, thus supplementing Lin.

Charles Altieri has written astutely on Snyder. In a chapter of his book on contemporary American poetry, *Enlarging the Temple* (1979), he observes that the lack of tension in Snyder's work has been censured while the lyric strategies that suggest harmony and interdependence have been ignored. He provides some superb close readings to bring out the ecological nature of Snyder's style. His essay "Gary Snyder's *Turtle Island*: The Problem of Reconciling the Roles of Seer and Prophet" (1976) asks some hard questions about the social criticism. Altieri asserts that Snyder is most effective as a visionary, a writer of contemplative poems, and that *Turtle Island* is weakened by a stridency and smugness when Snyder plays prophet in the wilderness.

Robert Kern's "Recipes, Catalogues, Open Form Poetics: Gary Snyder's Archetypal Voice" (1977) ambitiously places Snyder in relation both to William Everson's ideas about western American poetry and to postmodern literary theory. Everson has proposed that the distinctive quality of western poetry is an unmediated experience of reality: intensity is more important than hierarchy and form. Kern relates this idea to use of catalogs and recipes in Snyder's poetry: both forms show a trust in the orderliness of things as they are. Kern's "Clearing the Ground: Gary Snyder and the Modernist Imperative" (1977) discusses Snyder's poetics in the *Riprap* poems. Snyder's critics have sometimes discussed him rather simply as a neo-imagist or an imitator of Pound and William Carlos Williams. Kern is much more sophisticated, and the poetry at times gets lost in the glare of his erudition. But he usefully suggests that "these poems promote the value of the external world and of immediate experience. They do so, that is, by subordinating themselves to the world and by insisting on their own inadequacies" ("Clearing the Ground," p. 172).

David Robbins has his own kind of sophistication. His essay "Gary Snyder's 'Burning Island' " (1979) is concerned not with literary theory but with close reading. He examines one poem from *Regarding Wave* with great care and penetration to bring out its intricate texture. The clarity of Snyder's diction often leads critics to overlook the subtlety of his style. Robbins considers such aspects as the sound pattern of the poem, the use of style to suggest interconnections, and the typographical devices; the treatment is thorough. Like Kern, Robbins asserts that Snyder shows a trust in experience, but he also demonstrates how much art is required to let experience speak for itself.

L. Edwin Folsom provides a useful framework for discussing Snyder's "reinhabitation" of his country in "Gary Snyder's Descent to Turtle Island: Searching for Fossil Love" (1980). Folsom analyzes the quest for origins in *Turtle Island*, the attempt to uncover pre-Columbian realities under the palimpsest of American history. He relates Snyder's quest to the similar attempts by William Carlos Williams, Hart Crane, Theodore Roethke, and W. S. Merwin. The metaphor of descent is more Folsom's than Snyder's. But Folsom points out rightly that with the closing of the frontier, there is no place for western man to go but into the origins of what he has despoiled. It is time for Snyder's critics to make their own descent: into close readings of individual poems on Robbins's model and into the use of American Indian lore in the poetry. Relatively little has been published on Snyder's use of his primitive sources. But on the whole, his critics have done well by him.

Bibliography

Works by Gary Snyder

Riprap. Ashland, Mass.: Origin Press, 1959, expanded rpt. *Riprap & Cold Mountain Poems*. San Francisco: Four Seasons Foundation, 1965.

Myths & Texts. New York: Totem Press, 1960; New York: New Directions, 1978 [with a new preface].

Six Sections from Mountains and Rivers Without End. San Francisco: Four Seasons Foundation, 1965; *Six Sections from Mountains and Rivers Without End Plus One*. San Francisco: Four Seasons Foundation, 1970.

The Back Country. New York: New Directions, 1968.

Earth House Hold. New York: New Directions, 1969.

Regarding Wave. New York: New Directions, 1970.

Turtle Island. New York: New Directions, 1974.

The Old Ways. San Francisco: City Lights Books, 1977.

He Who Hunted Birds in His Father's Village. Bolinas, Calif.: Grey Fox Press, 1979.

The Real Work: Interviews & Talks 1964-1979. Ed. Wm. Scott MacLean. New York: New Directions, 1980.

Studies of Gary Snyder

Almon, Bert. "Buddism and Energy in the Recent Poetry of Gary Snyder." *Mosaic* 11 (Fall 1977): 117-25.

————. *Gary Snyder*. WWS. Boise, Idaho: Boise State University, 1979.

Altieri, Charles. *Enlarging the Temple*. Lewisburg: Bucknell University Press, 1979.

————. "Gary Snyder's *Turtle Island*: The Problem of Reconciling the Roles of Seer and Prophet." *Boundary 2* 4 (Spring 1976): 761-77.

Folsom, L. Edwin. "Gary Snyder's Descent to Turtle Island: Searching for Fossil Love." *Western American Literature* 15 (Summer 1980): 103-21.

Kern, Robert. "Clearing the Ground: Gary Snyder and the Modernist Imperative." *Criticism* 19 (Spring 1977): 158-77.

————. "Recipes, Catalogues, Open Form Poetics: Gary Snyder's Archetypal Voice." *Contemporary Literature* 18 (Spring 1977): 173-97.

Lin, Yao-Fu. " 'The Mountains Are Your Mind': Orientalism in the Poetry of Gary Snyder." *Tamkang Review* 6/7 (October 1975-April 1976): 357-91.

Lyon, Thomas J. "The Ecological Vision of Gary Snyder." *Kansas Quarterly* 2 (Spring 1970): 117-24.

————. "Gary Snyder, A Western Poet." *Western American Literature* 3 (Fall 1968): 207-16.

McCord, Howard. *Some Notes to Gary Snyder's Myths & Texts*. Berkeley: Sand Dollar, 1971.

Parkinson, Thomas. "The Poetry of Gary Snyder." *Southern Review* 4 (Summer 1968): 616-32.

Paul, Sherman. *Repossessing and Renewing*. Baton Rouge: Louisiana State University Press, 1976.

Robbins, David. "Gary Snyder's 'Burning Island.' " *A Book of Rereadings*. Ed. Greg Kuzma. Lincoln, Neb.: Best Cellar Press, 1979.

Rothberg, Abraham. "A Passage to More Than India: The Poetry of Gary Snyder."
    Southwest Review 61 (Winter 1976): 26-38.
Scott, Robert Ian. "The Uncollected Early Poetry of Gary Snyder." *North American
    Review* 262 (Fall 1977): 80-83.
Steuding, Bob. *Gary Snyder*. TUSAS. Boston: Twayne, 1976.
Wright, James [Crunk]. "The Work of Gary Snyder." *Sixties* 6 (Spring 1962): 25-42.

Glen A. Love

WILLIAM STAFFORD
(1914-)

Biography

William Edgar Stafford was born in Hutchinson, Kansas, on 17 January 1914, the eldest of three children of Earl Ingersoll Stafford and Ruby Mayher Stafford. He lived in Hutchinson through childhood, then moved to other Kansas towns with his father's changes of jobs. He graduated from high school in Liberal, Kansas, in 1933. Young Stafford grew up in close association with nature and with books. Fishing, camping, exploring, and reading were important pastimes for the family. Looking backward, he writes of these early days, "Our lives were quiet and the land was very steady. Our teachers were good" (*Writing the Australian Crawl*, p. 9).

Recalling the most important influence upon his writing, Stafford has cited his mother's presence and "her way of talking and a certain kind of not very assertive, but nevertheless, tenaciously, noncommital judgmental element that was in her. Not to assert very much, but on the other hand, to assert what she felt" (*Writing the Australian Crawl*, p. 87). Elsewhere he says of her, "My mother was my first editor and a very comforting and welcoming editor she was. She would ask me what happened at school that day, and I would answer her; that to me was just like publication" ("A Poet Responds" [1980], p. 176). It is Stafford's father, however, who appears more frequently in the poetry, a figure whose mid-American quests and beliefs, wherever they led, seem to have aroused in the young poet the powers of feeling and imagination. Of his father, the poet has written in his well-known poem, "Vocation," "I hear him say while I stand between the two,/ helpless, both of them part of me:/ 'Your job is to find what the world is trying to be.' " (This and all poems cited here are from Stafford's *Stories That Could Be True: New and Collected Poems*.)

After attending two junior colleges, Stafford transferred to the University of Kansas, from which hè graduated in 1937. Working for a time at various jobs, he returned to the University of Kansas and was close to receiving the master's degree in English when the United States entered World War II in 1941. Within a few weeks he was drafted. As a pacifist and a conscientious objector, he spent the years from 1942 to 1946 in work camps in Arkansas and California. During these years in the camps he was assigned to such jobs as fighting forest fires, building and maintaining roads and trails, and reclaiming land from soil erosion. "I was more a social objector, with benevolence but no firm doctrinal bent," Stafford writes of this time (Lensing and Moran, *Four Poets and the Emotive Imagination*, p. 197). In California he met Dorothy Hope Frantz, whom he married in 1944. They have four children.

After the war, Stafford taught in high school for a year and spent another year working for Church World Service, a relief organization. He completed the master's degree at the University of Kansas in 1947. His thesis was a book of prose, *Down in My Heart*, about his experiences as a conscientious objector. In 1948 he was offered a teaching job at Lewis and Clark College in Portland, Oregon, where he has remained during his academic career, with time out to earn the Ph.D. in creative writing from the University of Iowa. He received the degree in 1954, his thesis being a collection of poems entitled "Winter Words." Stafford has taught as visiting professor and has read and lectured at a number of domestic and foreign universities. In 1970-71 he was poetry consultant for the Library of Congress. He lives with his family in the Portland suburb of Lake Oswego, Oregon, where, recently retired from teaching, he remains an active composer and reader of poetry, as well as an avid biker and photographer.

Stafford's verse began appearing in magazines in the 1950s, but his first book of poems, *West of Your City*, was not published until 1960, when he was forty-six years old. His principal collections of poetry since then include *Traveling Through the Dark* (1962), winner of the National Book Award for Poetry in 1963, *The Rescued Year* (1966), *Allegiances* (1970), *Someday, Maybe* (1973), and *Stories That Could Be True: New and Collected Poems* (1977).

William Stafford is also the author of *The Achievement of Brother Antoninus* (1967), a critical study and selection of the poems of the California poet, now William Everson, who also spent World War II in conscientious objector camps. Many of Stafford's opinions on the craft of writing are collected in his *Writing the Australian Crawl: Views on the Writer's Vocation* (1978), which includes a number of earlier published essays and interviews.

Major Themes

One way to approach William Stafford's poetry is to think of it as an overheard dialogue between the poet's inner and outer life. The central element of Stafford's verse is the communicative process, a kind of listening to, and answering of, primal forces—the earth, revered places, natural creatures, memories, the self.

> This is the hand I dipped in the Missouri
> above Council Bluffs and found the springs.

> All through the days of my life I escort
> this hand. Where would the Missouri
> meet a kinder friend?
> [*Stories That Could Be True*, p. 242]

As in this first stanza from "Witness," Stafford characteristically opens with an encounter between some part of an invited or bidden natural world and the receptive poetic self. "I usually welcome all kinds of impulses and ideas, not making an effort, during that first moment of encounter, to restrict the cadence or pace or flow of the language" ("Finding the Language" [1969], p. 82). Here, the poet's own hand, familiar and commonplace as it is, is sufficient to begin the interchange of numinous energy that is typical of Stafford's art. "This is the sort of feeling you get when doing a poem," Stafford says. "It is not so much like telling someone something that I have already decided to tell them. It is more like watching the language do it." As he conceives the poet's task it is not a boring in upon preconceived ideas but "being distracted in a positive direction.... The more you let yourself be distracted from where you are going, the more you are the person that you are. It is not so much like getting lost as it is like getting found" ("A Poet Responds," pp. 175-76).

Once the process of creation and discovery is begun, Stafford imagines himself going where it leads. The poem's opening encounter is, then, followed outward in a series of reverberating images and reflections:

> On top of Fort Rock in the sun I spread
> these fingers to hold the world in the wind;
> along that cliff, in that old cave
> where men used to live, I grubbed in the dirt
> for those cool springs again.
> [*Stories That Could Be True*, p. 242]

Stafford believes, as the images of prehistory—the old cave, the earlier men, the springs—suggest here, that there is "a kind of resonance among our experiences. The key word might be myth. Every now and then we find ourselves encountering some story or pattern that wields more power over us than we would expect." Stafford's poems and his process of composing them reflect his belief that these patterns are present all around us. "If we follow our tentative impulses outward, we may blunder upon one of those reverberating patterns" (Gerber and Gemmett, "Keeping the Lines Wet," pp. 124-25).

Perhaps the word *myth* is too specialized to describe what is happening in this and most of Stafford's other poems. But certainly we can see that the poet of "Witness" has luckily set the reverberations of "hand" stirring in his mind, and thus in our own. "That's what a poem is about," says Stafford. "It starts out to be something and it keeps ever more being that something: it focuses, it reinforces," ("Ten Little Questions," pp. 30-31) as we see in the rest of "Witness":

> Summits in the Rockies received this diplomat.
> Brush that concealed the lost children yielded
> them to this hand. Even on the last morning
> when we all tremble and lose, I will reach
> carefully, eagerly through that rain, at the end—
>
> Toward whatever is there, with this loyal hand.

The poem has concluded with an arresting of the resonances in a final line that becomes the furthest outreach of the work's impulses. The poem's process is, then, a mutual exploration between poet and subject. The central image of the hand yields more to the receptive poet than would be expected had the process never been invited to begin. Correspondingly, the image is in turn graced and rendered memorable by the poet's apprehension and expression of the reverberations that have taken place. He has listened well and thus he has spoken well. And we are enriched by being "witness" to this revelation of significance.

In a like manner, the single word of the poem's title, "Witness," partakes of this expanding of our experience. *Witness*, in its oldest root meaning, from the Anglo-Saxon *witan*, "to know," suggests the calm sureness of the poem's tone. The testimony of a witness is expressed in the work's succession of images. We see how these images present a range of experiences, encompassing many aspects of the title, from the formal and legal ("I escort this hand....received this diplomat") to the lowly and the familiar ("Where would the Missouri meet a kinder friend?"), and from the communal ("where men used to live, I grubbed...for those cool springs again...Brush that concealed the lost children yielded/ them to this hand") to the private act of fealty to the self ("this loyal hand"). These are "firsthand" accounts, in all senses of the word. Finally, these images provide evidence, as a witness might, to what has previously been in question.

As Stafford says of poetry, "It's like any discovery job; you don't know what's going to happen until you try it. You don't make life be what you've decided it *ought* to be. You find out what life is *trying* to be" (*Writing the Australian Crawl*, p. 114).

While Stafford resembles the older, nineteenth-century romantics in his belief that the poet should not impose obstacles between himself and the natural world, he might differ from them in his emphasis upon the back and forth, oscillating aspect of the composing process. Indeed, the dramatization of this interchange between world and self is often at the very center of his poems. If he believes, as a proper romantic should, that we should prepare ourselves for what the natural world is telling us, and if he insists that encounters with this world must constantly be returned to throughout the process of composition, he also demonstrates that the poetic imagination, in its reverberating selection and shaping of elements in the forming poem, cannot be separated from this process. In practice the older romantics were probably closer to this than to being Aeolian harps themselves.

A clearer break with traditional romanticism will be found in the attitude with which Stafford, as a modern, approaches his task. He is no bardic seer, no unacknowledged legislator of the world. Although he goes to nature in the fashion of his predecessors to seek its meanings, he does so with assumptions that are far less grandiose. And he comes to realizations that seem not so much universal as quietly personal, although no less possessed of a firm integrity within their carefully defined limitations. If the essence of the older romanticism was its conception that the individual contains the potentiality of a god, the romanticism of this century has reduced its faith in the self to the possibility of its discovering its own authentic existence. Stafford, then, shares in the "Romantic Aestheticism" of modern poetry, as defined by M. L. Rosenthal: "The Self seeks to discover itself through the energy of its insights into reality and through the sensuous excitement generated by its experiences of reality" (*The New Poets*: *American and British Poetry Since World War II* [New York: Oxford University Press, 1967], p. 13).

But Stafford stands apart from most other exponents of this modern position in his refusal to accept the individual as mere victim or the world as hopelessly bleak or meaningless or self-destructive. He is not obsessed with private guilt or suffering, or with the construction of a personal shaping myth. The self does not take over his poems. He looks to the poetic self for values, but he also accepts the common bases of experience. He keeps coming back to particulars, to the repeated encounter with the otherness of the world. When asked during an interview how he managed calmness at a time when poets seem so neurotic in a neurotic world, Stafford replied, "Deranged senses don't bring in enough: arranged senses bring in plenty" (*Writing the Australian Crawl*, p. 124).

Stafford shares with the Imagist tradition of Ezra Pound and William Carlos Williams a belief in letting things reveal themselves: "No ideas but in things," as Williams's famous phrase has it. But Stafford is more interested in the dialogue between ideas and things than in the sharp and unadorned image. He stands apart, too, from the T. S. Eliot tradition with its belief in the extinction of the poet's personality, and its difficulty and obscurity. Stafford, indeed, is reluctant to use figures like metaphor and simile in his writing: "I would like to be as clear and unambiguous as possible," he claims. In answer to those who would maximize the uncertainty of experience, Stafford argues for the opposite (Gerber and Gemmett, "Keeping the Lines Wet," pp. 129-30).

Stafford's poetic style is characterized by a relatively simple vocabulary, a muted, calm, understated manner, common speech rhythms, and, of course, by close observation and reflection upon observation. At its best this approach achieves quiet revelations of genuine power, as in his masterful "The Farm on the Great Plains," which ends with several perhaps uncharacteristic, but unforgettable, figures.

> My self will be the plain
> wise as winter is gray,
> pure as cold posts go
> pacing toward what I know.
> [*Stories That Could Be True*, p. 34]

What the Stafford manner falls into at its least successful moments is flatness and inconsequentiality:

> If you are oppressed, wake up about
> four in the morning: most places,
> you can usually be free some of the time
> if you wake up before other people.
> ["Freedom," *Stories That Could Be True*, p. 239]

Of the poets and writers for whom Stafford admits admiration, Thomas Hardy and Robert Lowell receive frequent mention. In addition, he may cite Emily Dickinson, Willa Cather, and Mark Twain from among the Americans, and Sir Walter Scott, Charles Dickens, and George Eliot from the British. Stafford's similarities to Robert Frost have been noted, but only in passing. They deserve further examination. Stafford has written a careful reassessment of Frost's work for the *New York Times Magazine*, "The Terror in Robert Frost" (1974), an essay that reveals Stafford's familiarity with the older poet's life and work. In an interview with Cynthia Lofsness, Stafford has given a less guarded response to Frost that indicates something of his reservations: "He lived a long time, he showed up well in photographs, . . . he came from the right part of the country. He was a tenacious old guy who wrote some interesting poems" (*Writing the Australian Crawl*, p. 99).

Despite Stafford's distaste for influence tracing and despite his coolness toward Frost, there are a number of interesting parallels between the two poets' work. In Stafford's best-known and widely anthologized poem, "Traveling Through the Dark," the Frostian overtones are particularly strong. Charles F. Greiner has mentioned the similarities between the "conversational tone" of the poem and Frost's "Stopping by Woods on a Snowy Evening" and "Mending Wall," as well as the connection between speaker and reader in the Stafford and Frost poems ("Stafford's 'Traveling Through the Dark': A Discussion of Style," p. 1017).

Looking further, one notes the close resemblance in theme and situation between "Traveling Through the Dark" and "Stopping by Woods." In both poems a traveler on an evening journey is drawn from his normal course of action by an appeal from the natural world for which he feels a deep and sympathetic response. In Frost's poem, this appeal takes the form of the lovely woods, "dark and deep," which compel the traveler to stop. ("Dark" and "deep" are a favorite pairing in Stafford's work, as Jonathan Holden points out in *The Mark to Turn*, pp. 13-14.) In Stafford's poem the appeal to the speaker is that of an unborn fawn, lying within its dead mother's body, struck by a car on a western road. In both poems this appeal arouses within the speaker a muted but unmistakable longing for the wildness or the "otherness" of nature that beckons him.

This beckoning forms the emotional climax of each of the poems, Frost's speaker gazing into the hushed and enchanted snow-covered woods, and Stafford's standing over the doe's body, listening to the wilderness. In both poems, the world of obligation and expectation waits in the background, with all of logic and common sense on its side, while the speaker hesitates. With Frost's poem, it is the horse who shakes his harness bells as if to remind his master of the miles to go and the promises to keep. The reverie of Stafford's speaker ("I thought hard for us all—my only swerving") is intruded upon by the waiting car with its purposefully aimed lights and droning engine. Finally, both speakers, accepting the justice of their obligations, shake off their reveries and return to the everyday world represented by the horse and the car, "masters" of their drivers after all. Both poems are profoundly pastoral, as are many of the best poems of both Frost and Stafford, in which a poetic speaker arrives at a critical awareness of his complex society by setting against it the vision of a simpler but deeper natural order.

Stafford was sufficiently interested in "Stopping by Woods" to parody it in a poem he called "Stopping by Frost" (William Stafford Issue of *Northwest Review* [1973], p. 86). Given the penchant of scholars for influence tracing, one may anticipate more studies of possible lines of connection from Frost to Stafford, these two rural poets in an urban society who avoid the experimental for the traditional, who study and adapt in their verse the vocabulary and the rhythms of ordinary speech, and who, for the early parts of their careers at least, found themselves quite unfashionable.

The word *swerving* near the end of "Traveling Through the Dark" illustrates another important element of Stafford's style. It is a feature that Richard Bridgman, in *The Colloquial Style in America*, identifies as typical of American prose: the emphasis upon the individual word (see also Holden, *Mark to Turn*, p. 10). "Traveling Through the Dark" would not be a poem without the "swerving," an act that defines the crucial action of the poem and lifts the experience from the ordinary into the memorable. The truth cannot be told except at such a slant. Stafford's continuing fascination with the word may be seen in its employment in his later poem, "The Swerve." Often a "swerve" word comes near the end of a Stafford poem, virtually reordering it into a new significance. One thinks of the verb *flame* coming in the final line of the poem "Near": "But nothing will happen until we pause/ to flame what we know, before any signal's given." Here the unexpected "flame" strikes at once at the images of coldness and isolation with which the poem begins and marshals the previous tentative glimpses of color and life ("Maybe there are trumpets in the houses we pass/ and a red bird watching from an evergreen—") into dramatic assertion. The word *incarnadined* in Stafford's poem "Ceremony" is another of these galvanic terms, Latinate and polysyllabic among its plain neighbors, and bringing startlingly to mind its original coinage by Shakespeare in *Macbeth* in a scene that plays upon the meaning of the Stafford poem.

The category regional as often applied to Stafford deserves explanation. He is regional in the sense that he responds to the place in which he finds himself, and he would welcome the designation as evidence that all of the best art is regional in being grounded in immediate sensory perception. He is a western poet partly because the sponge of his imagination has soaked its images from his western places. Set him down in the East and he would, as an incorrigible poet, begin soaking up eastern images. "I don't think the locale is crucial," says Stafford, "but it is crucial that wherever you are, you converge with it" ("A Poet Responds," p. 174). But he is a western poet in a more important sense because of certain habits of mind, such as his reflective concern for the frontier past and earlier Indian life, and his tendency to think in terms of western geography with its enormous distances and its assumptions of journeys and movement. And he is a universal poet because through the power with which he re-creates himself in his place, he, paradoxically, speaks to all people everywhere.

Finally, few other poets have written so engagingly about the process of composing poems as Stafford. Much of this material is collected in *Writing the Australian Crawl* and is worth the attention of students and teachers of creative writing. Stafford's practice of lowering the threshold of expectation in order to prevent a writing block is one that deserves further inquiry as a spur to invention.

Survey of Criticism

William Stafford's work is often considered part of the plain-style reaction of the 1960s to the "academic" verse, heavily influenced by Eliot and Pound, of the preceding generation. For the most part, Stafford's weaknesses as a poet have been seen as those of that plain-style school, as Paul Zweig points out in "The Raw and the Cooked" (1974). Calling Stafford "one of the finest poets of the conversational style," Zweig nevertheless finds Stafford poems in which there is naiveté without vision, insufficient energy, and "smallness of perception." At the same time, Zweig cites Stafford as "too good a poet to be defined by his failures" (pp. 605-6). Such judgments are typical of those critics who see Stafford's work as less than uniformly excellent, without denying the excellence of his best. William Heyen, for example, writes in "William Stafford's Allegiances" (1970), "In Stafford's best work there is a sense of studied artlessness; in his worst, just a sense of artlessness that does not reach out, does not intrigue" (p. 316). Roger Dickinson-Brown in "The Wise, the Dull, the Bewildered" (1975) similarly questions uncharged language and redundancy of expression. The great number of poems that Stafford writes doubtless gives rise to the complaints of redundancy. In Stafford's defense, poet James Dickey is quoted as saying that Stafford writes so much "not because he is glib and empty, but because he is a real poet, a born poet, and communicating in lines and images is not only the best way for him to get things said; it is the easiest!" (Heyen, "Allegiances," p. 309).

Critical essays concentrating upon Stafford's major strengths as a poet tend to classify themselves as general or specific. General evaluations (such as those by John Lauber, Stanley Moss, D. Nathan Sumner, and Laurence Lieberman) are likely to touch upon a number of common Stafford themes and ideas—nature, the family, the father, and childhood memories—and to comment upon the characteristic Stafford voice and stance, as well as principal stylistic traits.

Lieberman's essay, "The Shocks of Normality" (1973), while somewhat impressionistic, is also unerring in its insights into Stafford's gifts and perhaps the best of these general appreciative essays.

Of those critical articles dealing with specific themes, strategies, and poems, mention may be made here of several. J. Russell Roberts explicates the idea of wilderness and the relationship between the wild and the human in Stafford's early poetry ("Listening to the Wilderness with William Stafford" [1968]). His discussion includes treatment of "Traveling Through the Dark," which is also dealt with, at length, in Greiner's essay. Carol Kyle's essay on "Returned to Say," another poem from the same collection as "Traveling Through the Dark," also explicates Stafford's treatment of wilderness in some detail ("A Point of View in 'Returned to Say' " [1972]). The motif of the journey in Stafford is classified and analyzed by Dennis Daley Lynch in "Journeys in Search of Oneself" (1976). Stafford's sense of place is treated by fellow-poet Richard Hugo in an early essay, "Problems with Landscape in Early Stafford Poems" (1970), that argues convincingly that Kansas, not Oregon, is Stafford's blood's country and does so by comparing Stafford's haunting "The Farm on the Great Plains" with "Traveling Through the Dark," to the disadvantage of the latter. Tom Lyon finds both ends of the West home for Stafford in his fine essay "Western Poetry" (1980), in which Stafford is grouped with Robinson Jeffers and Gary Snyder as essential western poets. Lyon defines *western* as possessing a post-frontier view of the past, a nonexploitative view of nature, and a strong attachment to place.

In his review of poetry books by Stafford, Wendell Berry, and others, Lawrence Kramer writes sensitively of the "quiet language" of these poets ("In Quiet Language" [1979]). Linda W. Wagner analyzes this unadorned verse in greater detail on Stafford in her "William Stafford's Plain-Style" (1975).

Two books published in 1976, Jonathan Holden's *The Mark to Turn: A Reading of William Stafford's Poetry* and George S. Lensing and Ronald Moran's *Four Poets and the Emotive Imagination*, which studies Stafford along with Bly, Wright, and Simpson, deserve special mention. While neither is a full-scale treatment of Stafford, both represent the most thorough studies to date of his art. Holden, with welcome directness and clarity, argues that the imagination is Stafford's central theme and that through the imagination and its voice, language, we experience in Stafford the distinction between the human and the natural worlds. Less closely focused than Holden's book, Lensing and Moran's is a wide-ranging and perceptive explication of several of Stafford's principal themes within the general outlines of what the authors call "the Emotive Imagination," which is subjective, process oriented, colloquial and simple in vocabulary, and rhythmically imaged.

Students and scholars of Stafford's work are awaiting the appearance of James Pirie's bibliography from Garland Publishers, which promises to fill a growing need in Stafford study.

William Claire's conclusion in "Contemporary American Poetry at the Crossroads" (1980) that William Stafford "represents the modern spirit in American poetry at its best" (p. 10), will seem, to all who have heard or read this quiet, generous poet, a just tribute to him.

Bibliography

Works by William Stafford

Down in My Heart. Elgin, Ill: Brethren Press, 1947 (rpt. 1971).
West of Your City. Los Gatos, Calif.: Talisman Press, 1960.
Traveling Through the Dark. New York: Harper and Row, 1962.
The Rescued Year. New York: Harper and Row, 1966.
The Achievement of Brother Antoninus. Glenview, Ill.: Scott, Foresman, 1967.
"Finding the Language." *Naked Poetry.* Eds. Stephen Berg and Robert Mezey. New York: Bobbs-Merrill, 1969, pp. 82-83.
Allegiances. New York: Harper and Row, 1970.
Someday, Maybe. New York: Harper and Row, 1973.
William Stafford Issue of *Northwest Review* 13 (1973).
"The Terror in Robert Frost." *New York Times Magazine*, 18 August 1974. pp. 24-26, 31-38.
"Ten Little Questions." *Agenda* 14 (Autumn 1976): 30-31.
Stories That Could Be True: *New and Collected Poems.* New York: Harper and Row, 1977.
Writing the Australian Crawl: *Views on the Writer's Vocation.* Ann Arbor: University of Michigan Press, 1978.
"A Poet Responds." *Oregon Historical Quarterly* 81 (Summer 1980): 172-79.

Studies of William Stafford

Claire, William. "Contemporary American Poetry at the Crossroads." *American Studies International* 18 (Winter 1980): 5-18.
Dickinson-Brown, Roger. "The Wise, the Dull, the Bewildered: What Happens in William Stafford." *Modern Poetry Studies* 6 (Spring 1975): 30-38.
Gerber, Philip L., and Gemmett, Robert J., eds. "Keeping the Lines Wet: A Conversation with William Stafford." *Prairie Schooner* 44 (Summer 1970): 123-26.
Greiner, Charles F. "Stafford's 'Traveling Through the Dark': A Discussion of Style." *English Journal* 55 (November 1966): 1015-18, 1048.
Heyen, William. "William Stafford's Allegiances." *Modern Poetry Studies* 1 (Winter 1970): 307-18.
Holden, Jonathan. *The Mark to Turn: A Reading of William Stafford's Poetry.* Lawrence: University of Kansas Press, 1976.
Hugo, Richard. "Problems with Landscape in Early Stafford Poems." *Kansas Quarterly* 2 (Spring 1970): 33-38.
Kramer, Lawrence. "In Quiet Language." *Parnassus* 6 (Spring-Summer 1979): 101-17.
Kyle, Carol A. "A Point of View in 'Returned to Say' and the Wilderness of William Stafford." *Western American Literature* 7 (Fall 1972): 190-201.
Lauber, John. "World's Guest—William Stafford." *Iowa Review* 5 (Spring 1974): 88-100.
Lensing, George S., and Moran, Ronald. *Four Poets and the Emotive Imagination.* Baton Rouge: Louisiana State University Press, 1976, pp. 177-216.

Lieberman, Laurence. "The Shocks of Normality." *Yale Review* 63 (Autumn 1973): 453-73.

Lynch, Dennis Daley. "Journeys in Search of Oneself: The Metaphor of the Road in William Stafford's *Traveling Through the Dark* and *The Rescued Year*." *Modern Poetry Studies* 7 (Autumn 1976): 122-31.

Lyon, Thomas J. "Western Poetry." *Journal of the West* 19 (January 1980): 45-53.

Moss, Stanley. "Country Boy." *New Republic* 155 (19 November 1966): 23-24.

Roberts, J. Russell. "Listening to the Wilderness with William Stafford." *Western American Literature* 3 (Fall 1968): 217-26.

Sumner, Nathan D. "The Poetry of William Stafford: Nature, Time, and Father." *Research Studies* 36 (September 1968): 187-95.

Wagner, Linda W. "William Stafford's Plain-Style." *Modern Poetry Studies* 6 (Spring 1975): 19-30.

Zweig, Paul. "The Raw and the Cooked." *Partisan Review* 41 (1974): 604-12.

Merrill Lewis

WALLACE STEGNER
(1909-)

Wallace Stegner ended a 1976 interview by remonstrating, "I don't really want to be a western writer. I'd rather be a writer." While he found himself supporting regionalism in writing, he said, it was "always with a slight ironic distance" ("Time's Prisoners," p. 267). Stegner's responses to regional writing have always been equivocal. And for good reason. Certain kinds of western writers he is not. He does not write in the popular tradition and the mythic material of the wild West. Nor is he a historical novelist, mining the material of the Old West. He may on occasion talk and write of his work alongside that of the so-called serious western writers of his generation—A. B. Guthrie, Walter Van Tilburg Clark, Paul Horgan, or Wright Morris. But when he thinks of the writers who have most influenced his art, he mentions the late-nineteenth-century realists (William Dean Howells, Henry James, Mark Twain), or Joseph Conrad, Willa Cather and Sherwood Anderson, or William Faulkner—some of whom had regional attachments, some of whom did not.

A commitment to certain principles of fiction, therefore, shapes his work as much as or perhaps more than something called the western experience. He has admired, as Howells and James did, the giants of late-nineteenth and early twentieth-century European literature—Conrad in England, Chekhov, Turgenev, and Tolstoy in Russia—for their honest attempt to render life as it is actually lived. With such writers he also takes what he calls an incorrigibly moral view of literature. Stegner's kind of realism, like theirs, offers a lens on life as much as it offers a slice of life. The point of view of the story is always important. His narrator is often a *raissoneur*, and the world observed never totally separated from the act of observation. If the narrator is also the protagonist, then his *agon* is kept in the background of the story, feeding the observing eye and giving an edge to the judging mind—creating a tension between private and social worlds. It colors the narrative in innumerable ways but seldom takes center stage—and then only after careful preparation. It may motivate the story—in fact usually does—but Stegner never allows something so personal to dominate the story.

Yet good fiction, by Stegner's definition, is fiction based upon personal experience and consists of impressions of those experiences thoughtfully deliberated upon, often masked, so that the human truth embedded in them can be extracted or distilled, or developed from the raw negative. Like Henry James he believes fiction reflects the spirit, the sensibilities, and the total understanding of the writer. Since Stegner was born and raised through his adolescent and early years a Westerner, his spirit and understanding have been molded in part by the experiences of those years. He believes that the writer's world is especially and profoundly influenced by the period of preadolescence—from say age six to twelve—a period he spent in southern Saskatchewan—caught between life in the small, rough-hewn frontier village of East End and a prairie homestead on the Canadian-U.S. border some fifty miles to the south and west. The life of his youth and the life of the society in which he grew up offered a paradox: radical deculturation on the one hand and slavish worship of culture on the other. All of his western writing and much of his nonwestern writing is Stegner's artistic working out and working with the consequences of that paradox. The working out and the working with—the intellectual and artistic problems he faced as a writer—shape his work. If, then, Stegner is finally a western writer, it is by accident of birth and nurture, not intention—by accident of nurture *and* by critical and creative design.

Biography

The biography of Stegner that prevails today is one for the most part shaped since the decade of the 1950s, though his writing career began in the mid-1930s. His first short stories were published in 1934; his first major piece of nonfiction prose, *Clarence Earl Dutton: An Appraisal*, in 1935; and his first novel, *Remembering Laughter*, in 1937. The Dutton monograph was his Ph.D. dissertation completed at the University of Iowa under Norman Foerster. The novel won a prize from Little, Brown. This first work was published while Stegner was an instructor in English at the University of Utah. He quickly left, however, after the success of his first novel, for a position at the University of Wisconsin. Experiences at summer writers' workshops in the East, most notably Bread Loaf, gave him contacts at Harvard University, where he moved in 1939. His eastern connections came with eastern and academic friendships. The most important were those with Robert Frost, Theodore Morrison, Howard Mumford Jones, and the western expatriate, Bernard DeVoto. After six years as a Briggs-Copeland Instructor of English at Harvard, he became professor of English at Stanford University and then director of the Stanford Writing Program, a position he held until retirement in 1971.

The earlier years—prior to the sudden discovery of a vocation in the 1930s—are chronicled in part in the rambling family saga, *The Big Rock Candy Mountain*, published in 1943 in the middle of the war and in the middle of the Harvard years, indicating that separation by distance and time from the painful years described in that novel helped the creative process. Born on 18 February 1909 in Lake Mills, Iowa, the son of parents of Norwegian and German descent, Stegner and his older brother Cecil experienced a hectic and nomadic youth that later, in the autobiographical sections of *Wolf Willow* (1962), he would see as something like the last vain gasp of the frontier movement in North America with its tragic aftermath. The nomadic life of the Stegner family took them to several places in the West: to the Puget Sound in the far Northwest, to southern Saskatchewan, Montana, and Salt Lake City, Utah. While the family eventually spent some fifteen years in Salt Lake, years that allowed Stegner to get a public school education and graduate from the University of Utah, his father's restless quest for the main chance made him seek out yet other places for short periods of time, including Los Angeles and Reno. The slow disintegration of the family was culminated by three tragic deaths: Cecil's sudden death from pneumonia in 1931, the lingering illness and final death of Stegner's mother from cancer in 1933, and the suicide of his father in 1940. The series of trials that accompanied these events have influenced many of Stegner's finest stories, where disease and human suffering seem the final marks of human disintegration, the final rebuff to human dignity, and the final challenge to human integrity and the human spirit. By 1947, two years after leaving Harvard, Stegner had published six novels, had written or contributed to three books of nonfiction, and had written dozens of short stories and essays on the art of fiction. An engagement with the intellectual controversies of the times and the growing conviction of the importance of fiction mix with the remembered struggles of youth and adolescence to give all the work of this early period its peculiar, serious tone.

Stegner claims that he did not become a self-conscious western writer, as distinguishable from a self-conscious provincial, until after he had completed his most western book, *Beyond the Hundredth Meridian* (1954), a biography of John Wesley Powell. Indeed, between the publication of his fictionalized biography of Joe Hill, *The Preacher and the Slave*, in 1950 (the novel was later reprinted under the title *Joe Hill*) and *The Gathering of Zion: The Story of the Mormon Trail* in 1964, Stegner's direction was decidedly toward the writing of nonfiction. While he did publish two collections of short stories, *The Women on the Wall* (1950) and *The City of the Living* (1956), and toward the end of the period a novel, *A Shooting Star* (1961), with a contemporary setting and contemporary themes, his most characteristic work was in biography, cultural history, and critical and polemical essays. Some of the latter he later collected in *The Sound of Mountain Water* (1969), including the frequently anthologized "Wilderness Letter." But his best works in this period are the biography of Powell and the collection of childhood memories, fiction, and social history, *Wolf Willow*, and the literary essays collected in *Mountain Water*. In "Born a Square," "History, Myth, and the Western Writer," and "On the Writing of History," he presents his views on the relationship between history and fiction and the possibilities of serious western fiction. But his evaluations of writers who have failed (Bret Harte) or succeeded (Willa Cather) or helped give the region a voice (Bernard DeVoto) also help establish Stegner's critical assumptions about fiction.

Stegner's engagement with DeVoto's personality and ideas following Stanford University's acquisition of the DeVoto papers in 1956 seems more important than the friendship between the two writers itself, though it went back to the 1930s. Stegner's preoccupation in the 1950s and early 1960s with the idea of a western culture, environmental issues, and the problems facing western novelists and historians coincided with his rediscovery of DeVoto. The rediscovery culminated in Stegner's biography of the man in many respects his mentor, *The Uneasy Chair* (1974).

While the DeVoto biography is a major accomplishment of the last fifteen years, Stegner has also returned to the novel with perhaps even greater success. Most readers would cite *Angle of Repose* (1971) as his singular accomplishment in fiction since *Big Rock Candy Mountain*, and the most western of these last novels. But equally vital are the two concerning Joe Allston, *All the Little Live Things* (1967) and *The Spectator Bird* (1976). Undoubtedly Joe Allston is one of his great creations. His most recent novel, *Recapitulation* (1979), is a remarkably well-crafted and moving story of Bruce Mason's later life. *Angle of Repose* won the Pulitzer Prize in 1972; *The Spectator Bird* won the National Book Award for 1976.

Major Themes

In his essay, "History, Myth, and the Western Writer," Stegner indentifies a number of themes characteristic of serious western writing, as distinguished from the popular, formulaic story. There is the elegiac celebration of a past that was once "noble" but is now "lost." In stories about the more recent West, there is the author's attack upon provincial, small-town vulgarity—what Stegner calls the "village virus." A particular offshoot of this dichotomy (or separation) of the past and present in western fiction is the conflict between "the freedom-loving, roving man and the civilized woman." There is the related conflict between the law (as stated in books and maintained by sheriffs) and right "as defined by private judgment and enforced by gun, fist, or rope" (*Mountain Water*, pp. 195-96). And there is the tale shaped largely around the trial by ordeal of the western hero.

In passing, Stegner mentions the extent to which his writing sounds the same themes. One should add, in fact, that since the 1950s his writing has often deliberately tested the resilience of these themes—their capacity to speak to the contemporary man and woman with meaning and power. In the opening section of *Wolf Willow*, and in the praise of folk culture in the chapter "Specifications of a Hero," it is clear that Stegner knows and feels the magnetic charm of the nostalgic pull towards the past, both the freedom and wildness of youth. An "idyl of miniature savagery" he calls it in "The Making of Paths" (*Wolf Willow*, p. 275). But *Wolf Willow* also makes it clear that nostalgia is not enough. The last section of the book judges the contemporary village of East End, Saskatchewan, as a seat of civilization and concludes that because people like Corky Jones still live there, life is "not unhopeful" (p. 306). The double negative is hardly an endorsement of the contemporary West, nor is it a scathing attack on small-town rural America of the sort one identifies with Sinclair Lewis's *Main Street*.

The story "Genesis" in the same volume narrates the trial by ordeal of an English gentleman (Lionel Cullen) turned cowboy (Rusty) and caught in the fury of a Canadian prairie winter. The story that follows, "Carrion Spring," explores the conflicting desires of a young husband and wife whose ambitions for their own ranch barely survive such a winter. And Stegner notes that in Bo and Elsa Mason in *The Big Rock Candy Mountain*, completed almost twenty years earlier, he had presented the conflict between the freedom-loving man and the civilizing woman long before he was conscious that it was a western theme. He would develop the same theme almost ten years after *Wolf Willow* with Susan and Arthur Ward in *Angle of Repose*.

Stegner cites no instances in his work of the conflict between the law and right conduct, but variations on the theme run through many of his best stories. Brucie Mason in *The Big Rock Candy Mountain* does not know which is worse—his father's illegal liquor business or his conduct toward Elsa and the boys. The theme is also present in the early novel, *Fire and Ice*, and in the late novel, *All the Little Live Things*. In the latter novel Joe Allston must confront a squatter on his five-acre tract—both the legal and the moral issues created by the presence of Jim Peck in his back yard. Sabrina Castro in *A Shooting Star* faces both public and personal questions of responsibility: the proper disposition of a virgin tract of redwoods and the acceptance of a child conceived out of wedlock. Lyman Ward in *Angle of Repose* must renegotiate his judgment of a wife who has left him a cripple but wants to return. Stegner's fiction is rich in variations on all the themes he touches upon in his 1962 essay, but they often intermesh in the questions of right conduct and the conflicts between men and women, husbands and wives, who are different people with different values.

The fact that Stegner gives the themes a unique touch does not change their identity. Take, for example, the theme of trial by ordeal. Many of his novels explore a man's attempt or desire to escape a situation he cannot face or face a situation he has long tried to escape. In *On a Darkling Plain* (1940), Ed Vickers seeks sanctuary from war and the barbarism of the civilized world by escaping to a prairie homestead. But he cannot escape the plague of 1918, for the war touches the girl he has come to love and forces him out of hiding. In Stegner's most recent novel, *Recapitulation*, an older and wiser Bruce Mason must return to the un-marked grave of his father, Bo, and accept what he has inherited.

In the better stories, the ordeals Stegner's men face are not the physical ones faced by Rusty in "Genesis" but psychological and moral. Consequently, the physical settings of Stegner's stories, though firmly western, and often vividly realized, are moral as well as physical.

Two ideas color Stegner's treatment of these themes. First, he believes that the West was and is essentially a highly mobile society. This means that stability and the idea of tradition are not readily available. (Only in Mormon society can Stegner find them.) Moral questions must be renegotiated. The typical Stegner protagonist finds himself cut off, tries to go it alone, finds it hard to share experience or blame, but longs for the stability and certainty of community and belief.

Stegner also accepts the idea that the West is an arid and urban region. The aridity assures westerners that the possibilities of realizing the American dream here are severely limited. The urbanity assures the culture of a constant tension between provincial and cosmopolitan values. At the end of *Angle of Repose*, Lyman Ward says he has experienced "that old September feeling." The dilemma embodied in that feeling (to borrow from Robert Frost) is what to make of a diminished thing. How could a life be at one and the same time so rich and full, and so limited?

The emotion of that feeling pervades much of Stegner's writing and indicates in one sense at least how he hopes his writing is both western and contemporary. Stegner's greatest thematic accomplishment, therefore, may be that he has preserved the West from absolute provincialism by indicating how richly its experience represents the dilemma faced by contemporary America and by the region itself.

Survey of Criticism

Insofar as there is some shape to the criticism of Stegner's work, it divides itself roughly along two lines. Chronologically, there is that written before and after the successful *Angle of Repose*. The novel has served as a catalyst for reassessing all Stegner's writing—both the very substantial body of fiction, biography, and history that preceded it and the remarkable series of books that have followed in the last ten years. It is also the book that has received most attention. The other rough division lies in the approaches of Stegner critics. Some read him primarily as a regional writer committed to the use of place and history in fiction, while others are interested in the artfulness of his writing—be it fiction or history or biography or some mixture of the three. Again, *Angle of Repose* has served both readers well. No wonder, then, that Kerry Ahearn calls it Stegner's magnum opus.

Criticism prior to the publication of this Pulitzer Prize-winning novel is thin. Book reviews were frequent and sometimes insightful, but there were only two sustained studies of his work. The earliest, an essay published by Chester E. Eisinger in *College English* in 1958 (a shorter version is included in his book, *Fiction in the Forties*), is now helpful only insofar as it reminds us that Stegner need not be approached as a regionalist. He is approached as a regionalist, however, in the second essay, "*The Big Rock Candy Mountain*: No Roots—and No Frontier" (1971), written by Lois Phillips Hudson, herself a writer and a Westerner. Taking as her critical texts Stegner's comments in "Born a Square," "History, Myth, and the Western Writer," and the autobiographical portions of

Wolf Willow, Hudson argues that Stegner, like the western regionalists generally (the southern regionalist is another thing), is forced back upon factual
experience because he or she has no literary or historical tradition within which
to work. The western writer "cannot erect fiction on fiction" because there are no
precedents. The West has not given us any Holinsheds, only "the plaster Paul
Bunyans" and "plaster cowboys" (*"Big Rock Candy Mountain,"* pp. 7-8). Caught
in such a dilemma, as Stegner explained in *Wolf Willow*, the world "measures
itself from me" (p. 19). Stegner's major protagonists (up to 1970), Bruce Mason
of *Big Rock Candy Mountain* and Joe Allston of *All the Little Live Things*, feel, as
their creator does, the restless quest of identity. They yearn for a place, a home,
and a cultural tradition but fear that all there may be is "criss-crossed trails,"
hostility, and anarchy.

Two surveys of Stegner's work written in the early 1970s following the publication of *Angle of Repose*, and conceived independently of one another, offer a
more panoramic view. Merrill Lewis and Lorene Lewis in their Boise State
Western Writers pamphlet, *Wallace Stegner* (1972), survey the canon of Stegner's
work from *Remembering Laughter* through *Angle of Repose*. They point out the
thematic connections between Stegner's western and nonwestern books, the
history and fiction, and the autobiography: the quest for home and identity, and
the relation of sons to fathers (and mothers) in the early stories and novels as
opposed to the relations of fathers to sons (and daughters) in the later novels. But
they see Stegner primarily as a western writer, regardless, a writer attempting to
realize the correspondence between his family experiences and regional experience in general.

Robert Canzoneri, in "Wallace Stegner: Trial by Existence" (1973), is the
first critic really to approach Stegner from the literary side. He is also more
selective in his survey, centering his discussion for the most part on Stegner's
fiction but in doing so placing Stegner much more firmly in literary history than
does Eisinger. He explains the nature of Stegner's particular kind of "impressionistic
realism," which presents the objective world as "only what the eye observed with
all its uncertainties" (p. 798). Stegner also presents that reality in a manipulated
and fragmented form, and it is more readily confirmed by human experience than
by some reference point outside our immediate human experience. Canzoneri sets
off Stegner's kind of fiction from fiction based on absurdist, Jungian, Freudian, or
mythic premises. By implication Stegner's realism is also set off against the
reality that interests historians, since the principles that govern his re-creation of
character are aesthetic. On the other hand he portrays character not as a point but
as a line, a line dictated by his heritage and his environment (Stegner, "Trial by
Existence," p. 808). So Stegner's realistic aesthetic does lead him to explore the
relationship of past to present and character to place. In Joe Allston and Lyman
Ward, he has created sophisticated adults capable of realizing the importance of
the past in understanding their predicaments and that of contemporary society.

The most thorough, authoritative, and thoughtful study of Stegner to date is
the short book Forrest Robinson and Margaret Robinson contributed to Twayne's

United States Authors Series (1977). The first chapter, based on extensive inter-
views with Stegner, establishes clearly the contours and character of Stegner
Country, offers an extensive sketch of Stegner's early years, and allows us to
put the autobiographical material in *Big Rock Candy Mountain* and *Wolf Willow*
in clearer perspective. The chapter on Stegner's nonfiction clarifies as well
Stegner's concept of "the middle ground"—between history and fiction, Clio and
Calliope—a ground that attempts to fuse rather than separate them. Almost all of
Stegner's nonfiction seeks such a fusion and in so doing takes certain liberties
with historical persons and events. In some cases, as in *Mountain Water* and
Wolf Willow, the books begin with memory and argue back from memory to the
attendant facts and then flesh out fact in the form of fully realized fictions. In other
cases, as in *The Preacher and the Slave, Beyond the Hundredth Meridian*, and
The Gathering of Zion, the full power of historical events and the essential
character of historical persons cannot be grasped until rendered in ways similar to
fiction.

The Robinsons not only explore the concept of the middle ground and its
impact on Stegner's later work; they explain in considerable detail Stegner's use
of historical material in his fiction, particularly his use of the letters and personal
reminiscences of Mary Hallock Foote in *Angle of Repose*. They justify Stegner's
changes in the Foote material by arguing that the novelist of the middle ground is
obliged to go beyond the historical questions concerning the what of the past and
explore (if not finally answer) the more vital questions concerning the why of
human actions. To explore these questions Stegner had "to extrapolate and
invent" (*Stegner*, p. 153). The other side of this issue, the novelist's invasion of
history and biography and the altering of fact to suit his fiction, is explored in a
paper by Mary Ellen Williams Walsh, "*Angle of Repose* and the Writings of
Mary Hallock Foote: A Source Study" (forthcoming). The novelist, Walsh in
effect argues, cannot take liberties with the lives of real people. The argument
turns on the question whether the novel is about Susan and Arthur Ward, who are
fictions, or Mary Hallock and Arthur De Wint Foote, who were not.

The historical side of the middle ground, rather than the fictive and ethical,
interests Barnett Singer in "The Historical Ideal in Wallace Stegner's Fiction"
(1977) and Richard W. Etulain in "Western Fiction and History: A Reconsideration" (1979). Singer identifies a number of historical ideals in Stegner's fiction.
In early books such as *On a Darkling Plain, Big Rock Candy Mountain, Second
Growth,* and *The Preacher and the Slave*, Stegner re-creates a certain time and
place and moment and occasionally has characters argue over the relationship
between factual history and imaginative story. The later novels set in contemporary California, however, take as a major theme the danger of historical innocence—
the cultural need to be knowledgeable about the past. In *Angle of Repose* the
narrator Lyman Ward must imaginatively reconcile past and present and re-
create the several Wests known to his grandparents whose lives he is reconstruct-
ing. Singer finds that the characters of Susan and Arthur Ward have a historical
authenticity; we see them fully within their late-nineteenth-century world, actu-

ally and typically as both history and realistic fiction should want them. Susan's behavior is molded by the literary models that captivated so many Victorians; Arthur is one of the casualties of the age of growth. By his use of impressionistic realism and in his philosophical justification of historical knowledge, Stegner demonstrates that history is no antiquarian pursuit.

Richard Etulain believes that historians can learn much from Stegner's search for a usable past in the novel. The lessons are embedded in two themes: the conflict between eastern and western cultural values and the discovery of continuities between past and present. In a much less sympathetic interpretation of Susan Ward than the one given by Singer, Etulain sees her as the disoriented eastern woman of culture who becomes attached finally to the West, but reluctantly and too late to prevent tragic misunderstandings between her and her husband. While Lyman is not clearly a westerner, he is more willing to take the West as it comes and make of the new what he can. The continuity between past and present—Stegner's other great theme in the novel—is possible only because of the success the narrator Lyman Ward has as commentator and sympathizer in his impassioned attempt to comprehend the relationships between the old and the new Wests.

Singer and Etulain praise the history in *Angle of Repose* because Stegner gives the past its legitimate and all-but-autonomous voice and also makes the past relevant to the present moment. But past and present are never brought together in the novel except in Lyman Ward's mind, and there, past and present run parallel to one another, presenting contrasts as well as similarities, as Singer tells us. To point out that the philosophy of history advocated by Lyman Ward does not explain the narrative he tells or the way he tells it is to recognize the importance of point of view in Stegner's fiction. The Robinsons trace Stegner's gradual shift from third-person "Brucie" stories written in the 1930s and 1940s to first-person "adult" narrators in the late 1940s and 1950s to his invention of Joe Allston in the signally important short story, "A Field Guide to Western Birds" (1956). They note that Allston's character combines the self-preoccupation of the younger, earlier protagonists with a certain self-scrutiny and self-criticism. They also note that Allston's imagination is "instinctively allegorical" ("Interview," p. 142), an attribute of a moralist rather than historian, one could add, that links him with some younger protagonists like Edwin Vickers in *On a Darkling Plain* as well as with the more problematical character Lyman Ward.

Kerry Ahearn and Audrey C. Peterson find the artfulness of *Angle of Repose* summed up in Stegner's intricate handling of point of view and voice. Peterson, in an incisively argued essay, "Narrative Voice in Wallace Stegner's *Angle of Repose*" (1975), explains how fully Ward contrives, manipulates, and ultimately controls the narrative in the novel—sometimes as an omniscient third-person narrator, sometimes as a first-person commentator. In writing a narrative that is about both his grandparents and himself, Ward is more fictionist than historian. Even the story that takes place in the last century is not a frontier story but a story as perceived by a sophisticated twentieth-century intellectual. Peterson finds considerable ambivalence in Ward's motive and role as narrator. As a historian turned novelist, Ward tells his son Rodman he knows he is not writing history. But he can later tell his secretary, Shelly Rasmussen, that he is "still [enough of] a historian under the crust" to want to tell the story of his grandparents as it must have been for them (*Angle of Repose*, p. 130).

Kerry Ahearn's "*The Big Rock Candy Mountain* and *Angle of Repose*: Trial and Culmination" (1975) is, as the title suggests, a study of an artistic failure and a success. Stegner's earlier novel is weak, Ahearn argues, because the reader cannot determine what voice is intended to control the telling of the story. Stegner has different major characters (all members of the Mason family) relate different portions of the story, yet he identifies too easily with the anger and even vindictiveness of the younger son Bruce, who is determined to make a case against the brutality of his father. *Angle of Repose*, on the other hand, develops the same larger themes but with more unity and more "resonance" because Lyman Ward commands the story. While admitting that Lyman's primary function in the novel is to relate the "straight" narrative—"to picture the West as it probably was" through the biographies of his grandparents ("Trial and Culmination," p. 27), Ahearn, like Peterson, finds Lyman as unreliable as he is reliable. Stegner gives him a formidable mind and a persuasive voice, but he also makes him prejudiced, dogmatic, and willing to speculate freely and self-righteously—hardly qualities to trust in a historian. Ahearn calls the relationship between the narrator and his creator complex but ultimately ironic.

Lyman Ward's motives for tracking through the past, when they finally emerge, are certainly more personal than historical. He is interested in the relations of men and women and questions of fidelity and infidelity. Ahearn explores these themes in "Heroes vs. Women: Conflict and Duplicity in Stegner" (1977). While Stegner's male protagonists are never cast in the role of the mythic western hero, they come to realize by the end of their various stories that they must have diminished expectations of life. Stegner's women, with the exception of Sabrina Castro in *A Shooting Star*, are never allowed to have it or see it as otherwise. The men may have grandiose schemes or insist upon their self-reliance, as do Bo Mason and Arthur Ward. The women are victimized or patiently dependent and yet endure, often with a grace found missing in the men. In the combativeness between Joe and Ruth Allston in *The Spectator Bird* (1976), Ahearn sees an acceptance of the marriage bond missing in the relationships in earlier novels, and he sees a new maturity in the male protagonist, Joe Allston. These changes are possible because Ruth is a stronger and more complex woman and Allston is willing to lecture himself, not just others.

The sophistication of Stegner's recent critics indicates that he has found the readers he has long deserved. They have shown some sense of his art and identified some of the qualities found in individual stories and books. A forthcoming collection edited by Anthony Arthur will bring together the most perceptive reviews and essays of the past forty years. Richard Etulain plans a book-length set of interviews with Stegner to be published by the University of Utah Press.

These should indicate whether Stegner's views as represented by the critics or as scattered through over a half-dozen somewhat ephemeral interviews published elsewhere during the past ten years are accurate. Stegner has said some things about his intentions not entirely congruent with statements in the essays collected in *Mountain Water* or seemingly implicit in novels like *Angle of Repose*. He has made statements about his current writing sometimes at odds with the novels that have come out. He continues to challenge his readers.

Bibliography

Works by Wallace Stegner

Remembering Laughter. Boston: Little, Brown, 1973.
"A Democracy Built on Quicksand." *Delphian Quarterly* 22 (Autumn 1939): 11-15, 29.
"Regionalism in Art." *Delphian Quarterly* 22 (Winter 1939): 2-7.
" 'Truth' and 'Faking' in Fiction." *Writer* 53 (February 1940): 40-43.
On a Darkling Plain. New York: Harcourt, Brace, 1940.
Fire and Ice. New York: Duell, Sloan, and Pearce, 1941.
Mormon Country. New York: Duell, Sloan, and Pearce, 1942.
"Is the Novel Done For?" *Harper's* 186 (December 1942): 76-83.
The Big Rock Candy Mountain. New York: Duell, Sloan, and Pearce, 1943.
The Preacher and the Slave. Boston: Houghton Mifflin, 1950; reprinted as *Joe Hill: A Biographical Novel*. Garden City, N.Y.: Doubleday, 1969.
The Women on the Wall. Boston: Houghton Mifflin, 1950.
"Variations on a Theme by Conrad." *Yale Review* 49 (March 1950): 512-23.
Beyond the Hundredth Meridian: John Wesley Powell and the Second Opening of the West. Boston: Houghton Mifflin, 1954.
The City of the Living, and Other Stories. Boston: Houghton Mifflin, 1956.
A Shooting Star. New York: Viking, 1961.
Wolf Willow: A History, a Story, and a Memory of the Last Plains Frontier. New York: Viking, 1962.
The Gathering of Zion: The Story of the Mormon Trail. New York: McGraw-Hill, 1964.
All the Little Live Things. New York: Viking, 1967.
The Sound of Mountain Water. Garden City, N.Y.: Doubleday, 1969.
Angle of Repose. Garden City, N.Y.: Doubleday, 1971.
"This New Man, the American." *Stanford Magazine* 1 (Fall-Winter 1973): 14-19.
The Uneasy Chair: A Biography of Bernard DeVoto. Garden City, N.Y.: 'Doubleday, 1974.
"The Provincial Consciousness." *University of Toronto Quarterly* 43 (Summer 1974): 299-310.
The Spectator Bird. Garden City, N.Y.: Doubleday, 1976.
Recapitulation. Garden City, N.Y.: Doubleday, 1979.

Studies of Wallace Stegner

Ahearn, Kerry. "*The Big Rock Candy Mountain* and *Angle of Repose*: Trial and Culmination." *Western American Literature* 10 (Spring 1975): 11-27.

————. "Heroes vs. Women: Conflict and Duplicity in Stegner." *Western Humanities Review* 31 (Spring 1977): 125-41.

————. "Wallace Stegner and John Wesley Powell: The Real—and Maimed—Western Spokesman." *South Dakota Review* 15 (Winter 1977-78): 33-48.

Canzoneri, Robert. "Wallace Stegner: Trial by Existence." *Southern Review* 9 (Autumn 1973); 796-827.

Dillon, David. "Time's Prisoners: An Interview with Wallace Stegner." *Southwest Review* 59 (Summer 1976): 252-67.

Etulain, Richard W. "Western Fiction and History: A Reconsideration." *The American West, New Perspectives, New Dimensions*. Ed. Jerome O. Steffen. Norman: University of Oklahoma Press, 1979, pp. 152-74.

Hudson, Lois Phillips. "*The Big Rock Candy Mountain*: No Roots—and No Frontier." *South Dakota Review* 9 (Spring 1971): 3-13.

Lewis, Merrill, and Lewis, Lorene. *Wallace Stegner*. WWS. Boise, Idaho: Boise State College, 1972.

Peterson, Audrey C. "Narrative Voice in Stegner's *Angle of Repose*." *Western American Literature* 10 (Summer 1975): 125-33.

Robertson, Jamie. "Henry Adams, Wallace Stegner and the Search for a Sense of Place in the West." *The Westering Experience in American Literature*. Ed. L. L. Lee and Merrill Lewis. Bellingham, Wash.: Bureau for Faculty Research, 1977, pp. 135-43.

Robinson, Forrest G., and Robinson, Margaret G. "An Interview with Wallace Stegner." *American West* 15 (January-February 1978): 34-37.

————. *Wallace Stegner*. TUSAS. Boston: Twayne, 1977.

Singer, Barnett. "The Historical Ideal in Wallace Stegner's Fiction." *South Dakota Review* 15 (Spring 1977): 28-44.

Richard Astro

JOHN STEINBECK
(1902-1968)

Of the many writers whose works are typically included in discussions of western American literature, John Steinbeck is among the most prolific and the most accomplished. He alone has had a book reach the top of the best-seller list. He alone has been awarded the Nobel Prize for literature.

Biography

Steinbeck was born a westerner on 27 February 1902 in the agricultural community of Salinas, California. As a boy he roamed the Salinas Valley, observing its people. And he wandered west to Monterey Bay and explored the towns along its shore: Monterey, Carmel, and Pacific Grove. From his mother, who taught school in several valley communities, he developed a love of books, the fiction of popular writers and the classics: Milton, Flaubert, and, most of all Sir Thomas Malory. The *Morte D'Arthur* was his favorite book from childhood.

Steinbeck graduated a well-rounded if undistinguished student from Salinas High School and then attended Stanford University, leaving in 1925 without taking a degree. Between academic years (and sometimes during them) he worked as a rancher, a cotton picker, and as a bench chemist in the Spreckles Sugar Factory near Salinas. In 1926, Steinbeck went to New York and tried unsuccessfully to become a writer. He retreated to California a year later on a ship via the Panama Canal and completed work on his first novel, *Cup of Gold*, which is set in the Caribbean and in Panama. Published in 1929, it was a commercial and literary failure.

In 1930, he began his long association with Elizabeth R. Otis of the New York literary agency of McIntosh and Otis. In that same year, he married Carol Henning of San Jose, a woman of substantial intellect who would later influence his writing. He also met Edward F. Ricketts, the marine biologist who owned and operated the Pacific Biological Laboratory on Cannery Row in Pacific Grove and who became the novelist's closest friend during the two decades of his best work. So taken was Steinbeck with Ricketts's person and his ideas that the novelist used him as the persona in a half-dozen of his books. Additionally, the two men collaborated on *Sea of Cortez* (1941), the content of which is seminal to an understanding of Steinbeck's best fiction.

During the early 1930s Steinbeck completed his second and third novels, *The Pastures of Heaven* (1932) and *To a God Unknown* (1933). These failed to sell, though both were accorded more favorable critical receptions than *Cup of Gold*. Steinbeck's first notable success came in *Tortilla Flat* (1935), his story about the *paisanos* of old Monterey. The book was published by Covici-Friede after being turned down by a number of other editors. In the process, Steinbeck and Pascal Covici became close friends, and when Covici joined the Viking Press in 1938, he took Steinbeck's work with him. Steinbeck never had another editor. *Of Mice and Men* (1937) made Steinbeck a national figure. It was a Book-of-the-Month Club selection and was produced successfully for the stage. Of less significance but also successful are many of the stories in *The Long Valley* (1938), several of which were published separately in small magazines earlier in the decade.

Despite his successes in *Tortilla Flat* and in *Of Mice and Men*, Steinbeck's reputation was based on his ability to tell entertaining but otherwise inconsequential tales. Only with the publication of *In Dubious Battle* (1936) and *The Grapes of Wrath* (1939), novels about the complex sociopolitical problems of California agriculture, was Steinbeck recognized as a major American literary figure. Agriculture in California during the 1930s consisted largely of farm factories operated by corporations who employed migrant laborers at low wages to pick fruit and vegetables. During the winter of 1934, he had extensive conversations with two farm labor organizers who furnished him with many of the materials for *In Dubious Battle*, a book about a strike in a California apple orchard. *The Grapes of Wrath* is without question Steinbeck's most ambitious and his most successful novel. It won a Pulitzer Prize and was an immediate best-seller. A movie version, starring Henry Fonda and Jane Darwell, reinforced the book's popularity. It has been in print continuously and remains an American classic.

The experience of writing *The Grapes of Wrath* tired Steinbeck. Needing a change of scene, he embarked in early 1940 with Ed Ricketts on a scientific expedition to the Gulf of California. *Sea of Cortez: A Leisurely Journal of Travel and Research*, the record of that expedition, was written by both men and published in 1941. It is a valuable catalog of marine life in the Gulf of California, as well as a work of travel literature, a treatise on philosophy, and a critique of contemporary society.

Pearl Harbor was bombed by the Japanese just after *Sea of Cortez* was published, and Steinbeck quickly offered his writing talents to the war effort. His first contribution was *Bombs Away* (1942), a propagandistic piece for the Army Air Corps. In 1943, Steinbeck, whose first marriage had collapsed, married again, this time a singer named Gwendolyn Conger, and traveled to England as a war correspondent for the *New York Herald-Tribune*. He sent back dispatches that were later collected and published as *Once There Was a War* (1958). His most notable piece about the war is *The Moon is Down* (1942), a play-novelette about the invasion of a small Scandinavian village. It was translated into several languages and was popular among resistance armies throughout Europe.

Steinbeck's first postwar novel, *Cannery Row* (1945), is, as he claims, "a kind of nostalgic thing written for a group of soldiers who had said to me, 'write something funny that isn't about the war' " (Lisca, *Wide World of John Steinbeck*, p. 198). The book's casual tone and simple plot, which deals with the exploits of a group of Monterey vagabonds and Doc, their friend and protector, camouflage Steinbeck's indictment of so-called civilized society. That indictment is more apparent in his next novel, *The Wayward Bus* (1947), an allegory of modern life in which a diverse group of men and women are thrown together on a bus bound from one California community to another. Shortly before he began work on *The Wayward Bus*, Steinbeck wrote a story based on a fable about a Mexican boy who found a great pearl that he thought would bring him happiness and that almost destroyed him before he wisely threw it back into the sea. Steinbeck rewrote this, his parable of the vanity of human wishes, a number of times before it was finally published in 1947 as *The Pearl*.

By 1947, Steinbeck had established himself as a New Yorker and, living in a new city, he searched for new literary vistas. During that year he visited the Soviet Union with photographer Robert Capa and sent back essays that would later be the basis of a book with Capa entitled *A Russian Journal* (1948). In May 1948, Steinbeck was to join Ed Ricketts for another collecting trip, this time to the west coast of Vancouver Island and the Queen Charlottes, but the trip was cancelled when Ricketts was killed in a bizarre car-train accident. Steinbeck spent the better part of the next two years wrestling with the nature of his literary indebtedness to Ricketts. His writing during the period reflects more than anything else his close relationship with the marine biologist.

The period after Ricketts's death was also one of personal convalescence for Steinbeck. By 1948, his marriage to Gwendolyn Conger had deteriorated, and Steinbeck was deeply concerned about the welfare of his and Gwen's two sons. When Ricketts died, Steinbeck came apart emotionally, and it was not until mid-1949 that he began to feel a new sense of purpose and direction. What changed things most was a woman named Elaine Scott. He married her in 1950 and returned to his work with a heightened enthusiasm.

Among Steinbeck's first works written after Ricketts's death is "About Ed Ricketts," a statement of affection for a man who influenced him deeply and permanently. *Burning Bright* (1950), which Steinbeck wrote for the stage, is an unsuccessful attempt to convert a story about Ricketts's character into a morality play. It is less a work of art than an abstract piece of philosophizing that fails as theater and as fiction. While he was lamenting the failure of *Burning Bright*, Steinbeck completed the filmscript for *Viva Zapata!,* his story of the Mexican revolutionary that Elia Kazan made into one of the best movies of 1952. During this period, Steinbeck worked at intervals on what he called his big novel, a sprawling study of three generations of two California families. Five years of research, writing, and rewriting went into *East of Eden* (1952), and while it is not a great novel, it is impressive for the largeness of its scope, for the expansiveness of its design.

Steinbeck's last novels are slight in scope and design, as well as in quality. *Sweet Thursday* (1954) is a sequel to *Cannery Row* but was written with the theater in mind. It was a Rodgers and Hammerstein musical, which played the 1955 Broadway season as *Pipe Dream*. *The Short Reign of Pippin IV* (1957) is a sapless book about a middle-aged astronomer who is suddenly drafted to rule the unruly French. Steinbeck was aware that *Pippin* was a slight book, but he felt otherwise about his work on a modernized edition of Malory's *Morte D'Arthur*. He prepared for this task by reading dozens of books about Malory and by traveling extensively with Elaine through the English and Welsh countryside. In total, his translations include five of the six parts of the Tale of King Arthur: the Gawain, Ewain, and Marhalt sections of the First Romance, and all of the Noble Tale of Sir Launcelot of the Lake. These were published posthumously in 1976, and throughout, Steinbeck is faithful to the original. His text is readable, and had he completed it, his Arthur would likely have become a standard edition.

Though he would write one more novel (*The Winter of Our Discontent*) by 1960, Steinbeck realized that as a novelist he had nowhere to go. Moreover, there is evidence that he had lost interest in writing fiction, and in his last years he was more productive as a journalist and traveler. His interest in science, in hibernation since Ricketts's death, emerged afresh when he went to the Mohole drilling site off of Baja California. In addition to a lengthy piece he wrote about Mohole for *Life Magazine*, Steinbeck authored two volumes of nonfiction during the decade that reflect his life-style as journalist and traveler. *Travels with Charley in Search of America* (1962) is the record of Steinbeck's trip across the country with his French poodle. *America and Americans* (1966) is a short narrative about his country interspersed with many fine photographs. *Travels with Charley* is Steinbeck's most important work of travel literature; there are passages in the book as moving as any he ever wrote. The best are those in which he describes his native California—the majestic redwoods, the sprawling Mojave, his native Salinas. When he died on 20 December 1968, his widow Elaine took his body to his birthplace for burial in the Steinbeck family plot.

Major Themes

Steinbeck wrote his best fiction during the 1930s, and his masterpiece is *The Grapes of Wrath*, published during the last year of that decade. In that work he celebrated what he called man's proven capacity for greatness of heart and spirit, his ability to grow beyond his work, to emerge ahead of his accomplishments. But throughout the narrative portion of *Sea of Cortez*, his next book, he seems less certain about the strength of our species. He notes a strange duality in man that makes for what he calls an ethical paradox in that while we define certain qualities as good and others as bad and while we claim to admire the good and abhor the bad, the so-called good qualities are the concomitants of failure, while the bad ones are the cornerstones of success. Throughout the book, Steinbeck attacks man's self-interest, calling it a mutation that can end only in our extinction.

At the same time Steinbeck affirms that man possesses qualities that keep him reaching forward. And this, he insists, is the human dilemma. He notes:

Man might be described fairly adequately, if simply, as a two-legged paradox. He has never become accustomed to the tragic miracle of consciousness. Perhaps, as has been suggested, his species is not set, has not jelled, but is still in a state of becoming, bound by his physical memories to a past of struggle and survival, limited in his futures by the uneasiness of thought and consciousness. [*Sea of Cortez*, p. 87]

The tragic miracle of consciousness is, for Steinbeck, man's greatest burden and his greatest glory. And it was Steinbeck's central concern as a novelist throughout his career—from his characterization of Henry Morgan's quest for power in *Cup of Gold*, to Ethan Hawley's search for purpose in the spiritual wasteland of *The Winter of Our Discontent*.

Steinbeck accurately perceived the gap between man's dreams and his ability to bring those dreams to life. He argued that man can transcend his weaknesses if he will not surrender to despair but will struggle against the darkness that alienates and disinherits. He also argued that innocence has no place in contemporary society and that while man must play out the allegory of innocence lost, he must grow to a higher consciousness, knowing that his only reward might be the personal feeling of self-worth that comes from accepting things as they are.

Although Steinbeck believed in man's ability to break through his limitations, he is often more interested in the fallibility of individual man and specifically with the destructive nature of human fantasy and illusion. He contrasted ways of living: innocence and experience, primitivism and progress, self-interest and a commitment to community. Many of his best characters are innocents shrouded in illusion who are alienated from the world of possibility. Take, for example, the protagonists in *Of Mice and Men*, his parable about man's voluntary acceptance of responsibility for his fellow man. In this story of George Milton and Lennie Small, migrant ranch hands who harbor a dream of "a little house and a couple of acres" with rabbits where they will "live off the fatta the lan' " (p. 16), Steinbeck renders his version of the elemental conflict between the idealized landscape and the real world with its pain and its suffering. *Of Mice and Men* is a story of two men who want to live in pastoral repose. But while Steinbeck describes the beauty of the garden and even allows George and Lennie a momentary belief that it exists, he provides that necessary check against our fantasies by showing that the dream cannot be realized. It is shattered when Lennie, whose physical strength is not under the control of an adult mind, accidentally kills the flirtatious wife of the boss's son. Steinbeck's story ends when George mercifully kills Lennie to save him from an angry lynch mob. What is most painful about *Of Mice and Men* is that there is no reconciliation to Steinbeck's version of the pastoral. Lennie is destroyed and George reduced to a life of personal survival, alone, beaten, and powerless. Steinbeck asserts the inherent superiority of simple human virtues to the accumulation of wealth and power in *Of Mice and Men*, but his tribute to those virtues is decidedly ironic.

Steinbeck's most ironic stories are the loosely related collection of tales that make up *The Pastures of Heaven*. The characters in these stories are simple people who have sought out the quiet life in the Pastures as a refuge from a complex society that limits their personal freedom. But because they are engulfed in illusions and self-deceptions that make it impossible for them to adjust to the simple life patterns in the Pastures, they cannot achieve the conditions necessary for full and meaningful lives. Instead, they live on the edge of personal chaos. They hang on slender threads to a world they do not understand and with which they cannot cope.

The inability to cope is also the central theme in some of the best stories in *The Long Valley*. In "The Harness," Peter Randall's quest for freedom is meaningless because he cannot come to terms with the fact of his wife's death. In "The Chrysanthemums," Eliza Allen's neuroses prohibit her personal happiness. And in "The White Quail," Steinbeck creates in Mary Teller a character so engulfed in private fantasies that she cannot respond to the beauty of the environment in which she lives.

Throughout Steinbeck's canon, there are characters who fail in their quests for happiness because they cannot deal with the worlds in which they live. In *Tortilla Flat*, a tragic-comic masterpiece about the escapades of a group of Monterey derelicts, Steinbeck demonstrates the feeble ethic of escape; he shows there is nothing in the philosophic-moral system of the *paisano* brotherhood that will enable them to cope with the complexities of modern life. This is also true for the denizens of the waterfront in *Cannery Row* and *Sweet Thursday*. In both books, Steinbeck enjoys the indolent life-style of his vagabonds, but he simultaneously portrays their inability to deal with a materialistic world that will eventually destroy their self-indulgent bliss.

Despite the large number of his characters who cannot deal with the worlds in which they live, Steinbeck remained a novelist of affirmation throughout his career. And there are characters in many of his novels who transcend their limitations and so achieve a paradise of the mind and heart. For Steinbeck, the key to meaning comes in large measure from a recognition of the wholeness of life, an understanding of the subtle relationships and interrelationships in all experience. At the core of Steinbeck's vision is a holistic order in which strong individuals can fuse thought and feeling, intellect and energy, and work for worthwhile, purposive goals. Steinbeck's most successful characters face squarely the problem of their frailty and the incompatibility between the pastoral ideal and an urban-industrial society. They move through and beyond these recognitions to live a deeper reality and make sense of the nonsense around them.

Much of this vision he acquired from the ideas of Ed Ricketts. Ricketts believed in what he called the toto-picture. He did not study things in and for themselves but for the structure of relationships. He argued that specialistic visions are fragmentary and reductionist. He confronted life by feeling a deeper reality, a combination of science and myth, reason and mysticism. He sought wholeness by unifying experience. He regarded his most important task as making that essential leap of the imagination to discover, through the proof of hidden likenesses, the holistic order of things. He questioned our usual way of viewing life, and he insisted on perceiving deeper, more essential pictures.

In *Sea of Cortez*, Steinbeck portrays the intertidal life of the Gulf of California as a microfield of a complex, interrelated universe. He sees in the overall pattern of life in the gulf the fact that everything is related to everything else, and he ponders the sociological and biological patterns that underlie this unity. He points to the world's greatest thinkers: "a Jesus, a Saint Augustine, a Saint Francis, a Roger Bacon, a Charles Darwin, and an Einstein" who came to their greatness through a "profound feeling" that "man is related to the whole thing, related inextricably to all reality, known and unknowable" (*Sea of Cortez*, p. 217).

And so it is with his most successful characters. They recognize this unity and grow beyond their personal limitations to serve the larger community. In *The Grapes of Wrath*, Jim Casy's recognition of the unity of life leads him to act to bring together "the folks that don't know which way to turn" (p. 127). Casy understands "all men got one big soul ever'body's a part of" (p. 127), and he dedicates himself "to go where the folks is goin" (p. 33), to lead his fellows in the just struggle for human dignity and a decent standard of living. Casy's disciple is Tom Joad who also recognizes the interrelatedness of all experience. He sees that man does not exist alone "cause his little piece of a soul wasn't no good 'less it was with the rest" (p. 570). And so he breaks through the walls of his self-interest and dedicates himself to do battle against political and economic oppression.

In *Viva Zapata!* Steinbeck depicts Emiliano Zapata as a Mexican Tom Joad, a man who moves beyond himself in his quest for land reform. He rejects the position of authority he is given after leading a successful revolt against the tyrannical government of Porfirio Díaz to work alongside his own people. He is the creative rebel who rejects the power that corrupts. He is living proof of Steinbeck's belief in man's enduring capacity for greatness.

There are other Steinbeck protagonists who transcend self-interest and emerge with a vision of the interrelatedness of all experience that gives meaning and purpose to their lives. In *Burning Bright*, Joe Saul returns from an insanity of self-interest to an understanding that it is the race, the species that must go staggering on. In *The Pearl*, Kino rejects the region of outward possessions for one of inward adjustments by throwing a pearl, which he thought would bring him happiness, back into the Gulf of California. And in *East of Eden*, Steinbeck's epic affirmation of man's free will, the novelist notes that while "most men are destroyed, there are others who like pillars of fire guide frightened men through the darkness" (*East of Eden*, p. 309).

Steinbeck's most successful characters are those pillars of fire who guide frightened men through the darkness. All must go, as Steinbeck notes of Kino in

The Pearl, through pain in order to come out on the other side. And some, like Casy, Zapata, and Mayor Orden in *The Moon Is Down*, pay for their visions with their lives. In much of his fiction, the search for paradise occasions paradise lost. Still, Steinbeck's greatest characters come to terms with the tragic miracle of consciousness; they fulfill Steinbeck's belief in man's capacity for greatness of heart and spirit.

Over the course of a career that spanned four decades, John Steinbeck developed a coherent view of man and the world in which he lives, a perspective that gives depth and breadth to his memorable pictures of American life. At the same time, he wrote books not the way books are supposed to be written, as he once remarked about *The Grapes of Wrath*, but about the way lives are lived. Steinbeck believed in people. He treated their fumbling efforts to deal with life with sympathy and with compassion. The subject of his books is the human condition, and his central thesis is that we must transcend our own weaknesses and so help one another create the conditions necessary for full and meaningful lives.

Survey of Criticism

Steinbeck is one among a number of important American novelists whose achievements were not properly recognized until after his death. This is not to say that he was ignored during his lifetime; his person was the subject of periodic scrutiny, and for the better part of three decades, his books were reviewed in the major newspapers and periodicals. Some of these reviews were favorable, others not, but few dealt with anything more than plot summaries, thematic overviews, and brief commentaries on structure and style. With two notable exceptions, full-length critical surveys were sketchy, imprecise, and generally unimpressive. Harry Thornton Moore's *The Novels of John Steinbeck* (1939) and F. W. Watt's *John Steinbeck* (1962) are cases in point. The exceptions are Joseph Fontenrose's *John Steinbeck: An Introduction and Interpretation* (1963), a brief but useful volume by a classicist who successfully identifies Steinbeck's use of myth and legend, and Peter Lisca's *The Wide World of John Steinbeck* (1958), a thorough and insightful assessment of Steinbeck's achievements through the mid-1950s. Lisca's book remains the best critical study of the novelist.

Despite the important efforts by Fontenrose and Lisca, Steinbeck's reputation was in disarray at the time of his death. The paucity of his literary achievement since *East of Eden* brought him into disfavor with the critical establishment. Additionally, he was much maligned during the mid-1960s by the critical Left for his support of the American presence in Southeast Asia. But late in 1968, all that began to change. The driving force behind most major advances in Steinbeck criticism since 1968 has been Tetsumaro Hayashi, at Ball State University, who founded and edits the *Steinbeck Quarterly* published at that university. For more than a decade, Hayashi has published the works of such established Steinbeck scholars as Lisca, Fontenrose, and Warren French (who authored the Twayne volume on Steinbeck in 1961) as well as more junior people such as Robert

DeMott, John Ditsky, Richard Peterson, and Reloy Garcia. While the content of the *Steinbeck Quarterly* is occasionally uneven, most of its articles are of high quality—a tribute to Hayashi's editorial ability and the aggressive way in which he has encouraged promising Steinbeck scholars.

In addition to editing the *Steinbeck Quarterly*, Hayashi has supervised a variety of other Steinbeck projects, that have culminated in useful critical studies. The Steinbeck Monograph Series, issued yearly at Ball State University, contains a substantial piece by Lawrence Jones, *John Steinbeck as a Fabulist* (1973), *Essays on East of Eden*, edited by John Ditsky (1977), and essays on Steinbeck's women and his travel literature. Hayashi has also edited two works of comparative criticism—*Steinbeck's Literary Dimension* (1973), and *Steinbeck and Hemingway* (1980)—a two-volume comprehensive study guide to Steinbeck, and a dictionary of his fictional characters. He also has helped form a community of Steinbeck scholars by coordinating annual Steinbeck meetings, the papers from which have been collected and published in the *Steinbeck Quarterly* and elsewhere.

More books about Steinbeck's life and work have been written since 1968 than during the three decades of his greatest work. Some are much better than others; worst among them are those that purport to be biographies. *John Steinbeck: The Errant Knight* (1975) by Nelson Valjean is an uninteresting record of Steinbeck's early years, and *The Intricate Music* (1979) by Thomas Kiernan is sketchy, incomplete, and altogether unsatisfying. Jackson J. Benson of San Diego State University has authored a number of promising short biographical essays that give hope that his authorized two-volume biography (to be published by 1982) will fill the void. At present, the best information about the novelist's life is in a collection of his letters that Elaine Steinbeck, his widow, and Robert Walsten edited for the Viking Press in 1975. *Steinbeck: A Life in Letters* is particularly valuable in revealing Steinbeck's feelings about his works, particularly those written after he had moved to New York City and communicated regularly with friends in California.

In addition to the shorter critical studies that have appeared in the *Steinbeck Quarterly*, in other literary journals, and in a number of critical collections edited by Hayashi, Robert Davis, and Richard Astro, several new full-length studies have appeared. In *Thematic Design in the Novels of John Steinbeck* (1969), Lester Marks attempts to isolate those particular qualities of Steinbeck's literary genius. In *John Steinbeck: Nature and Myth* (1978), Peter Lisca provides valuable insights into Steinbeck's use of myth. Howard Levant authored a flawed but still useful volume on Steinbeck's craft as a stylist, *The Novels of John Steinbeck* (1974). Astro has written a comprehensive assessment of the way in which Steinbeck's thinking and writing were influenced by the person and ideas of Edward F. Ricketts; it is titled *John Steinbeck and Edward F. Ricketts: The Shaping of a Novelist* (1973).

Though book continues to beget book and article continues to beget article, more work needs to be done. Most significantly, there is need for a standard edition of his works, for an updated bibliography, for the publication of Benson's biography, and for additional work on *East of Eden* and the unfinished Arthurian romances. Taken as a whole, though, the state of Steinbeck criticism has improved dramatically since 1968. His work has been subject to the most careful critical scrutiny, and from that he has emerged as a major American novelist who in his own voice and in his own time gave meaning to the uniquely complicated nature of the American experience.

Bibliography

Works by John Steinbeck

Page numbers given in the text for *Of Mice and Men, The Grapes of Wrath*, and *East of Eden* refer to the paperback Compass Books editions.

Cup of Gold. New York: Robert M. McBride, 1929.
The Pastures of Heaven. New York: Brewer, Warren and Putnam, 1932.
To a God Unknown. New York: Robert O. Ballou, 1933.
Tortilla Flat. New York: Covici-Friede, 1935.
In Dubious Battle. New York: Covici-Friede, 1936.
Of Mice and Men. New York: Covici-Friede, 1937; New York: Compass Books, 1963.
The Red Pony. New York: Covici-Friede, 1937.
The Long Valley. New York: Viking Press, 1938.
The Grapes of Wrath. New York: Viking Press, 1939; New York: Compass Books, 1958.
The Forgotten Village. New York: Viking Press, 1941.
Sea of Cortez: A Leisurely Journal of Travel and Research. Written in collaboration with Edward F. Ricketts. New York: Viking Press, 1941.
Bombs Away: The Story of a Bomber Team. New York: Viking Press, 1942.
The Moon is Down. New York: Viking Press, 1942.
Cannery Row. New York: Viking Press, 1945.
The Wayward Bus. New York: Viking Press, 1947.
The Pearl. New York: Viking Press, 1947.
A Russian Journal. New York: Viking Press, 1948.
Burning Bright. New York: Viking Press, 1950.
East of Eden. New York: Viking Press, 1952; New York: Compass Books, 1970.
Sweet Thursday. New York: Viking Press, 1954.
The Short Reign of Pippin IV: A Fabrication. New York: Viking Press, 1957.
Once There Was a War. New York: Viking Press, 1958.
The Winter of Our Discontent. New York: Viking Press, 1961.
Travels with Charley in Search of America. New York: Viking Press, 1962.
America and Americans. New York: Viking Press, 1966.
Journal of a Novel: The East of Eden Letters. New York: Viking Press, 1969.
Viva Zapata! Ed. Robert Morsberger. New York: Viking Press, 1975.
The Acts of King Arthur and His Noble Knights. Ed. Chase Horton. New York: Farrar, Straus and Giroux, 1976.

Studies of John Steinbeck

Astro, Richard. *John Steinbeck and Edward F. Ricketts: The Shaping of a Novelist*. Minneapolis: University of Minnesota Press, 1973.

————, and Hayashi, Tetsumaro, eds. *Steinbeck: The Man and His Work*. Corvallis: Oregon State University Press, 1971.

————, and Hedgpeth, Joel, eds. *Steinbeck and the Sea*. Corvallis: Oregon State University Sea Grant Program Press, 1975.

Benson, Jackson J. "To Tom Who Lived It: John Steinbeck and the Man from Weedpatch." *Journal of Modern Literature* 5 (April 1976): 151-210.

————, and Loftis, Anne. "John Steinbeck and Farm Labor Unionization: The Background of *In Dubious Battle*." *American Literature* 52 (May 1980): 194-223.

Davis, Robert M., ed. *Steinbeck: A Collection of Critical Essays*. Englewood Cliffs, N.J.: Prentice-Hall, 1972.

Ditsky, John, ed. *Essays on East of Eden*. Steinbeck Monograph Series 7. Muncie, Ind.: Ball State University, 1977.

Fontenrose, Joseph. *John Steinbeck: An Introduction and Interpretation*. New York: Barnes and Noble, 1963.

French, Warren. *John Steinbeck*. TUSAS. New York: Twayne, 1961.

Hayashi, Tetsumaro. *John Steinbeck: A Dictionary of His Fictional Characters*. Metuchen: Scarecrow Press, 1973.

————. *Steinbeck and Hemingway*. Metuchen: Scarecrow Press, 1980.

————. *Steinbeck's Travel Literature*. Steinbeck Monograph Series 10. Muncie, Ind: Ball State University, 1980.

————. *Steinbeck's Women*. Steinbeck Monograph Series, 9. Muncie, Ind: Ball State University, 1979.

————. *A Study Guide to Steinbeck: A Handbook to His Major Works*. Metuchen: Scarecrow Press, 1974.

————, ed. *Steinbeck's Literary Dimension*. Metuchen: Scarecrow Press, 1973.

Jones, Lawrence. *John Steinbeck as Fabulist*. Ed. Marston LaFrance. Steinbeck Monograph Series 3. Muncie, Ind.: Ball State University, 1973.

Kiernan, Thomas. *The Intricate Music: A Biography of John Steinbeck*. Boston: Atlantic-Little, Brown, 1979.

Levant, Howard. *The Novels of John Steinbeck*. Columbia: University of Missouri Press, 1974.

Lisca, Peter. *John Steinbeck: Nature and Myth*. New York: Thomas Crowell, 1978.

————. *The Wide World of John Steinbeck*. New Brunswick: Rutgers University Press, 1958.

Marks, Lester. *Thematic Design in the Novels of John Steinbeck*. The Hague: Mouton, 1969.

Moore, Harry Thornton. *The Novels of John Steinbeck*. Chicago: Normandie House, 1939.

Steinbeck, Elaine, and Walsten, Robert, eds. *Steinbeck: A Life in Letters*. New York: Viking Press, 1975.

Valjean, Nelson. *John Steinbeck: The Errant Knight*. San Francisco: Chronicle Books, 1975.

Watt, F. W. *John Steinbeck*. New York: Grove Press, 1962.

John Caldwell

GEORGE R. STEWART
(1895-1980)

Biography

George Rippey Stewart was born in Sewickley, Pennsylvania, on 31 May 1895 and died in San Francisco on 22 August 1980. While he was an adolescent his family moved to southern California, and he grew to maturity there. Although he attended two major eastern universities, the West claimed him; it was his home and the subject of most of his work. Of the forty-four titles written or edited by Stewart, thirty are related to the West through subject, location, or theme. He turned constantly to the Bay Area of California and the valley, mountains, and plains directly east of it; he lived there, and he identified with the land and the people.

Stewart's father was a businessman who lost a major share of his resources in the financially troubled mid-1890s. The family lived in Sewickley, a western suburb of Pittsburgh, until George was two years old, when they moved to the small western Pennsylvania town of Indiana. This quiet farm center, largely Scotch-Irish in origin, was the home of Mrs. Stewart's extended family. Stewart received his first education at home, where he learned to read, and in the town's public elementary school. Although the cultural opportunities of the area were limited, he received a thorough grounding in language and history. Eclipsed in these preadolescent years by his older brother Andrew, George withdrew into reading in the family's extensive collection of the standard authors and in the adventure stories of George Alfred Henty.

It was not until the family moved to Azusa, California, in 1907 that George, in the freer atmosphere of the little western town, began to be more active in the outdoors. He first established bicycle contact with neighboring communities and then hiked and camped in the nearby Sierra Madre Mountains and in the canyon of the San Gabriel River. His father, after a severe bout with pneumonia, had moved his family to southern California to escape the colder winters of Pennsylvania. Investing successfully in orange groves, he moved the family to the more urban area of Pasadena. Here George completed the last two years of high school and prepared, through private tutoring, for admission to Princeton University, the college of his mother's Presbyterian relatives.

From 1913 to 1917 as an undergraduate at Princeton under the guidance of T. M. Parrot and J. Duncan Spaeth, he received a grounding in literature and decided to become a teacher. His pursuit of this goal was interrupted by two years of service in the United States Army Ambulance Service. Although he was never sent overseas, he contracted pneumonia, and the lung damage resulting from this bothered him for the rest of his life.

It was in one of Herbert Bolton's courses at the University of California, where he went to do graduate work after his discharge, that he first became aware of the American West as a subject for literary and historical study. He did his master's thesis on "Stevenson in California" and would have remained to complete the doctorate if the graduate program had been stronger at that time. He went instead to Columbia University where, with a dissertation entitled "Modern Metrical Techniques as Illustrated by Ballad Meter," he was awarded the doctorate in English in 1922.

He began his teaching career at the University of Michigan as an instructor in English in September 1922; in 1923 he accepted an instructorship at Berkeley. The most important result of the year at Michigan was his meeting Theodosia Burton, the daughter of the president. They were married in 1924.

As a new, young academician with a reputation and a career to build, he taught a variety of courses within the English department and published a number of articles based upon his dissertation research. His interest in western subjects persisted, and he began to do research in that area, especially in the career of Bret Harte. This led to a series of journal articles on Harte, an edition of his stories and poems, and in 1931 to the definitive biography, *Bret Harte, Argonaut and Exile*. Stewart had been advanced to assistant professor in 1925, but as depression came to the country, promotion was slow, and the general academic situation was discouraging. Within this frame Stewart decided to do a book that would be historically accurate, grounded upon fact but presented in a popular fashion. This led to the research that produced *Ordeal By Hunger* (1936). This story of the Donner Party weaves diaries and recollections of the survivors, contemporary newspaper accounts, and a study of the route and the topography of the mountains into a narrative that is thoroughly historical but reads like fiction. He was so successful that the book is sometimes mistakenly referred to as a novel.

From the 1930s until shortly before his death, George Stewart lived a varied and eventful life. Until he retired from teaching in 1962, he was at once an author of popular books, an active member of the university faculty, and a research scholar. During this period he produced seven novels and a textbook; wrote, edited, or compiled more than two dozen volumes of history and biography, geography, conservation, and onomatology; and published eighty-five articles and book reviews. History, geography, and language, always primary interests of Stewart, he combined in the study of names and naming. He was one of the

founders of the American Name Society and in 1945 published the first edition of
Names on the Land, which has become an American classic in this field.

During World War II he accepted a special appointment with the United States
Navy as a writer on a submarine project at Pearl Harbor and also served as an
editor with the University of California Division of War Research. He was
Resident Fellow in Creative Writing at Princeton University for the academic
year 1942-43. From 1944 to 1947 he was chairman of the advisory committee of
the California Place-Names Project.

A divisive struggle developed within the University of California in March
1949 when the Regents demanded a special noncommunist oath as a condition of
employment. From then until April 1950, signers and nonsigners marshalled
their forces. Stewart was in the center of the struggle. While the issue was still
being contested, he began, with a group of unnamed collaborators, to compile
*The Year of the Oath; The Fight for Academic Freedom at the University of
California* (1950). This is not so much a history as a view, by some of the
participants, of a great university in turmoil.

During the fall and winter of 1952-53, George Stewart was in Greece as
Fulbright Professor of American Literature and Civilization at the University of
Athens. After his retirement from active teaching he dropped trout flies into
many of the rivers of the world as he and his wife traveled widely, but they
always returned to the Bay Area, though now to San Francisco rather than
Berkeley. During the last years of his life Stewart was afflicted with Parkinson's
disease, but he continued to write and was working on a new book at the time of
his death.

Stewart was given many honors and awards. In 1936 the Commonwealth Club
of California awarded its Silver Medal to *Ordeal By Hunger* and in 1938 its
Gold Medal to *East of the Giants* as that year's best work of fiction about the
state. For distinguished attainment in history, Stewart was elected a Fellow of
the California Historical Society in 1960 and was given its Henry R. Wagner
Memorial Award Medal in 1972. In 1963 the University of California awarded
Stewart the honorary degree, Doctor of Humane Letters, then, in 1968, gave
him its Centennial Citation and made him a Berkeley Fellow. That same year
his ecological study, *Not So Rich As You Think*, was given the Sidney Hillman
Award. He was presented an Honors Award in 1980 by the Association of
American Geographers.

Major Themes

The subjects covered in the body of George R. Stewart's work range from
verse technique and literary criticism through geology, geography, conservation,
biography, onomatology, and American and European history. He had an insa-
tiable curiosity and a highly developed capacity to do research on whatever
interested him. Although his interests were universal, they returned more and
more often to the West. Stewart's West can be said to begin with the overland

trails through the Rockies across the Great Basin over the Sierra Nevada into the Sacramento Valley and on to San Francisco.

Although Stewart is perhaps best known for the novels *Storm* (1941) and *Fire* (1948), his western writing took many forms. He wrote the definitive biographies of two western writers, Bret Harte and George H. Derby, and he applied the technique of fiction to historical material to achieve what could be called historical reconstruction. Evident in all of his work is an interest in how people got to California; *The California Trail* (1962) is the principal study in this area, but his interests are evident also in the editorial work that he did on travel accounts of people who journeyed to California between 1841 and 1859.

Underlying all of Stewart's work is the belief that people are affected by place, that the land determines what life will be like, and that people who would live in a particular place must conform to the conditions as they exist. This principle was spelled out by Stewart in a talk given to the National Council of Teachers of English and published in *College English* as "The Regional Approach to Literature" (1948). In this paper he affirms that to be regional, a work must be more than located in an area: it must be of the area; it must reflect the speech and mores of the people; and the topography, ecology, and climate must be a true and integral part of it. People, he says, are influenced by, molded by, the area, and are distinctive because of the way in which they adjust to its conditions.

This principle is most easily seen in Stewart's fiction, but it is an essential part of his nonfiction as well. Both *Fire* and *Storm* were hailed as new and exciting because they made a great natural disaster the central character in a novel. This view misses the real novel in both cases, however. The storm and the fire are the occasion for these novels, not characters in them. In each work it is the interaction of the people with their area that makes the story.

The *Storm* is no surprise to the people of central California, nor is it an unmitigated disaster. The people have been expecting it; their lives have been disrupted because the winter rains and snow have not arrived. The operations officers of the services and utilities have been prepared for months. They know the region and accept its conditions. With this knowledge they prepare for winter; they know that it will come, and they know that if they are going to continue to operate, they must be prepared to handle freezing rain and snow, high winds, and floodwaters.

Stewart made a thorough investigation of the nature and effects of California weather. At the weather bureau in San Francisco he studied the reporting and compilation of data and learned to draw weather maps, and he traveled the highway into the Sierras during bad weather to observe highway, telephone, railroad, and electric company crews in action. *Storm* is the story of these people and of their effort to keep mid-twentieth-century society functioning in a land of violent weather.

Each of the twelve days of the storm is a chapter that begins and ends with weather lore and of mankind's interaction with the atmosphere, but this is only the framework of the novel. The important aspect of the storm is its effect upon the lives of the men and women who must deal with it, whose lives must be adjusted to conform to an environment the weather produces. Their stories, fragmented throughout the days of the storm, are both personal and corporate. They reveal, sometimes in a paragraph, sometimes in a narrative strung out over several days, the effect of the rain and snow on individuals: Jan and Max as they return to Reno from San Francisco, Johnny Martley inside the dam at French Bar Power House, Big Al Bruntton flying through a turbulent cold front into San Francisco. Another group of characters, identified only by their titles, represent the utilities and public agencies that must combat the storm so that the lives of others can continue undisturbed. At the weather bureau in San Francisco the Junior Meteorologist and the Chief Forecaster discover and plot the progress of the storm (which the Meteorologist names Maria); upon their reports and predictions depend the decisions of thousands of people in the area. The telephone company's District Traffic Superintendent routes calls around broken lines, and people gossip from one side of the mountain to another. The losing struggle led by the Road Superintendent to keep U.S. 40 through Donner Pass open to traffic provides some of the most dramatic incidents in *Storm*. Throughout the novel the storm is impersonal; there is nothing malevolent or vindictive about it; it is a natural event, part of the lives of those who live in the area.

Fire, located in the fictitious Ponderosa National Forest, also relates a natural event. Beginning from a lightning strike, a forest fire burns for eleven days through the California Sierra. Although it is seen as a disaster, it is nevertheless a normal part of living in this area of long, dry summers. Here, because of the weather conditions, grow coniferous forests that are susceptible to forest fires. If the weather were different, the forest would be different. Although the people who live in the mountains are afraid of fires, they accept them and prepare for them. In this expectation and preparation the normality of fire is demonstrated. Spitcat, the name given to the fire, is extraordinary in size and intensity, but is the 164th fire of the summer, not an isolated event.

As in *Storm*, each day of the *Fire* forms a chapter that relates specific events. Many people are affected by the fire and are drawn together to fight it: the professionals—the superintendent, rangers, dispatchers, and clerks; those drawn temporarily into its orbit—summer lookouts and laborers; and the hurriedly gathered firefighting crews—loggers, winos, students, paratroopers, farmers, and bulldozer operators. Stewart, who studied fires and the techniques of fighting them as an official collaborator with the U.S. Forest Service, appears briefly as "a tall professorial looking author working on a book."

Fire presents a cross-section of California life, but unlike *Storm*, it has a novelistic conflict between Superintendent Jones of the Ponderosa and John Bartley, ranger of the largest district in the forest. Both love the forest, but Jones, an educated, modern forester, wants to harvest the mature trees to give growing space to the younger ones; "Bart" insists that the forest must be maintained in its natural wild beauty. They have agreed to disagree until Bartley, as Fire-Boss directing the battle against Spitcat, repeatedly insists upon setting his fire line unreasonably close to the advancing flames. Finally, Jones has to remove him and bring the fire under control himself.

In *Sheep Rock* (1951), the confrontation between man and the land is still more obvious. The novel is set in the Black Rock Desert of northwestern Nevada, which spreads across one of the emigrant trails. Here, at the southern tip of a chain of barren mountains, is a large hot spring surrounded by desert. It is a starkly beautiful country, the home of salt grass and seepweed, of stone, sand, and sun. Although the coyote and mountain sheep eke out a living here, it is inhospitable to man. Geoffrey Archer, a young poet on leave from a university teaching position, brings his wife and two young daughters to live at the spring for one year. He intends to write a long poem about the Renaissance, for which he has received a foundation grant.

As in *Storm* and *Fire*, natural phenomena play a major role in *Sheep Rock*. Stewart presents the geologic and geographical history of this desert, now waterless but once a vast lake whose beaches are still visible on the sides of the surrounding mountains. Overwhelmed by the place, Geoffrey gives up his plan to write about the Renaissance and begins instead to study the spring and its surrounding desert and to write his poem about them. But he finds that the land is too vast, and he gives up the second poem. Unable to master the land but instead mastered by it, Geoffrey Archer is presented by Stewart as a contemporary American in a classic western situation, the newcomer who finds that the land determines his destiny. Using artifacts found around the spring by Archer and his children, Stewart ties the family to the people who have preceded them. In a series of vignettes and short stories he reveals that the Indians and overlanders, soldiers, and prospectors who passed this way had each in their turn been mastered by the land.

Stewart's first novel, *East of the Giants* (1938), was placed in the Bay Area, but a century earlier. It is a three-part story of Mexican California, the American occupation, and American California to the first years of the Civil War. Although the viewpoint shifts among the principal characters, the story is about Judith Hingham. A New England shipmaster's daughter, she arrives in Monterey in 1837, elopes with Juan Godoy, and goes with him to live on the eastern frontier. Here is worked out another western theme: the metamorphosis of the Wild West into civilization beginning with the arrival of the white woman.

Rancho Amarillo, granted to Juan's father to help secure the frontier, is held by Juan and his half-breed vaqueros as an outpost where they raise cattle for the hide trade; its real purpose is to keep the Indians away from the settled areas around the bay. Judith gradually brings order to this chaotic man's world. Raising a family, improving and expanding the ranch buildings, Judith changes from a small-town New England girl into a wife and mother at home on a California ranch. She learns to love the ripe brown hills, the spaciousness, and her position in the center of its activity.

With the Mexican War, the discovery of gold, and the influx of greater numbers of Americans, life changes. The frontier is gone. Juan, an Indian fighter with no

Indians to fight, seeks his excitement drinking and gambling in San Francisco and is killed in a fight over a card game. The day of the frontier caballero is over; in the transition from frontier to civilization, from the ranch to San Francisco, Judith marries Daniel Melton, one of the wealthiest men in the booming new city. The third section of *East of the Giants* is the beginning of a new story. The family becomes American, a utopian experiment on the ranch fails, the spirit of business grips the future. Judith, having become an anachronism in her own land, dies in a shipwreck off the coast of Mexico.

The very different novels *Doctor's Oral* (1939) and *Earth Abides* (1949) are both located in Berkeley, but neither is concerned with western themes. The former depicts the day that a mediocre graduate student passes his oral examination; it could quite easily be relocated to the campus of any American university. *Earth Abides*, awarded the International Fantasy Award in 1951, portrays the rebuilding of human society after a swiftly moving pestilence has killed all but a few people. *The Years of the City* (1955), a kind of frontier novel, describes the life cycle of Phrax, a colony city on the edge of the Greek world.

Stewart also wrote biographies of three western writers, all born in the East but shaped by the West. In a very brief book, *Take Your Bible in One Hand* (1939), he discusses the career of William Henry Thomes, an author of adventure stories who spent eight years between 1843 and 1851 in California, first as hide drogher and later as unsuccessful miner. Thomes's best book, *On Land and Sea*, is based on his earlier experiences.

When Bret Harte arrived in San Francisco in 1854 as a youth of seventeen, he had neither training nor experience. Stewart, in *Bret Harte, Argonaut and Exile*, shows him maturing in the open society of California, observing life and adapting to it. The gold camps along the Tuolomne and Stanislaus were finished when Harte arrived, but he did work on a newspaper in Union for three years during the Trinity River strike in northern California. Returning to San Francisco he worked as a typesetter and contributed sketches and poems to the *Golden Era*. Befriended by Jessie Benton Frémont and Starr King, he received political appointments in the surveyor-general's office and then in the San Francisco Mint, all the while writing and publishing in the local papers and magazines. Stewart portrays him as a young man willing to learn, developing his talent, making influential friends, establishing himself in the milieu of the city, developing a reputation as poet, humorist, and editor. Then, making full use of all that he had learned, he published in the *Overland Monthly* "The Luck of Roaring Camp," "The Outcasts of Poker Flat," and the other stories that made him famous. Bret Harte, shaped, supported, and launched in California, rides his first wave of success to the publishing centers of the East and then to Europe. He continued to write California stories, but, out of touch with the land that nurtured his art, he never wrote better than he had in the early stories and rarely wrote as well.

Bret Harte left California and never went back. George H. Derby, when transferred from the West by the army, asked to be returned. A topographical engineer, West Point graduate, and career army officer, Derby had an irrepressible wit. Assigned to San Diego and San Francisco between 1849 and 1856, where, as Stewart claims in *John Phoenix, Esq.* (1937) "a good joke was above the price of rubies" (p. 58), Derby could be an army engineer while his alter ego, John Phoenix, had the freedom to develop as a jokester and to publish the hoaxes and burlesques that made Californians roar. These, collected as *Phoenixiana* in 1855, were hailed by *Alta California* as the first work of literary merit to be written by a Californian. Stewart concludes, "The West had given him his opportunity, appreciated his efforts both written and acted, and fostered him" (p. 181).

Applying to the writing of history what he called a novelistic technique, Stewart retold the disaster of the Donner party in *Ordeal By Hunger* and, in *Committee of Vigilance* (1964), the story of the 1851 citizens' movement to suppress crime in San Francisco. In each of these he skillfully weaves journals, reminiscences, and newspaper accounts into a narrative that reads like fiction. Stewart, more comfortable in handling character and action in a historical situation than in a fictional one, produces in James Reed and William Eddy of *Ordeal By Hunger* and William T. Coleman of *Committee of Vigilance* characters as well rounded as any that appear in the novels.

In Stewart's retelling the tragedy of the Donner party was the result of poor judgment and human error, but above all it was caused by ignorance of the land and of the demands that it would make upon the group. Their final paralysis in the snow was the result of their decision three months before to leave the established trail and to strike out through unopened country without knowing that they had neither the skill nor the experience to cope with the problems that it would present. Stewart's heroes are the men of the rescue missions who, against all odds, forced their way through the snow to bring out some of those stranded in the mountains.

San Francisco, the commercial center of the Pacific coast, was gripped by fear and suspicion in 1851. Inept and corrupt law enforcement left organized criminals free to terrorize the community. A series of violent crimes drew the concerned merchants into the revolutionary step of creating their own police and judiciary and restoring order to the city. In *Committee of Vigilance* Stewart portrays men in a frontier city responding to a crisis in a way made necessary by their political and geographic isolation from the rest of the country.

A fourth group of books are those that deal specifically with the overland journey. *Ordeal By Hunger* details the Donners' part in this movement; *The California Trail* provides a general history of the crossing, describing each year of the 1840s and summarizing the 1850s. The emphasis is on the interrelationship between the people and the land across which they traveled. Between spring and fall they became familiar with a land the like of which they had never known. Every day brought a new wonder: mountains, deserts, hot springs, rivers that disappeared into the sand, endless herds of buffalo, and various tribes of Indians. If on arrival they had not become westerners, they were no longer eastern farmers. Stewart edited and wrote introductions for diaries, journals, or reminiscences of eight people who made the overland journey to California, seven of them during the 1840s. Each of these is carefully edited and placed within the historical frame of the migration and the history of early California. This is the time and place of Stewart's West—the trail across to the Bay Area of the 1840s and 1850s, and that place one hundred years later.

Survey of Criticism

Almost without exception, George Stewart's books were given good reviews in all of the general review media and in the appropriate scholarly journals. But except for some passing references in a few literary histories, his work has received little critical attention. Why this should be is not obvious. It may be that his diversity has worked against his reputation. If he had written on fewer subjects in fewer forms, he would be easier to classify and therefore easier to describe. Whatever the reason, there has been very little published about his work.

Elizabeth Cummins Cogell uses *Earth Abides* as an example of primitive apocalypse in "The Middle-Landscape Myth in Science Fiction" (1978), and Madison S. Beeler discusses Stewart's work on place names in "George R. Stewart, Toponymist" (1976). Ferol Egan's "In a World of Creation" (1980) presents an affectionate personal overview of the wide range of Stewart's work, paying particular attention to the books on California and the overland experience. The only study of Stewart as a western writer is John Caldwell's pamphlet in the Western Writers Series (1981). He argues that the western works meet Stewart's requirement that regional writing must be a true reflection of the geography of an area and of the relationship of its people to their time and place. Wallace Stegner ("George R. Stewart, Western Writer" [1982]) sees Stewart taking the long view of historical events, judiciously and deliberately examining and re-creating the western past in his novels and histories.

Bibliography

Works by George R. Stewart

Bret Harte, Argonaut and Exile. Boston: Houghton Mifflin,1931.
Ordeal By Hunger: The Story of the Donner Party. New York: Holt, 1936; new ed., with a Supplement and Three Accounts by Survivors. Boston: Houghton Mifflin, 1960.
John Phoenix, Esq., the Veritable Squibob; A Life of Captain George H. Derby, U.S.A. New York: Holt, 1937.
East of the Giants. New York: Holt, 1938.
Doctor's Oral. New York: Random House, 1939.
Take Your Bible in One Hand; The Life of William Henry Thomes. San Francisco: Colt Press, 1939.
Storm. New York: Random House, 1941; New York: Modern Library, 1947 [with a new introduction].

Names on the Land: A Historical Account of Place-Naming in the United States. New York: Random House, 1945; 3d ed., Boston: Houghton Mifflin, 1967.

Fire. New York: Random House, 1948.

"The Regional Approach to Literature." *College English* 9 (April 1948): 370-75.

Earth Abides. New York: Random House, 1949.

The Year of the Oath; The Fight for Academic Freedom at the University of California, by George R. Stewart, in Collaboration with Other Professors of the University of California. Garden City, N.Y.: Doubleday, 1950.

Sheep Rock. New York: Random House, 1951.

The Years of the City. Boston: Houghton Mifflin, 1955.

The California Trail, an Epic with Many Heroes. American Trails Series. New York: McGraw-Hill, 1962.

Committee of Vigilance: Revolution in San Francisco, 1851. Boston: Houghton Mifflin, 1964.

Not So Rich As You Think. Boston: Houghton Mifflin, 1968.

Studies of George R. Stewart

Beeler, Madison S. "George R. Stewart, Toponymist." *Names* 24 (June 1976): 77-85.

Caldwell, John. *George R. Stewart*. WWS. Boise, Idaho: Boise State University, 1981.

———. "George R. Stewart, Jr.: A Checklist." *Bulletin of Bibliography* 36 (April-June 1979): 99-104.

Cogell, Elizabeth Cummins. "The Middle-Landscape Myth in Science Fiction." *Science Fiction Studies* 5 (July 1978): 134-42.

Egan, Ferol. "In a World of Creation." *Westways* 72 (July 1980): 16-19, 80.

Stegner, Wallace. "George R. Stewart, Western Writer: An Appreciation of a Remarkable Author." *American West* 19 (March-April 1982): 64, 67-69.

Leedice Kissane

RUTH SUCKOW
(1892-1960)

Ruth Suckow is a western writer to the extent that Iowa is a western state, for not only was she born and brought up in Iowa, but she located virtually all her fictions within its borders. Sinclair Lewis called her stories and novels "genuinely native." The appeal she holds for midwestern readers undeniably owes much to the pleasure of recognition. Anyone who has lived in Iowa feels immediately at home in her pages, thanks to her exceptional powers of observation and devoted attention to detail.

Suckow's true Iowa quality, however, is by no means her chief claim to distinction. Among the literary stars of the 1920s, she ranked in the first magnitude; now fifty-some years later, her reputation maintains its quiet luster with the reissue of two of her early books, *Iowa Interiors* (1926) and *Country People* (1924). A realist in the best sense, she has been commended for her concern with universals, a way of saying that her simple narratives have a basis of profound meaning. She has won, over the years, a devoted though possibly not a large following, admirers of her true-to-life representations and thought-provoking themes.

Ruth Suckow's sudden literary success is hard to explain. The daughter of a minister, a shy, serious young woman with no money, no antecedents, and few connections, she had literally nothing going for her except her determination to be a writer. She had always been, she said, a "scribbling child," her home and school environment fostered her inclination, and, with maturity, she developed a firm character that bolstered her intense ambition. Her emergence as a recognized writer has something miraculous about it. In her first decade as a producer of fiction, she hardly experienced a single rejection.

Not to be overlooked is the young writer's fortunate connection with H. L. Mencken. Her literary associate in Iowa City, John T. Frederick, editor of *Midland* magazine, was a protégé of the illustrious critic. With Frederick's encouragement, Ruth sent three of her short stories to Mencken who at once recognized their merit. Their author's honesty and unpretentiousness, even her German-sounding name and midwestern origins, appealed to him. Mencken not only published Suckow's stories in *American Mercury* and *Smart Set*, which he edited with George Jean Nathan, but he also became the young Iowan's friend and adviser, urging her to further efforts in completing a novel and recommending her to publishers. "He was like a kind old uncle to me," she wrote in later years.

Biography

Ruth Suckow was born in Hawarden, Iowa, 6 August 1892. She spoke of her birthplace as "a place of new beginnings" ("Memoir" in *Some Others and Myself*, p.176), a raw little prairie town in the far northwestern corner of the state. Her father was minister of a newly established Congregational church: her mother, artistic and gentle, created an attractive home. Petite, very blonde Ruth and her adored older sister Ema were the only children.

Later the Suckows lived in a number of different localities in Iowa, some small to middle-sized towns, others approaching cities in size. The Iowa Suckow observed was predominantly agricultural, the landscape dotted with farms. Towns existed mainly to meet the farmers' needs and to furnish a place for their retirement.

Suckow frequently accompanied her father when he made parish calls on his bicycle, a small seat attached behind for his little daughter. She learned to know the physical traits of the countryside, its fertile soil and rich, moist atmosphere, with fields of growing crops everywhere. She also came to know Iowans: their ways of speaking and how they lived.

At home the small girl was often present in the room where the minister composed his sermons. Written composition, the activity she loved best, she grew into naturally. Her first stories were narratives revolving around her paper dolls. Occasionally she created a tiny booklet containing an original story, which she presented to one of her favorite ladies of the church.

The church represented one of the two cultural strains of the young writer's background. The Congregationalists had come from New England; in Ruth's mind they were associated with the Pilgrims and with the nation's founding (she described herself in those days as "a fiery American patriot"). But the Suckows were German, not New England, by inheritance, their grandparents having come onto Iowa farms from Germany. Ruth failed to identify closely with her Teutonic relatives until World War I, when rife anti-German attitudes outraged her sense of justice. Later her grandfather, ninety years old, became the subject of one of her early short stories, "Four Generations," in which she described the lovable old patriarch in black skull cap and with smiling blue peasant eyes, singing quaveringly an old German song.

Ruth broke with her father on his and the church's militaristic stand during the war; she left the church and remained an outsider for many years. But her mother's sudden death and her sister's illness reunited her with her father. William Suckow accepted a pastorate at Earlville, Iowa; he offered Ruth his help in a bee-keeping venture by which she hoped to subsidize her writing.

After three years of schooling at Grinnell College and courses at the Curry School of Expression in Boston, Ruth had completed the work for the master's degree at the University of Denver and had tried teaching English in Colorado. But she became convinced that writing was what she wanted most to do. By raising bees and marketing the honey from her Orchard Apiary at the edge of Earlville, she was able to earn enough in the summer months to provide leisure for her writing during the rest of the year. She continued in this activity for six years.

The Reverend Mr. Suckow by this time had remarried and moved away. Ruth, now the successful author of two novels and a book of short stories, sold her bee farm and, against the outspoken counsel of Mencken, moved to New York. She made many literary friends there including Ferner Nuhn, the young writer who became her husband. The two lived and wrote at Yaddo and at the MacDowell Colony. She published several more novels, another collection of short stories, and, as a culminating triumph, a long novel *The Folks*, which was the choice of the Literary Guild in 1934.

Though Suckow never again equaled the remarkable productivity of this first segment of her career, she devoted the rest of her life consistently to writing. The fact that her output decreased in later decades may be attributed to changes in her circumstances. Her marriage to Nuhn eventually occasioned a move to his home in Cedar Falls, Iowa, where she became virtually writer in residence at the State College. During World War II the Nuhns, who had joined the Quakers, were involved in teaching and lecturing in conscientious-objector camps; afterward Ruth's arthritis prompted their move west in search of a drier, more sunny climate. After a time in Arizona, they settled permanently in Claremont, California. The writer never regained vigorous health and suffered some interruptions due to illness, but she kept diligently at work, producing among other things several nostalgic pieces based on childhood memories of Iowa. Her last book, *The John Wood Case*, was published in 1959, less than a year before her death at her home in Claremont on 23 January 1960.

Major Themes

When Ruth Suckow in Earlville was teaching herself to write, she kept a journal. Fresh from Colorado's mountain scenery, she recorded her surprise that the plain Iowa landscape could move her so deeply. She wrote, "One does not need mountains, waterfalls, shining places. I think I love beauty even more when it is half imperceptible like this—nothing but a road and a sky, the smell of evening, and birds singing in the bushes. Then beauty is only a little part—a sign—of the something overpowering in Nature."

The young writer also found beauty in what she called "the strange, twisted lives of men." In the short stories she began to write, the characters were counterpoised against the natural scene. For instance, rainy, dismal weather underscores the unfriendliness of the Kruses in "A Start in Life"; flower imagery in "Homecoming" serves to point up the delicate frailty of the aging heroine.

These first stories portray fellow townspeople in Earlville, chiefly elderly retired farmers and their wives. Their lives were barren, restricted to their narrow environment, hampered by inarticulateness. Lifelong habits of thrift had forced them into a style of comfortless poverty. Yet to Ruth Suckow these old people furnished a mine of rewarding material. She thought their ways were the result of a certain kind of experience—that of wresting a living from the soil. Prevailing cultural attitudes shaped their behavior, and the inevitable sorrows of life endowed them with fatalistic resignation.

In representing the lives of these rural Iowans, the author implies that this is the way things are, not the way we would like them to be. Many of the stories leave a melancholy impression in that no solutions are offered. Either there are no remedies or, if there are, it is too late to apply them. The author's attitude is one of disciplined calm. Never sentimental, she lets the situation speak for itself.

When the early stories were collected under the title *Iowa Interiors*, the name suggested comparisons with Vermeer and other masters in their admirably conceived Dutch interiors. It was apparent that Suckow too was an artist and that she, like the painters, was concerned with more than merely surfaces.

Country People, Suckow's first published novel, was written in a remarkably short space of time and, according to her husband, without agonizing and revisions. The record of four generations of German farmers begins with an immigrant ancestor in the 1870s and ends about 1930. Without elaboration, the author tells their story with almost biblical simplicity. In fact, John Frederick expressed dissatisfaction with it on these grounds; he felt that *Country People* was almost too bare a chronicle. Suckow, however, asserted in later years that she thought the plain style suited the material and that it had held up well.

Country People represents the subculture of Iowa farmers in the years before and after World War I. They are motivated by one urge: to achieve material prosperity. Honest, doggedly determined, parsimonious, these people worked to exhaustion to get ahead, giving little consideration to mind and heart. They were outraged when persecuted as "Boche" during the war, taking for granted that their economic success in their adopted country proved that they were good Americans. Women, in their role of passive obedience, endured a hard lot, unrelieved by cultural solacing. In old age, their activity at an end, these retired farmers suffered from boredom and a sense of futility. Suckow introduces one exception: an old German ex-minister, despised by his son-in-law as "not much of a farmer," who at the end of his life has "something to think about," and is devout and contented (*Country People*, p. 197).

The Odyssey of a Nice Girl (1925) and *The Folks*, of all Suckow's books, seem most indigenous to Iowa. *Odyssey* is based on the author's memories of her childhood in the state, so abundant and detailed that the book originally ran to 220,000 words. (Knopf, her publisher, suggested she take six months off and cut it to 90,000.) Every word rings true to the physical features of the small home-like town, the simplicity and goodwill of its inhabitants, its church and school activities.

Marjorie, the nice Iowa girl who engages in a quest to find herself and fulfill her destiny, is shaped by her environment, at the same time longing to escape from its everyday-ness. Much as the young girl loves the "innocence and simple freshness" that her author feels are distinguishing traits of the Middle West, she is convinced that the region's provinciality thwarts her ambitions. The torment she undergoes is intensified by her affection for her home and her identification with her family.

Always interested in women's involvement with home and family, Suckow pursued this subject in three novels and a number of short stories. (Present-day critics have remarked that this interest in feminism places her ahead of her time.) The title of the collected stories, *Children and Older People* (1931), suggests the much-discussed generation gap; this she often dealt with from the child's point of view. The older people's difficulties spring from faulty communication between marriage partners, interference by in-laws, and the conflict in a woman's psyche between her two roles of wife and mother, to list a few of the problems.

The novels probe the newly emerging situation of the career girl—the woman who works outside her home. In *Cora* (1929) and *The Kramer Girls* (1931), women run their households concurrently with business positions. The author leaves the impression that such arrangements demand extraordinary tact and strength. Her women, moreover, tend to place their homes and domestic duties first. Sarah Bonney enters the lists of working women though actually her wish is to marry and manage her own home. Suckow is a feminist in that she champions members of her sex who are unfairly dealt with. But she is convinced that a woman's deepest desire is to mate and then to devote herself to nurturing and sustaining the family group that results from that mating.

Although Suckow inserts plenty of honesty and good sense into these feminist works, they are rather humdrum. For the most part they lack the poetic elements that distinguish the best stories in *Iowa Interiors*. An exception is the author's sensitive remarking on women's mystic attunement to nature. Toldine ("Toldine and the Cat") and Rose Kramer's mother-in-law (*The Kramer Girls*) exhibit this characteristic in some outstanding passages. Clearly the author believes this close kinship is a specifically feminine endowment, possibly related to procreation.

While asserting that motherhood is woman's true vocation, Suckow turns a critical eye on some of the examples of parenting she observes. Overambitious mothers of gifted children, she implies, can warp their youngsters' lives. As Sarah Bonney points out, even far-seeing and intelligent mothers, well intentioned toward their young, sometimes deserve blame for forcing children into ways not natural to them. The best mothers are those who simply love, she concludes.

During a period of popular interest in folk literature, Suckow presented her theory that "folk" ways and ideas exist in Iowa as in other regions but have become so submerged by education and affluence that they are not patently apparent. "The folk" in Iowa have become "the folks." Her novel *The Folks* grew out of this theory and may be said to exemplify it.

The family in the novel are typical Iowa folks. They live in substantial comfort with their four children in Belmond, where Fred Ferguson holds a position in the bank and in the Presbyterian church. Fred is conservative and thrifty. His son says, "Dad's religious, but not exactly idealistic" (*The Folks*, p. 132). Annie is a conscientious mother, loving, inclined to be artistic, and ambitious for her family. Her image in the eyes of her townspeople is of paramount importance to her. She desires her housekeeping to meet their high standards and the Ferguson family to be thought of as close-knit and invulnerable.

The Folks is divided into several sections, focusing on postwar social change as it touches each of the Fergusons in turn. The eldest son, Carl, married to a coldly proper wife, discovers Freud and the childhood repressions that lie at the root of his troubled marriage. The marriage then deteriorates further. His sister Margaret, who detests dull, boring Belmond, escapes to Greenwich Village, hedonism, and a hopeless affair with a married executive. Pretty Dorothy's marriage to her handsome college classmate, heir of a rich grandfather, appears less satisfactory when her husband borrows against his inheritance to keep from having to go to work. Bunny, the youngest, becomes indoctrinated with socialism when he falls in love with the daughter of Russian immigrants.

The folks are shaken by all these new ideas; the breakdown in conventional relations between the sexes and in family solidarity brought home to them in their sons' and daughters' predicaments. They use folk expressions when discussing the worrisome developments—wondering, for instance, if Margaret is "carrying on." They had fondly hoped their children would "do better" than they had done. Now it looks as if they might not do as well.

The parents maintain their staunch sense of responsibility, however. When catastrophe threatens, as when Carl's wife tries suicide and loses her unwanted child, Annie is a comforting source of strength, one of Suckow's Iowa women "never found wanting in any purely human emergency." Fred, always fair and just, hands over the same tidy sum to Margaret as to all his other offspring in his intention to give them a "start in life" (*Some Others and Myself*, p. 110).

The Folks takes a broad look at conditions of the time. When Fred visits his parents' fine old farm, now in the hands of renters complaining of their lot, he thinks of some of Bun's notions that he had formerly dismissed as heresy. Now he wonders if perhaps they contain some truth. "Land so good maybe oughtn't to belong to any one man, particularly if he wasn't going to live there" (*The Folks*, p. 719).

The church Fred has worked for all his life has voted to close its doors, an indication of the prevalent relaxation of interest in religion. Even the bank is adopting new financial practices. Fred, though retired and in a sense unaffected, is saddened by these developments: "He himself had never liked to make promises he wasn't reasonably sure of being able to keep." He does not care for "the new way of doing business" (*The Folks*, p. 706).

Ruth Suckow shows her Iowans maintaining their folk quality in spite of change. She seems to believe that their character, like that of Faulkner's people, will endure. Her familiar melancholy, however, asserts its minor undertone: "This is the way things are; not the way we would wish them to be" (*Some Others and Myself*, p. 110).

With this novel Suckow came as close as she ever did to writing a best-seller. *The Folks* won many praises—for its accuracy in representing the people of a region and period, for its style and symmetry, for its message. It is what is known as "a good book." Suckow was partial to it, expressing the hope that it would be reissued so that present and future readers could become acquainted with her Iowans.

New Hope, which followed *The Folks*, though not immediately, is nothing like its predecessor. Indeed, it is difficult to categorize. The town of New Hope is patterned after the author's birthplace; the minister, Mr. Greenwood, resembles her father. The book, however, is not simply autobiographical. It evokes a remembered world, conveying the enchantment of unfolding discoveries and fresh impressions felt by the very young. There is an allegorical suggestion in the name of the minister's imaginative daughter, Delight, and in the enchantment her storytelling and inventiveness bring to the children's play. Utopian over-tones are present in the democracy of the small new community—"everybody helping everybody"—and in its confident strivings for progress. One critic de-clared the book is a statement about our country: "This is what we were: this is what we can be again" (letter from John Farrar to Sterling North, 28 March 1942, Ruth Suckow Papers, University of Iowa Library).

Suckow wrote a tribute to her father after his death, remarking that she wished to bear witness to the direction she received in the household of a liberal minis-ter. It contains an account of the author's long estrangement from the church and of her ultimately finding her way back through her affiliation with the Quakers. Her father's nonsectarian attitude as well as his kind understanding helped her reconcile her difficulties. The tribute was later published with a group of Suckow short stories entitled *Some Others and Myself* (1952).

These stories, mostly written in first person, disclose the writer's quickening interest in individuality and in questions of personal accountability. They seem to be leading her to examine the questions asked in her culminating fiction, *The John Wood Case*.

"Mrs. Vogel and Ollie" gives a masterly and rather humorous depiction of an old woman who has "reverted" when left stranded in the rundown streets of her deadly small town. Her daughter, acting on her father's dying injunction to "keep Mother happy," indulges the matron's escapades and plays hostess to the riffraff she collects, while knowing full well that "Mother was a child." Suckow sympa-thizes with this middle-aged daughter in whom she discerns a heroic quality, ordinary though she is. In this story, as in "Eltha" (a busy farm wife devotedly cares for her completely paralyzed and insentient daughter), the author studies the problem of the handicapped person from a unique angle: that of the normal individual left to shoulder the burden of care. The mother in "Eltha" confides after the child's death, "I miss Eltha," a clear affirmation of the selfless spirit that motivated her. It would seem that the author, who has repeatedly dealt with the sacrifice of worthy people on behalf of less worthy ones, has reached an important conclusion: pure goodness—unselfish love—is the catalyst that can turn sacrifice into joy.

The John Wood Case (1959) revolves around the crime of embezzlement committed by a leading church member, John Wood. He had special needs—his adored and ailing wife Minnie would have died of tuberculosis without his pampering indulgences—and she declares that what he has done in the name of love, though a mistake, is forgivable. His employer, George Merriam, from whom he has embezzled, sees it differently. He determines to prosecute John, over the protests of Lydia, his wife, a long-time friend of Minnie who is worried about the effect of the wrongdoing on young Philip, the Woods's high school-age son.

The town is shaken by the crime, the church at a loss over the stance it should adopt toward John. The school is torn by a conflict over the question of Philip: should he deliver the class address at graduation now that his father is in disgrace? There are other complications.

Lydia Merriam resolves the crucial problems, and as she does so, the reader is treated to a philosophical study in the nature of love and in what constitutes good and evil. All is put in simple language and illustrated by the lives of everyday people in a commonplace setting.

Mrs. Merriam may be taken as an exemplar of Suckow's final conclusions, which are indeed not final in the sense of dogmatic, but seeking and tentative. A New Englander and a follower of Emerson, Mrs. Merriam has been an advocate of plain living and high thinking. But she has become convinced of the wrong in her firm stand. She has lost her two artistic daughters and alienated her son because of it. Even virtues, she has learned, must not be carried to extremes.

So it is with love. Excessive romantic love, as exemplified by John and Minnie Wood, is shown to be powerful, admirable to a point, but ultimately arrogant and selfish, disregarding the rights and property of others in its demands. Natural human love is better; giving and taking, it is capable of comforting in adversity and smoothing difficult relationships. Best of all is the higher love Mrs. Merriam has achieved, which selflessly seeks to make the good prevail.

Philip Wood is adrift in that his parents no longer serve as models for him. They look only to each other. Though allied with the church, they seem to have learned nothing from its teachings. Mrs. Merriam with her gifts brings back the boy's self-confidence and turns his thoughts to the future.

Survey of Criticism

Critical studies of Ruth Suckow's fiction are not numerous, although there are indications of a growing appreciation and interest. Ferner Nuhn has always been an understanding and competent critic of his wife's work; he has brought out a number of posthumous publications by her, with helpful comments. John T. Frederick, Suckow's earliest and most perceptive critic, wrote of her genuineness and her generosity, coupled with a vigorous intellect that she used "ruthlessly and fearlessly," while tempering it always with "profound understanding and sympathy" (letter from John T. Frederick to Leedice Kissane, 15 November 1964).

Leedice Kissane's *Ruth Suckow* (1969), the first published book-length study of the author, traces Suckow's development through analyses of her fiction, finding her early short stories poetic and her later works deeply meaningful. Margaret Stewart Omrcanin in *Ruth Suckow: A Critical Study of Her Fiction* (1972) pays careful attention to the social themes in the writer's work.

Abigail Ann Hamblen's *Ruth Suckow* (1978), in the Boise State Western Writers Series, is an appraisal full of warm admiration. Margaret Matlack Kiesel is the author of "Ruth Suckow in the Twenties" (1980). This energetic and able scholar has access to valuable Suckow materials; future work by her is anticipated. Elizabeth Hardwick, in the introductions to *Iowa Interiors* and *Country People*, calls Suckow "an unusually gifted and pure example of the realistic school developing in American fiction in the 1920's."

"The most remarkable woman now writing short stories in the Republic," H. L. Mencken wrote about Ruth Suckow in 1926. Other critics were almost as flamboyant. Ferner Nuhn, reviewing *The Bonney Family* in 1928, noted the extraordinary sensitivity of her style; Allan Nevins called hers "one of the best because one of the truest of all the literary voices of the Union" ("A Painter of Iowa" [1928]). Carl Van Doren in *The American Novel* (1962) judged that she came nearer than any other writer to representing American life on farms and in the small towns. Harlan Hatcher, in *Creating the American Novel* (1935), noted her honesty and the calm control with which she "elevates the commonplace" (p. 106).

On the other hand, John T. Flanagan, in a review of *Some Others and Myself* (1953), fails to find evidence of development in Suckow's later work. In a review of *Carry-Over* (1936), Josephine Herbst felt Suckow neglected the social implications of her background. Phil Stong in *Hawkeye* (1940) found her "too reserved" to be a suitable narrator for Iowa, and Joseph E. Baker thought she neglected intellectual interests and the masculine concerns with business and politics ("Regionalism in the Middle West" [1935]).

We can remind ourselves that Jane Austen, who was attacked on almost every one of the above points, is in our century still being read, still being learned from. One of the great Jane's admirers and emulators, Ruth Suckow, has something to say to us as well. She invites us to think about what lies beneath the surfaces of her truthful representations of Iowa scenes and people as she observed them in her time. She shows us more than we can see.

A Ruth Suckow Memorial Association has been organized in Earlville; Ferner Nuhn and Georgia Dafoe Nuhn and Margaret Matlack Kiesel are members of its board. The association *Newsletter* (Spring 1980) reports posthumous publications by Suckow, as well as recent books and articles about her. In August 1978 Ruth Suckow was named to the Iowa Women's Hall of Fame "for her contribution to the lives of Iowa women both in her writings and in her life."

Bibliography

Works by Ruth Suckow

Country People. New York: Alfred A. Knopf, 1924.
The Odyssey of a Nice Girl. New York: Alfred A. Knopf, 1925.
Iowa Interiors. New York: Alfred A. Knopf, 1926.
"Iowa." *American Mercury* 9 (September 1926): 39-45.
"A German Grandfather." *American Mercury* 12 (November 1927): 280-84.
The Bonney Family. New York: Alfred A. Knopf, 1928.
Cora. New York: Alfred A. Knopf, 1929.
"The Folk Idea in American Life." *Scribner's* 88 (September 1930): 245-55.
Children and Older People. New York: Alfred A. Knopf, 1931.
The Kramer Girls. New York: Alfred A. Knopf, 1931.
"Middle Western Literature." *English Journal* (College Edition) 21 (March 1932): 175-82.
The Folks. New York: Farrar & Rinehart, 1934.
Carry-Over. New York: Farrar & Rinehart, 1936.
New Hope. New York: Farrar & Rinehart, 1942.
Some Others and Myself (including "A Memoir"). New York: Rinehart, 1952.
"An Almost Lost American Classic." *College English* 14 (March 1953): 315-25.
The John Wood Case. New York: Viking, 1959.

Studies of Ruth Suckow

Baker, Joseph E. "Regionalism in the Middle West." *American Review* 4 (March 1935): 603-14.
Flanagan, John T. Review of *Some Others and Myself*. *American Literature* 24 (January 1953): 568-69.
Frederick, John T. "The Farm in Iowa Fiction." *Palimpsest* 32 (March 1951): 124-52.
———. "Ruth Suckow and the Middle Western Literary Movement." *English Journal* 20 (January 1931): 1-8.
———. "Town and City in Iowa Fiction." *Palimpsest* 35 (February 1954): 49-96.
———. "The Writer's Iowa." *Palimpsest* 11 (February 1930): 57-60.
———. "The Younger School." *Palimpsest* 11 (February 1930): 78-86.
Hamblen, Abigail Ann. "The Poetry of Place." *Cornell College Husk* 60 (March 1961): 75-79.
———. *Ruth Suckow*. WWS. Boise, Idaho: Boise State University, 1978.
Hardwick, Elizabeth. Introductions to *Country People* and *Iowa Interiors*. Rediscovered Fiction by American Women Series. New York: Arno Press, 1977.
Hatcher, Harlan. *Creating the American Novel*. New York: Farrar and Rinehart, 1935.
Herbst, Josephine. Review of *Carry-Over*. *New Republic*, 21 October 1936, p. 318.
Herron, Ima Honaker. *The Small Town in American Literature*. Durham, N.C.: Duke University Press, 1939.

Kiesel, Margaret Matlack. "Iowans in the Arts: Ruth Suckow in the Twenties." *Annals of Iowa* 45 (Spring 1980): 257-87.

———. "Ruth Suckow's Grinnell." *Grinnell College Magazine* 8 (November-December 1975): 7-10.

Kissane, Leedice. "D. H. Lawrence, Ruth Suckow and Modern Marriage." *Rendezvous* 4 (Spring 1969): 39-45.

———. *Ruth Suckow*. TUSAS. New York: Twayne, 1969.

Lewis, Sinclair. Introduction to *Country People* in *Three Readers*. Ed. Clifton Fadiman, Sinclair Lewis, and Carl Van Doren. New York: Readers Club Press, 1943.

Mencken, H. L. Reviews of Suckow's works in "The Library." *American Mercury*, July 1924-January 1930.

Nevins, Allan. "A Painter of Iowa." *Saturday Review of Literature*, 10 March 1928, p. 666.

Nuhn, Ferner. "The Orchard Apiary: Ruth Suckow in Earlville." *Iowan* 20 (Summer 1972): 21-54.

———. "A Real Family." Review of *The Bonney Family*. *New York Herald-Tribune Books*, 22 January 1928, p. 7.

Omrcanin, Margaret Stewart. *Ruth Suckow: A Critical Study of Her Fiction*. Philadelphia: Dorrance, 1972.

Paluka, Frank. "Ruth Suckow: A Calendar of Letters." *Books at Iowa* 1 (October 1964): 34-40; 2 (April 1965): 31-40.

Stong, Phil. *Hawkeye: A Bibliography of the State of Iowa*: New York: Dodd, Mead, 1940.

Van Doren, Carl. *The American Novel: 1780-1939*. New York: Macmillan, 1962.

Thomas J. Lyon

FRANK WATERS

(1902-)

The great, central theme in Frank Waters's work, spanning some twenty-one books from the early *Fever Pitch* (1930) to the current work in progress, is integration. More specifically, it is the movement from a dichotomous or dualistic state toward resolution, synthesis, and eventual unity. This movement is seen primarily as a matter of human consciousness and personality and the ultimate integration comprises the two major styles of consciousness (ratiocinative and intuitive), the Jungian principles of *animus* and *anima*, and in a larger, indeed final inclusiveness, consciousness and being itself—this last level of integration amounting to enlightenment. Secondarily, Waters's concern with integration moves outward from the human self to society and race; here he develops a dialectical theory of history in which the white, European cultures represent the rationalistic, masculine, and aggressive aspects of the self and the nonwhite cultures, particularly the American Indian, the nonrational, feminine, and passive-adaptive. The movement of both self and socially discrete humankind over time, ideally, is toward unity; polarity, however, remains the grand, explicatory principle of existence.

In his pursuit of this theme, Waters continues a long American tradition in literature. The historical fact that a race and culture that considered itself civilized invaded and colonized a continent that it considered primitive has helped to create a strongly dualistic and dialectical frame of reference for American thought: civilization versus wilderness; white versus red; order and repression versus chaos and release. In the West, this dialectic reaches quintessential sharpness because the West was considered the least known and wildest, and was the most obviously chaotic geologically, of the quadrants of the American compass. Moreover, in the West some Indian cultures survived intact into the era of white self-reflection, thus forming a living antithesis to the always-advancing white thesis. In this general philosophical setting, Frank Waters's interpretations are sympathetic to the Indian or "wild" point of view, as if he means to bring it out of the (white) unconscious and into the light where it may be assessed fairly and perhaps take its place in a needed, future complementarity. Thus he takes the side of meditative and intuitive consciousness, as against the "engineering mentality," and the side of the Indian, who in pain and loss must try to adjust to a wholly new, white world. What may save Waters from a single-minded polemicism is his vision of ultimate synthesis. Although synthesis can become somewhat programmatic in his work, his very espousal of it tends to make his approach both fairminded and penetrating. Perhaps no other author has tried to see the import of the American western experience in terms at once so profound, psychologically, and so far-reaching, historically.

Biography

Waters came to his theme honestly, by the facts of his heritage. For Frank Waters synthesis has been a deeply personal matter. Waters was born 25 July 1902 in Colorado Springs, Colorado. His mother, May Ione Dozier, came from a well-established and once fairly well-to-do Colorado Springs family; his father, who had been a boarder taken into the Dozier home when the family fell upon hard times, was part Southern Cheyenne—as nearly as Waters has been able to tell. As he describes it in his autobiographical novels *The Wild Earth's Nobility* (1935), *Below Grass Roots* (1937), and *The Dust Within the Rock* (1940), and in the redaction of those novels, *Pike's Peak* (1971), the duality of his parentage was strongly marked and emotionally demanding. In *Below Grass Roots* he shows a white mother and a part-Indian father fighting with each other for psychic possession of their son, a wrenching process that left the child, as Waters describes the autobiographical "March Cable," "wavering between both desires" (*Below Grass Roots*, p. 263). This emotionally divisive childhood reached great intensity and poignance when Waters's father was tempted into working for his father-in-law, Joseph Dozier, in Dozier's mine high on the shoulder of Pike's Peak. In the cold dampness of the mine, far from the open spaces of his background, he developed lung disease, deteriorated quickly, and died when Waters was twelve. Ever after, the search of the boy for his father (and Waters referred to himself as "the boy" into his fifth decade and twelfth book) was the sincere core of a philosophical pilgrimage that would lead him to a lifelong study of the primitive, an immersion into Jungian psychoanalysis and Buddhist thought, and a strong artistic preoccupation with resolution.

In 1911, Waters had been taken by his father to the Navaho Reservation in northern New Mexico, had stayed there several months, and had naturally been attracted by the down-to-earth life of the Indians. Here, close to the land, life had the grit of dirt and sandstone and was altogether different from the status-conscious, faintly unreal existence back in wealthy Colorado Springs. "The boy" knew the difference but did not know that he knew and only years later would work out the meaning of the contrast. The Indian side of things called deeply, inherently, to him.

Back home, while visiting the family mine on Pike's Peak—the "family folly," Waters calls it—the boy once experienced, all unbidden and unprepared for, a moment of transcendent identification with his environment, which, as a literal touchstone experience, may be seen as the spiritual center of his later books. A victim of push and pull at home down below the mountain, here above timber line he was free. And yet the high environment seemed oppressively boring. "He simply felt imprisoned between sky and earth in a waste of stone," Waters says (*The Colorado*, p. 22). In this curiously free yet restricted setting, "one lived a life of stone." There was nothing to think or talk about but stone: ore, samples, tailings, drift.

Then suddenly it happened, the boy did not know how. All this dead stone became intensely, vibrantly alive. Playing on the dump one morning after he had washed the breakfast dishes, he happened to pick up a pinch. In the bright sunlight he saw with microscopic clarity the infinitesimal shapes and colors, the monstrous and miraculous complexity of that single thimbleful of sand. In that instant the world about him took on a new, great and terrifying meaning. [*The Colorado*, pp. 22-23]

The meaning was that every rock on the mountain, and by extension every mountain and the entire earth, was alive in a "close-knit unity similar to the one in his sweaty palm" (p. 23). Waters had touched process—again, as in his experience of the Indian reservation, without knowing completely what to make of it—but he did now know that things were not the discrete, static entities they seemed.

Waters's years in high school in Colorado Springs and at Colorado College were not, as he describes them in the novels, happy ones. Occasional glimpses of wholeness were not enough to overcome the pressures of economics and social status and the engineering major that family tradition landed him in. He dropped out in 1924, first working in the oil fields of Wyoming and then traveling to California, finally to work for the telephone company in Imperial Valley. Here he came to know the border towns and their racially mixed populations; this was apparently an impetus to self-study, for he began almost immediately to write fiction strongly oriented toward autobiography and toward the great theme of integration. In an artistic choice that seems clearly significant, Waters began his writing career by describing a man's experience of mystical unity with the wild desert around him. After he had worked out this description of fulfillment and rightness to his satisfaction, he invented a plot that would more or less credibly place the man in the wilderness and in the proper frame of mind for transcendent experience.

Waters's next writing project, the novel *The Yogi of Cockroach Court*, which would go through three drafts before being published twenty years later in 1947, is again centered on the experience of wholeness or enlightenment. Waters had hit upon his theme and in these first attempts was trying to describe it frontally, immediately; *The Wild Earth's Nobility* (written in 1932), which is the first book in the autobiographical trilogy and deals mainly with Grandfather Dozier (called Rogier in the novel), may show a growth in patience. Waters here is taking the long view, in effect, by starting with the grandfather and the family relationships that preceded and later enveloped him; it is as if he had recognized that the karmic patterns of real life, just as much as the isolated moments of break-throughs in consciousness, may reveal ultimate truth. Still, the overriding concern is with those moments. Rogier is shown, for example, to be obsessed with penetrating into Pike's Peak not just to get gold but to lay bare what he thought would be a hidden principle of existence.

Waters's move from California back to the Cripple Creek mining district in 1936, his beginning then to write full time, and his eventual move before the end of the decade to northern New Mexico may also be seen as supporting reflection and consolidation. These are moves into the past and into the heartland, closer to the Indian and closer to what many have regarded as the magnetic center of the Indian way, the Taos area. By 1940, Waters had finished his autobiographical novels, had begun the study of Indian thought that has occupied the rest of his life, and had become close enough to the Indian way, perhaps largely through his friendship with the Taos Pueblo man, Tony Luhan, that he could venture general, comparative statements about red and white cultures. He had mastered at least the outlines of his lifework and was beginning to turn out fiction that was not only searching for, or promising of, deeper matters, but that was becoming more and more clearly expressive of a profound, achieved outlook. *People of the Valley* (1941) and *The Man Who Killed the Deer* (1942) both deal surely with a nonwhite, nonrational view of the world. In *People of the Valley*, Maria, the central character, attains the wisdom of an authentic seer, and Waters presents this wisdom convincingly—almost from the inside. In the very highly regarded *The Man Who Killed the Deer*, he portrays the monistic, Indian vision by means of italicized passages that are meant to be the collective, traditional, inner voice of the tribe. In addition, in both novels he makes direct, essay-like comparisons of the "perennial philosophy" of the folk and the Indians with the materialistic white world.

World War II intervened in Waters's study; he spent a brief period in the army and then worked as a propaganda writer for the coordinator of inter-American affairs. Perhaps characteristically, his first writing project upon the end of the war was a third draft of his novel about meditation, *The Yogi of Cockroach Court*. Perhaps the confused and violent world situation and his own uprooting from home ground in the West renewed and deepened the pursuit not just for peace but for the source of peace. *The Colorado* (1946), Waters's contribution to Rinehart's Rivers of America series, may show a certain hitch in his philosophical development or perhaps simply the distraction of the war, for while it works primarily from the viewpoint of land mysticism and celebrates the Indian and the wilderness with sincere closeness, it also describes dams and irrigation schemes, symbolic of opposite values, in tones of excitement and awe. However, by 1947 Waters had moved back to Taos and had begun an intensive examination of Navaho and Pueblo life, a study that resulted in the provocative nonfiction work, *Masked Gods*, in 1950. This book has none of the apparent conflict of *The*

Colorado in the sense of contradictory values within itself; indeed, it transcends conflict by suggesting that the dominant white civilization, as indicated by modern or relativity physics, appears to be coming to a world view astonishingly similar to that of the Indians of North America and the Buddhists of Asia. Mankind is one, ultimately, in the furthest reaches of consciousness; the various cultures may only be traveling different roads of life toward a great realization and a great, conscious unity.

Masked Gods marks Waters's entrance into the mature phase of his thought, wherein a world scale and historically inclusive synthesis is attempted. In the 1950s, he became deeply attracted by the story of Edith Warner, a woman who had operated a tea room at a symbolically charged location on the Rio Grande River in New Mexico, across the river from the San Ildefonso Pueblo and down the hill from the secret, atomic city of Los Alamos, and over the next ten years he wrote three drafts of a novelization of her career. His theme was to relate her own transcendence—Edith Warner had apparently had mystical experiences—to the great human duality embodied in her geographic circumstance. Somehow, Waters apparently thought, the enlightenment of the individual and the possible future harmony of seemingly diverse cultures are all of a piece, if we but see it. One principle runs through all levels of conflict and duality; the inner life is repeated and enlarged in history and in the multiplication of individuals in society, but it is all nevertheless one life. *The Woman at Otowi Crossing* (1966) occupied Waters, one might perhaps say tormented him, with its possibilities. During the 1950s, he edited a weekly newspaper in Taos, worked as a writer for the Los Alamos Scientific Laboratory, and tried his hand as a screenwriter in Los Angeles. But it is clear that the story of the woman on the Rio Grande was the drama that compelled his most profound interest.

By the end of the decade, Waters was living on the Hopi Reservation in Arizona, interviewing Indians and compiling (with their cooperation) a one-volume scripture of their beliefs, myths, rituals, and history. *Book of the Hopi* (1963), like *Masked Gods*, suggests a dialectic of history and a possible final harmony. Indeed, the impetus of the book seems to have been the Hopis' belief that its publication might serve historical resolution and harmony. But for Waters's own career, perhaps the important point is that while working with the Hopi, he underwent important personal experiences, described in detail in his account of the Hopi years, *Pumpkin Seed Point* (1969), which seemed to give the requisite insights, or the needed opening of consciousness, with which to complete the story of the woman at Otowi Crossing. The fact that *The Woman* (1966) is his last novel, leaving aside *Pike's Peak* (1971), which is mostly an editing of the earlier trilogy, may indicate that it presents Waters's most sought-after themes, finally, to his satisfaction.

Since *Pike's Peak*, his work has included a painstaking investigation of Aztec and Mayan civilization, the fruit of which is *Mexico Mystique* (1975). This is a speculative book reaffirming the concept of the rational-nonrational amalgam and arguing that the ancient Mexican cultures believed in and indeed predicted this synthesis for humanity at large. In 1981, Waters published a collection of essays, *Mountain Dialogues*, which treats the themes of polarity and synthesis in terms of his own locale and his own life. He has (wth Charles Adams) coedited W. Y. Evans-Wentz's *Cuchama and Sacred Mountains* (1982), which appeared under the Ohio University Press/Swallow Press imprint, as did *Mountain Dialogues*.

Major Themes

In *The Woman at Otowi Crossing*, Waters deals for the first time with a white person who develops an enlightened consciousness with no particular background or training for it. Martiniano, in *The Man Who Killed the Deer*, is in effect surrounded with a cultural tradition of the higher consciousness, and is expected and pushed to realize it. Tai Ling, in *The Yogi of Cockroach Court*, is Chinese and follows precisely an ancient Tibetan Buddhist practice of meditation. But Helen Chalmers, the Woman, has no such advantages or guides; she does live in a powerful location—in what Waters had referred to in *Masked Gods* as "the crucible of conflict"—and this will frame her experience, but in this characterization Waters is stripping the issues to their simplest and most inner level and attempting to show that anyone, of any race or background, may achieve the universal, integrated mind. The theme is that mysticism is not exclusive and not really esoteric. Therefore, the great task Waters sets himself in this novel, which might be seen as a kind of final test of his fictional career, is to make enlightenment realistic, to bring it home. The larger meanings and applications are inherent in the Woman's situation between the atomic city and the pueblo but will come to life only if we first believe in her.

The circumstances of Helen's initial awakening are predominantly personal. She has learned that the Chile Line, the narrow-gauge railroad whose customers are her lunchroom's main source of business, is to be torn up. The world is plunging deeper into World War II, and in this atmosphere of tension Helen learns that her daughter, whom she had deserted some twenty years before and has not seen since, is coming for a visit. Her life is heading toward a great watershed, she feels, and her discovery of an ominous swelling between her breast and shoulder crystallizes her deep sense of portent. At the same time, though, she feels strangely detached from what is happening, and in this confusing scene of new pressures and contradictory feelings she experiences something entirely unexpected. It is an internal event, an event of consciousness, but one that reveals a world of perception so suddenly brilliant as to be like an explosion.

In its blinding brightness all mortal appearances dissolved into eternal meanings, great shimmering waves of pure feeling which had no other expression than this, and these were so closely entwined and harmonized that they formed one indivisible unity. A selfhood that embraced her, the totality of the universe, and all space and all time in one immortal existence that had never had a beginning nor would ever have an end. [*The Woman At Otowi Crossing*, p. 30]

The experience is immediately transformative. In this great unity it would be trivial and incorrect to worry over the tribulations, or even the death, of the small self. Helen's small self, in fact, has just "died."

Having established the core of the story, Waters proceeds to enmesh the Woman in a complex and realistic set of circumstances, some of which (as her relationship with the Pueblo Indian, Facundo) parallel and substantiate her emergence, and some of which (for example her now-transcended affair with Jack Turner, a bluff, rationalistic newspaperman) offer counterpoint. Her daughter Emily turns out to be an academic climber seeking to establish herself as an authority on ancient Indian civilizations. Turner, for his part, thinks his former lover is having "spells" and tries to get her to visit a Freudian analyst. Suddenly freed from ego and its vision-fogging demands, Helen looks at these unenlightened people with a compassion that seems to them cool withdrawal. Meanwhile, up on the "Hill," physicists and engineers are preparing a weapon of horrifying destructive power, which in Helen's lifetime will be used twice against people and then retested repeatedly, these actions making an obvious symbol of a mentality and a culture gone—at best—off center, out of balance. The world is sweeping into a new, frightening, perhaps apocalyptic age.

It takes Helen some time to adjust to the vast and seemingly impersonal consciousness she has entered. How strange, when the vision is of a great unity, that one's oldest relationships may quickly dissolve. How interesting that the seemingly blank-visaged old Indian who has been working in her garden suddenly now seems to perceive her innermost life with a quick, penetrating glance. Facundo takes her into the kiva at the pueblo and explains the Indian thought to her, and she realizes her moment of illumination was not an "emotional upset," as Turner had said, but an avenue into a widely shared vision, an emergence.

In creating Helen and her world, Waters seems particularly intent upon avoiding abstraction. Facundo, in his ordinariness, keeps Helen close to earth; as they are leaving the kiva and she is ruminating upon the universal truths she has been led to see, the old Indian says simply,"This old kiva cold and dirty. Lots of work gettin' ready for them big doin's" (*The Woman*, p. 68). Waters's own imagistic technique, in which he presents the Woman's life in terms of meals to cook, firewood to bring in, or simply the warm New Mexico sun in which she longs to bathe, parallels Facundo's implied advice. Both mean to show enlightenment not as some sort of mystical flight but as straightforward, grounded awareness. Helen is led by Facundo to see that this world of pine cones, gathered in burlap sacks and brought home by wagon for winter fires, and of a heron standing immobile on a sandbar of the Rio Grande, is also precisely the world of illumination. It is seen as Helen would see it much of the time; its grit and grain and disappointment are the environment that we too know. Helen is not presented as an accomplished seer or worker of magic, but a human who has glimpsed, and then become more fully acquainted with, a totality that makes her earlier standpoint and perception seem merely partial. She is in both worlds simultaneously because they are indeed the same world. Waters's attempt is to penetrate stereotypes of mystical thought, to reveal the inner life. This is what is common to all, and, the novel argues, perfectly accessible.

The larger picture—actually not so very different from what goes on within consciousness itself—is the historical nexus represented by the Atomic City's having been set squarely in the land of the ancient ones. The trend toward an ultimate merging of thought outlined in *Masked Gods* is here represented in one character, Edmund Gaylord. He is a physicist working on the Bomb and believes above all in a rational, practical approach to life. Waters portrays him, in the early stages of the Los Alamos project, as emotionally stunted and rather amazingly naive: a clear case of one-sidedness. But through a relationship with Emily, and by observing and getting to know Helen, and finally by realizing (through two serious accidents) some of the shortcomings in "white" thought—particularly its lack of control over the powers it so familiarly handles—Gaylord begins to deepen. It is only a halting start, perhaps, but it seems more believable, more human-sized, than the outline program of *Masked Gods*. There are differences between the power of the Indians and the power of the whites. These are shown dramatically in juxtaposed passages late in the novel. In the first scene, Helen and Facundo are visiting an old Indian who is staying within a kiva for forty days and nights as part of a religious ceremony. Facundo and the old man sit in silence, their visit wordless but mysteriously powerful. What passes between them, Helen comes to realize as it sweeps out to include her also, is nothing less than the essential, unifying force of all creation. Immediately thereafter, Waters switches the scene to an experiment at Los Alamos, where scientists are pushing two lumps of fissionable material together to practice what they call "tickling the dragon's tail." Working with hardly any acknowledgment that what they are dealing with is a fundamental, universal power and should be treated with the greatest respect or at least the greatest caution possible, they push the blocks of enriched atomic fuel past the critical point. There is a release of radioactivity that is lethal to the chief experimenter and that injures Gaylord seriously. One power, carefully guided, leads to enlightenment and brotherhood; the same power, warped and made dangerous by a shallow or egoistic mentality, can destroy the world. At the end of the novel, Gaylord is beginning to see that what matters, what really guides history, is whether our hearts are right.

The Woman at Otowi Crossing is Waters's most ambitious novel, at once his most particular description of awakened consciousness and his most realistic, historically grounded portrayal of a possible human destiny. In its insistence that the integration of consciousness and the simultaneous discovery of the world itself as a great unity are not bizarre or even unusual phenomena but truly the human birthright, this novel summarizes Waters's thought and hope.

Survey of Criticism

Thought and hope, of course, do not necessarily make great writing; perhaps the most damning criticism of Frank Waters's fiction is, in fact, that it is too much ruled by ideas. Vernon Young, in almost the first extended critical treatment of Waters, "Frank Waters: Problems of the Regional Imperative" (1949), argues that the novelist had a program, a "regional imperative" toward land mysticism, which dominated his characters and forced them to assume the role of mouthpieces for ideas. This criticism is perhaps based upon the traditional novel, with its European, British, and eastern American background and its central concern with manners, morals, love, seduction, marriage, and so forth, and perhaps it is not quite germane to what Waters is attempting. He is trying to get underneath the social or egoistic plane of personality and to voice the wild or ultimate connections that unite people, and people and world, at a deeper level. This is an unusual if not entirely new approach (Mary Austin, for example, worked some of the same ground), and perhaps Waters may be granted a certain expository freedom.

Martin Bucco, *Frank Waters* (1969), and Thomas Lyon, *Frank Waters* (1973), emphasize Waters's ideas and judge their presentation artistically respectable; both are disposed to give Waters, as a writer venturing into little-known territory, freedom from older, indoor standards. In recent years, symposia organized by Charles Adams and presented at Modern Language Association meetings have explored Waters's work in terms of its relevance to ancient philosophical systems, modern psychological research, and many aspects of modern history. The range of Waters's books certainly justifies a broad-gauge critical appraisal. But more important, the depth and possible accuracy of his insights, which seem so purposefully applicable to the human condition in this polarized time, should compel our attention and our careful judgment. Clearly he is a writer who believes in the writer's role as a social and psychological force. At the close of the *The Woman at Otowi Crossing*, Waters quotes Helen Chalmers's "Secret Journal," an account she kept for Jack Turner in hope of communicating to him what he seemed so resolutely to be pushing aside. Realization, or enlightenment, or integration of consciousness—whatever we might want to call the deep recognition of the world as unity—is, Helen says, "a normal, natural experience that eventually comes to every one of us" (p. 300). The "Secret Journal," and the works of Frank Waters also, testify to the ancient human urge toward transcendence but emphasize that the desired state is both inner and linked to all else; not an escape from the world but a completion of it.

Bibliography

Works by Frank Waters

Fever Pitch. New York: Liveright, 1930; New York: Berkley Books, 1954.
The Wild Earth's Nobility. New York: Liveright, 1935.
Below Grass Roots. New York: Liveright, 1937.
Midas of the Rockies. New York: Covici-Friede, 1937; Denver: University of Denver, 1949; Denver: Alan Swallow, 1954; Chicago: Swallow Press, 1972.
The Dust Within the Rock. New York: Liveright, 1940.

People of the Valley. New York: Farrar and Rinehart, 1941; Denver: Alan Swallow, 1962.

The Man Who Killed the Deer. New York: Farrar and Rinehart, 1942; Denver: University of Denver, 1951; Denver: Alan Swallow, 1954; Chicago: Swallow Press, 1968, 1970; New York: Pocket Books, 1971.

"Relationships and the Novel." *Writer* 56 (April 1943): 105-7.

The Colorado. New York: Farrar and Rinehart, 1946; New York: Rinehart 1954.

The Yogi of Cockroach Court. New York: Rinehart, 1947; Chicago: Swallow Press, 1972.

Masked Gods. Albuquerque: University of New Mexico Press, 1950; Denver: Alan Swallow, 1962; Chicago: Swallow Press, 1970; New York: Ballantine Books, 1970.

The Earp Brothers of Tombstone. New York: Clarkson Potter, 1960.

Book of the Hopi. New York: Viking Press, 1963; New York: Ballantine Books, 1969.

Leon Gaspard. Flagstaff, Ariz.: Northland Press, 1964.

"The Western Novel: A Symposium." *South Dakota Review* 2 (Autumn 1964): 10-16.

The Woman at Otowi Crossing. Denver: Alan Swallow, 1966; Chicago: Swallow Press, 1971.

"Words." *Western American Literature* 2 (Fall 1968): 227-34.

Pumpkin Seed Point. Chicago: Swallow Press, 1969.

Pike's Peak. Chicago: Swallow Press, 1971.

Conversations with Frank Waters. Ed. John R. Milton. Chicago: Swallow Press, 1971.

To Possess the Land. A Biography of Arthur Rochford Manby. Chicago: Swallow Press, 1973.

Mexico Mystique: The Coming Sixth World of Consciousness. Chicago: Swallow Press, 1975.

Mountain Dialogues. Athens/Chicago: Ohio University Press/Swallow Press, 1981.

Cuchama and Sacred Mountains. Ed. Frank Waters and Charles Adams. Text by W. Y. Evans-Wentz. Athens/Chicago: Ohio University Press/Swallow Press, 1982.

Studies of Frank Waters

Bucco, Martin. *Frank Waters*. SWS. Austin, Tex.: Steck-Vaughn, 1969.

Lyon, Thomas J. *Frank Waters*. TUSAS. New York: Twayne, 1973.

Milton, John R., ed. "Frank Waters Issue," *South Dakota Review* 15 (Autumn 1977).

Pilkington, William T. "Character and Landscape: Frank Waters' Colorado Trilogy." *Western American Literature* 2 (Fall 1967): 183-93.

Young, Vernon. "Frank Waters: Problems of the Regional Imperative." *New Mexico Quarterly Review* 19 (Autumn 1949): 353-72.

OWEN WISTER
(1860-1938)

Biography

Owen Wister's life covers a remarkable range of history and experience. Although this man grew up amid the sophistication and culture of the eastern seaboard, he became famous for narratives filled with the adventures and vernacular figures of the American West. But besides the cultural bifurcation of his life, there was a dramatic historical shift as well as he saw firsthand the disappearance of antebellum American innocence in the dark post-World War I atmosphere of the so-called lost generation. From Whittier to Hemingway was a long reach.

Wister's family background was hardly democratic. Indeed his ancestry carries with it strong suggestions of aristocracy. Wister's father, Owen Jones Wister, was a well-known Philadelphia physician, with roots extending well back into the old German families that first settled Pennsylvania. Owen's mother, Sarah Butler Wister, was the daughter of the famous actress Fanny Kemble and Pierce Butler (whose grandfather had signed the Constitution). Wister's mother was in many ways the epitome of Victorian genteel culture; she was fluent in French and Italian, she wrote for leading magazines, she played the piano, and she entertained artists and novelists with aplomb. As Philip Durham reported in his introduction to *The Virginian*, "Owen's mother, was (in the son's words) 'very much aware of the fact that she was a personage, and on an occasion when Henry James was a dinner guest she carved while wearing white kid gloves' " (p. v.).

The only child of this couple, Owen was born in Philadelphia on 14 July 1860. His education was up to the highest Victorian cultural standards: travel on the continent, association with important writers and painters, private boarding schools in Switzerland and Hereford, England, and college preparation at the prestigious St. Paul's School in Concord, New Hampshire. Here Wister wrote essays and poems and became editor of the school magazine, where in 1873 he published his first piece, "Down in a Diving Bell."

His preparation finished, Wister enrolled at Harvard University. He joined enthusiastically in the select society of the Porcellian Club, the Dickey, and the intense social life of nineteenth-century Harvard College, where he formed lifelong and influential friendships. As he wrote later of this experience, "It opened hearts to each other, its rough and tumble, straight out of the eighteenth century, knit sophomores, juniors, seniors, graduates, into a Harvard texture closer than modern mechanisms or rotarian methods can compass" (*Roosevelt* [1930], p. 12).

Following his literary and musical interests, Wister was author, director, chorus master, and composer in a number of musical productions of greater and lesser quality. In 1882, he was elected to Phi Beta Kappa and that spring graduated summa cum laude with a degree in music.

By this time Wister's experiences had convinced him that he was a musician, and with letters of introduction from his famous grandmother in his pocket he left for Europe and the chance to prove that his talent was indeed genuine. In Wister's own words:

In Wagner's house at Bayreuth, that first summer of *Parsifal*, I played to Liszt my proudest composition, *Merlin and Vivien*. He jumped up in the middle and stood behind me muttering approval, and now and then stopped me and put his hands over my shoulders onto the keys, struck a bar or two, and said:

"I should do that here if I were you."

And he wrote his old friend, my grandmother, Fanny Kemble, that I had "*un talent prononcé*" for music. [*Roosevelt*, p. 22]

But at this moment there came one of the most important turning points in Owen Wister's career. The reasons are not entirely clear, but the father, Owen Jones Wister, wanted his son to come home and take up a career with Major Henry Higginson in the offices of Lee, Higginson, & Company. And so with the final plea of his teacher, Ernest Guiraud, in his ears, "*N'abandonnes pas la musique!*" Owen Wister returned to State Street. But business had nose dived, and instead of a prestigious position with Higginson and Company, the young musician was put to computing interest rates on daily balances on a high stool below stairs in the Union Safe Deposit Vaults. The frustrations must have been profound.

This did not mean, however, that Wister's artistic interests were completely subverted. William Dean Howells and a group of painters, writers, musicians, and doctors had organized the Tavern Club. Wister was a member, and he found entertainment and considerable outlet for his energies by cultivating his friendship with Howells, whom he came to know well, and by writing with his cousin, Langdon Mitchell, a semiautobiographical novel, *A Wise Man's Son*. Wister showed the novel to Howells, who was evidently impressed:

"so much young man never seems to have got into a book before," was the opinion he gave of *A Wise Man's Son*; and it convinced him that the clerk in the Union Safe Deposit Vaults could write novels if he chose. . . . And then, after many encouraging words, he became an adviser to the clerk, who was just twenty-four. He urged that *A Wise Man's Son* be never shown to a publisher; some publisher might accept it, and the clerk would regret such a book when he was older. [*Roosevelt*, p. 23-24]

At this point in his life, twenty-four years old and still "computing interest on daily balances" with "no prospect of the Vaults ending," Wister wrote to his father. As he explained the situation, "I would go to the Harvard Law School, since American respectability accepted lawyers, no matter how bad, which I was likely to be, and rejected composers, even if they were good, which I might possibly be" (*Roosevelt*, p. 27). So Wister went back to Philadelphia to begin preparation for Harvard Law School. By this time the tension and disappointment were too much for the young man, and in the first part of 1885, as he says, "My health very opportunely broke down. I was ordered by Dr. Weir Mitchell to a ranch of some friends in Wyoming. Early in July, 1885, I went there" (*Roosevelt*, p. 28).

In the company of two unmarried aunts, Wister went by train and stagecoach into the frontier cattle country of Wyoming where the three easterners were guests of "Major" Frank Wolcott, an important cattleman who was to play a significant part in the Johnson County war. But that summer the ranch was generally peaceful, and Wister's enthusiasm with his western experience is evident in the pages of the journal that he kept:

I can't possibly say how extraordinary and beautiful the valleys we have been going through are. They're different from all things I've seen. When you go for miles through the piled rocks where the fire has risen straight out of the crevices, you never see a human being—only now and then some disappearing wild animal. . . . Then suddenly you come round a turn and down into a green cut where there are horsemen and wagons and hundreds of cattle, and then it's like Genesis.

On 8 July he wrote, "This existence is heavenly in its monotony and sweetness. Wish I were going to do it every summer. I'm beginning to be able to feel I'm something of an animal and not a stinking brain alone" (*Owen Wister Out West* [1958], pp. 31-32).

While Wister was deeply impressed with the experience of Wyoming, there was as yet no sense of vocation involved with that experience. It was enough for him that the West refreshed him and lifted his spirits. So, in the fall of 1885, Wister returned home to study law at Harvard, graduating in 1888. He passed the Pennsylvania bar and found a position with Francis Rawle. He argued at least one case successfully before the circuit court, and as he says, "Francis Rawle saw symptoms of a lawyer in me...but I couldn't get Wyoming out of my head" (*Roosevelt*, p. 28).

By 1891 there had been at least five summer excursions into the West, each trip packed with "camps in the mountains, camps in the sage-brush, nights in town, cards with cavalry officers, meals with cowpunchers, round-ups, scenery, the Yellowstone Park, trout fishing, hunting with Indians, shooting antelope, white tail deer, black tail deer, elk, bear, mountain sheep—and missing these same animals" (*Roosevelt*, p. 28), and each trip had been faithfully recorded in the remarkably complete journals that Wister kept of each trip.

But by 1891 the western experience and the artistic sensibilities of this young man were coming together to form a sense of purpose. As Wister told his mother on 21 June, "After a while I shall write a great fat book about the whole thing. When I feel enough familiar both by time and knowledge. There's a story I've already begun, some fifty pages of manuscript lying at home. That is intended merely as a trial trip" (*Owen Wister Out West*, p. 114).

The first western tales were finished that fall, and "Hank's Woman" and "How Lin McLean Went East" were sent to Henry Mills Alden at *Harper's Magazine*. Alden immediately bought the two pieces for *Harper's Weekly*. And, as Wister recorded, "Francis Rawle was as proud of the check from Messrs. Harper and Brothers as I was; he kept me in his office, where I worked at fiction for twenty-five years, and at law nevermore" (*Roosevelt*, p. 30). Whatever may have been missing up to this point in Owen Wister's life, at least he could now claim not only a sense of vocation but a profession.

So in October 1893, Wister was bouncing along in a western stagecoach, a traveling writer whose commission from Alden and *Harper's Magazine* instructed him that he was to write a series of western stories: "Each must be a thrilling story, having its ground in a real incident, though you are left free scope for imaginative treatment" (Etulain, *Owen Wister*, p. 10).

There followed in the next months Indian tales, army stories, and eventually a volume, *Red Men and White* (1896), in which Wister still characterized himself as the observer-recorder: the stories, he said, "are about Indians and soldiers and events west of the Missouri....[The] occurrences, noble and ignoble, are told as they were told to me by those who saw them" (*Red Men and White*, pp. vii-ix). But the great work in Wister's plan was a book-length expression of his Wyoming experience.

From the very first, it was the cowboy that interested Wister most. To him the Indians were colorful and exotic, the military officers intriguing in their combination of erudition and adventure, but it was the American on horseback, the cowpuncher, who came to be the focus of Wister's creative attention.

So Wister's castle in the air, as he called it, was to write an episodic novel including the two cowboy figures who had become prominent in his early fiction. But as he reported years later, "After those first four sketches, such a book was my aim until 1897 when I found that a novel with both Lin McLean and the Virginian as chief characters would be too long. I separated them, letting *The Virginian* wait and completing *Lin McLean* [1897], which was published that year" (*Lin McLean* [1928 ed.], p. x.).

Other western stories and a volume of short stories, *The Jimmyjohn Boss* (1900), soon followed. Then in fall 1901 with the previously published episodes in hand, Wister moved with his small family to Charleston, South Carolina, the town where he and his wife had honeymooned in 1898. There he revised and reworked the chapters into the volume that was to become *The Virginian*, and in May 1902 the book was published. It became a marvelous success, appearing almost immediately on American best-seller lists. It made the hero and the author famous, and a new phrase entered the American vocabulary: "When you call me that, smile." A sure mark of popular notoriety, the stage version of the play began traveling around the country making the actor, Dustin Farnum, famous as he sang songs that Wister himself composed (all of this, long before Gary Cooper became famous playing the part of the Virginian in the first movie version). Without question the author was a famous man, and in the flush of this recognition as a writer, Wister must have felt the sense of vocation and profession that he had sought for so long.

Other volumes followed: a novel of manners set in Charleston, *Lady Baltimore* (1906), and a second volume of western short stories, *Members of the Family* (1911). But the author's confession—"this book is three years late;...its follower should even now be ready. It is not yet begun; it exists merely in notes and intentions"—suggests that there were other claims on his energies. To begin with, national and international interests captured his attention: he had already ventured into biography with a short study of Ulysses S. Grant (1900) and a brief biography of Washington (1907). There were political essays stemming out of his rising concerns with the international tensions, a voluminous correspondence, and almost annual trips to the continent where he cultivated literary friendships with Henry James and others and kept in touch with the Old World culture that he so obviously loved. On top of all this, there were serious bouts with illness.

Not that he lost interest in the West entirely; to the contrary, in 1911 he took his family on a summer vacation to Yellowstone Park and the Teton Basin, and in 1912 he bought a small ranch in Jackson Hole. But as his daughter reported, "Owen Wister never talked about the West to his family" (*Owen Wister Out West*, p. 24).

For a decade or so after that 1911 volume, Wister did very little with the West, and he published nothing about the time and place for which he had become famous. Then, with an obvious sense of nostalgia and with evident feelings of loss, Wister turned back to his western notebooks and, now in his sixties, recalled his and his country's younger years. Some of these last stories seem strangely formed, as though the writer were striving for something just beyond his reach. But many are touched with a sense of tragic loss that makes them perhaps more interesting than anything else he ever wrote. In 1928 he gathered together almost all his published works for a collected edition of his works. For each volume he provided a reminiscent preface that offers interesting insights to both the man and his work. After the death of his good friend Theodore Roosevelt, Wister wrote a narrative personal tribute, dedicated to the president's widow, *Roosevelt: The Story of a Friendship* (1930). It was his last book. Wister himself died 21 July 1938.

Major Themes

As one might imagine, the themes of Owen Wister's stories and novels derive mainly from his relationship with the American West. In his earlier writings, for instance, he shows a fascination with what he often referred to in his journals as the "characteristic thing," those elements of geography, of flora and fauna, of speech, dress, and social custom that for the city boy seemed so strange and exotic—a sort of eternal Saturday. The fictional center of "Em'ly" and "Specimen Jones" and many of the stories that went into *Red Men and White* and *The Jimmyjohn Boss* demonstrate this interest in local color. But while he was fascinated with the peculiarities of the West, he was also impressed with a certain significance in the experience itself. And so, for the most part, rather than elaborating on the strangeness, by his own admission he tried to preserve what he felt and saw. Of these first stories he says, "They are told as they were told to me by those who saw them" (*Red Men and White*, p. ix).

While this mode of writing may satisfy the cry for authenticity, it was not just verisimilitude that Wister was seeking. He was interested in the human part of the western experience that is the special province of literature. As he told Henry Mills Alden:

This life I am trying to write about [does not] seem to me to have been treated in fiction so far—seriously at least. The cattle era in Wyoming is nearly over, and in the main unchronicled, though its brief existence created a life permeated with eccentricity, brutality, and pathos [*sic*] not only of most vivid local color, but of singular moral interest. Its influence upon the characters of all grades of men—from Harvard graduates to the vagrants from the slums has been potent [?] and very special. I should say the salient thing it did was to produce in educated and uneducated alike more moral volatility than was ever set loose before. [Lambert, "Owen Wister's 'Hank's Woman,' " p. 40]

But Wister's problem was not just method; it was a problem as well of form. We must remember that in writing serious fiction about the American West, Owen Wister was working almost without literary precedent. Not only that, but his problem was further complicated by his ambivalence about the meaning and values inherent in the experiences about which he was writing. On the one hand, he recognized in the West certain possibilities for freedom, simplicity, and spontaneity—values that were being challenged by the eastern civilization from which he came. He saw in the West as well a certain cruelty, violence, and social chaos that were antithetical to the tradition, refinement, and culture that he also prized highly. It is the manner in which he wrestled to find appropriate forms for these contradictory and complex values that makes Wister's work so fascinating. Like James Fenimore Cooper before him, Wister was truly a literary pioneer.

Wister's stories, then, typically take form around two figures, or two sets of figures. One is eastern, or at least a representative of certain sensibilities that one might label "civilized" or "cultured." The other is western and representative of the common-sense and unrefined values that we associate with the West and its way of acting and speaking.

Frequently the Easterner is a first-person narrator, not far removed from Wister himself. The protagonist of the fiction is often a westerner sharing some of the values of both the civilized and the western world, and the antagonist may be from either the East or the West, but he or she usually is symbolic of the worst of one culture or the other—either fraught with the silly gentility and pseudorefinement of civilization or the gross cruelty and violence of the frontier. The interplay of Wister's favorable and unfavorable responses to both the East and to the West becomes the formative principle of his work.

Wister was fascinated with cowboy figures who spoke with the rhythms and syntax of the vernacular language of the frontier. Particularly in his early writings, the figure of Lin McLean looms large. He was for Wister "a man whom among all cowpunchers I love most" (*Owen Wister's West*, p. 114). But as Wister worked more and more with Lin as a protagonist, he seemed to feel less and less comfortable with this cowboy figure, and his place in Wister's stories became less and less significant as Wister developed other characters with whom he was more comfortable. What happened between that first enthusiastic adoption of Lin as Wister's best fictional hero and his abandoning of Lin for the figure that was to become the Virginian was the realization that Lin was incompatible with too many of the elements of life that Wister valued. Wister tried to use Lin McLean as the hero of a novel, but in developing that character from "culthood" to adulthood, Wister was confronted by the problem of what kind of man Lin McLean was to become. Wister never solved this difficulty, and consequently, at least so far as the writer was concerned, Lin McLean failed as a fictional center. Neither as a spokesman nor as participant could Lin McLean carry the burden of meaning that Wister hoped for. Lin could not become the philosopher of wilderness values or the astute commentator on eastern mores that Wister needed. The result was that Wister tended to make the West, of which Lin was a part, less appealing as a place and as a way of life. He also tended toward a qualification of Lin's own Westernness; that is, Lin became less ready with the quick answer, more comical in civilized situations, and finally less and less a part of the cowboy's way of life. The result was that Lin McLean, who was supposed to become a man, really became a kind of fictional neuter. He lost the essential and vital elements of frontier life and yet could never acquire the elements of civilization.

This does not mean that those stories and the novel in which Lin McLean is most prominently presented are failures; indeed there are some fine sections in almost all of these stories. For instance, the handling of the death of the biscuit shooter in the closing chapters of *Lin McLean* represents some of Wister's finest writing. The style here, though full of surprising and unconventional imagery, is exactly right. The cowboys, though acting in unconventional modes, show a spontaneity and integrity that gives high seriousness to this rendering of one of the most fundamental of human experiences. As they sing the "Cowboy's Lament" over the grave of the dead prostitute, we sense an integrity that is truly admirable. But there are only moments of brilliance in this and the other works that contain Lin McLean, and as Wister became more and more uncomfortable with his first figure, he turned more and more to the unnamed Virginian who was to become a cultural hero to a nation and the source of Wister's fame.

The character of the Virginian was an invention for Wister's third story, "Baalam and Pedro," written in March 1893. In that story the protagonist seems to have died, but a year later Wister revived the hero for "Em'ly," and by July 1893 he had decided to continue with the Virginian as a protagonist for a whole novel. Then, as the vernacular Lin McLean failed, Wister became even more interested in his rather exceptional cowboy hero. Shifting from a cowboy who was one of thousands to a cowboy who was one in a thousand, Wister created a figure larger than life, a hero superior to the other figures in the narratives not only in looks and perceptions but in abilities and prowess. Avoiding the worst of both East and West, Wister combined in the figure of the Virginian enough of a frontiersman to be subversive to eastern gentility yet enough of a gentleman to be acceptable to eastern culture. He presented in one character successful affirmations of the best that he had seen in his western experience and the common sense ideal that he recognized among his best eastern associates. Thus Wister created a figure who appealed not only to our love for adventure and romance, but he also struck a more profound note in the American psyche by creating a cultural symbol that involved both our notions about a beneficent wilderness and our commitment to the codes, laws, and human relations generally associated with civilization. In creating this character, Wister reached almost to the level of myth in presenting the nation a character who, as Leatherstocking does in the East, stands as a profound symbol of the national experience in the trans-Mississippi West.

The difference between *The Virginian* and *Lin McLean* is best seen in the difference between the two protagonists. Lin was never meant to assume the heroic proportions of the Virginian. Even his end is more prosaic. He takes his wife and retires to a ranch, chickens, and children. The Virginian takes Molly and retires to a ranch, enterprises, and affluence. But Wister is even more explicit in his delineation: Lin was not an exception; rather he was representative of the average. And as Wister wrote in the magazine version of "How Lin McLean Went East," "they gallop over the face of the empty earth for a little while and those whom rheumatism or gunpowder does not overtake, are blotted out by the course of empire, leaving no trace behind" (*Harpers* 86 [December 1982], p. 135). The cowboy's fate was, latent with tragic possibilities, but to this Wister's imagination simply did not respond. Instead of exploring the tragedy inherent in this material, Wister turned to a completely new situation. He abandoned his average cowboy and all the problems that went with him, and turned instead to the Virginian, who by virtue of his heroic prowess, his superior moral and historical insight, avoided the problems that Wister had encountered with the vernacular Lin McLean. The story of this unusual cowboy, his conflict with the villain Trampas and his courting of the eastern schoolmarm, Molly Stark, is as well known as any other story in American popular literature. In his creation, Wister was eminently successful in bringing together into one figure a complex system of American values that are at bottom contradictory. Yet as the success of the book over the years has shown, he touched a fundamental chord in the American psyche, presenting to the American public a hero who embodied the positive qualities of the wilderness experience and eastern civilization. In the end of the book he is obviously more at home in the wilderness, yet there is nothing in the man that the eastern aunt finds to object to. The Virginian seems as much at home on a Vermont settee as he had been in the Wyoming wilderness.

Shortly after the book was published, Wister wrote to Hamilton Mabey about his cowboy: "He embodies something that I have felt the throb of far and wide in our land, the best thing the Declaration of Independence ever turned out.... That is the fellow I mean; and the plains brought him again to perfections only latent in civilization" (Lambert,"Owen Wister's Virginian," p. 107). As this letter implies, Wister intended the Virginian to be not so much a unique character as the embodiment of an essential element of the American mind, an essence that "the plains brought him again to perfections only latent in civilization" (p.107). Insofar as this ambiguity between the plains and civilization, the violent frontier hero and the gentleman entrepreneur, is concerned, Wister did remarkably well in the creation of this cowboy hero who stands as a positive symbol of the nation's sense of its experience in the West. And as long as Americans, a civilized people, concern themselves with their residual wild places, both actual and imaginary, the figure of the Virginian will have vitality, relevance, and significance.

With this book, Wister had produced not only his most famous work; he had passed an important mark in his creative life: never again would his works carry the sense of a present, living West. From this point on, the sense of nostalgia and loss became more and more evident. As he wrote in the preface to his next group of stories (delayed until 1911):

So natural did everything [in my visit to the West] continue to look, surely [the antelope] must be just over that next rise! No; over the one beyond that? No,...but gone forever more!... What was this magic that came through the window? The smell of the sage-brush. After several years it was greeting me again. All day long it breathed a welcome and a sigh, as if the desert whispered: "Yes, I look as if I were here; but I am a ghost, too, there's no coming back." [*Members of the Family*, pp. 8-9]

Although many of the old characters are mentioned in these stories, neither the Virginian nor the eastern narrator takes the important roles that he had before, and the stories seem like fragments, leftovers, and leavings of a former and more successful effort. It was not until Owen Wister was in his sixties that he took up seriously the matter of the West again. By 1924 he was again revising, rework-ing, and most significant of all, completing some of his best work about the West (*When West Was West* [1928]). Two of these last stories—the best two in fact—deal explicitly and perhaps even profoundly with the frontier that had disappeared. "The Right Honorable the Strawberries" is a story that deals carefully with an analysis of the values of a closed frontier, and "At the Sign of the Last Chance" becomes a sort of coda, a quiet elegy to a West that is gone. In "Strawberries" the old conflict between tradition and civilization and the violence and spontaneous freedom of the American West is brought into clear focus. It is a sad tale of the degradation of an admirable younger son of a British peer and the tragic death of an innocent and admirable cowboy, Chalkeye, who tries to help. The end of the story makes clear that those values, which had first caught Wister's imagination forty years before, were gone forever. Only the funeral elegy remained to be written; "At the Sign of the Last Chance" is that elegy. The story is a memory piece written with the careful control that Wister might use in a musical composition. He takes his narrator back to one of his famous spots in the West for one last visit. Stopping for the night at the almost abandoned hotel, the Easterner sits down to talk with his old friends and watch their listless game of poker. In tight, spare, clean lines, Wister narrates the sad story of the acknowledgment by the participants themselves, that the true West was gone, that the "bright, brave, ripple" was past.

For Wister, the frontier came to mean not just a youthful age but a special way of life, a different way of viewing life. It was as though the frontier offered him a chance to discover a more fundamental, a more natural, and hence a better self. Wister is surely speaking for himself when the narrator of *The Virginian* says, "To leave behind all noise, mechanisms, and set out at ease slowly with one pack-horse into the wilderness, made me feel the ancient earth was indeed my Mother and I had found her again after being lost among houses, customs, and restraints" (p. 230). This was the frontier that Wister experienced: a free, simple, spontaneous, natural way of life. But he also had to watch that life disappear. He saw that wilderness and its mounted representative washed over by the floodtide of civilization. He had seen an age dying, and he had tried to preserve it; but to save the whole thing, the whole epic of the cowboy was impossible. Wister did fix much of the West in our national imagination, but the actual experience of the West was gone forever.

Survey of Criticism

Although he was not his own best critic, Wister must be considered an important commentator on his work, for if he does have significance as a western writer, that significance lies not so much in the actual achievement of his pieces as it does in the literary problems that he confronted. Indeed Wister was working, for the most part, without precedent, and the problems he confronted were enormously difficult and complex. Thus, it is important not only to understand what Wister accomplished but also to have some idea of what he was trying to accomplish. This is what makes *Roosevelt, The Story of a Friendship* so important, for in commenting to his Harvard friend about the pieces on which he was working, Wister reveals much about the conception, the development, and the intention of many of his early western writings.

The same is true of his correspondence, most of it unpublished. The literary discussions Wister carried on with his mother, for instance, are very helpful to the scholar trying to determine Wister's relationship with his material. Some of those letters have been published by Wister's daughter as connecting links to his western journals, but these represent only a small fraction of the considerable body of correspondence contained in the Wister papers. Indeed the Wister papers (the important collections that bear on his western experiences are in the Library of Congress, University of Wyoming Library, and the New York Public Library) contain much material, without which his writings cannot be given adequate assessment.

Besides the unpublished material, the most important biographical sources are the publications edited by his daughter, Fanny Kemble Wister. Even knowing that the editorial work is uneven, the scholar benefits greatly from *Owen Wister Out West: His Journals and Letters* and *That I May Tell You: Journals and Letters of the Wister Family* (1979).

While a number of dissertations make general assessments of Wister novels and stories, there are few broad studies that consider the whole of Wister's western pieces; however, much of the work we do have is very good. Richard Etulain's *Owen Wister* (1973) is the best short introduction available. It is a fine piece of work that presents a concise and succinct summary of recent commentary about Wister, as well as fine biographical and bibliographical material.

Other studies have placed Wister in the larger context of American culture. The best work to date in this regard is G. Edward White's *The Eastern Establishment and the Western Experience: The West of Frederic Remington, Theodore Roosevelt, and Owen Wister* (1968). It is a good example of the kind of thorough and resourceful research that a figure like Wister deserves.

Most of the scholarship about Wister focuses on *The Virginian*. Of the many pieces in this regard, I certainly recommend the introduction by Philip Durham to the Riverside Edition of *The Virginian* (1968). Other articles by Mody C. Boatright, Carl Bode, John A. Barsness, Joe B. Frantz, and Ben M. Vorpahl provide interesting insights that discuss the Virginian as an important figure, not only for American popular literature, but for American culture as well. In that regard, Neal Lambert's "Owen Wister's Virginian" (1971) may prove interesting. A provocative discussion that shows the wide range that Wister's fiction invites is Sanford Marovitz's "Testament of A Patriot: The Virginian, the Tenderfoot, and Owen Wister" (1973). Of more recent interest is the article by Forrest G. Robinson, "The Roosevelt-Wister Connection" (1979), which contains some notes on the West and the uses of history.

Wister scholarship is aided considerably by the availability of some fine bibliographies. Besides those by Dean Sherman and Richard Charles Weber, there is a very helpful issue of *American Literary Realism* (Winter 1974) devoted almost entirely to an annotated bibliography of secondary material prepared by Sanford

E. Marovitz and others. It covers 1887 to 1973 with a pleasing thoroughness that touches the scholar's heart.

With all the interest that Owen Wister has generated in the last two decades, one might assume that the best work has been done and that the richest materials are used up; this is not the case. Those interested in Wister still look for at least two works: a first-rate biography placing the man and his work clearly in the broader context of the modernization of America, and second, a careful and thorough analysis of his work as a whole, studying not only his most famous novel but his developing techniques and attitudes as they are reflected in the manuscripts, in the revisions, and in his work in general. It is interesting to note here, for instance, Wister's fascination with the vernacular figures who take such important places in his pieces: "Chalkeye," "Scipio LeMoyne," "Honey Wiggins," and the early "Lin McLean." It is also interesting to note that after the novel itself, the Virginian never really found a significant place in any of Wister's fiction, even though Wister continued to write and even though this cowboy was introduced into several western stories. It is safe to say, at this time at least, that although much good work has been written, the best work on Owen Wister remains to be done.

Bibliography

Works by Owen Wister

Red Men and White. New York: Harper & Brothers, 1896.

Lin McLean. New York: Harper & Brothers, 1897.

The Jimmyjohn Boss and Other Stories. New York: Harper & Brothers 1900.

"Concerning Bad Men: The True 'Bad Man' of the Frontier, and the Reasons for His Existence." *Everybody's Magazine* 4 (April 1901): 320-28

The Virginian: A Horseman of the Plains. New York: Macmillan, 1902.

Members of the Family. New York: Macmillan, 1911.

When West Was West. New York: Macmillan, 1928.

The Writings of Owen Wister. 11 vols. New York: Macmillan, 1928.

Roosevelt: The Story of a Friendship, 1880-1919. New York: Macmillan, 1930.

Owen Wister Out West: His Journals and Letters. Ed. Frances Kemble Wister. Chicago: University of Chicago Press, 1958.

Studies of Owen Wister

Barsness, John A. "Theodore Roosevelt as Cowboy: The Virginian as Jacksonian Man." *American Quarterly* 21 (Fall 1969): 609-19.

Boatright, Mody C. "The American Myth Rides the Range: Owen Wister's Man on Horseback." *Southwest Review* 36 (Summer 1951): 157-63.

Bode, Carl. "Henry James and Owen Wister." *American Literature* 26 (May 1954): 250-52.

Durham, Philip. Introduction and Textual Note. *The Virginian*. Riverside Edition. Boston: Houghton Mifflin, 1968.

Etulain, Richard. "Origins of the Western." *Journal of Popular Culture* 4 (Fall 1970): 518-26.

———. *Owen Wister*. WWS. Boise, Idaho: Boise State College, 1973.

———. *Western American Literature: A Bibliography of Interpretive Books and Articles*. Vermillion, S. Dak.: Dakota Press, 1972, pp. 134-36.

Frantz, Joe B., and Choate, Julian Ernest, Jr. *The American Cowboy: The Myth and the Reality*. Norman: University of Oklahoma Press, 1955.

Lambert, Neal. "Owen Wister's 'Hank's Woman': The Writer and His Comment." *Western American Literature* 4 (Spring 1969): 39-50.

———. "Owen Wister's Lin McLean: The Failure of the Vernacular Hero." *Western American Literature* 5 (Fall 1970): 219-32.

———. "Owen Wister's Virginian: The Genesis of a Cultural Hero." *Western American Literature* 6 (Summer 1971): 99-107.

———. "The Values of the Frontier: Owen Wister's Final Assessment." *South Dakota Review* 9 (Spring 1971): 76-87.

Marovitz, Sanford E. "Owen Wister: An Annotated Bibliography of Secondary Material." *American Literary Realism 1870-1910* 7 (Winter 1974): 1-107.

———. "Testament of a Patriot: The Virginian, the Tenderfoot, and Owen Wister." *Texas Studies in Literature and Language* 15 (Fall 1973): 551-75.

Robinson, Forrest G. "The Roosevelt-Wister Connection: Some Notes on the West and the Uses of History." *Western American Literature* 14 (Summer 1979): 95-114.

Sherman, Dean. "Owen Wister: An Annotated Bibliography." *Bulletin of Bibliography* 28 (January-March 1971): 7-16.

Vorpahl, Ben M. "Ernest Hemingway and Owen Wister." *Library Chronicle* 36 (Spring 1970): 126-37.

———. "Henry James and Owen Wister." *Pennsylvania Magazine of History and Biography* 95 (July 1971): 291-338.

———. *My Dear Wister: The Frederic Remington-Owen Wister Letters*. Palo Alto, Calif.: American West, 1972.

Walker, Don D. "Essays in the Criticism of Western Literary Criticism: II. The Dogmas of DeVoto." *Possible Sack* [University of Utah] 3 (November 1971): 1-7.

———. "Wister, Roosevelt and James: A Note on the Western." *American Quarterly* 12 (Fall 1960): 358-66.

Weber, Richard Charles. "Owen Wister: An Annotated Bibliography." Master's thesis, University of Northern Iowa, 1971.

White, G. Edward. *The Eastern Establishment and the Western Experience: The West of Frederic Remington, Theodore Roosevelt, and Owen Wister*. New Haven: Yale University Press, 1968.

Wister, Fanny K. "Letters of Owen Wister, Author of *The Virginian*." *Pennsylvania Magazine of History and Biography* 83 (January 1959): 3-28.

———. "Owen Wister's West." *Atlantic Monthly* 195 (May 1955): 29-35; (June 1955): 52-57.

———, ed. *That I May Tell You: Journals and Letters of the Owen Wister Family*. Wayne, Pa.: Haverford House, 1979.

INDEX

CONTRIBUTORS

KERRY AHEARN teaches American literature at Oregon State University. He has published work in *Atlantic, TLS, Texas Quarterly, Western Humanities Review*, and other journals and served for two years as a Fulbright Professor at the University of Ghana.

BERT ALMON, Associate Professor of English at the University of Alberta, earned a Ph.D. at the University of New Mexico with a dissertation on Gary Snyder. In addition to his works on Snyder, he has written four collections of poetry, most recently *Blue Sunrise* (1980).

JUDY ALTER, who holds the Ph.D. degree from Texas Christian University, is a freelance writer in Fort Worth. The author of works on Stewart Edward White and Dorothy M. Johnson, she has also published a novel, *After Pa Was Shot* (1978).

LUCILE F. ALY, Professor Emerita at the University of Oregon, received the doctorate at the University of Missouri (1959), where she became acquainted with John G. Neihardt. She is the author of *John G. Neihardt: A Critical Biography*, and of many articles about his work.

RICHARD ASTRO is Dean of the College of Arts and Sciences at Northeastern University. He is the author of *Steinbeck and Ricketts: The Shaping of a Novelist* (1973), and has edited books on Steinbeck, Hemingway, Malamud, and literary New England.

WILLIAM BLOODWORTH, Associate Professor of English at East Carolina University, holds the Ph.D. degree in American Civilization from the University of Texas. He is the author of *Upton Sinclair* (1978) and of articles on western American literature and native American autobiography.

M. E. BRADFORD is Professor of English and American Studies at the University of Dallas. A Senior Fellow of the National Endowment for the Humanities, he has written several books and essays and contributed to *Southwestern American Literature: A Bibliography*.

ROBERT BROPHY is Professor of English at California State University, Long Beach. He has published two books, edited three, and written thirty-five articles in various journals. Since 1968 he has been editor of the *Robinson Jeffers Newsletter*.

PAUL T. BRYANT is Professor of English and Associate Dean of the Graduate School at Colorado State University. Holding the Ph.D. from the University of Illinois, he teaches and has published scholarly work in western American literature, nature writing, and rhetoric.

JOHN CALDWELL is Director of the library, Augustana College. Previously he was head of Technical Services at California State College, Stanislaus, and librarian at California Lutheran College. He teaches colonial American history.

MICHAEL CLEARY teaches English at Broward Community College. His works include articles on Jack Schaefer, John Seelye's *The Kid*, Thomas Berger's *Little Big Man*, and Edward Albee's *Who's Afraid of Virginia Woolf?*

G. B. CRUMP is Associate Professor of English at Central Missouri State University. In addition to a book, *The Novels of Wright Morris: A Critical Interpretation*, he has published articles in *Midamerica*, the *D. H. Lawrence Review*, and *Contemporary Literature*.

FRED ERISMAN is Professor of English at Texas Christian University. A specialist in American Studies, he has written extensively on children's literature, detective fiction, and the Western. His works include studies of Len Deighton, Harper Lee, and Jack Schaefer.

RICHARD W. ETULAIN is Professor of History at the University of New Mexico and editor of the *New Mexico Historical Review*. A specialist in the American West, he has edited books on the Basques, Jack London, and the popular Western, and has compiled several book-length bibliographies.

JOSEPH M. FLORA is Professor and Chairman of English at the University of North Carolina, Chapel Hill. He is author of *Vardis Fisher* (1965), *William Ernest Henley* (1970), and *Frederick Manfred* (1974), as well as numerous articles on these and other authors.

JAMES K. FOLSOM is Professor of English at the University of Colorado. A long-time student of western American literature, he has written biographies of Timothy Flint (1965) and Harvey Fergusson (1969), and a study, *The American*

Western Novel (1966). More recently, he edited *The Western: A Collection of Critical Essays* (1979).

ROBERT FRANK is Associate Professor and Chair of English at Oregon State University, and coordinator of the Northwest Studies Area of the Humanities Development Program. He is author of *Don't Call Me Gentle Charles: A Reading of Lamb's Essays of Elia* (1976).

WARREN FRENCH is Professor of English and American Studies at Indiana University-Purdue University at Indianapolis. He is the author of books on Steinbeck, Norris, and Salinger and editor of the Twayne Theatrical Arts Series and a section of the Twayne United States Authors Series.

ROBERT L. GALE, a native of Iowa, holds the Ph.D. from Columbia University, and is Professor of English at the University of Pittsburgh. His monographs on Charles Warren Stoddard, Charles Marion Russell, and Luke Short represent his first ventures into western American literature.

EDWIN W. GASTON, JR., Professor of English and Dean of the Graduate School at Stephen F. Austin State University, is the author of *The Early Novel of the Southwest* (1961), *Conrad Richter* (1965), and *Eugene Manlove Rhodes; Cowboy Chronicler* (1967).

ROBERT GISH is Professor of English at the University of Northern Iowa. He is the author of *Hamlin Garland: The Far West* (1976) and numerous essays on Garland and western American literature. In 1977 he was a National Endowment for the Humanities Fellow in the history of the American West at the University of California, Davis.

DON GRAHAM, Associate Professor of English at the University of Texas, is the author of *The Fiction of Frank Norris: The Aesthetic Context* (1978) and coeditor of *Western Movies* (1979). He is currently working on a book on Texas in the movies.

DORYS CROW GROVER is Associate Professor of English at East Texas State University. A specialist in the American novel and novelists, she is the author of *Vardis Fisher: The Novelist as Poet* (1973) and essays in *American Literature* and *South Dakota Review*.

DICK HARRISON teaches Canadian and American literature at the University of Alberta. Author of *Unnamed Country: The Struggle for a Canadian Prairie Fiction*, he has also edited *Crossing Frontiers: Papers in American and Canadian Western Literature*.

GERALD HASLAM, a native of California's great central valley, is editor of *Western Writing* (1974) and author of *Jack Schaefer* (1976). He has also published three books of fiction: *Okies: Selected Stories* (1975), *Masks* (1976), and *The Wages of Sin* (1980).

LEEDICE KISSANE is Professor Emerita of English at Idaho State University, where she was cofounder of the American Studies program. Her interest in Ruth Suckow stems from her Midwest origins. For two years she was a Fulbright lecturer at the University of Iceland.

EARLE LABOR, Professor of English at Centenary College of Louisiana, has published two books and more than thirty shorter pieces on Jack London. He has also coauthored *A Handbook of Critical Approaches to Literature* (1966) and has published articles on Crane, Faulkner, and others.

NEAL LAMBERT was born, raised, and educated in Utah. His understanding of American and western literature comes from the University of Utah. At Brigham Young University, he directed the American Studies program, taught literature, and has become Associate Academic Vice President.

JAMES W. LEE, Professor and Director of Graduate Studies of English at North Texas State University, is author of five books and numerous articles. He edited the Steck-Vaughn pamphlet series on southwest writers and recently coedited *Southwestern American Literature: A Bibliography*.

MERRILL LEWIS is Professor of English at Western Washington University. He is coauthor (with his wife, Lorene) of the Boise pamphlet on Wallace Stegner and has coedited two books of criticism: *The Westering Experience* (1977) and *Women, Women Writers, and the West* (1979).

GLEN A. LOVE holds the Ph.D. in English from the University of Washington and is Professor of English at the University of Oregon. A Fulbright senior lecturer at Universität Regensburg in 1978-79, he is author of *New Americans* (1982).

THOMAS J. LYON teaches at Utah State University and has edited *Western American Literature* since 1974. The author of *John Muir* (1972) and *Frank Waters* (1973), he is currently working on a study of mysticism in western regional writing.

JOSEPH B. McCULLOUGH, Associate Professor of English at the University of Nevada, Las Vegas, is the author of *Hamlin Garland* (1978) and of articles in *American Literature* and the *Mark Twain Journal*. In 1980-81 he was a Fulbright lecturer to Finland.

JAMES H. MAGUIRE is Associate Professor of English at Boise State University, where he serves as coeditor of the Western Writers Series. His *Mary Hallock Foote* is the second title in the series. He was president of the Western Literature Association for 1980-81.

MICHAEL T. MARSDEN is a faculty member in the Department of Popular Culture and the graduate adviser for the American Culture program at Bowling Green State University. He has published a number of articles on popular western fiction and films.

BARBARD HOWARD MELDRUM, Professor of English at the University of Idaho, has published many essays on western American literature. She has been awarded a National Endowment of the Humanities fellowship to research and write a book on western American pastoral fiction.

PATRICK D. MORROW is Associate Professor of English at Auburn University, and associate editor of *Southern Humanities Review*. In addition to his works on Bret Harte, he has published three other books and many scholarly articles. In 1981 he served as Fulbright lecturer at the University of Canterbury, New Zealand.

JOHN J. MURPHY, Chairman of English at Merrimack College, has written widely about Willa Cather. He has edited *Five Essays on Willa Cather* (1974) and is the author of *A Teacher's Guide to Willa Cather's "My Antonia" and "O Pioneers!"* (1981).

T. M. PEARCE, Professor Emeritus at the University of New Mexico, holds the Ph.D. in English from the University of Pittsburgh. He has coauthored or written fifteen books, of which the best known are *Southwest Heritage* (1938, 1972) and *Literary America* (1979).

WILLIAM T. PILKINGTON is Professor of English at Tarleton State University. He is author of *My Blood's Country: Studies in Southwestern Literature* (1973) and *Harvey Fergusson* (1975), and coeditor (with Don Graham) of *Western Movies* (1980).

ANN RONALD is Associate Professor of English at the University of Nevada, Reno. Currently writing a book-length study of Edward Abbey, she is also author of the Western Writers Series pamphlet on Zane Grey and numerous articles on the contributions of women writers.

ALAN ROSENUS has been editor of the Urion Press since 1972. His first novel, *The Old One*, appeared in 1974; a book of short fiction, *Devil Stories*

(Modern Man in Search of a Resort), was published in 1979, and he has written numerous short pieces of fiction and criticism.

ORLAN SAWEY, who retired from Texas A and I University in 1977, is author of *Charles A. Siringo* (1981) and *Bernard DeVoto* (1969). Educated at Texas A and I and the University of Texas, he taught regional American literature and folklore for thirty-one years.

HELEN STAUFFER is Professor of English at Kearney State College. President of the Western Literature Association in 1980, she has specialized in studies of Mari Sandoz and women's writing. Her biography of Sandoz was published in 1982.

ROSEMARY SULLIVAN is Associate Professor of English at the University of Toronto. She is the author of *The Garden Master: Style and Identity in the Poetry of Theodore Roethke* (1975) and has published criticism and poetry in numerous journals.

GARY TOPPING is Curator of Manuscripts at the Utah State Historical Society. Holding the Ph.D. in history from the University of Utah, he has published widely in western local history, historiography, popular western literature, and western religious history.

MARTHA SCOTT TRIMBLE, Professor Emerita at Colorado State University, is a native of Fort Collins, Colorado. Her studies of native American traditions were stimulated by her work with Navaho and Ute students. She is the author of the Boise pamphlet on N. Scott Momaday.

BEN MERCHANT VORPAHL, Associate Professor of English at the University of Georgia, is editor of *My Dear Wister: The Frederic Remington-Owen Wister Letters* (1973) and author of *Frederic Remington and the West* (1978). He has also published several shorter works of criticism.

MAX WESTBROOK, Professor of English at the University of Texas, Austin, is author of *The Modern American Novel* (1966) and *Walter Van Tilburg Clark* (1969). He has also written a chapbook of poems, *Country Boy* (1979), and essays on Crane, Dreiser, Hemingway, and American culture.

DELBERT E. WYLDER, who is Professor and Chairman of English at Murray State University, is author of *Emerson Hough* (1981), *Hemingway's Heroes* (1969), and essays in *Western American Literature, New Mexico Quarterly*, and *Journal of the West*.